W9-CQM-318

THE GREAT AMERICAN COOKBOOK

WITHDRAWN

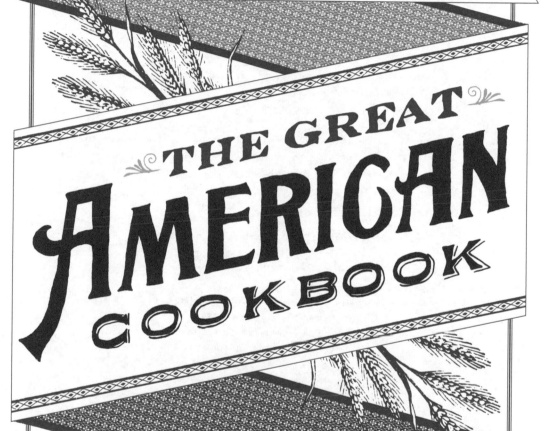

A REVISED EDITION OF THE CLASSIC COOKBOOK ⚜ HOW AMERICA EATS ⚜ BY

CLEMENTINE PADDLEFORD

THE GREAT AMERICAN COOKBOOK

500 TIME-TESTED RECIPES
FAVORITE FOODS FROM EVERY STATE!

ADAPTED AND WITH AN INTRODUCTION BY KELLY ALEXANDER
FOREWORD BY MOLLY O'NEILL

RIZZOLI
NEW YORK

Published *by*

RIZZOLI INTERNATIONAL PUBLICATIONS, INC.

300 PARK AVENUE SOUTH, NEW YORK, NY 10010

www.rizzoliusa.com

Original text from *How America Eats* © Estate of Clementine Paddleford
Adapted Recipes, Introduction, and Compilation © Kelly Alexander 2011
Foreword © Molly O'Neill 2011

All rights reserved. No part of this publication may be reproduced, stored in a retrieval system,
or transmitted in any form or by any means, electronic, mechanical, photocopying, recording,
or otherwise, without prior consent of the publishers.

2011 2012 2013 2014 / 10 9 8 7 6 5 4 3 2 1

Distributed in the U.S. trade by Random House, New York

Printed in the United States of America

Designer: ERICA HEITMAN-FORD *and* HANA ANOUK NAKAMURA *for* MUCCA DESIGN
Typesetter: TINA HENDERSON
Project Editor: CHRISTOPHER STEIGHNER
Copy Editor: LEDA SCHEINTAUB
Proofreader: SARAH SCHEFFEL
Indexer: CATHY DORSEY
Production manager: COLIN HOUGH-TRAPP

ISBN: 978-0-8478-3690-1

Library of Congress Control Number: 2011927161

Table of Contents

Foreword

I'd already logged several hundred thousand miles researching how America eats by the time I ran into Clementine Paddleford's opus *How America Eats*. After twenty years of writing restaurant criticism and food features in newspapers and magazines, I was gathering recipes and food stories to create my book *One Big Table: A Portrait of American Cooking*. Stumbling upon a signed copy of the book that documented Miss Paddleford's cross-country odyssey was like running into an earlier version of myself. A better, more adventuresome, more visionary, pioneering version. My inner journalist rent her garments and gnashed her teeth. I'd been scooped forty years before I'd even begun.

I'd found the volume at a garage sale outside Manhattan, Kansas, not far from the man-made lake that now covers Blue Valley Farm, the 260-acre sprawl where Miss Paddleford was born in 1878. I completely forgot about the chicken farmer I'd planned to interview that day. Instead, I sat in the car paging through the book, taking note of the dated photographs, the sometimes ingratiating prose, the occasional watered-down version of ethnic dishes. But I also took note of the regional specialties like San Francisco Cioppino and Lobster Newburg from Maine, Kentucky Burgoo, New Orleans Gumbo, and the vinegary Barbecue from South Carolina (a dish that I had thought was first introduced to a national audience by Craig Claiborne in the pages of *The New York Times*).

Only after I'd reassured myself of the obvious superiority of my own venture did I inhale sharply. Miss Paddleford had been writing about food for more than thirty years when Mr. Claiborne joined the staff of *The New York Times*. So who followed whom? After weeks spent comparing entries from *How America Eats* with Mr. Claiborne's work, I had little doubt. Clementine Paddleford was Lewis and Clark. She drew the map of American regional cooking that the rest of us are still following.

During her thirty-year reign as food editor of *The New York Herald Tribune* (from 1936 until the paper, eclipsed by the upstart *New York Times*, closed in 1966), Miss Paddleford wrote at least once and often twice per week for the *Tribune*, wrote a monthly column for *Gourmet* magazine, and published seven books. In the decades before highways, air travel, and regional train spurs made the far-flung corners of the country more accessible, Miss Paddleford flew her own Piper Cub to remote lumber camps in Washington State, fishing grounds in Alaska, and grazing areas in the high plains of New Mexico, as well as hundreds of other off-the-grid farming spots. Duncan Heinz cooked for her in his Kentucky home; so did the chefs aboard the submarine *Skipjack*. She roamed ethnic ghettos to chronicle immigrant cooking, attended the national hobo conference, dined with the Duchess of Windsor, and attended the coronation luncheon for Queen Elizabeth in 1953.

She built a readership estimated at 12 million people per week and became a household name. Bill Arno made her the subject of one of his cartoons in *The New Yorker*. Clementine Paddleford was, wrote R. W. Apple in *The New York Times*, "the Nellie Bly of culinary journalism." She was "a regal presence in the newsroom," the managing editor of the *Tribune* said in an interview with Mr. Apple, "a woman of enormous clout."

But after she died in 1967, her fame suffered a fate similar to that of the soufflé that she observed being served to Winston Churchill in 1946 before he made his Iron Curtain speech in Missouri. "With a rapturous, half-hushed sigh," wrote Miss Paddleford, the soufflé "settled softly to melt and vanish in a moment like smoke or a dream." By the time I enrolled in cooking school in Paris and began writing about food in 1978, I, like most of my contemporaries, had a vague and misbegotten knowledge of our predecessor. Years later when I rediscovered her, I decided I had to uncover her story.

Clementine Paddleford was a single mother who survived a youthful bout with throat cancer, speaking through a voice box that she concealed with a Gothish black velvet ribbon. She bent gender roles and minted a new way of writing about food when she refused to sit at her desk or stay in the kitchen. She and James Beard were the first to celebrate American cooking. She documented immigrant cooking, coined the phrase "regional cooking," and was a proponent of farm-to-table eating long before it was fashionable. But she paid a high price for being first.

I was unaware of how much she'd influenced me when I began my own American odyssey. But with two years down and eight to go, she became my constant companion. While driving around the United States, we time-traveled through a century of fashions in American food, the history of food writing, the nature of success, the definition of American cuisine, the loneliness of living far from home. Miss Paddleford toted her cat, Pussy Willow. I traveled with Tootsie, my dog. Everybody got along just fine.

Before Clementine Paddleford, there were two types of food writers in the United States. There were Ladies and there were Gentlemen.

The Ladies tended to focus on hearth and home and to observe the wider world through their kitchen windows. They wrote recipes, not prose, and they took their recipes very seriously. Beginning with the domestic science movement in the late nineteenth century, the Ladies of Food were all but willing to die defending the honor (read: accuracy) of the recipes they wrote. In addition to being *right*, they were prudent, efficient, sensible, health-conscious, buttoned-down, mildly creative, carefully generous, and economy-minded. They either were or did their best to sound like paragons of the established order and the settled life. Their recipes were instructions for life as it *should* be.

The Gentlemen, on the other hand, tended to range widely, to pride themselves on their adventuresome spirit, their worldliness, their knowledge of cuisine and their capacity to consume significant quantities of alcohol. Leaving the private sphere to the Ladies, the Gentlemen focused on food in public life, in restaurants, cafes, and bars, at newsworthy social events and affairs of state, at rustic rituals and regional feasts. While the Ladies' literary tone ranged from kindly grandmother to shrill school marm, the Gentlemen assumed either an ironic, avuncular tone or one of a sadly disappointed know-it-all. They wrote criticism and travelogues. Their stories were about life as it *could* be.

Miss Paddleford was neither a Lady nor a Gentleman. She was a woman grounded in the real world, a Kansas farm girl whose people fought in the American Revolution. Her mother warned her not to "grow a wishbone where a backbone ought to be." She did not escape a nostalgic longing for the home she left. In fact, fashionably spare and muscular modern writers criticize the overwrought sentimentality of her prose. Nevertheless, beneath the literary curlicues looms a rare reportorial thoroughness and heft. Miss Paddleford wrote about what should be and what could be, but mostly she wrote about what was.

Electing to record the external world rather than internal musings, she was a rarity among female food writers. In addition, her rigorous reporting set a high standard and cast a long shadow on secondhand reports and derivative work. It also paved the road for looking at food from both gustatory and cultural points of view, and this, in turn, demonstrated the power of the documentary approach to food that drives some of the best food writing today. To the best of my knowledge, Paddleford was also the first food writer to move easily between the public and private spheres of food.

Comparing the descriptions of the food she found in her midcentury travels to the American cooking I found four decades later was a constant lesson in cultural change. There was a lot less grilling, sautéing, and flash-frying going on when Paddleford roamed the countryside than when I hit the road. She was writing at a time in which there were still women at home to mind a slow-cooked pot,

and in an era in which the factory had not completely overtaken the farm. The bone-to-meat ratio in poultry, pork, and beef was much higher than it is today. Hence the best cooking techniques were ones aimed at melting cartilage and other connective tissue while coaxing flavor into the flesh from the bone: long, slow, moist heat. The denaturing (and consequent lessening of flavor) that occurred as food moved toward the mass-produced, processed, and pre-packaged in the mid- to late-twentieth century was not complete when Paddleford began to chronicle food in America. And so her recipes rely less on seasoning and flavor-enhancement than they do on the taste of the ingredient.

The most glaring difference, however, lies in the ethnic recipes she presents. Paddleford was writing about Enchiladas, Danish *Ebleskivers*, Chicken *Parikas*, and Greek *Dolmades* before most food writers knew they existed. Reporting before 1965 when immigrant cooking was only as successful as it was assimilated, Paddleford focused on dishes that she called "mixed and Americanized." A few years after her book was published, immigration standards shifted. The traditional European bias was replaced by a global mindset that welcomed Asian, African, Latino, and East Indian people. In the intervening decades, the standard of judging ethnic cooking switched from "how well has it become like everything else" to "how authentic is it." In this department, Paddleford-the-pioneer reads like Paddleford-the-bland. In a similar vein, the renditions of classic French and Italian dishes that Paddleford found lacked the sophistication that the same dishes acquired in the post-Julia, post-Marcella era when I began sampling and comparing iterations of the classics. Cooking, at least among the nation's best cooks, has improved dramatically in the past fifty years.

However, as imported dishes have become better and better, American regional dishes have begun to pale. Paddleford takes us back to a time when Mississippi stuffed ham was a three-day procedure and red beans and rice was only served on Monday. Her discovery and description loom so large that connoisseurs still recite her words, albeit unconsciously. Long after writing an entry about chowder evoking Ishmael and Queequeg, for *One Big Table*, for instance, I came across Paddleford's description of clam chowder as "equal that set forth to Ishmael and Queequeg by the hearty Mrs. Hussey." With twelve million readers, Paddleford's descriptions may have been repeated often enough to become part of the American food atmosphere, public domain, a given.

Recipes are family stories, tales of particular places and personal histories. They bear witness to the land and waterways, to technology and invention, to immigration, migration, ambition, disappointment, triumph, and, most of all, to the differences and similarities between people. Cooking is a way of telling the world who you are. It takes more energy than smarts to cover 50,000 miles and gather hundreds of good recipes a year. The tough part is figuring out what to keep and what to

toss, what is fleeting, what will endure, and what spirit and sensibility connects the crazy quilt of American cooking. That was Paddleford's genius.

From two thousand interviews, Paddleford identified the recipes and stories that best express these qualities. Her most successful selections reflect the simple calculus of place and what grows there and who lives there and how that all adds up to dinner. These regional recipes remain some of the less sullied and most tasty of the thousands of iterations that have been published since. Had I found the same cooks, I would have chosen them again. Had I not traveled with the ghost of Paddleford, I might still be driving around the country trying to figure out what these insanely diverse recipes hold in common.

Americans have a passionate belief in the future and they are also deeply committed to idealizing the past. The tension between the two creates a distinct yearning. Paddleford called it "hometown appetite." "We all have hometown appetites," she said in an interview in 1960. "Every other person is a bundle of longing for the simplicities of good taste once enjoyed on the farm or in the hometown [he or she] left behind." The farm or hometown is now likely to be several generations removed. But the yearning remains and many of the recipes that Paddleford gathered half a century ago continue to flatter, sate, and appease it.

MOLLY O'NEILL

Introduction

Maintaining frequent communication with the dead is a dicey business. At best, you feel slightly crazy, in an otherworldly sort of way. At worst, you feel codependent on a nonperson—deeply crazy, in other words. For more than ten years now, I've been heavily engaged in conversation with Clementine Paddleford (1898–1967), the late, great American food writer on whose work this book is based.

Telling the story of how I met Clem is so much a part of the weft and weave of my soul that I feel as if you, yes you, the collective reader, must already know it, but of course you probably don't. In a nutshell, I happened upon an ancient copy of Clem's seminal work, *How America Eats*, which is a collection of some of her columns written between 1948 and 1960. (The book was published in 1960.) It's a gut-busting anthology of more than eight hundred recipes that chronicles who Clem was and what she did, both for a living and for the concept of regional American food.

Clementine Paddleford was born on a farm in the now nonexistent town of Stockdale, Kansas, near Manhattan, where Kansas State University sits (both back then and now). She was one of those children who is always writing letters, pretending to be a reporter, annoying the neighbors with prying questions about their whereabouts. And she became a journalist, first for her college newspaper and then as a freelancer based in Chicago, and then finally for the *New York Herald Tribune*, which was then the most influential newspaper in the country, if not in the world. Her specialty was food. And here's the part that cannot be screamed loudly enough: Her specialty was food, and not because she loved to cook nor because she was a tremendously natural talent in the kitchen who invented her own sauces and baked two loaves of country bread by hand every day. Her specialty was food because she had a mother who did all of those things and more, and because of Clem's upbringing she understood that food was a way to talk about class and religion and culture and politics and, well, life in general. Food was her medium; telling stories was her passion.

And Clem was very successful, mostly because she was the first of her kind. Before her, newspaper food sections were run largely by home economists who were specialists at writing formulas but little else. Clem brought color to the proceedings, inserting into the recipes the narratives about the lives of the women who made them (and let's face it, in that era, which in some ways isn't so very different from today, almost all of the home cooks were women). She wasn't just telegraphing material from behind some desk, either: Clem was, as we would say today, "in the field," and she maintained an exhausting travel schedule as she headed from one home kitchen into another. "I have traveled by train, plane, automobile, by mule back, on foot—in all over 800,000 miles," she proclaims in the preface to *How America Eats*. And all the while her writing was breezy, smart, and sassy—often florid, yes, but never less than endearingly enthusiastic. Shrimp cocktail aboard the dining car of the Katy railroad are "tip-tilted over the glass like pink commas." Mushrooms are "pixie umbrellas." A bite of pecan cookie makes "a shower of nut-sweet crumbs crumble in the mouth." Crumbs crumble! And angel food cake is as "soft to the touch as a butterfly's wing."

It was the kind of copy that *moves*, full of action and energy and, most of all, a spirit of fun. Hard to believe now, in the days when any fool with a whisk and a laptop feels qualified to wax rhapsodic about a cupcake, but Clem was an original. In her prime, she commanded a huge salary, an audience of more than 12 million readers per week, and the title of "Best Known Food Editor," as bestowed by *Time* magazine.

She was tough, too, and tough in the way that counts: She never complained about the fact that as a young woman she survived throat cancer and had to speak out of a manually manipulated voice box instead of a larynx for the majority of her professional career (including while conducting interviews). She never complained that the advertising revenues generated by her columns were paying for the other news reporters' trips abroad and they got more respect in the newsroom than she did. Like her mother, whom she once described as a "Rock of Gibraltar," she simply carried on. For reasons that have largely to do with circumstance—Clem's health declined almost precisely with that of her newspaper, and her lack of voice rendered television appearances impossible just as that medium was becoming important—Clem's work was almost entirely lost when she passed away in 1967. (Her obituary was published in all of the country's major newspapers.) It was lovingly restored, finally and more than thirty years after the fact, chiefly by Cynthia Harris and other librarians and archivists at her alma mater, Kansas State University. Harris and I have worked closely together for years and co-authored an acclaimed biography on Clem, *Hometown Appetites*, published in 2008.

And then there's me: I started writing about Clem for Colman Andrews, the editor-in-chief of *Saveur* magazine, in 2001 (the initial article won a James Beard journalism award in 2003), and I have never really stopped. But sometimes it seems that there's only so much room in the world of food for things that aren't new, that the business is as ephemeral and fleeting as the subject matter itself—a good dish, like a good idea, has a shelf life. But just when I thought the conversation about Clem was on a permanent hiatus, so to speak, an enterprising editor named Christopher Steighner at Rizzoli managed to do the impossible: secure the rights to *How America Eats*, in the hopes of re-editing its iconic recipes for a public that is eternally aching, these days anyway, to define itself by what and how it eats.

So the question quickly became this: How can we keep the spirit of Clem's recipes alive while making them useful to a modern audience? Although these recipes were perfected in a test kitchen, the process happened more than fifty years ago—back when food editors didn't have to start recipes with the words "preheat the oven," or include pan sizes or indicators of doneness for cakes. Home cooks in those days would have known exactly what to do, because they practiced real cooking (which is to say making meals that often took longer than twenty minutes) every day. Cooking today is, of course, much different. And so that was challenge number one: adapting recipe language for the contemporary cook.

The second part of figuring out how to present Clem's vast recipe collection involved getting inside her head and attempting to determine why she chose various dishes and how we could create a balanced picture of "how America eats" that makes sense but also incorporates Clem's personal peculiarities. What am I talking about? Here's what: Clem was from Kansas. She grew up on a farm. She grew up in flatlands. When she finally went to Florida, she fell in love: As an avid naturalist with a keen interest in both flora and fauna, Clem practically worshipped the Sunshine State; to her it was incredibly exotic. And when she went to Hawaii, well, you can imagine: Here was a Midwestern daughter of the plains taking in the most luscious scenery known to man. She was in heaven. So that explains why she was the first food journalist to visit Hawaii after the announcement of its official statehood, and why Florida has a thirty-two-page chapter all its own in the original *How America Eats* (by comparison, the Southwest chapter, which includes Texas, New Mexico, and Arizona, is only twenty pages).

Another issue: Clementine embraced convenience foods. "Modern meal planners want the quick and easy, but with the plus of their own distinctive touches," Clem wrote. "Women have great need, in this automatic world, to express themselves creatively." Well, amen, sister: Even in the late 1950s, we still wanted to cook—we just needed a little help, a little advice of the kind your mother would have given you if you were raising your kids on a nearby farm. When women moved away from home and started going to work and were faced with getting dinner on the table, Clem became that collective mom.

The problem was that Clementine calls for things we don't necessarily endorse today. Because her readers were always writing to her with requests for time-saving tips and because the convenience food industry was so new and so exciting, she has no compunction calling for ingredients like processed cheese, canned crabmeat, and cream of chicken soup, and she had a propensity for gelatin-based so-called salad molds. I feel certain that if Clem were alive today, she would be a dedicated locavore—but one with the common sense to know what will do in a pinch (and this probably wouldn't include either canned mushrooms or bouillon cubes).

That said, every once in a while we included a recipe for its kitsch factor alone, to remind us of the way people really did eat in the 1950s. The most perfect example of this is Margaret Fisher's Asparagus Bake (page 541), which calls for both cream of mushroom soup and Cheez-It crumbs. "Oh my god," you might say. (In fact, that's what my editor, Mr. Steighner, said when I suggested keeping it in the text.) But I made that baked asparagus casserole, and it's good—and perhaps we should all get off our high horses every once in a while and benefit from a guilty pleasure. Not to mention the fact that this recipe gives a picture of what the Women's Alliance of the All Souls Unitarian Church of Tulsa, Oklahoma (still operational today, set to celebrate its centennial in 2021), actually served at their fundraising social in January 1959. Who knew? (Note: We also decided to include just one gelatin mold, the best of the lot, from Mrs. Thelma Brownfield, also of the All Souls Church: It contains two kinds of gelatin, cottage cheese, and crushed pineapple, and it turns out a lovely shade of soft mint green.)

Yet another rocky sea to navigate: Clem's personal peccadilloes. By this I mean, chiefly, her sweet tooth. What do you do when you inherit a recipe collection that contains sixty-one recipes for pie but just three for broccoli? How about thirty-eight cookie recipes but only one—one!—green salad. What it shows more than anything else is not only that American home cooks used to bake a lot more—and probably didn't refer to or require as many recipes for things like vegetable side dishes and salads as we do today—but also that the person choosing the recipes (Hi, Clem) was an unabashed dessert lover. This can be a problem when you are trying to present a universal picture of a national appetite and offer readers ideas for what to make for dinner in an age when obesity is a national crisis. (Even Americans today probably don't out-eat desserts to vegetables by twenty to one.) Our solution: One recipe for Perfect Pie Crust (page 13) and a significant narrowing down of the pies to the very best of the bunch.

Since I first read *How America Eats*, I have always felt the presence of Clem, like a voice whispering to me over my shoulder, urging me on, pressuring me not to be lazy, poking me to find a more muscular verb, encouraging me to rewrite, re-edit, revise—Clem was famous for her drafts, for writing columns until she got them just so—and she has informed my writing in ways both obvious and subtle. I have always felt that she left a powerful trail of breadcrumbs behind her, in the form of the tremendous archives at K-State, but mostly in *How America Eats*, so that we who came after could share these stories and could know both her and ourselves.

I have talked a lot about the quirky things in this book—all those damn pies!—but I haven't mentioned the fact that this is the place to find the recipes that we consider truly "American." Within these pages are the first nationally published recipes for the now-totemic dishes we all know and love: Key Lime Pie (page 355), New England Boiled Dinner (page 38), Southern Fried Chicken (page 269), New York Cheesecake (page 95), Caesar Salad (page 618), Oyster Pan Roast (page 84), Brunswick Stew (page 318). It was a revelation to publish recipes for foods like guacamole (page 806) and pizza (page 668) in those days; some people in this country still hadn't even heard of them, but Clem had. And Clem worked with both the homey (Red Flannel Hash, page 40) and the haute (Lobster Newburg, page 4). Finally, Clem also veered gingerly and gently into the "ethnic food" aisle, offering up recipes for dishes like *Hamantaschen* (page 642), Chicken *Paprikas* (page 632), and *Albondigas* (page 464).

It has been a great pleasure presenting the recipes that Clem so lovingly hunted down and committed to type. Now you can have the opportunity to virtually walk in her shoes, all across America's kitchens. But if you should hear a voice whispering to you the next time you're standing facing the stove, firmly directing you as you stir a pot of soup, don't say I didn't warn you.

KELLY ALEXANDER

Preface

THIS BOOK HAS BEEN TWELVE YEARS in the writing. It was in January 1948 I started crisscrossing the United States as roving Food Editor for *This Week Magazine*—my assignment, tell "How America Eats." I have traveled by train, plane, automobile, by mule back, on foot—in all over 800,000 miles.

I have ranged from the lobster pots of Maine to the vineyards of California, from the sugar shanties of Vermont to the salmon canneries in Alaska. I have collected these recipes from a wide variety of kitchens: farm kitchens, apartment kitchenettes, governors' mansions, hamburger diners, tea rooms, and from the finest restaurants with great chefs in charge. I have eaten with crews on fishing boats and enjoyed slum gullion at a Hobo Convention.

I have eaten many regional specialties I had never eaten before—cioppino on Fisherman's Wharf in San Francisco, Alaskan King Crab of the North Pacific in Seattle, mango ice cream in Tampa, chawed on cuts of fresh sugar cane in Louisiana, eaten roasted young goat in San Antonio, and roasted fresh trffles flown in from Italy at the Four Seasons in New York City.

This book is based on personal interviews with more than 2,000 of the country's best cooks. And I have eaten every dish in the book at the table where I found it. I have eaten each dish again when the recipes were tested by home economists in *This Week*'s kitchen.

Now a pause to look back. How does America eat? She eats on the fat of the land. She eats in every language. For the most part, however, even with the increasingly popular trend toward foreign foods, the dishes come to the table with an American accent.

From the very beginning, American dishes came from many countries, made from recipes German, Swedish, Italian, ad infinitum. . . . In some regions these dishes have kept their original character. But more often, over the years, they have been mixed and Americanized.

The pioneer mother created dishes with foods available. These we call regional. It is to these, perhaps, I have given the greatest emphasis here. However, I am not given to food favorites, hold no food prejudices. Good food is good food, wherever you find it. Many of these recipes were salvaged from batter-splashed, hand-written notebooks. The great majority had never been printed until they appeared in *This Week*. They are word-of-mouth hand-downs from mother to daughter. To get such recipes takes everlasting patience, and a dash of effrontery, too.

Recipes are included for the quick-cook artists, who love doing things the easy way. Some dishes are for gourmets who are happy to spend two days a week preparing one great dinner.

My files are bulging with America's best eating. I had a hard time to choose this small sampling, which I sincerely hope you will enjoy to the last mouthful.

CLEMENTINE PADDLEFORD
New York City
August, 1960

NEW

ENGLAND

MAINE

New England dishes are as devoid of fuss and feathers as a Puritan's hat. And although New England isn't of any great size she can claim more dishes to her credit than any other region in the United States. Her specialties are acclaimed nationwide, having traveled inland by waterway and covered wagon; New England food, like her houses and her furniture, followed with the frontier.

But taste these foods in their own home states; they have a flavor apart. Just why we don't know. Perhaps because New England cooks seem less inclined to take liberties with recipes. They seem to know, as their grandmothers before them, that the glory of the food lies in its robust simplicity.

Each summer New England plays host to thousands of visitors from all parts of the country, all of them eager to sample her traditional fare. Some know what they want: baked Indian pudding, real apple pandowdy, clam pie, and clam chowder.

To miss out on the good native eating is to forfeit half the pleasure of your holiday. But you must know what to ask for, then be willing to trail it far into the hills off main thoroughfares, or better yet, to be invited to sit down at a home table and eat with the family.

I have done just that, a hundred times and more, recipe-gathering through the New England states.

It was in Rockland, Maine, lobster capital of the United States, that I started my New England recipe hunt. Here fishermen boast of taking seven and a half million pounds of the handsome green crustaceans annually from the North Atlantic.

June lay gently on the shoulder. The fragrance of balsam mingled with the ocean's salty breath. Walter Stanley, fifty years a lobsterman, had invited me down to the bay to see how it goes, tending 125 traps. A long lean Yankee, with scraggly gray eyebrows and deep-set blue eyes cool with salt distance. He pulls his living from the sea at the end of 360 feet of warp. Come hell or high water, war or peace, Walter Stanley goes trawling.

His boat was heading for deep water. Stanley doesn't go for inshore fishing. He voiced his theories with decision: "Deep-water lobsters are harder shelled, larger sized, sweeter eating." Mingled with the smell of the sea is a bitter, lively smell from a barrel of dead fish, Stanley's bait, redfish today. He uses only natural bait like herring, mackerel, tuna, clams—none of that synthetic stuff!

We made a wide circle. Then our lobsterman let the engine idle. He put out his hand, took a lobster buoy and started pulling the warp over the snatch block, wrapping it around the winch head. The boat bucked and heaved. Slowly the trap came up from the ocean floor that lay anywhere from 200 to 300 feet down.

A fluttering inside the trap. Stanley opened the door and reached among the scissorlike claws. He brought out a lobster, next a crab, another crab. The crabs he hurled back into the sea. They went spinning, glinting in the sun like lighted pinwheels. Now a horny starfish. A crab, another crab, that was the catch. New bait from the barrel, the high-smelling redfish, was secured to the iron spike in the center of the floor, and the trap went back over the side.

From early morning until mid-afternoon the motor pounded away burning up gas, using oil. It wasn't good fishing. Stanley had but fourteen lobsters for his trouble. Going home he was in a reminiscent mood, saying that when he was a sprig of a lad lobsters had been so plentiful they raked them out of the water at low tide and one year piled them on the land to use as fertilizer. That was fifty years ago. And thirty years ago you could get them out of pools at low tide. Only twelve years ago Stanley,

with one helper, had sometimes made a hundred dollars a day.

We asked our Mr. Stanley how he liked his lobsters. "Steamed," he said, "and plenty of butter." He doesn't want pepper or even a smidgen of salt. A lobster steamed in seawater gets salt enough. And that's how he does it! Down Maine way even the prepared dishes are simple as simple—this to give the lobster a chance to make the most of its delicate flavor.

Back in the harbor town I went all out for recipes. "Who makes a crackerjack lobster Newburg?" I asked, and a dozen Rockland women told me to talk to Mildred Richardson, wife of the late John M. Richardson, her husband the former publisher of the *Courier Gazette*, and she too worked on the paper as society editor and clerk of the corporation. She had her finger in many a civic as well as lobster pie. The Richardsons both were born in the town; there was little going on that they didn't know.

Publisher John claimed his wife was weaned on the juice of the clam and her first solid food was lobster Newburg. Truth is, they both liked lobster so well they had it two or three times a week, at home or in a restaurant. They liked lobster as is, lobster in sauces, and lobster stew as a whole-meal dish with nothing else but dill pickles and oyster crackers.

When I caught up with the cracker-jack lobster Newburg I had been looking for I labeled it "Rockland's Best."

Rockland Lobster Newburg

9 large egg yolks, lightly beaten

3 cups heavy cream

¾ cup milk

¼ cup all-purpose flour

¾ cup (1½ sticks) unsalted butter, softened

3 cups cooked lobster meat
(or the cooked meat of 3 fresh lobsters, 1½ pounds each)

1 teaspoon salt

3 tablespoons sherry wine

Serves 8

In the top pot of a double boiler over medium heat, combine the egg yolks, cream, and milk and heat to very hot but not boiling, stirring occasionally. Remove from the heat.

In a medium bowl, using a fork to combine, blend the flour and soft butter to a paste. Gradually stir the paste into the egg yolk mixture until well blended. Add the lobster meat and salt.

Put the pot back on the stove over medium heat and stir constantly until thickened, about 10 minutes. At the last minute, add the sherry.

Spoon the lobster Newburg over buttered toast points.

THE RICHEST LOBSTER STEW I can ever remember was made by the late Robert P. Tristram Coffin, a Pierce Professor of English at Bowdoin College. Dr. Coffin was a Pulitzer Prize winner honored for his salty prose dealing with the rugged beauties of his state and its headstrong people. He was a major poet of America, an authority on modern poetry who had lectured and read his own works at hundreds of colleges and clubs from East coast to West. He was an artist as well, illustrating his own books. He had a green thumb for growing things. But the accomplishment in which he took greatest pride was the making of this lobster stew—a poem in the eating. Hearing that I was in Maine to collect lobster recipes, Dr. Coffin invited me for dinner at his salt-water farm in Pennellville, a few miles out of Brunswick.

Supper was a three-piece meal, the first course quahogs, which poet Coffin had spent the afternoon digging. Save room for the stew! In came broad soup plates, each holding a cupful. That was a stew! The flavors had melted together after a day of aging. There was a pink lobster blush on the surface that disappeared and came again as one plied the spoon. Down-east pilot crackers were passed and a bowl of dill pickles. Dessert was a platter of freshly made doughnuts with the coffee.

"About the recipe, Dr. Coffin," I had my pencil in hand.

"You must know the history of each lobster you cook," said my host. "But if you must pick your lobsters at the local market, the only alternative is to get them lively. Cook in Maine seawater," the Doctor directed. . . . Here we translate his directions into rules that will work anywhere.

Dr. Coffin's Lobster Stew

4 cups Maine seawater or 4 cups fresh water with 2 tablespoons salt, plus additional salt to taste

6 medium lobsters (about 1¼ pounds each)

½ cup (1 stick) unsalted butter

6 cups whole or 2% milk

2 cups heavy cream

Serves 6

Bring 2 cups of the saltwater to a boil in a 10- to 12-quart pot with a tight-fitting lid. Lay in 3 lobsters on their backs, shell side down, to steam in their own juices. Cover and steam over high heat 7 to 8 minutes. Remove from the pot and repeat with the remaining 2 cups saltwater and lobsters. The meat will be slightly underdone; pick it from the shell while hot. Remove the intestinal vein and lungs. Chop the meat into large bite-size chunks.

Melt the butter in a large pot over low heat and add the lobster meat; sauté gently for 2 to 3 minutes. Add the milk, stirring clockwise constantly to keep the mixture from coagulating; bring almost to a froth but not to a boil, then add the cream and once again bring almost to a froth. Check the meat for doneness; if not quite cooked through, simmer for a few additional minutes. Remove from the heat and season with salt to taste. Serve immediately.

STILL ON THE SEAFOOD trail I journeyed on in search of traditional recipes to Wiscasset, Maine, on the Sheepscot River, a lovely old town with architectural elegance and down-east flavor. This town forever looks back to the days when it was the biggest seaport north of Boston.

In Wiscasset I met the Burrage sisters, Madeleine and Mildred, artists both. Madeleine sets jewels, having the stones cut to her own specifications, setting only on order. Mildred, a painter, was well known for her murals. Both sisters were good cooks with a love for collecting recipes of the heirloom kind.

On a stifling June afternoon, by way of angling for an invitation for dinner, we rang the Burrage door bell and asked first thing for a look into their grandma's cookbook. We were invited into the green silence of the sleepy garden of the house.

Iced tea was poured, the pitcher wearing a bouquet of fresh mint. Madeleine brought out a box of her beautiful jewelry—rings, pins, bracelets. Mildred brought the cookbook and talked about the fish balls which had been a perennially popular supper dish at Grandma's house.

The sisters serve the whiskery brown balls for luncheon with cabbage, or sometimes they make tiny little ones to pierce on toothpicks and pass with cocktails.

The cookbook is an old copybook with a brown paper cover which someone used as a logbook between 1845 and 1850. Later Grandma took over, pasting in recipes clipped from newspaper and penning in those borrowed from friends. A bit of everything from cream of clam soup to perfect pie crust.

Grandma's Salt Cod Balls

1 pound center-cut skinless boneless
salt cod, rinsed well

2 cups diced uncooked peeled potatoes

2 large eggs, beaten

Salt and freshly ground black pepper

2 cups vegetable oil

Sea salt and lemon wedges

Serves 6 as an appetizer

Soak the cod in a large bowl with water to cover by 2 inches. Cover the bowl with plastic wrap and refrigerate overnight. When ready to cook, drain and cut the fish into bite-size pieces.

In a large pot, combine the fish with the potatoes and add water to cover. Place over medium heat, bring to a simmer, and cook until the potatoes and fish are cooked through, about 15 minutes. Drain the fish and potatoes in a colander, then return them to the pot and mash them together using a potato masher.

Add the eggs and beat until the mixture is smooth; no lumps should remain. Taste and add salt if needed. Season with pepper to your pleasure.

Heat the oil in a 5- to 6-quart heavy pot over medium heat until it registers 385 to 390 degrees on a deep-frying thermometer. Working in batches, drop the mixture by tablespoonfuls into the hot fat and fry until golden brown, about 1 minute. Remove from the oil with a slotted spoon or tongs and drain on paper towels. Sprinkle with sea salt and serve with lemon wedges, if you like.

I TRAVELED ON, LITERALLY hot on the trail; it was blistering summer weather. Even when I left the shore I found lobster, lobster everywhere. So it was a pleasant surprise to sip the raspberry shrub served at the home of Senator Margaret Chase Smith.

But Margaret Smith, the senator from the Pine Tree State, likes her lobster too. She puts it in a salad. Lettuce for the base, then big lobster pieces mixed with finely cut celery. Sometimes she adds grapefruit sections or she may garnish the salad with tomato quarters. An old-fashioned boiled mayonnaise is her first choice for dressing; or French is all right. Olives for the top decoration. This salad she serves usually for luncheon with medium-sized baked Maine potatoes. Ice cream for dessert with crushed strawberries.

"It's an old wives' tale," Senator Smith said, "that lobster and ice cream are bitter enemies. They go wonderfully together."

Now to that raspberry shrub. Growing raspberries was the beloved hobby of the senator's late husband, Congressman Clyde Smith. He grew the largest, sweetest red raspberries anywhere in the East, at their home in Skowhegan, Maine. The very finest of these berries were served with a dusting of sugar, wading in cream.

Mrs. Smith still makes her grandmother's Raspberry Shrub which she serves as a symbol of old-time hospitality: a joyous drink. Dilute the rich, vinous syrup with water, pour over cracked ice, a refreshment to cool and content the drinker!

Raspberry Shrub Syrup

4 quarts fresh raspberries

1 quart cider vinegar

5 cups sugar

Makes 5 cups syrup

Clean and pick over the berries. In a large bowl, cover the berries with the vinegar. Cover the bowl with plastic wrap and let stand in a cool, dry place for 4 days.

When the berries are ready, strain through a fine-mesh sieve into a bowl, pressing gently on the solids and then discarding them. What remains should be clear red raspberry juice with no pulp or seeds.

In a large heavy saucepan, combine the raspberry mixture and sugar and bring to a boil over medium-high heat. Reduce the heat and simmer uncovered for 15 minutes.

Pour the syrup into a bowl or bottle, cover, and chill in the refrigerator.

To make a shrub: Serve the syrup diluted, with three parts cold water to one part syrup. Fill a tall glass with crushed ice and pour in the syrup. Tinkle it, whiff it, sip it, and smile.

VERMONT

Oh to be in Vermont, now that April's there! The sun shines warm, the nights sting cold, it's sugarin' time in the great maple orchards of the northern tier states. Hang up the musical pails. It's speed work now, no recapturing the sweetness once the tree buds.

Feed the fires. Smoke curls from the sugar shanties. Inside there is filmlike gloom, made by the sweet-laden steam as the watery fluid boils into golden nectar. Sugaring, amateur or scientific, is but the process of taking sap from the maple and taking the water from the sap.

We travel to the north hills, to Derby Line Village, Vermont, a stone's throw from the Canadian border, to the 420-acre farm of Ira H. Aldrich for a sugar-on-the-snow party, our very first.

"Giddyap Nellie! Giddyap Chubb!" The tractor driven by twelve-year-old Bobby Aldrich gave a gasoline snort. We made a run, a jump for the edge of the sled, grabbed a firm hold on the sap-gathering tub and were off. The tractor nosed across the snow-covered meadow through muddy gullies into the woods heading for a violet smoke spiral curling from the chimney of a pitched-roof sugar house tightly hugging the hill.

Here we were; here was Ira smiling his welcome through the steam clouding the shanty door. The crowd tumbled off with cups, forks, and spoons, but we stayed on the sled for a ride through the bush to see the sap gathered. The buckets were like silver against the maples' grayness. Tall, proud trees, some still in their teens, and others there when Jefferson was signing the Declaration of Independence. Scurrying boys and men carried brimming pails to dump into the gathering tub. We were sloshed wet with sap. We drank sap fresh from the pail, a clear white liquid, like sweetish rainwater. It tasted of sun, of the earth and the weather.

Back at the sugar house the load was pipe-drained into a storage tank that, in turn, runs the sap to the evaporator, the biggest candy pan you ever did see, big enough to evaporate 300 gallons of sap in an hour.

Ira Aldrich was a ghost shadow in the steam, skimming the foam. Laughter and talk, rattle of spoon against cup, while the bubbling frothing syrup made a music quite its own: *oo-ieoo-ie,* like a faraway whistle heard through a fog. We heard Ira Aldrich tell his wife, "It's okay, Bea. Get a dipperful now and get it out on the snow."

Snow-filled pails waited on the outdoor table substituting for snow-banks. Mrs. Aldrich poured on drizzles of the thick syrup. Forks got busy stirring the mass. A half-warm, half-cold shiny brittle was formed, fine-tasting to the eager mouths. Syrup was poured into cups and stirred into soft cream. Dip in the yeast-raised doughnuts or dunk them in the hot syrup without the bother of "creaming" the cup. Ira Aldrich kept the syrup boiling, and now a fresh pouring. Stir it this time and a warm whitish sugar comes under the spoon. We ate on and on. But how differently this rich taste compared with the pale ghost taste of the sap. Scientists say the characteristic maple flavor is not in the sap as it comes from the tree, but is developed by the cooking.

When new-crop maple syrup goes to market it is bright, clear, fragrant, and the sugar light, hard, grainy. We learn the label language. "Fancy" means finest, made of pure maple sap containing not more than 35 percent water, a pale straw-colored liquid, clear as a dewdrop, not too heavy in body.

Other grades include A, B, and C and must meet the same standards except their color may run light to dark.

Maple syrup is handy to use. Pour a golden trickle over the cooked breakfast cereal, over the grapefruit. Use it occasionally to sweeten and flavor baked beans instead of molasses. Maple candy the sweet potatoes. Heat the syrup, mix with chopped nuts, a fine sauce for desserts. Apple-baking day, fill the cored centers with raisins, with nuts, add maple syrup for sweetness. Vermonters make a delicately thin pancake to roll and serve, three to a portion, deep in maple syrup, topped with whipped cream—a crêpe Suzette à la New England.

Everywhere we found native Vermonters almost swimming in syrup. Mrs. James Egerton says she uses eighteen gallons of maple syrup a season. The Egertons like maple syrup to sweeten cakes, candies and puddings. But the way they like it best is as a dunk for buttered bread.

One of Mrs. Egerton's nicest recipes is for a fluffy maple frosting.

Maple Frosting

1¾ cups maple syrup

1 large egg white, stiffly beaten

½ cup chopped walnuts

Makes about 2 cups, enough to cover one 9 x 13-inch cake pan or the tops and sides of two 8- or 9-inch cake rounds

In a 1-quart saucepan, bring the maple syrup to a boil over medium heat and boil for 5 minutes. Remove the pan from the heat. Gradually pour the hot syrup over the beaten egg white, beating constantly until the frosting forms soft peaks. Gently fold in the walnuts. The frosting may be stored in an airtight container or heavy-duty freezer bag in the refrigerator for up to a month.

Maple Syrup Pie

1 (8-inch) Perfect Pie Crust (page 13)

2 large eggs, separated

1 cup maple syrup

1½ tablespoons unsalted butter, melted

½ teaspoon vanilla extract

½ cup sugar

½ cup water

½ cup finely chopped walnuts

Serves 6 to 8

Preheat the oven to 325 degrees. Line an 8-inch glass pie plate with 1 rolled-out round of the Perfect Pie Crust. Trim the overhang to 1 inch, fold it under itself and crimp decoratively. Refrigerate until chilled, about 15 minutes.

Line the pastry with foil and fill with pie weights or dried beans. Bake for 30 minutes, or until nearly cooked through and dry to the touch. Carefully remove the foil and weights. Bake for 10 minutes longer, until golden. Let cool completely.

Make the filling: In medium bowl, whisk together the egg yolks, maple syrup, butter, ¼ teaspoon of the vanilla, ¼ cup of the sugar, and the water. Cook in the top portion of a double boiler over boiling water, stirring constantly until thick, about 10 minutes. Remove from the heat and stir in the walnuts. Allow the filling to cool, then pour the filling into the pie crust.

Make the meringue topping: In a medium bowl using an electric mixer, beat the egg whites until stiff. Add the remaining ¼ cup sugar, 1 tablespoon at a time, beating well after each addition. Continue beating until stiff peaks form. Blend in the remaining ¼ teaspoon vanilla. Spread the meringue over the filling. Bake for 25 to 30 minutes, until firm and lightly browned.

Perfect Pie Crust

1 cup all-purpose flour

¼ teaspoon salt

½ cup (1 stick) cold unsalted butter, cut into ½-inch pieces

2 tablespoons ice-cold water

Makes pastry for one 8- or 9-inch pie

In a large bowl, combine the flour with the salt. Add the butter, using your fingertips to break it up into the mixture until it resembles coarse meal. Use a pastry cutter to further cut the butter into the flour until pea-size clumps form.

Gradually add the cold water, stirring with a fork. Turn the pastry out onto a lightly floured surface. Using a pastry scraper if you like or just your hands, gather the pastry together and pat it into a disk. Wrap the disk in plastic and refrigerate for at least 30 minutes or up to 2 days.

When you are ready to use: On a lightly floured surface, roll out the pastry disk to a 10- to 12-inch round. Ease the pastry into an 8- or 9-inch pie plate. Trim the overhang to ½ inch and refrigerate until ready to fill and bake.

When you are ready to bake, follow the specific instructions for your pie recipe.

MISS SADIE F. HARD had a boardinghouse and a reputation for being the best cook in the maple country. One of her much-borrowed recipes was for maple graham bread.

Miss Hard said, tartly, "It don't amount to much," but let's pay her no mind. We already knew its local fame before we went begging.

Maple Graham Bread

2 cups buttermilk

½ teaspoon baking soda

1 cup maple syrup

1 teaspoon salt

½ cup sifted all-purpose flour

3½ cups sifted graham flour or finely crushed graham crackers

1 cup raisins

2 teaspoons baking powder

Makes 1 large loaf, 10 to 12 servings

Preheat the oven to 325 degrees. Generously grease and flour a large 10 x 5-inch loaf pan.

In a large bowl, whisk together the buttermilk, baking soda, and maple syrup. Stir in the salt with a wooden spoon, then the flours, and then the raisins. Add the baking powder and stir until well combined. The dough should be sticky but fairly smooth. Turn the dough into a loaf pan. Bake for 1½ hours, or until golden brown and a wooden pick or skewer comes out clean.

IT WAS EARLY IN April, the start of the season in "the sugar bush," that I skidded into luck. Back roads were softening. Melted snow from the deep ravines had turned brooks into rushing torrents. Late afternoon, rolling along near the Canadian border, the car skidded, a back wheel gently buried itself to the hub in soft earth.

Two miles to walk into Newport, a little town of 6,000, to find a garageman, a treasure of an inn, and a wonderful recipe for yeast-raised doughnuts to be dunked into the golden syrup of the maple.

The inn I stumbled into, foot-tired and hungry, was the Governor Prouty. Just a spacious old home, that of George H. Prouty, governor of Vermont back in 1908, a house built by his father. Now Nephew John Azro Prouty and wife Dorothy, a girl from the Pennsylvania Dutch country, have done the place in soft and cheerful colors. Only six bedrooms, but the food, that's the thing.

We dropped in unexpectedly, too late for lunch, too soon for dinner. It's good company manners up there to serve a caller coffee with raised doughnuts, these to dunk in warm maple syrup.

Mrs. Elizabeth LaRose, a tall akimbo sort of Vermont woman, was the pastry cook in the Governor Prouty kitchen. A tender heart she had for an admirer of her skill. She fed us these doughnuts in half-dozen sets and pressed the recipe into my hand when, car in order, I rolled on again.

Newport Raised Doughnuts

¾ cup milk

½ package active dry yeast (about ½ ounce)

1 cup lukewarm water

1 cup sugar

1 teaspoon salt

3 cups all-purpose flour

⅓ cup unsalted butter

1 large egg, beaten

½ teaspoon grated nutmeg

Vegetable oil for deep frying, 2–3 tablespoons or more as needed

Makes about 2 dozen

In a small saucepan over medium heat, heat the milk until it just begins to bubble. Immediately remove the pan from the heat, pour the milk into a medium bowl, and cool to lukewarm.

Dissolve the yeast in the lukewarm water until it becomes foamy, about 3 minutes, then add to the milk. To the mixture, add ½ cup of the sugar, the salt, and 1 cup of the flour, stirring together until smooth. Scrape the dough out onto a floured surface and use a pastry scraper to knead the dough until smooth. The dough should be soft and slightly sticky but smooth and elastic.

Gather the dough into a ball, transfer it to a lightly oiled bowl, and cover with a sheet of oiled plastic wrap. Let rise in a warm place until it doubles in bulk, about 2 hours.

Melt the butter and cool slightly. Meanwhile, punch down the dough. Add the melted butter to the dough. Add the egg, the remaining ½ cup sugar, and the nutmeg, mixing and kneading well. Add the remaining 2 cups flour. Using a pastry scraper, gather the dough into a ball again and place back into the bowl. Cover and refrigerate the dough for 2 hours or overnight. It should double in bulk.

Turn the chilled dough out onto a lightly floured board until smooth and elastic. Throw more flour down on surface and roll the dough out to a rectangle about ½ inch thick. Using a floured 3½-inch doughnut cutter, cut out as many doughnuts as possible and transfer them to waxed paper. Loosely cover the doughnuts with waxed paper and let them rise until soft and billowy, about 20 minutes.

In a large heavy saucepan or deep cast-iron skillet, heat the oil, at a depth of several inches, until it registers 350 degrees on a deep-frying thermometer. Working in batches, carefully add the doughnuts to the hot oil and fry until browned, about 1 minute per side. Mrs. LaRose uses an old-fashioned wire egg beater to turn the doughnuts; a wooden spoon with slots is a good utensil if you don't have a wire frying basket. Drain the doughnuts on paper towels. When almost completely cooled, sprinkle with sugar or leave plain if you plan to dunk them in syrup. Serve immediately.

OLD HOUSES ARE GENTLE THINGS

"If thou of fortune be bereft
And in thy store there be but left
Two loaves—sell one, and with the dole
Buy hyacinths to feed thy soul."

This quotation is the reason for the naming of Hyacinth House, the home and "inn of sorts" of Mrs. Mildred M. Rutherford of South Woodstock, Vermont.

It's an old house and old houses are gentle things; this one particularly so, built to beauty in 1812. It stands high on a knoll far back from the road, a stream between. The far side faces east into pine-covered mountains, soft green against the sky.

Mistress of the house was in her parlor-office-bedroom-den. She looked pert as you please propped high against the pillows of the broad bed. And pretty, too, the soft blue shawl around her shoulders, her white curls tight and trim, pinned high on her head. On every side cookbooks, account books, recipe files.

It was arthritis that put Mrs. Rutherford to bed but she didn't complain, she didn't give up. A strangely ingenious woman, she took a downstairs room within earshot of the kitchen and continued to be the mistress of the house. Here she plans her menus, keeps her accounts—everything possible is within reach of her hand. A smiling room without the feel of discontent, a room comforting and self-contained, a little world complete.

Her laughter came quickly into the tick-tock quiet of the place. She adjusted her glasses and looked through a small dilapidated book, yellowed with age. "I love this book," she said. "All of these are old New England recipes." Her eyes, hesitating between gray and blue, held a quiet smile.

The early winter twilight pushed thick and furry against the windows. Through the bedroom door came the smell of baking beans. Throughout the house a smell aromatic and stored, of wood, of chintz, of floors much walked upon.

These beans are a Saturday-night supper served with tomato-juice cocktail, boiled home-cured ham with homemade jellies, and mustard pickles and thick rich chili sauce. Always the homemade brown bread. Cole slaw for the salad; hot-milk sponge-cake the dessert or a lemon sponge pudding, this is nice.

Home-Baked Beans

4 cups dried navy beans

1 teaspoon baking soda

1 pound bacon, cut into ½-inch pieces

½ cup sugar

½ cup maple syrup

1 tablespoon salt

1½ teaspoons ground ginger

1 teaspoon dry mustard

1 small onion, peeled

Serves 8

Wash and pick over the beans and soak overnight in water to cover by 2 inches.

When you're ready to cook the beans, place them in a large stockpot with their soaking water and add the baking soda. Place over medium heat, bring to a simmer, and simmer until the skins ruffle when blown upon, about 1 hour.

Preheat the oven to 200 degrees.

Drain off the water and return the beans to the pot. Add the bacon pieces, sugar, maple syrup, salt, ginger, and mustard and bury the onion deep in the beans. Fill the pot with hot water. Cover and bake for 8 hours, adding more water if necessary and removing the cover and allowing the beans to brown during the last hour of baking.

Hot-Milk Sponge Cake

½ cup milk

1 tablespoon unsalted butter

2 large eggs

1 cup sugar

1 cup sifted cake flour

1½ teaspoons baking powder

¼ teaspoon salt

½ teaspoon vanilla extract

½ teaspoon lemon extract

Serves 8

Preheat the oven to 350 degrees. Generously grease an 8-inch square cake pan.

Combine the milk and butter in a small saucepan. Place over medium heat and bring almost to a boil. Remove from the heat and set aside.

In a medium bowl using an electric mixer, beat the eggs for about 2 minutes, until frothy. Add the sugar, beating thoroughly until well combined, 4 to 5 minutes. The mixture will turn light yellow and thicken. Add the flour and baking powder. Add the salt, the extracts, and the hot milk mixture. Quickly mix to just combine, only about 10 seconds, and quickly pour the batter, which will be very thin, into the prepared pan.

Bake for 30 minutes, or until the cake begins to come away from the sides of the pan and is golden brown and springy to the touch. Cool on a wire rack for about 10 minutes, then invert the pan to a platter (but don't remove the pan) and cool completely for about 1 hour. Lift off the pan. Serve the cake plain or with cocoa sauce (recipe follows), if you like.

Cocoa Sauce

1 cup heavy cream

3 tablespoons sugar

3 tablespoons cocoa powder

Makes 1 cup

In a medium bowl, whisk together all the ingredients well. Cover and refrigerate for a full 3 hours. When ready to serve, whip with a whisk or an electric mixer until stiff. Serve with sponge cake or fruit.

Note: This "sauce" is actually more like chocolate-flavored whipped cream.

Sponge Cookies

3 large eggs

¾ cup sugar

1½ cups cake flour

2 teaspoons baking powder

¾ teaspoon lemon or almond extract

Makes about 5 dozen

Preheat the oven to 400 degrees. Generously grease 2 large baking sheets with vegetable oil.

In a large mixing bowl using an electric mixer, beat the eggs until frothy. Add the sugar, beating until pale and thick.

Sift the flour and baking powder into a medium bowl and slowly stir into the egg mixture. Add the extract.

Drop the batter, ½ teaspoon at a time, on the prepared baking sheets, spacing the cookies about 3 inches apart.

Bake in batches for about 5 minutes each, until golden. Watch closely; these cookies scorch easily. Carefully transfer to wire racks to cool completely.

This cookie is quickly made and delicious with ice cream or to pass with a fruit compote.

NOT FAR AWAY, in Bethel, Vermont, I met a princess, a wonderful woman, the late Anna Maria Schwarzenberg. She invited me to dinner to try her pot roast. All the way there I kept saying to myself, "What a crazy idea to go to Vermont to eat a Viennese pot roast." What was good enough for Grandma is good enough for me, I thought. For my New England grandma and her league certainly could go to bat any day with one of those fellows in a tall white hat—French, Viennese, or a princess for that matter. I found out differently.

   This particular pot roast is a chef's creation taken from a family cookbook, written in 1824 by F. G. Zenker, first chef of His Highness Prince Joseph Schwarzenberg, great-grandfather of the princess.

   Grandma, I discovered, had a thing or two to learn. That royal roast has the Yankee variety beaten, if not by a mile, by an herb or two, or that heady baptism of wine.

   Ummm—something good cooking. The smell of it came creeping in from the kitchen reaching into every cranny and corner. "It's the pot roast," Miss Schwarzenberg said. "Shall we eat first and do the recipes later?"

   Dinner began with a clear chicken-stock soup, floating small farina dumplings. The pot roast came cooked with cabbage, passed with fried potatoes, with green beans slightly minted, a tossed green salad. Star guest, the famous Sacher torte of Vienna, served with whipped cream.

House of Schwarzenberg Pot Roast

3½ to 4 pounds chuck roast

Salt and freshly ground
black pepper

2 tablespoons vegetable oil

1 carrot

1 stalk celery

8 small sprigs parsley

1 bay leaf

2 tablespoons unsalted butter

1 medium onion, sliced

3 shallots

3 medium tomatoes,
peeled and chopped

2 cups beef stock

2 cups white or red wine

½ cup cognac or whisky

⅓ cup dry sherry wine

1 medium head green cabbage,
cut into 8 wedges

3 tablespoons heavy cream

Serves 8

Preheat the oven to 325 degrees.

Wipe the meat with a clean cloth or paper towel to dry. Sprinkle generously all over with salt and pepper and allow to come to room temperature.

Heat the oil in a Dutch oven or casserole over medium heat. Sear the meat on all sides to a deep golden brown, then add the carrot, celery, parsley, and bay leaf.

In a separate pan, melt the butter over medium heat. Add the onion and shallots and sauté until golden. Add to the meat, then add the tomatoes, stock, wine, cognac, and sherry. Cover tightly and bring to a low simmer.

Put the casserole in the oven and continue to cook for 3½ hours, or until the meat is fork-tender. About 10 to 15 minutes before it's done, add the cabbage and replace the cover. When the cabbage is just tender, remove the meat and cabbage to a warm platter. If the liquid remaining is more than 3 cups, reduce to roughly that amount, strain, then return to a simmer. Add the cream and stir well; adjust the seasoning. Serve with fried, mashed, or roasted potatoes, if you like.

Sacher Torte

1¼ cups (2½ sticks) unsalted butter, softened

¾ cup sugar

¼ teaspoon salt

6 ounces plus 1¾ cups semisweet chocolate chips, melted and slightly cooled

6 large eggs, separated

1½ cups all-purpose flour

½ to 1 cup raspberry or apricot jam

Serves 8

Preheat the oven to 350 degrees. Grease and lightly flour a 9 x 3½-inch springform pan.

In a large bowl using an electric mixer, beat together ¾ cup (1½ sticks) of the butter with the sugar until the mixture is fluffy. Add the salt and 1 cup of the melted chocolate, beating together well. Add in the egg yolks, one at a time, beating well after each addition. Set aside.

In a medium bowl using an electric mixer, beat the egg whites until stiff but not dry. Fold the egg whites into the chocolate-yolk mixture, then fold in the flour. Turn the batter into the prepared pan. Bake for 40 to 50 minutes, until a wooden pick or skewer inserted in the center comes out clean. Cool the cake in the pan for 20 minutes, then remove the ring and base and transfer to a rack to cool completely. (The cake may be made ahead up to this point and kept at room temperature for up to 2 days.)

When ready to serve, spread the jam over the top and sides of the cake. Set aside.

Make the glaze: In a small saucepan over low heat, melt the remaining ¾ cup chocolate and ½ cup (1 stick) butter, stirring constantly until blended. Remove the pan from the heat and cool until the mixture is of spreading consistency. Spread over the cake.

Serve immediately, with whipped cream, if you like.

NEW HAMPSHIRE

Something for a change. I went to Hanover, New Hampshire, to see what the young blades at Dartmouth like to eat when they are in cash and can afford an extra-good dinner. First I visited with C. Arthur Jones, Chef of the Hanover Inn. He told me steak and roast beef rate top of the list and the hot rolls disappear in half dozen sets. Salads, in recent years, are on the upswing in popularity. Caesar dressing is the one most ordered. The preferred desserts are such simplicities as cake and ice cream and rice pudding with fruit sauce. Dartmouth men are big soup eaters and the inn's cheddar cheese soup gets the laurel leaf.

———

Miss Jeanette Gill, Director of the Food Service for the college, invited me to the Outing Club to listen in while the boys gave their Sunday dinner orders. Miss Gill, who has been at the college since 1932, told me there have been radical changes in student eating habits over this period. She too notes a turn toward salads and less interest in over-rich desserts. The hamburger is more popular now than the hot dog, and the pizza is inching up on the burger. There are certain items on the menu the boys can't get enough of. One is the Dartmouth oatmeal bread, another the thick chocolate sauce and the butterscotch.

Oatmeal Bread

2½ cups boiling water

1 cup rolled oats (not instant)

2 tablespoons unsalted butter

½ cup dark molasses

2 teaspoons salt

Two ¼-ounce packages active dry yeast, about 5 teaspoons

5 to 6 cups all-purpose flour

Makes 2 loaves

In a large bowl, pour the boiling water over the oats. Stir in the butter and let the mixture cool to lukewarm. Stir in the molasses and salt. Sprinkle the yeast over the mixture and let stand until foamy, about 5 minutes.

Gradually stir in 5 cups of the flour until the mixture forms a dough. Turn the dough out onto a floured surface and knead the dough for 10 minutes, adding as much of the remaining flour as necessary to form a smooth, satiny, and elastic dough. Turn into a greased bowl, cover, and leave in a warm place to rest for about 1 hour, until doubled in bulk.

Lightly oil two 9 x 5 x 3-inch loaf pans. Shape the dough into 2 loaves and place in the pans. Cover the pans loosely with clean kitchen towels and let the dough rise until doubled again, about 1 hour.

While the dough is rising, preheat the oven to 350 degrees.

Bake the loaves for about 50 minutes, until well browned. Remove the bread from the oven and allow to cool in the pans for 10 minutes, then turn the bread out onto wire racks to cool completely.

Butterscotch Sauce

1 cup granulated sugar

1 cup firmly packed light brown sugar

1 cup light corn syrup

1 cup water

½ cup sweetened condensed milk

2 tablespoons unsalted butter (if using the sauce immediately)

¾ cup evaporated milk

½ teaspoon vanilla extract

Makes about 4 cups

In a small heavy saucepan, combine the sugars, corn syrup, and water and place over moderate heat. Stir to dissolve the sugar. Bring to a boil and then reduce heat to low and simmer over low heat without stirring for 10 minutes. Remove the pan from the heat and stir in the sweetened condensed milk. Add the butter if you will be using the sauce immediately. (If being stored for now-and-then use, omit the butter or the mixture will become granular.) Cool for 20 minutes; the sauce will thicken as it cools. Stir in the evaporated milk and vanilla.

If you're not using the sauce right away, cover and refrigerate; it will keep for up to 3 weeks. Serve it on ice cream, pudding, or cake.

Chocolate Sauce

8 ounces unsweetened chocolate

2 cups sugar

½ cup cocoa powder

1 cup hot water

1 cup light corn syrup

½ cup sweetened condensed milk

2 tablespoons unsalted butter
(if using the sauce immediately)

One 12-ounce can evaporated milk

1 teaspoon vanilla extract

Makes about 4 cups

In the top portion of a double boiler over low heat, melt the chocolate. In a small bowl, mix together the sugar and cocoa powder and stir into the melted chocolate. Add the hot water and corn syrup and stir until dissolved. Bring to a rolling boil while in the double boiler and cook for 10 minutes. Remove the sauce from the heat. Stir in the sweetened condensed milk. Add the butter if the sauce is to be used immediately. (If being stored for now-and-then use, omit the butter or the mixture will become granular.) Cool for 20 minutes; the sauce will thicken as it cools. Add the evaporated milk and stir well. Add the vanilla.

If you're not using the sauce right away, cover and refrigerate; it will keep for up to 3 weeks. Serve it on ice cream, pudding, or cake.

PRIDE IN HER TABLE

I journeyed next to peaceful little Durham, New Hampshire, to satisfy a great desire to meet Ella Bowles. She had written an excellent cookbook, *Secrets of New England Cooking,* co-authored with the late Dorothy S. Towle, a trained historian who provided the background of the good table set by early-day cooks. The book is now out of print, and that's a pity.

Ella Bowles told me about pie cupboards, and doughnuts, about taffy pulls, about that most typical of all New England meals—the Saturday-night baked-bean dinner. This is Mrs. Bowles's favorite meal, the beans served with steamed brown bread and all the pickles "I can gather together." Don't forget the cole slaw and for dessert, custard pie.

It's soldier beans that Hampshire cooks like best for baking. These beans look like yellow-eye beans, but instead of a yellow eye they have a distinctive dark brown marking said to appear as an armed soldier. This, of course, requires some imagination, like seeing the crucifix in the cross section of a banana, or the man in the moon. Unless you live in New Hampshire, forget about soldier beans—these are hard to find. Use pea beans instead.

This recipe is patterned after the earliest of New England baked beans, being sweetened with maple sugar. Molasses as a sweetener didn't become popular until the West Indian trade days. Even after cooks began pouring the dark syrup into bean pots, there were traditionalists who insisted that enough molasses to sweeten made the beans tough.

It was a delightful day I spent with Ella Bowles, enjoying not only her hospitality and the loan of her recipes but her modest tale of how as a young teacher she had married into the famed cooking family, the Bowleses of Franconia. Flo Bowles, who was Ella's mother-in-law, took pride in her table, and she cooked with a lavish hand. Daughter-in-law learned more about cooking from Flo, and handed on to me these family traditional treasures of the North Country.

Mother Bowles's Custard Pie

1 (9-inch) Perfect Pie Crust (page 13)

3 cups milk

3 large eggs, beaten

5 tablespoons sugar

¼ teaspoon salt

1 teaspoon vanilla extract

Grated nutmeg

Serves 6 to 8

Preheat the oven to 325 degrees. Line a 9-inch pie pan with the pastry and make a fluted standing rim around the edges, if you like. Set aside.

In a medium saucepan over medium heat, heat the milk until very hot but not yet boiling. Remove the pan from heat. Slowly stir the scalded milk into the beaten eggs a little at a time in a slow, steady stream. (The eggs should not be foamy.) Stir in the sugar, salt, and vanilla. Cool slightly, about 10 minutes.

Pour the filling into the unbaked pie shell and sprinkle the top of the pie with nutmeg. Bake for about 50 minutes, until the custard is set but still a little wobbly in the center and the crust is lightly browned. (Cover the edges of the pie with foil or a pie shield to prevent overbrowning during baking if necessary.) Let the pie cool completely on the rack, about 1½ hours, before serving.

Variation: To make Raspberry Custard Pie, add 1 cup raspberries to the filling and increase the sugar to ½ cup.

SPRAWLING PUMPKIN VINES

Pumpkin was a day-by-day food ranked by the Indians with corn and beans. Every patch of Indian maize had its sprawling pumpkin vines. Today we have a greater variety of squash and pumpkins and of finer quality than the Pilgrims enjoyed—but we haven't a single type that wasn't known to the prehistoric Indian races. Botanists have identified every last species from pottery reproductions taken from tombs built before the time of the Pyramids.

It was Squanto who taught the Pilgrim mothers what to do with the pumpkin and other food treasures of the New World. The Indians used dried pumpkin in soups and in stews. It was baked, it was boiled, and sometimes mashed to pat into cakes, to be fried in deep fat, a croquette of sorts. A pumpkin bread was made combining pumpkin flour with the Indian meal. Feast dinner food was pumpkin stewed and sweetened with the maple or wild honey.

Early settlers got sick and tired of this golden vegetable of the sterling assets. As an early-day poet wrote, "We have pumpkins at morning and pumpkins at noon. If it were not for the pumpkin we would be undone." They even made a drink, using the flesh of the pumpkin, if one can believe the old song: "Oh we can make liquor to sweeten our lips—of pumpkin, of parsnip, of walnut tree chips!"

It was the women of the early day colonies who turned pumpkin into pie. But those first pumpkin pies were mighty queer things made by cutting a hole in the side of the pumpkin, removing the seeds and fibrous matter, then stuffing the cavity with a mixture of apples, spices, sugar, and milk. The "plug" was stuck back and the "fruit" baked whole. Generations of cooks kept tinkering to make pumpkin pie better. One of the early-day recipes calls for thyme, sweet marjoram, rosemary, cinnamon, parsley, nutmeg, pepper, cloves, apples, currants, white wine, eggs, all to a half pound of cooked pumpkin. That conglomeration would make this honest-to-goodness 1953 pumpkin pie blush a deep orange.

Fluffy Pumpkin Pie

½ cup sugar

1 teaspoon ground cinnamon

½ teaspoon grated nutmeg

¼ teaspoon ground cloves

¼ teaspoon ground ginger

¼ teaspoon salt

1 cup cooked fresh or canned pumpkin

1 cup milk

2 large eggs and 1 large egg yolk, well beaten

1 large egg white, stiffly beaten

1 (9-inch) Perfect Pie Crust (page 13)

Serves 6 to 8

Preheat the oven to 425 degrees.

In a large bowl, mix together the sugar, spices, and salt. Add in the pumpkin and then the milk. Stir in the beaten eggs and egg yolk to combine. Fold in the beaten egg white.

Pour the filling into the pie shell. Bake for 45 minutes, or until the filling is set but trembles slightly (it will continue to set as the pie cools). Cool completely on a wire rack, about 1½ hours. (The pie can be refrigerated until ready to serve.) When ready to serve, top with swirls of whipped cream, if you like.

MASSACHUSETTS

Tell me where your grandmother came from and I can tell you
how many kinds of pie you serve for Thanksgiving. In the Midwest
two is the usual, mince and pumpkin. In the South no pie but
wine jelly, tender and trembling, topped with whipped cream.
Down East it's a threesome, cranberry, mince and pumpkin,
a sliver of each, and sometimes, harking back to the old days
around Boston, four kinds of pie were traditional for this
feast occasion—mince, cranberry, pumpkin, and a kind called
Marlborough, a glorification of everyday apple.

I had heard about Marlborough pie
but never met one face-to-face. Then
came a letter from Miss Susan L.
Ball of Lexington. She had lost one of
my recipes and offered to trade two
versions of her Marlborough pie if I'd
replace the loss. I sent the recipe along
and said, "Thank you very much, and
may I come to see you when I travel into
New England again?"

I found Miss Ball at home on
Bloomfield Street, Lexington, in the tall
white house under ancient elms where
she has lived for the past thirty years.
I had telephoned from Boston that I was
heading her way after the promised
recipes. She had them ready. One is
taken from an old Deerfield cookbook,
the second version a hand-down
belonging to Mrs. Helen Judd, who lived
with Miss Ball, this recipe from the
Judd family of Boston.

We sat in the library of the hundred-
year-old house to talk about pies. Miss
Ball said, "This house is no age at all
compared to the historic old houses
of Lexington."

I said, "Apple pies for Thanksgiving?"
Pumpkin, yes, and mince and cranberry.
But wasn't apple too everyday?

"But not just any apple pie went to
the holiday table," she explained. "It's
the Marlborough for celebration, sharp
of lemon rind and juice and thickened
with eggs."

She told me that where apple pie
to a modern cook means the ordinary
two-crust kind made of raw apples
sliced and sweetened, to our down-east
grandmothers the baking of apple pie
meant making a choice among a dozen
different recipes.

Boston Marlborough Pie

1 cup tart applesauce

3 tablespoons lemon juice

1 cup sugar

4 large eggs, lightly beaten

2 tablespoons unsalted butter, melted

½ teaspoon grated nutmeg

½ teaspoon salt

1 (9-inch) Perfect Pie Crust (page 13)

Serves 6 to 8

Preheat the oven to 450 degrees.

In a large bowl, stir together the applesauce, lemon juice, sugar, eggs, butter, nutmeg, and salt. Pour the filling into the pie shell.

Bake for 15 minutes, then reduce the oven temperature to 275 degrees and bake for 1 hour. The pie should be a rich yellow and cut like firm jelly. Cool completely on a wire rack. Serve with whipped cream or vanilla ice cream, if you like.

Variation: To make a Deerfield Marlborough Pie, use 2 cups of applesauce, omit the nutmeg, and add 1 teaspoon grated lemon peel.

THANKSGIVING BELONGS TO NEW ENGLAND

Thanksgiving belongs especially to New England and it was at Old Sturbridge Village I celebrated the occasion one year in the 1790 manner. It was to be a public dinner so I went a week ahead of time to watch the preparation. The village was a place all stir and doing. We met miller Roy Capen, a descendent of the Pilgrims, who was grinding the meal for the Thanksgiving corn sticks, for the turkey stuffing. At the cider mill a wagonload of apples was being dumped into the ox-driven crushers. The wooden pressers were squeezing out the sweet amber juice, a wine for Thanksgiving.

I took my time wandering around the old farm. I circled the village green. The oldest house dates back to 1735. At the Tavern on the Green I met Earl Newton, director of this gigantic museum, to talk about the celebration dinner which would be held here in the common room, the table lighted by fire shine and hand-molded candles. The foods planned were early Yankee dishes. We took a look into the Tavern Butt'ry where mincemeat was waiting in beige crocks, a rich fragrance of spice and liqueur, a mincemeat made when the first tart apples were barreled. Pumpkins are hard to peel, but for this colonial Thanksgiving dinner the pumpkin pies were made from scratch, rich with cream and molasses, eggs and spice.

The Bill O' Fare included only those foods typical of colonial tables. Old letters and diaries had been searched for authentic recipes. Dinner was one course, all the dishes coming to the table together. Cranberry juice was the cocktail, followed by oyster stew. Beautiful turkeys were stuffed with a corn sausage dressing, the freshly ground meal straight from the village gristmill.

Root vegetables predominated as in the old years when each winter bin sent a representative to the table. There were the buttered squash and the mashed turnips, and baked potatoes, their brown jackets amber-flecked from cooking in the hearth ashes. A bushel of silver onions had been boiled and then creamed. Of course, succotash, a dish certainly present at the first Thanksgiving. But a different dish in the Pilgrims' time. Then succotash was made of dried beans and dried corn cooked in huge batches in autumn, enough to last the winter. This was allowed to freeze solid, to knock off in sizable chunks as needed. Cornsticks for dinner, and cream of tartar biscuits. Cider is the drink, sweet but edged with a sparkling barm to nip the tongue and wash the palate clean for the next delicious forkload.

There will be three kinds of pie, the golden pumpkin of melting deliciousness, the mince pie of dark and spicy depth, and the Marlborough, a glorification of the everyday apple. In colonial times it was thought penurious and incorrect to offer company fewer than three kinds of pie.

THE PLACE I LOVED best in old Sturbridge Village was Minor Grant's store—it drew me in by the nose. Cookies were baking, the old-time favorites: hobnails, lumberjacks, pine-tree shillings, and these big Joe Froggers.

Black Uncle Joe who lived in a cabin by the frog pond in Marblehead, originally baked these spicy sweets for the local fishermen. They bought enormous batches to stock their galleys for long trips. Good keepers, these sweets! The name? It's just one of those things—the big flat cookies were remindful of the big fat frogs that sat on the lily pads in Uncle Joe's pond.

Joe Froggers

7 cups all-purpose flour

1 tablespoon salt

1 tablespoon ground ginger

1 teaspoon ground cloves

1 teaspoon grated nutmeg

½ teaspoon ground allspice

¾ cup water

¼ cup dark rum

2 teaspoons baking soda

2 cups molasses

1 cup (2 sticks) unsalted butter, softened

2 cups sugar

Makes 2 dozen 5-inch cookies

Sift the flour, salt, ginger, cloves, nutmeg, and allspice into a large bowl.

In a small bowl, combine the water and rum.

In another small bowl, whisk the molasses into the baking soda.

In a large bowl using an electric mixer, beat together the butter and sugar until creamy and light. Add half of the sifted dry ingredients, half of the rum-water mixture, and half of the molasses to the butter and sugar, beating well. Repeat with remaining dry ingredients, rum-water, and molasses, and beat well to combine.

Cover the bowl with plastic wrap and refrigerate for at least 4 hours or overnight.

When you're ready to make the cookies, grease 2 large baking sheets and preheat the oven to 375 degrees.

Turn out the dough onto a well-floured surface and roll out ¼ inch thick. Cut out cookie shapes with a floured 4-inch-round cutter. Using a spatula, carefully lift the cookies onto the prepared baking sheets.

Bake for 10 to 12 minutes, until edges are brown and crisp and center is just set. Let stand on the sheets for 2 minutes to prevent breaking, then carefully transfer the cookies to a wire rack to cool completely. Store the cookies in a lidded cookie jar.

A TWICE-A-WEEK JOY

The one-plate meal of early New England was the boiled dinner, a twice-a-week joy from the early autumn until the sap rose in the maples. The meal was cooked in the big iron pot swung from the crane and let bubble merrily over the maple log blaze; the pot lid heaved to the rhythm of regular breathing.

Dessert was the boiled pudding, a substantial sweet made with Indian meal steamed in a floured, flannel bag hung over the pot's side. Some preferred it baked in the hearthstones after the pies and the bread came out. Down East the pudding arguments are waged over the boiled pudding technique. Vermont women would add a few bay leaves and garlic to the sugar-sweetened water for boiling the beef and salt pork, Maine women would say no. Once the vegetables were boiled to death. Now these are added toward the end of the cooking when the corned beef is about one-half hour from done.

There are more pudding arguments. Should eggs be used? But why should thrifty New Englanders use eggs when a delicious pudding may be made without? Should the pudding whey or be of smooth consistency? Our choice is the whey type.

This boiled dinner recipe was given to me by the late Herman Smith, the writer of the "Stina" cookbooks. Herman Smith was living in the Westchester hills and for a brief period one winter was snowbound. Nearby friends with a large family who had been locked up together for days to the point of battle, implored him to let them come to his house for dinner, even though the drifts were waist-high. He warned that his larder was depleted. "No matter," they said, "we want a change." The idea occurred to Herman to give them the kind of food they would have had when such a predicament was a common lot not merely for days but often for weeks. Here is Herman's boiled pot with the Indian pudding. Also the red flannel hash which is to be enjoyed the day after to use up the leftovers. The essentials are corned beef, potatoes, and beets, to which may be added in small quantities carrots, cabbage, and anything else left from the meal.

New England Boiled Dinner

4 pounds corned beef

8 ounces salt pork with a big streak of lean or slab bacon

3 quarts boiling water

½ cup sugar

3 bay leaves

1 clove garlic, peeled

4 medium russet potatoes, peeled

3 yellow turnips, peeled and thickly sliced

8 carrots, scrubbed

4 white onions, peeled, leaving a bit of the root end, and quartered

6 parsnips, peeled

1 small head cabbage, cored and cut into 8 wedges, set on wooden skewers

6 small beets, peeled

Serves 8

Wash the corned beef in cold water and pat dry. Place the beef and salt pork in a large stockpot with the boiling water. Add the sugar, bay leaves, and garlic. Bring to a simmer and simmer covered for 4 hours. During the last 30 minutes of cooking, add the potatoes, turnips, and carrots, followed by the onions and parsnips. If a vegetable begins to overcook, remove from the broth with a slotted spoon and hold in a warm spot until ready to serve.

Transfer 2 cups of cooking liquid to another pot and add the cabbage; add enough boiling water to cover the cabbage. Cook until just tender, about 30 minutes.

Dip out another 2 cups of cooking liquid to another pot and add the beets; add enough boiling water to cover the beets. Cook until just tender, about 30 minutes.

Remove the corned beef and salt pork from the main pot and slice it. Arrange the dinner on a warmed platter, corned beef and salt pork slices in the center, the pink and white slices alternating. Slice the carrots, beets, and parsnips while hot to ring around the meat. Follow with the potatoes, halved, and the cabbage wedges. Moisten all with any remaining cooking liquid.

Accompaniments: English mustard, horseradish for
the corned beef, sweetened vinegar for the cabbage and
beets. By all means a dish of green tomato pickle. Serve
with cornbread squares, split and buttered. No salad, but
a big bowl of cottage cheese sprinkled with caraway.

Baked Indian Pudding

5 cups milk	1 teaspoon salt
⅔ cup dark molasses	¾ teaspoon ground cinnamon
⅓ cup sugar	¾ teaspoon grated nutmeg
½ cup yellow cornmeal	4 tablespoons (½ stick) unsalted butter

Serves 8

Preheat the oven to 300 degrees. Grease a 1½-quart
baking dish.

In a heavy large saucepan, combine all the ingredients.
Place over medium-high heat and whisk until the
mixture begins to thicken, about 20 minutes,
stirring frequently.

Pour into the prepared dish and bake for 3 hours, or until
pudding is golden on top and set. Pass with whipped
cream. Some prefer hard sauce, some like ice cream.

Red Flannel Hash

6 slices salt pork or bacon,
cut in ½-inch pieces

1 cup chopped cooked corned beef

¼ cup milk

3 cups boiled potatoes
cut into ½-inch pieces

1 cup chopped cooked beets

1 cup chopped leftover vegetables

1 onion, minced

Serves 6

Fry the salt pork in a large skillet over medium-high heat until crisp. Remove the pieces and reserve them for garnish. Do not drain the skillet.

In a large bowl, toss together corned beef, milk, beets, and leftover vegetables.

Heat the skillet the salt pork was fried in over medium heat. Spread the mixture smoothly over the bottom and brown slowly, about 10 minutes, until a crust forms. Flip the hash cake and continue cooking until browned and crisp on the other side, 8 to 10 minutes more. Serve on a hot plate garnished with the fried salt pork slices.

BEANS AND BROWN BREAD IN THE CRADLE

In Boston town, cradle of New England cookery, it's hunt in earnest among the restaurants to find the traditional foods still in full flower. The cosmopolitan influence has worked its way in. Beans and brown bread make the Saturday-night menus. Just occasionally come the aromas of the New England boiled dinner. But the cod is kept sacred. It shows up everywhere.

Ask any native why in heaven's name they have a cod carved in wood perched serenely over the Speaker's head in the Massachusetts House of Representatives, and he'll tell you in a hurry that the cod is the noblest of the finny families. So it is that codfish recipes remain as imperishable in the annals of New England as Bunker Hill and Plymouth Rock.

There is young cod they call the scrod, there are innumerable salt-cod specialties made with the same inexpensive salt fish you can buy in any corner grocery store from New York to Los Angeles.

I had eaten three codfish dinners in a row hunting very best recipes when Marjorie Mills, the *Boston Herald*'s Food Editor, suggested I try a "picked dinner." That started the search. The end was in the kitchen of Boston's old Parker House Hotel, an institution of the city since 1856.

Here we give you a dinner as it has been served at least once a week for almost a hundred years. Charles Dickens must have eaten salt cod in this manner when he used the Parker House as his headquarters during his visit to America. Certainly Longfellow ate salt cod in this fashion; so did Aldrich and Holmes.

It is said in the cooking circles of Boston that the City Women's Club kitchen makes fish balls as old-Boston as the Tea Party. That took us to No. 39 and No. 40 Beacon Street, to the twin mansions the club calls home.

I sat with Mrs. Susan Guiler, club manager, in the long drawing room of the Appleton House, the very room where Henry Longfellow had wooed and wed the Appletons' daughter Frances. There, facing the snow-covered Boston Common, I noted the ways of the codfish ball of tradition.

You notice I said ball, not cake? There is all the difference in the world between these two. Cakes are patted out, made regular in shape, rather solid in texture, lightly floured. The balls are a light puffy mixture whipped so furiously that when dropped from a spoon into the hot fat they come out wearing whiskers, all tenderly crisp. The secret of their making is disclosed in this recipe which is originally from Gloucester, the fishing village on Cape Ann. The balls come forth with a thin crisp crust and whiskery; inside they are light and tongue-melting as a puff of whipped cream.

Gloucester Codfish Balls

1 pound skinless boneless salt cod

1 pound russet potatoes

4 tablespoons (½ stick) unsalted butter

½ teaspoon freshly ground black pepper

1 large egg or 2 large egg yolks, lightly beaten

Salt (if needed)

3 tablespoons vegetable oil

Serves 6 as an appetizer

In a large bowl, soak the cod in cold water to cover by 2 inches in the refrigerator for at least 12 hours, preferably overnight. Change the water 2 or 3 times as it soaks.

The following morning pour off the water and shred the fish using a fork. Place the cod in a bowl and set aside.

Peel the potatoes and cut them into 1-inch pieces. Set a steamer over a large pot of boiling water and steam the potatoes until tender, about 20 minutes. Drain the potatoes, return them to the pot, and mash them thoroughly. Add 1 tablespoon of the butter and the pepper to the potatoes. Add the cod and the egg and stir until the mixture is light and fluffy. Season with salt if necessary. Cover the bowl and refrigerate for 30 minutes.

When ready to cook, preheat the oven to 250 degrees. Heat the remaining 3 tablespoons butter and the oil in a 10-inch heavy skillet over medium heat until the butter melts and the foam subsides. Drop tablespoon-size balls into the hot fat and cook in batches until lightly browned, 1 to 2 minutes. Drain on paper towels and transfer to a baking sheet as they are cooked. Keep warm in the oven.

Serve with ketchup or tartar sauce.

IT WAS IN MARBLEHEAD that I went calling on the Samuel Chamberlains, yes, that Samuel who is the famous photographer and writer, his wife Narcissa, co-author, collector of recipes. It was the Chamberlains who gave me this Spite House fish chowder, a dish of high standing in Marblehead.

When I visited the Chamberlains they had just completed a check-up of what's cooking in the United States. Mrs. Chamberlain had culled through hundreds of recipes to choose fifty-four she considered most typical. These they have used in their illustrated American cooking calendar edited by pretty daughter Narcisse.

Mrs. Chamberlain told me that she considers American cooking today under three divisions, the regional, the foreign, and the new. Heirloom recipes are the basic building blocks in our modern cuisine. It is estimated that two-thirds of all our recipes hinge back to old favorites of two types; the regional dish that grew up with the country based on products at hand; and the foreign, the international recipes which came to America with the immigrants from every corner of the world.

The other third of our cooking is strictly today's, making use of the new products—the little Rock Cornish hen of recent development, the time-saving ready mixes, the instants, the quick frozens. Modern meal planners want the quick and easy, but with the plus of their own distinctive touches. Women have great need, in this automatic world, to express themselves creatively.

Spite House Fish Chowder

12 ounces salt pork or bacon, diced

6 large onions, sliced

5 cups fish or chicken stock

6 small potatoes, peeled and
chopped ½ inch thick

2 pounds skinless haddock fillets,
pin bones removed, about
1 inch thick each

2 tablespoons all-purpose flour

1 quart milk

Worcestershire sauce

Salt and freshly ground
black pepper

Serves 6

Fry the salt pork in a large skillet over medium-high heat until crisp. Using a slotted spoon, remove the pieces and drain on paper towels. Add the onions to the fat remaining in skillet and sauté until browned, stirring occasionally, about 8 minutes. Remove the onions with a slotted spoon and set aside. Do not drain the fat.

Place the stock in a large pot and add the potatoes. Bring to a boil, then reduce the heat to low, cover, and cook for 10 minutes. Cut the haddock into 1-inch pieces and add to the pot. Add the browned onions.

Discard all but 1 tablespoon of the remaining fat from the skillet the salt pork was cooked in and heat the fat over medium heat. Stir in the flour just to combine and make a paste. Slowly stir in the milk until combined, stirring constantly, and cook for 5 to 7 minutes, until slightly thickened and well combined. Season the mixture with Worcestershire sauce, salt, and pepper to taste.

Pour the seasoned milk into the pot. Cover and simmer over the lowest possible heat for 3 hours without stirring. Stir the chowder, taste for additional seasoning, and serve in soup bowls with chowder crackers and a sprinkling of the crisp pork.

THOSE GREENS TASTED LIKE SPRING

In Marblehead, I came to Isabel Currier, "a good cook even if she is a book writer," as someone said, adding, "She does those lumberjack pies right down to perfection."

Isabel put aside her writing and gave me a warm welcome. She showed off her old house, the oldest in Marblehead, one half said to date back to 1640, the other half modeled after it a hundred years later. Right here we butted in with the question, "Do folks down there eat greens in the spring?" "By May," Isabel said, "everyone will be digging greens by the bushel. We like them, you know, with the cornmeal dumplings." I thought of my Grandpa Paddleford. "A labor of love," Isabel was saying, "to clean greens by the peck."

But I wasn't listening. I heard, instead, my grandfather, a shut-mouth man. Come early April when the sun swung high and to the north, when the Kansas lanes were greening, he would bring up his favorite culinary subject and talk at length about a mess-o'-greens dinner, topped off with cornmeal dumplings, a dish he remembered lovingly from down-east boyhood days. His talk started when the horseradish showed its first rapier blades. A few weeks later he'd spy the milder-flavored narrow dock and other edible weeds, the "pussly," the dandelions, and Grandpa was off with spade and basket on what Grandma called "one of Pa's expeditions."

Grandpa knew his Caroline was the best cook in Riley County, Kansas, and that she didn't need telling how to do things. But he told her anyhow. "My ma," he'd say, "cooked a hunk of salt pork and potatoes together, then put the greens over that. Right at the last she'd drop in the dumplings to sit on top of the mess and cook in the steam."

"Pshaw," said Grandma, "sounds like anybody's greens to me." "'Tain't," said Grandfather, with a hopeless shrug and a wistful look in his pale blue eyes. "Those greens tasted like spring."

That determined me at the ripe age of ten to go "back East" some day and learn about greens with corn dumplings and cook them for Grandpa. Now I know, but Grandpa is gone.

Better than greens is the lumberjack pie served in northern New England, its origin French-Canadian. These pies are usually made in batches of a dozen, frozen, then stored in a cold place, ready to stick in the oven as needed. In the North Country they are served all winter through, and are always a must for Christmas and New Year's Eve suppers.

French-Canadian housewives serve these pies hot on Christmas Eve after midnight Mass. Pickles and celery are the crunchy accompaniments. If used as a meat dish for supper, serve with a vegetable.

Lumberjack Pie

3 pounds ground pork

3 pounds ground beef

5 large onions, chopped

⅛ teaspoon dried thyme

⅛ teaspoon dried oregano

5 peppercorns

Salt

1 tablespoon ground cinnamon

1 teaspoon dried sage

3 cups mashed potatoes

2½ cups beef or chicken stock

8 (9-inch) Perfect Pie Crusts
(page 13)

Makes four 9-inch pies

In a large heavy stockpot, combine the ground pork, ground beef, and onions. Add enough water to just cover, bring to a simmer over medium heat, then reduce the heat to medium-low and simmer for 2 hours. Stir well and add the thyme, oregano, peppercorns, and salt to taste. Reduce the heat to low and cook for another 4 hours.

Remove from the heat and cool for 30 minutes. Pour the mixture through a colander to drain it of all liquid and fat.

Preheat the oven to 375 degrees.

Pour the meat and onion mixture into a large bowl. Stir in the cinnamon and sage. Add the mashed potatoes and stock and season with salt to taste. Divide the filling among the pie shells and top with a crust. Bake for 1 hour, or until the top of the pie is golden and the filling is set. Remove the pies from the oven and cool on wire racks for about 15 minutes. Serve warm.

Note: To freeze: Allow pies to cool completely, about 45 minutes, and then wrap well in plastic wrap and stored in the freezer for up to 3 months. (This recipe may easily be halved if you do not wish to stock your freezer with this many meals.)

FOLLOWING A BOILED-HAM DINNER, the northern New England cooks cook the peas in ham stock and have habitant soup. Otherwise the soup starts off with a piece of salt pork as we do it here.

A soup not soupy, but thick, a meal in a dish, its loving companion the hot Johnny cake served brown and crisp; salad to follow. Then apple custard pie for dessert (a recipe similar to that on page 33). It's the pie New England mothers in the nineteenth century taught their daughters to make as a show-off when beaux came courting.

Habitant Soup

1 pound dried yellow split peas

2 quarts water

8 ounces salt pork or slab bacon, cut into 1-inch cubes

3 onions, finely chopped

1 carrot, diced

⅛ teaspoon freshly ground black pepper

Salt

Serves 4

Rinse the peas and put them in a large heavy stockpot. Add the water, salt pork, onions, and carrot. Bring to a boil over medium-high heat, skim the froth from the surface, then reduce the heat and simmer until the peas are tender but not falling apart, about 4 hours. Add the pepper and season with salt to taste.

TWO GOOD COOKS,
TWO GOOD FRIENDS

"One if by land and two if by sea." The words came as a refrain—this was the road Paul Revere had taken the night the redcoats started marching. It was Route 2A out of Boston going toward Lincoln, Massachusetts. I was hunting Hartwell Farm and two good cooks, two good friends, Marion Fitch and Jane Poor.

That pair set a fine table, I had heard tell, and right along with the food was mentioned the historic old farmhouse, built in 1635. A minute's drive off the highway and I see the broad chimney. Under it the house sits solid, quietly taking its ease, seeming asleep in the shadow of the ancient elms. Miraculously on the instant there were Marion Fitch and Jane Poor at the door waving a welcome.

"Did Paul Revere stop here?" was almost my first question. No, Paul was taken captive half a mile down the road and had escaped later. It was Mary Flint Hartwell, mistress of the farmhouse, who flew across the fields to Captain Smith's place to report the British were coming.

It was in 1924 that Marion Fitch, a Boston schoolteacher, and Jane Poor, an architect whose specialty is the restoration of old houses, found Boston too crowded for leisurely living and bought the farm as a place for escape. Little by little over the years they restored the house to its original beauty. Old beams have been uncovered, wide floor boards refinished, the seven fireplaces reopened.

"About the food," I asked, "do you serve the down-east dishes ?" Jane said "Yes," Marion said "No," meaning "sometimes we do and sometimes we don't." "Our turkey is strictly New England," Jane put in. "We cook it in a flour-and-water-dough coat, baking it for six hours, sometimes longer, in the ole fireplace brick oven."

"This is the same idea as clay cooking," she explained, "and goes back to the time of the Indians." And the same dough blanket is used in baking their hams. But it's fried chicken and corn chowder which has won their table acclaim. It's been served daily ever since the day the dining room opened on Patriot's Day, April 19, 1925. Recipes for these two culinary menu leaders I give to you as they were given to me there by the fire glow in the living room.

Corn Chowder

4 to 6 ears corn

2 ounces salt pork or bacon, cut into ¼-inch dice

2 medium russet potatoes, peeled and chopped

1 medium onion, chopped

2½ teaspoons salt

⅛ teaspoon freshly ground white pepper

1 cup light cream

4 tablespoons grated sharp cheddar cheese

Serves 4

Preheat the oven to 350 degrees.

Shuck the corn and use a paring knife to strip the kernels into a bowl. Put the cobs in a pot with 4 cups water. Place over medium-high heat and bring to a boil; reduce the heat, cover, and simmer for 10 minutes.

Meanwhile, fry the salt pork in a large skillet over medium-high heat until crisp.

Add the potatoes and onion and cook, stirring occasionally, until the onion softens, about 7 minutes.

After the corn has cooked for at least 10 minutes, strain the liquid into the onion-potato mixture. Bring to a boil, then turn down the heat until the liquid is simmering. When the potatoes are almost tender, after about 10 minutes, add the corn kernels, salt, and pepper.

Pour the soup into a 2-quart casserole dish and cover tightly. Bake for about 1 hour, until the soup is thickened and the potatoes and onions are tender.

Preheat the broiler.

In a small saucepan, heat the cream, then add it to the chowder. Divide the soup into small casserole pans and top with toast sprinkled with grated cheddar cheese. Run under the broiler until cheese melts.

Boiled-Then-Fried Chicken

1 (5- to 6-pound) chicken, dressed

1 quart boiling water

1½ teaspoons salt, plus more
if needed

3 tablespoons unsalted butter

Freshly ground black pepper

Serves 6

Place the chicken in a large heavy stockpot, add the
water, and cover. Bring to a simmer, then simmer over
medium-low heat for 1 hour. Add the salt and continue
simmering covered for 30 minutes longer. Turn off
the heat.

Cool the chicken in the stock to room temperature,
about 45 minutes. Remove the chicken from the stock,
reserving the stock for later use. Refrigerate the chicken
and when it is thoroughly chilled, remove the skin and
pull the meat from the bones in large chunks. (Chilling
helps set the meat and makes it easier to handle in
frying.)

Melt the butter in a large skillet over medium heat. Add
the pulled chicken pieces and fry until browned, using
just enough fat so that the meat doesn't stick to the
bottom of the pan. Add more salt, if desired, and pepper
to taste.

UMM GOOD CHOWDER! The delight of steamed clams! Wonderful lobster! Indian pudding light as whipped cream! That was Sunday dinner in the H. O. Frye home for a party of nine with H. O. himself officiating as chef. Francie, that's Mrs. Frye, turned a hand here and there, but H. O. engineered the job. He's a born manager. Had practiced the managerial art for many years as head man of the Walter Baker Chocolate Company in nearby Dorchester. Chowder-making he claimed as a particular talent. It's "the best doggone chowder along the Rock-bound Coast."

Steamed clams the first course, the juice of the clam served in thin cups, a hot sip between bites. Now the chowder, a rich and creamy substance, a whiff of the sea. Afloat on each bowl was the cracker New Englanders know as "common cracker," a water biscuit of sorts. Cornbread was passed made of yellow meal, very thin and on the sweet side in the Boston manner.

Parade of the lobsters, the crimson crustaceans came plate-load by plate-load, one for each guest, caught that very morning off Minots Light on the Cohasset side.

The Indian pudding I thought nothing short of a masterpiece, it was so delicate! The secret is to boil very little corn meal in a vast amount of liquid.

Howard Frye's Chowder

5 pounds small to medium soft-shell clams (steamers)

2 cups water

4 ounces salt pork or bacon, diced

2 large onions, diced

4 large potatoes, peeled and cut into ¼-inch dice

4 cups bottled clam juice

2 quarts milk

¼ cup all-purpose flour

Salt and freshly ground black pepper

Serves 10

Thoroughly rinse and scrub the clams, making sure to take care with their brittle, fragile shells and to rinse and soak them in fresh water long enough to remove all dirt. It may take 4 or so soakings.

In a large heavy stockpot, bring the water to a boil. Gently slide the clams into the pot and cover. After about 4 minutes, remove the lid and stir the clams around to ensure even cooking. Cover and continue to steam the clams for another 4 to 5 minutes. All the clams should be open; if not, steam them a minute or two longer. Remove the clams to a large, clean bowl and cool to room temperature.

Remove the clams from the shells and cut off the siphons, as well as the protective skin that covers each siphon, and discard. Put the clams in a clean bowl, cover, and refrigerate until ready to use.

In a large pot or heavy skillet, fry the salt pork over medium-high heat until golden brown. Using a slotted spoon, transfer the pork bits to a small dish, leaving the fat in the pot, and set aside.

Add the onion to the pot with the remaining pork fat and sauté over medium heat, stirring occasionally, for about 10 minutes, until the onions are soft but not brown. Add the potatoes and clam juice, which should just cover the potatoes (if it doesn't, add a little water to cover). Turn up the heat to medium-high and bring the soup to a boil, cover, and cook for about 10 minutes, until the potatoes are soft on the outside but still firm in the center.

While the soup is simmering, in a small bowl, stir together 1 cup of the milk and the flour to make a paste. Remove the pot from the heat. Add the milk paste to the chowder and stir to fully incorporate. Stir in the clams and the remaining milk and season with salt and pepper to taste. The soup should be on the thin side but thicker than milk. Serve sprinkled with the fried salt pork pieces.

CLAMBAKES AND CRANBERRIES ON THE CAPE CALLED COD

It's no great occasion to find a new clam. Several hundred species are known. Only a few of these hundreds have become important commercially. But not long ago Cape Cod got all excited about a new mahogany quahog (spelled *quahaug* outside of New England). So I flew to Sandwich-on-the-Cape to join a group of Boston food reporters to see the clams caught, processed, and into the chowder bowl. We boarded the sixty-five-foot dragger *Gambler* for an hour's trip to the clam beds past beaches which curled into gentle harbors, on to the ocean, and off Mary Ann Rocks. There a dragger was dropped over either side, and then on for a thirty minute tow, before lifting. The haul was estimated at around fourteen bushels.

Picked up fresh from the ocean floor, the shell of this new commercial clam appears black, but it's actually mahogany and it's almost round in shape, and thick through. It's fun to watch an expert unfrock this big brother. A short knife rests lightly "along the ball of the thumb of the open hand." Now the dark quahog is placed expertly against the blade. A slight pressure and the succulent pink-fleshed clam is exposed, all a-quiver, firm, and flavorful, spilling its elixir, scattering the scent of the sea. It's a large clam, the yield about ten pounds of solid meat to a bushel of clams in shell.

The clams are eviscerated and quick frozen in five-pound packages packed in fifty-pound units for hotels, restaurants, hospitals, and schools.

After watching the processing of the clams we were invited to the loft of the plant to sample clam chowder made the New England way with salt pork, onion, and milk, a brew of honest, solid comfort. This was a chowder to equal that set forth to Ishmael and Queequeg by the hearty Mrs. Hussey of *Moby-Dick*.

THE WORLD'S MOST DELECTABLE SEAFOOD DINNER

After the clam diggers' party we ended the day at a clambake at the Treadway Inn in North Falmouth with Chef John B. Russel in charge.

The clambake is the world's most delectable sea-food dinner and Cape Cod claims her way with the ritual the most authentic. So does little Rhode Island; the same goes for Maine. Heaven only knows the truth!

I had gone to Coonamessett, the Treadway Inn, to report on their Friday bake given weekly throughout the summer. Anyone may attend, but hotel guests get the first chance. Vacationists come too from every direction up and down the Cape, but by reservation.

It was dusk as I waited on the terrace of the Inn for John Russel, the chef, my escort for the evening. Looking toward the beach I could see the bake steaming. It looked like a haycock ready to burst into flames. Down the grassy path to the water's edge. The crowd was gathering by the bar set up under a fancy open-sided tent facing the pond. There were cocktails if you wanted them, and beer of course. Every eye was glued to the bake and noses pointed toward the pungent steaming pit.

John Russel had briefed me on the preliminary details which start early in the morning. He uses a shallow pit dug into the earth one foot deep, four feet square, and bedded with stones about eight inches in diameter with smaller stones to fill in the crevices. Over this go hardwood logs of maple or oak and in between paper and kindling and more pebbles.

Then more logs laid crosswise, more paper, more little stones. Layer is laid upon layer to reach four feet aboveground. The fire is lighted some four hours before the bake goes on; cooking time is one hour and fifteen minutes. So absolutely simple the rules, yet in every little move there is a culinary cunning.

At the end of the four hours the logs unburned are raked away to avoid oversmoking. The small rocks now white with heat have dropped to ground level. Waiting is a stack of seaweed freshly gathered, this to be forked to the rock, in a 12-inch deep blanket. It is the weed that produces the humid heat which experts insist no other method can generate.

First layer, white or yellow potatoes tied in muslin bags, well cleaned but unpeeled. Clams over this, in wooden frames or in fish-net squares tied to make sacks. The clams are the soft shell, oval in shape and so fragile they can be crushed between the fingers. One peck of soft shell clams is about right to serve four. Remember quantity is the essence of the clambake. Next, sweet corn, one and one-fourth ears by nose count. Leave on thin jacket of husk, removing the silk; wet the corn well. Then come the lobsters tied in burlap sacks, one and one-fourth the average count to a guest. Top the pile with the appetite-whetting course, frankfurters and sausages wrapped in cheesecloth, or foil is better, but puncture, so the food can take on a rich smoked savoriness. Each individual package should contain one hot dog, one link sausage, two small onions that have been parboiled 10 minutes. Sometimes a piece of swordfish is included, or maybe haddock.

This mountain of food is covered with a wet canvas tarpaulin, the edge sealed with sand or earth. Nothing to do now but wait for an hour and fifteen minutes while the hot rocks and the salty steam from the marsh weed and the clams do their work. The seaweed scorches on the hot rocks and steam heat pours upward to the clams. They open their shells and the juice trickles down over the rocks. The increased steam pushes up, cooking the potatoes, the corn, and the lobster.

The unveiling is the high point. Hungry watchers wait while four workers wearing cotton gloves lift off the canvas. Everyone says "Ah-h-h . . ." Then a rush for the tables. First course: hot dogs, sausages, fish, then come the steamed clams in half-gallon waxed tub containers. There is a small waxed container of melted butter for each guest. Other things are there: bread, white and brown, platters of sliced tomato and cucumber, and such condiments as vinegar, salt, and pepper. There are plastic knives and forks, but who cares—futile tools. This is handwork.

After the first and second courses are removed from the bake it is canvas-covered again. Take it easy, bud, more things coming! When the crowd is ready, lobsters are handed out with corn and potatoes, and hurried table-ward. Cold beer and soda pop are circulating. Coffee for the end, along with the iced watermelon for those who can take it.

On the day following as an extra surprise John introduced me to a new dish, stuffed clams, made with the mahogany quahog.

Here's his receipt, to serve four.

Combine two cups of ocean clams, cleaned and chopped, with two cups coarsely ground dry bread crumbs. Add one teaspoon paprika, two tablespoons grated Swiss cheese (Parmesan, he thinks, is too strong for the delicate flavor of clams) two tablespoons melted butter, a sprinkle of salt. The sweetness of the clam, John tells us, needs a salty touch; now a dash of pepper. Mix in two ounces of dry white wine and the juice of one-fourth lemon. Toss together well and spoon into the washed, dried clam shells. Oven bake at 350 degrees for fifteen minutes. Add a dot of butter just before serving. Several of the food editor guests decided they would like a little onion or garlic added. But John warned, "Don't overdo on these or you lose the sweet flavor of the clam."

THE DAY AFTER THE clambake I drove on to Chatham, Massachusetts, for clam pie; my hostess, Mrs. John T. Russell, Jr.

A handsome lot of sunbrowned people young and old were gathered on the Russell terrace overlooking Pleasant Bay. Nothing here of flamboyant Florida, of plush Newport's aristocracy. Here were people who like the simple things, people accustomed to sports, and spacious, conservative living. We met Mrs. Russell's mother, Mrs. Richard W. Olney of Boston and the Cape. This is daughter Anne, just turned twelve; a big hello to bumptious Otis, almost six. Teddy, the oldest son, is off on a day's fishing trip.

Mrs. Russell's sister, Mrs. Charles H. Willard, joined the party with her twin boys Dickie and Albert. Friends from Boston, Mr. and Mrs. William Chase. Meet Mr. William Waugh, President of the Cape Cod Shellfish Corp., and our host Charles Russell, Jr., a senior member in a Boston—New York Stock Exchange firm, also a partner to Mr. Waugh, along with his brother Dr. Henry Russell, professor of marine biology

at Boston University. These three men call themselves the clamdiggers and are building a new business around the Cape's new clam, nicknamed the mahogany quahog. This new species, *Cyprina islandica,* is found in huge beds four to five miles off the Cape.

Charles Russell told me about the clams while the drinks were served, but our interest strayed when the scallops came hot from the fat pot, served with a most divine lemon butter.

Recipe: The luncheon was help-yourself from the dining-room table, a room opening to the terrace and the shining bay. There was a quartette of deep-dish pies filled to their pastry toppings with the clams, juicy and tender. There was cold sliced baked ham accompanied by a brown-sugar mustard. The two tablespoons of prepared mustard to one-half cup of the sugar, stirred together to make a thick paste. The avocado salad had a just-right richness to go with the pie. Dessert, the juicy Cranshaw melon, thick meated, of spicy flavor.

Clam Pie

4 ounces salt pork or bacon, cut into ¼-inch cubes

1 large onion, cut into rings

1 russet potato, peeled and cut into ½-inch cubes, boiled, and cooled

24 small clams, shucked and minced

1 tablespoon cornstarch

¼ cup cold water

Salt

2 (9-inch) Perfect Pie Crusts (page 13)

Serves 6

Preheat the oven to 375 degrees.

In a large heavy skillet over medium-high heat, fry the salt pork until crisp. Add the onion rings and sauté until golden brown, 6 to 7 minutes.

Transfer the pork and onion to a large bowl. Add the potato and clams and mix gently to combine.

In a small bowl, stir the cornstarch with the water using a fork to make a smooth paste. Stir the paste into the clam mixture. Season with salt to taste.

Turn the mixture into the pie crust. Cover with the top crust. Flute the edges and slit the top to allow steam to escape. Bake for 25 to 30 minutes, until the center is bubbly and the pastry is golden brown.

THE GOOD BERRIES ROLL ALONG

It was cranberry-picking time down on Cape Cod where 65 percent of the world's cranberries grow. Some 5,000 workers were combing 14,000 acres of bog land to bring in the scarlet harvest before old man winter could get his knife sharpened.

Stand on the ditched edge of a low-lying bog fringed with scrub pine. There, kneeling elbow to elbow, a dozen men work. It's the early blacks they're harvesting in Plymouth and Barnstable counties.

A dozen times we stopped to watch the pickers shuffling along on their knees pushing the broad wooden scoops with the 10-inch fingers. As the scoops filled they were emptied into bushel and half-bushel boxes. A worker with a wheelbarrow trundled the boxes ashore to the shed. There the fruit rests several hours to get out the field heat before trucking to the screen house to be groomed for the market. About 10 percent of the crop is dropped in the picking to be lost in the vines. To get the loose berries out, the fields are flooded and the berries floated off into the ditches and saved.

The Indians were the first to freeze the berry of the boglands. They bagged the harvest and winter did the job. It was a white man who put the first cranberry sauce into cans back in 1912. Marcus L. Urann of Hanson began canning cranberries in his home kitchen. He found that it was possible to market a sauce better than mother could make, darker in color, richer in flavor.

I visited one of the plants where the co-op members bring in their berries for milling and screening. Some growers have their own screen houses right at the bog, but all must ship through the Sales Company and abide by the inspector's decision, which berries to sell fresh, which must go to the processors.

The good berries roll along to a screening device which separates the smaller from the larger fruit. Undersize specimens are milled separately to sell as pie berries, going to processors. The fat and the fine go into boxes and cellophane bags for home use.

We go kitchen calling on the wives of cranberry growers to hand pick recipes. Mrs. Edward L. Bartholomew of Wareham, Massachusetts, wife of the owner of a sixty-acre bog makes ten-minute sauce by the quart to keep sealed in jars ready for instant use. She spreads the sauce between the folds of an omelet; stuffs it into baked apples; serves it parfait style in tall dessert glasses in alternating layers with creamy rice pudding.

Something else that's a favorite at the Bartholomews' table is this spiced cranberry-orange compote to be served as dessert and cold as zero.

Spiced Cranberry-Orange Compote

1 cup water

2 cups sugar

5 whole cloves

2 (2-inch) cinnamon sticks

3 large seedless oranges, peeled, white pith completely removed, and sliced ½ inch thick

4 cups fresh cranberries

Serves 4

Combine the water, sugar, cloves, and cinnamon sticks in a large saucepan. Place over medium-high heat, bring to a boil, and boil for 5 minutes. Add the orange slices, lower the heat to medium-low, and simmer for 3 minutes. Add the cranberries and continue to simmer for 5 to 8 minutes, until the liquid becomes syrupy and the cranberry skins pop open. Pour into a bowl, cover, and refrigerate for at least 1 hour.

Serve topped with whipped cream, or use as a topping for chocolate cake, pound cake, or vanilla ice cream, if you like.

IN EAST WAREHAM we met the energetic Mrs. Robert Hammond whose husband manages two hundred acres of berry land. Her three children, Papa too, go for mock cherry pie. A pie as old as New England, so is this recipe.

Mock Cherry Pie

3 cups fresh cranberries

½ cup raisins

1¼ cups sugar

1½ tablespoons all-purpose flour

½ cup hot water

Grated peel of ½ lemon

2 (8-inch) Perfect Pie Crusts (page 13)

Milk, for brushing

Serves 6 to 8

Preheat the oven to 400 degrees.

In a large bowl, combine the cranberries and raisins. Add the sugar and flour and gently stir together. Stir in the water and lemon rind.

Turn the mixture into the pie shell. Cover with the top crust, seal the edges, cut vents on top, and brush the top with a little milk. Bake for about 45 minutes. Cool completely on a wire rack for the filling to set, about 1 hour.

Let stand at room temperature for 2 hours before serving. The pie can be made a day ahead and refrigerated. Serve the pie warm or at room temperature.

To warm the pie: Cover with foil and heat in a preheated 325 degree oven for 10 to 15 minutes.

RHODE ISLAND

Go on to Providence, Rhode Island, to learn about johnnycake. Its making is one of the little state's most treasured arts, and an ancient art carried down the years to now.

Corn and cornmeal were important staples in colonial trade and the early New England settlers took quick advantage of the numerous streams with their short, sharp falls to set up gristmills. At the same time the women newly arrived from the Old World were quick to adapt Indian cooking. From the Indian corn they created dozens of new dishes. They developed the hominy of the South, the cornmeal mush of Pennsylvania, the hasty pudding of New Haven, Connecticut, the Indian pudding and brown bread of Boston, and the whitepot of poor man's custard of Newport, Rhode Island.

But the johnnycake of Rhode Island's south county has achieved more than local fame as a breakfast bread. In the colonial days in the old Narragansett County in Rhode Island where the gentry in their great houses, with their fine cooks and big fireplaces, lived luxuriously and leisurely, johnnycake was made daily. This was a halfway between Roger Williams with his "spoon full of meal and spoon full of water from the brook" and the present day of our "minute" made dishes.

Georgia W. Gardiner of Providence told me that in old times the ingredients included meal made from Rhode Island's white corn. No other kind would do. This corn was ground between stones of Narragansett marble, ground exceedingly fine. The meal had no harsh feeling of round, gritty granules. It was soft as the finest talcum powder. Many times the miller would run the meal through his fingers and adjust the stones until the product was perfect.

The element of time entered into the meal making. A hurried grinding produced hot meal with much of the life taken out. Slow grinding kept the meal cool and retained all of its vital statistics. Rhode Islanders care so much about this type of meal that there are still gristmills turning out stone-ground johnnycake meal and several brands of this product are on the market.

Mr. Gardiner takes his johnnycake with ham and eggs, with broiled bluefish, shad roe, steaks or chops. He names a long list, then added, "a well-buttered, golden brown, flaky crusted, soft-hearted Rhode Island johnnycake right hot off the griddle is the crowning glory of breakfast, lunch, or dinner." He approves it even as a solo dish with butter and a big pour of maple syrup.

One of the great traditions of the state is the johnnycake-eating contests held at Cole's Hotel in Warren. Queer thing is that few Rhode Island cooks ever agree on how to make this food of the gods. A native Rhode Islander, Mrs. E. T. G. Metcalf, a few years back gave a johnnycake luncheon for me at her lovely old home on Williams Street, Providence, a house she fondly refers to as "farmhouse" colonial. Mrs. Metcalf, a native of Rhode Island, had invited four johnnycake experts to give me the particulars regarding the honest-to-goodness way of this Rhode Island delicacy.

Talk went great guns; yet the five women at the table never did agree on one authentic method of johnnycake baking. They couldn't even agree on the spelling of the name. Likely the "H" doesn't belong. Originally the small oval corn cakes were journey cakes because travelers carried them in their saddlebags for refreshment along the way. Years of usage turned journey cake into jonnycake. No connection with the name John, but the dictionaries persist in the johnnycake spelling.

Disagreement again over the best corn for the meal; does it grow in Newport or in Washington County? Each guest at the luncheon gave me the name of the meal she prefers, five different meals! Five different millers.

Meet the guests: Mrs. Henry D. Sharpe, of Prospect Street, not a real Rhode Islander—she was born in Syracuse, New York—but she has lived in Providence thirty years.

Everyone listened politely to her way of scalding johnnycake meal in a double boiler, then to stand twenty minutes.

Next at the table, Mrs Charles C. Marshall, of Prospect Street. Her way is to scald the meal, then add cold milk to bring it to the right consistency. "Cold milk! Oh no, it's hot milk," someone put in. "With hot milk, there is much less stickiness."

Mrs. Gordon Washburn, wife of the former Director of the Providence Museum of Art, admitted she mixed the meal with milk and didn't bother to scald and that the cakes tasted all right.

Fifth guest: Violet B. Higbee, extension specialist in foods at the Rhode Island State College at Kingston, said that some women she knew put the cakes in the oven for a few minutes after the frying. Other women, she said, fry one side, then turn, then put the whole griddle into the oven to finish the baking.

Mrs. Metcalf was critical of the johnnycake she passed at her luncheon. I took a third helping and my hostess raised an eyebrow. "These cakes," she said, "didn't turn out right." A johnnycake, she explained, should be a glossy brown, thick crusted with a creamy soft center.

Reinforcements of hot cakes came from the kitchen. Nobody, I noticed, held back with the fork because of a lack in the gloss. Here we tread on dangerous ground but right or wrong we choose the Metcalf recipe to add to our regional files. Who can say it isn't the best? We are told that when the Rhode Island Federation of Women's Clubs held a contest to determine just what should go into the state's finest johnnycake, over one thousand recipes were submitted, no two alike.

Rhode Island Johnnycake

3 cups johnnycake meal or stone-ground cornmeal (preferably white)

2 tablespoons sugar

2 teaspoons salt

1 quart boiling water

½ cup whole or 2% milk

Vegetable oil for the pan

Serves 8

Sift the meal, sugar, and salt into a large mixing bowl. Slowly pour the boiling water into the bowl, stirring to combine. Pour in the milk, stirring to form a thin batter.

Heat a large nonstick griddle or skillet over medium-high heat and brush lightly with oil. Working in batches, spoon 1 tablespoonful batter for each cake onto the griddle, spreading a little with the back of a spoon. Cook until the cakes are golden brown on the bottom and firm at the edges, about 2 minutes. Turn the cakes over and cook until firm and golden brown, about 1 minute longer.

The johnnycakes can be made up to 1 day ahead. Cool, then cover with foil and refrigerate. Place on a baking sheet, cover with foil, and reheat in a preheated 350-degree oven until hot, about 7 minutes.

What to eat with a johnnycake at the breakfast hour? Sausage the first round, maple syrup the second.

RHODE ISLANDERS NEVER WASTE leftover johnnycake. Miss Higbee, who has made a study of the authentic old-time foods of the state, gave me this treasured recipe for johnnycake toast.

The cold cakes are split in half, laid in a spider or baking dish, dotted with butter or margarine and covered with milk or cream. Heat thoroughly on top of range or in oven. Have a care not to bring the milk to a boil. Salt to taste and serve like cream toast. Some families like johnnycake toast so much they make fresh cakes, let them cool, then toast just to serve in this fashion.

Johnnycakes are good at any meal with meat, fish or fowl. And try them with beefsteak fried in beef fat. Good all by themselves with a big spread of butter and swimming in syrup.

A BREATH OF SEA

The place was the home of the late John Howard Benson, Newport, Rhode Island. I stood on the sidewalk to bang the big knocker. Step out the back door, walk forty steps and you're into Narragansett Bay. Between front door and back is the beautiful house, nearly two hundred years old. The fireplaces are finished with tile brought over from England and Holland. That one in the living room occupies most of a wall. There you could spitroast a whole lamb, or maybe a steer. It's a room warm and pungent, busy with life. Here the sun slips in to play on the hearth and the wind talks big down the great chimney. Whoever opens the door lets in a breath of sea.

Next to the living room is the kitchen, built like the stern end of the dining room of the once-great steamer *Commonwealth*. A bay-windowed end, the windows facing the water. In one alcove is the broad table where friends sit to lap up the Bensons' good food. It's a room smelling kindly of drying boots, of drying herbs mingled with the ambrosial fumes of the chowder blending its flavors in the pot.

A good kitchen where Quaker Esther Fisher Benson, John's wife, cooked for her foursome—John, the lean Yankee with lion-colored hair, and three mighty sons, Thomas Tew, John Everett, and Richard, the youngest—all raring to go like wild horses. Simple foods cooked here—roasts without sauce and hearty stews and chowders and always more chowders.

John was a sculptor, a calligrapher, a cutter of commemorative stones, of memorial plaques. No one in this country, it is claimed, could match his ability in this particular field. And more to feed than the family—there was an endless procession of guests; they came by to call, they stayed on for supper.

"How do you manage always to have enough food?" I asked. Esther Benson quoted a Hindu proverb for an answer: "Five were invited, here come nine, water the porridge—all should dine." "But I don't," she said, "John goes out in the catboat and fishes more dinner—a mackerel, a bluefish, or a flounder to broil. If it's a big fish, then it's stuffed and baked. And when it's blackfish I make Thomas Tew's chowder."

This chowder goes back to Thomas Tew, a wood carver living in the years 1818 to 1874. Both Esther and John, like the famous chowder, are descended from the Tews. But as John put in, "The chowder is from my side of the family, we kept it going."

We have tested this dish once for accuracy, twice for pleasure, and Esther Benson has okayed the recipe just as it's given here.

Thomas Tew's Blackfish Chowder

2 ounces salt pork or bacon, sliced

2 medium onions, coarsely chopped

6 cups fish or chicken stock

4 potatoes, peeled and diced

1¼ pounds plum tomatoes, coarsely chopped

3 tablespoons canned tomato puree

1 small lemon, washed thoroughly

1 teaspoon dried sage

½ teaspoon ground cloves

1 teaspoon sugar

Pinch of cayenne pepper

½ teaspoon freshly ground black pepper

Salt

6 (7-ounce) blackfish, red snapper, or cod fillets

1 cup red wine

1 tablespoon unsalted butter

Serves 6

In a large, heavy skillet over medium-high heat, fry the salt pork until crisp. Add the onions to the pan and fry until they are limp and pale gold.

In a large stockpot, combine the fish stock with the fried salt pork and onion. Take ½ cup of the stock, pour it into the skillet, and stir to break up the browned bits and get every last bit of the flavor, then pour it into the chowder. Add the potatoes, tomatoes, and tomato puree to the pot. Simmer over medium heat until potatoes are just tender, 10 to 12 minutes. Reduce the heat to low and cover.

Thinly slice the lemon, discarding the tough ends. Quarter the slices, place them in a small saucepan, and cover with water. Place over medium heat and simmer for 10 minutes (do not let water boil or the flavor will be bitter). Add the sage, cloves, sugar, cayenne pepper, black pepper, and salt to taste. Stir to combine and pour the mixture into the stockpot. Add the fish fillets. Reduce the heat to low and cook for 10 minutes, until the fish is cooked through.

Just before serving, add the wine and butter and stir to combine. Heat the chowder until very hot but do not let it boil. Serve in deep bowls with oyster crackers.

TWO TEATIME SWEETS I want you to meet, Rhode Island beauties, a blond and brunette from a South County farm. The blond is a big, old-fashioned sugar cookie made thin and cut in curving oak-leaf pattern, the brunette a gingerbread, made in card shape, made to break into fingers.

Mrs. Mary Dye Whaley McBay of Providence, of the Homemaking Department in the Rhode Island School for the Deaf, served me these cookies with a tall glass of milk a midmorning in June, in her vine-shadowed workroom.

I met the same cookies later that day in the town of Kingston at the borne of Mrs. McBay's sister, Grace Cather Whaley, former supervisor of home economics in the State Department of Education.

The sisters learned to make the cookies in Grandma Catherine Douglas Dye's kitchen in the long ago when they lived with their grandparents on the South County farm during summer vacations.

Today the sisters make these old-time cookie favorites almost as often as did their Grandma Catherine.

Leaf Sugar Cookies

1 cup (2 sticks) unsalted butter, softened

1 cup plus 1 tablespoon sugar

1 large egg

3 cups all-purpose flour

1 teaspoon baking soda

¼ teaspoon grated nutmeg

Makes about 3 dozen

In a large bowl using an electric mixer, beat the butter and 1 cup of the sugar until fluffy. Beat in the egg. Sift the flour, baking soda, and nutmeg into a medium bowl and stir into the creamed mixture.

Preheat the oven to 425 degrees. Grease 2 large baking sheets and set aside.

Turn the dough out onto a lightly floured surface. Using a rolling pin, roll out the dough ⅛ inch thick. Using several different leaf-shaped cookie cutters, gently press down on the dough and carefully outline the inside of each one

with a very sharp knife. Sprinkle the cookies with the remaining 1 tablespoon sugar. Using a spatula, carefully place the cookies on the prepared baking sheets.

Bake in batches for about 8 minutes each, or until the edges are lightly browned. Cool for 1 minute on the sheets. Using a spatula, gently remove the cookies from the sheet to wire racks to cool completely.

Card Gingerbread Cookies

⅓ cup unsalted butter, softened

⅓ cup brown sugar

1 large egg, lightly beaten

½ cup dark molasses

2½ cups sifted all-purpose flour

½ teaspoon baking soda

Scant ½ tablespoon ground ginger

¼ teaspoon ground cinnamon

¼ teaspoon salt

Makes about 2 dozen

In a large bowl using an electric mixer, beat the butter and brown sugar until fluffy. Beat in the egg, then stir in the molasses. Sift the flour, baking soda, ginger, cinnamon, and salt into a large bowl and stir into the creamed mixture.

Preheat the oven to 325 degrees. Grease 2 large baking sheets and set aside.

Turn the dough out onto a lightly floured surface. Using a rolling pin, roll out the dough ¼ inch thick. Using a very sharp knife, cut oblong playing-card-shaped cookies, about 3 inches wide by 4 inches long. Score the "cards" with the knife in ½ inch parallel lines on the diagonal. Using a spatula, carefully place the cookies on the prepared baking sheets.

Bake in batches for about 10 minutes each, until the edges are lightly browned. Cool for 1 minute on the sheets. Using a spatula, gently remove the cookies from the sheets and transfer to wire racks to cool completely.

CONNECTICUT

From Colonial days when Connecticut was playfully named "The Wooden Nutmeg State," it has been famed for herbs and spices. Today none of them are phonies as were the early imitations fashioned of wood in the shape of nutmegs, soaked in extract of the real thing and sold by the Yankee peddlers.

It was my good fortune to spend a day in Medford at "Saltacres," the home of the late Rosetta Clarkson, known then as the state's outstanding herbalist. Herb lovers from everywhere have gone there to visit at one time or another to see the greenhouses, the demonstration garden, rosemary cottage, and Mrs. Clarkson's collection of hoary herbals dating back to the fourteenth century.

Rosetta Clarkson was an English teacher who made herbs her hobby and started an herbal renaissance in the United States. The herbs of grandmother's time were neglected, "yarb" cookery virtually forgotten, when Rosetta planted a city lot to herbs and savory seeds. A green enchantment grew. One amateur gardener after another fell under its spicy spell. Today, herb gardens are springing up everywhere.

Herbed Beef Stew

½ cup all-purpose flour

1½ teaspoons salt

¼ teaspoon freshly ground black pepper

1 pound stewing beef, cubed

3 tablespoons bacon fat or olive oil

4 carrots, sliced into ½-inch-thick rounds

1 large onion, chopped

6 potatoes, quartered

1 (28-ounce) can crushed tomatoes

1 tablespoon dried summer savory

1 tablespoon dried marjoram

1 tablespoon dried chervil

1 tablespoon dried basil

Serves 6

In a large baking dish, combine the flour, salt, and pepper. Pat the beef cubes dry and roll them in the flour mixture. Heat the bacon fat or oil in a large pan over medium-high heat until it shimmers. Brown the meat, without crowding, in 3 batches, turning the cubes to cook thoroughly, about 8 minutes per batch. Do not drain the fat.

Preheat the oven to 325 degrees.

Arrange the browned meat in a deep 2½-quart casserole or Dutch oven. Add the carrots, onion, potatoes, and the pulp drained from the canned tomatoes (reserve the tomato juice).

Stir the remaining seasoned flour into the fat left in the reserved pan and place over medium heat. When the mixture begins to bubble, gradually pour in the reserved tomato juice, stirring constantly, and cook until slightly thickened. Add the herbs and stir until just combined.

Pour the liquid over the meat and vegetables, adding, if necessary, enough water to come 1 inch from top of casserole. Cover and bake for 1½ to 2 hours, until meat is very tender and stew is very saucy and rich. Serve over biscuits, buttered noodles, or polenta, if you like.

THIS VERSION OF CONNECTICUT'S Election Cake came to me from Mabel Farnham Mangano who discovered it a few years ago when leafing through old cookbooks that had belonged to her great-grandmother Julia Gilette (1800–1830) of Suffield. The cake was popular in northern Connecticut one hundred years ago. It was a time when farmers drove into town to vote at the town meeting and do other business. They made it a holiday. The women cooked an ample dinner and this special cake was served—and so the name. It's a cake that is invariably a favorite with men. And the flavor—nutmeg—but the real thing—makes it a historical conversation piece.

Grandmother Gilette's Election Cake

⟡⟡⟡⟡⟡⟡⟡⟡⟡⟡⟡⟡⟡⟡⟡⟡⟡⟡⟡⟡⟡⟡⟡⟡⟡⟡⟡⟡⟡⟡⟡⟡⟡⟡⟡⟡⟡

2 packages active dry yeast, about 2 teaspoons

¼ cup lukewarm water

¾ cup lukewarm milk

1 teaspoon salt

2½ cups all-purpose flour

½ cup (1 stick) unsalted butter, softened

1 cup sugar

2 large eggs

¾ teaspoon grated nutmeg

⅓ cup seedless halved raisins or dried cherries

½ cup chopped citron, optional

⟡⟡⟡⟡⟡⟡⟡⟡⟡⟡⟡⟡⟡⟡⟡⟡⟡⟡⟡⟡⟡⟡⟡⟡⟡⟡⟡⟡⟡⟡⟡⟡⟡⟡⟡⟡⟡

Serves 10 to 12

⟡⟡⟡⟡⟡⟡⟡⟡⟡⟡⟡⟡⟡⟡⟡⟡⟡⟡⟡⟡⟡⟡⟡⟡⟡⟡⟡⟡⟡⟡⟡⟡⟡⟡⟡⟡⟡

In a large bowl, dissolve the yeast in the lukewarm water. Add the milk and salt, then add 1½ cups of the flour. Using an electric mixer, beat thoroughly. Cover the bowl with a clean kitchen towel and set aside in a cool, dry place. Let the batter rise until light and almost fluffy, 45 minutes to 1 hour.

Generously grease and flour a 9-inch tube or Bundt pan.

In a large bowl using an electric mixer, beat the butter and sugar until fluffy. Add the eggs one at a time, beating well after each addition. Stir in the yeast mixture. Add the remaining 1 cup flour and the nutmeg and beat until smooth. Stir in the raisins and citron, if using. Turn the batter into the prepared pan, cover gently with a clean kitchen towel, and set aside in a cool dry place to rise until doubled in bulk, about 1 hour.

While the dough is rising, preheat the oven to 375 degrees.

Bake the cake for 35 to 40 minutes, until pale golden and a wooden pick or skewer inserted near the center comes out clean. Place on a wire rack and cool the cake in the pan for 10 minutes. Invert the cake onto a rack and cool for 45 minutes longer. Top the cake with a generous dusting of powdered sugar or your favorite creamy vanilla icing, if you like.

SAY FOURTH OF JULY. Think of watermelon. Think of homemade ice cream. Middle Westerners and Southerners answer fried chicken, but those who hail from New England give first thought to salmon.

It's to honor George Washington that "Down-Easters" boil the salmon to serve with egg sauce, with new potatoes, green peas, and mashed potatoes. The story is that this particular combination was the favorite summer supper of the father of our country after he had come to battle with his notoriously ill-fitting false teeth.

More likely, this patriotic custom has its start in old years when July was peak month for this fish in North Atlantic waters. Now the East gets most of its salmon from the West Coast. And western salmon costs less—more abundant, that's why.

Hot Poached Salmon

⅔ cup water

1 tablespoon cider vinegar

1 medium onion, minced

1 small carrot, minced

4 peppercorns

1½ teaspoons salt

2 celery leaves

3 sprigs parsley

1 teaspoon dried thyme

1 bay leaf

6 (6-ounce) center-cut salmon fillets, either skinless or skin-on

1 hard-cooked egg yolk, diced, optional

Parsley for garnish, optional

Serves 6

In a large skillet, combine the water, vinegar, onion, carrot, peppercorns, salt, celery leaves, parsley, thyme, and bay leaf. Bring to a boil, then reduce the heat and simmer for 30 minutes.

Place the salmon fillets in the stock, skin side down if using skin-on fillets. Cover and cook over medium-low heat until the salmon is barely opaque in the center, about 10 minutes. Remove from the heat. Let stand covered for 5 minutes.

Using a slotted spatula or a long slotted spoon, remove the fish fillets from the skillet, straining gently, and arrange on a platter. Sprinkle with egg yolk and parsley, if using.

Serve with egg sauce (recipe follows), plenty of lemon wedges, or a simple dip made of sour cream blended with finely chopped scallions, if you like.

Creamy Egg Sauce

4 hard-cooked egg yolks

¼ teaspoon salt

¼ teaspoon paprika

½ cup (1 stick) unsalted butter, softened

2 tablespoons heavy cream

2 teaspoons lemon juice

Makes about 1 cup

In a small bowl, mash the egg yolks with a fork until they form a paste. Add the salt and paprika. Gradually work in the softened butter, cream, and lemon juice. Use immediately, or cover the bowl tightly with plastic wrap and refrigerate. This "egg sauce" can become a compound butter and can be used to spread on English muffins or toast, or to top hot fish or other meat dishes.

Salmon in Dill

1 large salmon steak or salmon fillet at least 1 inch thick (2½ to 3 pounds)

4 tablespoons (½ stick) unsalted butter

⅓ cup chopped fresh dill

¼ teaspoon salt

½ cup water

⅓ cup dry white wine

1 tablespoon lemon juice

1 tablespoon all-purpose flour

1 cup light cream

Serves 6

Cut the salmon steaks into 1-inch cubes.

Melt 2 tablespoons of the butter in a large skillet or saucepan over medium heat. Add the salmon cubes and sprinkle with the dill and salt. Add the water, wine, and lemon juice. Simmer uncovered for 15 minutes, stirring gently once or twice.

While the salmon is cooking, melt the remaining 2 tablespoons butter in a large skillet over medium heat. Whisk in the flour and continue whisking to form a smooth paste. Reduce the heat to low and gradually whisk in the cream until smooth and slightly thickened, stirring constantly, about 7 minutes. Set aside.

When the fish is cooked, pour the sauce directly into the skillet with the fish. Heat over medium heat until liquid begins to bubble, but do not allow to boil. Serve immediately, straining the salmon cubes onto serving plates and serving alongside roasted new potatoes or creamy mashed potatoes, if you like.

A PASTEL IN PINKS

With memories of marjoram, of basil, and of dill tingling the tongue, I munched my way through the Nutmeg State right up to Simsbury near the Massachusetts line, there to enjoy an exhibition of culinary masterpieces by an artist with food, the late Mrs. J. Kell Brandon, before her marriage Dorothea Belt of Boston and Pinehurst.

I can close my eyes and still see that picture luncheon—a pastel in pinks.

And when the dish was ready—the rich brown of the baked chickens contrasting so pleasantly with the rosy pink of ham. And then the rice was ready—shell pink, each grain separate. What finer color scheme, the rice banked around the sauce-laved birds, a silver tray for a picture frame. It was a dish as romantic in its conception as the *Pastorale* of Corot.

Picture dishes came regularly from Dorothea's kitchen but never fussed over, no filigree work with the parsnips, no cutting of carrot cameos. This was everyday food, perfectly prepared and presented with an eye for color effect. Pink color schemes were Mrs. Brandon's delight. Pink, she told me, has a special affinity with the fine old house in which she lived.

This was a strong old house of pink-brown stone from a local quarry, built in 1850, one year in the building. It stood well back from College Highway just across the street from that historical landmark, the Congregational Church, the white steeple to be seen for miles away.

On this summer day the luncheon table was moved to the screened terrace opening through floor-to-ceiling windows from the library. And beyond I could see King Phillip Mountain going up and up. The tablecloth was white and pink with a touch of blue to match the garden flowers. Background for the setting was the pink-brown stone of the house. Luncheon appeared, pink the accent color. The food was planned as always around the specialties of the area—young broilers for example, and in peach time the local peaches, in fall the apples. "And my baked apples with strawberries are one of the best things we do," Mrs. Brandon told me. "We use the Cortland apples, cored but never stuffed, just a sprinkle of sugar in the cavity, then baked slowly. Serve just warm, sauced with frozen strawberries defrosted to room temperature."

Pink again: a ball of ice cream with a brandied peach and over the ice cream this raspberry sauce. Defrost package frozen raspberries, then heat. Press through sieve to remove seeds; add one teaspoon unflavored gelatin, two tablespoons sugar, two tablespoons port wine and chill in the refrigerator until serving time.

Chicken Simsbury

3 (1-inch-thick) slices ham (about 2 pounds)

1 cup (2 sticks) unsalted butter

2 pounds fresh mushrooms, quartered

6 pounds whole chicken parts, about 2 chickens

½ cup chicken stock

Serves 8

Preheat the oven to 450 degrees.

Cut the ham into 1-inch cubes. Melt 1 stick of the butter in a large skillet over medium-high heat. Brown the ham cubes, remove from the skillet using a slotted spoon, and set aside in a bowl, covered in foil to keep warm. Add the mushrooms and sauté in the same hot butter until just beginning to brown. Remove the pan from the heat.

Place the chicken pieces in a large roasting pan. Pour the ham, mushrooms, and butter from the skillet around the chicken. Dot the chicken pieces with the remaining 1 stick of butter.

Bake uncovered for 10 minutes.

Remove the roasting pan from the oven, pour off about ½ cup of the fat, and add the stock to the pan. Return to the oven and bake for 45 minutes, or until the chicken is tender, basting the birds every 15 minutes. Remove the chicken from the oven, cover the roasting pan loosely with foil, and rest for 10 to 15 minutes. Serve the chicken alongside pink rice (recipe follows), steamed white or wild rice, and sautéed green beans, if you like.

Pink Rice

1 cup (2 sticks) unsalted butter

3 cups long-grain white rice

⅔ cup finely chopped onion

½ cup canned chopped tomatoes

2½ cups tomato juice

2 cups beef or chicken stock

1 teaspoon salt

¼ teaspoon freshly ground black pepper

Serves 8 to 10

Preheat the oven to 375 degrees.

Melt the butter in a large heavy skillet over medium-high heat. Add the rice and cook until the butter bubbles briskly, about 3 minutes. Add the onion, tomatoes, tomato juice, and stock. Stir the mixture gently, add the salt and pepper, and cover the pan.

Bake for 30 minutes. Uncover the pan and gently stir and separate the rice using a fork. Cover again and bake for 20 minutes more, or until the rice is tender but not mushy. Serve immediately.

TY LONG, THE YOUNG Wagnerian singer, once invited me to his birthday party, a fabulous feast given in his parents' home near Norwalk, Connecticut. The party was given in honor of his fellow artists. Ty did the cooking himself.

If Ty hadn't decided on a singing career he might have been an anthropologist. He could have been a great chef. It was during his student days at Columbia University, specializing in anthropology and foreign languages, that he became interested in the foods of other lands. He practiced cooking in his mother's kitchen. He searched for the unusual ingredients in foreign markets. Now Ty is in operatic work in Munich, Germany, but on last report he is still cooking exotic dishes for friends.

Ty's birthday dinner was menued in seven languages, not counting English. Six dishes for prelude, appetizers all, to go with the strawberry wine bowl. Polish borsch for the soup course. Five entrées followed with a great green salad. Last, this flaming dessert named in honor of Alexander Kipnis (Sasha). It's a party recipe planned to serve thirty people.

Sasha Flambé

For the torte:

10 large eggs, separated

2½ cups sifted confectioners' sugar

⅓ cup sifted all-purpose flour

½ teaspoon baking powder

1 teaspoon vanilla extract

2 tablespoons dark rum

¾ pound walnuts, finely ground

½ pound pecans, finely ground

Apricot brandy

For the mousse:

¾ cup lemon juice

2 teaspoons grated lemon peel

2 cups sugar

Dash of salt

½ cup water

6 large eggs, separated

4 cups heavy cream, whipped

¾ cup cognac, optional

Serves 30

Preheat the oven to 300 degrees. Grease and flour two 15½ x 10½ x 1-inch loaf pans.

Make the torte: In a large bowl, using an electric mixer, beat the egg whites until stiff. Set aside.

In another large bowl, beat the egg yolks until very thick and lemon-colored. Gradually beat in the confectioners' sugar. Add the flour, baking powder, vanilla, and rum. Gently fold in the beaten egg whites and ground nuts.

Divide the batter evenly between the 2 pans. Bake the cakes for 30 to 35 minutes or until brown and tester inserted in the center comes out clean. Cool on a wire rack for 10 minutes, then run a thin knife around edge of pan and turn the cake out onto the rack to cool completely, about 1 hour.

Cut each cake in half crosswise. Brush the cut sides of each well with apricot brandy. Set aside while you make the mousse.

For the mousse: In a large saucepan, combine the lemon juice, lemon rind, 1¼ cups of the sugar, the salt, and ¼ cup of the water. Place over medium heat and stir until the sugar dissolves; bring to a boil and simmer for 20 minutes. Remove the pan from the heat.

In a large bowl, beat egg yolks until thick and lemon-colored. Gradually add the remaining ¼ cup water and the lemon mixture, whisking constantly. Cook the mixture over a double boiler while stirring constantly until thickened, 5 to 7 minutes. Take the bowl off the heat and cool.

While the custard cools, gently fold the whipped cream into the lemon sauce. Turn the mixture into a 15½ x 10½ x 1-inch loaf pan, cover with plastic wrap, and freeze until very firm, about 1 hour.

Unmold and cut the mousse crosswise into 3 sections. On a plate, alternate layers of torte and mousse (4 of torte and 3 of mousse). Gently wrap the cake in plastic wrap and freeze again for 30 minutes.

Preheat the oven to 500 degrees.

While cake is freezing and oven is preheating, in a large bowl, beat the egg whites with an electric mixer until stiff but not dry peaks are formed. Gradually beat in the remaining ¾ cup sugar. Set the meringue aside.

Remove the cake from the freezer and cover the sides and top with meringue. Bake for 3 to 5 minutes, until lightly browned.

If you'd like to make this flambé, heat the cognac gently over medium heat, pour over the Sasha, and light.

THE

MIDDLE

ATLANTIC

STATES

NEW YORK

In New York City you eat around the clock, around the calendar;
East Side, West Side, all around the town, around the world,
and sometimes almost out of this world. And besides being our
eatingest city, this little old Manhattan, which we bought from the
Indians for a few bottles of rum, is still the drinkingest. Not only a
hot melting pot, but the world's greatest pot for all kinds of dishes.

For a soup-to-nuts feast begin with a
Ritz Carlton vichyssoise, a soup that's
really regal, and go on and on, course
by course, to cheesecake at Lindy's
come midnight.

Or, better still, start the eating with
oysters, right handy there as you get off
the train at the Grand Central Station.

Oyster stew for a light supper, oyster
stew after the theater, after midnight
caroling. His Majesty the Oyster is
indigenous to this city and New Yorkers
insist there are no oysters better than
the fat firm Long Island kind, no dish to
beat oyster stew as it's made at Grand
Central Oyster Bar.

Here come the oyster lovers from
all over the world. Stop at the bar any
time day or night and you might see Lily
Pons, for she likes to go there; so does
Gene Tunney; so does Bing Crosby, Tom
Dewey, and Mae West. So does everyone
who comes to town hungry for oysters.

The bar opened in 1913 as the first
Union News restaurant. It remains

unchanged except for minor repairs.
Here 25,000 oysters are dispensed
every day during the "R" season, which
brings the total for the eight-month
period to approximately ten million
bivalves. Oysters and clams are hand-
opened by thirty-six oystermen who
work in shifts, and twenty-six of these
experts have been Johnny-on-the-spot
for a quarter of a century.

How does the world want its oysters?
Half-shell and in stew. Half-shell
enthusiasts may take but a long squirt
of lemon, a dust of black pepper. But
most of the crowd prefer dunking the
oyster in the Grand Central Oyster Bar's
sauce, made some twenty gallons a day.
Opposite we give the recipe boiled down
to one quart of the lusty red mixture.
Hot enough to fire at thirty paces. A
good companion for shrimp, too.

Running neck and neck with oysters
on the half-shell is the oyster in stew.
Follows oyster pie, then oyster pan
roast. The experienced barman can

make a soup in exactly a minute and a half, thanks to the steam-pressure stew pots that heat in a wink. Turn on the steam, drop in a big lump of butter or margarine—a rounded teaspoonful—now a splash of the Worcestershire, a dash of celery salt, one of paprika, quickly in with the oysters, seven to a portion.

Give the mixture a stir and almost on the moment it comes to a bubble. At this point one-fourth cup of oyster juice is added and this brought to a bubble boil. Milk next, or milk and cream, or all cream—that's up to you. A skim around with the spoon, a second to rest. See, the surface is shivering. There it is next to boiling. Turn into a bowl, add a big pat of butter or margarine, a sprinkle of paprika; a milky sea-fresh smell curls up through the warm air.

Now you take a try. Here's the recipe developed in family style using home kitchen equipment. It takes more than a minute but tastes just as fine.

Oyster Stew

28 oysters, well chilled

6 tablespoons (¾ stick) unsalted butter

2 teaspoons Worcestershire sauce

1 teaspoon sweet paprika

½ teaspoon celery salt

1 cup whole milk

1 cup half-and-half

Salt

Serves 4

Shuck the oysters over a medium bowl to catch the oyster liquor, putting the shucked oysters into another bowl. Discard the shells.

Melt 4 tablespoons of the butter in a medium saucepan over medium-high heat. Stir in the Worcestershire sauce, paprika, and celery salt, then add oysters and bring to a simmer. Add 1 cup of the reserved oyster liquor to pan, discarding any remaining liquor, and bring to a boil. Add the milk and half-and-half to the pan and heat, stirring once or twice, until just about to boil (do not allow to boil, or the stew will curdle), 3 to 5 minutes. Season with salt.

Divide the remaining 2 tablespoons butter among 4 warm soup bowls just before ladling in the stew.

Oyster Pan Roast

4 dozen oysters, cleaned

1 cup (2 sticks) unsalted butter

6 tablespoons chili sauce

2 teaspoons Worcestershire sauce

1½ tablespoons lemon juice

1½ cups oyster liquor

½ teaspoon celery salt

1 teaspoon paprika

¼ cup heavy cream

Salt

Serves 6

Place the oysters in a large, deep heavy saucepan or skillet. Dot with the butter. Add the chili sauce, Worcestershire sauce, lemon juice, oyster liquor, celery salt, and paprika. Place over medium heat and bring to a boil. Cook, stirring constantly, for about 1 minute. Add the cream and bring to a simmer (do not let it boil). Season with salt. To serve, ladle the mixture over toast in soup plates.

Cocktail Sauce

1½ bottles (about 14 ounces) ketchup

½ (12-ounce) bottle chili sauce

6 tablespoons Worcestershire sauce

1 cup prepared horseradish

A few dashes of Tabasco sauce

Makes 1 quart

The day before you wish to use the sauce, mix all the ingredients together in a large bowl. Cover and let stand for 30 minutes to marry the flavors, then refrigerate for 24 hours. The sauce can be kept in the refrigerator for up to 3 days before using.

IT WAS THE GREAT Oscar Tschirky who created the Waldorf salad to take its social bow at a society supper at the preview of the original Fifth Avenue Waldorf, March, 1893. George C. Boldt, proprietor of the hotel, knew that if Waldorf guests were to include the "Four Hundred" he must gather them there for some festive first occasion. He planned the preview in connection with a benefit concert for society's pet charity, St. Mary's Hospital for Children. He offered the use of the rooms and served the supper without charge. In attendance came fifteen hundred social leaders from New York, Philadelphia, Baltimore, Boston. The evening was a great success with Walter Damrosch conducting the New York Symphony and Oscar ruling in the kitchen. From that night forth the hotel was society's rendezvous, the Waldorf salad the talk of the table, salad made as simply as this: two parts diced apple to one part celery, tossed in mayonnaise, served on crisp lettuce, the variations came later.

Waldorf Salad

1½ cups cored and diced unpeeled tart red apples

1 tablespoon lemon juice

1 cup diced celery

½ cup mayonnaise

Iceberg or other large lettuce leaves, chilled

1 cup chopped walnuts

Serves 4

Place the apples in a large bowl and sprinkle them with the lemon juice to keep from discoloring. Add the celery, then stir in the mayonnaise. Arrange the lettuce leaves on 4 salad plates and spoon in the salad mixture. Just before serving, sprinkle with the walnuts.

YEARS AGO WHEN THE old Ritz-Carlton opened its Roof Garden Restaurant, New York City was served its first vichyssoise. The late Chef Louis Diat, master of the hotel kitchen, sought to provide foods different for summer dining. His mother's potato and leek potage made with chicken stock came to mind. He remembered how in hot weather at home, when the children begged for something cool, the ingenious Madame Diat worked out the formula. Since the little town from which he came is almost unknown but close to the famous watering place Vichy, he called the soup vichyssoise. On the Ritz menu the name became Crême Vichyssoise Glacé which means that cream is included and that it is served very cold.

Today every New York restaurant of any rating serves the soup and no two alike, being built from anything that even approaches the original formula. Here we give you the Diat vichyssoise, which has a light delicacy that so many of the imitations lack.

Louis Diat's Vichyssoise

1 tablespoon unsalted butter

4 leeks, white and pale green parts only, cleaned well and cut into 1-inch pieces

½ cup chopped onion

1 quart boiling water or chicken stock

5 medium boiling potatoes, peeled and cut into ½-inch pieces

1 tablespoon salt

3 cups heavy cream

1 tablespoon chopped chives, optional

Serves 6

Melt the butter in a large saucepan over medium heat, then add the leeks and onions. Sauté until softened but not browned, 3 to 4 minutes Add the boiling water, potatoes, and salt. Simmer until the potatoes are tender, about 30 minutes.

Pour the mixture in a blender in 2 to 3 batches depending on blender capacity, and puree for 1 minute, or until smooth. Return the puree to the pan and add the cream.

Place over medium heat, bring the soup almost back up to a boil, then remove from the heat. Pour the soup into a large bowl, cool to room temperature, then cover and refrigerate for at least 6 hours or overnight. For a bright garnish and extra flavor, sprinkle with the chives.

Note: Serve in a large bowl set in a bed of ice, or "simply in a cup set in a wide soup plate filled with ice cubes," to use Mr. Diat's suggestion for home service.

ONE OF GOD'S BEST GIFTS

Manhattan dotes on Vichyssoise, but there are other notable soups which favor the leek, "one of God's best gifts to man." The leek is a favorite vegetable with the European-born New Yorkers and those who learn from them the ways of this root, a relative of the onion, cultivated for the thickened lower part of its stem. Blanchette Arnaud of Jackson Heights, New York, wife of Leopold Arnaud, Dean of the School of Architecture of Columbia University, learned of the leek from her husband's family. Her father-in-law was Spanish and her husband, though born here, lived much of his life in France and that explains why many of her specialties are Continental in origin. The Arnauds do a round of entertaining each winter and friends are lavish in their praise of Blanchette's menus. Dishes for the most part are inexpensive, made of everyday foods, but the unusual ones.

When I met Mrs. Arnaud she was a part-time teacher, lecturing on world history at the Private Collegiate School in New York City. She had also been a part-time guide in the Metropolitan Museum of Art giving gallery talks. Cooking, however, was her greatest interest. Being academic-minded, she likes to research, so had investigated the background of the leek. As I said, it resembles the common green onion, but is smaller in size, sweeter in flavor. Mrs. Arnaud adds, "It has been eaten since the dawn of history and was greatly relished by the Romans, Greeks, and Egyptians. Leek soup was a favorite dish of Nero. It is the emblem of Wales."

The plant has broad, dark green leaves, straight, thick stalk, white neck, long white thread-like roots resembling witch's hair. It is sold in bunches, priced slightly higher than the green onion. Remove root and outer skin and wash thoroughly as earth packs between the leaves. Remove green tops and boil stalks in salted water for fifteen minutes. Drain and serve buttered with a cream sauce. Mrs. Arnaud uses leeks in many recipes as a substitute for asparagus.

Leek and Potato Soup

3 large or 4 small leeks, white and pale green parts only, thinly sliced (4½ to 5 cups)

3 medium or 2 large russet potatoes, peeled and diced

4½ cups strong beef broth or stock

Salt and freshly ground black pepper

1 to 2 teaspoons unsalted butter, optional

Serves 4

In 2 large pots, bring about 3 cups of salted water to boil over medium-high heat in each. Add the leeks to one and the potatoes to the other. Reduce the heat and simmer for about 20 minutes, until tender.

Turn off the heat under both pots and place a strainer or colander over the leek pot. Pour the contents of the potato pot into the strainer and mash the potatoes through the holes. Add the beef stock and season with salt and pepper. Bring the soup to a boil over medium heat, reduce heat, and simmer the soup for 5 minutes. Stir in the butter, if you like. Serve immediately.

IN NEW YORK CITY you can dine around the clock on a million or a dollar. At Jack and Charlie's famous "21" Club a main course for a party luncheon or a midnight bust is frequently this crown of lobster served with toasted French bread and a green salad.

This dish is extravagant. It requires expensive materials, it takes time to make. The can opener isn't going to help you much except to come by a truffle.

Crown of Lobster is a yours-from-scratch creation, a glamorous recipe. It is a dish for gourmets and gourmet cooks, a recipe originated by Escoffier, something to make just once in a long, long while when you feel in the mood to do the elaborate.

The recipe here is developed for the home cook by the talented Yves Louis Ploneis in charge of the "21" kitchen. A very great chef is this French-born

Yves who came to the United States in 1930, going first to the Greenbrier Hotel in White Sulphur Springs, West Virginia, later to the French Pavilion at the World's Fair, and from then to now at the "21" except for those years he served his adopted country as a mess sergeant in the army.

Crown of Lobster

4 cups cooked lobster meat, cut in small chunks

1 cup heavy cream

2 large egg whites, stiffly beaten

¼ cup brandy, sherry, or white wine

Salt and freshly ground black pepper

Dash of Worcestershire sauce

Cayenne pepper

2 or 3 truffles, thinly sliced

White of 1 hard-cooked egg, sliced

Serves 4

Butter a round 2-quart metal food mold and chill in the refrigerator.

Place the lobster meat in a large bowl. Settle the lobster bowl inside another bowl filled with chopped ice, so that the lobster bowl is effectively buried to the rim in another bowl of chopped ice. Slowly pour the cream into the lobster and mix well. Using a rubber spatula, gradually fold in the egg whites, then add the brandy. Season with salt and pepper, the Worcestershire sauce and cayenne. Set aside.

Remove the buttered mold from the refrigerator. Decorate the bottom with sliced truffles arranged alternately with pieces of egg white. Pour the lobster mixture into the mold, cover, and refrigerate for 3 hours.

Preheat the oven to 375 degrees. Remove the lobster mold from the refrigerator and cover the bottom with waxed paper; fasten it tightly. Place the mold in a large roasting pan filled with an inch of boiling water. Bake for 35 minutes, or until firm. Remove from the oven and turn the mold upside down onto a warm platter. Let rest for about 10 minutes, then unmold. Slice and serve with sauce cardinal (recipe follows) or any other sauce you may prefer.

Sauce Cardinal

4 tablespoons (½ stick) unsalted butter

Meat of 1 (2½-pound) lobster, diced

¼ cup diced truffles

1 cup brandy

3 cups Fish Velouté (see Note)

1 cup heavy cream

3 tablespoons Lobster Butter (recipe follows)

Makes enough for 1 Crown of Lobster

Melt the butter in a medium saucepan over medium heat. Add the lobster meat and truffles and sauté for 3 minutes. Add the brandy and cook for about 2 minutes. Add the fish velouté and cream, reduce the heat to medium-low, and cook until the sauce is of medium thickness, stirring constantly, 7 to 8 minutes. Add the lobster butter and mix well. Serve hot.

Note: Fish velouté is a classic French sauce made like béchamel: Blend together 2½ tablespoons unsalted butter and ⅓ cup flour in a saucepan over medium-low heat, then slowly add 3 cups hot fish stock. Whisk together and simmer until thickened, about 15 minutes.

Lobster Butter

2 cups (4 sticks) butter

lobster shells from 3–4 lobsters

lobster lungs from 3-4 lobsters

Makes enough for 1 Crown of Lobster

Melt the butter in the top part of a double boiler over simmering water. Skim the top, then let rest. Pound the lobster shells and add to the butter along with the lobster lungs. Simmer for 3 hours in the double boiler, then strain. Any leftover butter may be frozen, if desired, for up to one month.

ANYONE INTERNATIONALLY FAMOUS can be found at some time or other, in, or visiting New York City. It was here I interviewed the cook of the great, late Arturo Toscanini. I was told soup was the dish he enjoyed above all else. He was a man almost Spartan in his eating habits. Food was the last thing he would fuss about, but it might be the first thing if he didn't get the soup.

The recipes here were given to me by cook Anna, given word of mouth, onion by carrot by cup of beef broth.

Escarole Soup

½ pound escarole (about ½ head), cut crosswise into ½-inch strips (about 6 packed cups), washed well and spun dry

2 large eggs, beaten

2 tablespoons grated Parmesan cheese

3½ cups beef stock

Serves 2

Bring a large, heavy saucepan of salted water to a boil, add the escarole, and cook until tender, about 10 minutes. Drain the escarole, finely chop it, and return it to the pan. Stir the eggs into the escarole, then stir in the cheese. Gradually add the stock, stirring constantly. Warm the soup to a bare simmer and serve immediately. A quite different soup, one you'll enjoy.

Minestrone

¼ cup dried French green lentils

1 tablespoon olive oil

1 tablespoon unsalted butter

¼ cup chopped onion

½ cup chopped celery

½ cup diced carrot

2 large tomatoes, chopped

1 small turnip, chopped

⅓ cup coarsely chopped Savoy cabbage

1 small russet potato, peeled and chopped

2 quarts beef stock

½ cup fresh or frozen and thawed green peas

½ cup red kidney beans

½ cup uncooked rice

Serves 6

In a small bowl, soak the lentils in 1 cup of water for 1 hour.

Melt the butter in the oil in a wide, heavy stockpot over medium heat. Add the onions and cook until transparent, about 3 minutes. Add the celery, carrots, and tomatoes; cook for 3 to 5 minutes to soften. Add the turnip, cabbage, and potato, along with 1 quart of the beef stock and the drained lentils. Simmer gently until the lentils are almost tender, about 25 minutes. Add the green peas and kidney beans. Add the remaining 1 cup stock and the rice and simmer for 15 minutes. Remove from the heat, let stand for 10 minutes, and serve with bread sticks or crusty rolls.

Gnocchi

3 cups mashed russet potatoes
(from about 1½ pounds potatoes),
cooled to room temperature

1 cup all-purpose flour

2 large egg yolks, beaten

¼ cup grated Parmesan cheese,
plus more for serving

Melted unsalted butter

Serves 4

Turn the mashed potatoes onto a lightly floured surface. Work in the flour, egg yolks, and cheese with your hands to form a dough. Roll the dough into 3 or 4 ropes, each about ¾ inch thick. Cut each rope into 1-inch lengths and press with the floured tines of a fork. Place the gnocchi on a baking sheet in rows.

Bring a large pot salted water to a boil. Drop in the gnocchi and boil just until they float on the water's surface, then remove with slotted spoon and carefully transfer to bowls. Serve with melted butter and dust with grated Parmesan cheese, that to please the maestro. His family prefers the following tomato sauce as the accompaniment. Pass separately, each guest helps himself.

Tomato Sauce

½ cup (1 stick) unsalted butter

1 small onion, chopped

¼ cup chopped celery
(about 1 large stalk)

2 tablespoons chopped carrots (about
1 medium carrot)

1¼ cups canned tomatoes

1 (8-ounce) can tomato sauce

Salt and freshly ground black pepper

Makes enough for 1 recipe of Gnocchi

Melt the butter in a large saucepan over medium heat.
Add the onion, celery, and carrots. Cook for about 5
minutes to soften the vegetables but do not let them
brown. Add the tomatoes and tomato sauce. Cover,
reduce the heat to very low, and cook until thick, about
45 minutes. Strain and season with salt and pepper. Pass
with the gnocchi.

PROUD THE CHEESECAKE, a Broadway
favorite. It stands half a foot tall, it
measures one foot across. Its top is
shiny as satin and baked to the gold
of the frost-tinged oak. Trim and
smooth are the sides. The knife slips
through, it comes out clean. Fluffy,
velvet soft, the filling dry, but not too
dry, an extravaganza in richness.
Cheese and eggs are the body and soul
of its substance.

This is the Lindy cheesecake,
beloved by the Broadway celebrities,
by all people who go to Lindy's to feast.

There's cheesecake for luncheon, it's
an afternoon filler, starred as dinner
dessert. But to see the cheesecake
full bloom, go around midnight when
the theater crowd pushes in. Then the
orders for cheesecake and coffee are
as a refrain.

The late Mr. Lindy, full name Leo
Lindeman, was a lovable, laughable,
unpredictable little man. If he liked you
he would give you virtually anything
except the way of the cheesecake. Then
the impossible happened. "Have a piece
of the cherry cheese pie," he urged as

I finished a wedge of cheesecake plain. "How about serving up the recipe?" I asked. It was our way of saying it was a wonderful cake. Mr. Lindy snapped his fingers for a waiter. "Call the baker," he ordered. From the hinterland of the huge restaurant came little Paul Landry. He couldn't believe his ears. The cheesecake recipe was being handed over by the big boss. I give it to you as Paul Landry gave it to me.

Lindy's Cheesecake

For the cheese filling:

2½ pounds cream cheese, at room temperature

1¾ cups sugar

3 tablespoons all-purpose flour

1½ teaspoons grated orange peel

1½ teaspoons grated lemon peel

Pinch of vanilla bean (inside pulp) or ¼ teaspoon vanilla extract

5 large eggs

2 large egg yolks

¼ cup heavy cream

For the pastry:

1 cup sifted all-purpose flour

¼ cup sugar

1 teaspoon grated lemon peel

Pinch of vanilla bean (inside pulp)

1 large egg yolk

½ cup (1 stick) unsalted butter or margarine

Serves 12

To make the filling: In a large bowl, combine the cream cheese, sugar, flour, grated peels, and vanilla. Beat in the eggs and egg yolks one at a time, stirring after each addition. Stir in the cream and set aside.

To make the pastry: Preheat the oven to 400 degrees. Oil the bottom of a 9-inch springform cake pan. In a large bowl, combine the flour, sugar, lemon peel, and vanilla. Make a well in the center and add the egg yolk and butter. Work together quickly with your hands until well blended and to form a ball. Wrap the ball in waxed paper and chill thoroughly in the refrigerator, about 1 hour.

Roll out the pastry ⅛ inch thick and place over the prepared springform cake pan. Trim any overflow dough by running a rolling pin over the sharp edges. Reserve the trimmings.

To bake: Place in the oven and bake for 20 minutes, or until light gold in color. Place on a wire rack and cool completely. Increase the oven temperature to 500 degrees.

Butter the sides of the cake form and snap over the base. Roll the remaining dough ⅛ inch thick and press inside the band. Fill the form with the cream cheese mixture and bake for 10 minutes. Reduce the oven temperature to 250 degrees and bake for 1 hour. Set on a wire rack and cool for at least 2 hours before unmolding and cutting.

ISLAND LONG ON DUCKS

Snuggling close to the famous island of Manhattan is a big sister island 130 miles long and 20 miles wide known as Long Island. It contains about half the population accredited to the city of New York and over one-fourth the population of the State.

Henry Hudson, English captain of the Dutch ship *Half Moon,* on a Northwest sea route searching the riches of the Indies, made history when he landed in 1609 on a Long Island beach. He laid claim to the island in the name of Holland. The first deeds for its purchase, bought from the Indians by the Dutch settlers, were dated 1636.

By 1640 English settlers had established homes in Eastern Long Island at Southold and Southampton. The island was of foremost importance in Colonial times. Today the flats and farms are a part of Brooklyn. The beach is known as Coney Island.

There was a period around the turn of the century when the Island was covered with vast estates owned by some of the most famous names in politics, business, and finance. Now it belongs mostly to the workaday world. Here are huge factories, flourishing farms, and, in the boroughs of Brooklyn and Queens, thriving businesses. Long Island has a large fishing industry. She is famous for oysters, scallops, clams, and for cauliflower and potatoes. Her duck farms are doing a land-office business. The Long Island duckling is known nationwide.

This duckiest capital of the world comes to quacking life around the first of April.

Banks of creeks and inlets are edged with ducks like drifts of lingering snow. Mile after mile of ducks are paddling the waterways. The ducks have a monopoly of the air. It vibrates with their talk.

Great batteries of incubators, electrically controlled, turn eggs into ducklings in twenty-eight days. Ducks are hatched hungry. In ten weeks a duckling eats five times its weight in food. Then behold, fresh duckling for dinner. But a fat duck doesn't mean layers of fat. It means a duck of rounded body, no pelvic bones sticking out and up, no angles or sharp points showing.

Long Island ducks are not native Long Islanders. They are descendants of ducks that as recently as 1872 waddled about the imperial aviaries in Peking, China. The story is that a member of the importing firm of Fegg and Company was on a business trip to China in the spring of '72. There he saw ducks of unusual size and obtained a few eggs, which he took to the Shanghai office to have incubated. Fifteen ducklings hatched and grew. The same spring came a clipper from Stonington, Connecticut, with James E. Palmer, poultry breeder and financier searching the Orient for new poultry products. He bought the ducks to bring to America. Six died at sea, but the other nine were safely landed in 1873. Those nine are the "Mayflower" ancestors of all Long Island ducklings.

Duck growers' wives are partial to this recipe for duckling in orange juice. And did you ever have duckling fried?

Roast Duckling in Orange Juice

1 (5- to 6-pound) Long Island duck

Salt

1 onion

1 tablespoon vegetable oil

½ cup orange juice

2 tablespoons all-purpose flour

1 cup water

Peel of 1 orange, blanched and finely shredded

12 to 16 small orange sections, optional

Serves 4

Preheat the oven to 500 degrees.

To prepare the duckling for roasting: Rub salt over the surface and in the cavity and place the onion inside. Rub the outside surface with the oil. Place on a rack in a roasting pan. Bake for 15 minutes, basting with orange juice every 5 minutes, then reduce the oven temperature to 350 degrees and continue baking for 15 to 20 minutes longer, still basting every 5 minutes with orange juice, until a thermometer inserted in the thigh registers 170 degrees.

Transfer the duck from the pan to a cutting board; remove the onion from the cavity and discard it. Let the duck rest, covered lightly with aluminum foil.

In the pan, skim the fat from the drippings. To 2 tablespoons of the fat, whisk in the flour. Add the water, gradually stirring until the mixture is smooth. Add the remaining orange juice and the zest. Simmer very gently for 5 minutes, but do not let it boil. Carve the duck for serving, cover with the sauce, and garnish with orange sections, if you like.

Fried Duckling

1 (5- to 6-pound) duckling

1 large egg, beaten

3 tablespoons milk

Salt and freshly ground black pepper

½ cup fine dry breadcrumbs

2 tablespoons water

Serves 4

Preheat the oven to 350 degrees.

First, cut up the duck: Thoroughly wash and pat it dry. Cut off the fatty flap of neck skin and reserve it. Insert a sharp knife into one breast near the shoulder joint and slice around the wishbone in a semicircle. Slide your finger in back of the wishbone and pry it out. To remove the legs, lift the duck by one leg and cut through the skin all around the thigh, including the meaty piece along the backbone, called the "oyster." Grasp the leg at the knee and pull back the thigh to expose the joint. Cut through it and pull the leg off the carcass in one piece. Repeat to remove the other leg. Cut the drumsticks from the thigh pieces. To remove the breast halves, slice along both sides of the breastbone. Lay the duck on its side and cut through the upper shoulder joint. Hold the carcass down by the neck with one hand, grasp the shoulder section with the other, and pull off the entire breast half, in one piece. Repeat on the other side. Pull out the two slim meaty fillets that remain on either side of the breastbone. Chop off the wing tips. Cut around the wing on one breast piece to free it from the breastbone; separate the largest wing joint from the other two. Repeat on the other side. You should now have 12 pieces. Cut the trimmed skin and fat into very small pieces.

Melt the duck fat in a large saucepan over medium heat. Meanwhile, in a wide shallow pan, whisk together the egg and milk. In another wide shallow pan, mix together the salt and pepper and breadcrumbs. Dip the duck pieces, one at a time, in the egg wash, then the breadcrumbs, and then fry until golden brown, turning the pieces as needed, about 20 minutes total. Remove the pan from the heat. Pour the excess fat out of the pan and add the water. Cover and bake for 50 minutes, removing the cover during the last 10 minutes of cooking. Let rest covered for 10 minutes, then serve.

OYSTERS ARE THE OPENING PRAYER

East Hampton on the far end of the island is a tidy little town with a village green and a white steepled church. It is a town boastfully proud of its Colonial-day homes, its traditional foods. It has every right to be proud. In East Hampton is that old famous home built in 1660, the gray-shingled cottage, that inspired John Howard Payne to write "Home Sweet Home."

It was a week before Thanksgiving during the darkest years of World War II that I went knocking at East Hampton's kitchen doors asking for recipes that have come down through the local families, mother to daughter, for three centuries. These are recipes with a New England flavor, for the town was united in 1657 with the Connecticut colony. During three days I walked into the old kitchens of the gray-shingled, slope-roofed houses built in the seventeenth century. I talked to the women whose ancestors built the houses, and whose Thanksgiving dinner would be the traditional dinner of the island. I picked through the treasured receipts of the Edwardses, the Daytons, the Lawrences, the Mulfords, the Osbornes. Give us a menu, I said, as typical of Long Island as the breath of fog in the face, or an Island field of potatoes. Give us the dish-by-dish setup of an early American dinner that might have been cooked in the great fireplace in the kitchen of the "Home, Sweet Home" when John Payne was a boy. This is what they gave me:

Gardiner's Bay Oysters
Turkey Amagansett with
Sausage-Apple Stuffing
Napeague Beach Cranberry Sauce
Long Island Whipped Potatoes
Giblet Gravy
Glazed Onions
Baked Squash
Mashed Turnip or Cauliflower
Light Oatmeal Rolls
Montauk Hills Wild Grape Jelly
Red and Green Relish Garlic Pickles
Celery Radishes
Brown Sugar Pumpkin Pie
Stone Jar Mince Pie
Coffee Jericho Cider

Gardiner's Bay oysters are the opening prayer. Lemon, please, and just a dash of pepper, and very little salt, for these are oysters extra salty, extra tanged, due to the close proximity of the beds to the open sea.

That tantalizing odor of browning bird is turkey, hand-picked from local flocks. Divers ways to stuff a bird, yet East Hampton women are mostly agreed that there is no better dressing to be made than that which Mrs. N. N. Tiffany dips out of her turkey on Thanksgiving Day. Bread crumbs, sausage, celery, apple, all perfumed with sage—a stuffing bound to make a bird almost burst with pride, a stuffing pleasingly moist yet crumbly when dipped to the plate.

The Long Island potato is the first-ranking crop. Only in Aroostook, Maine, are more potatoes grown annually than in Suffolk County. Light snowy drifts of mashed potatoes heap Thanksgiving bowls. Whip potatoes light as cream, the women insist.

Long Island is cauliflower's favorite home. Some grow in California, some in Colorado, but the island grows the most and Long Island grew it first. The plants were brought from Europe by the Duryea family at least seventy-seven years ago. Many ways to cook the cauliflower but for the Thanksgiving Day it will be cooked just tender and served with drawn butter and a sprinkling of buttered crumbs or a halo of paprika or a golden crown of American cheddar.

Go to the kitchen of Mrs. E. T. Dayton for a glazed onion recipe.

The marshes of Amagansett and Napeague supply the cranberries. Every family in these parts picks enough for a few special jars for holiday dinners. High brier blackberries make a jelly with a bouquet like a song. Wild grapes are gathered at Montauk. From Napeague come the beach plums to cook down to a purple loveliness, to tumble into cut-glass jelly bowls.

Mrs. Beck's Cauliflower à la Polonaise

1 large head cauliflower
(2½ to 3 pounds)

1 teaspoon salt

1 quart water

3 tablespoons unsalted butter
or margarine

6 tablespoons dry breadcrumbs
or cracker meal

Serves 4 to 6

Remove the leaves and stalk of the cauliflower and wash it well. Bring the water to a boil in a 5-quart wide heavy pot and add the salt. Place the cauliflower in the pot, cover, and steam until just tender, about 15 minutes. Drain and place on a warm platter.

Melt the butter in a small saucepan over medium-high heat. Add the breadcrumbs and cook until golden and crisp, 3 to 5 minutes. Spread over the cauliflower.

Mrs. Dayton's Glazed Onions

Salt

4 pounds small white onions, unpeeled

½ cup sugar

⅔ cup water

½ cup (1 stick) unsalted butter, cut into pieces

1 or 2 sprigs fresh parsley

Serves 6 to 8

Bring a large pot of water to a boil over high heat and add 2 generous pinches of salt. Add the onions and cook until soft when pierced, 15 to 20 minutes. Drain the onions in a colander and set aside until cool enough to handle. Peel the onions by trimming the root ends and slipping them out of their skins, then spread them out over a single layer in a large heatproof baking dish.

Preheat the broiler. Combine the sugar and water in a medium heavy-bottom saucepan, cover the pot, and bring to a boil, swirling the pan over the heat several times until the sugar dissolves, about 5 minutes. Add the butter and 1 teaspoon salt and heat, swirling the pan occasionally, until the butter melts, about 5 minutes more.

Pour the sugar-butter mixture over the onions and broil, basting and turning the onions frequently, until the onions brown and the syrup turns pale golden, 20 to 30 minutes. Transfer the onions and syrup to a warm serving dish and garnish with the parsley sprigs.

Mrs. Lawrence's
Brown Sugar Pumpkin Pie

1 (9-inch) Perfect Pie Crust (page 13)

2 cups pumpkin puree

¾ cup firmly packed brown sugar

½ teaspoon salt

1 teaspoon grated lemon peel

½ teaspoon ground ginger

¼ teaspoon ground mace

¼ teaspoon grated nutmeg

⅛ teaspoon vanilla extract

3 large eggs, lightly beaten

1¾ cups milk

Serves 6 to 8

Preheat the oven to 450 degrees.

Line a 9-inch pie pan with the pastry and make a fluted standing rim.

Place the pumpkin in a medium bowl. Add the brown sugar, salt, lemon peel, ginger, mace, nutmeg, and vanilla and blend thoroughly with the pumpkin. Stir in the eggs.

Warm the milk in a small pan over medium heat until just bubbling but not boiling and gradually add the milk to the pumpkin mixture, stirring continuously. Pour the mixture into the prepared crust and bake for 10 minutes. Reduce the oven temperature to 350 degrees and bake for 30 to 40 minutes longer, until a wooden pick or skewer comes out clean when inserted in the custard.

JEANETTE RATTRAY GAVE GENEROUSLY of her recipes, hand-downs from the Edwardses on her father's side who came to the town in 1648 and from the Hunttings on her mother's side who settled in East Hampton fifty years later in 1699. Until 1924, when Jeannette's brother married a girl from Idaho, and 1925, when she married Arnold Rattray of California, no member of her family had married outside the village.

East Hampton's chowders are all made from heirloom recipes that go back for centuries. Jeannette says that soup, as it is served there today (she doesn't mean chowder), also the salads, are imported frills brought in by the summer people, the New York City folks who first invaded the village as a vacation spot back in the 1840's.

The day I had luncheon in the Rattrays' cottage it was Jeannette's mother who provided the Long Island clam chowder—much thicker than a Manhattan chowder, thick enough to catch with a fork but always served with a spoon and big pilot crackers. Followed a green salad scented with a trio of herbs: thyme, basil, and dill. Hot from the oven came the yeast rolls. Then iced tea and these molasses cookies—each one as big as the palm of your hand.

East Hampton Crullers

3½ cups all-purpose flour

4 teaspoons baking powder

¼ teaspoon baking soda

¼ teaspoon salt

1 teaspoon grated nutmeg

⅛ teaspoon ground ginger

½ cup egg yolks
(about 6 extra-large yolks)

½ cup buttermilk

½ cup half-and-half

1 cup sugar

1 to 2 quarts vegetable oil

Makes 2 dozen

Sift the flour, baking powder, baking soda, salt, nutmeg, and ginger into a large bowl. Beat the egg yolks in a large bowl and add the buttermilk and half-and-half. Stir in the sugar. Add the dry ingredients and beat until almost smooth.

Turn a portion of the dough at a time onto a lightly floured surface and roll or pat out ½ inch thick. Cut with a 3-inch doughnut cutter or use a 3-inch biscuit cutter, then make a hole in the center of each round with a 1-inch cutter or the end of a wooden spoon handle.

Fill a heavy 6-quart pot halfway with oil and heat the oil to 365 degrees. Fry the doughnuts for 45 seconds to 1 minute on each side, until golden brown. Drain on paper bags and serve immediately.

Great-Grandma Joan Huntting's Soft Molasses Cookies

½ cup evaporated milk

1 teaspoon white vinegar

½ cup (1 stick) unsalted butter, softened

½ cup sugar, plus 3 tablespoons for sprinkling

1 cup molasses

2 large eggs

2 teaspoons ground ginger

1¾ teaspoons baking soda

Pinch of salt

3 cups sifted all-purpose flour

Makes about 40 small cookies

Sour the milk: Combine the evaporated milk with the vinegar and allow to sit at room temperature for at least 30 minutes but not more than 1 hour.

Preheat the oven to 400 degrees. Grease and flour 2 cookie sheets.

In a medium bowl using an electric mixer, cream the butter with ½ cup of the sugar until thoroughly blended, 1 to 2 minutes. Mix in the molasses, eggs, ginger, baking soda, and salt. Stir in the flour.

Drop the batter from a teaspoon onto the prepared cookie sheets in batches, spacing the cookies 1½ inches apart. Sprinkle with the remaining sugar. Bake for about 8 minutes, rotating the sheet once, until the cookies are crisp around the edges and still a bit soft in the center. Transfer cookies with a metal spatula to wire racks to cool.

Montauk Berry Duff

2 cups sifted all-purpose flour

1 cup sugar

2 teaspoons baking powder

2 large eggs, beaten

1 cup milk

2 cups blueberries or blackberries, fresh or canned and well drained

Serves 6 to 8

Generously butter and flour a 1½-quart casserole.

In a medium bowl, stir together the flour, sugar, and baking powder. In another medium bowl using an electric mixer, beat the eggs and milk until light and frothy. Pour the milk mixture in the flour mixture and blend together to make a batter.

Spread half of the berries in the bottom of the prepared casserole. Pour the batter over the berries. Spread the remaining berries on top.

Place a wire steaming rack in the bottom of a large saucepan. Place the casserole in the pot and add boiling water to come halfway up the sides of the casserole. Cover the pot and steam the pudding for about 1 hour, until the pudding is firm to the touch and a wooden pick or skewer inserted in the center comes out clean. Remove the covered pan from the heat and let cool for 15 minutes. Unmold the pudding onto a platter. Serve with whipped cream, if you like.

Long Island Clam Chowder

48 hard-shelled clams, shucked

3 slices salt pork or bacon,
cut into ¼-inch dice

2 large onions, cut into ¼-inch dice

2 medium russet potatoes,
peeled and cut into ½-inch cubes

3 tablespoons finely chopped parsley

½ cup diced celery (about 1 stalk)

½ cup diced green pepper

6 cups water

1 (28-ounce) can chopped tomatoes

Salt and freshly ground black pepper

Serves 6

Wash the clams well under cold running water in a colander. Place the clams in a large pot and add enough water to cover the clams by 2 inches. Cover the pan and place over high heat.

When the water comes to a boil, shake the pot to evenly distribute the clams. Remove from the heat and, using a slotted spoon, take out all the clams that have opened. If any clams remain closed, put back on the heat, cover the pan, and cook for another 1 to 2 minutes. Remove the remaining clams and reserve.

In a large heavy stockpot, fry the salt pork pieces over medium heat until they begin to brown, about 3 to 5 minutes. Add the onions and sauté until golden, about 10 minutes. Add the potatoes, parsley, celery, and green pepper with water to cover. Bring to a simmer and simmer until the potatoes are just tender, 10 to 15 minutes. Add the tomatoes, simmer for 10 minutes more, and season with salt and pepper. There should be 2 quarts of liquid remaining.

Remove the clams from their shells and coarsely chop them. Add them to the chowder, reduce the heat to low, and simmer for 30 minutes.

Note: This chowder tastes best made a day ahead and reheated.

SCOUTING RECIPES IN GREENPORT, Long Island, we met Captain Chris Jensen who had been in the oyster business for half a century. Folks told me the captain had been a leader in the development of the Long Island oyster grounds. But what I asked the captain was how he liked his oysters. He said, "The way the missus does them. In a deep dish pie."

Captain Chris's Oyster Pie

3 tablespoons unsalted butter

1 cup sliced mushrooms

3 tablespoons all-purpose flour

1 cup milk

½ teaspoon salt

¼ teaspoon celery salt

Dash of freshly ground black pepper

1 teaspoon lemon juice

1 quart oysters, cut in half if large, well drained with ¾ cup liquor reserved

2 (8-inch) Perfect Pie Crusts (page 13)

Serves 6

Preheat the oven to 450 degrees.

Melt the butter in a large saucepan or skillet over medium heat. Add the mushrooms and sauté until slightly tender, about 3 minutes. Stir in the flour. Gradually add the milk, whisking to thicken and stirring constantly, 3 to 5 minutes. Add the salt, celery salt, pepper, lemon juice, and oysters. Cook, stirring, until the oysters just start to curl, 1 to 2 minutes more.

Fill the bottom of the prepared pie crust with the oyster mixture and cover with the remaining dough. Press the edges of the dough together with fork dipped in flour. Make slits in top to allow escape of steam. Bake for 15 minutes, then reduce the oven temperature to 350 degrees and bake for 10 to 15 minutes more, until the top is golden brown and the filling is bubbly. Remove from the oven and place on a wire rack to cool for 15 minutes before serving.

REMEMBER THAT HALF DOZEN barrels of real native oysters Sam Pickwick carried in the coach to the Christmas party at Dingley Dell? How were they served? Mr. Dickens doesn't tell. But guessing is easy: à la half shell, eaten as the Walrus and the Carpenter ate them in Alice's Looking Glass Land—only pepper added, a few drops of vinegar, with bread on the side.

Here's an improvement on that long-ago sauce. It's called Mignonette and we give it exactly as it was made by Théophile Kieffer, chef of the Sherry Netherlands Hotel back in the thirties.

Mignonette Sauce

⅔ cup white wine vinegar

3 teaspoons coarsely cracked pepper

3 or 4 shallots, finely chopped

Makes about 1 cup

Combine all the ingredients in a glass bowl or jar. Cover and refrigerate for 3 days before serving as an oyster dunk. The sauce grows better with age; cork it and store in refrigerator for up to three weeks.

ONE OF AMERICA'S ORIGINAL masterpiece recipes—a dish literally fit for a king—was created in the Brighton Beach Hotel, Brighton Beach, Long Island, adjoining Coney. Dining in this coastal resort section of the City of Cities was once upon a time something very special.

It was at the Brighton Beach Hotel, a summer evening, that Chef George Greenwald prepared a different dish for his boss, E. Clarke King II and his lady. He presented the breast meat of chicken in a sauce sherry-flavored, showing bits of dark mushroom, glints of green pepper, the flame of pimiento.

"Seconds please," but the chef had made only two servings. Delighted that his dish was well liked he asked permission to include it on the following day's menu and name it for his chief. It appeared as Chicken à la King. This is the original recipe.

Chicken à la King

❖❖

1 ¾ cups chicken broth

1½ boneless skinless chicken breasts

5 tablespoons unsalted butter

½ green pepper, seeded and cut into ½-inch pieces

1 tablespoon chopped onion

Salt and freshly ground black pepper

2 tablespoons all-purpose flour

2 cups heavy cream

1 cup thinly sliced mushrooms (¼ to ½ pound)

3 large egg yolks

1 tablespoon lemon juice

2 tablespoons dry sherry

½ teaspoon sweet paprika

1 tablespoon shredded pimiento peppers, optional

❖❖

Serves 6

❖❖

Bring the chicken broth to a gentle simmer in a 2- to 3-quart heavy saucepan over medium heat. Add the chicken breasts and simmer uncovered until just cooked through, about 10 minutes. Using a slotted spoon, transfer the chicken to a cutting board to cool. Reserve the chicken broth.

Heat 2 tablespoons of the butter in a 4- to 5-quart wide heavy pot over medium-high heat until the foam subsides, then add the green pepper and cook until softened but not browned, about 6 minutes. Transfer to a bowl and season with salt and pepper.

Add the onion and the remaining 3 tablespoons butter to the pot, reduce the heat to medium-low, and cook, stirring, until softened but not browned, about 3 minutes. Add the flour, season with salt and pepper, then reduce the heat to low and continue cooking, stirring, for

2 minutes more. Whisk in 3 cups of the reserved chicken broth. Pour in the cream and add the mushrooms. Simmer until the mushrooms are tender, about 5 minutes.

In a medium bowl, whisk together the egg yolks, lemon juice, sherry, and paprika. Whisk in ½ cup of the cream sauce, then stir the yolk mixture into the remaining sauce in the pot. Cook over low heat, stirring, until the sauce is slightly thickened, about 2 minutes. Remove from the heat and reserve.

Cut the chicken into ½-inch cubes. Add the chicken and green peppers to the sauce. Cook over low heat (do not let simmer), stirring occasionally, until the chicken and peppers are heated through.

Spoon the chicken à la king over hot buttered toast in 6 bowls. Garnish each with shreds of pimiento peppers, if you like.

FROM ALL AROUND THE TOWN TO ALL AROUND THE STATE

It was in Purchase, that elegant suburb of New York, I met Mrs. Abraham Elkon who told me, "Cooks in America are neglecting a wonderful winter vegetable—I mean the endive."

This is a Belgian export and it does get the nod occasionally as a salad green, I hastened to say. But Mrs. Elkon answered right back that only our professional chefs know how to cook the ivory spears. "Yet in Europe," she said, "endive is a vegetable of note as commonly used as the carrot, and every cook has her own little repertoire of recipes."

I had gone to see Juliette Elkon to talk about the new *Honey Cookbook* she had authored, the first general book to sing the virtues and benefits of the world's oldest sweet. We never did get around to the subject of cooking with honey. We talked instead about the endive. She mentioned her endive soup, delicate and distinctive. She uses endive in a salad also, but in a Continental manner, combining the crisp stalks with shredded red cabbage.

Endive arrives in the States twice weekly throughout the winter. But we use only a dribble compared to the countries in Europe. Mrs. Elkon thinks this vegetable will come into popularity here when Americans learn more ways to prepare it as a hot dish.

Endive Soup

1 pound Belgian endive (2 to 4), cut crosswise into 1-inch pieces, cores discarded

5 cups chicken stock

¼ teaspoon cayenne pepper

1 beef bouillon cube

1 tablespoon unsalted butter, softened

1 tablespoon all-purpose flour

3 large egg yolks

2 tablespoons heavy cream

Serves 6

Combine the endive, chicken stock, and cayenne pepper in a large stockpot. Bring to a simmer and simmer until the endive is very tender, about 20 minutes. Using a slotted spoon, remove the endive from the broth and puree in a blender until smooth, 2 to 3 minutes. Return the pureed endive to the broth. Add the bouillon cube and bring to a boil, stirring until the bouillon cube is dissolved.

In a small bowl, combine the butter and flour with a fork to make a paste. Stir into the soup and simmer gently for 5 minutes. Meanwhile, in another bowl, beat together the egg yolks and cream. Gradually pour the egg yolk mixture into the soup, stirring constantly just until soup comes to a boil. Remove from heat immediately and serve.

IT WAS IN SHERBURNE, New York, that I heard about Mrs. Austin Carpenter the local dessert queen. "Yes," she admitted when I telephoned, "I do make a lot of desserts. I married a two-dessert man. He wants homemade desserts two times a day and doesn't mind two kinds at one meal. When I think of the puddings, the cakes, the pies I have baked for my husband, it's a miracle he doesn't weigh a ton and a half."

Austin and Florence Carpenter were young folks together in Cattaraugus County, New York, and have the same eating tastes. Now those were the days! But these too are the days, for Mrs. Carpenter is a fine cook and a hostess of the old school.

Cherry Cake

½ cup (1 stick) unsalted butter

1 cup sugar

2 large eggs

3 tablespoons sour cream

2 cups all-purpose flour

1 teaspoon baking soda

½ teaspoon salt

2 teaspoons ground cinnamon

1 cup canned sour red pitted cherries and juice

Serves 8 to 10

Preheat the oven to 350 degrees. Grease and flour 3 (8-inch) round layer pans.

In a large bowl using an electric mixer, cream the butter and sugar. Add the eggs one at a time, beating well after each addition. Stir in the sour cream and set aside.

Sift the flour, baking soda, salt, and cinnamon into a large bowl. Add to the creamed mixture and stir with a wooden spoon to combine thoroughly. Add the cherries and juice.

Pour into the layer pans and bake for 25 to 30 minutes, until a skewer inserted in the center of the cakes comes out clean. Cool the cakes in their pans on a wire rack for 5 minutes, then turn out onto cake racks. Cool completely, then put the layers together with your favorite frosting or whipped cream, if you like.

EN ROUTE TO CANAJOHARIE, for a tour through the state's largest baby food—packing plant, I was met at Albany by Edward James, then by car the fifty miles up the Mohawk Valley. We stopped in Schenectady for a bite in a sixty-year-old German place called Nicholaus Delicatessen Restaurant. Here all manner of early-day German dishes are served against a background of red-checked tablecloths, old posters, weathered walls saturated with the steam of wursts and sauerkraut, and sighs of satisfaction. The menu was starred with knackwurst, Nuremberg Bratwurst, fresh pig hocks, and, always and again, potato salad. It's a salad selling annually by the thousands of pounds, either to eat on the spot or to carry home in a carton.

"My wife Gladys can make this salad just as well," said the quiet Ed James. "The late Mr. Nicholaus told her how to do it in a general way, and she worked out her own version. If you like collecting recipes," he added, "let Gladys tell you how."

Nicholaus Potato Salad

8 large potatoes

1 cup thinly sliced celery

3 medium onions, thinly sliced

3 tablespoons minced parsley

½ teaspoon celery seed

⅔ cup cider vinegar

⅓ cup water

¼ teaspoon prepared mustard

2 teaspoons salt

¼ teaspoon freshly ground black pepper

4 slices bacon

Serves 6

Bring a large heavy stockpot of salted water to a boil. Add the potatoes and boil them in their skins for 30 to 35 minutes until just tender but not falling apart. Drain and as soon as they are cool enough to be handled, peel them and slice them ⅛ inch thick. Put the potato slices in a large bowl and add the celery, onions, parsley, and celery seeds.

In a small saucepan, combine the vinegar, water, and mustard and heat, stirring, just until bubbles appear. Immediately pour over the potatoes. Add the salt and pepper.

Fry the bacon in a large skillet over medium heat until crisp; drain on paper towels and keep warm. Pour the hot bacon drippings over the potatoes and mix thoroughly. Stir in the crumbled bacon. Place the salad on a platter; then let stand at room temperature for about 2 hours before serving.

IN THE MOHAWK VALLEY I met the Pickle Queen, Mrs. Ada Nellis of Palatine Bridge.

Mrs. Nellis still made her own pickles as in the old days to serve on her own table, to bring to the church bazaars and to donation sales, to give as presents at Christmas time.

"How many kinds of pickles do you make?" I asked.

"Glory be, I never got around to counting them all," she answered

But the nine-day pickles are her greatest pride because they can be opened and let stand indefinitely and never "work." "I can swear by this recipe," she told me, "for I have made nine-day pickles by the hundreds of jars. The recipe for the dills sounds too simple to be any good but don't let this fool you." The pickle maker added, "I make a batch every year and I've never eaten dills that tasted any better."

Dill Pickles

12 pickling cucumbers

1 quart water

1 tablespoon pickling spice

6 slices peeled horseradish root

1¾ cups distilled white vinegar

1½ tablespoons coarse sea salt or kosher salt

6 sprigs of fresh dill

Makes three (24-ounce) jars

Sterilize 3 (1½-pint) wide-mouthed jars. Wash the cucumbers well.

Combine the water, pickling spice, horseradish, vinegar, and salt in a large bowl. Let stand at room temperature for 2 hours for the salt to dissolve.

Transfer 4 cucumbers to each of the sterilized jars. Pour the pickling mixture over to cover. Cover jars tightly and store in a warm place for 2 to 3 weeks. Add new brine (a vinegar, water, and salt mixture) when necessary to keep the cucumbers covered, removing any scum as soon as it forms. When gas formation ceases (after 2 to 3 weeks), cover with lids and seal tightly. The pickles will keep, refrigerated, for up to a month.

Mrs. Nellis's Chili Sauce

8 pounds skinned ripe tomatoes, finely chopped

6 medium onions, finely chopped

6 green peppers, seeded and finely chopped

1½ cups sugar

2 tablespoons salt

1 quart distilled white vinegar

¼ cup whole cloves

¼ cup ground allspice

4 sticks cinnamon

Makes three 1-pint jars

Sterilize three 1-pint jars according to manufacturer's instructions.

In a large heavy pot, combine the tomatoes, onions, and green peppers. Add the sugar, salt, and vinegar. Tie the spices securely in a cheesecloth bag and place in the pot. Cook the mixture over low heat until thick, about 2½ hours, stirring occasionally. Discard the cheesecloth. Ladle the sauce evenly into the sterilized jars. Cover with lids and store in a cool, dry place for 2 to 3 weeks. After the jars are opened, they may be stored in the refrigerator for up to 2 months.

SPEAKING OF PICKLES, let me tell you about the best watermelon pickles I have ever eaten. They came in a gift jar a translucent green with an occasional blush of pink. Crisp to bite, yet so tender and wonderfully redolent of the vinegar and sweet spices congenially "osmosified" with the rind. Bearer of my gift was a wiry, energetic young man of sixty-five named Harry McGibbon. His card read, "Ella and Harry: Jellies, Jams and Pickles." This was their after-sixty career—a Brooklyn, New York, couple.

I wrote about their good things a few times, speaking of the old-fashioned goodness of their elderberry jelly, of the peach preserves, and always with a special bouquet for my favorite, the watermelon pickles.

A few summers ago I had a letter from my friend Mrs. McGibbon, a woman I remember as tall and gray and straight as a lath. The letter came from Ward Manor, Red Hook, New York, a private hotel for our elder citizens. "This month," she wrote, "I am eighty years old. I'm not making the pickles any more but I remember how much you liked them, so I am sending you my recipe—it was our best money-maker. Keep it for yourself or give it to others."

Spiced Watermelon Rind

4 pounds white portion of watermelon, pink bits scraped off, cut into ¾-inch squares

8 cups sugar

4 cups cider vinegar

4 cups cold water

1 tablespoon whole cloves

1 tablespoon whole allspice

1 tablespoon broken-up cinnamon stick

1 lemon, sliced

Makes 5 pints

In a large bowl, let the watermelon stand in salted water to cover overnight (2 tablespoons salt to 1 quart fresh water).

When ready to prepare, drain the watermelon, put the cubes in a large saucepan, and cover with fresh cold water. Cook over medium heat until tender, about 30 minutes. Drain and set aside.

In the same saucepan, combine the sugar, vinegar, and cold water. Tie the cloves, allspice, cinnamon, and lemon slices in a cheesecloth bag; add to the pot. Place over medium heat, bring to a boil, and stir constantly until the sugar dissolves, about 5 minutes. Add the watermelon rind and cook until the rind is transparent and the juices are syrupy, about 45 minutes.

Sterilize 5 (1-pint) jars according to manufacturer's instructions, then ladle the mixture into the hot jars, cover, and seal.

NEXT STOP PAWLING, and patriotic vittles by the expert hand of a popular New York governor's lady.

Home-born delicacies, American as Uncle Sam's hatband, that's the kind of eating Thomas E. Dewey's family likes best—and gets! Fried chicken with mashed potatoes fluffed to a marvel, pot roast and rich brown gravy, crispy corn sticks, all those old palate teasers made by Mom Dewey when Tom was a young fellow in Owosso, Michigan.

Baked ham, in a brown-sugar overcoat, homemade lemon ice cream, moist apple cake make frequent appearances on the Dewey table, all the good things Frances Eileen learned how to cook under her own Mama's watchful eye in Sapulpa, Oklahoma.

Down on the farm in Pawling, New York, pot roast is the favorite supper of the three Dewey men, meaning Dad and the boys. What for dessert? Maybe lemon ice cream, freezer-made, the kind Mrs. Dewey explained, "That was served when I was a girl." As for Mr. Dewey, he said, "Make mine applesauce cake."

Farm Pot Roast

1 (4-to 6-pound) piece of beef, round or boneless chuck

¼ cup plus 2 tablespoons all-purpose flour

1 tablespoon salt, plus more for the pan

¼ teaspoon freshly ground black pepper, plus more for the pan

3 tablespoons unsalted butter

1 clove garlic

2 large onions, sliced

2 large carrots, sliced

1 cup diced tomatoes

½ cup room-temperature water

¼ cup cold water

Serves 8

Wash and thoroughly pat the roast dry. In a large bowl, sift ¼ cup of the flour with the salt and pepper. Dredge meat in the mixture.

Melt the butter in a large heavy saucepan or skillet over medium heat. Add the garlic to the pan and brown the roast slowly on all sides, about 12 minutes total. Watch that garlic—when it's brown, lift it out!

Add the onions, carrots, and tomatoes to the pan, return the garlic to the pan, and season with salt and pepper. Add ½ cup water and reduce the heat to low. Cover and gently simmer the roast until tender, about 3½ hours, turning it occasionally and adding more water if needed.

Remove the meat to a cutting board, cover, and let rest until ready to serve.

To make a pan sauce, measure the broth in the pot and add enough meat stock to make 2 cups. Blend and add the remaining 2 tablespoons flour and the cold water. Cook, stirring constantly, until thickened. Season with salt and pepper, strain, and pour over the meat.

A BROILER ROAST ON CAYUGA LAKE

Down the Elmira road, heading south out of Ithaca, watch for a white Colonial place, the one with the stately pillars. Easy to find is this hundred-year-old house sitting there calm on its knoll, well back from the road. But that Sunday in June the place was a beehive of action; young people everywhere. There were the McMillans' three, there were school friends of the young McMillans; there were cousins galore.

Meet the lady of the house—Ruth McMillan. A little taller than she is short, more comely than she is plain, eyes a little grayer than they are blue, mouth more merry than serious—that's Mrs. William D. McMillan, everybody's good friend. Extension authorities at Cornell University, where Ruth is a home-economics graduate, sent me to the McMillan farm. Ruth, they said, is one of the finest cooks in upper New York State. She certainly knows how America eats in her neck of the woods.

Ruth's kitchen was hustle and bustle. Her brothers, the Rice boys, and their families, the McMillans and Grandpa McMillan, Daddy James E. Rice, then eighty-four, who started Cornell's Poultry Department back in 1903, were having a broiler roast at the Rice cottage on Cayuga Lake.

Rice brothers John and Jim live nearby, operating a large poultry farm; the McMillans raise a few broilers, about three hundred a year, just for home eating. When the Rice clan gets together at the lake place, sure as shooting there is chicken—a broiler apiece and a few halves for good measure. Twenty-five chickens as a rule are dressed for the party.

It's Ruth McMillan who officiates at the barbecue fireplace, chicken the mainstay. These are prepared the night before, the halves rubbed thoroughly with a mixture of lemon juice and oil. Other doodads in plenty, but they're considered merely extras—platters of fresh garden relish, green onions, rosy little radishes, young carrots cut into sticks, and homemade ice-water pickles. Always a bowl of garden greens, dandelions, lettuce, and young spinach tossed with sour cream dressing. Always a heaped mound of the homemade cottage cheese from the McMillan farm, sour cream cookies for the sweet bite and coffee.

Anyone can duplicate the Rice broiler roast in the home oven or at the backyard barbecue. Save the giblets for the giblet stew, the recipe from Ruth McMillan's Aunt Alice Van Buren Price, who lived in Valatie, near Kinderhook, on the Hudson. I can't mention the McMillans' table and fail to tell you about a rhubarb recipe that Mrs. Rice says her mother originated. This sometimes goes to the broiler roasts in spring instead of fresh fruit.

Picnic Chicken

½ cup vegetable oil

2 tablespoons lemon juice

¼ teaspoon salt

⅛ teaspoon dried marjoram

6 chicken breast halves, with skin and bones

10 whole chicken legs

Serves 12

In a large bowl, whisk together vegetable oil, lemon juice, salt, and marjoram. Divide the mixture evenly into thirds. Place two thirds of the mixture in a bowl, cover, and refrigerate. Brush the remaining third of the mixture all over the chicken breasts and legs. Place the chicken pieces in containers or large zip-top bags. Marinate the chicken overnight in the refrigerator.

When you're ready to cook, brush the chicken with half of the remaining refrigerated oil mixture.

Open vents on the bottom and lid of a charcoal grill. Light a large chimney starter of charcoal briquettes (80 to 100) and pour them evenly over one side of bottom rack (you will have a double or triple layer of briquettes).

When the charcoal turns grayish white (15 to 20 minutes), place legs on an oiled grilling rack and sear the chicken legs in 3 batches, uncovered, turning once, until well browned, 6 to 8 minutes total. Transfer to a tray as cooked.

Put all the browned legs on the side of the grill that has no coals underneath, cover with the lid, and cook, turning occasionally, until just cooked through (the flesh will no longer be pink when cut near the joint), 15 to 25 minutes more. Transfer the legs to a platter and loosely cover with foil to rest and keep warm while cooking the breasts.

Add 10 to 15 new briquettes to the coals and wait until they light, about 5 minutes. (They will not be grayish white yet but will give off enough heat with the other briquettes to maintain the correct cooking temperature.)

Sear the chicken breasts, skin-side down first, in two batches on a rack over the coals, uncovered, turning once, until well browned, 6 to 8 minutes total. Transfer to a tray as cooked.

Put all the browned chicken breasts on the side of the grill with no coals underneath, cover, and cook, turning occasionally, until just cooked through, 12 to 15 minutes. Transfer the breasts to a platter with legs.

Just before serving, brush the bird with the final amount of the refrigerated herb-oil mixture and season with salt and pepper.

Rice Farm Rhubarb

1½ cups sugar

¼ cup all-purpose flour

1½ pounds rhubarb stalks, cut into ½ -inch pieces (about 6 cups)

2 large eggs, lightly beaten

1 lemon slice

2 whole cloves

1 tablespoon unsalted butter, cut into small pieces

Serves 6

Preheat the oven to 300 degrees. Grease a 2-quart casserole.

Combine the sugar and flour in the casserole. Add the rhubarb pieces and toss until well coated. Add the eggs and stir lightly. Add the lemon and cloves and dot with the butter.

Bake for about 1 hour, until the mixture thickens and the rhubarb is tender but not falling apart. Cool until warm, about 30 minutes. Serve the rhubarb and its juices over vanilla or another favorite ice cream, if you like.

MRS. ALVORD BAKER of Freeville, New York, is an expert candymaker. Chocolate dipping is one of her special accomplishments. She did her first chocolate dipping her senior year in the Home Economics Department of Cornell University.

Mrs. Baker is a farmer's wife who once made sweets as a pin money business. Not anymore. She hasn't the time now with the 180-acre farm humming with varied activities. But at Christmas Mrs. Baker, with the help of daughter Gertrude, makes pounds and pounds of candy to fill the gift boxes.

The chocolate creams are wonderful but her fudge is perfection. Soft, tongue-melting, rich as Croesus. Give the gold star to the caramel fudge; a silver star to the kind made with sour cream.

I took Trudy's advice and got the recipe also for her mother's nut torte. "The best thing she makes," said the young daughter. And just for good measure I took the recipe for the steamed fig pudding that graces the Bakers' table each Christmas Day.

Vanilla Caramels

1 cup sugar

1 cup heavy cream

1 cup light corn syrup

¼ cup sweetened condensed milk

4 tablespoons (½ stick) unsalted butter

1 teaspoon vanilla extract

Makes about 64 (1-inch) pieces

Generously grease an 8-inch square baking pan.

Combine the sugar, cream, and corn syrup in a large saucepan. Place over low heat and stir constantly until the mixture reaches the thread-spinning stage on a candy thermometer (230 degrees). Add the condensed milk and continue cooking and stirring until a small amount of syrup forms a firm ball in cold water (about 240 degrees on a candy thermometer). Add the butter and vanilla and remove from the heat. Pour into the prepared pan and cool completely. Cut into 1-inch pieces and wrap the pieces in waxed paper and twist the ends, if you like.

Sour-Cream Fudge

2 cups sugar

½ cup sour cream

⅓ cup light corn syrup

2 tablespoons unsalted butter

1 teaspoon vanilla extract

2 (1-ounce) squares unsweetened chocolate or 6 tablespoons cocoa powder

Makes about 64 (1-inch) pieces

Grease an 8-inch square baking pan.

In a heavy saucepan, combine the sugar, sour cream, corn syrup, and butter. Place over medium heat and bring to a boil, stirring, until the temperature on a candy thermometer reaches 232 to 234 degrees, or until a small amount of syrup dropped in cold water just holds together. Remove the pan from the heat. Very gently stir in the vanilla and chocolate, but do not stir again after adding them. Set the pan on a wire rack and cool for 20 minutes.

Beat the fudge with a wooden spoon until it thickens and loses its gloss. Pour into the prepared pan. Spread evenly and set aside to cool. Cut into 1-inch squares.

Nut Torte

3 large eggs, separated

1 cup sugar

1 tablespoon all-purpose flour

½ teaspoon baking powder

1 cup chopped black walnuts

1 cup heavy cream, whipped

Serves 8

Preheat the oven to 325 degrees. Grease a 9-inch springform pan and line the bottom with parchment paper.

In a large bowl, beat the egg yolks. Beat in the sugar and continue beating until the mixture becomes light and ribbony. Set aside.

In a medium bowl using an electric mixer, beat the egg whites until stiff peaks form.

In a small bowl, combine the flour and baking powder. Fold into the egg mixture. Stir in the nuts. Fold in the stiffly-beaten egg whites. Pour the mixture into the prepared pan. Bake for 40 minutes, or until a wooden pick or skewer inserted in the middle of the torte comes out clean. Place on a wire rack and cool completely in the pan. Cut around the sides of the pan to loosen the torte. Remove the sides of the pan. Cut the torte into wedges and serve with the whipped cream.

The torte may be made 1 day ahead, cooled completely, covered, and stored in the pan at room temperature until ready to serve.

HAMMONDSPORT, NEW YORK—the wine bowl of the East—it's the Finger Lake country of west central New York. October is the month. I came to see the grape harvest—grapes into wine. I had come to find cooks who understand the use of wine in fine dishes.

Here in Hammondsport I came to meet Mrs. Greyton Taylor whose husband is one of three brothers who run The Taylor Wine Company, a family firm now in the third generation. I came because friends had told me

"Muriel does wonderful wine-flavored hors d'oeuvres."

Mrs. Taylor graciously invited me for an afternoon snack fest along with a small group of her neighbors. Behold, a profligate array of little hot things which were passed with dry sherry. Men go plenty for these Beef Burgundy Balls; women prefer the ham-stuffed mushroom caps. But my choice is the delicate cheese balls filled with wine jelly.

Beef Burgundy Balls

½ pound ground round

1 large egg

2 tablespoons all-purpose flour

2 teaspoons finely chopped onion

¼ teaspoon Worcestershire sauce

1 tablespoon Burgundy wine

Salt and freshly ground pepper

¼ cup dried breadcrumbs

3 tablespoons vegetable oil

Serves 6

In a large bowl, combine the ground beef, egg, flour, onion, Worcestershire sauce, wine, and salt and pepper to taste. Form into small balls about the size of a tablespoon. Roll in the breadcrumbs.

Heat the oil in a large skillet over medium-high heat. Add the meatballs and brown them for about 5 minutes, then drain on paper towels. Serve hot on toothpicks.

AFTER THE GUESTS HAD gone, Muriel Taylor and I settled down in her cozy kitchen to talk recipes. Cooking, she told me, had been one of her dearest hobbies ever since she has had a home of her own. And baking bread, it turned out, is the thing she does best. These breads, we find on testing, are slightly different from the usual in the proportions of their ingredients—the salt, sugar, shortening, and yeast. But the finished loaves taste simply perfect to us, as they do to the young Taylors and their friends.

Mrs. Taylor's chicken pie is a miracle of hearty tenderness and flavor, the best pie I know for those who like chicken flavored with wine and not too many other distractions.

White Bread

2¾ cups milk

2 envelopes active dry yeast (about 4½ teaspoons)

8 cups all-purpose flour

2 tablespoons sugar

4 teaspoons salt

3 large eggs, lightly beaten

4 tablespoons (½ stick) unsalted butter, plus additional for tops of loaves, optional

Makes three 8 x 4-inch loaves

In a small saucepan, heat ¾ cup of the milk over medium heat until lukewarm. Pour the milk into a medium bowl and stir in the yeast. Let stand until the yeast dissolves and the milk begins to bubble, about 5 minutes. Stir in 1½ cups of the flour. Cover with plastic wrap and let stand until slightly risen, about 20 minutes.

Scrape the yeast-flour mixture into the bowl of a standing electric mixer fitted with a dough hook. Add the sugar, salt, eggs, and the remaining 2 cups of milk and beat at medium speed until blended. Carefully add the remaining 6½ cups of flour and beat at low speed until the flour is just incorporated. Beat at medium speed until dough is well combined, about 5 minutes. Add the butter and continue to beat until the dough is very soft, about 10 more minutes.

Lightly grease a large bowl. Turn the dough into the bowl, cover with plastic wrap, and put in a warm place to rise until doubled in bulk, about 1 hour. Punch down the dough, then cover again and let the dough rise until doubled in bulk again, about 1 hour more.

Punch down the dough and turn it out onto a heavily floured work surface. Divide the dough into 3 equal pieces. Form into balls; cover gently with an oiled piece of plastic wrap and let rest and rise on a floured work surface for about 15 minutes.

Butter three 8 x 4-inch loaf pans. Shape each piece of dough into a loaf about the same size as the pans. Gently ease the loaves into the pans. Cover the pans with oiled plastic wrap and let rise until the dough is rounded above the edge of the pans, 50 to 60 minutes.

Preheat the oven to 350 degrees. Bake the loaves for 50 minutes to 1 hour, until the tops are golden and the loaves sound hollow when tapped on the bottom. Cool completely on wire racks before slicing. For a soft crust, rub the tops of the loaves with a little butter.

The Taylors' Chicken Pie

1 (4-pound) chicken, cut into pieces

2 tablespoons salt

2 stalks celery, cut into 1-inch pieces

1 large onion, coarsely chopped

3 tablespoons unsalted butter

¼ cup all-purpose flour

2 cups chicken stock

¼ cup heavy cream

Freshly grated nutmeg

Salt and freshly ground pepper

Paprika

1 (9-inch) Perfect Pie Crust (page 13)

¼ cup Sauternes

Serves 6

Place the chicken pieces in a large stockpot and cover with cold water. Add the salt, celery, and onion. Place over medium-high heat and bring to a simmer, then reduce the heat to low and cook until the chicken is tender enough to slip from the bones, about 1½ hours. Let the chicken cool in its stock, 45 minutes to 1 hour. Remove the chicken and take the meat from the bones in large pieces. Set aside.

Preheat the oven to 400 degrees.

Melt the butter in a large saucepan over medium heat. Add the flour, gradually whisk in the stock (fat removed first), and cook until thickened, about 8 minutes. Add the cream, cooked celery and onion, and seasonings to taste. Line the sides only of a deep 9-inch pie pan with part of the pastry. Put the chicken pieces in the pan, starting with the white meat. Add the dark meat until the pan is half filled. (If you have any remaining chicken, reserve for another use, such as chicken salad or soup). Pour over the sauce and add the Sauternes. Cover with the remaining pastry; cut openings to allow the steam to escape. Bake for 20 to 25 minutes, until the inside is bubbling and the top is golden brown.

BISHOP'S BREAD HAILS FROM the shores of Lake Chautauqua in the western extremity of New York State. But I discovered recently when cookbook reading that a similar hot bread is made in Austria and it has the same name. It's a bread sweet and rich enough to use as a pudding when served with a sauce. Mrs. Frank Robinson came by the recipe fifteen years ago when she and her husband moved from Florida to the New York resort to open a summer hotel.

"Would you give it to me?"

Mrs. Robinson wrote it out willingly, remembering that it was her good luck to borrow it from Mrs. Dorothy Bierly who once owned a hotel in the town and served the bread daily.

Bishop's Bread

½ cup (1 stick) unsalted butter, melted

2 cups brown sugar

1 large egg

2½ cups sifted all-purpose flour

2 teaspoons baking powder

½ teaspoon baking soda

½ teaspoon salt

1 teaspoon ground cinnamon

¾ cup buttermilk

1 cup chopped dates

Sugar and cinnamon, for topping

Makes one 9 x 9-inch loaf

Preheat the oven to 375 degrees. Grease a 9 x 9-inch square baking pan.

In a large bowl using an electric mixer, cream the butter and brown sugar. Add the egg and beat on low speed until smooth.

Sift the flour, baking soda, baking powder, salt, and cinnamon into a large bowl. Add the dry ingredients, alternating with the buttermilk, to the creamed mixture, beating well after each addition. Fold in the dates.

Pour into the prepared pan and bake for 35 to 40 minutes, until a wooden pick or skewer inserted into the center comes out clean. Sprinkle the top of the loaf with sugar and cinnamon. Cool the bread a little on a wire rack. Serve hot slices as a dinner bread.

PENNSYLVANIA

Not too many years ago the H. J. Heinz Company, famous
Pennsylvania food processors, entertained 140 newspaper food
editors who were holding their annual conference at the Waldorf-
Astoria in New York City. The dinner given was Pennsylvania-
Dutch, a sampling of what a housewife of the old school might do
when company came.

Here's the menu for the evening:
sauerbraten in rich brown gravy,
geschmelzte nudle, oven-baked beans,
tomatoes, fried eggplant, sweets and
sours, shoo-fly pie, cheesecake, cider
and coffee. On every table a lazy
Susan gaily painted with Dutch design
was loaded with a tempting array of
the traditional seven sweets and
seven sours.

The sweets, of course, were
the jellies and jams, spiced fruits,
marmalades, and fruit butters. The
sours, the pickles, relishes, and tangy
sauces, with any number of vegetables
marinated in vinegar and spice. One
of the best of the best of these is the
sweet and sour beans. Also, I want you
to have the sauerbraten recipe, as no
dish is more typical of Pennsylvania
than this spicy pot roast.

Sauerbraten

For the marinade:

1½ cups cider vinegar

½ cup red wine

1 cup water

12 peppercorns

2 tablespoons sugar

2 large onions, sliced

4 bay leaves

12 whole cloves

1 teaspoon mustard seeds

2 teaspoons salt

3½- to 4-pound round or rump of beef

½ cup plus 2 tablespoons all-purpose flour

1½ teaspoons salt

Dash of freshly ground black pepper

¼ cup vegetable oil

1 onion, sliced

½ teaspoon mustard seeds

6 whole cloves

½ teaspoon peppercorns

⅓ cup finely crushed gingersnaps (about 7 cookies)

Serves 6 to 8

Two to four days before serving, combine the marinade ingredients in a heavy-duty zip-top bag. Place the beef in the marinade and let stand for 2 to 4 days in the refrigerator. Remove the meat from the marinade and dry on paper towels.

Combine 2 tablespoons of the flour, the salt, and pepper and coat the meat on all sides with the mixture.

Heat the oil in a Dutch oven over medium-high heat, add the meat, and brown on all sides. Strain the marinade and add to the meat along with the additional sliced onion, mustard seeds, cloves, and peppercorns. Cover and simmer for 3½ hours, or until the meat is fork-tender.

Remove the meat to a heated platter, slicing it beforehand, if desired. Strain the liquid from the pot. Add the remaining ½ cup flour and the crushed gingersnaps to the Dutch oven and slowly return the liquid to the pot. Simmer, stirring constantly, until thickened. Pour some of this gravy over the meat and serve the remainder at the table.

Sweet-Sour Beans

2 pounds fresh green beans, ends trimmed

3 quarts water

1½ tablespoons salt

3 tablespoons unsalted butter

1 medium onion, sliced

½ cup cider vinegar

¼ cup water

½ cup sugar

Serves 6

Fill a large pot with the water and bring to a boil. Add the green beans, cover, and cook until tender, 10 to 12 minutes. Drain into a large bowl. While hot, toss the green beans with the salt and butter and let stand for 5 minutes. Add the onion.

In a small bowl, whisk together vinegar, water, and sugar and pour over the green beans. Cover and marinate in the refrigerator for 3 to 4 hours or, better yet, overnight. Store the green beans in a covered jar in the refrigerator. They will keep for up to 3 weeks.

LATER I DOUBLED IN Dutch when the American Spice Trade Association spread a Penn-Dutch meal for this same group of newspaper food writers—this time at the Hotel Astor. That evening in company with guests brought over from Lancaster County, Pennsylvania, the heart of the Penn-Dutch country, we ate our way from *flaish un kais* (curried turnovers) to *lotwarrik meringue boi* (apple-butter meringue pie). In between were such dishes as *bretzel supp mit clams* (hand-twisted clams) and *hairnhutter rinsflaish mit doonkes* (Moravian beef with gravy). True to the Dutch tradition there were fourteen different relishes, sweet and sour.

The dinner was the result of numerous visits made by members of the Spice Trade Association to the Pennsylvania Dutch country, gathering authentic recipes which they felt would be practical for homemakers everywhere. Here are the dishes we enjoyed most.

"Sye Noof-Gawickelt" (Oysters Wrapped in Bacon)

½ cup fresh lemon juice

1 teaspoon freshly ground black pepper

24 small to medium shucked oysters

12 slices bacon, cut in half

Serves 6 as an appetizer

Preheat the broiler.

In a shallow bowl, combine the lemon juice and pepper. Add the oysters and toss to coat. Cover and marinate in the refrigerator for 20 minutes.

Place the bacon flat on a work surface, place 1 oyster on each piece of bacon, and roll up to enclose. Secure with a toothpick and place on a foil-lined baking sheet. Place on the top rack of the oven and broil for 3 to 5 minutes until the bacon is crisp and the edges of the oysters have curled, turning once to cook both sides evenly. Remove from the oven and serve hot.

"Hairnhutter Rinflaish Mit Doonkes" (Moravian Beef with Gravy)

1 (4-pound) boneless chuck roast

1 teaspoon dried sage or poultry seasoning

½ teaspoon dried thyme

1 teaspoon salt

½ teaspoon freshly ground black pepper

2 teaspoons whole cloves

2 teaspoons whole allspice, crushed

2 bay leaves, crumbled

4 cups beef bouillon

2 tablespoons grated or finely slivered lemon peel

3 tablespoons lemon juice

2 tablespoons vegetable oil

1 medium carrot, quartered

1 medium onion, sliced

1 tablespoon all-purpose flour

⅓ cup sour cream

Serves 6

Pat the beef dry with paper towels and place in a large container or stockpot. In a large bowl, combine the seasonings, bouillon, lemon peel, and lemon juice. Place over medium heat and bring to a simmer; do not let it boil. Pour the marinade over the meat and cool, about 30 minutes. Cover and marinate in the refrigerator for 24 hours, turning several times.

Preheat the oven to 350 degrees. Remove the meat from the marinade and pat dry. Reserve the marinade for later use.

Heat the oil in a 5-quart wide heavy ovenproof pot or Dutch oven over medium-high heat until hot but not smoking. Brown the beef on all sides, about 15 minutes total. Add the carrot and onion to the pot. Pour in the reserved marinade, cover, and braise in oven until the meat is tender, 2½ to 3 hours total.

Transfer the meat to a cutting board and cover loosely with foil. Let rest for 30 minutes. Meanwhile, strain the cooking liquid, pour it back into the pot, and bring to a gentle simmer over medium heat. Whisk in the flour to thicken. Stir in the sour cream, being careful not to bring the sauce to a boil. Serve the meat with the gravy immediately, with *Groombeera Fillas* (recipe follows), if you like.

"Groombeera Fillas" (Potato Filling)

5 pounds yellow-fleshed potatoes, such as Yukon gold

2 large eggs, well beaten

4 tablespoons (½ stick) unsalted butter or margarine, melted

4 cups dried breadcrumbs

2 teaspoons grated onion

1 tablespoon dried parsley

1 teaspoon garlic salt

1 teaspoon celery salt

¼ teaspoon freshly ground black pepper

Serves 6

Peel and quarter the potatoes. Place them in a 5-quart heavy pot and cover with cold salted water by 1 inch. Bring to a simmer over medium-high heat, then reduce the heat and simmer uncovered until tender, about 25 minutes. Drain the potatoes in a colander, return to the pot, and stir in the eggs and butter.

In a small bowl, combine the remaining ingredients and fold into the potatoes. Serve hot.

"Shnitzel Boona Mit Tamats" (Snap Beans with Tomatoes)

4 strips bacon

1 large onion, chopped

1 pound tender young green beans, ends trimmed and snapped in half if large

2 cups chopped fresh tomatoes

About 1 teaspoon salt

1 teaspoon whole basil leaves torn into bits

⅛ teaspoon freshly ground black pepper

1 cup hot water

Serves 6

Fry the bacon in a large heavy saucepan over medium heat until crisp. Drain the bacon on paper towels and set aside. Add the onions and sauté until softened but not browned, about 5 minutes. Add the remaining ingredients, bring to a simmer, cover, and simmer for 15 to 20 minutes, until the green beans are tender. Serve immediately, topped with the crumbled bacon.

Ginger "Gapickelti Roata Reeva" (Ginger Pickled Beets)

1 cup cider vinegar

½ cup water

½ teaspoon ground mace

½ teaspoon ground ginger

¼ teaspoon ground cloves

2 tablespoons prepared horseradish

2 tablespoons sugar

3 beets (about 1 pound without tops)

Makes about 3 cups

Place all the ingredients except the beets in a 2- to 3-quart saucepan and bring to a boil, stirring until the sugar is dissolved. Reduce the heat, cover, and simmer for 30 minutes. Cool the marinade, transfer to a jar or container, and refrigerate for 1 day for the flavors to marry.

When you're ready to make the beets, cook them in a saucepan of boiling salted water until tender, about 1 hour. Drain them and cool. Slip off the skins and cut the beets into ½ inch pieces. Add the beets to the marinade, cover, and marinate in the refrigerator for 1 day before serving. They will keep, refrigerated in an airtight container, for 4 days.

"Gapickelti Beera" (Spiced Pears)

4 Anjou pears, peeled

¾ cup sugar

¼ cup water

1 (1-inch) cinnamon stick

5 whole cloves

1 teaspoon ground allspice

Serves 4

Cut each pear in half and core each half. Combine the sugar and water in a large heavy saucepan. Place over medium heat and heat until the sugar dissolves. Add the cinnamon, cloves, and allspice to the syrup and simmer gently for 10 minutes.

Using a slotted spoon, remove the pears from the liquid and place into a large bowl. Pour the hot liquid over the pears. Cool to room temperature, cover with plastic wrap, and refrigerate for 1 hour, then drain before serving.

"Hairnhutter Booder Semmel" (Moravian Butter Rolls)

1 envelope active dry yeast
(2½ teaspoons)

¼ cup warm, not hot, water

3 tablespoons sugar

7 tablespoons unsalted butter

1 cup milk

4½ cups all-purpose flour,
plus more as needed

1½ teaspoons salt

1 large egg, well beaten

½ teaspoon grated nutmeg

1 large egg white

1 tablespoon water

1 tablespoon poppy seeds

Makes 18 rolls

In a large bowl, stir together the yeast, warm water, and 1 tablespoon of the sugar until the yeast dissolves, then let stand until foamy, about 5 minutes.

Melt 6 tablespoons of the butter in a small saucepan over medium heat, then add the milk and heat to lukewarm.

Add the remaining 2 tablespoons sugar, the butter mixture, 2 cups of the flour, and the salt to the yeast mixture and stir with a wooden spoon until well combined. Then add the remaining 2½ cups flour, which should make a sticky dough. Cover tightly with plastic wrap and let the dough rise in a cool, dry place until doubled in bulk, about 1 hour.

Butter a large bowl. Knead the dough on a lightly floured surface, kneading in more flour as needed to keep dough from sticking, until smooth and elastic, about 10 minutes (the dough will be slightly sticky). Form the dough into a ball and put it in the buttered bowl, turning to coat.

Butter 18 muffin cups with the remaining butter.

In a small bowl, combine the beaten egg with the nutmeg. Turn the dough out onto a lightly floured surface and work in the mixture. Divide the dough into three equal-size pieces. Working with one piece at a time, cut off tablespoon-size pieces of dough and form the pieces into balls. Put 3 balls into each muffin tin. Cover loosely with a clean kitchen towel and let the rolls rise in a cool, dry place until doubled in bulk, 30 to 40 minutes.

Preheat the oven to 400 degrees.

In a small bowl, beat the egg white and water until foamy but not stiff. Brush the rolls lightly with the egg wash, sprinkle the tops of the rolls with poppy seeds, and bake until golden, 15 to 20 minutes. Serve warm.

SHOO-FLIES ARE OF THREE KINDS

See Edna Eby Heller," that's what they told me at The Pennsylvania Dutch Folklore Center in Bethel where I went asking for help in finding Dutchland recipes. "But I want more than recipes," I explained. "I want to visit in Penn-Dutch kitchens and actually see some of these foods prepared." Again it was "See Edna Heller, she will take you around."

This Edna, I discovered, was born in Lititz in Lancaster County and this fact alone gave her a real head start in the cookery art. Then, a few years ago, *The Pennsylvania Dutchman*, a quarterly publication of the Folklore Center of Franklin and Marshall College, asked Edna to be their food editor, writing on traditional dishes. That's been Edna's job since.

I went visiting Edna in her Buena Vista home two miles east of Hershey, Pennsylvania. It's there in her colorful kitchen that she spends one day a week testing old-time good things, translating pinches and handfuls into accurate measurements. Chicken corn soup, for one. Sugar cakes stand high on the preferred list as they do with most Dutch families. "Some of you come-a-visiting folks," Edna told me, "call sugar cake coffee cake, but my goodness, we have the cake with coffee, of course, but come Sunday afternoon, what could be more welcome than a piece of sugar cake with a glass of lemonade? Mother baked the sugar cake in pie tins and sprinkled over granulated sugar just before baking—this formed a crust rather similar to icing. The layers were cut into wide wedges to serve."

"What's an honest-to-goodness shoo-fly pie?" I asked. "I know in general that the pie is a combination of brown sugar and molasses flavor in a cake baked in a pie crust," I said. "But what has had me confused over the years is that sometimes shoo-fly pie is dry, sometimes it's very wet on the bottom, and sometimes it's a little wet all the way through."

"There you have it," said Edna. "Shoo-flies are of three kinds. A dry pie is good for dunking and the men love this for breakfast. It has a slightly moist base with crumbs on top. Then there is the very gooey type with a truly wet bottom and again crumbs on top. The third is a real cake in type. Crumbs and liquid are alternated and this kind is usually called shoo-fly cake despite the fact that it is baked in a pastry shell."

Shoo-Fly Pie (Dry)

1½ recipes Perfect Pie Crust (page 13)

For the crumb mixture:

1½ cups all-purpose flour

1 cup brown sugar

4 tablespoons (½ cup) unsalted butter

For the liquid:

½ cup molasses

½ cup hot, but not boiling, water

½ teaspoon baking soda

¼ teaspoon cream of tartar

Makes three 4-inch pies

Preheat the oven to 350 degrees. Line three 4-inch pie pans with pastry.

In a large bowl, combine ingredients for crumb mixture, using your hands to blend the mixture into coarse crumbs.

In another large bowl, combine liquid ingredients and pour into the pie pans. Top with the crumbs. Bake for about 25 minutes until center is set and top is brown and cool on wire racks to room temperature or slightly warm. Serve with softly whipped cream, if you like.

Shoo-Fly Pie (Wet)

1 (9-inch) Perfect Pie Crust (page 13)

For the crumb mixture:

¾ cup sifted all-purpose flour

½ teaspoon salt

½ teaspoon ground cinnamon

½ teaspoon ground ginger

⅛ teaspoon grated nutmeg

⅛ teaspoon ground cloves

½ cup brown sugar

2 tablespoons unsalted butter

For the liquid:

½ cup dark molasses

¾ cup hot water

1 large egg yolk, well beaten

½ teaspoon baking soda

Makes one 9-inch pie

Preheat the oven to 400 degrees. Line a 9-inch pie pan with the pastry.

In a large bowl, combine the ingredients for the crumb mixture, using your hands to blend the mixture into coarse crumbs.

In another large bowl, combine the liquid ingredients and beat with an electric mixer until smooth. Pour into the pie pan and top with the crumbs. Bake until the pie starts to brown, about 10 minutes. Reduce the oven temperature to 325 degrees and bake until firm, about 30 minutes. Cool on a wire rack to room temperature or warm. Serve with softly whipped cream, if you like.

Shoo-Fly Pie (Cake Type)

1 (8- or 9-inch) Perfect Pie Crust
(page 13)

For the crumb mixture:

1½ cups all-purpose flour

¼ cup granulated sugar

¼ cup brown sugar

1 teaspoon baking powder

2 tablespoons unsalted butter

For the liquid:

½ cup dark molasses

¾ teaspoon baking soda

½ cup hot water

Makes one 8- or 9-inch pie

Preheat the oven to 350 degrees. Line an 8- or 9-inch pan
with pastry.

In a large bowl, combine the ingredients for crumb
mixture, using your hands to blend the mixture into
coarse crumbs.

In another large bowl, combine the liquid ingredients.
Add one third of the liquid to the pie pan, followed by one
third of the crumbs. Continue alternating, ending with
the crumbs. Bake for about 30 minutes or until center is
set and top is brown. Remove from the oven and cool on
a wire rack to room temperature or slightly warm. Serve
with softly whipped cream, if you like.

PIE FOR BREAKFAST, FOR DINNER, FOR SUPPER

There are always pies in the Pennsylvania Dutch country. Pie for breakfast, for dinner, for supper, for the bedtime bite. It's there that pie has been developed to its last possibility. Every kind of food has been used as pie timber. There are fruit pies, cake pies, molasses pies, custard pies, milk pies, vinegar pies. In the early days, pies were the real test of the good cook. Pies were a challenge to the imagination and seldom were fewer than fifteen baked at a time in outdoor Dutch ovens.

One of the everyday reliables was *schnitz* or dried-apple pie. Sour green apples were used—cored, quartered, sun-dried. I had heard, all my life, about *schnitz* pie, but had never tasted one until the autumn when I was in Hungerford, Pennsylvania, to see a vegetable canning operation. Mr. William Free, the owner, insisted I come to his house for luncheon as Mrs. Free, he said, had baked a *schnitz* pie just for me

to try. Mrs. Free talked about the glories of Pennsylvania Dutch cooking. "I can brag about their art," she explained, "because I'm not one of them. They consider modesty a prime virtue. Next to being lazy or untidy, the greatest crime is 'bragging on yourself.' Born and raised here in York County, I know food from my Penn-Dutch neighbors."

I wanted the *schnitz* recipe but Mrs. Free warned, ". . . You can't buy this exact kind of dried apples anywhere else." She gave me a pound of *schnitz* for recipe testing. We tried the pie using also the regular commercial dried apples—and good!

Now I have discovered a *schnitz* pie filling being packed commercially by a Pennsylvania firm, in jars of one pound, one ounce net content, one jar holding the exact amount for an eight-inch pie. Write to the Hungerford Packing Co., Inc., Hungerford, York County, Pennsylvania.

Schnitz Dried-Apple Pie

1 pound dried apples

1 quart cold water

1 tablespoon ground cinnamon

1 to 1½ cups sugar

4 teaspoons grated orange peel

½ cup orange juice

2 (9-inch) Perfect Pie Crusts
(page 13)

Makes one 9-inch pie

Place the apples and water in a heavy 5-quart
stockpot. Bring to a simmer and gently simmer until
the apples turn into a soft pulp, about 45 minutes,
stirring occasionally.

Preheat the oven to 450 degrees.

Pour the apples into a large bowl. Add the cinnamon,
sugar, grated orange peel, and orange juice.

Line a pie pan with pastry, fill with the *schnitz*
makings, and cover the top with pastry; make slits
in the top crust. Bake for 10 minutes, then reduce the
oven temperature to 350 degrees and continue baking
for 30 minutes or until golden brown. Cool the pie in
the pan on a wire rack. Serve with whipped cream or
ice cream, if you like.

PAST THE TIME-MELLOWED STONE houses, past the tremendous red barns which tell of fat farms, past green pastures where red cows graze knee-deep in lush meadows. Now the corn is waist-high, the contoured rows banding the low hills. In the limestone valleys where creeks meander the wheat turns golden, nearing its harvest.

Down to Kutztown we go, nestled in the shadow of the Blue Mountains in the County of Berks. This is a folk festival town where the largest regional cookery exhibition in American history is held each Fourth of July weekend.

Here I stepped into a new world of Old World feasting. Exhibited was everything from apple butter making in huge outdoor cauldrons to the manufacture of farm cheeses. The major sects bring their food specialties as a part of the educational side of the festival.

That year I counted over three hundred dishes arranged down narrow plank tables, each with its hand-written recipe propped alongside, each with its maker present to answer visitors' questions and hand out samplings. It was early morning when I started my stop, taste, and talk tour. "Just love your lemon butter," I told Mrs. Palma Clifford Baker of Cochranville, Pennsylvania.

She said, "It's a recipe over a hundred years old." Her folks spread it on the breakfast toast and also take it on picnics.

"Lemon Booder" No. 1 (Lemon Butter)

4 large eggs

1½ cups sugar

¾ teaspoon ground mace

Zest of 2 medium lemons

Makes 2 cups

In a small bowl, beat the eggs. Stir in the sugar, mace, and zest. Place in the top portion of a double boiler and cook over hot water until thick, stirring constantly, about 20 minutes. Cool, transfer to a jar, cover, and store in the refrigerator. Spread on breakfast toast, if you like.

Lemon Butter No. 2

3 large eggs, beaten

2 cups sugar

Juice and grated peel of 3 lemons

½ cup (1 stick) unsalted butter

Makes 3 cups

In a medium saucepan, combine all the ingredients. Place over low heat and cook, stirring constantly, until just thickened, about 5 to 7 minutes. Serve hot or pour into a bowl, cover, refrigerate until chilled, and serve cold.

Plow Lines

2 large eggs

1 cup half-and-half

4 cups all-purpose flour

2 teaspoons salt

3 tablespoons vegetable oil

Molasses for dipping

Makes 8 pieces

In a medium bowl using an electric mixer, beat the eggs with the half-and-half. In another medium bowl, combine the flour and salt and add to the egg mixture. Knead well and roll the dough out onto a floured surface to a ¼-inch-thick rectangle. Cut into pieces 4 to 5 inches wide and 6 inches long. Using a pastry wheel, cut ½-inch strips in each piece, leaving a ½-inch border.

Heat the oil in a large skillet over medium heat until hot and shimmering but not smoking, about 375 degrees. Fry one or two dough pieces at a time until lightly browned. Dip in molasses. Serve as bread for supper, if you like.

LITTLE CLOUDS OF TANTALIZING STEAM

Next taste, hot salad dressing thick with crumbled bacon, made by Mary Bohn of the London Grove Grange. "It's wonderful good," she told me, "for potato salad, or lettuce, or hot slaw, or on the cold meats."

The things I tasted in less than two hours! Old-fashioned brown soup, potato-stuffed dumplings, creamed tomatoes, Amish vanilla pie, vinegar candy. I was halfway down the line when my hostess, Edna Eby Heller, insisted, "It's dinnertime now."

Dining tents had been set up all around the fair grounds. Some tents seated three hundred people at a time. At each entrance the day's menu was posted.

Everything but dessert crowded the tables—all I could see was a solid mass of platters, covered dishes, relish, *smearkase,* plates piled with homemade bread, huge cuts of butter. . . . And rising from everywhere were little clouds of tantalizing steam.

After soup, I helped myself to dried corn, fresh lima beans, boiled beef, boiled ham and potato filling, and noodles yet! Pepper cabbage, that was my favorite.

That pepper cabbage recipe we have from the maker, Mrs. Claude F. Moyer, who lives near Allentown, Pennsylvania, one of the three women on the kitchen committee. Mrs. Moyer was born in Berks County and has been making pepper cabbage (sometimes called pickled cabbage) as long as she can remember. Dinner over, I went sampling down the midway. There were fifty-one booths preparing traditional dishes, cakes, pies, apple butter, dumplings—everything to sell. Take it home or "eat yourself full" right on the spot. Signs announced *Hinkel Welsh Karn Suppe,* that's chicken corn soup with noodles, homemade, a meal in a cup. *Boova Shakel,* dumplings stuffed with potato filling. Drink stands offered local birch beer.

Mrs. Viola Miller, wife of a dairy farmer and living near Kutztown, was making "plow lines." "Nice for afternoon tea?" I asked. She said, "My six boys and man like plow lines for breakfast dunked in thick molasses."

Pepper Cabbage

1 cabbage, about 2 pounds

1 green pepper, seeded and diced

1 red pepper, seeded and diced

1 stalk celery, diced

1 cup sugar

2 tablespoons salt

½ cup water

About ½ cup vinegar

Serves 6

Finely grate the cabbage into a large bowl. Add the peppers and celery.

In a small bowl, whisk together the sugar, salt, water, and vinegar. Taste to see if you have enough vinegar and add more if needed. Add to the vegetables, toss, and serve.

Potato Filling

½ pound white bread

2 cups milk

4 pounds potatoes

1 medium onion, diced

3 stalks celery, minced

1 cup (2 sticks) unsalted butter

2 large eggs, beaten

1 cup chopped parsley

Serves 12

Preheat the oven to 350 degrees. Generously grease a 3-quart casserole.

In a medium bowl, crumble the bread into pieces and pour the milk on top. Set aside to soak while you prepare the remaining ingredients.

Fill a large heavy stockpot with salted water. Add the potatoes, place over medium-high heat, and bring to a simmer. Reduce the heat and simmer until tender, about 25 minutes. Drain and mash the potatoes. Set aside.

Melt half the butter in a large skillet over medium heat. Add the onion and celery and sauté until the celery is tender, about 8 minutes. Add to the mashed potatoes. Add the bread and milk mixture to the mashed potatoes. Melt the remaining butter. Add the eggs and the melted butter. Beat the potatoes with an electric beater until smooth. Keep beating and add the parsley. Turn into a 3-quart casserole and bake for 30 minutes, or until heated through.

Mary Bohn's Hot Salad Dressing

4 slices bacon

⅓ cup cider vinegar

⅔ cup water

1 tablespoon all-purpose flour

2 tablespoons sugar

½ teaspoon dry mustard

Pinch of salt

1 large egg, beaten

Makes enough for 6 salads

Fry the bacon in a large heavy skillet over medium heat until crisp. Remove the bacon to a plate and add the vinegar and water to the fat; bring to a boil.

In a small bowl, combine the flour, sugar, mustard, and salt. Add to the liquid and whisk to a smooth paste. Stir in the egg and heat for a minute more. Use as a warm dressing for potato salad, coleslaw, or another vegetable salad. Crumble the reserved bacon to garnish the salad.

I MET MRS. MARTIN A. MOORE at the festival. She was on the morning food program demonstrating the Pennsylvania-Dutch method of making a pickling syrup for summer fruits.

I came late to the program tent and didn't catch all the details of her talk. I wanted to know more.

But Mrs. Moore had to hurry back to the farm. "Come along," was her invitation, "we can talk there." The lovely old farmhouse was a cool oasis after the heat of the road. My hostess rushed to her kitchen and back in a hurry with a beaded pitcher of homemade grape juice. Up came the subject of old-time fruit shrubs.

All through the Dutch country, Mrs. Moore said, shrubs are still being made using raspberries, blackberries, elderberries, black currants, and other small fruits.

And that pickling syrup? I didn't forget.

Fruit Shrub

About 4 to 5 cups currants, black or red raspberries, blueberries, grapes, or elderberries

¼ cup water

1 pound sugar

Makes 3 cups

Thoroughly wash the fruit. Place in a saucepan, add the water, bring to a simmer, and cook until the fruit juice is released. Remove from the heat and let cool. Empty into a colander and drain off the juice. Strain the juice (you should have about 2 cups) through 1 layer of cheesecloth back into the pan. Add the sugar and boil for about 15 minutes. Skim and pour into sterilized bottles (Mrs. Moore saves empty vinegar bottles for this purpose). Cover tightly and set aside in a cool dry place for 1 month.

To serve, pour the shrub over ice and dilute with still or sparkling water or ginger ale.

Pickled Peaches

3 pounds sugar

1 quart cider vinegar

¼ cup water

6 pounds small ripe fresh peaches

Makes 3 quarts

In a large heavy stockpot, combine the sugar, vinegar, and water. Place over medium heat, bring to a boil, and boil until the sugar is dissolved. Wash the peaches, add them to the syrup, and boil gently until the fruit is fork-tender, 3 to 5 minutes. Pack the peaches in hot sterilized jars and fill with the pickling liquid. Serve as a relish with meats.

Note: This pickling liquid also may be used with cantaloupe cut in 2-inch pieces with the thin outer part of the rind removed. It's a Dutch thrifty idea to use melons of little flavor. After pickles are eaten, the remaining juice may be reused by adding an equal portion of newly made pickling syrup. Or add the leftovers to mincemeat for an added smack of flavor.

IT'S "PASS THE *FASTNACHTS*" for Shrove Tuesday breakfast in the Pennsylvania Dutch country. But the hour doesn't matter—pass these raised doughnuts any time the day long. No one ever will pass a *fastnacht* by. Eating the rich fried cakes on the last day before the beginning of Lent stems from early Christian times of rigid fasting. Then it was customary for cooks to use all leftover fats in the house. In some lands pancakes were made; the Germans made doughnuts. Whatever the origin of the *fastnacht,* in the Pennsylvania Dutch country it is made purely for pleasure in the eating because the Dutch never fast.

"Fastnachts"

3 medium potatoes, peeled and quartered

2 cups salted water

1 cup sugar, plus more for sprinkling

1 teaspoon salt

7 to 8 cups sifted all-purpose flour

1 envelope active dry yeast

¼ cup warm, but not hot, water

½ cup (1 stick) unsalted butter, softened

2 large eggs

½ teaspoon grated nutmeg

Vegetable oil for frying

Makes about 4 dozen doughnuts

In a large heavy stockpot, boil the potatoes in the salted water until tender, 15 to 20 minutes. Drain and set the potatoes aside; reserve 1 cup of the boiling water and pour it into a large bowl. Stir in the sugar, salt, and 1 cup of the flour. Using an electric mixer, beat until smooth. Dissolve the yeast in the warm water; beat it into the batter. Cover the bowl with a cloth and let rise in a warm place free from draft until the dough is light and full of bubbles, about 4 hours.

In a large bowl, mash the hot potatoes with a fork or potato masher until smooth. Measure 1 cup of the mashed potatoes into a large bowl and, using an electric mixer, beat in the butter, eggs, and nutmeg. When the batter is full of bubbles, stir in the potato mixture and enough of the remaining flour to make a firm, stiff dough.

Turn out on a lightly floured surface and knead for 8 to 10 minutes, until smooth and elastic. Place in a greased bowl, brush the top with melted butter, cover, and let rise in a warm place free from draft until doubled in bulk, about 2 hours.

Punch the dough down, cover the bowl, and refrigerate until 2 hours before serving time. Remove from the refrigerator and cut the dough in half. Roll each half ⅓ inch thick on a floured surface. Cut with a doughnut cutter or into 2-inch squares with a sharp knife. Place the doughnuts on a floured surface, cover with a cloth, and let rise in a warm place until doubled in bulk, about 20 minutes.

In a large heavy skillet, pour enough oil to reach a depth of 2 inches. Heat the oil to 365 degrees. Slip the doughnuts into the deep hot fat. When they rise to the top, turn with a long-handled fork to brown the other side. Drain on absorbent paper towels and sprinkle with sugar.

PATRIOTIC PEPPERPOT PUDDING

Pepperpot is a patriotic dish originating in Pennsylvania and still much served in Philadelphia. It has a romantic history to tell. It was that bitter winter at Valley Forge; George Washington's soldiers were in rags, food was ever lacking. Cooks made ends meet where there was nothing but ends and they met just over the starvation line. Soldiers began to think longingly of home; desertions were frequent. General Washington put his faith in the inner comfort of man. He called the head cook of the Revolutionary armed forces and explained the seriousness of the hour. He demanded a stomach-filling dish. The chef protested.

"I have only tripe, a few hundred pounds, the gift of a nearby butcher. I have peppercorns the gift of a Germantown patriot; all the rest is but scraps."

"From nothing," said the general, "you must create."

By early dark great pots sent up a heart-warming, comforting fragrance. Came the bugle call, men ate their fill of the fortifying food. They laughed again. They joked, "Bring on the redcoats."

The general called for the cook. "This dish is the stuff of heroes, what is its name?"

"I have conceived it but not called it," the cook replied. "But pepperpot would be my humble suggestion, sir."

"Call it Philadelphia pepperpot," said the general, "in honor of your own hometown."

In old years this savory soup was hawked through the Philadelphia streets by vendors calling "Peppery pot, smoking hot," dipping it from milk cans covered with snowy white towels.

Cooks argue what to put in, what to leave out. Tomatoes in our recipe, but these certainly were missing in the original for then tomatoes were known as love apples and were considered dangerous eating.

Philadelphia Pepperpot

¾ pound honeycomb tripe

2 pounds veal knuckles
(about 3 knuckle bones)

3 quarts cold water,
plus more if needed

1 tablespoon salt

1 small bunch parsley

10 whole cloves

16 peppercorns, crushed

3 green peppers, seeded and cut into
¼-inch dice (about 3½ cups)

3 medium onions, cut into ¼-inch dice
(4 to 5 cups)

3½ tablespoons unsalted butter

2 teaspoons vegetable oil

3 medium beets, cut into ¼-inch dice
(about 4 cups)

1½ cups canned tomatoes,
finely chopped, liquid reserved

⅓ cup uncooked rice

Makes 8 main-course or 12 first-course servings

Wash the tripe thoroughly and cut it into ¼-inch cubes.
Place in a large pot with the veal knuckles; add the water.
Place over low heat and slowly bring to a simmer. Simmer
for 10 minutes, then skim the fat from the surface. Season
with salt. Cover the pot and cook gently for about 2 hours.
Combine the parsley, cloves, and peppercorns in a
cheesecloth bag and add it to the pot. Cover the pot and
continue cooking for 1 hour. Remove the bag of spices.

Meanwhile, melt 1 tablespoon of the butter in ½ teaspoon
of the oil in a medium skillet, add the peppers, and sauté
until golden brown, about 5 minutes. Season lightly with
salt. Remove from the pan and set aside. Repeat the process
with the onions. In the same pan, melt the remaining
1½ tablespoons butter in the remaining 1 teaspoon of oil.
Add the beets and sauté until slightly softened, about
3 minutes. Remove the beets from the pan and set aside.

Deglaze the pan with tomatoes and their juices; add
this to the soup pot. Then add the reserved vegetables to
soup mixture along with the rice. Cover and simmer for
30 minutes. After 10 minutes, check the consistency and
adjust seasoning: The soup should not be too thick; if the
rice is absorbing liquid quickly, add ½ to 1 cup water.
Remove the veal bones, skim the fat, and serve.

SCRAPPLE WAS THE CHIEF DISH

Breakfast was the prelude to the opening of the Republican National Convention one June morning in 1948. Scrapple was the chief dish. It was served with syrup, or with poached or fried eggs, served with fried apples. A humble food but locally famous in the City of Brotherly Love. The close relationship was best expressed by Edward VII when he was Prince of Wales. Describing Philadelphia to friends, he said, "The city has a remarkably fine breakfast food and a famous old family. Their names are Biddle and Scrapple, but I'm damned if I know which is which."

What is this scrapple? It's a Pennsylvania-Dutch concoction. Its ancestor was called *pawn-haus* and made two hundred years ago, a kind of mush made of cornmeal with pork trimmings. In the early nineteenth century some smart meat man added marjoram, sage, and pepper, and scrapple was born. Until fifty years ago it was made only by local butchers. Then a packing plant was opened to introduce mass production. Today three companies make most of the 10,000,000 pounds of scrapple produced yearly.

In the early days scrapple's season was set to match that of the oyster. There was no way to keep it fresh. The season opened the first week of September and closed the middle of March. Now it is sold in pound molds, wrapped in cellophane during the winter. But canned scrapple makes it a year-round seller, available in cities everywhere.

Open both ends of the can to give a smooth edge. Force out the scrapple about three-eights to one-half inch and slice. Sprinkle with flour or cracker dust, or cornmeal to give more crust and keep the sputtering fat to a minimum.

Don't turn scrapple more than once. That makes it hash. Something else to be fussy about: scrapple needs to be drained on absorbent paper towels, then into a hot oven to reheat. No good to eat unless served hot as flame. Philadelphians want the ketchup bottle handy when eating scrapple. Upstate Pennsylvanians like it with brown-sugar syrup, also with poached eggs. New Yorkers like their scrapple with hot applesauce touched up with cinnamon.

Sausage Fruit Scrapple

4 pigs' knuckles

1 pound lean pork sausage

1 large onion

3 quarts water

1½ teaspoons salt

1 tablespoon freshly ground
black pepper

1 teaspoon ground sage

1 cup wheat cereal, such as
cracked wheat cereal or
cream of wheat

2 cups cornmeal

1 tablespoon chopped parsley

All-purpose flour for dredging

3 tablespoons butter

Fried bananas, optional

Serves 6

Grease two 9 x 5 x 3-inch loaf pans.

In a heavy 5-quart stockpot, combine the pigs' knuckles,
sausage, onion, and water. Place over medium-low
heat and slowly bring to a simmer. Cover and cook for
2½ hours. Drain, reserving the broth and sausage and
onions. Transfer the knuckles to a small bowl, cover, and
refrigerate for 30 minutes. Remove and separate the meat
from the bones. Chop the meat. Place the meat with the
reserved sausage and onions in a saucepan. Add 2 quarts
of the reserved broth. Add the salt, pepper, and sage and
bring to a boil.

In a medium bowl, combine the cereal and cornmeal with
the remaining 1 quart reserved broth and stir into the
boiling mixture. Cook over medium heat until thickened,
stirring constantly. Cover, reduce the heat to very low,
and cook, stirring occasionally, for 20 minutes.

Pour into the loaf pans. Cool, cover with plastic wrap,
and refrigerate overnight.

When ready to cook, cut the scrapple into ¼-inch slices
and dredge each slice in flour.

Melt the butter in a large skillet over medium heat. Add
the scrapple and fry until browned, about 4 minutes on
each side. Serve hot with fried bananas, if you like.

RECIPES PRIVATE AS STATE SECRETS

The select Philadelphia Club for men at the corner of Walnut and Thirteenth Streets has through the years kept its recipes private as State secrets. Then came the promise, red tape involved, that I could have maybe three of the favorites. The appointment was set. I felt a little awed passing through the broad classic door with the lovely old fanlight into the calm of a building no woman ever enters except a housekeeper and a few anonymous helpers.

Like the famous London clubs, White's, Brooks's, and Boodle's, the Philadelphia Club had started as a coffeehouse, the outcome of a gentlemen's reading and chess room going back to the time of Benjamin Franklin.

Legends abound of its groaning board. It's a kitchen set in its ways—clam chowder is made without tomatoes; cottage cheese is only cottage cheese when it's made with real cream; mincemeat always must have a brandy breath.

A look into the dining room before visiting the kitchen. It is a large room of classic simplicity.

Nine small tables around the walls and stationed in the center, one tremendous board, made of two tables of English mahogany and set for luncheon the morning of our visit. Here was a room that for one hundred years had been dedicated to one purpose—to do honor to the gastric juices of Philadelphia's leading citizens. Even the waiters exhibit a reverence for the place.

It was in the kitchen, on the third floor, that I felt most at home and most welcome. Chef Vincent Maiocco told me that "The gentlemen favor a soup before meals. It's quite a sight," he said, "to see forty men or more bending to their soup bowls. A sturdy soup may be the luncheon, such a one as the French onion, or the crab gumbo, or the snapper stew terrapin, or chicken mulligatawny, or the black bean. If it's oyster stew, there must be hard water crackers. These are as much a part of the stew as the oyster itself."

Lamb kidney in casserole is a menu regular. So is the English mutton chop stuffed with a kidney and girdled with bacon. And seldom if ever a refusal for curry of shrimp with the steamed rice. Winter and summer veal-and-ham pie is made two times a week.

Black Bean Soup

1 pound dried black beans

2 tablespoons bacon drippings or vegetable oil

1 cup minced onions

1 carrot, minced

2 tablespoons minced celery

3 sprigs parsley

⅛ teaspoon dried thyme

Pinch of dried hot pepper seeds

1 bay leaf

2 tablespoons Worcestershire sauce, plus more if needed

Salt and freshly ground black pepper

6 cups ham stock or water with ham bone or bacon skin

¼ cup sherry

Slices of lemon, hard-cooked egg, or chopped hard-cooked egg, optional

Serves 8

Place the beans in a nonreactive pan, cover with cold water, and soak for at least 6 hours or overnight. Discard any beans that float; drain and rinse the remaining beans.

In a large heavy pot, melt bacon drippings or heat the oil over medium heat; add the onions, carrot, celery, parsley, thyme, hot pepper seeds, and bay leaf. Sauté until the vegetables are golden brown, about 15 minutes Add the Worcestershire sauce and season with salt and pepper. Add the beans and stock. Bring to a simmer, then reduce the heat to very low, cover, and simmer slowly for 5 hours. Add more stock or water if the soup becomes too thick. Remove from the heat, cool, cover, and refrigerate overnight.

When ready to cook, place the pot over low heat and slowly bring to a boil. Transfer the soup to a blender and puree until smooth. Pour the soup back into the stockpot. Taste and add more salt, pepper, or Worcestershire sauce, if needed. Add the sherry. Serve with a slice of lemon or hard-cooked egg or 1 tablespoon chopped egg sprinkled over each cup.

A STICKINESS INCARNATE

Sticky cinnamon buns belong to Philadelphia as much as Independence Hall and the Twelfth Street Market. Not just any cinnamon bun, this bun of Quaker City, but a bun unique, of true cinnamon flavor, of a stickiness incarnate.

Time was when every bake shop in the city made the buns daily, the very rich ones baked in ring pans, these for tea and eating at dinner; the less rich in square pans, these buns made bigger—a breakfast bread. Bakery buns in olden days were just about perfect. Times change and today only a few commercial bakers turn out these buns of tradition.

There is no one recipe for this cinnamon bun because the home cooks can't agree. They argue minor matters. Which syrup for soaking? Shall it be raisins or currants, or maybe half and half? And should there be nuts? About the raisins: the only right kind is the seeded, never the seedless.

A pilgrimage to Philadelphia in search of the bun traditional led down Race Street to the kitchen of Harriet E. Worrell, scarcely more than a stone's throw from Rittenhouse Square. The Ogdens and the Worrells, she told us, are cinnamon-bun families from away back—meaning they like sticky buns daily, baked at least three times a week.

Harriet's buns are baked in a glass casserole so she can peek to gauge the right shade of brown. She tucks six buns around the outside and one in the middle. Enough syrup goes into the dish to soak half an inch up the bread. The outside fold of the bun is about a quarter of an inch thick, but after one unwind the layers are thin as cardboard. There is no argument whatever about when to serve sticky buns; good for any occasion.

A birthday party isn't a party unless sticky buns are there, light as a feather, served with Philadelphia ice cream.

Recipe: What is this Philadelphia ice cream? It means ice cream "Simon pure," made of the richest ingredients. This real-thing ice cream has but three ingredients in it: basic cream, sugar, and a touch of the vanilla bean. Fruits and other flavors can be added as you will.

In the old days Philadelphia families were often divided about the best place to eat ice cream around town. Of all these great ice-cream places, only Bassett's remained and there it was, bar and all, in the Twelfth Street Market. Here we give you the basic recipe as it was made at Bassett's and in Philadelphia home kitchens. Yes, ma'am, freezer-made served on the soft side, for then it's more flavorsome.

Philadelphia Cinnamon Buns

1¼ cups milk

1 envelope active dry yeast

¼ cup warm water

5 cups all-purpose flour

1½ teaspoons salt

¾ cup plus 1 tablespoon sugar

½ cup shortening

2 large eggs

4 tablespoons (½ stick) unsalted butter, at room temperature

½ cup packed brown sugar

2 teaspoons ground cinnamon

½ cup chopped walnuts

½ cup raisins or dried currants

2 cups corn syrup

Makes 2 dozen

Scald the milk in a medium saucepan over medium heat. Cool to lukewarm. In a large bowl, dissolve the yeast in the water in a large bowl and add the milk. Make a sponge by adding 2 cups of the flour, the salt, and 1 tablespoon of the sugar and beating until smooth. Set aside in a warm place.

In a large bowl, using an electric mixer, whip the shortening until light. Whip in the remaining ¾ cup sugar. Add the eggs, one at a time, beating each in thoroughly. Gradually beat this mixture into the bubbly sponge. Stir in enough of the remaining flour to make a soft dough.

Cover and let rise in a warm place until doubled in bulk, 1 to 1½ hours. Divide the dough in half and roll each portion ¼ inch thick. Spread with the butter. Combine the brown sugar and cinnamon and sprinkle over the dough. Scatter on the nuts and currants and dribble with 1 cup of the syrup. Roll each piece as for a jelly roll. Cut each roll into 1½-inch lengths, about 12 pieces per roll. Grease 2 deep 9-inch-square pans well with ½ cup syrup each. Stand the buns on the cut end in the pans.

Cover and let rise until doubled in bulk, 1 to 1½ hours. Top the buns with the remaining syrup.

Preheat the oven to 350 degrees.

Bake for 30 to 40 minutes, until browned. Turn out of the pans immediately.

Philadelphia Ice Cream

4 cups half-and-half

¾ cup sugar

⅛ teaspoon salt

1 vanilla bean or 2 teaspoons vanilla extract

Makes 1 quart

In a medium heavy saucepan, combine 2 cups of the half-and-half, the sugar, salt, and split vanilla bean in the top portion of a double boiler over boiling water. Stir constantly for 10 minutes, until the half-and-half is scalded and thickened. Remove from the heat and scrape the seeds and pulpy part from vanilla bean, discarding the pod. Mix the seeds with the half-and-half mixture and cool. (Store the remaining pod in your sugar jar to subtly flavor the sugar, if you like.) If vanilla extract is used, add after the half-and-half mixture is removed from the heat. Add the remaining 2 cups half-and-half and pour into a large stainless steel bowl. Set the bowl in an ice-water bath and chill thoroughly.

Pour the mixture into an ice cream maker and freeze according to the manufacturer's instructions. Store the ice cream in airtight containers in the freezer for up to 3 days.

Note: To make strawberry ice cream: To the custard, add 2 cups mashed strawberries that have been mixed with ¾ cup sugar and allowed to stand 2 hours. Freeze as above.

THE VERY SYMBOL
OF NEIGHBORLINESS

Quaker City Philadelphia is one of the food-lovingest of all the U.S. cities I have visited. Their special love is for foods traditional—snapper and oyster stew served with hard water crackers, pepper hash, sticky cinnamon buns, lamb kidneys in wine (for the Sunday breakfast), Philadelphia ice cream. And ask any native to name foods characteristic of the hometown—he'll rattle off a list that never fails naming Sautter's Old-Fashioned Pound Cake.

Man and times may pass. Rittenhouse Square is no longer a holy of holies; the great houses of yesterday are being torn down or rebuilt into apartments. But one thing as lasting as the Liberty Bell is that pound cake of Sautter's.

This dates back to the first Sautter's ice-cream parlor opened in 1864 when young Louis and his wife set up for business on Locust Street, directly across from the Academy of Music. Just a little place, but by 1916 there were three restaurants all humming like beehives. The pound cake was baked by Mrs. Sautter—to serve with the famous ice cream that the music-loving townspeople came to eat after concerts.

The ice-cream ingredients were country born, rich and wholesome. Nothing unusual, either, about the recipe for the cake but unusually good because it was honestly made: a pound of butter, a pound of sugar, a pound of eggs, a pound of flour. In olden days this type of cake was the very symbol of neighborliness in Philadelphia homes. It was served to wintertime callers with the pot of hot tea, to summertime visitors with the chilled pitcher of raspberry vinegar.

And other famous sweets in Sautter's cake cases—the most delicate of ladyfingers, meringue glacés, and macaroons—a kind you could chew instead of having them break into tasteless crumbs in the mouth. Old Philadelphians remember Sautter's "pies with windows" and the pretzels, golden, thin, and salty.

Times change, dynasties and restaurants close their doors. It was 1939, after more than fifty years catering to the Best Philadelphia Families, that the last of the Sautter restaurants was on the way out. But that didn't quite happen. Gaspar G. Lopez, a hotel man of long years' experience, was prevailed upon by the citizens of the town to continue the operation. He agreed, providing the Sautter recipes went along with the deal. They did, and so did Jacob Yackle, the baker who had been in the firm since 1918. I tried to borrow one of those recipes and Jacob said, "No." It was on bended knee that I begged for this pound cake recipe, and got it too. And the original way of the ladyfingers.

Sautter's Old-Fashioned Pound Cake

2 cups (4 sticks) unsalted butter, softened

2 cups sugar

9 large eggs

1 tablespoon vanilla extract

2 teaspoons orange extract

1 pound all-purpose flour

Makes 2 pound cakes

Preheat the oven to 325 degrees. Butter two 9 x 5-inch loaf pans.

Using an electric mixer at medium-high speed, cream the butter and gradually beat in the sugar until pale and fluffy, about 8 minutes. Add the eggs bit by bit and continue beating until thoroughly blended. Add the extracts. Gently and slowly beat in the flour. Pour into the prepared pans and bake for 1½ hours, or until a tester inserted into the center of each cake comes out clean. Cool in the pans on a wire rack for 30 minutes. Remove from pans and cool completely.

Ladyfingers

¾ cup all-purpose flour

10 tablespoons cornstarch

Pinch of salt

6 large eggs, separated

¾ cup granulated sugar

½ teaspoon vanilla extract

¼ cup cream of tartar

Sifted confectioners' sugar, for dusting

Makes about ninety 4-inch cookies

Preheat the oven to 425 degrees.

Sift the flour, cornstarch, and salt into a small bowl and set aside. Line 3 baking sheets with parchment paper.

Using an electric mixer, beat the egg yolks, ¼ cup of the granulated sugar, and the vanilla until thick and lemon-colored, about 5 minutes. Set aside.

Clean the beaters. In a clean bowl, beat the egg whites with the remaining ½ cup granulated sugar and the cream of tartar until stiff glossy peaks form.

Using a rubber spatula, gently fold the egg-yolk mixture into the egg-white mixture. Gently fold in the flour mixture. Transfer to a pastry bag fitted with a ½-inch round tip. Working in batches, pipe 4-inch cookies onto the prepared baking sheets, leaving about 1 inch between the cookies. Dust the cookies with confectioners' sugar.

Bake until the fingers are pale gold and just beginning to brown around the edges, 10 to 12 minutes. Immediately remove the paper with the ladyfingers from the sheet to prevent drying and transfer onto wire racks to cool. Turn upside down on a table; wet the back of the paper and remove the fingers. Arrange in rows and lightly dust with confectioners' sugar. Serve immediately, with jam or curd sandwiched between two cookies, if you like. The ladyfingers may be stored at room temperature in an airtight container for up to 2 weeks.

A FRAGRANT SIDE TRAIL

West of Philadelphia I followed a fragrant side trail that led me directly into the mushroom country, straight into Coatesville, Pa., to the kitchen door of Arece Lambert Anderson.

That Arece is a chip right off the old block. The old block is the late Louis Ferdinand Lambert, for many years known as the Dean of the mushroom industry. Father Lambert produced the first all-white mushroom and named it Snow White. Today the white princess has descendants galore. All the white mushrooms are of this family, representing 95 percent of the market varieties.

Today Arece and her husband Forrest Anderson run the Keystone Mushroom Co., selling spawn, growing mushrooms to sell fresh, and putting mushrooms into cans.

Arece uses the mushroom as much as most women do the onion. Sometimes she uses the fresh, but just as often it's the canned, which she keeps on hand to add to Welsh rabbit, stuffings, scrambled eggs, meat pies, spaghetti, and à la King dishes.

I asked Arece for the mushroom dish that ranks first with her family. Chipped creamed beef with mushrooms, she said, to serve over waffles. It's a dish her mother made for Saturday luncheons when daughter came home from college bringing her friends. Arece made the waffles at the table, crisp and golden, and Mother carried in a soup tureen filled to the brim with creamed mushrooms and dried beef.

She has a mushroom hors d'oeuvre recipe I liked especially. At your next club party bring on little sandwiches filled with Arece Anderson's mushroom spread and glory in the compliments.

But before I tell the recipes, just a word about kind treatment to fresh mushrooms, if that's what you use. Never, never peel the white beauties; just cut off the stem tips and wipe the caps with a damp cloth. But if you feel they need washing, do it in a hurry or you wash away the flavor. Arece thinks that many many people who insist they don't like mushrooms are prejudiced because they don't prepare them correctly. They cook them to death. Low heat, quick cooking—otherwise the vegetable shrivels and toughens. Use very little water—the fungus itself is 90 percent moisture.

Chipped Creamed Beef with Mushrooms

3 tablespoons unsalted butter

½ pound dried beef slices, shredded

3 tablespoons minced onion

3 tablespoons minced green pepper

3 tablespoons all-purpose flour

2 cups milk

1 tablespoon chopped parsley

¼ teaspoon paprika

2 tablespoons sherry wine

2 (4-ounce) cans mushrooms, drained

Serves 4 to 6

Melt the butter in a large skillet over medium heat. Add the beef and sauté until lightly browned and beginning to crisp, about 5 minutes. Add the onion and green pepper and cook until tender, about 5 minutes. Blend in the flour. Slowly add the milk, stirring constantly. Simmer until thickened and creamy but still somewhat liquid, about 5 minutes. Add the parsley, paprika, sherry, and drained mushrooms. Serve immediately, ladled over hot buttered waffles or toast.

Mushroom Sandwich Spread

½ cup (1 stick) unsalted butter

1½ pounds white button mushrooms, very finely chopped

1 tablespoon cornstarch

1 teaspoon salt

¼ teaspoon freshly ground black pepper

1 tablespoon chopped parsley

Makes about 2 cups

Melt the butter in a large saucepan over medium-high heat. Add the mushrooms and sauté just long enough to draw out the juices, about 5 minutes. Remove the pan from the heat. Remove 2 tablespoons of butter from the pan, cool slightly, and blend in a small bowl with cornstarch to make a smooth paste. Add to the mushrooms. Add the salt and pepper and return the pan to medium heat, stirring until thick and smooth. Add the parsley and transfer to a medium bowl. Cover and chill in the refrigerator. Spread between thin slices of crustless white bread and cut each slice into 3 thin fingers. The spread may be covered and kept in the refrigerator for up to 2 days or frozen, wrapped in foil, for a month. Bring to room temperature before serving.

IT WAS DOWN IN the mushroom country I heard tell of a pair of chocolate cakes, so famous people drive one hundred miles and more to eat a slice fresh-cut from one or the other. The cakes stand shoulder to shoulder in popular favor. The kinds—chocolate icebox and Aunt Sabella's black chocolate.

Chocolate cake, now that's my meat. I headed the car east out of Coatesville, took a left turn, second crossroad on Lincoln Highway, Route 30. Then to the Dutch Cupboard's door, home of the chocolate-cake twins. I ate a light luncheon, then settled for double dessert, one slice of each cake.

Want my honest opinion? I liked the chocolate icebox cake a wee bit better. But as everyone says, Aunt Sabella's black chocolate "is out of this world."

I talked to Eleanor Taylor of the Eleanor-and-Jackson-Taylor (Mr. and Mrs.) team who own the Dutch Cupboard. Aunt Sabella, Eleanor told me, was her father's sister, Sabella Nye Chapman, of Cayutaville, New York. She gave the recipe to Eleanor's mother who gave it to Eleanor when the restaurant was opened.

Aunt Sabella's Black Chocolate Cake with Fudge Icing

For the cake:

5 tablespoons plus 1 teaspoon unsalted butter, softened

2 ounces unsweetened chocolate, chopped

1¼ cups sifted all-purpose flour

1 teaspoon salt

1 cup buttermilk

1 teaspoon baking soda

1 cup sugar

2 large egg yolks

For the frosting:

2¼ cups confectioners' sugar, sifted

5 tablespoons cocoa powder

6 tablespoons unsalted butter, melted

5 tablespoons hot freshly brewed coffee

1½ teaspoons vanilla extract

Serves 6

Preheat the oven to 350 degrees. Grease an 8-inch square cake pan with 1 teaspoon of the butter and set aside.

To make the cake: Melt the chocolate in a small heatproof bowl set over a small pot of gently simmering water, stirring occasionally with a wooden spoon. Remove the bowl from the heat and set aside to cool.

Sift the flour and salt into a small bowl and set aside. In another small bowl, combine the buttermilk and baking soda and set aside.

In a large bowl using an electric mixer, beat the sugar and the remaining 5 tablespoons butter on medium speed until light and fluffy, about 2 minutes. Beat in the egg yolks, then add the melted chocolate and beat until thoroughly combined. Add one third of the flour mixture, then one third of the buttermilk mixture, beating well after each addition. Repeat until all the ingredients are used, then pour the batter into the prepared pan and bake until a toothpick inserted in the center of the cake comes out clean, 40 to 50 minutes. Transfer the cake to a rack and cool in the pan, then invert onto a cake plate.

To make the frosting: Sift the confectioners' sugar and cocoa into a medium bowl. Stir in the butter, then the coffee, then the vanilla, mixing well with a wooden spoon after each addition until the frosting is smooth. Ice the top and sides of the cake with the frosting.

MAKE FRIENDS WITH THE COOK

Pittsburgh once was a steamboat town, and at least part of its fame rests on steamboat pudding. Helen Ruch, a Pittsburgh advertising writer, likes to recall vacation trips down the Ohio and Mississippi Rivers, piloting with Grandpa George Gibson. He was one of the very few licensed to pilot all the way from Pittsburgh down to New Orleans. The memory comes gently—the churning of the water made by the great wheel, the lonesomeness of the whistle reverberating against the low cliffs, the stevedores singing their hearts into the night.

"Floating palaces," Grandpa said. "Finest of everything. And the food! No hotel in the land sets up better fare." Grandpa told how the ladies of the river towns vied with each other copying the dishes they had eaten when taking the grand tour.

The abundant table precedent was set by Cap'n Jim Rees when he warned the cabin crew of his famous *Kate Adams*, "I don't want to see an inch of tablecloth showing during a meal." When river-boat guests came to the table it was already crowded with relishes, condiments, jellies, nuts, fruits. All the food except the meat was served in kidney-shaped side dishes and often a dozen of these "shells" flanked a guest's plate. Hot breads were rushed continuously to the table. And no matter how many other desserts, a layer cake for the ending.

"Honey," Grandpa would say when he took little Helen aboard, "be polite to the captain, but make friends with the cook."

That's just what she did. How well she recalls Cook Jim's warning, "Never use sour cream in them flannel cakes, missy. Buttermilk—that's what gives 'em the flavor." It was Jim who taught her the verse about steamboat pudding. "Here comes the Cap'n wid a snicker and a grin, wheelhouse puddin' all over his chin."

Flannel Cakes with Chicken Hash

For the chicken hash:

3 tablespoons unsalted butter

2 tablespoons diced onion

3 tablespoons all-purpose flour

1 cup chicken or turkey broth

⅓ cup diced celery

2 teaspoons minced parsley

½ cup half-and-half

2 cups cold cubed or shredded chicken or turkey

Salt and freshly ground black pepper

For the flannel cakes:

2 cups all-purpose flour

¾ teaspoon baking soda

1 teaspoon salt

2½ cups buttermilk

2 tablespoons unsalted butter, melted

2 large eggs, separated, whites stiffly beaten

Serves 6 to 8

To make the chicken hash: Melt the butter in a large heavy skillet over medium heat. Add the onion and sauté until tender, about 3 minutes. Add the flour and cook for 4 minutes, stirring constantly. Add the broth, celery, and parsley and simmer gently for 5 minutes. Add the half-and-half and stir well. Add the chicken. Heat to the boiling point and season with salt and pepper. Set aside to thicken while you make the flannel cakes.

To make the flannel cakes: Preheat the oven to 250 degrees. Grease a large baking sheet.

Sift the flour, baking soda, and salt into a large bowl. Using an electric mixer, beat in the buttermilk and melted butter. Beat in the egg yolks until smooth. Fold in the stiffly beaten whites.

Heat a griddle or large nonstick skillet over medium heat. Spread a thin coating of butter over the griddle and let melt. Working in batches, drop the batter by ⅓ cupfuls onto the griddle, spacing them apart. Cook the pancakes until browned on the bottom and bubbles form on top, about 3 minutes. Turn the pancakes over and cook until the bottoms are browned and the pancakes are barely firm to the touch.

Place a generous tablespoon of hash on the cakes, roll the cakes, and fasten with a toothpick. Place in rows on the prepared baking sheet. Heat in the oven until ready to use.

Steamboat Pudding

2 cups large dry bread cubes (about 10 slices home-style white bread, preferably slightly stale, crusts removed)

1 quart milk, scalded

1 tablespoon unsalted butter, melted

½ teaspoon salt

¾ cup sugar

4 large eggs, lightly beaten

1 teaspoon vanilla extract

½ cup seedless raisins

Serves 6

Preheat the oven to 350 degrees. Grease a 1½-quart casserole.

In a large bowl, soak the bread cubes in the milk until most of the liquid has been absorbed, about 45 minutes. Stir in the remaining ingredients and pour into the prepared casserole. Place the baking pan in a roasting pan; pour enough boiling water into the roasting pan to come halfway up the sides of the baking pan. Bake for 1 hour, or until a knife inserted in the center of bread pudding comes out barely clean (do not overbake). Let stand for 5 minutes. Serve warm, with crushed sweetened fruit, if you like.

READING, PENNSYLVANIA, is center of the modern pretzel world. There pretzels are made by the millions a day by machinery processing. If you would see them done in the old fashioned way, visit the Lititz, Pennsylvania, Pretzel House, open daily to visitors. Youngsters are invited to try their hands at pretzel twisting and diplomas are given for their best efforts.

There are two schools of thought regarding the pretzel's origin, but both start at the church. The crossed dough ends of the bread are said to represent the crossed arms of the priest or the acolyte at prayer. From this point forward pretzel authorities differ. (Don't smile, there are pretzel experts, and they take themselves quite seriously.) One story is that glazed hard pretzels encrusted with coarse salt were given out at monastery doors to passing pilgrims. The hole in the center had a functional purpose—pretzels could be strung on a pilgrim's staff.

A more charming theory is that the name pretzel is derived from the Latin "pretiola" meaning a small reward, and the bread was made by the monks of southern Europe to give to those children who learned their prayers perfectly.

The art of pretzel making was brought to this country by the Germans and Austrians. The first American pretzels were baked in home kitchens on open hearth fires. Then in 1861 came the first commercial pretzel bakery established in Lititz. Soon pretzels were baking in near-by Reading. Soon every little Dutch hamlet had its pretzel maker.

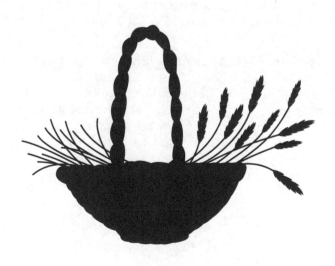

"Bretzel Supp Mit" Clams (Pretzel Clam Soup)

1 (7-ounce) can minced clams and liquor

2 tablespoons diced onion

2 cups canned clam broth

2 cups milk

½ teaspoon dried thyme

½ teaspoon salt

1 teaspoon garlic salt

¼ teaspoon freshly ground black pepper

2 tablespoons dried parsley flakes

4 tablespoons (½ stick) unsalted butter

2 tablespoons all-purpose flour

½ cup heavy cream

Paprika

12 large pretzels

Serves 6

Drain the clams and pour the liquor into a medium heavy saucepan. Add the onion, broth, milk, thyme, salt, garlic salt, pepper, and parsley. Place over medium heat and simmer very gently for 5 minutes. Do not allow to come to a full boil.

Melt 2 tablespoons of the butter in a large saucepan over medium heat. Stir in the flour. Remove from the heat and gradually stir in 1 cup of the milk mixture. Add the remaining milk mixture; heat and stir until slightly thickened, about 5 minutes. Add the minced clams, the cream, and the remaining 2 tablespoons butter and heat through. Serve sprinkled with paprika. Crumble the pretzels over the soup just before serving.

NEW JERSEY

The budding maple was stretching its branches over bulbous Bill Kotze and that small inferno of sputtering coals he tended with a garden rake. It was the evening of the big shad fry and the Hudson River shad men were expecting Bill to plumb outdo himself on the tenth anniversary of their feast, the year 1946.

Everything sitting pretty, Bill assured himself, squinting an investigating eye. The shad were nailed to their planks, the planks one on another piled the garden bench. Bags of charcoal made a barricade to the south of the tree. Bill counted four pairs of white cotton gloves for firemen and plankers. He checked the salt and pepper in the big kitchen shakers. The night settled down. It threw a velvet blanket over the tree, turning the shad kitchen into a firelighted crypt.

The place was the Homestead, Union City, New Jersey. It was George Edward Jester's Inn. Betty Burns the cook. Bill Kotze is the shad fisherman who held the distinction of being America's top shad-fry artist. He is the only one aside from his brother George who can run such a racket. The Kotze boys learned the art in their teens from their father, old Joseph. It was Bill who supplied the roe shad for the party, these taken from his own nets strung into the Hudson just above Edgewater. Steve Cuomo, the speed boner of New York's Fulton Fish Market, did the dissecting.

A shad to a plank, that's the allotment. The two fillets are crossed with three strips of bacon, then nailed tight to the board. The oak planks measured two feet in length, about fifteen inches in width and were fitted on a prop like a shaving mirror, so they stood at any angle desired. Planks can be used two seasons only, then they dry out and will go up in a whiff of flame to ruin a party. .

I had been to many a fish fry, but this shad fry—oh my! a tricky business laying the fire, built as it was on top of the ground. Newspapers were put down to cover the chosen spot which measured three feet wide and six to seven feet long, the length depending, of course, on the number of planks to be set. Bill had twenty planks, enough to serve sixty people. One big shad will serve four, only a few hearty eaters can manage second helpings. Over the newspaper was laid kindling wood intermingled with paper to get it off to a good start. About an hour before the planks were set, the kindling was fired. Spears of fire rose to jab at the darkness. Bill officiated with his rake. A fire bed must be made just so, tucked in nice and neat around the edges, mitered at the corners.

White smoke plumes curled. A north breeze sent the smoke rolling south; when a west wind came it ran to the east. Big Bill, ambling like a bear, traveled always in the opposite direction to keep the smoke from his eyes. A rake here, a poke there, and at last he shouted, "Mack (that was Mack McGlone, one of Bill's shad crew), lay on the charcoal." A couple of bags for the beginning, more as needed. It figures out a bag to a plank.

"Set 'em up, Mack," Bill's voice was mighty. That was the signal to set the shad planks.

Some one passed the word along to the kitchen. "They're starting now." Guests at the bar came out to watch.

Captain Bill hoisted up his sagging trousers, moistened his throat with a glass of beer and gave out the orders. Mack ran the circle. "Move it back, Mack. That one forward." Bill was in his element. Another glass of beer. "Straighten that one, Mack, turn her over."

The kitchen exhaled savory undulations of food. Betty Burns in a yellow and lavender flowered blouse with helpers Frances Miche, Sadie Penrice, and Clara Emerson, were giving that last-minute touch to the dinner. There's more to a shad fry than the shad. There's always the chowder, clam chowder.

Good-natured Betty, right in the middle of the hubbub, obligingly told us how she made that ten-gallon batch. She made it Manhattan style. She made it without water.

Betty will never be popped in the eye frying shad roe for a crowd. She wraps the roe in wax paper and bakes it in bundles. Roe is placed in a sieve and cold water run over. Then arranged on clean towels and let dry. It is salt and pepper seasoned, rolled in the paper, the ends twirled for a tight closure. The rolls are spread over a baking sheet to wait for the moment the shad planks are set by the fire; then into a slow oven. The roe and shad cooking the same time, one hour and fifteen minutes.

Captain Bill gave an appraising glance at the shad and sent word to the kitchen that Betty dip the chowder. A runner carried the shad planks from fire to kitchen. A strong man pulled out the nails with the back of a hammer. The blistering fillets were sliced across the middle, servings for four, a quarter of a shad to a plate. The roe was pulled from the oven and each cut in half. A spoonful of green beans, a hot potato boiled in its jacket. The green salad came along next. No dessert, no coffee, but beer flowed as if from some inexhaustible source.

Shad is an east coast fish featured on restaurant menus from Maine to Florida. The season starts around the first of December. By January the Florida run is on big and by the middle of the month even Georgia is sending shad from the Savannah and Altamaha Rivers. Before the last week of January South Carolina and North Carolina are contributing, and so up the coast. North Carolina is the big shipper. Next, Maryland and Virginia. Delaware shad is considered a specialty in Philadelphia, coming to season in late March. One of the street cries of the city nearly one hundred years ago was "Shad oh! Oh shad ! Delaware shad!"

Late March, early April shad appears off the New Jersey shore. Not many years back there were exceptional runs in the Hudson River. In recent years almost no shad, as the river is polluted. It is May when the shad start running in the Connecticut River, then members of the Quinnipeock Club at New Haven can stop their ceaseless questioning as to "When will we have Connecticut shad on the menu?" Rhode Island, too, has shad in May, and New Brunswick sends out a few hundred pounds.

Some women assert they can bone their own shad. Every year women write to us telling their way of cooking a shad by dissolving the bones. It can be done, for we have done it, but the long, long cooking seems to take away something of the pristine freshness of the fish. So we thought, until one Sunday eating a shad cooked in Marcia Garrick's kitchen at Saw Mill Farm, Rockland County, New York. Marcia has been gone a dozen years, but I still remember her gay self as of yesterday and her fine cooking with herbs. This shad she cooked with its bones, cooked the day long, cooked on a feather-soft bed of wild sorrel. Marcia started with a recipe from *Madame Prunier's Fish Cookery Book*. But Marcia, being Marcia, she did it quite her own way. The five and one-half pound "lady" shad (the roe appeared at breakfast) was prepared with the head on, only its innards and backbone came out. The cleaned fish was massaged with olive oil, salt and pepper, seasoned, then herbal additions, and over all a sprinkle

of sweet Spanish paprika. From the herb garden came the wild sorrel, almost two pounds to clean, then brown in duck fat with one clove of minced garlic, one onion thinly sliced. When the sorrel was well wilted Marcia chopped it fine to bed down the shad in the big pottery dish. Sorrel, you know, must never be cooked in aluminum. Fish on the greens, more sorrel over top, then sliced tomatoes over all. Then the cut parsley. Dampened parchment paper was laid over the baking dish in lieu of a lid and this fastened secure with the top of the aluminum roaster.

Ten hours in the oven, that shad's surely done! The sorrel is scraped to one side of the fish, creamy mashed potatoes mixed with finely cut chives, dotted with butter, flanked the opposite side. Into a hot oven for the potatoes to brown and straight to the table.

Dinner was preceded by a number of cocktails to bolster our courage for feasting on bones, but bones truly melted into the sweet flesh of the fish. A mushroom sauce made with vermouth accompanied the dish, a sort of gilding of the lily. Watercress was the green salad, fresh picked from the brook, with a few spears of cooked asparagus thrown in for good measure. This was tossed in Marcia's herb garden dressing.

OUTSIDE A LITTLE WIND ruffled the new leaves along DeForest Avenue, Summit, New Jersey. Inside, the piano made music like laughing.

"In closing, Ann Bartleson will play a duet with her sister Susan," and Mrs. Helen Chrystal Bender, standing tall with a gentle Quaker dignity, smiled her teacher's smile at the two young girls. Music in hand, they squeezed their way out of the second row back, heading for the grand piano where the tall tapers made the golden light.

In the pause of waiting, a solid, compact little girl's voice from the front row queried, "Do we eat the cakes next?" This child was as patiently expectant as everyone else for the recital's grand climax: supper with Mrs. Bender and the feast of cakes.

Wonderful cakes! For thirty years these cakes had been baked by teacher Bender to help celebrate the school's Sunday afternoon musicals. After music the ham and bean supper, then the cake cutting. Mrs. Bender cooked the meal, she baked the cakes, over two hundred a year. There were nine on the table the evening I visited. Now Mrs. Bender is retired and lives in Hawaii. At long last she has put her famous cake recipes into a book.

Teacher Bender's favorite of the cake collection is the gold cake, which goes along with the angel food to use the yolks left behind by the whites. Spice cake—that's for me any old time!

Gold Cake

For the cake:

½ cup (1 stick) unsalted butter

1¼ cups sugar

11 large egg yolks (about ⅞ cup)

½ cup milk

1¼ cups cake flour

½ teaspoon salt

¼ teaspoon orange extract

¼ teaspoon lemon extract

¼ teaspoon almond extract

2 teaspoons baking powder

For the icing:

4 tablespoons (½ stick) unsalted butter

1 pound confectioners' sugar

2 to 3 tablespoons orange juice

Makes one 9-inch cake

Prcheat the oven to 350 degrees.

To make the cake: In a large bowl using an electric mixer, cream the butter and sugar. Add the egg yolks, beating until creamy. Add the milk alternately with the flour, beating well after each addition. Beat in the salt. Add the extracts, and at the very end the baking powder. Turn the mixture into an ungreased 9-inch tube pan and bake for about 45 minutes, until a wooden pick or skewer inserted in the middle of the cake comes out clean. Invert onto a wire rack and cool for about 20 minutes. Run a spatula along the sides and remove the cake.

To make the icing: In a large bowl, blend the butter with the confectioners' sugar and add just enough orange juice to give the icing a nice spreading consistency. Ice the cake with the icing.

Angel Cake

11 large egg whites (about 1½ cups)	1 cup all-purpose flour
½ teaspoon salt	1½ cups sugar
1 teaspoon cream of tartar	1 teaspoon vanilla extract

Makes one 9-inch tube cake

Preheat the oven to 375 degrees.

In a large bowl using an electric mixer, beat the egg whites until foamy but not stiff. Add the salt and cream of tartar and continue beating until the whites are just stiff enough to form soft peaks.

Sift the flour and sugar into a small bowl. Gently fold into the egg white mixture, sifting in 2 tablespoonfuls at a time. Fold in the vanilla. Pour the batter into an ungreased 9-inch tube pan. Bake for 40 minutes, or until a tester inserted in the center comes out clean. Invert the pan onto a wire rack until cooled, about 1½ hours. Run a spatula along the sides and remove the cake.

Spice Cake

½ cup (1 stick) unsalted butter, softened

1 tablespoon molasses

1½ cups sugar

1 teaspoon salt

½ teaspoon ground cloves

½ teaspoon grated nutmeg

⅛ teaspoon ground allspice

1 teaspoon vanilla extract

2 large eggs

1 cup milk

1¼ cups cake flour

1 tablespoon baking powder

Makes one 9-inch cake

Preheat the oven to 375 degrees. Line 2 (9-inch) round cake pans with greased waxed paper.

In a large bowl using an electric mixer, cream the butter, molasses, and sugar. Add the salt, cloves, nutmeg, allspice, and vanilla. Beat in the eggs. Add the milk alternately with the flour, beating well after each addition. Blend in the baking powder. Pour the batter into the prepared pans. Bake for 25 minutes, or until a tester inserted in the center of each cake comes out clean. Cool the layers on a wire rack for 10 minutes, then turn out to cool completely, about 30 minutes. Frost with your favorite icing.

DELAWARE

It's a monster contraption, the double submarine that nosed into sight along the East Coast late in the war. The original spot of its sighting is a matter of contention, but nobody argues over its present home base. Biggest submarine-sandwich fleet in dry dock is built by Jack Twilley's stand-up-and-at-'em snack bar at Rehoboth Beach, Del., most proper summer-resort town.

Far off the beaten path of epicures is Twilley's little bar, its front opening on Rehoboth's main street. Four Sundays back, we stood there, notebook in one hand, pencil in the other, recording who came by to buy "subs" and to get the details of "giant sandwich" construction.

Listening in, we learned that submarines never miss a beach picnic. They go out to summer suppers, to beer parties, off on boat trips.

Women with home freezers buy "subs" in sets of a dozen to freeze, then defrost and serve when the crowd gathers. Another trick with these "Paul Bunyan" tidbits is to wrap tightly in wax paper, chill a few hours, slice crosswise with a sharp knife, eight cuts to a sandwich. Even "sub-divisions" are four-bite affairs served as snack fare when the drinks are poured.

Want to introduce the submarine to your town? Take a long, soft finger roll, the longer the better, nine inches the length. If you can't get the long rolls, whack off nine-inch cuts of French flute bread or use the long Italian hard rolls.

Rehoboth Beach
Submarine Sandwiches

1 (9- or 10-inch) sub roll, baguette, or other sandwich roll

3 to 4 ounces thinly sliced deli ham

2 ounces thinly sliced provolone cheese

4 crisp leaves of iceberg lettuce or ½ cup shredded

4 thin slices ripe tomato

Dried thyme

Ground celery seed

Salt

2 teaspoons olive oil

4 or 5 thin rings raw red onion

4 (½-inch) slices dill pickle

4 sliver-slices hot pickled peppers

Serves 1 to 2

Split the rolls lengthwise, almost into halves but not quite. Flatten them like an open book, and now to your building. Lay on the following ingredients, one thing on the other, exactly in this order: three thin slices of pressed ham, arranged overlapping; two thin slices provolone cheese; four crisp leaves of lettuce or the shredded lettuce if you prefer; four slices of tomato. Sprinkle with thyme, celery seed, and salt. Drizzle over the olive oil. Add the onion rings; overlay with 4 slices of dill pickle and a few sliver slices of hot pickled peppers— to set a fire in the mouth. Cut the sandwich through the center into two halves and quickly snap it together. Wrap in waxed paper and into the refrigerator until picnic time. Figure one to a person or maybe two people. On one submarine you can dine, and dine well.

THAT WAS THE BEST Sunday dinner I ever did eat. So it seemed at the moment! We were hungry as threshers, Harriet Arnold and myself. We had left New York City on a Friday evening seeking good cooks and had picked up a few Pennsylvania Dutch recipes. We visited a Maryland hostess, then someone suggested Mrs. Sheldon F. Potter at Rehoboth Beach, Del., a former Philadelphian.

I telephoned and Mrs. Potter said, "Fine! Come down for Sunday dinner; the house is only half built—but the kitchen is finished!"

Mrs. Potter is Margaret Yardley Potter, writer of the cookbook "At Home on the Range," that drew lifted eyebrows among the family's most proper friends. "Such an odd woman," they said. "She likes to bake her own bread and you know what she did? Instead of giving her daughter Madeline a coming-out party she repainted the kitchen; that's where the young Potters do their entertaining."

The Potters' table is long; it is broad; it has extra boards. The Potter children could ask friends to dinner without a formal invitation or asking Mom first. Mrs. Potter made a habit of dishes expandable.

Now the children are married and gone from the home coop, but Mrs. Potter as ever welcomes the visitor. That's why our telephone call out of the blue brought a prompt invitation to "Little Wiser" there at Road End.

Fried turkey on the menu with new corn on the cob; fresh snap beans in the salad; Delaware soft-top rolls, hot from the oven—we ate four in a row. Dessert was a blackberry mush.

Fried turkey Mrs. Potter thinks will eventually give fried chicken a run for the money. This Delaware soft-top roll recipe detailed below is one Mrs. Potter borrowed from Edith Holland, who is from Lewes, Del., now pastry cook at the Corner Cupboard, a popular guest house run by Mrs. Potter's good friend Alice Gundry. Rolls almost as soft as marshmallows, airy light, tender.

Delaware Soft-Top Rolls

¼ cup vegetable shortening

½ cup mashed potatoes

1 teaspoon salt

⅓ cup sugar

½ envelope active dry yeast

1 cup warm milk

1 large egg

3 cups all-purpose flour

Makes about 30

In a medium bowl, combine the shortening with the mashed potatoes, salt, and sugar. In a small bowl, dissolve the yeast in the milk and let it rest for 5 minutes or until foamy; stir into the potato mixture. Beat the egg in a large bowl. Pour in the potato mixture and stir well with a wooden spoon. Pour in the flour slowly, stirring to form a soft dough.

Cover the bowl loosely with plastic wrap or a clean kitchen towel and leave in a warm place to double in bulk, about 3 hours.

Generously grease several muffin pans. Form rolls about 1 tablespoon in size using your hands; place each in a cup of the prepared pans. Cover the rolls loosely with plastic wrap or a clean kitchen towel and let rise until doubled in bulk, about 1 hour.

Preheat the oven to 450 degrees. Bake the rolls for about 10 minutes, until golden and puffy. Transfer from the pans to a wire rack to cool. Serve warm.

Blackberry Compote

2 quarts fresh ripe blackberries

1 cup sugar

3 tablespoons cornstarch

Serves 8

Wash the berries, removing the hulls and any imperfect specimens. Place in a stockpot and cover with water. Bring to a simmer over medium heat and simmer until you can almost see the seeds and the berry juices are released, 5 to 7 minutes. Drain, then mash the berries with a potato masher and press through a fine sieve, but easy; press too hard and the seeds break and get into the puree. There should be about four cups of liquid, which you should turn into a saucepan. Stir in the sugar.

In a small bowl, blend the cornstarch with an equal amount of the blackberry juice and stir well to combine. Add the mixture to the remaining juice. Cook the mixture over low heat, stirring constantly, until thick and clear, almost a jelly consistency, about 10 minutes. Pour over vanilla ice cream or serve in bowls topped with freshly whipped cream, if you like.

DISTRICT OF COLUMBIA

When the all-American salad was introduced in the Senate dining room on Capitol Hill I attended the luncheon. The salad came cradled in the largest salad bowl in the world, and filled to the brim, carried in the arms of four stalwart waiters. Senate salad is the name and it may well appear daily on the restaurant menu to give Senate bean soup and Senate rum pie a run for the money. The salad is a ten-ingredient recipe, this inscribed on silver and inlaid on one side of the bowl.

This salad recipe was made in conference with seven states trying to mix garden wares. The problem was which state would give what? Nobody argued when Senator Margaret Chase Smith announced, "Maine adds the lobster." And beautiful it was with the claw pieces laid in a wide band over the top and more sweet lobster lumps waiting the fork interwoven through the greens.

New Jersey put in the plump red tomatoes. California lettuce, the standard salad greenery bed. Why California? Because California grows lettuce every month of the year and 90 percent of the lettuce consumed in this country comes from there. Arizona, too, is a lettuced state, but she added romaine; she put in the grapefruit, and surprisingly good it is with the lobster, giving exactly the right tang. The spicy watercress was grown in West Virginia.

Here's California again slicing in the avocado. Great Texas contributed little green onions. Texas could fill that bowl with the salad of the centuries. They grow everything!

Senate salad is prepared with a salad-dressing mix, the quintessence of the French kind and with just the right kiss of garlic. Louisiana poured the oil.

Here you are, ladies—try it yourself. The Senate restaurant recipe has been pared down to family size. It's an adjustable salad—instead of lobster, use chicken or shrimp or crab meat. Or leave out the extras and make it a salad of greens.

Senate Salad

For the salad:

1 cup bite-size pieces of Bibb lettuce

1 cup bite-size pieces of romaine or escarole lettuce

½ cup bite-size pieces of watercress

1½ cups diced fresh lobster meat

1 cup diced celery

½ cup thinly sliced green onions and stems

2 medium tomatoes, cubed

1 medium avocado, peeled, pitted, and cubed

5 large pimento-stuffed olives, sliced

8 to 12 segments from half a grapefruit

Salt and freshly ground black pepper

Senate Salad Dressing (recipe follows)

Makes 4 entrée salads

Combine the lettuces and make a bed with them on 4 individual plates. Place the ingredients in rows or separate piles on the lettuce beds. Season with salt and pepper. Pass with Senate salad dressing.

Senate Salad Dressing

½ cup olive oil

1 tablespoon plus 2 teaspoons white wine vinegar

1 small clove garlic, chopped

3 hard-cooked eggs, finely chopped

½ cup mayonnaise

1 tablespoon thinly sliced chives

½ teaspoon salt

Makes 2 cups

In a medium bowl, combine the oil and vinegar and whisk in the remaining ingredients.

Congressional Apple Pie

2 (9-inch) Perfect Pie Crusts (page 13)

½ cup sugar

¼ cup honey

½ teaspoon ground cinnamon

¼ teaspoon salt

1 tablespoon lemon juice

8 large tart apples (about 3½ pounds), peeled, cored, and sliced about ¼ inch thick

1 tablespoon unsalted butter

Makes 1 double-crust 9-inch pie

Preheat the oven to 450 degrees. Line a 9-inch pie pan with pastry.

In a large bowl, combine the sugar, honey, cinnamon, salt, and lemon juice. Add the apples and toss lightly. Arrange in the pastry-lined pie pan. Dot all over with the butter. Moisten the edges of the crust and cover with the top crust, which has been gashed to allow steam to escape. Fold the upper crust under the lower crust and seal the edges with a fork.

Bake for 10 minutes, then reduce the oven temperature to 350 degrees and bake for 40 to 50 minutes longer, until the apples are tender and the filling is bubbling, covering the edges with foil if it is browning too quickly.

Remove from the oven and cool on a wire rack for 30 minutes. Serve warm or at room temperature. The pie can be made 1 day ahead, covered loosely, and stored at room temperature.

Senate Rum Pie

¼ cup all-purpose flour

2 tablespoons cornstarch

2 cups milk

5 large egg yolks, lightly beaten

¾ cup sugar

Pinch of salt

½ cup (1 stick) unsalted butter, melted

2 tablespoons dark rum

1 Graham Cracker Crust (recipe follows)

Whipped cream

Chopped pecans

Grated unsweetened chocolate

D.C.

Makes one 9-inch pie

In a medium bowl, whisk together the flour and cornstarch. Stir in ½ cup of the milk and the egg yolks; mix until smooth and set aside.

In a large heavy saucepan combine the remaining 1½ cups of the milk, the sugar, and salt. Place over medium-low heat and bring almost to the boiling point. Stir in the flour and egg yolk mixture. Cook slowly until thick and smooth, stirring constantly, 10 to 12 minutes. Remove the pan from the heat and cool to room temperature. Whisk in the melted butter. Gently whisk in the rum. Pour into the graham cracker crust, cover, and chill thoroughly in refrigerator for several hours.

When ready to serve, top with whipped cream and sprinkle with nuts and chocolate. Serve cold.

Graham Cracker Crust

1½ cups finely ground graham cracker crumbs (about 12 crackers)

½ cup confectioners' sugar

½ teaspoon grated nutmeg

½ cup (1 stick) unsalted butter, melted

Makes one 9-inch pie crust

In a large bowl, combine the crumbs, confectioners' sugar, and nutmeg. Slowly pour in the melted butter and mix thoroughly.

Line a 9-inch pie pan with mixture and press firmly into place. Cover and chill in the refrigerator for 30 minutes before filling.

U.S. Senate Bean Soup

1 pound dried navy, Great Northern, or marrow beans

4 quarts cold water

1 meaty smoked ham hock

1 tablespoon unsalted butter

1 small yellow onion, finely chopped

Salt and freshly ground black pepper

Serves 4 to 6

Sort through the beans, discarding any small stones. Place in a pan, add 2 quarts of the water, and soak overnight. Drain, then rinse under cold running water. Put the beans, ham hock, and the remaining 2 quarts cold water into a medium heavy-bottomed pot. Place over high heat, cover, and bring to a boil. Uncover, reduce the heat to medium-low, and simmer until bean skins are tender and the interiors are soft, about 1 hour.

Meanwhile, melt the butter in a medium skillet over medium heat. Add the onion and cook, stirring frequently with a wooden spoon, until soft and just beginning to brown, 3 to 5 minutes. Remove the skillet from the heat and set aside.

Reduce the heat to low on the beans and stir in the onions. Cook for 2 hours, stirring occasionally to prevent scorching. Retrieve the ham hock from the pot and set aside until cool enough to handle. Remove and discard the skin, bone, and excess fat, dice the meat, and add it to the soup. Mash some of the beans against the side of the pot with the back of the spoon to make the soup a little thicker and a bit creamy, then season with salt and pepper. Serve in individual earthenware pots with garlic bread, if you like.

MARY TURNER HAS STAYED in one place but she's influenced the eating habits of the nation. Just try her baked crab imperial. Mary wouldn't say so—she would think the idea simply ridiculous—that she, Mary E. Turner, Washington, D.C., has done more, perhaps, than any other one person to influence the eating habits of cross-country America.

Her job had been the same one for twenty-seven years: Director of the Home Service Bureau of the Potomac Electric Power Company. Through all of these years she had taught women cooking, the tried and true and things brand-new.

Mary's influence has been nation-wide. True, she hadn't moved out of Washington but the capital city has a shifting population. Women come, women go. They come from every state in the Union, live for a period, then home again to show the neighbors how it's done.

A joy in life to Mary is company for supper, preferably summer company with supper in the garden.

In June, July, and August, when the garden is in its glory, Sunday-evening buffets come almost weekly. The start-off usually is tomato-juice cocktails with appetizers. No fiddle-faddle with the finger foods; simple good eating, blessed by the magic touch of originality. Example: the little spring onion wearing a cheese wrap-around. Men coming to supper? Then a savory substantial, raw meatballs.

"Is there any one food belonging especially to Washington?" we wanted to know. Mary Turner said, "Yes, the blue crab of the Chesapeake."

Casserole of Baked Crab Imperial

2 cups milk	2 tablespoons sherry
3 tablespoons unsalted butter	1 cup soft breadcrumbs
2 tablespoons all-purpose flour	2 tablespoons minced fresh parsley
1 teaspoon salt	1 tablespoon minced onion
⅛ teaspoon freshly ground black pepper	1 pound jumbo lump crabmeat
Dash of cayenne pepper	¼ cup toasted buttered breadcrumbs
1 large egg yolk, beaten	1 teaspoon sweet paprika

Makes 4 entrée or 6 appetizer servings

Preheat the oven to 400 degrees. Grease a shallow 1½-quart casserole well.

In a small pan, warm the milk over low heat. Meanwhile, melt the butter in a medium pan over low heat. Whisk in the flour, raise the heat slightly, and continue to cook until blended, about 2 minutes. Gradually whisk in the warmed milk, the salt, pepper, and cayenne and bring to a low simmer, stirring constantly, until thickened, about 2 minutes. Gradually add the egg yolk, tempering to prevent scrambling, and continue cooking for 2 minutes more. Remove the pan from the heat. Add the sherry, soft breadcrumbs, parsley, and onion; mix gently. Season with additional salt and pepper to taste and add the crabmeat.

Pour into the prepared casserole. Top with the buttered crumbs, sprinkle with the paprika, and bake for 20 to 25 minutes. Serve with a green salad and toasted bread, if you like.

DR. WILLIAM M. MANN, Director of Washington's National Zoo, is on speaking terms with everyone of his 2,800 animal wards—even though his specialty is ants. He has penetrated some of the least-known parts of the world to learn more about ants and to collect wild game.

His collections are more varied than the public knows. His secondary interest is collecting recipes. Gray-haired, stocky Dr. Bill Mann takes time out always to investigate the foods of the lands he visits. He eats of native dishes with an observing eye, with a curious palate. Invariably he can guess the ingredients. Home again, the doctor tries reproducing these dishes, searching foreign shops for exotic seasoners and odd groceries; then to prepare a little dinner to amaze his friends.

Mrs. Mann once thought of writing a book about her husband's recipes but he hasn't any. She said, "The trouble is, Bill cooks off the top of his head, beautifully and comprehensively inexact."

Mexican dinner is one of their most applauded. Turkey broilers for this, prepared in a sauce made with mole powder—a below-the-border seasoner you can buy in Spanish stores, hot with chilis, containing some twenty balanced herbs and spices. Black beans with rice, in the Cuban manner, go with this dinner. Tortillas take the place of bread. These are sold fresh in some cities ready to toast or fry; also sold canned in Spanish stores. Garlic bread might be served instead.

Black Beans, Cuban Style

1 pound dried black beans	3 medium onions, chopped
1 tablespoon plus 1 teaspoon salt	½ teaspoon ground sage
4 cloves garlic	2 bay leaves, crushed
½ cup vegetable oil	3 tablespoons cider vinegar
3 green peppers, seeded and chopped	Freshly ground black pepper

Serves 4 to 6

Wash and pick over the beans. Place in a heavy-bottomed saucepan, cover with water, and soak overnight. Drain and return to the saucepan with fresh water to cover. Add 1 tablespoon salt and 1 clove of garlic, cut in half. Bring to a simmer over medium heat, then reduce the heat to medium-low and cook until tender, about 3 hours, adding more water as needed.

Just before serving, heat the oil in a large heavy skillet over medium heat. Add the remaining garlic, the green peppers, onions, sage, and bay leaves. Cook until the vegetables are softened, 5 to 7 minutes. Add the vinegar, the remaining 1 teaspoon salt, and pepper to taste. Place the beans in a serving dish and pour the vegetable mixture over all. Serve with steamed white rice, if you like.

Pavo Picante

½ cup (1 stick) unsalted butter

¼ cup olive oil

One 1 pound boneless turkey breast, sliced into 8 even medallions (about 2 ounces each)

2 cups chopped onions

2 cups chopped red or green pepper

2½ cups chopped tomatoes

2 bay leaves

1 cup beef stock

1 tablespoons sweet paprika

4 cloves garlic, chopped

1 tablespoon hot sauce

1 teaspoon cayenne pepper

Serves 4

Melt the butter in the oil in a large skillet over medium heat. Add the turkey and brown evenly on all sides, about 9 minutes total. Remove the turkey from the pan and drain on paper towels.

In the same pan, add the onions and pepper and sauté for 4 to 5 minutes. Add the tomatoes and bay leaves and cook for 5 minutes, stirring occasionally. Add the beef stock, paprika, garlic, hot sauce, and cayenne. Reduce the heat to low and simmer uncovered for 20 to 25 minutes, until slightly thickened and reduced. Add the turkey medallions and continue to simmer for about 5 minutes, until the turkey is tender and excess liquid is evaporated. Serve with rice, Cuban-style black beans (see page 193), and a big avocado salad, if you like.

D.C.

THE
SOUTH

MARYLAND

I had never traveled in the South until I started my recipe search around the United States for *This Week Magazine*. All of my growing-up days I thought of the Mason-Dixon line as something akin to the great wall of China. It had never occurred to me to vacation in the Southland. Now for twelve years I have made a southern pilgrimage at least once a year. I have learned about mint juleps and syllabubs, southern hams, grits and gravy, hot breads and innumerable ways to do the yam and the ham. I learned about mustard greens cooked with a streak o' lean. I learned that contrary to general opinion real southern cooking does not have an excess of grease. I can cheer with my southern friends about the peas that look like beans. I have eaten Brunswick stew and been to a burgoo party. I know about evening picnics and the right kind of southern fried chicken that is deliciously crusty and golden on the outside yet meltingly sweet within. I have gathered dozens of ways of doing the chicken, simply by dredging in flour or first dipping in egg and milk and sautéing in hot fat, or do it in batter, then deep fat fry. The chicken may be served with smoking hot fried cornmeal mush or mounds of snowy rice or be smothered in cream gravy made from the savory leftover in the skillet. Or pass the beaten biscuits or waffles or batter cakes.

In the South I learned to love squash. There it is picked young and treated with all the delicate elegance a northern cook gives to the first garden peas or the season's first fresh asparagus. I learned to my dismay the truth of those lines in "Dixie" in reference to buckwheat cakes and injun batter, "make you fat and a little bit fatter."

But let's not get into a serious discussion of southern cooking whys and wherefores. There are books enough already telling these things. Let's just go south.

I've been in the home kitchens of every southern state and in many restaurants to meet first-hand the authors of the dishes given here. Although there are many subtle differences in the cooking between states, one thing they have in common is the lavish tradition of plantation days, which is evidenced in all of their recipes. The bountiful meals were rich and elaborate, not only in the number of ingredients, but in the technique of preparation.

In collecting these Southern Souvenirs I made a good beginning with the Fred Stieffs who easily sold me on the idea that no state sets a better table than merry old Maryland.

The early settlers there came from the landed gentry of England. As their estates in the new world prospered they dined more and more luxuriously. Their menus evidenced understanding of flavors and textures. Wines, brandies and herbs were components of everyday cooking. Meals began with soups seasoned with a "bouquet" of parsley, thyme, sweet basil, marjoram, clove and bay. It was brought to the table in a huge tureen equipped with cover, ladle, and always the element of surprise, for nowhere was there greater variety. In addition to artfully seasoned broths there were okra soup,

onion, mulligatawny, cream of corn, asparagus, beef, blackberry, chicken, clam, terrapin, green pea with veal and onion-mushroom. Let's not forget tomato and oyster combined with chopped lean bacon, butter, onion, and cream; there is rabbit soup with bits of sliced, smoked ham, flavored with thyme. The Eastern Shore with all its rich supply of seafood was prominent in the culinary history of Maryland. Chicken and turtle were preferred to duck and geese. Game has always occupied an important place.

Wine and food sage Frederick Philip Stieff met me on a fine May morning at my downtown hotel to talk old Maryland recipes. "But we can't talk here," Mr. Stieff said firmly. "You must see Villa Fiesole, my home in Roland Park."

"The most gracious dining rooms in the world," he stated with a square-toed positiveness, "are in the old Maryland manors . . . the colonial pillars, the great sideboards, cellarette beneath, always a museum display of glassware in the corner cupboard."

Frederick Stieff knows the food of his state, great house by great house. He spent a year driving from near to yonder visiting twenty-three counties tracking down family recipes to include in his book *Eat, Drink and Be Merry in Maryland*, which was published in 1932. His recipes were taken at source, given word of mouth by family cooks or copied from handwritten cookbooks of over a hundred years ago. Frederick Stieff's own background is Old Maryland, of the Stieff piano family in business in Baltimore from 1842 until 1952. Food and wine for years had been his hobby.

Villa Fiesole, of dark brown stucco with bright blue shutters and tiled roof, is of Italian architecture. It was named for a little town near Florence where the Stieffs once had a most happy holiday. Their house stands on a cliff surrounded by gardens overlooking a tree-shaded glen. The locust and dogwood trees were in full bloom. It was a day of bird singing. The cardinals, orioles, robins, and wrens were busy setting up housekeeping. We sat in the kitchen facing the dell to have coffee and muffins and talk.

"If you want an authentic old Maryland recipe take the stuffed ham," Mr. Stieff urged. Stuffing of a ham is almost a lost art and is confined, generally speaking, to southern Maryland. The recipe given here, he told me, came from Colonel John Douglas Freeman. It requires first of all a Maryland ham smoked with all the tribal ceremonies of the old manor smokehouse.

One of Maryland's major scenic glories, the Chesapeake Bay, is also the source of some of her greatest gastronomic delights. This bay is the natural habitat of the blue crab, wholly delicious in either its hard- or soft-shell states. One of Mr. Stieff's best soft-shell recipes is from Mrs. R. D. Bradley, Sr., who died at eighty years of age.

The Stieffs served these crabs to André Simon of London, founder of the Wine and Food Society, when he came to Baltimore in 1946 to organize the local chapter of which Mr. Stieff served as the first president.

His prize recipe is this plum pudding handed down from Mrs. John Moale (Ellin North) to her great-grandson the late Walter de Curzon Poultney. Ellin North's birth date was in 1740 and she is reputed to have been the first white child born in Baltimore. The recipe came to Mr. Stieff from Dr. J. Hall Pleasants who is Ellin's great-grandson. Each Christmas the Pleasants have a southern cook of reputation come from Anne Arundel County to make the pudding for their holiday dinner.

Ellin North's Plum Pudding

For the pudding:

1 pound raisins

1 pound currants

½ pound citron, finely chopped

1 pound white suet, chopped
(sour cream may be substituted)

4 or 5 apples, peeled, cored,
and cut into small pieces

2 cups soft breadcrumbs
(preferably from day-old bread)

1 tablespoon salt

1½ tablespoons grated nutmeg

1½ tablespoons ground ginger

1 tablespoon all-purpose flour

8 large eggs, well beaten

2 cups milk

2 cups sugar

½ cup brandy

For the sauce:

¾ cup sugar

½ cup (1 stick) unsalted butter,
softened

2 large eggs, well beaten

1 cup sherry

Makes one 3-quart pudding

Generously grease a 3-quart mold.

In a small bowl, combine the raisins, currants, and citron.

In a medium bowl, combine the suet or sour cream and apples. Mix in the breadcrumbs, salt, nutmeg, ginger, and flour.

In a large bowl, whisk together the eggs, milk, and sugar. Add the breadcrumb mixture. Add the brandy. Pour into the prepared mold. Tap the mold gently to settle and level the pudding. Cover the mold with a piece of oiled parchment paper, followed by a piece of foil crimped tightly around the edges.

Set the pudding on a rack in a large pot. Pour enough boiling water into the pot to reach two thirds of the way up the side of the pudding. Cover the pot and bring to a boil. Reduce the heat to low and simmer for 2 hours; add more boiling water if the water evaporates.

While the pudding is cooking, make the sauce: In a medium bowl using an electric mixer, cream the sugar and butter. Whisk in the beaten eggs. Pour into a medium saucepan and warm the sauce over low heat until smooth and well blended. Take the sauce off the heat and whisk in the sherry.

Carefully remove the pudding from the pot and cool slightly. Uncover the pudding and invert it onto a plate. Slice the pudding and serve warm with the sauce.

Maryland Stuffed Ham

1 (15-pound) smoked ham

3 pounds spinach

3 pounds kale

1 large handful of shallots, chopped, or 2 onions, chopped

1 teaspoon garlic powder

Salt and freshly ground black pepper

Serves about 30

If the ham is strongly cured, soak overnight in a large pot filled with enough cold water to cover. In the morning, drain the water, refill the pot with fresh water to cover, place over medium heat, bring to a simmer, and simmer for 1 hour.

Wash the spinach and kale thoroughly; remove and discard all the stems and finely chop the leaves. In a large bowl, combine the spinach, kale, shallots, and garlic powder and season with salt and pepper.

After the hour of simmering, remove the ham from the pot, leaving its skin on. With a long sharp knife, make as many crosshatch incisions in the surface of the ham as possible and as deep as possible.

Lightly dampen the stuffing (greens and seasonings) with the liquor the ham boiled in and fill the incisions with as much stuffing as you can get in. Spread the remaining stuffing over the top of the ham. Wrap the ham tightly in a large piece of cheesecloth; tie together well with kitchen twine or secure in many places with toothpicks. Return the stuffed ham to the pot and simmer over medium-low heat until tender, about 3½ hours (or 15 minutes per pound).

Remove the ham from the liquid, cool to room temperature, cover, and refrigerate for 24 hours before serving. When ready to serve, remove the ham from the refrigerator 1 hour before serving. Serve slightly chilled or at room temperature.

Mrs. Bradley's Soft-Shell Crabs

12 small soft-shell crabs	1½ cups all-purpose flour
Salt and freshly ground black pepper	1 cup (2 sticks) unsalted butter

Makes 12 appetizer or 6 entrée portions

Clean the crabs thoroughly and wipe them dry. Season heavily on both sides with salt and pepper. Dredge the crabs in the flour, tapping off any excess.

Bring the butter almost to a boil in a large skillet over medium-high heat. Place the crabs in the pan, in batches, and turn frequently until nicely browned and crisp, 3 to 4 minutes on each side. Using a slotted spoon, transfer the crabs to paper towels to drain. Serve at once with tartar sauce and plenty of lemon wedges, if you like.

JUST THE RIGHT WHIFF OF SAGE

Sophie Kerr, one of America's best-known novelists and short story writers, seasons much of her fiction with fine food—East Shore Maryland food. Miss Kerr was born in Denton where the fruits and vegetables simply leapt from the soil, where the bay and rivers were crowded with soft crabs and oysters, abundant shad in its season and always the wonderful terrapin. Game birds flocked over field and marsh. "And there were many, many families," Miss Kerr told me, "who smoked hams of their own raising and who put just the right whiff of sage and black pepper into the pork sausage." There were biscuit blocks for beating biscuits and water mills to grind meal and buckwheat flour and even a local distillery that made apple and peach brandy—page "Southern Comfort"! And as Miss Kerr explains, "That's where I learned my best recipes."

So magic are her words in describing a dish, that the mere mention of old-fashioned cornmeal dumplings boiled with cabbage and served instead of potatoes with a corned beef dinner, brings a mailbag of letters from women of the fifty states begging the recipe.

I asked Miss Kerr (Mrs. Sophia Kerr Underwood) if she would choose one of her best East Shore souvenir dishes for me to use in this around America cookbook. She said, "All of my best dishes are in a cookbook already, the one I did with June Platt, food writer and designer, and titled *The Best I Ever Ate*. But you are welcome to include one of these in your book because everyone should know East Shore Maryland at its best."

She suggested fried oysters as made by Mrs. Doctor Smithers, ". . . a substantial eastern shore of Maryland matron of agreeable manners and easy hospitable ways." Miss Kerr tells me, "These are fried oysters as never were before and never will be again."

Fried Oysters

3 dozen fresh shelled oysters
and their juice

2 cups (4 sticks) unsalted butter

2 cups vegetable oil

2 large eggs, beaten

½ teaspoon salt

½ teaspoon coarsely ground
black pepper

1¼ cups finely crushed saltines or
other favorite crackers

Serves 6 to 8

Preheat the oven to 200 degrees.

Make sure the oysters have some juice. When you are ready to cook them, strain the liquid through cheesecloth and save about ¼ cup of it. Wash the oysters and drain them well.

In a deep cast-iron skillet, medium heavy-bottom saucepan with high sides, or deep-fat fryer, melt the butter in the oil but do not bring it to the smoking point.

In a large bowl, combine the beaten eggs, the reserved oyster juice, the salt, and pepper. Place a generous pile of crushed crackers on a sheet of waxed paper. At this point, heat the fat until it becomes smoky hot or registers 350 degrees on a deep-fat thermometer. Roll a few oysters at a time first in the cracker meal, then into the egg mixture, again in the cracker meal, and then place in the hot fat. Watch out, for they may splatter a bit. Fry for 3 to 4 minutes, turning once, until they are a rich, golden-brown color. Remove from the pan with a 2-pronged fork or slotted spoon and drain on paper towels.

Slide the oysters onto a nonstick baking sheet and keep warm in the oven until all the oysters are fried. Serve immediately on a hot serving platter accompanied by homemade mustard pickle, if you like.

A "MARINADE COOK"

One of the pleasures of my gustatory wanderings is that I never know what to expect. A weekend stop in Washington, D.C., and I hear from a friend who has it from a friend that James R. Dunlop, a commercial photographer and his wife June are a cooking team famous around Chevy Chase. A telephone call and the invitation is to "drive right out and see our house."

The setting turned out to be a rambling nine-room domain, designed for leisurely living for two without benefit of servants. Avid collectors of early Americana, the Dunlops admit laughingly that they built their house to house their collection. The kitchen, heart of the home, is planned for entertaining and was ten years in the planning. Cooking, the Dunlops both enjoy so they divided the kitchen into "his" and "hers." Jim's side has a colonial fireplace equipped for barbecuing by grill or spit. It's a fireplace with a twin, however, located on the closed porch for use in hot weather, one chimney serving both.

Jim is meat chef; June prepares the rest of the meal in her modern-as-tomorrow working space opposite the colonial fireplace.

Steaks are Jim's first vote. He'd have steak always but June insists on a variety of meats including spareribs, chicken, lamb. But whatever the meat, it gets lavish praise from every guest for its special flavor and tenderness. It's just the same meat anyone can buy, Jim says: that is, if he chooses top quality. But Jim adds a touch—he's a "marinade cook."

A marinade, as you know, is a seasoned liquid of acid base to be poured over meat, and the meat let soak in this several hours before broiling. The acid works the tenderizing effect and the seasonings give the extra flavor. He varies the marinade according to the meat. Vinegar is the standard acid, this diluted with water, then seasoned to taste. But he may use wine or tomato juice, and even ketchup can tenderize. So does the juice of grapefruit and lemon—these citrus juices are used for the delicate meats.

So does pineapple juice; that's Jim's choice for a duckling. Cider he thinks is the best for pork. Buttermilk can coax a leg of lamb into a milk-fed succulence.

Two cups of liquid cover three pounds of meat, that is, it will if the meat is placed in a small enough bowl to avoid excess space. Fit in the meat, pour over marinade to cover, and into the refrigerator. After soaking remove the meat and proceed with the preparations in the usual manner.

Oven-Roasted Spareribs

1 (3½- to 4-pound) slab of pork spareribs, excess fat trimmed

1 lemon, thinly sliced

1 large onion, thinly sliced

2 cups water

1 cup ketchup

⅓ cup hot sauce

1 teaspoon salt

1 teaspoon chili powder

Serves 4

Preheat the oven to 450 degrees.

Place the spareribs in a shallow heavy roasting pan, meaty-side up, fat-side down. Arrange the lemon slices and onion slices over the top of the ribs. Roast for 30 minutes.

Meanwhile, whisk together the remaining ingredients in a medium saucepan. Place over medium heat, bring to a boil, and take off the heat. Pour the sauce over the ribs. Reduce the oven temperature to 350 degrees and continue roasting the ribs until tender, about 1 hour, basting the ribs with the sauce every 15 minutes. If the sauce gets too thick, add more water. Let the ribs stand for 15 minutes. Using a very sharp knife, cut the rack into ribs and arrange on a platter.

Marinade for Steaks

9 tablespoons bourbon whisky
or red wine

6 tablespoons soy sauce

2 tablespoons red wine vinegar

2 tablespoons vegetable oil

½ teaspoon plain salt or smoked salt

½ teaspoon any favorite herb,
such as sage, thyme, or rosemary

½ teaspoon seasoned salt

½ teaspoon freshly ground
black pepper

Makes 1 cup

In a large bowl, whisk together all the ingredients and
use it to marinate steaks. The marinade may be stored in
the refrigerator for up to 1 week.

Note: The bourbon imparts a special flavor and the
Dunlops prefer it to wine.

Basting Sauce for Birds

2 tablespoons unsalted butter, melted

2 tablespoons sherry wine

Salt

Sweet paprika

Makes enough sauce for 1 large chicken

In a small bowl, whisk together all the ingredients. Brush
over chicken every few minutes during cooking time,
whether oven-roasting, grilling, or smoking.

DOWN ON THE DELMARVA Peninsula, a finger of land made up of bits of Delaware, Maryland, Virginia, chickens are machine-hatched. They come by the millions out of the hatcheries to take their place on the assembly lines of the broiler-meat factories. A chick's life work from dawn to dark, is to eat its way in a hurry to the frying pan. Seasons no longer count, young chickens come to the market right around the calendar.

Proud of their industry the Delmarva Growers decided in 1947 to hold a Chicken Festival—everybody come! And everybody did, and has been coming ever since. The latest crowd count was fifty thousand visitors. Each year a different town in the tri-state area plays host to the industry and the industry's many friends.

The festival is a three-day event with parades, concerts, chicken-eating contests, a chicken-fry in the world's largest frying pan, a talent show, a beauty contest. But the most spectacular event, one that has attracted an ever-widening national interest, is the chicken-cooking contest when the champion home chicken cooks of the nation are chosen, both senior class and junior. The contest has attracted top contestants from thirty-five states. But more than fifty percent of the winners have been the chicken growers' wives of the area. Here I give two winning recipes, which have been my favorites; both winners are from Maryland.

Chicken in Sherry Sauce

For the chicken:

1 (3-pound) Delmarva or other high-quality fresh chicken

2½ cups water

2 teaspoons salt

⅓ pound flat, wide egg noodles

1 tablespoon unsalted butter

3 tablespoons grated Parmesan cheese

For the sherry sauce:

4 tablespoons (½ stick) unsalted butter

6 tablespoons all-purpose flour

3 cups chicken stock

½ teaspoon salt

¼ teaspoon sweet paprika

1 (4-ounce) can sliced mushrooms, drained

⅔ cup sherry wine

Serves 4

In a large heavy stockpot, submerge the chicken in the water. Add the salt. Place over medium-low heat, partially cover, and bring to a simmer. Simmer until tender, about 1 hour.

While the chicken is cooking, make the sherry sauce: Melt the butter in a medium saucepan over medium heat. Whisk in the flour. Slowly whisk in the chicken stock and cook until creamy, whisking constantly, about 7 minutes. Add the salt, paprika, mushrooms, and sherry.

When the chicken is done, transfer it to a cutting board. When cool enough to handle, discard the skin and bones; reserve the cooking liquid. Slice the chicken and set aside on the cutting board.

Preheat the oven to 425 degrees. Grease an 8 x 11-inch baking pan or 2-quart casserole.

Cook the noodles according to the package directions in a medium pot of boiling salted water until tender; drain. Pour boiling water over the noodles and drain again. Return the noodles to the pot and add the butter. Spread the buttered noodles in the prepared pan or casserole and arrange the chicken over the noodles. Pour the sherry sauce over the chicken and noodles and sprinkle with cheese. Bake for 30 minutes, or until lightly browned and bubbling. Remove from the oven, cool for 15 to 20 minutes, and serve.

LITTLE MRS. CORA HANCOCK of Girdletree, Maryland, with her smiling bright eyes, is in her seventies. She cooks a handsome platter of chicken. And her husband looks on nervously to make sure it will be exactly like "last time."

Miss Cora's Fried Chicken

1 (3-pound) Delmarva or other high-quality fresh chicken, rinsed well and cut into 10 pieces

1 tablespoon salt

⅛ teaspoon freshly ground black pepper

1 teaspoon baking powder

½ cup water

¼ cup milk

1 cup all-purpose flour

¾ cup vegetable oil or shortening

Serves 4

Put the chicken pieces in a large bowl. Sift the salt, pepper, and baking powder into another large bowl. Add the water and milk and pour in the flour all at once. Stir well to form a batter.

Dredge each piece of chicken in the batter, making sure to coat them well. Heat the oil or shortening in a heavy 10-inch skillet over medium heat to the smoking point or until the temperature registers 350 degrees on a deep-fat or candy thermometer. Place the chicken in the hot fat and cover the pan with a heavy lid. Fry until golden brown, then turn and brown on the other side. The entire cooking time is 25 to 30 minutes. Transfer the chicken from the fat to paper towels to drain. Transfer to a platter and serve hot or cold with hot rolls, salad, and vegetables. This chicken carries well for a picnic, too.

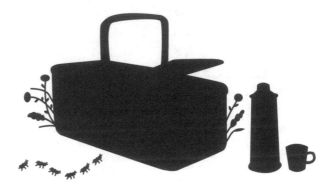

VIRGINIA

Virginia was the scene of the first English settlement in the New World and had its share of hardships, burdensome overseas government and Indian massacres. However, there was an important difference in the background of these Southern provinces as compared with the colonists in New England and Pennsylvania. Their immigration was not inspired by rebellion against the established laws of England. To them the wilderness was not an escape but a challenge. The climate proved friendly. Tobacco was a profitable crop early in their history, and as the plantations prospered the first families founded what was to be known as Tidewater Aristocracy, reverting to the way of life they had known at home. Colonial Virginia was celebrated for its bountiful larder, the sea and forest contributing.

My first Virginia trip was to Williamsburg over a Christmas holiday. The celebration there was in the old manner when Christmas wasn't a day but a period of festivals starting December 16 and continuing through until Twelfth Night. Then schools and colleges were dismissed, slaves were excused from most of their labor, and were given new clothes. Public and private business was set aside for a tremendous round of visiting. Great dinners were planned. Open house to everyone and eggnog served. There were balls and diversions and much revelry. The inn kitchens hummed for weeks in advance preparing fruit cakes, plum puddings, pies galore and innumerable sweetmeats.

Now each year in Williamsburg old Christmas lives again. Churches shine with candlelight, doors of the fine houses are decked with swags of green brightened with fruits. Wax tapers are in every window, lighted at dusk. Hundred of visitors come to the town from every state in the union, and so warmly welcomed, made to feel a part of the community festivities.

The celebration starts a week before the holiday with a pageant and Christmas musicals, dinners, dances, tea, a candlelight procession. There is nightly caroling in the streets. December 21 comes the big hunt for the Yule Log. Two days later the firing of the Christmas guns. Between day's end and the dark on Christmas Eve Yule log ceremonies are staged. Follows the lighting of the giant Christmas tree set up on the green in Market Square. There facing the street is the George Tucker house where the first lighted Christmas tree in Virginia was displayed in 1842. Charles Frederick Minnigerode, a guest of the Tuckers, a professor of Latin and Greek at William and Mary College and a political refugee from Germany, suggested the tree and attended to its decoration.

The tree-lighting service is a signal for the entire community to light up for the holiday season. A candle is set in every window and as the tapers are touched to flame all the bells in Williamsburg ring out and Christmas is ushered in.

By day I visited the colonial shops on Main Street, which is named Duke of Gloucester. I stayed a long time in the bakery with its wood-fired brick ovens where master baker Parker Crutchfield in colonial costume was making the gingerbread men. Such a fine collection of molds. Some were two feet tall.

Christmas dinner is the day's concern. Every inn includes colonial holiday fare. The King's Arms Tavern goes all out for authenticity. This inn catered originally to dignified Williamsburg gentry. The dinner is in many courses. Waiters are students from William and Mary College wearing ruffled shirts and yellow frock coats and shoes with big buckles. The moment you are seated at the candle-lighted table a waiter is tying a yard square linen napkin around your neck. Notice the table setting. China, silver, and glass are in reproduction of colonial table fittings. Water glasses are hand blown, knives have pistol handles, easy fitting to the hand, forks are three-tined. Spoons have a rat tail where the handle fastens to the bowl.

The dinner I enjoyed had nothing to do with calorie counting. Yet not so many courses were served as in the days when Washington and Patrick Henry walked the streets of Williamsburg. Then there would have been two main courses of ten to fifteen dishes each with dessert to follow plus wine or a tankard of beer to round out the repast. My dinner started with cranberry shrub. Savory tomato soup followed, a combination of two parts stock to one part tomato soup seasoned with marjoram, thyme, and tiny red peppers. The herbs of the day were grown in kitchen gardens. Soup was sipped from sippets, long slender, crisp fingers of toasted bread to dunk, then eat.

A relish tray was passed with numerous fruit conserves and pickles. Turkey held the place of honor over ham, this stuffed with a fragrant dressing of sage. There was giblet gravy, escalloped oysters. Onions and peanuts came creamed together, a sweet-potato soufflé, creamy smooth, and green beans sauced with butter.

The breads at this meal were of several kinds including corn muffins and a superb Sally Lunn, like a rich coffee cake.

There was a choice of seven desserts. Have one, have two or three as you feel inclined. Plum pudding of course, with brandy sauce. The second most important sweet a fresh coconut cake which belongs to a Virginia Christmas as the angel to the top of the Christmas tree. Add hot mince pie and greengage plum ice cream. Assorted nuts and fruits arrived with the coffee. The drink of the day, of course—hot spiced cider.

Wherever one eats in Williamsburg soup has an important menu rating. In the old capital city the soup tureen was on every table. The day after Christmas at the Williamsburg Inn, at the lodge, at the King's Arms Tavern, old-fashioned turkey soup is the featured event.

Here I give you bountiful dishes offered by the Williamsburg Inn and the Travis House, a prize selection from thousands of old recipes culled from early-day cookbooks and home files. Things like the greengage pie and Albemarle County possum gravy were as necessary to the revival of the history of the period as holly hedges and the Governor's palace.

Virginia's school children were asked to ask their mothers and grandmothers for the oldest recipes in the family cookbooks. Of course prizes were offered and the contributions rolled in. These recipes called for "butter the size of an egg", a "generous goblet of sugar," "as much saleratus as would lie on a penny." . . . They measured molasses by gulps, and spices by pinches. One famous spongecake recipe read, "as many eggs as you please, their weight in sugar and one-half their weight in flour."

For three years the food historians dug into the age-worn cookbooks that Martha Washington and her contemporaries had studied with such devotion "for the way to a man's heart," they told each other gravely. No idler's job, adapting these old menus and recipes to modern appetites.

VIRGINIA

Herb-Celery Dressing

1 (1-pound) loaf white bread, unsliced

1 cup minced celery

½ cup minced onion

½ cup (1 stick) plus 2 tablespoons unsalted butter

1 tablespoon poultry seasoning

Serves 6

Preheat the oven to 350 degrees. Generously grease a 1½-quart baking dish.

Cut the crusts from the bread and coarsely grate the loaf into a large bowl. Set aside.

Melt ½ cup of the butter in a medium skillet over medium heat, add the celery and onions, and sauté for about 2 minutes, until translucent. (It must *not* brown, merely soften.) Add the cooked vegetables and poultry seasoning to the breadcrumbs. Turn into the prepared dish and dot with the remaining 2 tablespoons butter. Bake for about 45 minutes, until browned and set.

Brandied Sweet Potatoes

2½ pounds sweet potatoes

½ cup (1 stick) unsalted butter

½ cup light brown sugar

1 teaspoon ground cinnamon

½ teaspoon salt

¼ teaspoon grated nutmeg

½ cup brandy

Serves 6

Preheat the oven to 375 degrees. Grease a 2-quart casserole or shallow baking dish.

Wash and dry the sweet potatoes and prick them all over with a fork. Place on a rimmed baking sheet and bake until very tender when pierced with a knife, about 1 hour. When cool enough to handle, cut them in half. With a spoon, scoop out the flesh (discard the skins); transfer to a bowl and mash well. Place in the prepared dish and dot with the butter.

In a small bowl, combine the brown sugar, cinnamon, salt, and nutmeg. Sprinkle over the sweet potatoes and pour the brandy over. Bake for about 30 minutes, until browned and bubbly. Serve immediately.

King's Arms Tavern Escalloped Oysters

1 quart oysters, including their liquor

½ cup (1 stick) unsalted butter

¾ cup all-purpose flour

1 tablespoon sweet paprika

1 teaspoon salt

½ teaspoon freshly ground black pepper

¼ cup chopped onion

¼ cup finely chopped green bell pepper

½ teaspoon chopped garlic

2 teaspoons lemon juice

1 tablespoon Worcestershire sauce

2 tablespoons cracker crumbs

VIRGINIA

Serves 6 to 8

Preheat the oven to 400 degrees. Grease a 1½-quart baking dish.

Drain the oysters, reserving their liquor, and set aside. (You will need 1½ cups liquor; if you don't have quite enough, add water.).

Melt the butter in a large saucepan over medium heat and add the flour; cook for 5 minutes, stirring constantly. Add the paprika, salt, and pepper and cook for 3 minutes. Add the onion, green pepper, and garlic and cook for 5 minutes. Remove from the heat and add the lemon juice, Worcestershire sauce, oysters, and liquor; gently stir together to thoroughly combine. Transfer to the prepared dish and sprinkle the crumbs on top. Bake for about 30 minutes, until bubbling and thick. Serve piping hot.

Williamsburg Inn
Old-Fashioned Turkey Soup

3 large onions, finely chopped

3 stalks celery, finely chopped

2 medium carrots, finely chopped

1 cup cold water

3 quarts turkey or chicken stock

1 pint half-and-half

1 cup (2 sticks) unsalted butter

1½ cups all-purpose flour

¼ cup minced cooked turkey
or chicken

¼ cup uncooked long-grain rice

Salt and freshly ground white pepper

Serves 8 to 10

In a medium pot, combine the onions, celery, and carrots with the cold water. Place over medium-high heat, bring to a simmer, then reduce the heat and simmer for 20 minutes, or until tender.

In another medium pot, combine the stock and half-and-half and heat until just warm.

In a large heavy stockpot, melt the butter over medium heat and whisk in the flour. Cook, whisking, for 5 to 7 minutes. Gradually and slowly whisk the stock mixture into the butter and flour mixture, stirring until any lumps disappear. Add the vegetables, water and all, to the pot, then add the rice. Cook, stirring, over low heat for 16 to 18 minutes, until the rice is tender. Season with salt and pepper and add the turkey at the last minute.

Baked Carrot Soufflé (Williamsburg Inn)

2 pounds medium carrots,
cut into 1-inch pieces

4 large eggs, lightly beaten

3 tablespoons sugar

1 teaspoon salt

3 tablespoons unsalted butter,
melted

1 tablespoon cornstarch

¾ cup water

1 pint half-and-half

Serves 10

Preheat the oven to 350 degrees. Generously grease a
1½-quart baking dish.

Place the carrots in a large pot and cover with water by
2 inches. Bring to a boil, then reduce the heat and simmer
until tender, about 35 minutes. Cool slightly and mash
thoroughly with a potato masher. Add the eggs, sugar,
salt, and melted butter to the mixture.

In a small bowl, dissolve the cornstarch in the water and
stir to make a paste. Stir into the carrot mixture. Stir
in the half-and-half. Pour into the prepared dish and
submerge the dish in a large pan of hot water filled about
halfway up the carrot dish. Bake for about 45 minutes,
until steaming hot and lightly brown on top. Serve hot.

Martha Washington's Light Potato Rolls

2 large russet potatoes, peeled and cut into 2-inch pieces

3 tablespoons unsalted butter, plus more for brushing the dough

2 tablespoons sugar

1 teaspoon salt

1 envelope active dry yeast

¼ cup warm, but not hot, water

½ cup lukewarm milk

6 to 7 cups sifted bread flour

Makes 3 to 4 dozen

Place the potatoes in a medium saucepan and cover with water. Bring the water to a boil, then reduce the heat and simmer until the potatoes are tender, about 15 minutes. Drain, reserving 1½ cups of the liquid; set the liquid aside to cool.

Place the potatoes in the bowl of an electric mixer fitted with the dough hook attachment. Add the butter, sugar, and salt to the hot potatoes and beat well. Stir in the reserved potato cooking water. Set aside.

Dissolve the yeast in the reserved potato water and set aside until foamy, about 10 minutes. Beat it into the potato mixture, then beat in the milk. With the mixer on low speed, gradually beat in 4 cups of the flour. Add enough of the remaining flour to make a stiff dough. Knead the dough on a floured surface until smooth and elastic, about 2 minutes. Brush the top with melted butter and place in a large bowl. Cover the bowl with buttered plastic wrap and set the bowl aside in a cool, dry place so that the dough may rise slowly, until doubled in bulk, about 5 hours.

Preheat the oven to 400 degrees. Line 3 large baking sheets with parchment. Turn the dough out onto a floured surface and roll out ¾ inch thick. Cut the dough into 2-inch-wide strips. Cut the strips into triangles or squares and place them at least 1¼ inches apart on the prepared baking sheets. Brush the tops with melted butter and cover with buttered plastic wrap. Let the dough rise until it is very light and does not spring back when pressed with a finger, about 20 minutes. Bake for 20 minutes, or until golden, and serve hot.

Sally Lunn Bread

1 (¼-ounce) envelope active dry yeast	1½ tablespoons sugar
¼ cup warm, but not hot, water	2 large eggs
¾ cup warm milk	3½ cups sifted all-purpose flour
3 tablespoons unsalted butter, softened	1¼ teaspoons salt

Makes one 9-inch tube bread

Generously butter a 9-inch tube pan.

In a small bowl, dissolve the yeast in the warm water; add the warm milk and set aside until foamy, about 10 minutes.

In a large bowl using an electric mixer, cream the butter and sugar. Add the eggs.

Sift the flour and salt into a medium bowl and add to the creamed mixture alternately with the yeast mixture. Cover the batter with a clean kitchen towel and place in a cool dry place to rise until doubled in bulk, about 1 hour. Stir down the batter and scrape evenly into the prepared tube pan. Cover with a clean kitchen towel and let rise in the pan for about 1 hour, until doubled in bulk again.

Preheat the oven to 300 degrees. Bake the bread for 1 hour, or until it is brown on top and sounds hollow when tapped. Serve warm with butter, if you like.

Eighteenth-Century Ginger Cookies

½ cup (1 stick) unsalted butter, softened

2 tablespoons ground ginger

½ tablespoon grated nutmeg

½ tablespoon ground cinnamon

Dash of salt

½ cup sugar

1 cup dark molasses

½ cup light cream or evaporated milk

4 to 5 cups sifted all-purpose flour

Makes 4 dozen

Preheat the oven to 375 degrees. Line 4 baking sheets with parchment paper.

In a large bowl, combine the butter, ginger, nutmeg, cinnamon, and salt. Add the sugar and, using an electric mixer, cream thoroughly. Set aside.

Combine the molasses and cream in a small pan. Place over medium heat and heat until warm and little bubbles just begin to come to the surface. Remove the pan from the heat and gradually pour the molasses mixture into the butter mixture; mix well. Stir in the flour with a wooden spoon until a fairly stiff dough is formed.

Roll out onto a floured surface ⅛ inch thick and cut with a 3-inch cookie cutter. Transfer the cookies to the baking sheet and bake for 10 to 12 minutes, until firm around the edges but slightly soft in the center. Cool on a wire rack. Store in an airtight container for up to 3 days.

Note: This recipe makes a very hard cookie, like a gingersnap.

Cranberry Shrub

1 quart cranberry juice cocktail

1 quart grapefruit juice

1 quart apricot nectar

1 quart pineapple juice

Orange slices or orange sherbet, optional

Makes 4 quarts

Combine all the juices in a large bowl and refrigerate for at least 1 hour. When ready to serve, pour over ice in a punch bowl. Garnish with orange slices or spoonfuls of orange sherbet, if you like.

Chowning's Hot Spiced Punch

1 quart apple cider

Juice of 1 lemon

3 cinnamon sticks

1 whole nutmeg

1 teaspoon whole cloves

Serves 8

In a large pan, combine the cider, lemon juice, and cinnamon sticks. Place over medium-low heat, bring to a simmer, and simmer for 30 minutes. In the meantime, make a cheesecloth bag, fill it with the nutmeg and cloves, and tie it well. Drop the little sack into the cider mixture and steep until the punch is spicy enough to suit your taste, at least 9 minutes.

Note: This punch was served on Christmas Eve at Yule log ceremonies.

Greengage Plum Ice Cream

1 cup ripe greengage or other plums, peeled and pitted

⅔ cup sugar

2 tablespoons lemon juice

1⅓ cups heavy cream

2 cups milk

Makes about 1 quart

In a large bowl, combine all the ingredients. Using an electric mixer, mix until sugar is dissolved. Transfer to an ice cream maker and freeze according to the manufacturer's instructions.

Pickled Oysters

2 dozen large shucked oysters and their liquor (about 1 quart)

1 tablespoon black peppercorns

1 tablespoon whole allspice

1 lemon, very thinly sliced

½ cup cider vinegar

Salt

Cayenne pepper

Makes 1 quart

Put the oysters and their liquor in a large nonreactive saucepan. Place over medium-high heat and cook just long enough to curl the edges of the oysters, 3 to 5 minutes. Using a slotted spoon, transfer the oysters to a deep nonreactive bowl. Wipe off the oysters with a clean cloth and set aside. Add the peppercorns and allspice to the oyster liquor, place over medium-high heat, and bring to a boil. Lower the heat and simmer until a strong infusion is made, about 30 minutes. Pour over the oysters and add the sliced lemon. Add the vinegar and season with salt and cayenne. Cover and refrigerate for at least 24 hours before serving. Serve the oysters in small glasses or bowls along with their liquid, if you like. They will keep in the refrigerator for about 3 weeks.

RECIPES FROM THE TIME OF NOAH

Near Williamsburg, in James City County, Virginia, I spent a winter afternoon with a fascinating woman, Mrs. Archibald McCrea of Carter's Grove. Her home, a historic Georgian mansion, named as America's most beautiful house by the noted author and photographer Samuel Chamberlain. Something Mr. Chamberlain overlooked was to credit part of the charm of this plantation to its delightful hostess, the beloved "Molly" to her hundreds of friends. Her real name, Mary Dunlop McCrea, a throwback to her colonial ancestry, tracing her family descent from the Virginia Spottswoods and the Carters.

Here is a woman who has mixed her guests with a clever knowing, who has entertained in the eighteenth-century manner, planning meals typical of those served in the days when colonial Williamsburg was one of the world's most important capital cities.

This Molly, a tiny person with eyes as mischievous as a gamine's, resembles the châtelaine of a manor as painted by Sargent. As a celebrity in the realm of hospitality she has attracted to her table countless visitors of fame. Her visitors' books, a dozen or more, read like a *Who's Who* of the distinguished of America and Europe.

The house stands as a sentinel, shaded by great tulip poplars looking down on the James River. There is the central mass flanked on either side by lesser buildings, a kitchen at one end, a guest house at the other. One of the chief glories of Carter's Grove is its doorway with a pediment and side pilasters fashioned with molded brick. There are two of these, one facing the river, the other to the land side.

The house is approached by an avenue bordered by venerable cedar trees that antedate the Revolutionary War. This avenue circles an island of boxwoods as it approaches the house.

Mrs. McCrea has kept a continuous file of the recipes she has served on important occasions. "My recipes," she told me, "date from the time of Noah."

Many of the menus she serves are by the request of guests. Some are straight out of her collection of cookbooks brown with age. One's appetite is whetted on hearing her tell of dinners with terrapin stew flavored with sherry, of wild duck from the river, venison with wild rice and herbs, planked shad, creamed mushrooms and peas, aspic salad served with fresh garden asparagus and Virginia ham.

Molly keeps her hand in by making many of the dishes herself. The pickled oysters (recipe opposite) are a specialty, a great favorite with the men.

Hyden Relish Salad

2 quarts finely chopped cabbage

1 quart green tomatoes, finely chopped

¾ cup brown sugar

1½ tablespoons yellow mustard seeds

1½ tablespoons celery seeds

1½ tablespoons salt

1 tablespoon ground cinnamon

1 teaspoon ground cloves

1 quart cider vinegar

Makes 2 quarts

In a very large stockpot, combine all of the ingredients. Place over medium heat and bring to a boil. Reduce the heat and cook at a gentle simmer, stirring occasionally, until the vegetables are tender, about 25 minutes. Cool to room temperature, then cover with plastic wrap and refrigerate for at least 1 hour before serving. Serve cold. The relish will keep, refrigerated, for up to 3 months.

Note: This relish is delicious on deli sandwiches and hot dogs.

AMERICA'S FIRST GOURMET

Thomas Jefferson, one of our trio of greatest presidents, was America's first gourmet. Cooking interested the tall quizzical sage of Monticello almost as much as statesmanship.

It was Mrs. Helen Duprey Bullock who told me these things. I listened carefully, for Mrs. Bullock is an authority on colonial-day cooking. It's a part of her job as historian for the National Trust for Historic Preservation.

Each year on April 13, Helen Bullock invites guests for a little dinner in her apartment on Capitol Hill, Washington, D.C. The menu is in honor of Mr. Jefferson's birthday, featuring the spring dishes he served most often on his Monticello table.

This Jefferson birthday menu Mrs. Bullock plans has many French touches. When Thomas Jefferson left the United States for France in 1785 as Minister to the Court of Louis XVI, he was saying farewell to the Virginia tradition of fried chicken, ham, and hog jowls with greens and discovering the more subtle cooking of the French.

The food of France he found both a joy and a revelation. Despite his love for things American he was greatly instrumental in introducing French cooking into the United States. It was Thomas Jefferson who introduced vanilla here, who brought from France such ideas as blanc mange, wine jelly, biscuit de Savoy, and meringues. During Jefferson's time in the White House, its cuisine as well as the wines became the talk of the food world.

Jefferson's birthday menu features baked shad, a very plentiful dish and inexpensive once. This is prepared with a roe soufflé in the French style. Mrs. Bullock serves scalloped potatoes with this and fresh asparagus with butter sauce. Follows a green salad and crisp corn sticks. Dessert is the old-fashioned pound cake with brandied peaches or apricots.

"But asparagus," I objected, "wasn't in the market back in that time."

"Oh yes it was," our hostess said. "It was grown in the garden at Monticello."

Baked Shad

1 (5- to 6-pound) shad with roe

1 tablespoon vegetable oil

1 extra shad roe

1 tablespoon mild vinegar

1½ teaspoons salt, plus more to taste

1 bay leaf

2 or 3 sprigs of parsley

6 tablespoons unsalted butter

1 onion, minced

¾ cup all-purpose flour

1 cup plus 1 tablespoon milk

1 cup chopped parsley

¼ cup white wine, optional

3 large eggs, separated, whites stiffly beaten

Sweet paprika

Juice of 1 lemon

Serves 8 to 10

Have the fish market prepare the shad by splitting the fish fillets open (not dividing in half) and removing the spine and bones.

Lightly oil a broiler pan or baking sheet. Put the fillets in the pan, skin-side down, and rub the surface with the oil.

Meanwhile, prepare the roe: Place the shad roe in a large saucepan and pour in just enough water to cover. Add the vinegar, ½ teaspoon of the salt, the bay leaf, and parsley sprigs. Place over medium heat and bring to a very gentle boil. When the roe becomes firm, after 2 to 3 minutes, drain. Remove the membrane and set the roe aside.

Melt 4 tablespoons of the butter in a large, heavy skillet over medium heat. Add the onion and sauté until translucent, about 3 minutes. Add the roe, breaking it up gently with a fork, and cook until the small eggs are separated and well coated with butter. Add ½ cup of the flour and the milk. Cook, stirring, until thickened, 5 to 7 minutes more. Remove the pan from the heat, add the chopped parsley, wine, and the egg yolks, lightly beaten (stir some of the warm mixture into yolks before adding to prevent curdling). Add the remaining 1 teaspoon salt, then fold in the 3 stiffly beaten egg whites.

Meanwhile, preheat the oven to 350 degrees. Sprinkle the shad in the reserved pan with some salt and paprika and the lemon juice, then dot generously with 1 tablespoon of the remaining butter and sprinkle lightly with the remaining ¼ cup flour. Bake for about 12 minutes to the pound. Remove from the oven, spread the roe mixture over the inner portions of entire fish, dot with the remaining 1 tablespoon butter, and sprinkle with paprika. Return to the oven and bake for about 10 minutes, then turn on the broiler and broil until the soufflé is delicately browned, about 3 minutes.

Note: If you are one who must keep a strict eye on the budget, substitute buck shad for the roe shad or use any large white fish. Buy fresh herring roe to pinch hit for the shad roe. Roe of herring comes in 12-ounce tins; drain well. Prepare as the recipe directs after the boiling.

PIGS OF PIGS

Colorful is the history of the Smithfield ham. It came originally from an English breed of razorback hogs that ran wild in the Virginia woods. They rooted for their living, growing fat on beechnuts and grass nuts, and later as the colony began raising peanuts they nosed deep for those still in the ground after harvest.

The original razorbacks are not any more, but a few of the venturesome cast their pearls before swine of lesser importance and so today these "pigs of pigs" that make the "ham what am" are still rooting for a living in the peanut belt.

Let the Virginia State Legislature tell exactly what a Smithfield ham must be to wear the proud label: "Meat to be branded genuine Smithfield must be cut only from the carcass of peanut-fed hogs raised in the peanut lands of Virginia and North Carolina, and cured within the corporate limits of the town of Smithfield." Formula for the hams of old are still cherished and have been handed down to be used to the last detail, the dry salt cure, the many spices, the hickory smoke, all in the manner which immortalized those hams of the colonial era.

Virginians do a lot of talking about their Smithfields. I'm not going to give a recipe. I prefer to pay more for a Smithfield ham and receive the specialty prepared by the expert chefs in the processor's kitchens.

Some of the old school insist on buying a Smithfield as it comes from the smokehouse, and I'm sure these women know exactly what to do with it.

GEORGE STICKNEY, of Fredericksburg, Virginia, gave me this recipe he calls "a circuitous regional." His father took his Kentucky bride to Michigan where he was engaged to design locks for the Sault Ste. Marie Canal. There numerous young couples "from away" lived in the local boardinghouse. On cold nights after a snowshoe outing or an evening of cards, the chafing dish would come out and something filling, something quite different from daily fare, would be in the making. Torquemado was one of the stand-by dishes. Mr. Stickney has never encountered this "little mix-up" outside his own home. There it is served as a one-dish supper, filling, inexpensive and to everyone's delight.

Torquemado

2 tablespoons bacon fat or unsalted butter

3 medium onions, sliced and separated into rings

2 cups canned tomatoes

Salt and freshly ground black pepper

2 large eggs

4 slices buttered toast, cut in half diagonally

Serves 2 to 4

Heat the fat in a large heavy skillet over medium heat. Add the onions and cook until translucent, about 3 minutes. Add the tomatoes and simmer for about 20 minutes, until the onions are tender. Season with salt and pepper. Remove the pan from the heat and quickly stir the eggs into the tomato mixture. Serve over buttered toast triangles.

DANCE AND BUBBLE AND PUFF

VIRGINIA

When I met Miss Sue Tokes she wasn't young anymore. "There was a time," she told me, "when I could cater two flossy events in a day and cook everything myself." But at this point of her career nephew George Davis and his Addie had shouldered the responsibility. They were trying to keep Miss Sue out of the kitchen. Fifty-five years of cooking! Isn't that enough?

But Miss Sue was a handful. Cooking had been her life, she couldn't stop now, and who else, she'd like to know, makes apple pie so good, or the apple dumplings? And her puffs, no cookbook's got that recipe because "I just make them, but you can watch if you want to," and so I did.

A wedding within a hundred miles of Winchester, Virginia, and Miss Sue would get a call to oversee the menu.

In the summertime she gave fried chicken parties in the long built-on room back of her kitchen.

It was a lovely blue-haze morning that I knocked on the door of her modest frame house. A tall woman, Miss Sue, she seemed to fill the doorway. She was wearing a starched pink dress and a hand-knitted shawl folded around her shoulders. "You sit there," She indicated a rush-bottomed chair. She sat opposite facing in an old-fashioned rocker.

She cleared a rattle out of her throat. "I've catered picnics for Senator Harry F. Byrd. His apple orchards in Berryville are just a piece from here. Sometimes over three thousand people are at the Apple Blossom Festival. Last crowning day I cooked seven hundred and thirty chickens and thirty hams."

"What would you serve, Miss Tokes, for a real nice country dinner?"

"My tomato bouillon with the puffs," she said without even thinking.

"What do you mean, 'puffs'?" I asked.

"Ain't no other name, just puffs, yeast dough fried crisp on a griddle. Goes nice with the fried chicken. And I'd have lima beans and corn pudding and apple dumplings with my rum sauce. I take whole apples for dumplings."

Then, Miss Sue told me, she rolls the dough thin, cuts it into squares, sets a peeled and cored apple on each square, bringing the dough up and around the apple, pinching it together. Each dough-wrapped apple is tied in cheesecloth, little squares being kept just for the purpose. Now drop the dumplings into a pot of boiling water where they dance and bubble and puff.

"Or it could be apple pie," Miss Sue was still planning our menu. "I'm old-fashioned with my cooking, never use store stuff and I want lard in pie crust and fresh cooking apples. Now Addie here uses all the new fangles and she has good luck, but I couldn't, never will."

Miss Sue's Puffs

2 cups sifted all-purpose flour

½ teaspoon salt

1 teaspoon unsalted butter, softened

1 teaspoon active dry yeast

¼ cup warm, but not hot, water

1 cup lukewarm milk

2 tablespoons vegetable oil

Makes 24

In a large bowl, combine the flour and salt, then cut in the butter.

In a small bowl, dissolve the yeast in the water until it gets foamy, about 10 minutes. Add the yeast to the flour mixture, along with the milk, and stir together to form a dough. Turn the dough out onto a lightly floured surface and knead until the dough is smooth and rounded, 2 to 3 minutes. Using a well-floured rolling pin, roll the dough out about ¼ inch thick and cut with a 3-inch cutter. Cover with a clean kitchen towel and place in a warm place to rise until doubled in bulk, about 30 minutes.

Heat a griddle over medium-high heat. Add the oil and cook the puffs until browned on each side, 2 to 3 minutes per side. Serve with butter and tomato bouillon (recipe opposite), if you like.

Tomato Bouillon

1 quart chopped fresh tomatoes (about 6 large tomatoes)

1 cup chicken stock

1 teaspoon salt

⅛ teaspoon freshly ground black pepper

Dash of red pepper flakes

Serves 6

Combine the tomatoes and chicken stock in a large heavy stockpot. Place over medium-high heat, bring to a boil, then reduce the heat and cook until the tomatoes are soft, about 20 minutes. Press through a sieve. Reheat the liquid, add the salt, pepper, and red pepper flakes, and bring to a gentle simmer. Serve hot.

THE CAROLINAS

"Spice Islands," cried the sailors as the sweet fragrance came floating over the waters from the dark, wooded shore. The year was 1584 and Captain Arthur Barlow was looking for a landfall. He turned toward the perfumed sand banks to discover a woven ambuscade of vines bearing golden brown fruit. This site in what is now called North Carolina was the "mother vineyard," home of America's first grape, the scuppernong. Captain Barlow had been commissioned by Sir Walter Raleigh to find a suitable site for a colony. Upon discovering the home of the scuppernong he became so enchanted with the spot that he proposed it to Sir Walter. It was settled soon after, to become tragically famous as the Lost Colony, the birthplace of Virginia Dare.

Down the years the scuppernong has been used extensively throughout the South for jellies and preserves. It is frequently put down in brandy. Wines are made of the grape. Every southerner lauds the fragile, rusty colored scuppernong. No other fruit except maybe peaches is as all-southern as solidly southern as the old Confederacy itself. Little known elsewhere as the grape is a poor traveler. Fill a truck with this fruit and forty bumps from the vine the load is running dribbles of juice. Each grape (and each grows separately, not in bunches) is like a tiny skin of wine. It tastes like no other grape, although in a way it resembles the Niagara. Wonderfully sweet the meat, exceedingly spicy, each berry holding one big drop of juice to tingle the tongue and the fancy. The aroma is irresistible; tropical in its musty heaviness.

The very stick of chance stirred the pudding for me. Quite by accident I met Mary Huguenin, who told me of a cookbook the senior members of the Charleston, South Carolina, Junior League had put together as a moneymaking venture. Some four hundred old families of the city had given seven hundred of their finest dishes, heirloom "receipts" heretofore cherished as secrets.

I wanted to borrow from this collection to pass the good eating on to my readers—and not just the recipes, I wanted to introduce some of the people who serve these traditional foods of the Old South. Mary Huguenin said, "Come to Charleston, meet everyone, eat the book if you like. Take your pick of the dishes; I'll arrange for the parties."

My visit started on a Saturday noon and then followed three wonderfully exciting days, eating, just eating. There were leisurely meals at candle-lit tables behind the carved doors of the beautiful old houses. There were breakfasts with potted birds and hominy, with hominy and shrimp paste, or do you like mullet roe? There were little suppers, guest of honor the Old South ham, sliced paper-thin. Beaten biscuits, of course.

Okra soup was perhaps my greatest pleasure—this is the first dish I met—served at the Huguenins' dinner table. Husband Tom was home for the midday meal, so deft with his carving of a pair of wild ducks. The soup was made with okra, fresh from the freezer, grown last summer on the Huguenins' plantation, Halidon Hill. The soup, Mary said, should be made enough at a time to last several days, for it's a dish long-cooked—five to six hours—and improves on standing.

Down the Ashley River Road with Ann Montague Stoney, one of the cookbook editors, to Middleton Place to meet Mr. and Mrs. J. J. Pringle Smith, their gardens a show spot of the world. These sixty-five acres of broad-sweeping terraces, of mirror pools, of camellias and azaleas, were the dream of Henry Middleton, whose leadership in

the colonies won him the presidency of the Continental Congress.

Walk and talk, then back to the house to drink Sherry Bolo and eat hot benne biscuits. Only one wing of the original home remained after the passing of Sherman's troops. But this single wing is house enough, a mansion in size.

The Sherry Bolo came in old English wine cups and made in this manner: three glasses of sherry with the juice of one lime, sugar to taste; pour over crushed ice for six small drinks. The benne biscuits were passed hot from the oven, made with benne seed grown on the place. The true name of the seed is *Sesmum indicum,* better known as sesame, and not related to Ali Baba's "Open Sesame." It was brought into the South by the Africans in slave days. The rich spicy seeds they loved to eat raw with sugar and milk, they used them in gravies, stirred them into cakes, waffles, and candies. Benne seed today is a pantry staple in the old city.

A tremendous meal, that supper with Admiral and Mrs. William S. Popham at their 1797 house on Tradd Street, supervised by the faithful Faber. Bulls Bay oysters came on the half shell, little things, no larger than cherrystone clams. Then Popham's shrimp pie with artichoke pickle, with pumpkin chips, with Faber's cornbread, tossed greens and heavenly anchovy dressing. Every dish served was a cookbook recipe, somebody's treasure. Dessert was sweet-potato pone, spirited with rum, topped with hard sauce.

Early morning and off to Mrs. Stuart Dawson's to sample shrimp paste. Mrs. Dawson was born Mae Elliott Hutson, daughter of a cotton planter. Shrimp paste is a frequent breakfast dish on their table. Little river shrimp for this, made into a rich paste pounded fine with fresh butter, patted thin, cut into strips to serve cold with hot hominy.

Grits in Charleston are hominy. And every home serves this plain boiled for breakfast, not as a cereal with sugar and cream but to mix with butter to eat as a relish with such hearty foods as bacon and eggs or fish cakes or mullet roe, or those potted birds that were sent in by a friend as our special treat for Sunday morning breakfast at the Francis Marion Hotel.

Mrs. Dawson gave us a taste of a shrimp mold also, which she makes to spread on crackers with cocktails. The chief difference between the spread and the paste is that celery seed is used in the paste; mace flavors the cocktail blend.

Well, this was a day. Hurry on now to the Footlight Players Work Shop, a remodeled cotton warehouse on Queen Street, where the play *Syllabub* had its opening night and a bowl of syllabub waited, the traditional Charleston holiday-dinner ending, half drink, half dessert.

It's like eating air with a spoon. The last foamy fluff becomes a spirited liquid, milky white. Turn up the glass and drink it down. In olden days a syllabub chum was used for the whipping. In Charleston many a kitchen still possesses such a churn—but never mind, these have been copied and are available in stainless steel. Recipes vary for syllabub. Some say bourbon, some say sherry. One feature on which all old English recipes agreed was that after the spicing and sweetening of the cream the milk should be added not from the bottle but direct from the cow.

Mrs. Lionel K. Legge did us proud at dinner with a cooter soup, a cooter being a freshwater rice-field turtle, yellow-bellied. Turtle eggs in my bowl. Deer steak for this dinner and beautiful rice. Speak of rice and a Charlestonian's

face lights, his eyes take on a dreamy look and you can hear him saying, "Every grain must be separate and plenty of butter."

On every table pickles galore; always the artichoke and the pumpkin chip, a wonderful preserve—the recipes are in the cookbook, of course. And there was eggplant at the Legge dinner, this called guinea squash in the South, and creamed Jerusalem artichokes. A wine jelly for dessert, clear amber, vibrant of sherry, topped with whipped cream.

I ate my first pine-bark stew at the Otranto Club, fifteen miles from Charleston on Goose Creek, near the St. James Goose Creek Church, which was built in 1711. The clubhouse was the former rectory. Mr. and Mrs. L. Y. Dawson gave the party, made the stew. Don't let the name pine bark scare you off; it refers to the fuel. The cooking is done over an open fire, pine bark providing the slow, slow heat. This bark burns for hours aided by little oak sticks to sparkle and crackle.

It's when the bream are running that South Carolinians yearn for this treat. But other fish do as well. The night Patsy cooked our dinner she used blackfish, a saltwater species that isn't quite the ticket but all right. The freshwater fish included were bream and pike and the bigmouth bass. This is an open-fire dish made in a three-legged frying pan fifteen inches across. The secret of it all, as Patsy told me, is the secret of the sauce. She has a pot at the side of the fire and into this go the butter and seasonings. Now and again she pours in the juice which collects in the pan. Pine-bark stew was the first course of supper. It came on a square platter, garnished with crisply fried bacon with a parsley border, a complicated perfume. Then came country ham that had been soaked overnight in beer and baked with orange juice and grated rind of lemon and orange. Honey-glazed at the last.

It's Lady Baltimore cake for dessert made by the original recipe. Adelaide R. Read baked this cake for the party about as perfectly as anyone can and told me its story. Mrs. Alicia Rhett Mayberry, a great lady of the town, was the first to introduce Lady Baltimore cake, a creation of her own. In later years at the urging of friends she baked cakes on order. When Owen Wister chose the old city as a setting for a novel, his heroine was Mrs. Mayberry, who had been a famous belle in her day. Much impressed with her cake, rich and luxurious he took its name *Lady Baltimore* as the title of the book.

Charleston Okra Soup

6 cups beef stock

½ cup diced okra

1 slice bacon, chopped

2 cups canned crushed tomatoes, with juice

2 bay leaves

½ cup diced onion

Salt and freshly ground black pepper

Steamed white rice, optional

Serves 6

In a large stockpot, combine the beef stock, okra, bacon, tomatoes, bay leaves, and onions and season with salt and pepper. Place over medium heat and bring to boil. Reduce the heat and gently simmer for 30 minutes. Serve over steamed white rice, if you like. Hot buttered cornsticks are a tasty accompaniment.

Sesame Seed Wafers

1 cup sesame seeds

1 cup all-purpose flour

¼ teaspoon baking powder

¼ teaspoon salt

¾ cup (1½ sticks) unsalted butter, softened

1½ cups firmly packed brown sugar

1 large egg, beaten

1 teaspoon vanilla extract

Makes about 4 dozen

Preheat the oven to 375 degrees. Grease 2 or 3 baking sheets.

Place the sesame seeds in a pie pan and toast in the oven for about 10 minutes, stirring occasionally, until deep golden. Transfer to a plate and cool. (They burn easily, so watch closely.)

Sift the flour, baking powder, and salt into a small bowl.

In a large bowl using an electric mixer, cream the butter and sugar until light and fluffy. Beat in the egg. Stir in the flour mixture. Add the vanilla and toasted sesame seeds, stirring just enough to incorporate.

Drop the batter by ½-teaspoonfuls onto the prepared baking sheets, allowing 2 inches between each cookie (bake only a few at a time, in batches, noting that they spread a lot while baking). Bake for 5 to 6 minutes, until the edges are lightly browned. Cool a minute or two before removing the wafers from the baking sheet, then remove them gently and quickly with a spatula and transfer to a wire rack to cool completely. If the cookies get too crisp to remove easily, return them to the oven for a minute or so to soften. Serve the wafers warm or at room temperature. They may be stored in an airtight container for up to a week.

Popham Shrimp Casserole

1 cup (2 sticks) unsalted butter, softened

½ pound onions, finely grated

1 quart canned crushed tomatoes

2½ pounds shrimp, peeled and deveined

1 teaspoon Worcestershire sauce

½ teaspoon paprika

Pinch of red pepper flakes

Pinch of ground mace

Salt

4 cups dry and fluffy cooked white rice

6 strips bacon

Serves 8

Preheat the oven to 375 degrees. Generously grease a 2-quart casserole or baking dish.

Melt the butter in a large heavy saucepan over low heat. Add the onions, tomatoes, shrimp, Worcestershire sauce, paprika, red pepper flakes, mace, and salt. Cook, stirring occasionally, for about 30 minutes, until the mixture thickens and the flavors have melded. Stir in the rice. Turn the mixture into the prepared dish and arrange the bacon strips on top. Bake for about 25 minutes, until the bacon is crisp. Serve immediately.

Shrimp Pâté

1 pound shrimp

½ cup (1 stick) unsalted butter, softened

3 tablespoons mayonnaise

1 teaspoon Worcestershire sauce

¼ teaspoon lemon juice

A few drops of Tabasco sauce

Pinch of ground mace or celery seed

Salt and freshly ground black pepper

Serves 6 to 8

In a medium saucepan, bring 2 cups of salted water to a boil and add the shrimp. When the water returns to a boil, turn off the heat, cover the pot, and allow the shrimp to sit for 5 minutes. Drain, peel, and devein the shrimp.

Place the shrimp in the bowl of a food processor and pulse 8 to 10 times, until finely chopped but not mushy. Transfer to a large bowl and add the butter. Stir until well blended. Add the mayonnaise, Worcestershire sauce, lemon juice, Tabasco, and mace and season with salt and pepper. Line a 2-cup mold or glass bowl with plastic wrap, leaving lots of overhang. Place the shrimp mixture into the mold, packing tightly with a spatula. Cover with the plastic wrap overhang and refrigerate for at least 2 hours or overnight.

When you're ready to serve, unwrap the overhang and invert the mold onto a plate. Remove the plastic wrap. Serve with crackers or thin, crisp toast, if you like. This dish is delicious served with hominy for breakfast.

Syllabub

Peel of 2 lemons

1 cup sweet wine

1 cup Madeira wine

1 quart heavy cream

6 tablespoons lemon juice

6 tablespoons sugar

Pinch of grated nutmeg

Makes 3 quarts

In a large bowl, soak the lemon peel in the sweet wine and Madeira until the flavor is extracted, about 1 hour. Discard the lemon peel.

In another large bowl, whip the cream until it just begins to hold its shape; it should be thickened but still soft and billowy. Gradually whisk in the wines, lemon juice, sugar, and nutmeg. Heap in glasses and serve with spoons.

Wine Jelly

2 (¼-ounce) envelopes unflavored gelatin

½ cup cold water

1 cup boiling water

⅔ cup sugar

Pinch of salt

¼ cup lemon juice, strained

¼ cup orange juice, strained

2 cups sherry wine

Serves 6

In a large bowl, combine the gelatin with the cold water. Let stand for 5 minutes, then stir. Whisk in the boiling water. Add the sugar, salt, lemon and orange juices, and sherry. Pour into a 1½-quart mold, cover with plastic wrap, and refrigerate overnight to set. To serve, unmold onto a plate and cut into slices.

Lady Baltimore Cake

3½ cups sifted cake flour

3½ teaspoons baking powder

1 cup (2 sticks) unsalted butter, softened

3 cups sugar

4 large eggs

1 cup milk

½ cup water

2 teaspoons vanilla extract

2 teaspoons almond extract

Makes one 9-inch layer cake

Preheat the oven to 350 degrees. Generously grease 2 (9-inch) cake pans and line with rounds of parchment paper. Set aside.

Sift the flour and baking powder into a medium bowl; set aside.

In the bowl of an electric mixer, beat the butter until soft. Gradually beat in 2 cups of the sugar until the mixture is light and fluffy. Add the eggs, one at a time, and beat thoroughly. With the mixer on low speed, add the flour mixture, alternately with the milk, blending until smooth after each addition.

Divide the batter evenly between the prepared pans. Bake for 30 to 35 minutes, until the cakes are golden brown and a wooden pick or skewer inserted into the center of each comes out clean.

While the cakes are baking, in a medium saucepan combine the remaining 1 cup sugar with the water, place over medium heat, and cook, stirring continuously, until a thick syrup is formed, about 3 minutes. Stir in the extracts.

When the cakes are done, transfer them to wire racks to cool in the pans for 15 minutes. Invert the cakes onto wire racks and remove the parchment. Use a serrated knife to trim the tops of the cakes and make them level. Brush the tops of the cakes with the syrup mixture. Let the syrups set on the cake for about 1 hour. Frost and fill with Lady Baltimore frosting (recipe follows).

Lady Baltimore Frosting

2 cups sugar

⅔ cup water

2 teaspoons corn syrup

2 large egg whites

2 cups raisins, finely chopped

12 figs, finely chopped

2 cups pecans, chopped

Dash of almond extract

Dash of vanilla extract

Makes about 3 cups

In a small saucepan, combine the sugar, water, and corn syrup. Place over low heat and stir until the sugar is dissolved. Simmer until the syrup reaches 234 to 238 degrees on a candy thermometer (soft-ball stage). Remove from the heat and set aside.

In a medium bowl using an electric mixer, beat the egg whites until stiff but not dry. Slowly and carefully pour the syrup in a fine stream over the egg whites, beating constantly. Continue to beat until the frosting has cooled and is a proper spreading consistency, about 3 minutes.

To make the filling, transfer one third of the frosting to a medium bowl. Stir in the raisins, figs, and pecans. Add the extracts. Use the remaining frosting to frost the tops and sides of the cake.

Note: The raisins and figs may be soaked overnight in a small amount of sherry or brandy if desired.

OH, SHRIMPY, ROE, ROE, ROE

At the very outset of my culinary meanderings I had observed that up North, lobster is the Maine thing. Now in the South I discover lobster's baby brother, the shrimp, is the sure thing. Skipping down the coast this favorite food refrain kept singing in my head . . .

"Oh shrimpy roe, roe, roe, roe
Up to your door, door, door, door
Bet you'll want more, more, more
Of shrimpy roe, roe, roe."

The soft coaxing voice fades into the distance, into the still morning. "Shrimpee-ee-ee-ee-ee," and the voice of the vendor is lost far down a street in old New Orleans.

It was afternoon in late January that I again heard the "shrimpy roe" call this time coming from a New York apartment kitchen. The crier was singer Adelaide Van Wey, busy preparing a party dinner with shrimp-avocado bake as the main dish. Adelaide is a native of North Carolina and all her growing up days she had listened to the soft, lush calls of the food vendors. The peddlers, she told us, use every imaginable means to bring their products to town—trucks, mules, wagons, baskets, pushcarts. Vendors have their regular routes but "just in case" still cry their wares. There are watermelons to be sold, peaches, blackberries, sweet oranges, strawberries, vegetables, flowers; years of calling wares in heat, rain, and wind go into perfecting their cries. To lessen the tiresome hawking, a variety of words are used and a little tune becomes easier to repeat than a sharp yell or a loud call.

The street vendor is passing from the American scene but Adelaide Van Wey has written down these cries and has sung them into an album of records.

It was after she came north to study with New York's finest vocal teachers and coaches that she came to realize the "unconscious" music of the street cries. It was then she began collecting them from memory, from friends, from books. Adelaide likes to sing while she cooks and she cooks as she sings, in an effortless, easy way. She loves entertaining and never a paid caterer to prepare the food for the Van Wey parties. Adelaide does it herself and serves it, too, without aid of maid.

Here we give you the supper menu she prefers when both men and women are invited for an evening at cards. The first course is usually tomato juice sherbet, the main dish this avocado-shrimp bake, which she calls simply, My Very Own Favorite.

My Very Own Favorite

5 medium avocados

About ¾ cup French Salad Dressing
(recipe follows)

3 pounds peeled and deveined
cooked shrimp

4 tablespoons (½ stick) unsalted butter,
melted and cooled

1¾ cups cornflakes, crushed

5 slices bacon

2 cups rock salt

Serves 10

Preheat the oven to 350 degrees.

Using a very sharp knife, cut the avocados into halves
and remove the pits. With your fingers, rub the inside of
the avocados with some of the French dressing, pressing
gently not to bruise the flesh.

Pack the shrimp into the avocado halves and dribble
1 tablespoon of the dressing over each "cradle." Pour the
melted butter over the halves. Sprinkle the tops of the
avocados with cornflakes, tucking them around and
over the shrimp. Lay on half a slice of raw bacon atop
each shell.

Spread rock salt on the bottom of a large baking pan.
Place the filled avocado halves on the salt. Bake for
15 minutes, then run under the broiler for 2 minutes to
brown the bacon. Serve immediately.

French Dressing

¼ cup cider vinegar

½ to ¾ cup olive oil

½ teaspoon salt

½ teaspoon sweet paprika

1 tablespoon ketchup

Freshly ground black pepper

Makes 2 cups

In a large bowl, whisk all the ingredients together.
Scrape into a glass jar, cover, and refrigerate until ready
to serve. The dressing can be kept refrigerated for up to
3 weeks. Shake well before using.

WITH THIS PASS FRENCH fried potatoes
cut in long, thick pieces, no brittle
shoestrings for Adelaide. To fry, place
potatoes into a sieve before their dip
into hot fat. "So easy to take from the
pot," the singer explains. When cooked
turn sizzling sticks into a paper bag
along with salt. Now shake until every
little piece is salt-tinged and the bag
has soaked up the excess fat. Into a
fresh bag, into a warm oven to keep
hot until serving. A green salad with a
Roquefort cheese dressing is served
right on the supper plate. French
bread is passed. The loaf is sliced just
to bottom crust, but not through, and
the slices brushed with garlic-scented
butter. The loaf is wrapped in foil and
placed in a moderate oven to heat.

Dessert? Adelaide's weakness, Apple
Honey Crunch. "Lord have mercy, but
that crunch is rich stuff," she explains,
"and here I am," she laughs, "weighing
much too much. I daren't eat it more
than once a month."

Apple Honey Crunch

4 large Granny Smith apples, peeled, cored, and cut into ¼-inch slices

Juice of 1 lemon

15 whole cloves

¼ teaspoon ground cinnamon

½ cup honey

1 cup packed brown sugar

3 tablespoons unsalted butter, softened

¼ cup all-purpose flour

1 cup salted peanuts

Serves 6

Preheat the oven to 350 degrees. Generously grease a 9-inch glass baking dish.

Arrange the apples in the prepared dish. Sprinkle with the lemon juice, cloves, and cinnamon. Drizzle 2 tablespoons of the honey over the apples. Bake for 30 minutes, or until the apples are tender.

While the apples are baking, in a medium bowl using an electric mixer, beat together the brown sugar, butter, and flour. Stir in the remaining honey, then stir in the peanuts. When the apples are tender, spread the sugar mixture over them. Place under the broiler and broil until the topping melts and browns, 3 to 4 minutes. Serve hot with ice cream or whipped cream, if you like.

Black coffee is a must with this rich-as-Croesus dessert, "coffee as black as bayou," Adelaide explains. Add a piece of cinnamon bark to each cup before pouring the brew.

THE OYSTERS START POPPING

This Yankee had never set foot on a southern plantation until the invitation to come to Buckfield, home of Mr. and Mrs. C. Wesley Frame, Yemmassee, South Carolina. It was one of my happiest adventures. It's an exciting experience to visit a farm 10,000 acres big, 8,000 acres in timber, 1,000 in pasture, 1,000 in grain.

Here's a plantation that hums with activity. Mr. Frame sees to that. Beef cattle his pride—he raises three hundred head. He operates a dairy milking one hundred Holsteins.

Mrs. Frame does the work of three women. No small chore being a mother of three and running a home. There's help in the kitchen but Rosalind Frame is big chief. She plans the menus, she does the day's marketing, and she's a career woman to boot.

Several years ago she discovered a salad dressing right to her taste at The Hitching Post Inn in Aiken, South Carolina. After mulling over the idea a few months she contrived to buy the name, formed a company and built a small manufacturing plant. Today she makes numerous products, selling her wares in twenty-one states.

How can any one person get so much done? She lives her life on a schedule planned for each hour of the day. She even schedules her parties, entertaining *en masse* once every three months with a crowd jamboree.

Roast oysters are the first course in the "R" months. There is a special roasting pit to do the job, this dug one foot deep and covered with a sheet of metal that stands on short legs, six inches aboveground. Oysters are bought by the bushel, fresh-dug from local creeks, one bushel allowed to fifteen guests. The mud is washed off with a hose, the oysters then scrubbed with a brush and dumped on the sheet iron, red hot over a bed of glowing coals. When the oysters start popping, it's time for eating. Workers shovel the feast to a table built with rimmed edge.

Bring on the dunk sauce: two kinds coming up—plain melted butter, the other any good oyster sauce. Cotton work gloves are passed out to guests, for those oysters are hot.

Off season for oysters, it's the boiled shrimp that gets the party off to a galloping start. Ten pounds of shrimp, well-washed, are dropped into two gallons of boiling water to which is added one-half cup vinegar and two tablespoons of black pepper. The shrimp are boiled until tender when pierced with a fork. These are dipped out and thrown to the big table, newspaper-covered. The crowd peels its own shrimp to hand-dunk in butter or a spicy shrimp sauce.

Plantation goulash for the main course: lusty bracing fare that men tuck into with a real glint in the eye. Mrs. Frame makes this in quantity for seventy to one hundred people, dips it into freezer bags in amounts to serve ten, then to freeze. The goulash is always at hand. Add a tossed green salad with garlic toast, coffee, ice cream, and cupcakes. What more could one ask?

Plantation Goulash

⅓ pound bacon

⅔ cup diced green bell pepper

2 onions, finely chopped

1½ cups diced celery

2 pounds ground beef

1 tablespoon salt

1 teaspoon freshly ground black pepper

1 (28-ounce) can crushed tomatoes

1 teaspoon sugar

1 bay leaf

Serves 12

Cut half of the bacon into small pieces and place in a large heavy skillet along with the peppers, onions, and celery. Place over medium heat and cook until the bacon is crisp. Remove the pan from the heat and set aside.

Cut the remaining bacon into strips and in another large skillet, fry the bacon until crisp. Transfer to paper towels to drain. Cool and crumble the bacon into pieces and set them aside. Leave the bacon fat in the pan and set it aside.

Place the ground beef in a large bowl and work in the salt and pepper. Mix in the crumbled bacon, taking care not to overhandle the beef. Form the ground beef mixture into balls about 2 inches wide in diameter.

In the pan with the reserved bacon fat, turn the heat up to medium-high. Brown the meatballs quickly in the hot bacon fat. Immediately transfer the browned meatballs to the pan with the sautéed vegetables. Add the tomatoes, sugar, and bay leaf. Reduce the heat to low, cover, and simmer until the sauce is medium-thick, 40 to 45 minutes. Discard the bay leaf. Allow to sit for 30 minutes before serving. Served over hot buttered noodles or steamed white rice, if you like.

ROSY-CHEEKED PEACHES

Blistering hot it was that July day I drove to the loading platform of the long peach-packing shed.

"Where's Mrs. David Hughes?" I asked a young worker who was nailing peach crates.

"There." With a jerk of his thumb—he didn't stop working—he pointed out his boss lady in a spotless brown percale, blond hair loosely waved. She was right on the line, her capable hands rolling over the rosy-cheeked peaches passing on a broad conveyor belt.

There were seventy-five men and women packing peaches that afternoon and Vera Hughes was working with them to know exactly how the fruit was running in the orchard they had started picking that morning. Vera is a licensed broker, sells her own fruit, and packs and sells for her neighbors.

She suggested we drive to the orchards for a look at the picking. She has a hundred acres, thirty thousand trees. There was the dusty flavor of dry earth in the air. She lifted and snicked a peach from the branch held out for me to see. "Beautiful," I said.

Mrs. Hughes said, "Nobody but a grower knows the days and months of worry back of every peach packed. I begin my real worry in March and never get peaches out of my mind until the crop is sold." Any trick of the weather may ruin the harvest. A high wind can whip the peaches to the ground; hail can cut the fruit to the pit. One night of frost at blossoming will defeat months of work.

During the picking season Vera has no time for her friends or her home. When peaches are over she celebrates with a series of little dinner parties, four to six guests, and does her own cooking. Company coming, the help gets the night off. Her favorite dinner is steak. A thick T-bone and there is always prime beef in her twenty-foot locker. French-fried potatoes, or French-fried onions with the steak, a tossed salad and a bleu-cheese dressing, good crusty homemade bread, fresh peach ice cream for dessert. Every year Vera freezes eight gallons of fresh peach ice cream, which she packs into quart containers to use during the winter. She makes usually eighteen quarts of pickled peaches to serve with cottage cheese as a salad, and the pickled peaches are just right with a roast beef dinner.

Vera's deep-dish pie, a very special one, is her mother's masterpiece, made with whole-wheat flour. It's one of the best pies I have tasted.

Peach Pickle

2 cups sugar

1 cup cider vinegar

2 (3-inch) pieces cinnamon stick

12 small firm but ripe peaches, quartered, pitted, and skinned

1 teaspoon whole cloves

Makes 1 quart

Combine the sugar, vinegar, and cinnamon in a large heavy saucepan and place over medium-high heat. Bring to a boil, then reduce the heat to medium and simmer for 20 minutes, stirring occasionally to dissolve the sugar. Add the peaches and simmer for 5 to 10 minutes, until just tender. Using a slotted spoon, transfer the peaches into a hot, sterilized jar and place the cloves in the jar. Fill the jar to overflowing with hot syrup. Adjust the covers and seal at once according to the manufacturer's instructions. Refrigerate and serve the peaches cold. The peaches may be stored in the refrigerator for up to 2 weeks.

Peach Ice Cream

4 large ripe fresh peaches, peeled, pitted, and cut into bite-size pieces

¾ cup sugar

½ cup peach preserves (not jelly)

1 cup half-and-half

1 cup heavy cream

1 cup whole milk

1 teaspoon vanilla extract

1 teaspoon almond extract

Makes 6 cups

In a large bowl, toss the peaches with the sugar. Cover and let stand for at least 10 minutes or up to 2 hours.

Pour the rest of the ingredients into a medium saucepan. Heat over medium heat and bring the mixture just barely to a simmer; as soon as you see a bubble come to the surface, remove from the heat and strain into a lidded container. Cool to room temperature, then refrigerate for about 2 hours to chill.

Freeze in an ice cream maker according to the manufacturer's instructions. Once the volume has increased by half and reached a soft-serve consistency, add the peaches and any accumulated syrup and continue churning. Scrape the mixture into a lidded container and let harden in the freezer for at least 2 hours before serving.

My Mother's Deep-Dish Peach Pie

1 Perfect Pie Crust (page 13)

1 tablespoon all-purpose flour

1 cup plus 1 teaspoon sugar

8 large fresh ripe peaches, peeled, pitted, and cut into ½-inch slices

1 teaspoon ground cinnamon

1 teaspoon grated nutmeg

4 tablespoons (½ stick) unsalted butter

5 tablespoons warm water

1 cup heavy cream

1 teaspoon almond extract

Makes one 8-inch square pie

Using a floured rolling pin on a lightly floured surface, roll out the Perfect Pie Crust pastry ⅛ inch thick. Using a floured serrated knife, cut the pastry into 1-inch strips.

Preheat the oven to 450 degrees. Generously grease an 8 x 8-inch baking dish.

Lay one third of the strips in a crisscross fashion across the bottom of the prepared dish. Sprinkle with the flour and 1 tablespoon of the sugar. Lay in half of the peaches; sprinkle with the cinnamon, nutmeg, and ½ cup more of the sugar. Cover with another third of the pastry strips; add the remaining peach slices and sprinkle over all but 1 teaspoon of the remaining sugar. Dot the top with butter and pour in the warm water. Cover the top with the remaining pastry. Bake for 20 minutes, then reduce the oven temperature to 350 degrees and bake for about 20 minutes longer, until the filling is thick and bubbling and the crust is golden brown. Cool the pie on a wire rack for at least 20 minutes to fully set before serving.

In a small bowl, whip the cream until slightly thickened; gradually add the remaining teaspoon sugar and beat until stiff peaks form; fold in the almond extract. Serve over the warm pie.

GEORGIA

The South loves a picnic in the evening, or it may be a barbecue over a Fourth of July weekend. I visited Sea Island, Georgia, traveling 820 miles for a fish fry, or call it southern barbecue, because it was both. Word had come from friends who vacation in the sun that the most dramatic eating event in their life was this Sea Island picnic.

Sea Island is one of these "Golden Isles" lying off the Georgia coast from the town of Brunswick, one of those charming islands whose shrimp and crab and other sea dishes are all but out of this world. This particular island is corporation-owned, just one hotel, The Cloister, of red-tile roof and stucco walls set amid a grove of sighing palms.

On Friday night there's scarcely a visitor who doesn't go a piece down the island to eat fried fish and hush puppies with rice and shrimp mull.

I arrived at the barbecue grounds just after sundown; the air was soft with the gentle warmth of the South. Ben McIntosh was a dark shadow tending the chicken over a pit of red-eyed coals. The long plank tables under the moss-hung oak were lantern-lighted.

The crowd lined up cafeteria-style for the feast. Every inch of the tables was spread with food. The takeoff: pickles, olives, cole slaw; next a cauldron of lobster bisque. Next rice, dry and fluffy,

every grain separate. A dip of this and over the rice a helping of shrimp mull. Thank you, sea trout, deep-fat-fried sizzling hot from the pot. A hush puppy, this fried in the fat after the fish came out.

Have some of Ben's barbecued chicken, our companion was urging. The chicken made a stack three feet high and blistering hot. I took a half. Over this a waiter sloshed barbecue sauce, a sauce famous to the island. After that, coffee. Buckets of coffee awaited the guests and a regiment of pies, cut into wedges, each piece chumming with Cheddar. With my tray-load I slipped away from the crowd and down to the water's edge to eat alone.

The moon held a semi-tropical beauty to make the heart ache for things gone by. I remembered what I'd read about the history of this place. Here on the islands during colonial days flourished a luxurious and colorful life. The islanders formed an aristocracy of wealth and power and dwelt each to himself, confessing allegiance only to King Cotton of whom they held their domains in fief. Gone! All is gone. But the legends remain.

I hurried back to the crowd circling the blazing driftwood fire. I had work to do. I retreated to the cook's area to meet Ben McIntosh. He had worked thirty years with John Life, who for half a century wore the island's crown as barbecue king. Today Ben is the only man in the know of John Life's recipes.

John Lucas, assistant manager at The Cloister, who runs the barbecue, introduced me. "Tell her how you do that sauce, won't you, Ben?"

"Yassir," said Ben, hiding his eyes in the weed patch of his brows. But Ben doesn't measure and he doesn't believe in giving recipes away even if the big boss gives the order. He said, "I takes some vinegar, I takes some ketchup."

It was H. C. Smith, better known as Smitty, chef at The Cloister then for twenty-two years, who helped us get Ben's guesswork into definite amounts. Smitty said, "I've seen that sauce made hundreds of times. Do it this way."

Barbecue Sauce for Chicken

1 quart cider vinegar

2 cups ketchup

2 cups Dijon mustard

1 to 2 teaspoons Tabasco sauce

Freshly ground black pepper

½ teaspoon red pepper flakes, or more to taste

2 cups (4 sticks) unsalted butter, melted

Makes 10 cups

In a large stockpot, combine the vinegar, ketchup, mustard, and Tabasco. Place over medium heat and bring to a boil. Turn the heat down and whisk in the black pepper and pepper flakes. Whisk in the butter. Reduce the heat to low, just hot enough to keep the mixture warm. Using a new dish cloth, swab the chicken with sauce when it comes hot from the smoker, grill, or old-fashioned barbecue pit. The sauce may be stored, covered and refrigerated, for up to 1 week.

Shrimp Stew

3 slices bacon

1½ cups diced onion

1 green bell pepper, cored,
seeded, and diced

2 stalks celery, finely chopped

1 pound medium shrimp,
peeled and deveined

About 1 quart water

1 cup diced tomatoes

Freshly ground black pepper

1 teaspoon Worcestershire sauce

Salt

1 tablespoon hot sauce

Serves 4 to 6

Fry the bacon in a large heavy skillet over medium heat
until crisp. Add the onion and sauté until golden, 3 to
4 minutes. Add the green pepper and celery, cover, and
simmer for 5 minutes. Add the shrimp and pour in the
water. Add the tomatoes, black pepper, Worcestershire
sauce, salt, and hot sauce. Bring to a boil, then reduce the
heat and simmer until thickened, about 30 minutes. Serve
over steamed white rice, if you like.

PASSING THE SHRIMP SANDWICH

GEORGIA

Once at Sea Island I found it hard to get away and decided to spend several days and visit around to make a sojourn of it. From the flood of clams and crabs offered to me in every style I thought the place might as well be called "C" Island; but that wouldn't be fair to the overwhelming shrimp supply, so I compromised on Sea Food Island and it certainly was that!

Shrimp sandwich is the local party refreshment. I met the native shrimp at least seven times in a sandwich and each time tasting differently.

This shrimp mixture goes to tea parties; it's served as an hors d'oeuvre, open-face style, coming along with the cocktail and the popular cola. A cola party in Brunswick—and these number thirteen to a dozen—is simply unthinkable without passing the shrimp sandwich.

Mrs. James D. Compton, wife of the president of the Sea Island Company, invited me to try her version of the pink party repast, a mixture she has been making for twenty-eight years. Her first sandwich was tasted the second day of her arrival. Mrs. Compton had one, she had two, she had three.

The next party she attended there was that sandwich again! And again it came different. Then and there Mrs. Compton began a comparative study of shrimp combinations. Now she has a recipe that even the island's old-timers—meaning the descendants of the original families—ask her to share.

Mrs. Compton figures three pounds of fresh shrimp for about one hundred hors d'oeuvres. The bread circles she cuts in advance, packages, and into the deep freeze to take out as needed. A flavor secret: the shellfish are shelled and the intestinal vein removed before cooking, which gives a new sweetness.

Shrimp Canapés

1 pound fresh shrimp, peeled, deveined, and cooked

1 tablespoon minced onion

1 teaspoon minced celery

1 teaspoon minced green bell pepper

2 teaspoons lemon juice

½ teaspoon grated lemon peel

¼ teaspoon salt

4 to 5 drops hot sauce

Dash of freshly ground black pepper

¾ cup mayonnaise

About 12 slices white bread

2 tablespoons unsalted butter, softened

Chopped parsley, optional

Makes about 3 dozen

Finely chop the shrimp and place in a large bowl. Add the onion, celery, green pepper, lemon juice, lemon peel, salt, hot sauce, black pepper, and mayonnaise. Taste and add more seasoning if desired. Cover and refrigerate to set, at least 30 minutes.

Meanwhile, lightly toast the bread slices and spread a little of the butter on each. Using a very small cookie cutter, cut 36 rounds, each about the size of a half dollar, from the toast. Remove the shrimp mixture from the refrigerator and pile a heaping teaspoon of the mixture on each round. Garnish the canapés with parsley or pretty green leaves, if you like. Pass for hors d'oeuvres.

LEAVE YOUR SHOES ON THE PORCH

Neighbor to Sea Island is St. Simon, another of the Golden Isles off the Georgia coast, and that's where I learned about crabbing. We made the trip over a causeway by car to Edwin Fendig's house. Just across the patch of lawn was the white sandy beach lipped by the water of St. Simon Sound.

"Ready? Let's go. Here's a crab basket. Leave your shoes on the porch," Mrs. Fendig orders. Barefoot we cross the lawn to the beach and wade in to the knees, traps in hand. The peck basket soon fills and we are off to the kitchen to hose down the catch, then to cook in a cauldron half filled with boiling, salted water. Once the crabs go pink they are dipped out to cool; Mrs. Fendig breaks off the backs and the claws, she takes out the devils' fingers. One-half pound of butter is put to melt in a deep pan over low heat. The main bodies of the crabs are dropped into this, the pan covered and the feast let steam thirty minutes. To serve, the crabs are centered on a large platter, the claws, which have been cooked separately in the boiling pot, are laid around as a border.

Time to eat, folks! Each guest helps himself, picks out the royal meat to dunk into butter sauce. Crackers, pickles, celery, cold beer, that's all it takes to make a never-to-be-forgotten beach supper.

Mrs. Fendig has other ways of using the crab, which is caught at all seasons in Georgia's coastal waters. She uses the boiled, picked meat in soups, in salads and casseroles. Crab soup is a Sunday-night regular at the Fendigs' table. The rich, filling soup, a green salad, French loaf bread—buttered and oven-heated—and a hearty dessert.

Sunday Supper Crab Soup

3 tablespoons unsalted butter

½ cup minced celery

3 tablespoons all-purpose flour

2 cups whole milk

2 cups half-and-half

1 pound crabmeat, picked free of shell

2 teaspoons salt

¼ teaspoon freshly ground black pepper

¼ cup sherry

2 lemons, thinly sliced

2 hard-cooked eggs

Serves 6

Melt the butter in a large heavy saucepan over medium heat. Add the celery and cook until just tender, about 3 minutes. Stir in the flour until well blended. Slowly add the milk and continue to cook until smooth and bubbly. Slowly add the half-and-half, stirring constantly. Stir in the crabmeat, salt, pepper, and sherry. Heat until piping hot.

Into each service plate, place 2 thin slices of lemon and 2 slices of hard-cooked egg. Pour the soup into bowls and serve immediately.

BRUNSWICK, GEORGIA, IS a town famous for its cooks and its seafoods, a town that basks in the reflected glory of neighboring Sea Island.

Maud E. Boyd, born and raised in Brunswick, had invited me to a little get-together with local cooks to talk recipes. I had written to Mrs. Boyd a few weeks before regarding her mother's recipe for a nut bread that, I had heard, tasted different from any other nut bread.

Mrs. Boyd had promised me the recipe and also suggested I meet Mrs. Paul Morton whose apple crisp pudding, a marvel of translucent tenderness, and her sea-scented clam chowder get the nod of approval from the ladies of the area.

"And that clam chowder," she told me, "doesn't need to be made with fresh clams if you haven't got them handy—canned clams do."

Mrs. Irving Harned—she is Mrs. Morton's daughter—came to the luncheon. She's a good cook like her mom, one who cooks just for the love of it.

These recipes are traditional of the hospitality of the region's romantic past. From the days of the wealthy rice and cotton planters to the present resort centers, the bountiful table has characterized the life of the section.

Brunswick Clam Chowder

2 slices bacon, diced

1 medium yellow onion, chopped

2 cups clam juice

1 pound russet potatoes, peeled and diced

2 pounds littleneck clams, shucked and chopped

1 teaspoon salt

Freshly ground black pepper

1 quart whole milk

2 tablespoons unsalted butter, softened

2 tablespoons all-purpose flour

Oyster crackers, optional

1 tablespoon finely chopped parsley, optional

Serves 6 to 8

Fry the bacon in a heavy stockpot over medium-high heat until crisp, about 8 minutes. Stir in the onion and sauté until it starts to soften, about 2 minutes. Add the clam juice and potatoes, bring to a boil, then reduce the heat, cover, and simmer until the potatoes are just tender, about 12 minutes. Add the clams to the pot along with the salt, pepper, and milk.

In a small bowl, blend together the butter and flour with a fork to make a paste; stir in a teaspoon or so of the soup liquid, then add the mixture to the chowder. Cook until slightly thickened, about 3 more minutes.

Line the bottom of a large soup tureen with oyster crackers, if you like. Pour over the chowder and sprinkle with chopped parsley, if you like. Serve immediately.

Mrs. Boyd's Nut Bread

6 cups all-purpose flour

2 cups sugar

2 tablespoons baking powder

1 teaspoon salt

2 cups finely chopped pecans

2 large eggs, beaten

2 cups milk

1 tablespoon unsalted butter, melted and cooled

Makes 2 loaves

Preheat the oven to 350 degrees. Generously grease two 8½ x 4½ x 2½-inch loaf pans.

Sift the flour, sugar, baking powder, and salt into a large bowl. Add the pecans.

In a medium bowl, whisk together the eggs, milk, and butter. Quickly stir the mixture into the dry ingredients. Divide the batter evenly between the prepared pans. Bake for 50 to 60 minutes, until a wooden pick or skewer inserted into each loaf comes out clean. Cool the bread in the pans on wire racks for 5 minutes. Turn out onto the racks and cool completely. Wrap the breads in plastic wrap and store in a cool dry place at room temperature.

Mrs. Morton's Apple Crisp Pudding

4 cups peeled and sliced
Granny Smith apples

1 teaspoon ground cinnamon

½ cup water

½ cup (1 stick) unsalted butter,
softened

1 cup sugar

¾ cup all-purpose flour

1 cup whipped cream or 1 pint
vanilla ice cream, optional

Serves 4

Preheat the oven to 375 degrees. Generously grease a
1½-quart casserole.

Place the apple slices in the prepared casserole. In a small
bowl, whisk the cinnamon into the water and pour over
the apples. In a medium bowl, using a fork, stir together
the butter, sugar, and flour until crumbly. Sprinkle the
mixture over the apples. Bake for 35 to 45 minutes, until
the top is golden, the apples are tender, and the mixture
is bubbly. Serve warm in bowls topped with whipped
cream or ice cream, if you like.

THE ROISTERING ERA
OF THE SAILING SHIP

It's only a two-hour drive from Sea Island to Savannah and still on the sea. No city we have visited blends more palpably the old and the new. Broad shaded streets are lined with stately homes. Even the newer residences avoid the sophisticated modern and have instead aristocratic graciousness. A city laid off into squares mathematically exact, with commanding parks at regular intervals. A city of statues and monuments to greet one with historic memories. The past is the living present and that goes, too, for the food.

Hotel De Sota is a chapter "out of the gone." Halls are broad as U.S. Route 1. Our suite of rooms was a match measure for Grand Central Station. Hospitality here blossoms as a fine art. Breakfast for example: broiled ham steak, grits with red-eye gravy, and a pair of wide-eyed eggs.

That breakfast was just what was needed after the night before. We speak in awed reverence of Artillery Punch (recipe follows). The Hansel Hillyers gave a party Sunday evening at their home on East Broad Street in Trustees Garden. That garden, by the way, is a miniature Williamsburg. It ranges several blocks in area, a section that a few years ago was counted as Savannah's most disgraceful slum; today a show place, the houses restored to the original beauty of their period.

A woman's idea—credit Mrs. Hansell Hillyer, wife of the president and general manager of the South Atlantic Gas Company. The company, wanting property near the plant to use as headquarters, found that to get the location they must buy a city block both sides of the street. Hansell Hillyer hesitated over such heavy spending.

"Buy it, Hansell," Mrs. Hillyer said. "Buy several blocks and let's rebuild the entire section, have a little Williamsburg of our own right here in Savannah."

Mr. Hillyer said, "Sweet, you're crazy." Then he got to thinking maybe she wasn't. He would buy the block and remodel one house and see if it rented. So the work started. A company was formed to finance the venture and Mrs. Hillyer was asked to do the job of directing. Now they have fifteen houses complete, in all, fifty apartments, and this is but the beginning.

The Pirate House is one of the restored group again in operation, the authentic relic of a tavern that belonged to the roistering era of the sailing ship. The place is situated a scant block from the Savannah River, a rendezvous once for sailors from the seven seas.

Here the ghost of Cap'n Flint, bloodthirsty pirate of *Treasure Island* fame, is said to haunt the area on the moonless nights. Tradition has it that the prototype of the Robert Louis Stevenson character died in an upstairs bedroom of the old inn.

I was the Hillyers' guest in one of those back-to-glory houses. First, a sight-seeing turn with Mrs. Hillyer, then back to the party to drink Artillery Punch as a salute to the Fourth of July. The punch was created by the Chatham Artillery National Guard unit in 1819 when President James Monroe was a visitor in the Scarborough House from May 8 to May 13. The mixture was made with one purpose: to banish inhibitions. It's nothing less than dynamite.

Artillery Punch

1 gallon rum

½ gallon Hennessey's
Three Star Brandy

½ gallon gin

½ gallon rye whisky

1 gallon unsweetened iced tea

½ pound pineapple,
cut into small cubes

1 quart maraschino cherries

Makes 5 gallons

In a very large bowl or pot, combine all the ingredients. Cover and refrigerate for 2 weeks. When ready to serve, place a large ice block in a punch bowl and pour the mixture to half full, then serve in champagne glasses, very well chilled, if you like.

BUT NEVER MIND THE punch; it's old South victuals I want to talk about, these served at the Pirate House in the garden court under the sassafras trees. I helped myself to a sampling of every dish present; deviled crabs, baked hominy grits, corn pudding to eat with the fried fish. Barbecued lamb with a tongue-tingling barbecue sauce, hushpuppies—crisp outside and inside all-a-melting—and hot cinnamon rolls that looked something like a popover but had the texture of brioche.

We were nicely settled to the feast when a spatter of rain flipped the sassafras leaves; drops fell and flattened on the paved court. The crowd was hustled inside to the "Captain's Room." It was here negotiations were made by short-handed ship's masters for the shanghaiing of unwary seamen to fill out the crews.

I wanted recipes. Frances McGrath and Hilda Norris, the restaurant managers, invited me to the kitchen and detailed the way of the deviled crab, the secrets of corn pudding and of the almond mold that came for dessert.

It was Mrs. T. H. Gignilliot, a guest at the party, who gave the recipe for the hot cinnamon rolls. Several women guests brought their specialties for me to taste. Mrs. Hillyer made a salad; she baked the grits.

Almond Mold

9 tablespoons sugar

3 tablespoons cornstarch

2 large eggs, lightly beaten

1 quart hot milk

1 (¼-ounce) envelope
unflavored gelatin

¼ cup cold water

2 teaspoons almond extract

1 pint heavy cream

14 graham crackers, crumbled

Serves 10

Combine 6 tablespoons of the sugar, the cornstarch,
and eggs in a large saucepan. Place over low heat and
stir until smooth. Do not let the mixture boil. Gradually
stir in the milk and bring to a very gentle simmer, being
careful not to let it boil, and continue cooking, stirring
constantly, until the custard is thick and smooth, about
10 minutes.

Meanwhile, soften the gelatin in the cold water for
5 minutes; add to the hot mixture and stir until
thoroughly dissolved. Remove from the heat and cool to
room temperature. Stir in the almond extract.

While the custard is cooling, in a large bowl, combine the
remaining 3 tablespoons sugar and the cream and whip
until soft peaks form. Gently fold the whipped cream into
the custard, reserving about 1 cup to use as a topping.
Pour the mixture into a 9 x 12 x 2½-inch pan. Coat with
the graham cracker crumbs. Cover and refrigerate until
ready to serve. Top with the remaining 1 cup whipped
cream when ready to serve.

Deviled Crabs

1 pound crabmeat, picked over

1 cup fine dry breadcrumbs

2 large eggs, lightly beaten

½ cup minced celery

½ cup minced green bell pepper

2 tablespoons lemon juice

1 tablespoon white wine vinegar

1 tablespoon Worcestershire sauce

1 teaspoon dry mustard

½ teaspoon salt

½ teaspoon freshly ground black pepper

½ teaspoon hot sauce

1 cup (2 sticks) unsalted butter, melted

8 blue crab shells, well cleaned, optional

Serves 8

Preheat the oven to 375 degrees.

In a large bowl, mix together all ingredients. Stuff into 8 crab shells or ramekins. Lay the crab shells on a large baking sheet and spoon the mixture into the shells. Bake for 10 to 12 minutes, until piping hot, golden brown, and bubbly. Remove from the oven and serve hot.

Corn Pudding

4 cups fresh or frozen corn kernels

2½ tablespoons sugar

½ tablespoon salt

¾ tablespoon baking powder

2 large eggs, lightly beaten

1½ cups whole milk

3 tablespoons unsalted butter, melted

¼ cup all-purpose flour

Serves 6

Preheat the oven to 350 degrees. Generously grease a 1½-quart casserole.

In a large bowl, stir together the corn, sugar, salt, and baking powder. In a small bowl, whisk the eggs with the milk and butter. Add the egg mixture, alternately with the flour, a little at a time, to the corn mixture. Turn into the prepared casserole. Bake for about 50 minutes, until golden brown. Let stand for at least 5 minutes, then serve warm.

HAVING COVERED THE WATERFRONT from Maryland's East Shore and Chesapeake Bay to Georgia's Seafood Isle, I headed inland for a final recipe roundup of the deep South. Now through Georgia and Alabama bound with more chicken dinners than anywhere else I'd been. Here the old saying of poor folks: "Chicken one day, feathers the next," was miraculously changed to: "Chicken one day and twice as much tomorrow." Southern fried chicken, of course, running neck and neck with those shrimp along the coast.

It was my lucky day. I had arrived quite by accident at the Henry Grady Hotel in Atlanta, along with a hundred or so food specialists from all parts of the state. The Georgia Home Economics Association was holding its annual meeting in the hotel ballroom—a roundup of the experts who preach, teach, and demonstrate the state's favorite dishes.

Elizabeth Parker, Home Service Director of the Georgia Power Company, with forty-seven home economists under her direction working in all parts of the state, came across with this fried-chicken recipe. Miss Parker said chicken done in this manner is exactly what a southerner expects fried chicken to be.

Southern Fried Chicken

1 (2½ pound) broiler chicken, cut into 8 pieces

1 teaspoon salt

½ teaspoon freshly ground black pepper

½ cup all-purpose flour

1½ cups vegetable shortening or lard

Serves 4

Wash the chicken pieces thoroughly and pat dry with paper towels. Season with the salt and pepper and dredge in the flour. Melt the fat in a large heavy skillet. Keep the heat just below the smoking point. Lay in the thick meaty pieces first—these take the longest to cook. Brown quickly on one side, then on the other. Cover the pan, lower the heat, and cook until done; that is, until there is no pinkness of meat at the bone, about 10 minutes. Using a slotted spoon, transfer the chicken pieces to paper towels to drain. Serve immediately.

Note: To make a gravy, after the chicken is removed from the pan, pour off all but ¼ cup of the fat, add ¼ cup flour to the fat in the pan, and whisk to blend; slowly pour in 1 cup milk and 1 cup heavy cream and season with salt and pepper. Cook the gravy until smooth and thick, whisking constantly, 5 to 7 minutes.

IN ATLANTA I TASTED a dreamy light sponge cake, ethereal as magnolias and moonlight, the recipe from Mrs. Henrietta Dull, one of Georgia's leading cake artists. Mrs. Dull was a slender eighty-six-year-old careerist still in the food business right up to her elbows, a consultant for southern food firms.

Atlanta women in old days had the town bakers do their holiday fruit cakes by the family's own formula. Henrietta Dull had the idea of baking for her friends and the very first Christmas turned out three hundred pounds. The next year she bought a gas range and began baking cakes of all kinds and catering for parties. The local gas company, hearing of her success, asked her to work for them as a cooking teacher for clients. For ten years Mrs. Dull served as a home-service worker. Followed twenty years with the Atlanta *Journal* as cooking-page editor. During this period Mrs. Dull's recipes became known near and far.

Mrs. Dull liked to talk cake. I like to talk cake and once we got started we talked till it was time to eat supper. Fried chicken on the menu, with biscuits and gravy and green beans cooked with salt pork.

I ate this perfection sponge cake served with fresh strawberries and a great glop of whipped cream. A cake just as good as angel cake, just as light, but golden, and it takes but six eggs.

Mrs. Dull's Perfection Sponge Cake

6 large eggs, separated

⅛ teaspoon salt

½ teaspoon cream of tartar

1¼ cups sugar

1½ tablespoons lemon juice

1¼ cups sifted cake flour

Makes one 10-inch cake

Preheat the oven to 300 degrees.

In a large bowl using an electric mixer, beat the egg whites with the salt until foamy. Add the cream of tartar and continue beating until the whites are shiny and stiff. Gradually add the sugar and beat for about 3 minutes, until the mixture holds its shape. Set aside.

In a medium bowl using an electric mixer, beat the egg yolks until light and creamy; add the lemon juice. Fold in the whites using a rubber spatula. Fold in the flour a little at a time. Pour into an ungreased 10 x 5 x 3-inch loaf pan. Bake for about 1 hour and 10 minutes, until a wooden pick or skewer inserted in the center of the loaf comes out clean. Invert the cake on a rack and cool for 10 minutes before removing from the pan. The cake can be wrapped in plastic and stored at room temperature for up to 3 days. Serve with strawberries and whipped cream, if you like.

FOUR STATES CLAIM PECAN pie for their own—Alabama, Tennessee, Mississippi, and Georgia. I have eaten this incarnate richness in each of its homelands and my choice goes to the Georgia pie made by Callie Williams, who, when I found her, had been making 100 to 150 pies daily for twenty-five years.

Callie was pecan-pie baker for the Magnolia Tea Room in Rich's Department Store in Atlanta, the biggest and the busiest store, they claim, in the Southeast. Some three thousand people a day eat at its tables and snack bars. Out of this number, at least one thousand wrap themselves around a wedge of Callie's nut pie.

This pecan-pie formula has been polished and brought to perfection by a six-days-a-week workout for a quarter of a century. The recipe reads like a poem; it eats like a dream. A rich conglomeration of eggs, of corn syrup, of nut halves encased in tender crust and baked to pigskin brown.

But one can't dine on just pie. I had Southern beef hash and fritters of brisk corn flavor, neck-and-neck items.

Callie's Pecan Pie

3 large eggs

2 tablespoons unsalted butter, melted

2 tablespoons all-purpose flour

¼ teaspoon vanilla extract

⅛ teaspoon salt

½ cup sugar

1½ cups dark corn syrup

1 (8-inch) Perfect Pie Crust (page 13)

1½ cups broken pecan halves

Makes one 8-inch pie

Preheat the oven to 425 degrees.

In a large bowl using an electric mixer, beat the eggs. Beat in the melted butter, flour, vanilla, salt, sugar, and corn syrup. Set aside.

Line an 8-inch pie plate with the pastry and crimp to fit. Sprinkle the nuts over the bottom of the unbaked pastry shell. Gently pour over the syrup mixture. Bake for 10 minutes. Reduce the oven temperature to 325 degrees and bake for about 40 minutes more, covering the top and rims with foil if they begin to brown before the center sets. When done, the filling should be puffed and set but still slightly wiggly. Cool completely on a wire rack.

Corn Fritters

1 large egg, separated

½ cup milk

½ cup canned cream-style corn

½ cup sifted all-purpose flour

½ cup stone-ground cornmeal

1 teaspoon baking powder

1 teaspoon sugar

½ teaspoon salt

3 tablespoons unsalted butter, melted

3 tablespoons vegetable oil

Serves 4

In a medium bowl using an electric mixer, beat the egg yolk with ¼ cup of the milk. Stir in the corn. Set aside.

Sift the flour, cornmeal, baking powder, sugar, and salt into a large bowl. Add to the corn mixture. Add in the remaining ¼ cup milk. Stir in—do not beat—the melted butter.

In a small bowl, beat the egg white until stiff. Fold the egg white into the batter.

Heat the oil in a large heavy skillet over medium-high heat until hot but not smoking. Drop the batter by tablespoonfuls into the oil and fry until golden brown, turning once, about 4 minutes. Drain on paper towels. Serve with fried country ham, crisp bacon, or link sausage. Pass the cane syrup and a big pat of butter. Garnish the plate with glazed apple rings, if you like.

Southern-Style Beef Hash

2 tablespoons unsalted butter

½ cup diced green bell pepper

½ cup diced white onion

1 cup diced potatoes

2 cups minced cold roast beef

1 cup beef stock

Salt

Freshly ground black pepper

2 tablespoons minced parsley

Serves 6

Melt the butter in a large heavy skillet over low heat. Add the green pepper and onion, cover, and cook for 10 minutes. Uncover and add the potatoes, beef, and beef stock and season with salt and pepper. Cook over low heat for about 40 minutes, until the potatoes are tender, stirring occasionally and adding water as needed if the mixture beings to stick to the bottom of the skillet. Fold in 1 tablespoon of the parsley. Remove the hash to a serving dish and garnish with remaining 1 tablespoon parsley. For a backyard supper, serve the hash right from the skillet, resting it on a large wooden plate or iron griddle, if you like.

ALABAMA

I was Alabama-bound to Birmingham. The day of my arrival the glory of the Old South lived anew. It was Confederate Memorial Day below the Mason-Dixon Line. Atop Birmingham's city hall the Stars and Bars rippled in the breeze. Dinner parties were underway. Menus were planned in the colonial manner; lace tablecloths came out of blue-paper wrappings; heirloom silver and glass came down from high cupboards to do the day honor.

ALABAMA

Frances Bomer, born in Tennessee and raised in Louisiana, Old South to the core, had invited me to take a drive around the city, then to luncheon at the Mountain Brook Club where regional food is the specialty. First dish of the luncheon a hillock of shrimp. A rusk for the base, this spread with anchovy paste and bedded on fine lettuce shreds. Next a thick sliver of tomato and on this a half deviled egg rested cut-side down. Then in a pink pyramid, eight fat shrimp marinated in sauce rémoulade.

Fried chicken with the dinner and without the least coating of batter. Along with the chicken came fluffy white rice and rich chicken gravy, came the candied yams—candied in their own golden juices, no spices to distract from the true flavor. Came the turnip greens with a garden relish, a truly remarkable mixture. The corn pone, too, was wonderfully good. The grand finale, fried apple pies served piping hot with a big dip of ice cream.

Turnip Greens with Garden Relish

4 pounds young turnip greens

1½ tablespoons coarse salt

1 quart water

1 (2-inch) square salt pork or 1 slice thick-cut bacon, cut into small pieces

Pinch of cayenne pepper

Serves 6

Strip the turnip leaves from their stems, leaving the sides of the leaves and the top portion in one piece. If the greens are very young, merely pinch off the stem end and leave the leaf intact. Put the leaves in a colander, sprinkle the coarse salt over, and start dousing under running water. It takes several minutes of constant washing to get out the grit. When the leaves are clean, drain well.

Pour the water into a large heavy-bottomed pot. Add the salt pork or bacon. Place over medium-high heat, bring to a boil, and boil for 10 minutes. Stir in the cayenne and dump in the greens. Cover, reduce the heat, and simmer for about 10 minutes, until the leaves have withered. Taste and add salt if necessary. If the greens are young, 15 to 20 minutes' cooking is sufficient. If old and on the tough side, cook for 30 to 40 minutes. Drain, reserve the pot liquor, and serve as a bouillon, with a slice of lemon, to drink with the main course. Cut the greens a few times across with a knife, place in serving dish, and pass with Garden Relish (recipe follows).

Garden Relish

2 medium ripe tomatoes, cut into ¼-inch dice

¾ cup chopped celery

1 large cucumber, peeled and cut into ¼-inch dice

1 green bell pepper, cored, seeded, and cut into ¼-inch dice

2 tablespoons finely chopped onion

1 tablespoon French Dressing (page 246)

2 to 3 tablespoons cider vinegar

Salt

Freshly ground black pepper

Makes 2 cups

In a large bowl, combine all the ingredients. Cover and refrigerate for 2 hours or until the flavors are blended.

Corn Pone

3 cups white cornmeal

1 teaspoon salt

3 tablespoons bacon fat or unsalted butter, melted

About 5 cups boiling water

Makes about 2 dozen corn sticks

Preheat the oven to 400 degrees. Generously grease 2 cast-iron corn-stick molds or a 9-inch cast-iron skillet.

Place the cornmeal in a large bowl and add the salt and fat. Pour in the boiling water until the meal absorbs all it can hold, stirring with a wooden spoon and bringing it to the consistency of a thick batter. Pour the batter into the prepared pans. Bake for 40 minutes, or until a wooden pick or skewer inserted into the sticks comes out clean. Cool in the pans for 10 minutes, then gently lift the corn sticks from the mold. Serve warm.

Fried Apple Pies

1 cup sugar

1 tablespoon ground cinnamon

2 cups all-purpose flour

1 tablespoon baking powder

1 teaspoon salt

4 tablespoons (½ stick) unsalted butter, softened

⅔ cup whole milk

1½ cups thick applesauce

½ cup vegetable oil

Makes 8 to 10 individual pies

Prepare a large rimmed baking sheet by sprinkling the bottom with the sugar and cinnamon. Set aside.

Sift the flour, baking powder, and salt into a large bowl. Cut in the softened butter until well blended. Gradually stir in the milk and stir to make a soft dough. Turn the dough out onto a lightly floured surface and knead with a light touch.

Using a floured rolling pin, roll out the dough very thin, to about ¼ inch. Using a standard saucer placed atop the dough, gently cut around the edge with sharp-pointed knife; make 8 to 10 circles. On one side of each circle, place 3 tablespoons of the applesauce, then fold the circles in half and moisten and seal the edges with a fork.

Heat the oil in a large heavy-bottom skillet over medium heat until it reaches 350 degrees on a candy thermometer. Slide the apple pies into the pan. When browned on one side, turn and brown the other, 5 to 8 minutes total. Lift the pies from the fat, drain on paper towels, and then very gently dredge them through the prepared pan with the sugar-cinnamon mixture, giving both sides a good sugar coating. Quickly serve while hot with plain cream or vanilla ice cream, if you like.

THE AIR IS SWEET with an indefinable sugar. A wonderful day to talk about wedding dishes. I walk up a steep driveway to Grandmother Elmore's snug little house with its grandfather-graybeard shrub by the door. Here lives the wedding-meal expert for Birmingham, Alabama, today busy at her table painting flowers on a bread tray. Mrs. Ewing Hulsey Elmore chatted about her catering career. "I plan and do all kinds of parties," she told me, "but I do weddings best. Shall we talk about wedding feasts?"

If there is room Mrs. Elmore usually suggests a sit-down meal; otherwise a buffet affair. The supper calls for baked ham or roast turkey, sliced beautifully thin, then reassembled for cold service along with a hot casserole such as asparagus with almonds, or a mushroom casserole to go with turkey or chicken. A green salad, or have one of mixed fruits and ice cream for dessert, frozen into miniature fruit forms.

Southern grits is a popular dish for breakfast surrounded with a garland of bacon curls or fat little sausages; or both may be used and fried apple rings with parsley betwixt and between.

Baked Southern Grits

3 cups water

1½ teaspoons salt

1 cup stone-ground grits
(not instant or regular)

½ cup whole milk

2 large eggs, lightly beaten

4 tablespoons (½ stick)
unsalted butter, melted

½ cup grated cheddar cheese

Serves 6

Preheat the oven to 350 degrees. Grease a 2-quart casserole dish.

Pour the water into a large heavy saucepan over medium-high heat, add the salt, and bring to a boil. Slowly sprinkle in the grits, a little at a time, and whisk until completely combined. Reduce the heat to low, cover, and simmer for 1 hour, or until the grits are soft, stirring occasionally. If the grits cook stiff, stir in a little boiling water. Remove from the heat and cool to lukewarm, 15 to 20 minutes. Stir in the milk, eggs, and butter. Pour into the prepared casserole. Bake for about 40 minutes, until set and a knife inserted comes out clean. Ten minutes before the dish is done, sprinkle over the grated cheese and let it melt and brown.

ONE OF THE SOUTH'S most successful herbalists is Mrs. Luther Simms of Birmingham. When I met her a few years ago she was growing 210 varieties of herbs in her hillside garden on Montevallo Road.

Enjoy these tips from her kitchen. When you're pan broiling chops or steaks add one sprig tarragon, one sprig winter savory, one sprig basil. Give distinctive flavor to a soft-boiled egg by putting a sprig of English or common thyme in the cup before the egg is dropped in. A salad idea is to make cottage cheese balls the size of English walnuts and roll in finely chopped chives and parsley with a small sprig of tarragon. Make blush pink with paprika. Stuffing a chicken Mrs. Simms adds a little thyme or rosemary to a sage dressing. When her platter piece is roast beef she scatters fresh or dried tarragon leaves over the meat before it goes into the oven.

MISSISSIPPI

Mississippi, a Gulf state like her neighbor Louisiana, makes great use also of the abundant seafood and again shrimp. But drive north and one comes to the cattle-raising lands with the cooking more general by southern standards than in the Gulf area. First a stop to visit in a hundred-year-old mansion at Pass Christian, which had recently been restored and opened on occasion to the public for tea and sightseeing.

Melanie is my hostess—the house belongs to her. This exuberant, small woman charged with a joy for living is the wife of the late Colonel Hubert de Ben, a New Orleans businessman. And New Orleans was home until one summer day when Melanie and daughter went house hunting for a weekend place in the nearby coastal city of Pass Christian.

Places proved few. A real-estate agent suggested that the old mansion was for sale. The Greek temple façade facing the Gulf held to its beauty, the Greek and Italian marble fireplaces were lovely as ever, but after twenty-five years of neglect the house had gone to seed. The rooms were large, once gracious, but now dilapidated. Boards creaked and sometimes sagged; here and there chunks of plaster had fallen and the laths showed.

"Make me an offer, any offer," the agent kept urging. "Call tomorrow."

Melanie's daughter was thoughtful on the drive home. "You like doing things, Mother, why not buy and restore it?" Melanie telephoned and made her offer, expecting a refusal. Before she could think twice and back out of the deal, the mansion was hers with twenty acres of garden. Six months later Pass Christian couldn't believe its eyes. The old place had been returned to its early-day beauty. The fourteen-room house, built in 1848 by Seth Guion of Louisiana, was livable again, furnished in three periods: French Victorian, this furniture having belonged to Melanie's New Orleans grandmother, and odd pieces of French Empire and Louis XIV.

One of the large convention hotels on the Gulf Coast suggested to Mrs. de Ben that she open a part of her home to convention visitors. The hotel would pay her for the sightseeing privileges and she would serve tea in the Old South manner. Melanie saw in this arrangement a way to pay herself out of the debt.

The fires burned brightly in the old fireplaces, the candles were lighted in the crystal chandeliers, the tea table was dressed in a Chantilly lace tablecloth and laden with bounty. Hot from the oven came the dollar-size biscuits filled with a satiny honey butter. There were fragile cheese ribbons well peppered to heat-prick the tongue. The French-Swiss cookies were made from a hundred-year-old recipe, rolled tissue thin, so tender and crisp.

These are no more. Three years ago, this beautiful mansion burned to the ground. Now Melanie lives in the garden house. But these recipes have been carried home by many a visitor, to be enjoyed down the years. Here are three we enjoyed with Melanie in her top-floor apartment in the old mansion.

Nettie Rose's Cheese Straws

2 cups all-purpose flour

1½ teaspoons salt

1 teaspoon cayenne pepper

1 cup (2 sticks) unsalted butter, softened

2 cups finely grated sharp cheddar cheese

Makes about 5 dozen

Preheat the oven to 300 degrees.

In a large bowl, combine the flour, salt, and cayenne. In a large bowl using an electric mixer, cream the butter with the cheese. Add the flour mixture ½ cup at a time and stir until the batter is smooth.

Scrape the batter into a 1-gallon plastic bag. Cut a corner from the plastic bag and pipe out straw shapes onto a large ungreased baking pan, making 2 rows that are about 5 inches long and 2 inches wide. Bake for 10 to 15 minutes, until lightly browned and crisp. Remove the straws to wire racks to cool.

Note: The cheese straws can be stored in an airtight container for up to a week.

THE HAND OF HISTORY lies heavily on Vicksburg, Mississippi, sitting so proud there, high on the bluffs overlooking the Big River. This is a city of antebellum houses, of historical churches; it's the graveyard of heroes, both the Blue and the Gray. Here is the largest military memorial park in the world, covering 1,323 acres. A city most modern, yet it cleaves to its past, especially so at the table. Recipes are handed down from old family servants. I speak of home cooking; little of the sort could be found in the restaurants, not until Mary McKay opened the Old Southern Tea Room.

Mrs. McKay was born and brought up at Millbrook, the old family plantation, constructed by slave labor in 1840. Aunt Elvira presides over Mary's kitchen just as her ancestors did at the plantation hearth during the lavish days of the Old South. Elvira can't tell a recipe—she cooks by inspiration. I watched these dishes made, then had them translated into cup and spoon measurements.

Old Southern Baked Oysters

2 quarts shucked raw oysters, drained well and patted dry on paper towels

½ cup finely chopped parsley

½ cup finely chopped shallots or onions

1 tablespoon Worcestershire sauce

2 tablespoons lemon juice

½ cup (1 stick) unsalted butter, melted

2 cups fine cracker crumbs

Salt and freshly ground black pepper

Tabasco sauce

Paprika

¾ cup half-and-half

Serves 12 to 15

Preheat the oven to 375 degrees. Generously grease a shallow 2-quart baking dish.

Place a layer of oysters over the bottom of the prepared dish. Sprinkle with half of the parsley, shallots, Worcestershire sauce, lemon juice, butter, and cracker crumbs and season with salt, pepper, and Tabasco. Make another layer using the remaining half of the above ingredients and again season with salt, pepper, and Tabasco. Sprinkle with paprika.

Just before baking, make evenly spaced indentations in the casserole and pour the half-and-half into the holes, being careful not to moisten the crumb topping. Bake for about 30 minutes, until the casserole is bubbly and golden brown on top.

Old-Fashioned Sweet Potato Pone

2½ pounds sweet potatoes
(about 3 large sweet potatoes)

2 tablespoons sugar

3 tablespoons unsalted butter, melted

2 large eggs, beaten

1 teaspoon ground cinnamon

1 teaspoon ground allspice

1 teaspoon grated nutmeg

1 teaspoon ground cloves

1 cup golden raisins

Serves 6

Preheat the oven to 400 degrees. Generously grease an 8 x 8-inch casserole.

Put the sweet potatoes on a baking sheet and pierce each one 2 or 3 times with a fork. Bake for 45 to 50 minutes, until tender. Set aside to cool.

Reduce the oven temperature to 250 degrees. Scoop the sweet potato flesh out of the skins and into a medium bowl. Discard the skins. Mash the sweet potatoes until smooth. Add the remaining ingredients except the raisins and whisk until smooth. Stir in the raisins. Transfer the mixture to the prepared pan.

Bake for 1 hour, or until the mixture is browned on top and piping hot with steam coming off of it. Serve immediately.

Vicksburg Baked Ham with Herbed Dressing

For the dressing:

1 cup (2 sticks) unsalted butter

2 medium onions, finely chopped

4 celery stalks, finely chopped

1 pound crackers, very finely crushed

6 cups crumbled toasted bread

2 tablespoons sugar

1 teaspoon mustard seeds

1 teaspoon dry mustard

½ cup pickle relish

1 tablespoon chopped parsley

4 large eggs, beaten

1 cup sherry wine

4 dashes of Tabasco sauce

1 tablespoon cider vinegar

Salt and freshly ground black pepper

For the ham:

1 (10- to 12-pound) smoked ham
on the bone

1 tablespoon cider vinegar

2 tablespoons brown sugar

1½ cups lukewarm water

Serves about 20

To make the dressing: Preheat the oven to 350. Generously grease a 2½- to 3-quart deep casserole.

Melt the butter in a large skillet over medium-low heat. Add the onions and celery and sauté until soft, about 20 minutes. Transfer to a large bowl, add the remaining ingredients, and spoon into the prepared casserole. Bake for 40 minutes, or until golden brown on top and set.

To make the ham: Reduce the oven temperature to 300 degrees. Trim the tough outer layer of skin and excess fat from the ham. Place the ham, meat-side down, in a large roasting pan and score, making crosshatch incisions with a sharp knife. Roast for 2 hours, or until an instant-read thermometer inserted in the thickest part of the ham registers 120 degrees.

In a medium bowl, whisk together the vinegar, brown sugar, and lukewarm water until the brown sugar dissolves. Remove the ham from the oven and glaze with the vinegar–brown sugar mixture, brushing all over the surface of the ham. Bake for about another 1½ hours, until glossy, brushing with glaze at least twice. Transfer the ham to a cutting board or serving platter and allow to rest for about 30 minutes before carving, reheating the dressing while the ham rests. The ham may be served warm or at room temperature with its dressing alongside.

Stuffed Bell Peppers, Creole

½ cup (1 stick) unsalted butter

2 cloves garlic, chopped

1 small onion, chopped

1 cup chopped ham

½ cup water

½ cup tomato juice

1 (14½-ounce) can stewed tomatoes

1 large egg, well beaten

4 cups fine breadcrumbs

1 teaspoon sugar

Salt and freshly ground black pepper

3 red bell peppers, cut in half lengthwise, cored, and seeded

Serves 6

Preheat the oven to 350 degrees.

Melt the butter in a large saucepan over medium heat. Add the garlic and onions and sauté until softened, about 5 minutes. Add the ham, water, tomato juice, and tomatoes and cook until most of the liquid is absorbed, about 10 minutes. Stir in the egg, breadcrumbs, and sugar and season with salt and pepper.

Arrange the pepper halves cut-side up in a 9 x 13-inch baking dish and fill each pepper half with the ham-tomato mixture. Bake for about 20 minutes, until the peppers are piping hot.

THE INEFFABLE FRAGRANCE OF BREAD

Rolling down the Delta country—first stop Greenville, Mississippi. "What's cooking here, who cooks it best?"

I was told to see Mrs. Phil Mayhall. "She's the town's leading hostess. She serves wonderful meals and can cook what she plans."

Twenty minutes later I'm ringing the doorbell. The door was opened and instantly I felt the happy spirit of the house and the woman who lived in it. Came a rush of warm air laden with the ineffable fragrance of bread. I looked at my hostess, she looked at me, radiating good cheer.

"I'm baking my cornbread, we'll have it hot for dessert with cane ribbon syrup." This syrup, I discovered, is to the Southerner as maple syrup is to the tables of New Englanders. It is a syrup clearer colored than molasses and lighter in consistency.

"It's your recipes for homemade light breads that I came to borrow." Her neighbors had tipped me off to this idea.

"It's all just one recipe, my mother's," Mrs. Mayhall explained. "My light bread I turn into coffee cake, apfel kuchen, any number of things. . . ."

Our hostess is Pennsylvania-born and learned cooking in the Dutch country, but after thirty years in the Delta her dishes speak with a Southern accent. Her pickle-relish cupboard is a sight to behold, with at least twenty sweets and sours waiting for dinner. The freezer is stocked with extra batches of cakes, cookies, and pies. If company comes unexpectedly Mrs. Mayhall can shake up a ravishing meal while another woman would be debating whether she could invite them to stay.

Mississippi Corn Muffins

½ cup stone-ground cornmeal

1½ teaspoons baking powder

1 teaspoon salt

1 teaspoon sugar

1½ cups whole milk

1 large egg

4 tablespoons (½ stick) unsalted butter, softened

Makes 1 dozen

Preheat the oven to 425 degrees.

Sift the cornmeal, baking powder, salt, and sugar into a large bowl. Add the milk and beat in the egg until just blended.

Coat each of 12 medium muffin cups with 1 teaspoon of the softened butter and place the muffin pan in the oven. When the butter is smoking hot, in 2 to 3 minutes, remove the pan and add enough batter to half-fill each cup. Return the pan to the oven and bake for 25 to 30 minutes, until the muffin tops are crisp and a wooden pick or skewer inserted into the center of the muffins comes out clean. Immediately unmold the muffins and serve them piping hot, with butter and honey, if you like.

AN "EX" AT EVERYTHING

In Hattiesburg, Mississippi, I met Mrs. Howard S. Williams. Children watch for her coming. Her pocketbook is a Santa's sack stocked with hard candies, with chewing gum. She never goes anywhere empty-handed. The flowers in her garden, the daisies and daffodils, the jonquils and dahlias are raised for one purpose—to carry to friends. Banana bread she bakes by the half-dozen loaves, gift bread for neighbors.

When Emma Ray Smith of Meridian, Mississippi, married Howard Williams of Columbia, Tennessee, he was a newspaper reporter, an Associated Press correspondent. His job took him to Mexico to live for nine years. It was there Mrs. Williams tried her hand at cooking Mexican, rice and shrimp, her best dish.

Mr. Williams gave up newspapering to turn evangelist, traveling America holding revivals in nineteen states—over three hundred meetings in twenty-eight years.

Pressed to tell of her many civic activities, she said, "I'm an 'ex' at everything"—meaning that she had once won the gold medal as the state's woman golf champion, that she was the first Mississippi woman to serve on the Democratic Executive Committee, that she and Mr. Williams opened the first business and professional women's club in the state, that she started the first of these clubs in Hattiesburg, and that she was a charter member of the town's home and garden club and garden council.

"And I'm an ex-cook," she added, when the questioning turned to the foods friends around the state had recommended I sample at the Williams table. "When our three children were at home and we lived in the big house, then cooking was my big job. Now I cook by streaks when the mood moves me, then I cook up a storm." That is, all in one day she bakes cookies, cakes, pies, does a roast—food enough to last a week. It's then she bakes this banana bread to carry to neighbors or convalescing friends.

Committee groups meeting at her house for luncheon get rice and shrimp as the main dish, by request. Asparagus or peas for the vegetable along with buttermilk biscuits.

Banana Bread

½ cup (1 stick) unsalted butter

1 cup sugar

2 large eggs

2 cups all-purpose flour

1 teaspoon baking soda

½ teaspoon salt

1 cup ripe mashed bananas (about 3 bananas)

Makes one 9-inch loaf

Preheat the oven to 350 degrees. Grease a 9 x 5 x 3-inch loaf pan.

In a large bowl using an electric mixer, cream the butter and sugar until light and fluffy. Add the eggs, one at a time, beating well after each addition. Sift the flour, baking soda, and salt into a medium bowl. In a small bowl, mash the bananas thoroughly with a fork. Add the flour mixture alternately with mashed bananas to the creamed butter and sugar.

Pour the batter in the prepared pan and bake for 55 to 60 minutes, until a wooden pick or skewer inserted in the center comes out clean. Cool in the pan on a wire rack for 15 minutes, then invert the bread onto the rack and cool completely before slicing and serving.

Buttermilk Biscuits

1½ cups sifted all-purpose flour

1 teaspoon baking powder

½ teaspoon baking soda

½ teaspoon salt

2 tablespoons unsalted butter, softened

½ cup buttermilk

Makes 16

Preheat the oven to 400 degrees. Grease a large baking sheet.

Measure 2 heaping tablespoons of the flour and use it to dust the work surface. Put the remaining flour in a large bowl, make a hole in the center of the flour, and put the baking powder, baking soda, and salt into the hole. Add the butter and pour in the buttermilk. Use your fingertips to gradually mix the flour and liquid into a soft dough.

Turn the dough onto the prepared floured surface and pat out gently ½ inch thick, using your fingers rather than a rolling pin. Cut the dough using a 2-inch floured biscuit cutter and place the dough circles on the prepared pan. Bake until risen and golden brown, 12 to 15 minutes, watching carefully at the end. Remove the biscuits from the pan and cool on a wire rack for a few minutes before serving.

Individual Lemon Puddings

3 large eggs, separated

1 cup sugar

1 cup milk

2 tablespoons all-purpose flour

Pinch of salt

Grated peel and juice of 1 lemon

Whipped cream, optional

Serves 6

Preheat the oven to 350 degrees. Grease six 1-cup ramekins.

In a large bowl using an electric mixer, beat the egg yolks, gradually adding the sugar. Gradually beat in the milk. Add the flour a little at a time, stirring until smooth. Stir in the salt and lemon peel and juice.

In a small bowl using an electric mixer, beat the egg whites until stiff and shiny. Gently fold the egg whites into the egg yolk–lemon mixture. Pour the batter into the prepared ramekins and place them in a large baking dish. Fill the baking dish with hot water to come halfway to the top of the ramekins. Bake for 45 minutes, or until a wooden pick or skewer inserted in the middle comes out clean. Let the puddings rest for a couple of minutes in the water bath, then remove them and serve warm, with whipped cream, if you like.

Mexican Rice with Shrimp

1 cup uncooked long-grain rice

4 tablespoons (½ stick) butter, softened

1 medium onion, chopped

¼ cup chopped green bell pepper

1 (14½-ounce) can diced tomatoes

1 cup chicken stock or water

1 teaspoon salt

Dash of cayenne pepper

1 dozen shrimp, peeled, deveined, and cooked

Serves 4

Wash the rice and dry it on a clean dish towel.

Melt the butter in a large heavy saucepan or skillet over medium heat. Add the rice and cook, stirring constantly until it is a deep golden brown, about 5 minutes. Add the onion and cook until transparent, about 3 minutes. Add the green pepper and cook, stirring, for a few seconds. Add the tomatoes, stock, salt, and cayenne. Reduce the heat to low, cover, and cook, without stirring, until every grain is separate and the rice is fluffy, 15 to 20 minutes, stirring in the shrimp 3 minutes before serving.

TENNESSEE

One hot August I spent a week visiting a Tennessee camp meeting, the Taylor family's kinsfolk revival held near Brownsville, sixty miles north of Memphis. This meeting has been a family tradition for over one hundred years. Here the good eats came next to godliness.

The camp hummed with voices. There was the shrill shouting of children, merry-mouthed as young guinea hens, the scraping of deck chairs, the creak-squeak of swings. A calling of greetings. "Well, if it isn't Cousin Bessie! When did you get in?"

There was the clatter of dishes. Came the good eating smells, all fittin' to stir the hunger of a stone man. Southern ham was frying, buttermilk biscuits were baking; rich simmerings gave off their varying scents as cooks lifted pot lids.

Late August, as in the olden times, when the crops are laid in, it's meeting time at the church. Here come the Tennessee Taylors from every part of the nation, to worship together, to eat fried chicken, to christen the year's crop of babies, to pay their respects to their dead.

Tabernacle is strictly a family affair with a few invited guests. Get invited three times and you are considered a "fixture." Averil Taylor, that's Mrs.

Edmund Taylor, invited me to come and sample the camp-meeting cooking. Food served at Tabernacle is the talk of the countryside. Cooks there strive to outdo one another.

At the Edmund Taylor camp, "Dick" runs the kitchen with a firm and batter-smeared hand. Dick's been coming to Tabernacle since she was nine years old. Her mother and grandmother had cooked here in their day.

"Dick's calling supper," said Averil, cocking an ear. The long table for grownups was set for twenty places. In the lean-to off the kitchen the children's table packed them in ten strong.

Pan-fried steak for supper, and green beans, whipped potatoes, steak gravy. Of course, hot biscuits to make one more background for good gravy. Sliced tomatoes, big thick slices, the color of Christmas, a spaghetti dish as an extra filler, and Dick's candied apples, corn on the cob, chess pie for dessert. Taylors on local farms bring their own hams, beef, lamb, and chicken for this occasion. They have freezers in town and drive in almost daily for fresh supplies. Each summer a special garden is planted to bear in late August: sweet corn, field peas, butter beans, turnip greens.

The last mouthful of chess pie, the last sip of coffee, the cow horn was tooting the signal for evening meeting.

The church on the rise seats three hundred people, and on this August night the place overflowed. Chairs were put up; Taylors sat on the porch, spread out on the lawn. Front rows were reserved for the little shavers. The drugstore set, the twelve- to eighteen-year-olds, some forty-odd, sat on the platform. This was the choir. And everyone sang, whether he could "hyst a hymn" or not.

The benediction, then gaiety took over. Hand-shaking on the lawn. "Come to our camp, we're cutting a melon." "Come to our camp, we're having a sing." "Can't you drop in for a cake and coffee?" And the cakes they pass! Averil cut a melon.

Women gathered around to tell me who is who among the good Taylor cooks. They were eager to help me get recipes, believing there is nothing good to eat north of Washington. Nobody in our camp went to bed before three.

At six came the sound of the horn, a signal for rising. I skipped prayer meeting but was on hand for the big breakfast; pink-brown slices of ham afloat in red-eye gravy. There was· beef hash undefiled, nothing in it but potatoes, beef, and onions—not a catchall. Plateloads of whole-wheat muffins came by, and homemade blackberry jam.

Back to Averil's table for Sunday dinner featuring home-cured lamb with chili sauce. No one around Haywood County eats lamb without chili. Guests from six states were at the dinner table. Children from other camps peeking in to ask, "What are you folks having? Car'mel cake? Can I have a piece, Aunt Averil?"

In two days I didn't get around to everybody's table but I did try to call on the best of the cooks and have borrowed some of the most unusual of the Taylor family recipes. Dick's apples for one—most wonderful, rich as candy, shining as polished crystal. But your modern stove can't do these apples to quite the same perfection as Dick's old wood-burning range. And we give you Zaidee's Jelly Pie; we give you Lib's Chicken Pie, for after all, at this pleasant revival there was more pie than piety. Additional Taylor specialties are the peach ice cream blackberry-jam cake, chess pie, the chili sauce, the corn pudding. . . .

Lib's Chicken Pie

1 (3½- to 4-pound) fresh chicken, cut into 8 pieces

1½ teaspoons salt, plus more for the pie

1 Perfect Pie Crust (page 13)

⅛ teaspoon freshly ground black pepper

4 tablespoons (½ stick) unsalted butter

Serves 6

Grease an 11 x 7 x 1½-inch baking dish.

Place the chicken pieces in a large stockpot and cover with about 1 quart of water, just enough to submerge them. Add the salt. Place over medium-high heat, cover the pot, and bring to a simmer. Reduce the heat to low and simmer until the chicken is just tender, about 30 minutes. Cool the chicken in its liquid until it's ready to handle, about 30 minutes.

Meanwhile, using a floured rolling pin on a floured surface, roll out half of the pie dough to a ⅛-inch-thick rectangle and line the bottom of the prepared pan with it.

Preheat the oven to 400 degrees. When chicken is cool enough to handle, pick off all of the meat with your fingers. Discard the skin and save the bones for stock. Lay the pulled chicken meat on the dough. Season the chicken with salt and the pepper and dot with the butter. Cover with the broth that was used to cook the chicken (the dough will absorb some of the broth as it bakes).

Using a floured rolling pin on a floured surface, roll out the remaining dough to a ⅛-inch-thick rectangle. Cover the top of the baking dish and seal the edges; prick the top with a fork. Bake the chicken pie for 30 to 35 minutes, until the top is golden brown and the liquid is bubbling. Rest for 10 minutes and serve warm.

Zaidee's Jelly Pie

1 (8-inch) Perfect Pie Crust (page 13)

½ cup (1 stick) unsalted butter, softened

1 cup tart plum or currant jelly

3 large eggs, beaten

½ cup sugar

2 tablespoons finely crushed butter crackers (such as Ritz crackers)

Makes one 8-inch pie

Preheat the oven to 350 degrees.

Using a floured rolling pin on a lightly floured surface, roll out the dough into an 11-inch round and fit into an 8-inch glass pie plate. Trim the excess dough and crimp the edges decoratively. Line the dough with parchment, pleating it as necessary to fit the pan. Fill with rice or dried beans, making sure they are pushed up against the sides of the parchment. Bake for 20 minutes, then lift out and remove the parchment with the rice or beans and prick the bottom of the crust all over with a fork. Return the dough to the oven and bake for 7 to 10 minutes, until pale golden brown, checking after the first 3 minutes and pricking again if the upper layer of dough bubbles up. Remove the crust from the oven, cool completely, and refrigerate for 30 minutes.

Increase the oven temperature to 425 degrees while the crust is chilling.

Meanwhile, in a medium bowl using an electric mixer, cream the butter and gradually add the jelly, blending well. In another bowl, beat together the eggs, sugar, and cracker crumbs thoroughly. Gradually blend the crumb mixture with the butter and jelly. Pour the mixture into the chilled pie crust and bake for 10 minutes. Reduce the oven temperature to 350 degrees and continue baking for 25 to 30 minutes longer, until the center of the pie is set and the crust is golden. If the crust begins to burn before the center is set, cover the pie with foil. Remove the pie from the oven and cool completely on a wire rack before serving.

Spoon Bread

1 cup yellow cornmeal

1 teaspoon salt

1 cup milk, scalded

1 cup boiling water

2 teaspoons baking powder

2 large eggs, well beaten

3 tablespoons unsalted butter, melted

Serves 4 to 6

Preheat the oven to 350 degrees. Grease a 9-inch square baking pan.

In a medium saucepan, combine the cornmeal and salt; place over medium heat and gradually stir in the scalded milk and boiling water. Cook, stirring constantly, until thick and smooth, about 5 minutes. Stir in the baking powder, eggs, and melted butter.

Pour the batter into the prepared pan and bake for 30 to 35 minutes, until the center is set and the top is golden brown. Remove from the oven and serve immediately.

Butterscotch Pie

1 (8-inch) Perfect Pie Crust (page 13)

¼ cup cornstarch

2 cups packed light brown sugar

5 large eggs, separated

2 cups whole milk

3 tablespoons unsalted butter

1 teaspoon baking powder

Makes one 8-inch pie

Preheat the oven to 350 degrees.

Using a floured rolling pin on a lightly floured surface, roll out the dough into an 11-inch round and fit it into an 8-inch glass pie plate. Trim the excess dough and crimp the edges decoratively. Line the dough with parchment, pleating it as necessary to fit the pan. Fill with rice or dried beans, making sure they are pushed up against the sides of the parchment. Place in the oven and bake for 20 minutes. Lift out and remove the parchment with the rice or beans and prick the bottom of the crust all over with a fork. Return it to the oven and bake for 7 to 10 minutes more, until pale golden brown, checking after 3 minutes and pricking again if the upper layer of dough bubbles up. Remove the crust from the oven and cool completely, then refrigerate for 30 minutes while you make the filling.

In a small bowl, combine the cornstarch and brown sugar. In a large bowl using an electric mixer, beat the egg yolks until thick and lemon-colored; add the brown sugar mixture. Add in the milk and beat well; set aside. Melt the butter in a large saucepan over low heat, and cook for 5 to 7 minutes, stirring constantly, until lightly browned. Pour the custard into the pan with the butter and stir constantly until thick; start over low heat and gradually increase to medium. This will take about 20 minutes. Remove the mixture from the heat and cool to room temperature, uncovered, about 30 minutes.

While the mixture is cooling, preheat the oven again to 350 degrees. When the mixture has cooled, pour it into the prepared crust.

In a medium bowl, beat the egg whites until frothy; gradually add the baking powder. Continue beating until the whites are stiff and shiny and stand in peaks. Top the pie with the meringue, spreading to the edges. Bake until lightly browned, about 5 minutes. Cool completely on a wire rack, cover, and refrigerate until ready to serve.

Capp's Blackberry Jam Cake

1 cup raisins

1 cup Burgundy wine or grape juice

3½ cups all-purpose flour

1 cup finely chopped citron

1 cup finely chopped pecans

2 teaspoons baking powder

1 teaspoon baking soda

1 teaspoon salt

1 cup (2 sticks) unsalted butter

1 cup granulated sugar

5 large eggs

1 cup seedless blackberry jam

¾ cup buttermilk

1 tablespoon confectioners' sugar

Serves 10 to 12

Preheat the oven to 350 degrees. Generously grease and flour a 10 x 4-inch tube pan.

Place the raisins in a small bowl, cover with the wine or grape juice, and soak at room temperature overnight. The following morning, strain the raisins, reserving the soaking liquid. Pour ½ cup of the flour into a medium bowl and dredge the raisins, citron, and pecans through it. Set the pieces aside. Sift the remaining 3 cups flour, the baking powder, baking soda, and salt into another medium bowl.

In a medium bowl using an electric mixer, cream the butter and granulated sugar until fluffy. Beat in the eggs one at a time. Add the jam and beat until smooth. Add the flour mixture alternately with buttermilk, beating until smooth after each addition. Blend in the reserved wine or grape juice. Add the dredged fruit to mixture and mix thoroughly. Pour the batter into the prepared pan and bake for 65 to 70 minutes, until the cake pulls away from the sides of the pan and a wooden pick or tester inserted into the center of the cake comes out clean. Cool the cake in the pan on a wire rack for 10 minutes, then unmold the cake onto the rack and cool completely. Dust the top of the cake with the confectioners' sugar just before serving.

Chess Pie

1 (8-inch) Perfect Pie Crust (page 13)

½ cup (1 stick) unsalted butter

1 cup sugar

3 large eggs

1 teaspoon vanilla extract

Makes one 8-inch pie

Line an 8-inch pie plate with the crust, cover, and refrigerate for 30 minutes.

Preheat the oven to 450 degrees.

In a large bowl using an electric mixer, cream the butter with the sugar. Add the eggs one at a time, stirring well after each addition. Add the vanilla. Pour into the prepared chilled pie shell and bake for 10 minutes. Reduce the oven temperature to 300 degrees and bake for 20 to 25 minutes longer, until the custard is golden and the filling is firm but not completely set and still a bit jiggly; if necessary, cover the edges of the pie crust with foil about halfway through baking to avoid burning the crust. Cool on a wire rack completely before serving. The pie can be prepared 1 day in advance, covered, and refrigerated. Bring to room temperature before serving.

PIES A-PLENTY I ENJOYED as guest of the Taylor clan and then fared forth to sample others. I'll never forget these little molasses picnic pies made by Mrs. Leslie W. Smith of Gibson County, Tennessee, the sweet of sweets in her bend of the creek. Tempting little treasures, brown and flaky, spicy and sugary, comforting to the stomach. Maybe the proudest moment of Mrs. Smith's life was at the county fair when she won fifty-three first prizes for her culinary entries.

Molasses Pie

2 cups molasses

¼ cup lemon juice

2 tablespoons all-purpose flour

3 tablespoons water

½ teaspoon ground cinnamon

½ teaspoon grated nutmeg

2 tablespoons unsalted butter, melted

3 large eggs, separated

½ cup sugar

1 (8-inch) Perfect Pie Crust (page 13)

Makes one 8-inch pie

Preheat the oven to 425 degrees.

In a medium bowl, combine the molasses with the lemon juice. In the large bowl of an electric mixer, moisten the flour with the water and add the cinnamon, nutmeg, and melted butter; add the molasses mixture. In a medium bowl, beat the egg yolks with the sugar until light, about 3 minutes. Add the eggs to the molasses mixture, mixing well. Set aside.

In a medium bowl, beat the egg whites until stiff peaks form. Gently fold the egg whites into the molasses mixture.

Line an 8-inch pie pan with the crust. Poke holes in the crust with a fork and bake for 5 minutes. Pour in the filling, reduce the oven temperature to 350 degrees, and bake for 30 to 40 minutes more, until the filling is set and the top is golden brown. Cool completely on a wire rack before serving.

IN MEMPHIS, TENNESSEE, long famous for its dishes, it was suggested I try the Tennessee Club Chicken which is almost as old as the club itself. And that club is no youngster—it was founded in 1875, the oldest organization in the state and with the possible exception of one club in Richmond, one in New Orleans, it's the oldest club in the South. The chicken dish is as much a part of the place as the picture of General Lee on his horse, and like the club's various rooms the dish is built round as a silver dollar.

The building overlooking Court Square was erected in 1890, designed by architect Edward Terrell, of Columbus, Ohio. Terrell had a passion for circles. Windows, card rooms, dining rooms, all are round as Rome's Pantheon.

Who dreamed up Tennessee Club Chicken? Nobody knows, but that dish goes on forever like Mr. Tennyson's brook. It's a tradition at suppers served for the town's society belles who make their debut in the famous ballroom. It's a pip of a recipe if you can find time to go through all the rituals. What you need is a running start of three days.

"And don't be changing the Roquefort cheese dressing either," is the order that came along to George Anderson, experienced hotel man who had taken over the management.

"You bet I didn't," he confided to me. "I've been living in this city twenty-nine years and I know what tradition means around the table." He admits this dressing is a queer one. But get it together and it's "truly wonderful eating"—the club's lunchtime favorite spooned over a big bowl of the chef's salad.

Roquefort Salad Dressing

6 egg yolks

¼ cup olive oil

¼ cup vegetable oil

¼ cup lemon juice

Dash of Tabasco sauce

½ teaspoon Worcestershire sauce

1 teaspoon salt

¼ teaspoon sweet paprika

1 cup crumbled Roquefort cheese

¼ cup half-and-half

Makes 3 cups

In a large stainless-steel or glass bowl, beat the egg yolks with until thick. Slowly pour in the oils and continue the beating until the mixture starts to thicken. Keep thinning with lemon juice, adding a dribble at a time. When completely smooth, add the Tabasco, Worcestershire sauce, salt, and paprika. Crumble in the cheese. Add the half-and-half and beat until fairly smooth, about 5 minutes. The dressing should be thick but still pourable.

Serve over greens or a chef's salad; it's also delicious sauce for shrimp cocktail and a love match with the avocado.

Tennessee Club Chicken

6 boneless skinless chicken breast halves

9 tablespoons all-purpose flour

6 tablespoons vegetable shortening

6 slices country ham

2 tablespoons unsalted butter

2 cups whole milk

½ cup sherry wine

Salt and freshly ground black pepper

6 slices plain white toast, crusts removed

Serves 6

Preheat the oven to 300 degrees.

Dredge the chicken breasts in 6 tablespoons of the flour, shaking the breasts well to avoid clumps.

Heat the shortening in a large heavy-bottomed saucepan or skillet over medium heat.

Brown the breasts in the shortening, but do not fully cook; using a slotted spoon, transfer them to paper towels to drain.

In a separate large heavy-bottomed and ovenproof pan, cook the ham slices over medium heat until browned and crisp. Remove from the pan and drain on paper towels. To the remaining fat in the pan, whisk in the butter. Blend in the remaining 3 tablespoons flour, add the milk, and cook until thickened, whisking constantly, 5 to 7 minutes. Add the sherry, stir well, and season with salt and pepper. Place the reserved chicken pieces into the sauce and cover the pan tightly. Place in the oven and bake until the chicken is tender, about 30 minutes. The sauce should have the grace of proper consistency, too thick to run, too thin to clot, just thick enough to cling to the meat.

Lay one prepared toast round on each of 6 ovenproof plates and lay a slice of country ham, trimmed to fit the toast, over the toast, followed by one of the chicken breast halves. Pour over the remaining sauce from the baked chicken. Place the plates in the oven until everything is piping hot, 3 to 5 minutes. Serve immediately.

DURING THE HUNTING SEASON it's dinner party time for Mrs. William Kent of Memphis, Tennessee. Then her palatial home on South Willett Street is lively with guests who come from all parts of the country, friends of the family invited for shooting. Quail and duck in the bag, quail and duck on the table.

Mrs. Kent knows what the men like to eat and plans menus to please. Entertaining is Mrs. Kent's forte, and it's based on long years of practice.

Hunters home from the hills with a quarry of quail. What for a quail dinner? First the oysters Rockefeller, a recipe of Mrs. Kent's own devising after eating the dish many times in New Orleans at Antoine's. Quail to follow,

each bird parked on a toast square. Wild rice and sharp currant jelly the perfect accompaniment; green peas the vegetable.

Even a hunter gets fed up with game. Roast beef, Mrs. Kent finds, is the perfect alternative. This she serves on the rare side with a rare sauce. Mr. Kent, a carving maestro, carves the roast at the table. "Sauce?"

"My, yes!" everyone answers, "if it's that sauce we had the last time we came."

Big-crowd parties Mrs. Kent puts in the hands of a caterer. But the chicken soufflé, served no matter what else, is cook Julia's concern.

So are the hot corn muffins which come in regiments from the oven.

Roast Beef Sauce

1 bunch watercress (about 5 ounces), tough stems removed

1 cup tomato sauce

¼ cup packed light brown sugar

2 tablespoons cider vinegar

¼ teaspoon ground cinnamon

Dash of ground cloves

Dash of allspice

¼ teaspoon Tabasco sauce

1 tablespoon finely grated fresh or prepared horseradish

Makes enough for one (6 pound) roast

Wash the watercress, dry it well, mince it, and place it in a medium bowl. In a separate bowl, whisk the remaining ingredients together and toss with the watercress. Cover and refrigerate for at least 1 hour and up to 3 hours before serving. Serve cold, with roast beef.

Chicken Soufflé

For the chicken:

2½ cups diced cooked white chicken meat

1 cup finely chopped cooked dark chicken meat

¼ teaspoon freshly ground black pepper

Salt

1 teaspoon Worcestershire sauce

1 onion, finely chopped

2 large eggs, separated and yolks beaten

1 cup heavy cream, whipped

For the sauce:

¼ pound fresh mushrooms, quartered

2 tablespoons unsalted butter

2 cups chicken stock

3 tablespoons all-purpose flour

Salt and freshly ground black pepper

Preheat the oven to 325 degrees. Generously grease an 8½ x 2-inch ring mold.

In a large bowl, combine the dark- and white-meat chicken. Add the pepper and season with salt. Add the Worcestershire sauce, onion, and beaten egg yolks. In a small bowl, beat the egg whites until stiff but not dry and gently fold into the chicken. Pour the mixture into the prepared mold and bake for 40 minutes, or until the center is set and firm. Serve immediately, with sauce.

While chicken is baking, make the sauce: Melt the butter in a medium saucepan over low heat. Add the mushrooms and sauté until the liquid the mushrooms release has evaporated, about 5 minutes. Turn the heat up to medium and cook, stirring occasionally, about 5 minutes more, until the mushrooms are lightly browned. Turn off the heat and set aside.

Heat the chicken stock in a large heavy saucepan over medium heat. Slowly and carefully whisk in the flour and cook until slightly thickened, 2 to 3 minutes. Season with salt and pepper and continue cooking, whisking constantly, for 10 minutes, or until thick. Stir in the prepared mushrooms. Serve alongside the chicken soufflé.

PAPPY WAS MIGHTY GLAD to see me, but not in the least surprised. "Yes, Ma'am, I figured you'd be coming this way because everyone in Tennessee knows about Pappy's southern rolls."

Folks go to Pappy's place in Memphis to eat ham and red-eye gravy and Tennessee catfish and two-pound lobsters and "T"-bone steak and French fried potatoes. But they no more than sit down before they are saying, "Bring along a plate of hot rolls."

The place is called Pappy and Jimmie's Lobster Shack and was intended primarily as a seafood house. Pappy, that is L. C. Sammons—he does the meal planning and the cooking. Jimmie, that's J. G. Mounce—he does the managing. Pappy had spent long years with the Madison Seafood Cafe,

TENNESSEE

then he retired and went crazy nearly, just twiddling his thumbs. He got the restaurant idea, teamed up with Jimmie. Pappy is a man long and slim as a squirt of Vichy water, blue eyes framed by steel-rimmed glasses. His life is a dash from baking board to stove and into the dining room asking, "How you folks coming? Is the steak to your liking?"

"Just lovely, just lovely, Pappy. May we have another plate of those rolls?"

Pappy's Southern Rolls

1 tablespoon active dry yeast

⅓ cup warm, but not hot, water

3 large eggs

½ cup vegetable shortening, melted

⅓ cup milk, at room temperature

1 tablespoon sugar

1 teaspoon salt

3 cups all-purpose flour

3 tablespoons unsalted butter, melted

Makes 2 dozen

In a small bowl, dissolve the yeast in the warm water and let stand until foamy, about 5 minutes.

In a large bowl of an electric mixer fitted with the dough hook, beat together the eggs, melted shortening, milk, dissolved yeast, sugar, and salt. Gradually add the flour and beat at medium speed until a smooth, elastic, and silky dough forms, about 10 minutes. Transfer the dough to an oiled bowl, cover with plastic wrap, and let rise in warm place, 45 to 60 minutes, until doubled in bulk.

Grease two 12-hole muffin pans. Punch down the dough and divide it into 24 walnut-size pieces. Place the dough pieces in the greased muffin pans and let rise in a warm place, covered loosely with plastic wrap, until the rolls are as high as the pan, about 1 hour more.

Preheat the oven to 400 degrees. When dough has risen, bake for 8 to 12 minutes, until the rolls are fluffy and golden. Transfer the pans to wire racks and cool for 15 minutes. Invert the rolls onto a platter, then invert again back onto the wire rack. Hot from the oven, brush the tops of the rolls with butter and serve.

SPINDRIFT WITH A SPOON

TENNESSEE

I was eating spindrift with a spoon. Now the last of the foamy fluff diluted into a spirited liquid, milky white. I turned the glass to drink it down. That was syllabub, a dessert drink from the old South.

Mrs. Jack Wilkinson of Signal Mountain, Chattanooga, Tennessee, taught me the syllabub etiquette. The Wilkinsons serve syllabub for holiday occasions like Thanksgiving and Christmas and for family celebrations such as anniversaries and christenings.

No mamby-pamby fare. Ingredients: one pint whipping cream, one pint milk, one-half cup sugar and bourbon to taste, one-half cup a guest. That gives service for eight. It takes a syllabub chum to whip the stuff to a fluff and these churns are rare things. Mrs. Wilkinson has her grandma's chum, meaning Grandma Hatcher Hughes Riley of Amelia Courthouse, Virginia. But the chum was an heirloom even in Grandma's day, brought over from England. Now if you are syllabub making use your egg beater.

Mix all ingredients in a deep bowl, place beater in center and get busy. When the top of the bowl is well covered with froth, skim with a spoon and dip into tall glasses. Continue beating and skimming until the mixture is used. Syllabub can be beaten over and over again as long as it lasts. To serve, sprinkle with grated rind of lemon and a dust of nutmeg.

Sherry may be used instead of bourbon, then serve over fruit. The one feature in which all old formulas agree is that after spicing and sweetening the cream, milk should be added, not from the bottle, but warm and frothing from the cow. About 150 years ago in London syllabub was vended in the parks and the cooperative cow went along with the vendor to be milked into the bowl to give the big splash. The cow was frequently admitted into society, led in at fetes and milked into the fine china bowl that contained the ingredients for syllabub. The mistress did the milking if she dared officiate. Otherwise a dairymaid did the work. Squeamish guests drank mulled wine instead.

Today syllabub can be a party sensation all without the help of "Mrs. Elsie." Make your syllabub light and bubbly. If it goes thick and creamy, thin the mixture by adding more milk. Serve it with fruit cake, with tea cakes or wedges of angel food. Side dishes of salted pecans, stuffed dates, or crystallized fruit are all in good taste.

Syllabub was known as early as the sixteenth century and has been frequently mentioned in literature. In a diary in 1694, a treasury of early American manners, Judge Dewall recommends a syllabub with a basis of "syder." "Put in as much thick cream by two or three spoonfuls at a time, as hard as you can, as though you milk it." (Here the syllabub tradition of milk fresh from the cow is plainly preserved, if not her bodily presence.) "Stir it together exceedingly softly, once about, and let it stand two or three hours at least."

In *Tom Brown at Oxford:* "We retire to tea or syllabub beneath the shade of some great oak."

KENTUCKY

Duncan Hines, who for three decades was America's number one food connoisseur, traveling the nation's highways in search of good food and good recipes, belonged especially to Kentucky. He made Kentucky his home. I went to Bowling Green several years ago to visit Duncan and his wife Clara in their ranch-style house set amid flower beds and blue grass just a few miles out of town. When I arrived my host and hostess were at work in their kitchen, fixing a green salad and omelet for supper. Mr. Hines was busy with a dressing, adding pinches of herbs, tasting as he worked. He liked fussing in the kitchen and considered himself an Escoffier when it came to a salad. He collected spices as some folks collect stamps or rare jades. He had a fine assortment of knives, which he kept sharp as daggers. "A man is no better carver," he explained, "than the knife in his hand."

The Hineses were home for a breather after two months of cross-country touring. At home they ate their own cooking, simple food, to try to lose pounds. Their big meal was at midday, then a light supper. Mr. Hines got the breakfast toast and orange juice. If guests were on hand he added bacon and eggs or maybe fried ham.

"Aren't you scared to cook for him?" we asked Mrs. Hines, who was rolling out biscuits.

"No," she said, "He's easy to please."

"But Clara's a good cook," Duncan said.

"When I strike a snag with menu planning," Mrs. Hines explained, "I ask Dunc what's for dinner today and his reply is 'Oh, anything,' just like any husband. Then he adds, 'hot biscuits, of course?'"

"Clara's buttermilk biscuits are the very best," Duncan Hines said, trying to get a word in edgewise through woman chatter. "That goes for her fried chicken, too. But you can taste that for yourself. We'll have fried chicken tomorrow."

Clara fried the chicken while she answered our questions about Duncan Hines's favorite dishes. We sat on a high stool in her immaculate kitchen overlooking the pasture that loafs lazily down to Barren River. One eye for our notes, one eye for the chicken. Each piece was wiped carefully with a damp cloth, dried, then dusted with salt and pepper and rolled lightly in flour. The frying fat was one-third butter, one-third vegetable shortening, one-third bacon drippings. The big iron skillet held the whole chicken; pieces slightly overlapping. No cover on the pan. When the fat was good and hot, the chicken went in. The fat was still sizzling as the last piece was placed. Then the heat was turned down and the chicken cooked slowly to brown. It was turned, the other side browned, then out to drain.

With the chicken came yellow squash, this fresh from the garden. It was washed, cut into thin slices, boiled in salted water until tender, drained and placed in a casserole. Butter was added, a little grated onion, salt and pepper to taste and all stirred with a fork. In went a half cup of heavy cream and over the top Parmesan cheese. Into the oven until the cheese browned.

The salad was a tomato stuffed with cottage cheese, blended with grated onion and cucumber. The hot biscuits with dinner were eaten wading in gravy. Apple pie for dessert, the recipe from Mr. Hines's sister. The Hineses didn't lose any pounds at that meal—we didn't either.

Duncan Hines wasn't keen for cocktail appetizers. He thought they took the edge off the pleasure of dinner. But sometimes he liked crackers with homemade cheese spread to go along with his late-afternoon whiskey sour. The spread was a combination of Roquefort, a sharp American cheese, and Camembert with heavy cream "and cayenne pepper, a recipe Mrs. Hines introduced to her champion eater. It's cooked over low heat until the cheeses are melted, then strained into jars, sealed and held in the refrigerator until needed. This has a good spreading consistency and is wonderfully nice for stuffing celery stalks.

The soup Clara told me her husband liked best was Crême St. Germain, a pea soup; this recipe from the chef at the Cameo Restaurant in Chicago. There Duncan Hines went for dinner every time he had a chance. Another dish is guinea squash pie made with eggplant, with milk-soaked toasted bread, egg, onion, cream, butter, and seasonings. Pretty as a picture when it comes golden brown from the oven.

Fried eggs with Kentucky ham were one of the Hineses' specialties. What ham? One cured by the Hines hand. Before the meat shortage during World War II he had sidelined his tasting with the preparation and curing of hickory-smoked hams, which he sold in every state in the Union. His recipe is for those long-cured, country-style hams of the South.

Hines Hickory-Smoked Ham

1 (10-pound) hickory-smoked
bone-in ham

6 medium onions, chopped

2¾ cups packed light brown sugar

2 cups cider vinegar or cooking wine

2 bay leaves

24 whole cloves

1 cup dry breadcrumbs

2 teaspoons dry mustard

1 teaspoon ground cloves

Serves 10 to 15

Preheat the oven to 250 degrees. Place the ham facedown
in a roasting pan. Cover loosely with foil and bake
for 1 hour and 15 minutes, or until an instant-read
thermometer inserted in the thickest part of the ham
registers 120 degrees.

Meanwhile, prepare the glaze: In a large heavy saucepan,
combine the onions, 2 cups of the brown sugar, the
vinegar, bay leaves, and whole cloves. Bring to boil over
medium heat, whisking constantly; reduce the heat to
low and simmer gently, stirring occasionally, for 20 to
25 minutes. Set aside.

In a small bowl, combine the remaining ¾ cup brown
sugar, the breadcrumbs, mustard, and ground cloves.
When the ham is ready to be taken from the oven, remove
the foil. Brush all over with the brown sugar–onion glaze,
making sure to get the sides and the bottom. Then pour
the breadcrumb mixture over the top and pat it into
the glaze.

Return the ham to the oven and bake uncovered for
30 to 45 minutes, until the internal temperature reaches
150 degrees and ham is glazed and browned. Place the
roasting pan on a wire rack and let the ham rest for 15 to
20 minutes. Carve the ham off the bone in very thin slices
and serve.

Clara's Buttermilk Biscuits

2 cups all-purpose flour

1 teaspoon baking powder

¾ teaspoon salt

¼ teaspoon baking soda

¼ cup vegetable shortening

¾ to 1 cup buttermilk

Makes 14

Preheat the oven to 450 degrees.

Sift the flour, baking powder, salt, and baking soda into a large bowl. Using 2 knives or just your fingers, cut in the shortening until the mixture resembles cornmeal. Pour in enough buttermilk for the dry ingredients to come together into soft dough. On a lightly floured surface using a floured rolling pin, roll out the dough ½ inch thick. Cut out biscuit shapes with a floured 2-inch biscuit cutter and place them on an ungreased baking sheet. Bake for 15 minutes, or until the biscuits are golden brown on top. Serve immediately.

Note: This recipe makes 14 biscuits. In Duncan Hines's opinion that's servings for 2.

HINES CALLED PLAIN UNITED States cooking the best in the world. Traditional foods he found survived in all sections and he urged cooks everywhere not to let these provincial treasures die by nonuse. Much of our best cooking, he told me, is of native origin, deriving its authority from the preservation of natural, rather than from the invention of artificial, flavors.

New England, he believed, had done the best job bringing her local dishes to fame. "It makes my mouth water," Mr. Hines told me, "to think of the baked Indian porridge as it is prepared at Toll House, Whitman, Mass. That's the kind of dessert, he says, "that makes a fellow wish for hollow legs."

Baked Indian Pudding

3 tablespoons yellow cornmeal

3 cups milk

⅓ cup molasses

1 large egg

½ cup sugar

1 tablespoon unsalted butter, melted

½ teaspoon ground ginger

½ teaspoon ground cinnamon

½ teaspoon salt

Serves 6

Preheat the oven to 300 degrees. Grease a 1½-quart baking dish.

Scald the milk in a large heavy saucepan. Gradually add the cornmeal to the scalded milk and cook, stirring constantly, until slightly thickened and the mixture just comes to a boil. Remove from the heat and stir in the molasses. Set aside.

In a large bowl, beat the egg with the sugar, butter, ginger, cinnamon, and salt. Gradually add the mixture to the hot cornmeal mixture; mix well. Pour into the prepared dish and bake for 2 hours. Serve in small cups or bowls.

ANOTHER KIND OF PIE that got the Hines' blessing was the tamale, the one he discovered in Los Angeles at La Palma Cafeteria and known throughout the Southwest. This holds a delectable filling of ground steak with ripe pitted olives, with grated cheese, with green peppers of the hot, hot kind, yet not hot enough to make the mouth smoke.

Cornmeal is the nutritious backbone of the dish.

Upside-Down Tamale Pie

2 tablespoons vegetable oil

1 medium onion, minced

1 clove garlic, minced

1 green bell pepper, cored, seeded, and minced

1 pound ground beef

¼ pound ground pork

1 (28-ounce) can chopped tomatoes

½ cup chopped black olives

2 teaspoons salt

1 teaspoon freshly ground black pepper

1 teaspoon cayenne pepper

½ cup grated cheddar cheese

1½ cups yellow cornmeal

1 teaspoon chili powder

3 cups boiling chicken stock or water

3 tablespoons unsalted butter

Serves 6 to 8

Heat the oil in a large heavy-bottomed skillet over medium heat. Add the onion, garlic, and green pepper and sauté until lightly browned, 4 to 5 minutes. Add the ground beef and pork to the pan and brown lightly, about 5 more minutes. Add the tomatoes, olives, 1 teaspoon of the salt, the black pepper, and cayenne. Bring the mixture to a boil, then reduce the heat to low and simmer uncovered for 1 hour, stirring occasionally to prevent sticking on the bottom.

Preheat the oven to 375 degrees. Grease a 2-quart casserole.

In a large saucepan, whisk together the cheese, cornmeal, chili powder, chicken stock, and the remaining 1 teaspoon salt. Place over medium-high heat and bring to a boil, whisking constantly. Reduce the heat to medium-low and simmer, whisking occasionally, until thick and smooth, 6 to 8 minutes. Remove from heat and stir in the butter. Pour the cornmeal mixture into the prepared casserole. Pour the meat mixture over the top. Bake for 20 minutes, or until the filling is bubbling. Serve immediately.

IN A MORE DELICATE mood is the crab custard, another California Hines' choice, as it was made in Orick, at the Valley Green Lodge. Sweet lumps of crabmeat are baked in a rich sauce, scented of onion, zested with Tabasco, and bedded under a blanket of well-buttered crumbs.

Crab Custard

4 tablespoons (½ stick) unsalted butter

1 teaspoon finely chopped onion

¼ cup all-purpose flour

1 teaspoon salt

Freshly ground black pepper

4 cups whole milk

½ cup half-and-half

Dash of Tabasco sauce

1 teaspoon A.1. or other steak sauce

4 large eggs

1 tablespoon sherry wine

3 cups jumbo lump crabmeat

1 cup crushed butter crackers such as Ritz crackers

Sliced avocado and olives, optional

Serves 4 to 6

Preheat the oven to 325 degrees. Grease a 1½-quart casserole.

In the top portion of a double boiler over simmering water, melt the butter. Add the onion and cook until translucent, about 3 minutes. Whisk in the flour, salt, and pepper, then whisk in the milk, half-and-half, Tabasco, and steak sauce. Raise the heat and cook over boiling water until thickened, 5 to 7 minutes, stirring constantly. Remove from the heat and set aside to cool slightly.

In a large bowl, beat the eggs. Slowly whisk in the sherry and then, even more slowly and gently, the milk mixture, stirring constantly. Line the bottom of the prepared casserole with the crabmeat. Pour the sauce over and sprinkle with the cracker crumbs. Bake for 1 hour, or until a knife inserted comes out clean. If desired, garnish the top with avocado slices and olives. Serve immediately.

EVERY SOUTHERN STATE HAS a stew of note and inevitably a masterpiece. But in Kentucky give the laurel to burgoo, the national dish. It is the stew for celebrating the Kentucky Derby, election day, or any victories and all auspicious events of the sporting and political world. And burgoo picnics are famous in the annals of Kentucky life.

Burgoo is a vegetable soup made thick with beef and chicken cooked for long hours outdoors in iron kettles and served in tin cups.

Burgoo events are usually managed by burgoo masters and stew chefs who seldom cook anything else.

Here is a recipe we have from Cissy Gregg, food home consultant for the Louisville *Courier Journal,* taken from her cookbook and a guide to gracious living. Cissy is an authority on special Kentuckian fine dishes and their history.

Cissy's Kentucky Burgoo

2 pounds pork shank

2 pounds veal shank

2 pounds beef shank

2 pounds lamb breast

1 (4-pound) hen, cut into 8 pieces

8 quarts water

1½ pounds russet potatoes, peeled and diced

2 medium onions, diced

2 cups diced carrots

1 cup diced green bell pepper

2 cups fresh or frozen okra rounds

1 cup diced celery

2 cups chopped cabbage

2 cups fresh or frozen whole corn kernels

1 cup fresh or frozen lima beans

1 medium fresh hot red pepper, quartered

1 quart tomato puree

1 tablespoon Tabasco sauce

1 tablespoon A.1. or other steak sauce

1 tablespoon Worcestershire sauce

Salt and cayenne pepper

½ cup chopped parsley leaves

Serves 25

Combine all the meat in a very large heavy stockpot and add the water. Place over medium-high heat and bring to a boil. Reduce the heat and simmer until the meat is tender enough to fall from the bones, about 2 hours. Remove the meat from stock.

When the meat is cool enough to handle, discard the skin and bones and chop the meat. Return the meat to the stock and add the remaining ingredients except the parsley. Return the mixture to a boil, then reduce the heat and simmer until thick, 25 to 30 minutes, stirring frequently with a long-handled wooden paddle or spoon during the first part of the cooking and almost constantly after it gets thick. (Burgoo should be very thick, but still "soupy.") Season along the way with salt and pepper, but not too much, until it is almost done. Add chopped parsley just before stew is served.

Fred's Brunswick Stew

1 (3- to 5-pound) hen (stewing chicken)

3 tablespoons salt, plus more to taste

½ pound salt pork or bacon

Corn cut from 6 medium ears

5 medium onions, chopped

1 pound fresh or frozen sliced okra

2 pounds fresh or frozen lima beans

2 medium green bell peppers, cored, seeded, and chopped

5 large tomatoes, quartered

¼ teaspoon Tabasco sauce

Freshly ground black pepper

Serves 10

Wash the hen thoroughly and pat it dry. Place the hen in a large heavy stockpot and cover with water. Add the salt and salt pork. Bring to a boil over medium-high heat, then lower the heat and simmer gently until the meat separates from the bones, about 3 hours.

Transfer the hen from the stock to a cutting board or bowl and set aside until cool enough to handle, about 20 minutes. Pull the meat from the bones, saving the bones for stock and discarding the skin. Put the hen back into the reserved cooking liquid and add the remaining ingredients. Place over medium-high heat and bring to a boil, then reduce the heat to low so that the stew barely simmers and cook uncovered, stirring often to prevent sticking, until it is thick and mushy, about 3 hours. Season with salt and pepper and serve in warm bowls.

A TEN-GALLON IRON WASHPOT

Just mention old-fashioned Brunswick stew, one of the deep South's regional dishes, and if there are as many as two southerners within earshot get ready for an argument with strong opinions expressed on both sides. We know that talking about a favorite Brunswick stew is heading for trouble. So pretending complete ignorance of the subject, saying not a word that we have a favorite Brunswick stew recipe in hand from Virginia, we asked our friend Conrad Frederick Smith, born in Trenton, Tennessee, a fine cook and first-class trencherman, for his recipe. Although he lives in New York he describes himself in a slightly homesick tone as a transplanted southerner.

Fred wrote us nearly a chapter on Brunswick stew, originated in Brunswick County, Virginia, Brunswick County, North Carolina, or maybe Brunswick, Georgia. Fred admits that Brunswick stew is a kissin' cousin to the Kentucky burgoo that has both chicken and squirrel. He tells, "When I get that run-down feeling New Yorkers call 'nerves' I take the Brunswick stew cure in Tennessee and they make it plenty good.

"In Augusta, Georgia, in the midst of the barbecue belt, I had the stew served from a ten-gallon iron washpot in which it was made. It requires several hours' cooking time. If it's a big southern barbecue young hogs sixty to ninety pounds are dressed out and laid on green poles over a pit of coals, late afternoon, say four o'clock. After slow cooking and frequent basting the meat is just about right at noon next day. Regarding the burgoo, the chickens go in first to be simmered down until the meat is ready to slip from the bones. Then the vegetables are added to be cooked down slowly until they lose identification. A good stew master doesn't mind an occasional grain of corn or a solitary butter bean showing up, but he insists that the onions, okra, tomatoes, peppers, and other vegetables be cooked into a thick mushy substance. By this time the piece of salt pork or cured ham and the chicken are as one. The stew is served in bowls or deep paper plates and eaten with a spoon. Brunswick stew is served in many restaurants in the South, but you have to know just where to find the right one." So closing, Fred enclosed his own recipe.

WEST VIRGINIA

Creating new dishes, the quick-to-do and lovely-to-eat kind, is the hobby of Helen Pavlech, a career girl of Morgantown, W.Va. Helen is a microbiologist at the West Virginia University Medical Center and shares a home with a sister and brother. They take turns at housework and cooking. When it comes to Helen's turn at the range, everybody's happy, especially Helen.

———————————

She enjoys entertaining small groups. Her first rule in cooking is that a minimum of time and effort be required. Frequently, she impulsively invites guests for dinner when she hasn't the slightest notion what there is to serve until she gets home. Even before she takes her coat off, she scans the pantry supplies, the refrigerator, the freezer.

As a rule she plans to serve an hour after she gets in from work. She has a ready-for-anything supply shelf stocked with canned and dehydrated foods, and a choice of frozen foods in the freezer. So entertaining is never an ordeal. She boats, "I can prepare a meal for 12 people without notice." After scanning the stockpile, she plans the dinner while she changes from her office clothes to a housecoat. It is then that she creates the delightful surprises for her guests, and in fact, the dish is often a surprise even to herself. The recipe here is one she invented using leftover vegetables, tuna fish, and eggs.

Helen's Hot Tuna

1 (7½-ounce) can good-quality tuna fish, preferably imported Italian, drained and flaked

1 pound leftover vegetables, chopped (15 ounces frozen vegetables, thawed, may be substituted)

¼ pound mushrooms, thinly sliced

1 tablespoon onion powder

½ teaspoon dried parsley

4 large eggs, lightly beaten

½ teaspoon seasoned salt

Salt and freshly ground black pepper

2 tablespoons unsalted butter

Serves 4

In a large bowl, combine all the ingredients except the butter. Stir until well blended. Melt the butter in a heavy 8- or 9-inch skillet over medium heat. Pour in the fish mixture, reduce the heat to medium-low, cover, and cook, stirring occasionally, until firm, about 30 minutes. Cut the casserole into quarters. Serve hot with a tossed salad and hot biscuits.

FLORIDA

FLORIDA

There is a tendency to classify as southern all cooking done below the Mason-Dixon line. A mistaken idea. Every section of the South, I find, has its own particular recipes, and of these they are mighty proud, mighty proud. . . .

Florida, for example, has cooking completely different from her next-door neighbor. Georgia tells of her Brunswick stew, fried chicken, beaten biscuits, brandied peaches. A far cry from Florida's hushpuppies, mullet and other fish favorites, such as the pompano. the king fish, red snapper and hard crab.

There are other fish which the amateur fisherman catches from time to time, and most excellent. One is the beautiful dolphin of delicate flesh, to serve with a Hollandaise sauce or melted butter. Another is the common bonita which, when small, may be served split and broiled, accompanied by a sauce sharp of mustard.

Florida cooking on the west coast and the southern tip has a Spanish flavor. It was in Tampa I started my tasting of the state's specialties, then east and south to Miami and on to Key West where things are grown, caught, and raised like nowhere else. Not only fish—it's a coconut, pineapple, banana country. You can pick and eat your fill of mangoes, papayas, sapodilla, loquats, as well as oranges and grapefruit.

There are avocados, guavas, limes, and the sea grapes. Every dooryard has a few fruit trees for shade, avocado and mango being the most common.

When you visit Tampa, Florida, hail a taxicab, say "Ybor City." In less than fifteen minutes you are in the heart of America's little Spain. There on the outskirts of Tampa is a truly Spanish community where only a few years ago señoritas wore mantillas to the public marketplace.

Little Spain came into being before the turn of the century when Y. M. Ybor, a cigar tycoon of Havana, moved his business to Tampa. With him came thousands of Cuban cigar makers to live near the factory, and Ybor City was born.

The colorful Latin atmosphere has dimmed in recent decades. But several of the original Spanish cafés and restaurants remain, catering to the Spanish taste with pungent viands. The largest of these is the Columbia, serving Spanish food in six ornate dining rooms, serving more than half a million meals in a year.

This restaurant was started as a corner bar by Casimiro Hernandez, of Havana, who came to Ybor City in 1905. Soon he added a room and called it La Fonda, "the meeting place," to serve chicken with rice and his Spanish bean soup.

Casimiro's four boys were brought up helping Papa and took over the business when the father died. Papa's little corner place is now three stories high and half a block long. The decoration is more Spanish than Spain. In the room called La Fonda there are two hundred squares of tile portraying the life of Don Quixote.

I ate dinner in the patio where palms grow in tubs. In the center of this room is a fountain statue that came from Naples, a terracotta replica of the original one found in the ruins of Pompeii. Here decoration is a part of the show but so are the dark-faced waiters who speak in rippling Spanish. Best lure of all is the excellent food.

I had many, too many, dishes. First Florida's stone crabs with the magnificent red and onyx claws, thoughtfully cracked, holding their little miracles of sweet meat. Next black beans and rice, a hearty dish served in a soup bowl. The waiter put in rice and over this a tablespoonful of chopped mild onion; next the beans, now a dash of vinegar and olive oil. I ate that and went right on to chicken and yellow rice, which is one of the house's favorite dishes, done Valencia style.

Dessert was a Mexican custard flavored with anisette and I am giving you this recipe. Also the chicken dish is detailed.

Arroz con Pollo

½ cup vegetable oil

4 chicken drumsticks or thighs

1 tablespoon salt, plus more for seasoning the chicken

Freshly ground black pepper

1 onion, chopped

2 cloves garlic, minced

1 medium green bell pepper, cored, seeded, and chopped

¾ cup chopped tomatoes

3 cups water

1 bay leaf

Pinch of saffron

1 cup uncooked white long-grain rice

¼ cup cooked small green peas, optional

1 tablespoon pimiento peppers, optional

Serves 4

Preheat the oven to 350 degrees.

Heat the oil in a large deep skillet with a lid over medium-high heat. Season the chicken pieces with salt and pepper and fry, turning, until well browned, about 8 minutes total. Transfer the chicken to paper towels to drain; let the rendered fat remain in the pan. Reduce the heat to medium-low and add the onion, garlic, and green pepper; cook, stirring occasionally, until the vegetables soften, about 5 minutes. Add the tomatoes and water, bring to a simmer, and cook for 5 minutes. Add the bay leaf, 1 tablespoon salt, the saffron, and rice. Lay the chicken pieces on top of the mixture, cover, and bake for 20 to 25 minutes, until the chicken is tender and the rice is just done. Garnish with the peas and pimientos, if you like.

Flan

3 cups sugar

½ cup water

6 large eggs

1 tablespoon anisette or
other favorite liqueur

1 teaspoon vanilla extract

Dash of grated nutmeg

Dash of salt

2 cups boiled milk

Serves 8

Preheat the oven to 350 degrees. Set eight 6-ounce ramekins in a large roasting pan.

In a medium saucepan, combine 1 cup of the sugar and the water and place over medium-high heat. Cook, stirring, until the sugar is dissolved and the mixture becomes amber in color, about 6 minutes. Immediately pour the caramel into the ramekins, tilting them to coat the bottoms. Let the caramel cool completely in the ramekins.

In a large bowl, beat the eggs until frothy. Add the remaining 2 cups sugar, the anisette, vanilla, nutmeg, and salt and beat well. Gradually whisk in the milk and pour the custard mixture into the caramel–coated ramekins. Carefully pour enough hot water into the roasting pan to reach halfway up the sides of the cups. Cover the roasting pan with foil and bake for 30 to 40 minutes, until the custard is firm and set but the centers are still jiggly. Transfer the pan to a roasting rack and let cool for 10 minutes in the water. Transfer the cups out of the roasting pan to wire racks to cool completely, then cover the flans with plastic wrap and refrigerate overnight.

When ready to serve, loosen edges of custard with a sharp knife and turn the ramekins upside down so that the caramel tops the custard.

WITH FOND FEELINGS FOR La Fonda feasting I wanted to eat Spanish again, and home-style for a change, not always in restaurants. So I called my friend Barbara Clendinen, Food Editor of the Tampa *Tribune* there, to ask advice. She said Mrs. Eliot Fletcher entertains beautifully and knows Spanish foods. Mrs. Fletcher was Bertha Corral, daughter of the late Manuel, one of Tampa's leading cigar manufacturers, the family prominent in the city. Husband Eliot Fletcher is rated as one of Florida's top-notch architects. It was with Barbara's help that a dinner party was planned at the Fletcher home in Beach Park, the menu to center around the famed local dish, the Spanish *boliche*.

The Fletchers' kitchen is sun-bright; it's copper-bright with a long row of shiny copper-bottomed utensils. Here Mrs. Fletcher spends hours experimenting with new recipes, for she dearly loves cooking, an art she learned from her mother. Her deep-fat fryer is her favorite piece of equipment. This she used to make the plantain chips, passed crisp and salty with the cocktails.

Dinner was served family style, Mr. Fletcher carving the *boliche,* which is a fixed-up eye of the round. Mrs. Fletcher gave me the recipe, also this chicken *cerola* (recipes follow). Both dishes she learned in her mother's kitchen, both dishes came from Spain.

"Boliche"

8 strips salt pork or bacon
(each strip about 1 x 3 x ¼ inch)

1 (3½- to 4-pound) brisket of beef

8 strips ham (each strip
about 1 x 3 x ¼ inch)

32 pimiento-stuffed olives

4 cloves garlic, finely chopped
and crushed to a paste

4 tablespoons olive oil

¼ cup lime juice

½ cup white wine

¼ cup chopped parsley

1 cup coarsely chopped onions

1 teaspoon salt

About 2 cups beef stock

Serves 6 to 8

Bring a medium saucepan of water to a boil; add the
salt pork or bacon and simmer for about 2 minutes to
soften. Drain and set aside. Remove the silver skin and
fat from the beef and wipe the beef with a damp cloth
or paper towels.

Take a sharp, slender knife and, holding it at a 45-degree
angle from the beef, make 16 deep incisions, wide enough
to accommodate the strips of pork and ham, almost
through the meat from end to end. Fill the incisions
with strips of salt pork and ham. Make 8 more incisions
and fill with the olives, stuffing the fillings in with
your fingers.

In a small bowl, combine the garlic with 1 tablespoon
of the oil and rub it over the beef. Place the beef in a
shallow pan. Pour the lime juice over the beef, then add
the wine, parsley, onions, and salt. Cover and refrigerate
in the marinade for at least 8 hours or overnight, turning
occasionally so that all sides are marinated.

When ready to cook, preheat the oven to 325 degrees.
Remove the meat from the marinade, scraping off all
of the onions and reserving them for later. Reserve the
marinade and pat the beef dry. Heat the remaining
3 tablespoons oil in a Dutch oven with a tight-fitting lid
over medium-high heat. Brown the meat on all sides,
10 to 12 minutes total. Pour the marinade back over the

meat and add enough beef stock to cover the meat about halfway. Cover the pot tightly and bring to a simmer. Remove from the stovetop and bake for 3½ to 4 hours, until fork-tender. Remove the meat, skim the excess fat from the gravy, and strain into a blender or food processor along with the onions and puree the mixture until smooth. Let the meat rest for a few minutes, then slice it across the grain ½ inch thick and serve on a warm platter, topped with the pureed onion-gravy mixture.

Chicken "Cerola"

1 (2- to 3-pound) chicken, cut into 8 pieces

1 clove garlic, cut in half

1 teaspoon salt

3 tablespoons lemon juice

¼ cup white wine

1 bay leaf

3 tablespoons vegetable oil

1 tablespoon all-purpose flour

¼ cup chopped onion

¼ cup chopped green bell pepper

1 cup diced carrots

½ cup sherry wine

Serves 2 to 4

Wash and dry the chicken pieces completely. Rub the pieces of chicken with the cut side of the garlic and sprinkle with the salt. Arrange the chicken pieces in a large heavy-bottomed pot. Mince the cut garlic and add it to the pot, along with the lemon juice, wine, and bay leaf. Cover and marinate in the refrigerator for about 2 hours, turning a few times if the marinade doesn't completely cover the pieces.

When ready to cook, preheat the oven to 350 degrees.

Remove the chicken pieces from the marinade and reserve the marinade. Heat the oil in a large pan over medium heat and brown the chicken on all sides, turning as needed, about 8 minutes total. Transfer the chicken to paper towels to drain. Add the flour to the drippings remaining in the pan, stirring until smooth, and cook for 3 to 5 minutes. Add the onion, green pepper, and carrots and cook for 1 minute more. Pour in the reserved marinade and heat through, 1 to 2 minutes. Arrange the browned chicken in a 2-quart casserole and pour the contents of the skillet over the chicken. Add the sherry to the casserole, cover, and bake for about 40 minutes, until no pink shows at the bone of the chicken pieces. Serve immediately.

THE WAY LED ACROSS Tampa Bay by Gandy Causeway where the pelicans rocked on the waves under the open sun. Into St. Petersburg and through the town proper, and then beyond to Gulf Boulevard. There, behind a barricade of plantings stretched a long, low house facing the Gulf of Mexico, its water-ward side made with glass walls.

This is the home of Mrs. Whitney Payne and daughter, Mrs. Eleanor O'Shea. And it's home to a parakeet family, home to Corky, a toy Boston bull, ruler of the ranch. It's a home to friends innumerable down from the North for a few winter weeks.

On a sunny Sunday, the Paynes' curve of sand is a posy bed; red and blue flash the beach pads, candy-striped the beach umbrellas; white wicker furniture on the terrace, cool-looking as ice cream. Green water breaks on the shore, wave upon wave in endless repetition. The living-room and dining-room doors open wide to terrace and beach. The clink of ice is a merry sound; long, cool drinks are in the making. When the sun slides into the sea, and the west runs out of gold, the breeze comes chilly.

Appetites are braced. Everybody is ready for a piping-hot dish. It's always a casserole Eleanor makes for the crowd. Here is one of her most borrowed recipes.

Seafood Casserole

3 sticks (1½ cups) unsalted butter

3 tablespoons all-purpose flour

3 (12-ounce) cans evaporated milk

2 tablespoons plus 1½ teaspoons salt

¼ teaspoon freshly ground
black pepper

1 tablespoon Worcestershire sauce

1 tablespoon capers

6 tablespoons grated
Parmesan cheese

1 teaspoon sweet paprika

2 quarts water

1 pound medium raw shrimp,
peeled and deveined

2 cups scallops

1 pound flounder fillet

½ pound canned or fresh crabmeat

2½ cups cooked lobster meat

2 tablespoons sherry wine

½ cup dry breadcrumbs

FLORIDA

Serves 6

Generously grease a 3-quart casserole.

Melt the butter in a large heavy-bottomed saucepan
over low heat. Gradually stir in the flour and whisk to a
smooth, thin paste. Pour in 1 can of the evaporated milk
and cook, stirring constantly, until the mixture begins
to thicken, 3 to 4 minutes. Gradually add the remaining
2 cans of evaporated milk and cook for 5 minutes longer,
stirring occasionally. Add 1½ teaspoons of the salt, the
pepper, Worcestershire sauce, capers, 2 tablespoons of the
cheese, and the paprika; the mixture should be pale pink.

In a large pot, bring the water to boil, then reduce the
heat to a simmer and add the shrimp, scallops, and the
remaining 2 tablespoons salt. Simmer for 2 minutes;
add the flounder and cook for an additional 3 minutes,
or until all the shellfish and fish are tender. Drain and
transfer to a bowl and add the crabmeat and lobster.
Using a fork, flake the scallops, flounder, crabmeat, and
lobster into bite-size pieces. Add the seafood to the cream
sauce and stir in the sherry. Pour the mixture into the
prepared casserole and refrigerate for 40 minutes.

Preheat the oven to 300 degrees.

When ready to cook the casserole, remove it from the refrigerator, top it with the breadcrumbs and the remaining 4 tablespoons cheese, and bake for 40 minutes, or until bubbling and browned on top. Serve immediately, piping hot.

DRIVE EAST FROM St. Petersburg to Miami, right across the state. On the eastern side one discovers that the original flavor of Florida's cooking has become submerged by an influx of people from everywhere. Search for native foods and you can find them of course, *coquina* broth, the stone crab and dishes like *bollos calientes* showing the Spanish influence. But the day-by-day eating, and particularly so in vacation city Miami, is much the same as one would eat in Junction City, Kansas. Winter visitors at the beach hotels eat exactly as they would in the big hotels the world over—the Ritz in Paris, Excelsior in Rome, the Palace in San Francisco. The real-estate boom, the retirement lure to the land of sunshine to bake an arthritic knee, has brought food to Florida from every state.

But these "dishes from home" take on a new character over a period of time, a Florida flavor influenced by the abundance of easily available fruits. Mrs. L. K. McCormick told me that this has happened to her since she and her husband moved from Cleveland, Ohio, to North Miami.

"My four-egg sponge cake," she said, "I have made for years, but only after I moved here did I start using a fresh orange-juice frosting. Apple pudding I now serve with an orange sauce." She pointed to her backyard. "You see why? We have our own orange trees—four of them." In a half-acre plot back of the kitchen I counted in addition to the orange trees, three grapefruit trees, one kumquat, several coconuts. But women everywhere can buy these same fruits fresh from their corner grocery store.

"Try a piece of my coconut candy," my hostess invited. "This too is something I have made only since living here. Fresh coconut is what I use," she said, "but the wet-pack canned coconut would be all right."

Four-Egg Sponge Cake

4 large eggs, separated

½ teaspoon salt

2 tablespoons cold water

½ cup hot water

1½ cups sugar

1 teaspoon vanilla extract

1½ cups all-purpose flour

½ teaspoon cream of tartar

Orange Icing (recipe follows)

Makes one 10-inch tube cake

Preheat the oven to 325 degrees. Grease a 10-inch tube pan.

In a 3½-quart mixing bowl, beat the egg yolks and ¼ teaspoon of the salt until very thick and light-colored. Add the cold water and beat for 1 minute. Add the hot water and beat for about 5 minutes, until the mixture fills the bowl three quarters full. Gradually beat in the sugar and vanilla until very fluffy, then gradually beat in the flour.

In a medium bowl, beat the egg whites until frothy; add the cream of tartar and the remaining ¼ teaspoon salt and continue beating until stiff but not dry. Using a rubber spatula, gently fold the whites into the egg-yolk mixture.

Pour the batter into the prepared pan and bake for 1 hour, or until a wooden pick or skewer inserted into the center of the cake comes out clean. Invert the pan onto a wire rack and cool for 20 minutes. Cut the cake away from the pan with a sharp knife and turn out on a rack to cool completely. Frost with orange icing.

FLORIDA

Orange Icing

4 tablespoons (½ stick)
unsalted butter

2 cups sifted confectioners' sugar

1 tablespoon grated orange peel

4 to 6 tablespoons orange juice

1 cup sweetened shredded coconut,
finely chopped, plus more
for decoration

Makes about 2 cups

In the medium bowl of an electric mixer, cream the butter with the confectioners' sugar. Add the grated orange peel and enough orange juice to bring the icing to an easy spreading consistency and beat until fluffy. Cover the top and sides of your cake with icing and sprinkle the top with grated coconut.

Apple Pudding

For the apple pudding:

4 tablespoons (½ stick)
unsalted butter, softened

1 cup sugar

1 large egg, well beaten

½ cup sifted all-purpose flour

½ teaspoon ground cinnamon

½ teaspoon grated nutmeg

¼ teaspoon baking soda

1½ cups peeled and chopped Golden Delicious apples (about 2 apples)

For the orange sauce:

½ cup sugar

1 tablespoon cornstarch

½ cup boiling water

½ cup orange juice

2 tablespoons unsalted butter

Serves 4

Preheat the oven to 350 degrees. Grease a 1½-quart baking dish.

In the medium bowl of an electric mixer, cream the butter with the sugar. Beat in the egg. Sift the flour, cinnamon, nutmeg, and baking soda into a small bowl. Beat the dry ingredients into the creamed mixture. Using a rubber spatula, gently fold in the chopped apples. Turn the batter into the prepared dish and bake for about 35 minutes, until the pudding is puffed and browned on top and a wooden pick or skewer inserted into the center comes out clean.

While the cake is in the oven, make the orange sauce: In a medium saucepan, combine the sugar with the cornstarch. Slowly pour in the boiling water, stirring constantly. Place over low heat, bring to a boil, and cook until the liquid is clear, stirring frequently, 5 to 7 minutes. Remove the pan from the heat and whisk in the orange juice and butter until the butter is melted.

Pour the hot sauce over the apple pudding straight from the oven.

MRS. HARRY BEST WAS born in Barcelona, Spain, lived twelve years in Cuba, and then moved with her family to North Miami, where she was married and has lived ever since. I visited this busy little homemaker to talk about cooking. The Home Demonstration Agent for Dade County told me that Mrs. Best was one of her women who cooked with real imagination and with Spanish accents. "Maybe you would like to try my favorite way of using the avocado," my hostess suggested. We sipped iced coffee and balanced a guacamole salad on the arm of our chairs. It's a perfect luncheon dish to serve with bread-and-butter sandwiches.

Mrs. Best invited me for dinner, to sample her family's favorite rice-and-pork combination, savory and filling, a meal in itself.

Cuban Guacamole

2 medium avocados, peeled

1 cup small fresh pineapple chunks

⅓ cup olive oil

⅓ cup lime juice

2 cloves garlic, minced

Salt and freshly ground black pepper

Serves 4 to 6

In a medium bowl, mash the avocados with a fork, allowing some chunks to remain. Stir in the pineapple chunks and set aside. In a small bowl, whisk together the oil, lime juice, and garlic and season with salt and pepper. Pour the dressing over the fruit and chill in the refrigerator for about 20 minutes, stirring occasionally. Serve on lettuce or with corn chips, if you like.

Arroz con Puerco

2 tablespoons vegetable oil

2 small cloves garlic, minced

1 pound lean pork shoulder, cubed

2 pounds salt pork or bacon, cubed

1 medium onion, sliced

1 medium green bell pepper, cored, seeded, and sliced

1 cup uncooked white rice

1 (28-ounce) can chopped tomatoes

¾ cup cooked green peas

¼ cup chopped roasted salted peanuts

Serves 4

Heat the oil in large skillet over medium-low heat. Add half of the garlic and the pork shoulder and brown slowly, stirring occasionally, about 30 minutes.

In a separate skillet, render the salt pork over medium-low heat until translucent and soft, about 12 minutes. Add the remaining garlic, the onion, and green pepper and sauté until the vegetables are golden, about 7 minutes. Pour off all but ½ cup of the fat. Add the rice to the skillet with the vegetables and cook until the grains begin to brown, about 5 minutes. Add the tomatoes and the pork mixture, cover tightly, and simmer until the rice is tender, about 20 minutes. Just before the dish is done, stir in the peas and peanuts. Serve immediately.

Coconut Dulce

3 cups sugar

4 cups water

1 fresh coconut, grated
(about 2½ cups grated coconut)

Makes 4 cups

In a large saucepan, combine the sugar and water, place over medium heat, and bring to a boil; cook, stirring constantly, until the mixture reaches a thin-syrup consistency, about 10 minutes. Add the coconut and cook, stirring occasionally, until it becomes transparent, about 25 minutes. Scrape the mixture into a bowl, cover, and refrigerate until the mixture is chilled and spreadable, at least 2 hours. Serve with cream cheese and saltine crackers or use as a cake filling.

AN ARTIST WITH THE "BOLLOS"

The farther south I traveled the more dishes I met that had their roots in Cuba, Puerto Rico, and other islands southward. *Bollos calientes* are one such novelty, deep-fat-fried fritters made with black-eyed peas, sold hot at street stands.

It was through the state extension department that I heard of Mrs. Mario Martinez, an artist with the *bollos*. A phone call to the lady in Hialeah, a suburb of Miami, resulted in an invitation to see her make the fritters from scratch, or almost.

Mrs. Martinez is a native of the state, born in Live Oak, but married to a Spaniard up from Key West. She learned Spanish cooking as a bride, just to please her man.

Bollos calientes are among his favorite tidbits, but a dish that takes practice. "In the beginning," Mrs. Martinez said, "I made them as a labor of love, but once you get the knack, these are no more bother than making angel-food cake."

Mrs. Martinez makes the fritters once a week for her husband and son, and friends too enjoy the treat. "And sometimes," she admitted, "I make *bollos* just because I like them myself."

It was three years in a row Mrs. Martinez won prizes in Dade County's home-demonstration-club exhibits for her coconut "put-ups." Her coconut palms usually harvest over two hundred fruit in a year. The coconut meat she processes both in moist and dried form.

To pack moist, she grates the meat of a medium-size coconut, adds one-half cup sugar, mixing well, adds one-fourth cup of water (about), just enough to have the meat moist but not wet. This mixture is packed into sterilized pint jars and processed in a hot-water bath forty-five minutes.

She dry-cans by dividing the grated fresh coconut into three parts, one part left natural, one part tinted light pink, one part made pale green with vegetable coloring.

Now spread coconut thinly over a cookie sheet, a light sprinkle of sugar, and into a slow oven (275 degrees) for twenty minutes. The coconut should be thoroughly dry but not brown. Pack into sterilized pint jars, white in middle, green on bottom, pink on top. Process in a hot-water bath thirty minutes.

These two excellent desserts Mrs. Martinez makes with fresh coconut. The *dulce* (see previous page) she serves with a two-inch square of cream cheese and pass the saltines.

Coconut Meringue Pie

1 (9-inch) Perfect Pie Crust (page 13)

3 tablespoons cornstarch

3 tablespoons cold water

3 large eggs, separated

⅛ teaspoon salt

1 teaspoon vanilla extract

1 cup sweetened shredded coconut, finely chopped

2 cups milk

¾ cup plus 6 tablespoons sugar

1 tablespoon unsalted butter

Makes one 9-inch pie

Preheat the oven to 350 degrees. Line a 9-inch glass pie plate with the pastry. Trim the overhang to 1 inch, fold it under itself, and crimp decoratively, if you like. Refrigerate until chilled, about 15 minutes.

Line the pastry with foil and fill with pie weights or dried beans. Bake for 30 minutes, or until nearly cooked through and dry to the touch. Carefully remove the foil and weights and bake for 10 minutes longer, or until golden. Cool completely on a wire rack.

Increase the oven temperature to 425 degrees.

In a small bowl, dissolve the cornstarch in the cold water. In another small bowl, beat the egg yolks with the salt and vanilla. In the top portion of a double boiler over simmering water, heat the coconut and milk, stirring to combine. Add ¾ cup of the sugar and the butter, then add the dissolved cornstarch. Cook, stirring constantly, until the mixture thickens to the consistency of sour cream, about 8 minutes. Add the egg yolk mixture and cook for 1 minute longer, stirring constantly. Pour the mixture into the prepared pie shell and let it cool for 5 minutes.

In the meantime, in a medium bowl of an electric mixer, beat the egg whites at medium speed until foamy; gradually add the remaining 6 tablespoons sugar and beat until the whites are stiff but not dry. Spoon the meringue onto the top of the pie and spread it to the edges of the crust. Bake until the meringue is golden brown, about 7 minutes. Cool completely on a wire rack before serving.

THE MOBILE WAY OF LIFE

One can't talk about cooking in Florida and overlook our modern gypsy queens who cook in trailer kitchens. Trailer parks cover hundreds of acres and each park is a model town in itself with a manager-mayor, recreation hall, garden club, swimming pool.

How do these trailer cooks cook? With a bit of conniving, it was arranged for me to visit with the women in the Bell Haven Park in northwestern Miami.

I couldn't believe my eyes! No wonder two million Americans have adopted the mobile way of life. I don't know what I expected to see, certainly not three-legged gypsy pots over open fires. Yet not what I saw—efficient, compact little kitchens designed for easy cooking, for effortless work. Most of the trailers I looked into, half a hundred at least, have automatic dishwashers, garbage disposers, eye-level ovens, double sinks, huge refrigerators, automatic washing machines. Trailer cooks have it better than kitchenette cooks. But like the gypsies of old, one-dish meals are preferred: done top-stove or in the oven depending on the weather.

First stop was to visit park manager Frederick J. Bird and his wife Selma. They lived in a thirty-six-foot cruiser—three rooms, over seven feet wide, wall to wall; two porch enclosures, north side, south side. Spaciousness is the first impression on entering the living room, efficiency next, then the luxuriousness of the furnishings. There was wall-to-wall carpet, built-in television, radio, fold-away tables, comfort-able sofa, easy chairs, complete electrical equipment including air conditioner.

But I came to see the kitchen. Mrs. Bird stood in the center of her workroom and pivoted a half turn in each direction to show me that she could reach sink, range, refrigerator, work counter, and cupboards and never take a step. "No bend, no stoop, no squat," she said. Mrs. Bird had a job in the city, so like any career woman, she planned supper menus that get together in a jiffy. Her Sunday dinners are more elaborate. A favorite is a three-dish meal: fried chicken, scalloped potatoes, this from her Norwegian mother, and a green vegetable salad. Fresh fruit for dessert; add a beverage and dinner is served.

Mr. Bird took me touring his town down streets palm-lined. We stopped to talk with Mrs. James Raferty. She and her husband, a commercial photographer, have been trailering since 1937. Mrs. Raferty does all her housework and the washing and ironing; she does all the dressmaking for her teenage daughters Judy and Jean. In fifteen years the Rafertys had had five trailers, lived in five cities and made five thousand friends. Mrs. Raferty cooks one-dish meals, mostly top-stove. "I'm quite proud of my chili," she admitted modestly. "It's easy to make and doesn't need watching."

Mr. and Mrs. George Haydu of Plainfield, New Jersey, leave their twelve-room stand-still home in mid-January to enjoy Florida's semitropical winter. The two children are taken along and enrolled for the spring term of school in Miami. The Haydu trailer is three-and-a-half-room size with two bedrooms, with combination living room, dinette, and kitchen, with enclosed all-aluminum patio.

Mrs. Haydu calls cooking her recreation. Her husband is Hungarian and just to please him she makes a meatball casserole (recipe follows), the recipe one of his mother's.

The Arthur A. Yatkins of Hartford, Connecticut, had one of the park's most luxurious trailer homes with patio and porch and fenced-in yard—you enter by gate. In the back the children had their sandpile and Daddy his barbecue.

Mr. Yatkin is owner of a drugstore chain, headquarters Hartford, but he was a week-end commuter to Miami where his family was living five months in the year, taking chaffeur and cook. Sunday was help's day off, and Mr. and Mrs. Yatkin did the meal-getting. Spaghetti and meatballs were Arthur's specialty. It's the sauce, he admitted, that is terrific!

Selma's Scalloped Potatoes

6 medium russet potatoes, peeled and cut into ¼-inch slices

6 tablespoons unsalted butter

Salt and freshly ground black pepper

2 tablespoons all-purpose flour

8 ounces sharp cheddar cheese, grated

2 cups whole milk

Serves 4 to 6

Preheat the oven to 350 degrees. Grease a 2-quart casserole.

Place one third of the potato slices in the bottom the casserole, dot the tops of them with one third of the butter, season with salt and pepper, dust with 1 tablespoon of the flour, and cover with one third of the cheese. Use one third of the remaining potatoes to make a second layer, top with one third of the remaining butter, season with salt and pepper, and add the remaining 1 tablespoon flour and one third of the remaining cheese. Add a third and final layer of potatoes and butter and season with salt and pepper. Pour the milk over the casserole and top with the remaining cheese. Bake for 1 hour, or until the potatoes are tender and the casserole is golden and bubbling. Remove from the oven and let rest for 5 minutes. Serve hot, with fried chicken and a mixed green salad, if you like.

Mrs. Haydu's Hungarian Meatballs

2 pounds ground chuck

1 teaspoon salt

¼ teaspoon freshly ground black pepper

1 onion, minced

1 clove garlic, crushed

¾ cup tomato juice

1 large egg

1 cup finely ground breadcrumbs

3 tablespoons vegetable oil

Serves 6 to 8

In a large bowl, combine all of the ingredients except the oil and ½ cup of the breadcrumbs. Using a tablespoon, form the mixture into balls and roll the bolls in the remaining breadcrumbs.

Heat the oil in a large skillet over medium heat, add the meatballs, and cook, turning, for 3 to 4 minutes total, until the meatballs are browned and cooked through. Drain on paper towels and serve immediately.

Mrs. Raferty's
Oatmeal Macaroons

1¼ cups sugar

⅓ cup vegetable shortening

1 large egg

1½ teaspoons vanilla extract

⅔ cup all-purpose flour

5 tablespoons cocoa powder

2 teaspoons baking powder

½ teaspoon salt

⅓ cup whole milk

2½ cups quick-cooking oats

Makes 42 cookies

Preheat the oven to 350 degrees. Grease 2 or 3 large baking sheets.

In the medium bowl of an electric mixer, cream the sugar with the shortening; add the egg and cream again. Blend in the vanilla. Sift the flour, cocoa powder, baking powder, and salt into a medium bowl and add to the shortening mixture alternately with the milk. Stir in the oats.

Drop the batter by tablespoonfuls onto the prepared baking sheets and bake for 12 to 15 minutes, until lightly golden but still moist inside. Cool completely on a wire rack before serving. The macaroons can be stored in an airtight container at room temperature for up to 3 days.

CONCH CHOWDER TO LIME PIE

To Miami and beyond, to that bony finger, the Florida Keys, pointing the way 150 miles south to Key West. It's a four-hour drive down the spectacular overseas highway, U.S. No. 1, to come to a different kind of eating from what I had sampled in any other corner of the nation. I knew what to expect: conch stews, turtle steaks, crawfish dishes, the fresh lime pies. Promises had been given by Annette, wife of artist Robert Eugene Otto, to provide me with real Key West dishes from the Otto family files.

Riding down the Keys, island linked to island by a series of causeways, is like a journey by boat. The world is all water in a scramble of colors—blue into green, pink into lavender, ever-changing as the light changes over coral reefs, over deep undersea ravines, over the shallows of golden sand and the dark seaweed. A ribbon of road and the wind singing in your ears.

At the tip of the Keys is the little coral and limestone island, four miles long and two miles wide, the southernmost point of the United States. Here the plant and animal and bird life is different from that on the mainland—so is the food, Spanish in its seasoning.

It was early morning when I rang the Ottos' doorbell. The beautiful Annette answered, her wavy platinum-blond hair combed severely back and twisted into a bun low on her neck. Her blue-green eyes, I noticed, were as changing as the Gulf waters. She said, "I'm getting dinner. Let's talk in the kitchen."

I had thought a midday meal meant a light luncheon, but real Key Westers, she told me, eat dinner midday, and a real hearty dinner.

By early afternoon the crimson hibiscus are on fire and the heat drives the lizards under the leaves. The bees are still working, but humming "Siesta! Siesta!" It's too hot then to be in the kitchen for more than fixing a cool limeade.

This was a company meal. Luis Marden was coming, a writer for *National Geographic* magazine, visiting the island to report on the annual flower show. Any moment he was due to take pictures of Mrs. Otto in her postage-stamp garden back of the kitchen. Only room there for a table, a few chairs, but see what grows in this brick-paved Eden! Palms of several kinds, the West Indian pavender, the Australian banana, a breadfruit tree, two kumquat trees, and flowers. The African daisies were in bloom; so were the iris; more flowers than I could name!

Our hostess went calmly ahead getting the midday meal despite interruptions. I was underfoot note-taking while she cooked. Her excitable artist-husband was on hand giving background bits regarding Key West's history. He talked about this house his father had built in the West Indian manner, a porch in front, a side porch, and porches upstairs.

The menu on this day was crawfish, that is, rock lobster, done in Newburg, served in a fried-rice ring. Fried plantains and fried breadfruit with this to amaze us visitors from the North. A green salad followed; dessert was the rich guava tarts.

After luncheon in the cool, shaded garden, Mrs. Otto brought out her recipe files to give me her mother-in-law's pot roast, the dried lima bean soup, and exact ingredient amounts for the dishes served at the dinner.

Rustic Lima Bean Soup

2 cups dried lima beans

4 tablespoons vegetable oil

2 tablespoons unsalted butter

½ pound meaty salt pork (rinsed if crusted with salt), cut into ½-inch cubes, or a meaty ham bone or ham hock

4 onions, peeled and quartered

1 cup canned tomatoes

1 clove garlic

1 cup finely chopped celery

2 quarts boiling water

1 teaspoon salt

1 tablespoon Worcestershire sauce

Dash of freshly ground black pepper

Croutons, optional

Serves 6 to 8

Place the beans in a large bowl, pour enough cold water over them to cover, and soak overnight. Drain the beans and put them in a 4-quart saucepan with the oil, butter, salt pork or ham hock, onions, tomatoes, garlic, and celery. Pour in the boiling water and add the salt, Worcestershire sauce, and black pepper. Place over medium–high heat, bring to a boil, then reduce the heat to low and simmer gently for 3 to 4 hours, stirring occasionally to prevent scorching and adding additional boiling water if needed to prevent sticking. Don't strain; serve as is, and garnish with croutons, if desired.

Crawfish Newburg

3 tablespoons unsalted butter

2 tablespoons all-purpose flour

1 cup half-and-half

½ cup whole milk

2 pounds peeled crawfish tails

3 tablespoons tomato paste

2 teaspoons Worcestershire sauce

¼ teaspoon sweet paprika

¼ teaspoon garlic salt

3 tablespoons sherry wine

One-One Fried Rice (recipe follows)

Serves 4

Melt the butter in a large saucepan over medium heat. Add the flour and cook, stirring constantly, for 4 to 5 minutes to form a paste and to begin to brown the flour. Gradually stir in the half-and-half until smooth and slowly pour in the milk. Cook, stirring constantly, until thickened, 3 to 4 minutes more. Add the crawfish tails and cook, stirring occasionally, until they give off some of their liquid, 6 to 8 minutes. Add the tomato paste, Worcestershire sauce, paprika, and garlic salt and cook, stirring constantly, for 3 minutes more. Just before serving, add the sherry. Serve on a mound of one-one fried rice.

One-One Fried Rice

4 tablespoons vegetable oil

1 cup uncooked long-grain white rice

1½ teaspoons salt

2½ cups boiling water

Serves 4

Pour the oil into a large heavy-bottomed skillet, tipping the pan to coat its entire surface. Add the rice, place over low heat, and cook, stirring occasionally, until all the kernels are opaque, 20 to 25 minutes. Add the salt. Increase the heat to medium and cook until the kernels are golden brown, stirring constantly, about 5 minutes more. Reduce the heat to low and add the boiling water. Increase the heat and bring to a boil for 1 minute. Reduce the heat again and cook about 20 minutes longer, until the rice comes out each grain "one-one," as the Key Westers say, meaning each kernel separate. Fluff the rice and serve immediately.

Guava Tarts

2 (½-pound) pieces of puff pastry

2 teaspoons grated nutmeg

1 (15-ounce) bar prepared guava paste, cut evenly into eighths

8 teaspoons unsalted butter

2 teaspoons ground cinnamon

Serves 8

Grease 8 muffin cups from a standard 12-cup muffin pan.

On a lightly floured surface using a rolling pin, roll out the pastry ⅛ inch thick. Using a floured 5½- to 6-inch round cookie cutter, cut the dough into 16 circles. Fit 8 of the pastry rounds into the greased muffin cups. Fill each disk with a slice of the guava paste, then sprinkle each tart with ¼ teaspoon cinnamon and ¼ teaspoon nutmeg and place 1 teaspoon of the butter on top. Fold the remaining circles of puff pastry in half and place over the first pieces. Unfold the circles to enclose the filling, being careful not to trap any air beneath. Gently press the top and bottom edges of the pastry together and refrigerate for about 25 minutes, until the pastry is completely chilled. Make sure there are no open seams or guava paste will leak out.

Preheat the oven to 400 degrees.

Transfer the pan from the refrigerator to the oven and bake for about 30 minutes, until puffed and golden brown on top. Cool the muffin pan on a wire rack for 15 minutes, then gently remove the tarts by sliding 2 large spoons around them. Serve warm.

IT IS THREE BLOCKS from the south end of U.S. 1 to the Caroline Lowe House, the hundred-year-old historic landmark of little Key West, today a restaurant. Here we were headed to eat grouper chowder, to try turtle steak, to indulge in lime pie.

This is the home of Trade Winds, the dining room built to the rear, its kitchen providing the best in conch cookery. What is the meaning of conch cookery? That's difficult to explain except to say its a sort of combination of English and Cuban methods of preparing foods with the recipes changed to meet each cook's needs.

Sitting in the Trade Winds restaurant open to the garden, the air came soft and warm-scented of jasmine, of frangipani. The fragrance was mingled with the odor of turtle steaks broiling over charcoal in the barbecue kitchen, which occupies one corner of the big room.

We started our meal with Key West sautéed shrimp (recipe follows), then followed the turtle steak and hot garlic bread. Eight out of every ten tourists order the turtle steak just to go home and tell neighbors that it tastes very much like veal. Grouper chowder is a meal in a bowl; nevertheless, we had that too. A thick, thick, chowder, hot, wafting the salty aroma of the sea.

Grouper Chowder

1½ cups tomato juice

5 cups water

¼ cup chopped green bell pepper

1 sweet onion, chopped

¼ cup chopped celery

1 clove garlic, minced

2 tomatoes, chopped

2 pounds skinless grouper fillets, cut into 1-inch chunks

½ teaspoon dried thyme

Salt and freshly ground black pepper

¼ cup Sauternes or other sweet wine

Serves 6

FLORIDA

In a large heavy stockpot, combine the tomato juice, water, green pepper, onion, celery, garlic, and tomatoes. Place over medium heat and bring to a boil, then reduce the heat and simmer for about 10 minutes, until the vegetables are soft. Add the fish and continue cooking for 5 minutes, or until the fish is tender. Gently beat the mixture with a wire whisk until the fish is flaked and the vegetables are softened. Add the thyme and season with salt and pepper. Add the Sauternes and serve hot.

Note: For Second-Day Chowder: Reheat the chowder and add 1 cup heavy cream and 1 cup tomato juice. Whisk 2 tablespoons flour with some of the chowder to make a smooth paste, add it to the soup, and cook, stirring, for 5 minutes.

Key West Shrimp Sauté

½ cup (1 stick) unsalted butter

1 clove garlic

4 dozen jumbo shrimp,
peeled and deveined

3 tablespoons finely chopped parsley

½ cup sherry wine

Serves 6

Melt the butter in a large heavy saucepan or skillet over medium heat. Add the garlic and cook for 2 minutes, then remove and discard the garlic. Add the shrimp and sauté for 5 minutes, or until the shrimp are pink. Using a slotted spoon, transfer the shrimp to a warm platter. Add the parsley and sherry to the butter, increase the heat, and sauté for 30 seconds more. Serve the sauce over the shrimp.

Conch Chowder

Juice of 2 small limes or 1 large lime

2 pounds cleaned conch meat, diced

¼ cup vegetable oil

1 green bell pepper, cored,
seeded, and diced

1 onion, diced

2 cloves garlic, minced

1 (6-ounce) can tomato paste

6 cups water

Salt and freshly ground black pepper

1½ pounds new potatoes, quartered

Serves 6

In a medium bowl, toss the lime juice with the conch and cover with plastic wrap. Heat the oil in a large heavy saucepan over medium heat. Add the green pepper, onion, and garlic and sauté until golden brown, about 10 minutes. Add the tomato paste and simmer, stirring occasionally, for 10 minutes. Add the water and season with salt and pepper and bring to a boil. Add the potatoes and simmer until about half done, 10 to 15 minutes. Add the conch meat and cook until the conch and potatoes are tender, 15 to 20 minutes more. Season with salt and pepper again and serve hot.

WRITIN' LADIES NEED A HOT LUNCH

The real point of this Key West visit was to steal a holiday with my long-time friend the late Thelma Strable and eat of Bessie's famous chowder made with the conch, with onions and sweet peppers, "two plugs" of garlic and West Indian magic.

Thelma's novel *Reap the Wild Wind*, first serialized in the *Saturday Evening Post* and later made into a picture produced by Cecil B. De Mille, would never have been written, she told me, "except for Bessie and her cooking, and conch chowder in particular." This combination made a vacation stay in the little town such a thrilling adventure that Thelma decided to build a home there on the farthest point south in the United States. Living there and loving the place is how she came to write the book, its plot laid in that period when Key West was the center of the salvage operations along the Florida Keys.

During the weeks the writing was in progress Bessie took over. "Writin' ladies," she would explain, "need a hot lunch." Conch chowder with a salad appeared day after day.

We have that conch recipe first as Bessie told it, beginning, "The Missus uses six conches. I beats them into bits." Bessie doesn't bother to tell how to get them out of the shell. That's a job she didn't need to do because down on the Keys conches are cooked on the wharves, taken from their shells and peddled "unhoused" to back doors. I am giving you Bessie's directions translated into a recipe for anyone to use in any kitchen provided she can buy a conch.

A COCONUT TO A KEY WESTER means the graceful coconut palm, it means the freshly grated white meat axed from the brown-whiskered nut, the shreds moist of their own rich and flavorsome milk. It means a coconut marshmallow cake baked by Miss Etta Patterson.

It was late afternoon, the trade winds freshening the palms, that I sauntered over to Miss Etta's for a date with a cake. Miss Patterson could tell me more about her house than she could about the cake. She just picked the recipe up somewhere, then went on doing it in her own way.

"I baked it for President Truman when he came on his second visit," she said. "Remember he brought Mrs. Truman and Margaret." She was off to find Mrs. Truman's thank-you note and the recipe.

"But fresh coconuts," I objected, "not everyone can get them."

"I use them, of course," she said, "we grow them here, but 'wet pack' does as well."

Coconut Marshmallow Layer Cake

For the cake:

1 cup (2 sticks) unsalted butter, at room temperature

2 cups sugar

6 large eggs, separated

2 teaspoons lemon juice

2 teaspoons vanilla extract

4 cups pastry flour

2 tablespoons baking powder

½ teaspoon salt

1½ cups whole milk

For the coconut frosting:

1½ cups sugar

½ cup water

6 large egg whites

¼ cup cream of tartar

6 large marshmallows, minced

1 tablespoon lemon juice

10 large marshmallows, thinly sliced into rounds

1½ cups grated sweetened coconut

Serves 12

Preheat the oven to 375 degrees. Grease and flour three 9-inch layer cake pans with removable bottoms.

In a large mixing bowl using an electric mixer, cream the butter; add the sugar, egg yolks, lemon juice, and vanilla. Sift the flour, baking powder, and salt into a separate bowl; add alternately with the milk to the butter mixture. Stiffly beat the egg whites and fold them in.

Pour the batter into the prepared pans and bake for 20 to 25 minutes, until golden brown on top and a wooden pick or skewer inserted into the center of the cake comes out clean. Cool the cakes on wire racks in their pans for 10 minutes, then remove the cakes from the pans and cool completely on the racks.

While the cakes are cooling, make the frosting: In a small pot, combine the sugar and water. Place over medium heat and gently swirl the pot to dissolve the sugar without stirring. Raise the heat to medium-high and bring the mixture to soft-ball stage (238 degrees on a candy thermometer), washing down the inside of the pot with a wet pastry brush as needed to keep sugar crystals from forming.

Toward the end of the boiling, start beating the egg whites: Place them in a medium bowl and, using an electric mixer, beat on low until foamy. Add the cream of tartar, raise the speed to medium-high, and beat until stiff but not dry peaks form.

Add the minced marshmallows to the sugar syrup, but do not stir. With the mixer running on medium, pour the hot sugar syrup with the marshmallows in a thin stream over the beaten egg whites. Raise the speed to high and beat until cooled, stiff, and glossy, about 10 minutes. Stir in the lemon juice.

Trim the tops of the cakes if needed to make flat disks. Ice the cake, distributing the icing, sliced marshmallows, and coconut in between each layer, saving enough to garnish the top.

A MAZE OF CONFLICTING TESTIMONY

Destination: Lime Pie! This trip to Florida I had resolved to search out the finest lime pie in the state and the finest recipe for it. Lime pie followed lime pie punctuated with a maze of conflicting testimony. There is no agreement in the state as to the best way of making the dulcet filling.

The great wrangle regards the kind of limes for juicing. Down in the Keys, where the wild limes grow, everyone uses the little yellow-green fruit with a tang that no other lime can boast. In the citrus-producing areas, especially in Polk County where three-fourths of the citrus of the state is raised, the Persian lime, which grows to a mighty size and green as a jealous eye, is the pie-baker's favorite. And in Polk County I found my blue-ribbon lime pie.

The baker was Mrs. Thomas Swann, wife of one of the state's leading citrus growers. The Swanns' home, Tara Hall, is in Winter Haven on Lake Eloise. A house walled with the pink brick of colonial days, brick 150 years old, brought from England as ship ballast. But what I wish you could have seen was Mrs. Swann's dinner table. At one end a tall epergne, its tiered bowls filled with summer flowers. At the opposite end of the table, handy to our host, a southern ham, which had spent two mellowing years in the smokehouses on the Swanns' farm near Knoxville, Tennessee. With the ham came a baked papaya dish that was new to me; baked sweet potatoes, mashed, seasoned, served half-shell.

After the main course came the pie. "Isn't it a beauty?" Tom Swann said with a nod. It stood four inches high, capped with peaks of meringue wearing an even sun tan. The knife cut through the soft filling, through the tender crust, as smoothly as scissors cut through silk. Mrs. Swann lifted a slice for our admiration. I tasted hopefully. The filling was fragile as spindrift, rich and soft, a delicious custard, tart and sharp with a zestful zing. Here was lime-pie perfection.

Lime Chiffon Pie

1 (9-inch) Perfect Pie Crust (page 13)

4 large egg yolks

1 (14-ounce) can sweetened condensed milk

⅓ cup lime juice

¼ teaspoon salt

6 large egg whites

½ cup sugar

Serves 6

Preheat the oven to 350 degrees. Line a 9-inch glass pie plate with the pastry. Trim the overhang to 1 inch, fold it under itself, and crimp decoratively, if you like. Refrigerate until chilled, about 15 minutes.

Line the pastry with parchment and fill with pie weights or dried beans. Bake for 30 minutes, or until nearly cooked through and dry to the touch. Carefully remove the foil and weights. Bake for 10 minutes longer, until golden. Cool completely on a wire rack.

Preheat the oven to 400 degrees.

In a medium bowl using an electric mixer, beat the egg yolks until thick and lemon-colored. Stir in the condensed milk, lime juice, and salt. In a separate medium bowl using an electric mixer, beat the egg whites until foamy; gradually add in the sugar and continue beating until the meringue stands in stiff but not dry peaks. Fold ¼ cup of the meringue into the egg-yolk mixture. Pour the filling into the prepared baked pie shell and cover the top with the remaining meringue. Bake for 8 to 10 minutes, until lightly browned and just barely set in the center. Transfer the pie to a wire rack to cool completely, then cover and refrigerate until chilled, or overnight, before serving.

THE NAME SNIVELY IN Florida means citrus groves, it means citrus plants, it means cattle lands and barbecue parties. The name Snively means the brothers John and the late Tom, Sr., and sons John, Jr., and Tom. It means eight grandchildren, and all of these Snivelys live within shouting distance in the Winter Haven area.

A hot summer day in March, the Snively family was host to a group of ten food editors from New York City and Canada on tour of the citrus country. A barbecue was set to follow our visit to the Snively packing plant.

Hot and foot-weary we left by car for John Snively, Jr.'s, cattle ranch. Our caravan came to a halt at a luxurious log cabin facing Lake Clear, a place built for one purpose—to have a good time.

In a clearing to the rear was the barbecue pit, the meat cooking, and Mr. John, Jr., overseeing the job. The pit was about one and a half feet deep, covered with a wire-netting grate. Hams and sirloin steaks and the shoulders and ribs of four young hogs were coming to a succulent tenderness over the slow, slow, ash-gray coals. More coals were shoveled in as needed from the nearby fire pit. Every half hour an attendant had swabbed the meat with Mr. John Jr.'s own barbecue sauce.

The sun went down in a flame-red glow; dinner was announced. The meat came, a platter load to a table, each seating six. Came a casserole of green beans done with a Chinese touch, a special recipe concocted by Mrs. John, Sr. Always the Brunswick stew at a Snively barbecue, orange shortcake for dessert. I was so busy getting recipes I had scarcely time to eat.

Florida's Best Barbecue Sauce

8 cups cider vinegar

5 cups ketchup

½ cup Tabasco sauce

1 (6-ounce) bottle A.1. or other steak sauce

1 (10-ounce) bottle Worcestershire sauce

¼ cup freshly ground black pepper

½ cup (1 stick) unsalted butter

½ cup sugar

½ medium garlic head (about 4 large cloves), mashed

¼ cup orange juice

¼ cup grapefruit juice

Salt

1½ onions, diced

1 bay leaf

1 tablespoon dried oregano

Makes 1 gallon

In a large heavy stockpot, combine all of the ingredients. Place over medium-high heat and bring to a boil. Reduce the heat and gently simmer for 30 minutes. Remove from the heat and discard the bay leaf.

Note: Leftover sauce keeps for 3 weeks in the refrigerator. When you are barbecuing with this sauce, you can make a mop for it by fastening a new dish mop to a stick and swabbing the meat on the grill or in the smoker every 30 minutes over a 6- to 8-hour period.

FLORIDA

Green Bean Casserole

2½ tablespoons unsalted butter

½ cup diced onion

½ cup sliced fresh mushrooms

2 cups sliced green beans

1 cup water chestnuts, sliced

1 (10¾-ounce) can
cream of mushroom soup

Salt

1 cup grated cheddar cheese

1 (2.8-ounce) can French fried onions, crumbled

Serves 6

Preheat the oven to 400 degrees. Grease a 2-quart casserole.

Melt the butter in a large skillet over medium heat. Add the onions, mushrooms, and green beans and sauté until the vegetables soften, 7 to 8 minutes. Add the water chestnuts and soup and season with salt.

Pour the mixture into the prepared casserole, bake for 20 minutes, then top the casserole with the grated cheese and fried onions. Bake for 5 to 10 minutes longer, until the casserole is bubbling hot and the cheese is completely melted. Serve hot.

BY BOAT UP THE Indian River, a river four miles wide in many places. We stopped along the way to visit A. B. Michaels, Deerfield Groves, on Orchard Island; these groves said to be the oldest on the river. Mrs. Michaels entertained our party in the big, cool house serving chilled orange juice and grapefruit juice and a pound cake, exquisite. Every food writer in our party asked for the recipe and it was gladly given. Shortly after this visit Mrs. Michaels was killed in a car accident. Knowing she was no longer there I couldn't bring myself to test her recipe. But I did for this book and give it to you as she gave it so proudly to us that sun-dappled afternoon.

Beulah Michael's Pound Cake

2 cups (4 sticks) unsalted butter, softened

3⅓ cups sugar

2 cups eggs (about 9 large eggs)

4 cups all-purpose flour, sifted

Makes one 10-inch cake

Grease a 10-inch angel food pan.

In the medium bowl of an electric mixer, cream the butter and sugar until very light and fluffy. (The sugar must be completely absorbed.) Add the eggs, one at a time, and beat well to combine after each addition. (The entire beating process takes about 1 hour.) Fold in the sifted flour, a cupful at a time, and be careful that no white streaks remain.

Pour the batter into the prepared pan and place the cake in a cold oven. Set the oven to 250 degrees and bake for 1½ hours. Increase the oven temperature to 300 degrees and bake for 1 hour, or until the cake is cracked down the center, golden on top, and a wooden pick or skewer inserted into the center comes out clean. Cool the cake in the pan on a wire rack for 10 minutes, then unmold the cake and cool completely. Serve plain or toasted. The cake can be kept at room temperature, covered, for up to 3 days.

FLORIDA TO THE NORTH

How to live on fish and love it might be the subject of my little visit with Mrs. Charles Cook Howell, Jr., of Jacksonville. Even if she told you how, you probably wouldn't! But remember, here's a woman to know if you ever want to serve fish each meal, each day in the week. She has a recipe for every fish that swims and most of her dishes are from her girlhood home in Gothenburg, Sweden.

Sigrid Jonsson came to America to visit relatives in Jacksonville. There she met the up-and-coming young lawyer, Charles Howell, Jr.—and she didn't go home. A perfect man, Sigrid figured, except he didn't like fish. But when his bride cooked the dish her mother had prepared so often for Gustaf V, the late King of Sweden, when he came visiting, Charles Howell, Jr., called it wonderful eating.

Mrs. Howell's mother, Mrs. Folke Jonsson, back in Sweden, still makes the king's dish using *gratinerad sjotunga,* one of Sweden's finest fish. Here, her daughter uses Florida's finest, the delicate pompano. This pompano is a poor traveler, it doesn't get far from home, so Sigrid suggests substituting fillets of flounder or trout which one can buy anywhere.

Sigrid's father was one of Sweden's shipping and lumber kings and his home was well staffed. Pretty young daughter with the green eyes, the dark hair, hadn't a household care, except one—like all Swedish girls, she had to learn to cook. It came natural to Sigrid. With food, she had the touch

of an artist, the skill of a craftsman. Eat at her table and know she cooks with loving hands because she loves cooking.

A smorgasbord, done as it is in her homeland, is her favorite way for party entertaining, something different for the guests. When it's a buffet supper the hot main dish is frequently curried chicken. A fowl is boiled until tender enough to slip the meat from the bones. Large pieces are arranged in the center of a silver platter, the dark meat underneath, the white meat on top. Around this a ring of fluffy rice; over the chicken she pours the curry sauce. A big sprinkle of finely cut parsley and to the table.

It's for the children Sigrid keeps a well-filled cookie jar with the kind of sweets she thinks youngsters should eat. These Swedish oatmeal cookies for one thing, and it's for them she makes this rich chocolate pudding (recipes follow).

Jacksonville is a fish-eating town and Mrs. Howell came from a fish-eating country with numerous clever tricks to make even a quite ordinary "swimmer" sit up and take a bow. Broiled fish and fried fish are something else again when served with a fish sauce made with fish stock, to which Sigrid adds parsley, a great handful, finely cut, plus lemon juice to taste. Another day she may dress the fried fish with a sauce of melted butter combined with chopped hard-cooked eggs and that parsley again! This fish dish she wants to share is "fit for a king."

Fish au Gratin

2 pounds pompano or flounder, filleted

2 tablespoons lemon juice

2 teaspoons salt

6 tablespoons (¾ stick) unsalted butter

3 tablespoons all-purpose flour

½ cup heavy cream

1½ cups fish or chicken stock

2 large egg yolks

2 teaspoons finely chopped parsley

2 dozen small shrimp, peeled, deveined, and boiled

2 tablespoons grated cheddar cheese

Serves 6

FLORIDA

Preheat the oven to 425 degrees. Grease a shallow casserole.

Place the fish fillets in the casserole and sprinkle them with the lemon juice and salt, then dot with 2 tablespoons of the butter. Cover loosely with waxed paper and bake for 7 to 10 minutes, until the flesh is tender and the tops are browned. Remove the casserole from the oven and set it aside. Do not turn off the oven.

Melt 2 tablespoons of the remaining butter in a large heavy saucepan over medium heat. Add the flour, stirring constantly to combine. Gradually add the cream, mixing to form a smooth paste. Pour in the stock. Bring to a boil, then reduce the heat to low and simmer for 10 minutes, stirring occasionally.

In a small bowl, beat the egg yolks and gradually add them to the sauce. Add the remaining 2 tablespoons butter and the parsley. Pour the sauce over the cooked fish fillets. Garnish with the shrimp and sprinkle with the cheese. Return to the oven and bake until the cheese is browned, 4 to 5 minutes.

Swedish Oatmeal Cookies

½ cup (1 stick) unsalted butter, softened

3 cups quick-cooking oats

½ cup sugar

1 large egg, beaten

1 teaspoon almond extract

Makes 2 dozen

Preheat the oven to 325 degrees. Use 1 tablespoon of the butter to grease a large cookie sheet.

Place the remaining butter in a large bowl and, using your fingers, knead it with the oats and sugar. Add the egg and the almond extract. Form the batter into tiny balls the size of marbles and place on the prepared sheet. Press down each cookie with the tines of a fork to make crosshatch marks on top. Bake for 10 to 15 minutes, until golden around the edges and just set. Let the cookies cool on the sheet for 5 minutes, then transfer to a wire rack to cool completely.

Note: Our kitchen changed this recipe, adding the egg and almond extract. Mrs. Howell used only butter, oats, and sugar, in slightly different proportions. The cookies were delicious but too crumbly to store.

Swedish Chocolate Pudding

1 large egg

½ cup sugar

¼ cup cocoa powder

⅔ cup whole milk

½ tablespoon unflavored gelatin

1 tablespoon warm water

1¼ cups heavy cream, whipped, plus more for serving, optional

Serves 6

In medium saucepan, whisk together the egg, sugar, cocoa powder, and milk. Place over medium-high heat and cook, whisking constantly, until thick, about 10 minutes. Remove from the heat. Put the gelatin in a small bowl and add the warm water; let it stand for 1 minute to soften. Stir the gelatin mixture into the pudding mixture and cool completely, about 10 minutes, stirring occasionally. Fold in the whipped cream and pour into a 1-quart glass dish or individual ½-cup ramekins.

Press plastic wrap directly on the surface of the pudding and refrigerate for at least 1 hour, until firm and chilled. Garnish with whipped cream, if desired, and serve.

FLORIDA

THE "COFFEE" IS A popular daytime party with Jacksonville women. This isn't a breakfast, it isn't a luncheon, but something of both, a stand up and walk around, overeat occasion.

When Mrs. Lawrence Adams entertains her Friday Musicale, one of the oldest and largest cultural organizations in Florida, founded in 1890, she gives a coffee, twenty guests, more or less between the hours of twelve and two. Favorite dish for this party is the French chicken loaf, this to cut into thick slices, each slice to recut into three fingers. It's accompanied by hot rolls, these filled with tangerine marmalade spread into the folds before the rolls go to the oven. A choice of fancy sandwiches is on hand and a green salad, a rich, rich dessert, and coffee.

The dishes given here are typical of Jacksonville tables. Mrs. Adams told me, and she ought to know, having lived here always. Music is Mrs. Adams' first interest, cooking her favorite recreation; gardening comes next. She spends long hours in the garden back of the twelve-room home overlooking St. Johns River. This is a remarkable river, one of the few in the world to flow toward the north, whirling its miniature whitecaps.

Eggnog Pie

1 (8-inch) Perfect Pie Crust (page 13)

1 envelope unflavored gelatin

¼ cup cold water

4 large eggs, separated

1 cup sugar

½ teaspoon salt

½ cup hot water

¼ cup dark rum

1 teaspoon grated nutmeg

Whipped cream for garnish

Makes one 8-inch pie

Preheat the oven to 350 degrees. Line an 8-inch glass pie plate with the pastry. Trim the overhang to 1 inch, fold it under itself, and crimp decoratively, if you like. Refrigerate until chilled, about 15 minutes.

Line the pastry with foil and fill with pie weights or dried beans. Bake for 30 minutes, or until nearly cooked through and dry to the touch. Carefully remove the foil and weights. Bake for 10 minutes longer, until golden. Cool completely on a wire rack.

Put the gelatin in a small bowl and add the cold water; let it stand for 5 minutes to soften. Meanwhile, in a medium heatproof bowl, beat the egg yolks with ½ cup of the sugar and the salt. Gradually stir in the hot water. Place the bowl over a pot of simmering water to form a double boiler and cook, stirring constantly, until the mixture thickens, forms a custard consistency, and coats the back of a spoon, about 10 minutes. Add the softened gelatin and stir until completely dissolved. Remove from the heat and cool, about 1 hour.

Stir the rum and ½ teaspoon of the nutmeg into the custard. In a medium bowl, beat the egg whites until foamy; gradually add the remaining ½ cup sugar and beat until stiff but not dry peaks form. Fold the egg-white mixture into the custard. Turn the custard into the prepared pie shell, cover, and refrigerate to set completely, at least 4 hours or overnight. To serve, garnish with whipped cream and sprinkle with remaining ½ teaspoon nutmeg.

Tangerine Marmalade

3 medium firm tangerines
(about 1½ pounds)

3 medium lemons (about 1½ pounds)

8 cups cold water

3 cups sugar

4 ounces pectin, optional

Makes five half-pint jars

Rinse the fruits and pat them dry. Cut each piece of fruit in half and juice them, reserving the juice. Scrape the pulp and seeds from the fruit and discard. Using a sharp knife, slice the peels ⅛ inch thick and reserve.

Place the zest strips in a large heavy saucepan, add the water, place over medium-high heat, and bring to a boil. Boil for 2 minutes. Drain the strips and return them to the saucepan.

Add the reserved fruit juices and the sugar. Place over medium heat, bring to a simmer, and cook, stirring to dissolve the sugar, until the marmalade sets, about 30 minutes.

If a firmer marmalade is desired, stir in the pectin. Spoon the marmalade into 5 hot ½-pint canning jars, leaving ¼ inch of space at the top of each. Close each jar with the lids and rings. To process, boil the jars in a large heavy stockpot in just enough water to cover for 15 minutes. Cool and let stand at room temperature for 2 days before opening.

Candied Grapefruit Peel

Peel of 1 medium grapefruit   1 cup sugar

3 cups water

Makes about 40 pieces

Wash the grapefruit well and pat it dry. Using a vegetable peeler, remove 10 wide strips of zest from the grapefruit. (Take care to remove only the surface and not the white pith underneath.) Slice the zest into ¼-inch-wide strips. Place the strips in a saucepan, cover with 2 cups of the water, place over medium-high heat, bring to a boil, and cook for about 10 seconds. Drain the strips in a colander and rinse them under cold water.

Return the zest strips to the saucepan with ⅔ cup of the sugar and the remaining 1 cup water. Place over medium-high heat, bring to a boil, and cook uncovered until the mixture starts to thicken, about 8 minutes. At this point, the syrup should be gooey and the zest strips should be nearly transparent.

Spread the remaining ⅓ cup sugar over a large baking sheet. Using a slotted spoon, transfer the strips to the sheet and toss them in the sugar, separating the pieces so that each strip is coated with sugar. Transfer the strips to a plate and let stand until completely dry, at least 30 minutes. Store the strips in the refrigerator in a jar with a tight-fitting lid.

QUICKLY MADE AND QUICKLY EATEN

There was a buzz of conversation around the tea table, and the talk was all food. Mrs. Marian Adams Mitchell, of Bishop Gate Lane, in Jacksonville, had invited a few friends in to give me the low-down on regional dishes of the town.

"There's Mrs. Robert Adams' fig pudding," someone was saying.

"Our Yacht Club does a fried chicken to make the South proud." The air was criss-crossed with suggestions, and I wasn't listening. My eyes were glued to Marian's tea table, a pretty sight!

What tawny toast, and glistening—as if old-rose shellacked—with strawberry jam. Small muffin-size tea cakes had their tops puffed and spread like a chef's high hat, so neatly arranged on a pedestal cake plate. Still another sweetmeat—sugared grapefruit peel, moist and tender, but in long strips.

Marian Mitchell was pouring tea from an heirloom silver pot, fragile the cups, and gay in an all-over flower design.

"This toast," she said, "is whole-wheat bread, buttered, then spread with strawberry preserves and run under the broiler. That gives the glazed look." The butter cooks into the jam, or maybe it's the other way around, giving an appetizing candied effect.

"Have cake? It's still oven-warm."

"Absolutely!" It melted away in the mouth as one bit in. I asked about the cake recipe.

"That's Mother's," Marian said. "Mother is the cook in the family, and I always use her recipes." A cake to be served in different ways, sometimes teacake style. Again, made as a layer cake, or a loaf cake, or one single thick layer to be cut into squares and served with sauce. Best of all strawberry hard sauce.

The grapefruit peel is another of Mother Adams' specialties (see opposite). It's a peel unlike the usual, being more tender, more moist, like a jelly candy. It is quickly made and should be quickly eaten, not kept around to get hard.

FLORIDA

Simple Yellow Cake

1½ cups sifted cake flour

2 teaspoons baking powder

½ teaspoon salt

½ cup (1 stick) unsalted butter

1 cup sugar

1 teaspoon vanilla extract

2 large eggs, separated

½ cup whole milk

Frosting of choice

Serves 8

Preheat the oven to 350 degrees. Grease two 8-inch cake pans and line the bottoms of each with parchment paper.

Sift the flour, baking powder, and salt into a medium bowl. In a separate medium bowl using an electric mixer, cream the butter and sugar until very fluffy. Beat in the vanilla and the egg yolks. Add the flour mixture alternately with the milk, beating well after each addition. Beat the egg whites until they form stiff but not dry peaks and fold them into the batter.

Turn the batter into the prepared pans and bake for 30 to 35 minutes, until springy in texture and a wooden pick or skewer inserted into the center of the cakes comes out clean. Cool the cakes in their pans on wire racks for 15 minutes, then run a knife around the edges and invert them onto a rack. Peel off the paper, turn the cakes upright, and cool completely. Cover the layers with your favorite frosting, let stand for 1 hour, then serve.

Note: For a loaf cake, pour the batter into a greased and floured 10 x 5 x 3-inch loaf pan. Bake at 350 degrees for 50 to 60 minutes. Follow the doneness and cooling instructions above. Slice and serve with ice cream.

Note: For tea muffins, pour the batter into greased and floured small-hole muffin pans. Onto each muffin cup of batter, drop 4 or 5 raisins and a half pecan. Bake at 400 degrees for about 15 minutes. Follow the doneness instructions above and serve warm. Makes 1½ to 2 dozen small muffins.

Note: For cake to serve with a sauce, pour the batter into a greased and floured 9-inch square pan. Bake at 350 degrees for about 45 minutes. Follow the doneness instructions above. While still warm, cut and serve immediately, dolloping each square with strawberry hard sauce (recipe follows).

Strawberry Hard Sauce

½ cup (1 stick) unsalted butter, softened

2½ cups confectioners' sugar

1 cup muddled fresh strawberries

Makes 2 cups

In the medium bowl of an electric mixer, cream the butter. Gradually beat in the confectioners' sugar until smooth and well blended. Gradually add the muddled strawberries and beat until light and the berries are completely incorporated. Serve over warm cake.

A FIRST COUSIN TO THE FISH FRY

igh up in north Florida and way down upon the Suwannee River, far, far away, at White Springs, near the famed Stephen Foster Memorial, I learned about the "perlo supper."

Perlo in local parlance is a chicken pilau, which is made in a huge pot, enough to feast a crowd, the great dish of the area for community picnics, for money-making church affairs and for political shindigs.

I had gone to White Springs to visit the Stephen Foster Memorial and was staying at the Colonial Hotel run by Floridians Mr. and Mrs. W. A. Saunders. It was Lillian, Mrs. Saunders, who showed me the sights of the countryside.

The "perlo supper," Mrs. Saunders told me, is a social event of the early days that has carried down the years. Before the War Between the States, several wooden hotels were built at White Springs, Florida, which was then a popular watering spot. Then, too, the perlo supper was an everybody-come social. Before that the Indians had the springs to themselves.

The suppers were usually held on the banks of the quiet-flowing Suwannee under the tall pines and the spreading live oaks where Osceola and his forbears had camped.

The supper is a first cousin to the fish fry, but pleasantly different. The food is cooked in a tremendous pot over coals of oak and hickory. First in are the fat hens to cook until tender. Remove from the stock and add long-grain rice, about one and one-half cups to a bird. When the rice is almost tender, the cooked chicken is returned to the pot for the final heating. Stir, gently stir, not to break the rice kernels.

The pilau is served usually with sour pickles, with homemade cabbage slaw and hot buttered yeast rolls. Coffee is made over the coals. Homemade fruit pie is the perfect dessert, or cake, or both.

Fish fries, too, are common in the area, using the Suwannee River catfish cut in good-size pieces. The freshwater trout and the bream, averaging about one and one-half pounds apiece, are cleaned and cooked whole. The fish is salted, rolled in corn meal and then into hot fat. Hushpuppies accompany the feast.

Chicken Pilau

6 small bone-in chicken breast halves, skin removed

I large onion, thinly sliced

3½ teaspoons salt

Boiling water

1½ cups uncooked long-grain white rice

4 tablespoons (½ stick) unsalted butter

⅛ teaspoon freshly ground black pepper

Dash of cayenne pepper

Serves 6

Put the chicken breasts, onion, and 2 teaspoons of the salt into large pot. Add just enough boiling water to cover the chicken. Place over medium heat, bring to a simmer, and simmer until the chicken is tender, 30 to 35 minutes. Transfer the chicken to a cutting board. Add the rice to the liquid in the pot (there should be about 3 cups of liquid; if there isn't, add a little more). Add the butter, the remaining 1½ teaspoons salt, the black pepper, and cayenne. Cover the pot and simmer until the rice is tender and the water is absorbed, about 20 minutes. Return the chicken breasts to the pot and heat until warm and the juices run clear when the chicken is pierced with the tip of a knife, about 5 more minutes. Serve immediately, with hushpuppies (recipe follows), if you like.

FLORIDA

Hushpuppies

2 cups yellow cornmeal

1 tablespoon all-purpose flour

1 teaspoon baking powder

1 teaspoon salt

½ teaspoon baking soda

3 tablespoons finely chopped onion

1 cup buttermilk

1 large egg, beaten

Vegetable oil for frying

Makes about 30

Sift the cornmeal, flour, baking powder, salt, and baking soda into a large bowl. Make a well in the center and add the onion, buttermilk, and egg. Whisk well until smooth. Cover and refrigerate the batter for 1 hour to set.

When ready to cook, heat 2 inches of oil to 375 degrees. Set a rack over a large rimmed baking sheet and place it near the stove. Stir the hushpuppy batter and drop it by tablespoonfuls into the hot oil and fry it until cooked through and golden brown, about 3 minutes each. Drain the hushpuppies on the prepared rack and serve them very hot.

Devil's Food Cake

3 large eggs

1½ cups sugar

1½ cups milk

4 ounces unsweetened chocolate

½ cup (1 stick) unsalted butter, softened

1 teaspoon baking soda

2 cups sifted all-purpose flour

⅛ teaspoon salt

2 teaspoons vanilla extract

Frosting of choice (see Note, page 374)

Makes one 9-inch layer cake

Preheat the oven to 350 degrees. Grease and flour two 9-inch cake pans.

Separate one of the eggs. In a medium bowl, whisk together 1 egg yolk and ½ cup of the sugar. Gradually whisk in ½ cup of the milk.

In a large heatproof bowl set over a large saucepan of simmering water, melt the chocolate. Slowly pour the egg mixture into the melted chocolate and cook until thick, stirring occasionally, about 7 minutes. Set aside to cool before using.

In a medium bowl using an electric mixer, cream the remaining 1 cup of sugar with the butter. Beat in the remaining egg white and whole eggs. Dissolve the baking soda in the remaining 1 cup of milk and add alternately with the flour to creamed mixture, beating well after each addition. Blend in the chocolate mixture, the salt, and vanilla.

Pour the batter into the prepared pans and bake for 25 to 30 minutes, until a wooden pick or skewer inserted into the center of each cake comes out clean. Transfer the cakes to wire racks and cool completely in their pans. Invert the cake layers onto a work surface and peel off the paper. Set one layer on a large plate and spread ¼ inch your favorite frosting on top. Stack and frost the remaining cake layers. Spread the remaining frosting all around the sides of the cake.

Note: When the cake has cooled, Mrs. Saunders recommends frosting it with this icing: Whisk 3 cups sugar and 9 tablespoons cold water in the top portion of a double boiler over rapidly boiling water. Add 3 egg whites and beat with a handheld mixer for 7 minutes or until stiff enough to spread. Add a pinch of salt, 2 teaspoons vanilla extract, and 2 teaspoons fresh lemon juice and beat until cool.

THIS RECIPE ROUNDUP ENDED at the state capital, Tallahassee, about as far north in Florida as Key West is south. Skidding over a pair of roller skates, quick dodging a coaster wagon, I arrived breathless up the steps to ring the doorbell of the Governor's Mansion.

"Hello," said a small voice, "did you come to see Mama? I'm Darby."

"Come in, Ma'am," said the white-aproned maid, chock-full of dignity. "Won't you rest your wraps?"

Came the slender Mary Call Collins, brown hair, warm brown eyes, a working partner to her lawyer husband, the thirty-second governor of the State of Florida.

"Luncheon can wait, come and see 'The Grove.' That's our own home. It's just over there," Mary Call nodded toward a columned mansion across the grounds shadowed by a grove of live oaks dripping Spanish moss.

The home of the Collinses is from Mary Call's side of the family, built in the 1820's by Richard Keith Call, a lieutenant on General Jackson's staff who came to Florida to fight the Indians.

Here romance and history walk hand in hand. Richard Keith Call loved Mary Kirkham of Nashville, Tennessee, but Mary's mother disapproved of a marriage that would take her daughter into the Florida wilds.

It was by Jackson's connivance that Call and Mary eloped to marry in his home, "The Hermitage," outside of Nashville.

"The Grove" was started soon afterward, with young Call determined to make it a mansion comparable to the one where his bride had lived. The husband of the first Mary Call became a general and later served two terms as territorial governor of the state, appointed by President Jackson.

"Luncheon will be waiting," and Mary Call Collins whisked me through the wide hall back to the Governor's Mansion. Fresh Florida fruits in a salad for the first course. With this came Mary Call's famous cheese straws. The main dish was baked oysters and a platter of country-cured ham, sliced thin; the vegetable, broccoli. Dessert, a fudge pie with ice cream.

We were in the middle of talking recipes when a voice came from the back entrance. "Mary Call, you there?" It was the Governor. He joined in to tell me the foods he likes best. "I'm inclined toward country-cured ham," he said, "and beefsteak rare, and orange sauce for the wild duck."

Orange-Blossom Punch

2½ cups sugar

2½ cups water

1½ quarts fresh, frozen, or canned grapefruit juice, chilled

1½ quarts fresh, frozen, or canned orange juice, chilled

1½ cups fresh lime juice

1½ quarts ginger ale, chilled

Makes about twenty 1-cup servings

Combine the sugar and water in a large heavy saucepan. Place over medium heat and stir until the sugar is dissolved, then bring to a boil and boil for 5 minutes without stirring. Turn off the heat and cool to room temperature, 20 to 30 minutes. Add the fruit juices. Just before serving, add the cold ginger ale. Pour over ice cubes flavored with fresh orange juice, if you like.

Duck with
Florida Orange Sauce

1 (4- to 5-pound) duckling

2 tablespoons sugar

1 tablespoon cornstarch

1 teaspoon minced fresh ginger

½ teaspoon salt

1⅓ cups orange juice

1 tablespoon fresh lime juice

2 teaspoons slivered orange peel

⅔ cup hot water

1 orange, sectioned

Serves 4

Preheat the oven to 350 degrees. Wash the duck inside and out with cold water; dry it carefully. Place the duck on a rack in a shallow roasting pan. (Do not cover or add water and do not prick the skin.) Roast for 2 hours.

While the duck is roasting, combine the sugar, cornstarch, ginger, and salt in saucepan. Stir in the orange and lime juices and the orange peel. Place over medium heat and cook, stirring constantly, until the mixture thickens and comes to a boil. Remove the pan from the heat.

Remove the roasting pan from the oven and take the duck off the rack. Pour off all the fat from the pan, reserving it for another use if you like; add the hot water to the pan and stir to dissolve any browned bits on the bottom of the pan. Stir these pan juices into the orange sauce. Return the duck rack to the pan and pour the orange sauce over the duck. Arrange the orange sections over the top of the duck, return to the oven, and roast for 10 to 15 minutes longer, until the meat is very tender and the skin is crisp. Let the duck rest for 20 minutes, then carve it and transfer the pieces to a warm serving platter.

Fudge Pie

½ cup (1 stick) unsalted butter

1 cup sugar

2 large eggs

2 ounces unsweetened chocolate, melted

¼ cup all-purpose flour

¼ teaspoon salt

1 teaspoon vanilla extract

½ cup chopped pecans

1 pint vanilla or other favorite ice cream, optional

Serves 6

Preheat the oven to 350 degrees. Grease an 8-inch pie pan.

In the medium bowl of an electric mixer, cream the butter with the sugar. Add the eggs, one at a time, beating after each addition. Stir in the melted chocolate. Add the flour, salt, and vanilla and beat briefly to just combine. Stir in the pecans.

Spread and scrape the batter into the prepared pan. Bake for 20 to 25 minutes, until the edges of the fudge are dry. Let the pie cool slightly in the pan on a wire rack. Serve in wedges, warm, topped with ice cream, if you like.

FLORIDA

QUEEN OF THE SUMMER fruit stalls is the big Persian lime, glossy and shining. It's the size of a lemon and offers just as much juice, just as refreshing its tang, but more gentle in its sourness. Once this fruit was prized by the Ancients of Persia, now it's happily at home in semi-tropical Florida. It was there I first tasted these "Lime Lovelies" in a roadside tearoom, and found them as refreshing as the kiss of a wave.

Lime Pavlovas

For the pavlovas:

3 large egg whites

¼ teaspoon cream of tartar

⅛ teaspoon salt

¾ cup sugar

For the lime filling:

3 large egg yolks

¼ cup sugar

¼ cup fresh lime juice

1½ teaspoons grated lime peel

1 cup heavy cream, whipped

Green food coloring, optional

Serves 6

Preheat the oven to 275 degrees. Line a large baking sheet with parchment paper.

In the large bowl of an electric mixer, beat the egg whites at low speed until foamy; add the cream of tartar and salt and beat at medium speed until stiff but not dry peaks form. Gradually add the sugar, beating until very stiff and glossy. Spoon the meringue into 6 mounds about 3 inches in diameter on the prepared baking sheet. Using the back of a spoon, make a 2-inch well in the center of each mound. Bake for 1 hour, or until slightly dry to the touch and just set. Turn the oven off and leave the meringue shells in the oven with the door closed to cool for 1 hour.

Meanwhile, make the filling: In a medium heatproof bowl, beat the egg yolks; add the sugar and lime juice. Place the bowl over a pan of boiling water and cook, stirring constantly, until thick, 8 to 10 minutes. Add the lime peel. Remove the bowl from the pan and cover it with plastic wrap; refrigerate for about 1 hour, until set. When ready to serve, fold the lime custard into the whipped cream. Tint the filling with a small amount of green food coloring, if you like.

Set the meringue shells on dessert plates, spoon the lime filling into the wells in each one, and serve.

THE CREOLE COUNTRY

LOUISIANA

Creole cookery is the best-known single type of cooking in the nation, but to tell you the honest truth I was tired of hearing, "When you get to New Orleans . . . !" Then at last I was there, and good gracious—I stayed three weeks, and that wasn't long enough. I visited in homes, ate in the famous restaurants, answered the "Morning Call" for café-au-lait and doughnuts at the old French Market. Now I know that no matter what they say about Creole cookery it isn't exaggerated. It's a cuisine unique, based on the belief that eating should be a pleasure and not a task to be hurried through, that food and drink are fine things to be talked about, and that recipes are meant to be shared.

Such a variety of recipes and each with some distinctive touch that trademarks it as Creole cooking! And what does that mean? To understand I had to learn a few things regarding New Orleans history and geography. The French *émigrés* who came in the eighteenth century were both aristocrats and peasants. They brought their recipes, which ran the gastronomic scale from the elegant *daube froid* (a cold meat jelly) to something as simple as *grillades*. They brought their flair for subtle blending of flavors and their remarkable ability to create dishes, such as *pot-au-feu,* from the thriftiest of ingredients.

Spanish rule introduced the hotter, more pungent seasonings. It was when Louisiana was under Spanish dictatorship that the Choctaw Indians brought medicinal herbs to the old French Market, the filé powder, for one, the tender pulverized leaves of sassafras. Originally the Indians had used this for medicinal purposes only, but the Negro cooks soon discovered its magic in making gumbos. These old Negro mammies from the wilds of Africa wrought their own particular spell over food by the uncanny knowledge of using rare flavoring herbs. They didn't actually employ witchcraft and sorcery in concocting their specialties, though the effects achieved have suggested just that.

It was later the famous chefs of France, seeking safety and to make their fortunes in the New World, invaded New Orleans because of its French-speaking ancestry. Before the French Revolution every noble family in France had its own private chef with his small army of assistants and its secret file of ingenious dishes for which he was personally famous. But the guillotine ruined so many royal and noble appetites, and having one's own personal cook became so unpopular in the Reign of Terror, that many of the greatest chefs in the world either opened their own restaurants or fled with their masters to the West Indies, then to Louisiana. The majority gravitated to the Little Paris of America to add to Creole cooking the finesse of sauces and the recipes of royalty.

Nature too has done her share in making Louisiana cooking distinctive. The tabasco peppers that flourish on Avery Island fire a vast number of dishes and there are other ingredients that grow in this area and nowhere else. One is a unique variety of mustard seed used in preparing creole mustard, the indispensable zest in the sauce rémoulade.

New Orleans has an abundance of fish, many of which are found but rarely anywhere else. They have crawfish and river shrimp, soft-shell turtles, red fish, sheeps head, terrapin, black fish, sting ray. The port of New Orleans makes it easy to bring in tropical fruits and vegetables from Central America.

In choosing these recipes for the classical Creole dishes, I have attempted to use products that you can buy in the markets of the larger cities anywhere in the States.

My first morning in New Orleans I went at daybreak to the picturesque old French Market to make my leisurely way around the market stalls. It was with a made-to-order appetite that I arrived at the "Morning Call" and climbed on a high stool ready for coffee and doughnuts. There I sat for an hour rubbing elbows with workmen in overalls and market women who sell "soup bunches" of assorted vegetables and hot herbs in "bouquets." How exciting to discover I was there elbows away from the very stool where Jenny Lind perched at midnight after her concert at the St. Georges Theatre. That was a hundred years ago when the colorful little coffeehouse was already a rendezvous, the select night spot for men and women in evening dress who sat all in a row with the workers to share the same heavenly brew and celestial sinkers, which were served around the clock.

Now I was learning first hand about *croquignolles* with café-au-lait. These "cracknels," as the name translates, were like doughnuts, deliciously crisp, light, and luscious little *bonnes bouches,* good mouthfuls. The coffee was made creamy with hot milk, half-and-half, an exhilarating beverage with a pleasing flavor and a deep rich color; this because chicory is added. The big round bowls of long ago have given way to modern cups, but the drink hasn't changed. It is still the same, I was assured, that had flowed across the counter in the "Mocha and Java" days of our forefathers. Turn the page to learn how it is made.

THIS DEVIL'S BREW IN THE MAKING

The good Creole cook never boils coffee. Her method is to boil the water instead, and "furiously," before pouring it over finely ground coffee dust. And you pour it on in small splashes, only, so the coffee can swell and start the essential oils flowing.

Originally the dripper was set in a pan of boiling water so the brew couldn't cool with the slow drip, drip, drip, until the very last black tear of full flavored essence was out. But in these hurried days they nudge along the operation by pouring on about one third of the total amount of boiling water to be used, allowing this just one-half minute to moisten and "settle" the fresh grounds before adding the remaining deluge. Then—and this is important—when the dripping is all done, the pot should be picked up and rhythmically rotated so the heavy and light oils in the brew will swirl together to make a uniform beverage.

A dark or "high roast" coffee is the favorite in the Crescent City and a goodly amount of chicory is stirred in before the roasting, which is done daily. Chicory is the making of the breakfast cup, and added to coffee gives a greater depth to its color, more body, more pungency. It can be likened to the use of salt in the right amounts, giving that something extra to palatability, something of magic to those who learn to enjoy its subtle flavor.

Chicory isn't a grain, you know, but a humble root that for use in coffee must be washed, dried, sliced, toasted, and ground. It was introduced in France centuries ago as an adulterant, and probably because it

made a cheaper, sharper potion the thrifty French acquired a speedy and special liking for it.

Today the Creole mixture is vacuum-packed and sold nationally for just what it is—French market–style coffee and chicory. Where this is unobtainable, the nearest thing to it is "high roast," "Italian type" or "double" drip coffee, roasted as black and ground as fine as the New Orleans kind, but of chicory not a trace.

Small cups of black coffee, café noir or demitasse, are downed as eye-openers by the old-timers who still call this straight shot "Morning Joy." These are drunk not only before the standard café-au-lait for breakfast but also as after-dinner demitasse. The strong, straight quaff has long been universal. In many sophisticated places it is taken with a spot of brandy or Kirschwasser, but in New Orleans the after-dinner coffee (Joy of the Evening) is lavishly laced with brandy and spices, and sumptuously served forth in a blazing brûlot bowl.

The Café Brûlot Diabolique capped the climax of my Creole adventures in a dinner at Antoine's, where I found it all that Lafcadio Hearn had advertised in his great cookbook *La Cuisine Creole:* "The crowning of a grand dinner . . . the *piece de resistance,* the greatest *pousse-café* of all."

Watching the preparation of Café Brûlot Diabolique by the practiced hands of Roy Alciatore, owner of Antoine's, is an experience to remember. There in the 1840 Room, directly under the watchful eyes of Grandfather Antoine and Father Jules looking down from their paintings, we saw this devil's brew in the making.

This ceremonial rite, we were told, developed from the custom of the French *bans vivants* of the olden days who liked to poise a spoon holding a sugar lump drenched in cognac over their demitasse of dripped coffee. This was set alight and kept burning until just before the sugar began to caramelize, then it was lowered into the cup, stirred an instant, and the beverage sipped most gratefully.

It was Mr. Jules who conceived the idea of placing the brandy in the dish with peel of lemon, lumps of sugar, and spices, then the fireworks. But watch son Roy make magic with flame. Into the silver brûlot bowl, a tall urn-like affair, Mr. Roy placed the spices, the lemon peel, the lumps of sugar. The brandy was poured into the ladle. At this point the lights were dimmed that the eyes might feast. The brandy was ignited. Slowly it was poured into the bowl in a flaming cascade. Slowly the ladle was lifted, again the burning essence, blue and orange, spilled into the bowl, the procedure was repeated until the sugar dissolved. Nothing in the room was visible save the illuminated faces of the party at our table.

Everywhere the sweet odor of spice. At the last, strong, freshly dripped coffee was added, but very gradually. The brûlot ladle lifted, dipped as the flames died, the air was saturated with exotic odors, pungent yet sweet.

Lights on! Immediately the beverage was ladled into the tall narrow cups that had been designed especially for the service.

A delicious melody, the flame bringing the various ingredients into one harmony of taste. Serve this at your table or by the fireside following dinner. Remember to flick out the lights if you would make the most of the fiery display. The late John Ringling of circus fame, on tasting the brew, remarked, "What could be more sublime than to taste the delights of heaven while beholding the terrors of hell?"

Café-Au-Lait

2 cups half-and-half

2 cups hot chicory coffee, brewed in a French drip pot or press

Sugar cubes

Serves 2

Heat the half-and-half in a small saucepan over low heat to the boiling point while your coffee is dripping in a French drip pot. The dripping must be slow, "as slow as New Orleans molasses in January," for according to a Creole saying that still serves: "Honey, if you can hear it drippin', it's drippin' too fast."

When the last drop has dripped, fill the cup halfway with the boiling hot half-and-half and add the jet-black coffee until it's the coffee-and-cream shade you like. Add sugar cubes to your taste.

Café Brûlot Diabolique

1 (1-inch) stick cinnamon

8 whole cloves

Peel of 1 lemon, thinly sliced

3 lumps sugar

3 jiggers brandy

3 cups strong hot coffee, brewed in a French drip pot or press

Serves 4

Combine the cinnamon, cloves, lemon peel, and sugar in a silver brûlot bowl or chafing dish. Place the bowl directly over a heat source such as a Sterno with the flame turned to low. Add the brandy, and just as the liquid starts to simmer, half fill a large metal ladle with the liquid and ignite it with a long thin candle-lighting butane torch. Return the flaming liquid to the dish to ignite the rest and stir until the sugar dissolves. As the flames begin to subside, slowly stir in the coffee, ladling the mixture until the flames fade. Ladle the coffee into special brûlot or demitasse cups and serve immediately.

THE *CROQUIGNOLLES* **ARE OF** many recipes but the one I like best, after testing several from around the state, is that of Mrs. Leota Edwards Claudel. Her reminiscences of the French lore of her native parish, Avoyelles, have inspired many of her son Calvin Claudel's articles on Louisiana-French folklore. Mrs. Claudel is of French-English extraction, her family one of the oldest in the parish, which was itself one of the first to be settled in Louisiana by Frenchmen who came across the ocean and by French-Canadians who came down through the Midwest to the Red River—rich lands.

In Avoyelles, *croquignolles* they were and are. And this is a recipe I have right from Mrs. Claudel, a splendid cook. The amount of sugar she uses will seem a lot, and the use of water instead of milk may strike one as perhaps a loss of richness, but actually this makes for lightness and crispness. Little more water is needed besides that required to melt the sugar or wet it thoroughly. Also she stiffens the flour, if necessary, to roll out the dough, then cuts the cakes round with a hole in the center.

With traditional French disregard for scientific measurements and a mild contempt for anyone who asks for them, she advises a hint of freshly ground nutmeg and a drop or two of fresh vanilla bean to flavor.

The word *croquignolles* comes from the French verb *croquer,* "to crunch," and Mrs. Claudel's sweet fried cakes have an irresistible, crunchy exterior and a light, tempting interior.

Ah me, five pounds later I had learned a lot about those *croquignolles*.

"Croquignolles"

2¾ cups all-purpose flour

1 teaspoon baking powder

½ teaspoon grated nutmeg

1 cup sugar

2 tablespoons water

2 large eggs

Vegetable oil for frying

Confectioners' sugar, optional

Makes about 2 dozen

Sift the flour, baking powder, and nutmeg into a medium bowl. In another bowl, whisk the sugar with the water. Beat in the eggs, one at a time. Add the dry ingredients to the wet ingredients in two additions, beating well after each addition. Lightly flour a work surface. Roll or pat out the dough on the surface to somewhere between ¼ and ⅛ inch thick. Cut out rounds with a floured 2½-inch doughnut cutter.

Fill a deep fryer with 2 inches of oil and heat it to 370 degrees. Fry the dough rounds in batches until light golden brown and crisp, turning as needed, about 4 minutes each. Drain on paper towels. Dust with confectioners' sugar, if you like, and serve immediately.

NEW ORLEANS DARES TO be different at breakfast. Staying at the Roosevelt Hotel, we saw cream cheese on the morning menu. We ordered and it came neatly molded, turned into a soup dish with cream to pour over and sugar to be added. Unlike the cream cheese of the North and the French petit Suisse, which doubtless served as a model, it has a slightly sour tang. It is to be eaten with a spoon, accompanied by crusty hard rolls, or, more adventurously, with the typically Creole *calas*.

Calas are toothsome rice fritters to rival muffins, croissants, and even brioche, the French breakfast cake that went native in New Orleans centuries ago. Until recently *calas*,

like pecan pralines, were sold on the streets by Creole vendors in the French Quarter.

The *calas*, piping hot, were wrapped in a clean towel and packed in bowls or baskets well covered to keep in the heat as the *cala* women toted them around the Vieux Carré on top of their "tignon" cushioned heads. The little rice cakes were made either in their home kitchens or cooked fresh and crisp over charcoal braziers by partners who held down every busy street corner in town.

These cakes are somewhat of a chore to make and take time, for the rice sponge must be set in the evening and allowed to rise overnight. But so easy to eat!

"Calas"

3 cups boiling water

½ teaspoon plus a pinch of salt

½ cup uncooked long-grain white rice

½ envelope active dry yeast

2 tablespoons warm, but not hot, water

3 large eggs, well beaten

¼ cup granulated sugar

⅛ teaspoon grated nutmeg

About ¼ cup sifted all-purpose flour

Vegetable oil for frying

Confectioners' sugar

Makes 16 to 20

Bring the water and a pinch of salt to a boil in a large saucepan. Add the rice, reduce the heat, cover, and simmer until the rice is very soft, about 40 minutes. Drain the rice in a fine colander or sieve, then transfer the rice to a large bowl and mash it against the side of the bowl with the back of a spoon until it is smooth and of a relatively consistent texture but not completely uniform.

Meanwhile, in a small bowl, dissolve the yeast in the warm water until foamy, about 10 minutes. Add to the mashed rice and mix completely. Cover the bowl with plastic wrap and let it rise overnight.

In the morning, add the eggs, granulated sugar, the remaining ½ teaspoon salt, and the nutmeg. Add the flour and stir to make a thick batter. Cover again with plastic wrap and let the dough rise again in a warm, draft-free place for at least 20 minutes or up to 1 hour, until the dough doubles in bulk.

Fill a Dutch oven or large heavy-bottomed skillet with at least 4 inches of oil and heat it to 360 degrees. Dip a tablespoon into the hot oil, then into the batter and scoop out a heaping tablespoonful. Hold the spoon close to the oil and let the batter roll off and into the oil. Fry until golden brown on each side, about 2 minutes per side, repeating with the remaining batter and using a slotted spoon to remove the *calas*. Briefly drain on paper towels, sprinkle with confectioners' sugar, and serve immediately.

ALL THINGS TO ALL MEN

In this most epicurean of all our cities, among all of its unusual dishes there is one that is even more so—the delicious meal-in-one gumbo.

Lafcadio Hearn immortalized one traditional type—green gumbo or gumbo of herbs in the title *Gumbo Zhérbes,* for his collection of sapid Creole sayings, because everything goes into the gumbo. And in New Orleans instead of bidding a friend good-bye with "See you in church," it is still funny to say, "Au revoir, meet you in the gumbo."

The praises of this delightfully gelatinous, gummy creation have come down to us in quotes like this:

"With a good gumbo prepared by Sylvia Without any scolding I could pass my life."

Gumbo is all things to all men, described as a soup dish, a stew, or a "hodgepodge," as Balzac dubbed the delicious bouillabaisse of Marseilles that later made its home away from home in New Orleans. Gumbos are on the lavish, too-much-is-plenty side. They go beyond the limits of definition. I found them so good, indeed, that I never quite got my fill as I meandered and munched my way from private homes to restaurants and back again, past old walls and green-shuttered dwellings under quaint balconies and through grilled iron gates into patios with cool fountains and luxuriant vines.

Gumbos are based on two sorts of gelatinous ingredients—filé powder, or the okra, but mostly filé that so happily unites and gums together any gumbo combo in one hotly spiced, thick, and salubrious stew. It may be made of crab, shrimp, oysters, or all three, or turkey, chicken, pigeon, squirrel, or rabbit, in a lush wild plenty. There are vegetable gumbos, too. The Creole cook never wastes anything, the gumbo pot is her catchall. She will make a gumbo to use leftover chicken, or wild turkey. Even turkey bones are cooked in it to extract that extra last bit of goodness. That's the thrifty touch of the French, economy married to flavor.

In the New Orleans of nearly two centuries ago there was gumbo every day and often twice a day at most tables. By now the frequency of serving has dwindled, but three veteran types hold their ground and we give recipes in this order:

First, Creole gumbo or gumbo filé, distinguished by the prime ingredient. Many people think gumbo isn't gumbo without filé powder.

Second, green or herb gumbo, made with almost every vegetable and spice *except* filé and okra.

Third, plain crab or shrimp gumbo of the okra gumbo family, gumbo fevi, that combines chicken, onion, tomatoes, ham, spices and butter with "fifty counted okra."

One might go to New Orleans many times and never meet that old time favorite gumbo *d'zerb (gumbo des herbes)* considered a tonic for spring. This is a sort of "throw-together" of spinach, mustard greens, beet tops, turnip tops, outside leaves of Creole lettuce, green cabbage, green celery leaves, green onion tops, green anything, a thick messy delight. Gumbo *des herbes* in the old days was made only on Holy Thursday and unfortunately today only a few cooks bother with the dish. Originally it was prepared in commemoration of the Last Supper, which Jesus ate with his disciples. Correctly made there should be thirteen kinds of greens, one for Jesus and one for each disciple. It is a "poverty" dish but it tastes like a king's feast. The greens are to be chopped fine, fine, never ground, that spoils the flavor. One old French lady who lives along the Bayou Lafourche told me that only wild greens should be used.

I had the green gumbo served to me when I went visiting Mrs. Ray Samuels (Martha Ann Brett is her writing name), who then lived in Mirabeau Gardens. Martha used but nine greens and one of them roquette. You may not know it, but parsley substitutes nicely for this sharp pepper leaf of the watercress family. Martha, formerly a newspaper reporter, is an outlander, but married to a New Orleans newspaperman.

Gumbo "d'Zerb"

2 tablespoons vegetable shortening

1 pound thick-sliced bacon,
cut into ½-inch dice

3 pounds coarsely chopped mixed greens, such as mustard greens, spinach, turnip greens, or a favorite lettuce such as frisée or arugula, washed, stemmed, and trimmed

1 pound finely shredded
green cabbage

½ cup finely chopped parsley

2 onions, chopped

2 tablespoons all-purpose flour

1 ham hock (about ½ pound)

2 quarts water

Salt and freshly ground black pepper

1 bay leaf

Pinch of dried marjoram

Pinch of dried thyme

1 whole clove

9 whole allspice

Dash of Tabasco sauce

¾ cup steamed long-grain white rice

LOUISIANA

Serves 6

Melt the shortening in a large heavy stockpot over medium-low heat. Add the bacon and brown it, about 20 minutes. Using a slotted spoon, transfer the bacon bits to paper towels to drain. Add the chopped greens, cabbage, parsley, and onions and cook until they are wilted, about 10 minutes, stirring frequently. Stir in the flour. Return the bacon to the pot along with the ham hock and add the water. Season with salt and pepper, then add the bay leaf, marjoram, thyme, clove, allspice, and Tabasco. Bring to a simmer, then cook for about 1½ hours, until the ham is tender at the bone. Remove the ham hock using a slotted spoon, cool slightly, then chop the meat from the bone and return it to the pot. Cook for 5 minutes to heat through, then ladle the gumbo into large warm bowls along with 2 tablespoons cooked rice for each portion.

Seafood Gumbo with Okra

2 tablespoons unsalted butter

1 large onion, minced

½ jalapeño pepper, minced

½ pound small okra, stem ends trimmed and sliced ½ inch thick

2 cups chopped tomatoes

2 quarts fish stock

3 pounds medium shrimp, peeled and deveined

½ pound blue crab claw meat, picked over, or 6 prime soft-shell crabs, tops peeled off, chopped

Salt

1 cup steamed long-grain white rice

Serves 8

Melt the butter in a large heavy stockpot over medium-high heat. Add the onion, pepper, and okra and sauté for 2 to 3 minutes, being careful not to let the okra scorch. Stir in the tomatoes and cook for 5 minutes. Gradually add the fish stock, then add the shrimp and crabs. Bring to a simmer, then reduce the heat to low and simmer for about 2 hours, until the fish is tender and falling apart and the shrimp is firm. Season with salt. Ladle the gumbo into warm bowls with 2 tablespoons cooked rice for each portion.

Note: Since okra is easier to come by than filé in anyplace except New Orleans, this simple sort of seafood gumbo is recommended for beginners. The slippery, mucilagenous quality of okra simulates the gumminess of filé, but the flavor is milder.

I INTERVIEWED MRS. FRANCES Parkinson Keyes, the distinguished author, a few weeks after she had finished her novel *The River Road*. The action of the story is laid in Louisiana's Grand Parade, that road along the Mississippi between Baton Rouge and New Orleans. When Mrs. Keyes decides upon a locale for a novel there she goes to live, to do her research and write, to observe her neighbors, to learn of their local customs and the good things of their table. To Mrs. Keyes's way of thinking the most ingratiating dish of the region was the chicken gumbo, succulent with tender pieces of the fowl and the fat sweet oysters curling their edges. A fragrant soup, which with rice, makes a hearty meal. The recipe came to her from the files of Mrs. Allain Hebert, whose Christian name and characteristics were given to Merry, the book's heroine. The name D'Avery, surname of the leading family of the story, came from the maternal side of Mrs. Hebert's family, as did this gumbo recipe.

YOU'LL NEVER RUE IT

Roux is a basic recipe in every Creole cook's repertoire. So many dishes begin, "First, make a *roux* . . ." (pronounced *roo)*. It's a foundation mixture of flour blended with melted butter or other shortening that starts almost any sauce on the right track.

There are just two kinds of *roux,* white and brown. For white *roux* the flour is only lightly colored. And for the brown there are just two *roux* rules—never let the flour overbrown, and keep stirring it carefully so it won't burn. From either of these shades of *roux* you can build up the best of sauces by frying chopped onion, minced bell pepper, parsley, or mixtures thereof, with other seasonings, and adding tomatoes, soup stock, water, wine, or other liquid as your sauce recipe may direct.

Learn to make a good *roux* and you'll never rue it.

After that the next lesson for those who aspire to majoring in all that is most typically Creole is to prepare rice properly. For almost any tried-and-true recipe specifies this most popular of grains grown in Louisiana, either in or as an accompaniment to the main course. There are several methods for its cooking, but only those which can bring rice to the table with each grain plumply apart from the other can be considered acceptable.

One good method is to drop rice into briskly boiling salted water, cook for about fifteen minutes until the grains are tender, wash in a colander under running water, drain, and steam dry over a pot of boiling water until ready to serve. Another method is to steam washed rice in one and a half times its own measure of water in the top of a double boiler. And remember the one and only rule for rice—never touch a spoon to it or stir it once cooking has started.

Mrs. Herbert's Creole Gumbo

1 tablespoon unsalted butter

1½ tablespoons all-purpose flour

1 (4½- to 5-pound) chicken,
cut into 8 pieces

2 teaspoons salt

1 large onion, diced

2 quarts chicken stock or water

3 dozen oysters, shucked,
with their liquor

7 tablespoons minced parsley

Red pepper flakes

1½ tablespoons gumbo filé powder

¾ cup steamed long-grain white rice

Serves 6

Melt the butter in a large heavy pot over medium heat until bubbling. Stir in the flour and cook until browned, stirring, about 5 minutes. Season the chicken with the salt and brown the pieces in the roux, about 4 minutes per side. Add the onion and sauté until transparent, about 3 minutes. Add the stock, bring to a boil, then reduce the heat to low and cover the pot. Cook for 2½ to 3 hours, until the chicken is tender. Add the oysters and their liquor and the parsley and season with red pepper flakes. Cook until the oysters curl at the edges, 3 to 5 minutes more. Remove from the heat and stir in the filé powder; do not reheat. Serve immediately in warm bowls with 2 tablespoons cooked rice in each portion.

Note: This to remember—filé powder is so delicate and gummy it should never be cooked or even warmed over. It must always be added to the dish just before serving, and it must be added gradually while the mixture is still boiling. Filé might be called an indigenous American curry powder, along with chili, its opposite number on the Tex-Mex border.

LOUISIANA

SINCE GUMBO SUGGESTS SHRIMP we might as well finish off now with that succulent subject. For here in the queen city of the Mississippi, shrimp is king. It is omnipotent, omnipresent. Shrimp wiggles into every course of the menu. It swims in the soup, parades in an appetizer, stars in main dishes and salads. It is the backbone of innumerable sauces.

A magnificent morning. The sun and the moon both hung in the sky. The car rolled down the planked gangway to Louisiana Avenue's wobbly little ferry. With a chuck, chuck, chuck, it plowed straight across the Mississippi's dark oily water to the town of Harvey.

Here I went to see the shrimp canned, visiting the plant of the Southern Shellfish Company, one of many such canneries scattered along the waterfront from Florida to Texas. From these coastal waters come 90 percent of all shrimp caught, and of this, 35 percent go to market in cans. Now these plants freeze shrimp in vast quantities.

Smell of shrimp, of steam, of water-drenched wharf greets me. Hum of voices, rasp of shovels, mark the unloading of ice boats that bring the catch to the plant direct from the shrimp fleet.

The day is full blown. We recross the big river headed for a late-afternoon party being catered by Marie Natalie Therese Paola Castanedo Copeland Grafton of an old French-Spanish family, meaning Creole. One of the many small tidbits she served was this shrimp canapé, which we have met nowhere else than in New Orleans.

Shrimp Canapés

Salt

1 pound medium shrimp

¼ teaspoon dried thyme

Dash of cayenne pepper

1 bay leaf

½ cup fresh celery leaves (yellow leaves)

½ envelope unflavored gelatin

¾ cup vegetable juice

1 loaf white sandwich bread

2 tablespoons unsalted butter, softened

1 bunch watercress, optional, for garnish

Makes 25 hors d'oeuvre servings

Bring a large heavy stockpot filled with 1 quart of salted water to a rapid boil. Drop the shrimp into the water; add the thyme, cayenne, bay leaf, and celery leaves and cook for 5 to 8 minutes, until the shrimp turn pink. Drain, and when the shrimp are cool enough to handle, peel and devein them, then mince them.

Soften the gelatin in 1 tablespoon of the vegetable juice for 10 minutes. Heat the remaining juice in a small saucepan over medium heat, add the gelatin, and stir until dissolved. Stir in the minced shrimp. Pour the mixture into a glass bowl, cool, then cover with plastic wrap and refrigerate for at least 8 hours or overnight.

When ready to serve, cut out twenty-five 2-inch rounds from the sandwich bread using a biscuit cutter or a glass. Toast the bread on one side only and spread a little butter over the slices. Stir the chilled shrimp mixture and mound it on the toasts. Garnish each canapé with watercress leaves, if you like.

TO CROSS THE PORTAL of Arnaud's Restaurant in the heart of the Vieux Carré is to enter a gustatory paradise. But to go at the invitation of the late Count Arnaud Cazenave was virtually to sit in the laps of the gustatory gods. Count Arnaud is no longer there. Daughter Miss Germaine Wells has taken over, but on this gay evening of which I write the Count was our most genial host. He ordered the dinner, the first course shrimp Arnaud (Shrimp Rémoulade), boiled shrimp blended with a spicy sauce that seemed to defy imitation. The recipe was created by Arnaud's first chef, Lows Pickett La Mothe, and long claimed a secret. But here it is as the Count detailed it to us. A secret, but of course!

Shrimp Rémoulade

French Dressing (recipe follows)

1 tablespoon prepared Creole mustard or good-quality coarse-ground mustard

1 teaspoon prepared horseradish

6 shallots, chopped

¼ teaspoon garlic salt

¼ teaspoon sweet paprika

1½ pounds cooked peeled and deveined medium shrimp

Serves 6

Pour the French dressing into a large bowl. One at a time, whisk in the all of the ingredients except the shrimp. Add the shrimp and mix thoroughly. Cover and refrigerate for 30 minutes to 2 hours before serving so the shrimp flavor permeates the sauce and the dish is completely chilled.

French Dressing

1 tablespoon vinegar, preferably tarragon or basil

1 teaspoon salt

¼ teaspoon freshly ground black pepper

1 teaspoon prepared Creole mustard or good-quality coarse-ground mustard

3 tablespoons olive oil

Makes 4 tablespoons

In a small bowl, whisk together the vinegar, salt, and pepper. Place the mustard in a medium bowl. Add the oil, at first drop by drop, then in small quantities, beating constantly with a whisk. Add the vinegar mixture, a few drops at a time, beating constantly to emulsify and being careful not to let the dressing curdle. When the last of the oil and the last of the vinegar mixture have been beaten in, the dressing is ready to use as a base for a rémoulade.

THE LAST DAY OF my New Orleans visit I spent with Mrs. Caroline Weiss, who was growing and packing Creole herbs on the family farm, Kiskatom (sixty miles out of New Orleans near Madisonville), a paradise place of three hundred acres spreading in leisurely beauty along Lake Pontchartrain. A farm with its own bayous, its own ageless oaks. To give us a sampling of her herbs at work Caroline served this stewed shrimp dish. Try it and agree with Brillat Savarin that "Good food is not a matter of money but of manner."

Shrimp Creole

2 tablespoons unsalted butter

1 tablespoon all-purpose flour

2 onions, finely chopped

2 pounds large shrimp, peeled and deveined

6 fresh tomatoes or 1¼ cups canned tomatoes

1 cup water

1 green bell pepper, cored, seeded, and diced

1 teaspoon fresh thyme leaves or ½ teaspoon dried thyme

2 teaspoons chopped fresh parsley or 1 teaspoon dried parsley

1 bay leaf

1 teaspoon garlic salt

Salt and freshly ground black pepper

1½ cups steamed long-grain white rice

Serves 6

Melt the butter in a large skillet or saucepan over medium-high heat. Gradually stir in the flour and cook, stirring, until it turns light brown, about 3 minutes. Add the onions and sauté until golden, 3 to 4 minutes. Add the shrimp and toss well to coat. Add the tomatoes, water, green pepper, thyme, parsley, bay leaf, and garlic salt and season with salt and pepper. Cook, stirring frequently, for about 10 minutes, until the shrimp are pink. Divide the rice among warm soup plates, top with the shrimp, and serve.

THERE ARE OTHER SHELLFISH than shrimp in Louisiana. Crayfish is abundant in lagoons and bayous. I saw whole families fishing for a crayfish dinner, using crude poles, the lines baited with little chunks of salt pork.

This Creole crayfish dish comes from Amite, from Victoria Touchtone, and with the good advice to use shrimp or frozen crayfish tails if you can't get the genuine freshwater kind.

Crayfish à la Creole

½ cup vegetable oil

1 large onion, chopped

2 cloves garlic, minced

1 (6-ounce) can tomato paste

1 (14-ounce) can chopped tomatoes

3 cups chicken or fish stock

Salt

Dash of cayenne pepper

2 pounds fresh crayfish tails, peeled, or large shrimp, peeled and deveined, or rock lobster, peeled and cut into small chunks

Serves 4

Heat the oil in a large skillet or Dutch oven over medium heat. Add the onion and garlic and sauté until softened, about 3 minutes. Stir in the tomato paste and tomatoes. Cook until the fat spreads over the top of sauce, about 30 minutes, stirring occasionally. Add the stock, season with salt, and add the cayenne, then the crayfish tails (or shrimp or rock lobster). Bring to a boil, then reduce the heat to low and simmer until the sauce is medium-thick, 1 to 1½ hours. Serve hot with steamed rice.

NEXT TO GOING TO heaven to dine on ambrosia is going to New Orleans to eat at Antoine's. The fame of the foods of this century-old restaurant has belted the globe. Recipes have been handed down word-of-mouth from the founder Antoine Alciatore to his son Jules, to Jules' boy Roy, now maestro of the house.

Nowhere else in the world is eating so surrounded by mystery, by legend; restaurant of a thousand dishes, and each a guarded secret, that is, until now. But have patience, take care. A majority of Antoine's specialities require a ritual too involved to be practical for home use. Home cooks lack the necessary seasonings, stockpots, and sauces to produce masterpieces. "How many women would want to make sauce marchand de vin?" Mr. Alciatore asked.

"Not one," we agreed when we heard the step-by-step procedure that takes a full day. And who would want to make the bisque d'écrevisse cardinale, a six-hour routine? But it's different with the oysters en brochette. Anyone can make them with gratifying results. Roy Alciatore himself gave me a choice from the famous recipe collection of the house.

Here I'm giving a few of the simplest, which I feel home cooks can try and prepare with good luck.

Oysters en Brochette

36 freshly shucked raw oysters

12 slices bacon, cut into thirds

1 cup all-purpose flour

Salt

Freshly ground black pepper

½ cup (1 stick) unsalted butter

⅓ cup olive oil

12 toast triangles or rounds

1 teaspoon chopped parsley

1 teaspoon lemon juice

Serves 6

Pat the oysters dry with paper towels. Wrap each oyster with a piece of bacon and secure with a toothpick. Put the flour in a shallow bowl and season it with salt and pepper. Toss the oysters, a couple at a time, in the seasoned flour, coating each side completely. Shake off the excess flour.

Melt the butter in the oil in a large heavy-bottomed skillet over medium-high heat. Add the skewered oysters and fry, turning to cook on all sides, until golden brown, 3 to 4 minutes. Drain the oysters on paper towels. To serve, lay 6 skewered oysters onto 2 toast triangles; repeat with the remaining oysters and toast triangles. Add the parsley and lemon juice to the butter in the skillet and spoon over each portion. Serve immediately.

"Oeufs Sardou"

8 artichokes, stems peeled and trimmed, tough outer leaves removed

Salt

16 anchovy fillets

8 eggs, poached

1 cup Antoine's Hollandaise Sauce (recipe follows)

½ cup chopped cooked ham

1 tablespoon *glace de viande* or rich beef stock

4 slices truffle, optional

Serves 4

Preheat the oven to 200 degrees.

Cook the artichokes in a pot of boiling salted water until tender, about 20 minutes. Drain and remove the petals and choke; reserve the bottoms. Place the artichoke bottoms on a baking pan and put 2 anchovy fillets on each. Keep warm in the oven.

Have the poached eggs and Hollandaise sauce ready and warm.

Now assemble the dish: On each artichoke, over the anchovy fillet, place a poached egg. Cover with Hollandaise sauce. Sprinkle with the ham and drizzle with a few drops of the *glace de viande*. Place a slice of truffle on top and serve immediately.

Antoine's Hollandaise Sauce

2 tablespoons tarragon vinegar

1 tablespoon water

1 tablespoon minced onion

3 peppercorns

4 large egg yolks

1 cup clarified butter (see Note)

Juice of ¾ lemon

Salt

Makes about 1 cup

In a small saucepan, combine the vinegar, water, onion, and peppercorns. Place over very low heat and cook until reduced to 1 teaspoon. Remove the peppercorns, pour into a medium metal bowl, and cool. Add the egg yolks and place the bowl over a medium pan of barely simmering water and whisk until lemon-colored. Whisking constantly, drizzle in the butter, then add the lemon juice at the end. Season with salt and serve immediately.

Note: To clarify butter, slowly melt the butter over low heat. Let stand until the clear part can be skimmed off easily.

Fresh Mushrooms "Sous Cloche"

1 cup water

½ cup white wine

3 tablespoons unsalted butter

1 pound fresh mushrooms

1 tablespoon all-purpose flour

Juice of ½ lemon

1 large egg yolk

¼ cup half-and-half

4 slices toast, buttered and cut into large circles

Serves 4

Combine the water, wine, and 1 tablespoon of the butter in a large skillet. Place over medium heat, add the mushrooms, and bring to a boil. Reduce the heat, cover, and simmer for 10 minutes. Drain, reserving the stock, and thinly slice the mushrooms.

Melt the remaining 2 tablespoons butter in the hot skillet, place over medium-low heat, and stir in the flour until combined, about 3 minutes. Do not let it brown. Pour in the reserved mushroom stock and cook, stirring constantly, until slightly thickened, about 5 minutes. Add the sliced mushrooms and lemon juice and cook for about 5 minutes, stirring occasionally, until the sauce is smooth.

Meanwhile, in a large bowl, beat the egg yolk and whisk in the half-and-half. Gradually pour in the mushroom mixture and mix well. Arrange the toast rounds on 4 small plates and evenly spoon the mushroom mixture over the toasts. Cover with a glass bell. Serve hot, removing the glass bell in front of the guests.

LOUISIANA

Chicken Creole

1 (3½-pound) chicken,
cut into 8 pieces

¼ cup olive oil

1 (14-ounce) can chopped tomatoes

2 tablespoons unsalted butter

1 teaspoon salt

Pinch of freshly ground black pepper

Pinch of cayenne pepper

1 sprig thyme

1 tablespoon minced parsley, plus
parsley sprigs for garnish, optional

1 bay leaf

3 cloves garlic, minced

1 tablespoon all-purpose flour

6 shallots, chopped

5 tablespoons chopped
green bell pepper

½ cup white wine

Avocado slices, optional

Serves 4

Wipe the chicken pieces dry with a damp cloth. Heat the oil in a large skillet or Dutch oven over medium heat. Add the chicken and cook, turning to brown both sides, about 7 minutes total. Transfer the chicken pieces to paper towels to drain. Add the tomatoes and 1 tablespoon of the butter to the skillet and simmer for 10 minutes, stirring occasionally. Add the salt, pepper, and cayenne and cook for 10 minutes more. Add the thyme, parsley, bay leaf, and garlic and cook for 15 minutes, or until the sauce is thick.

Meanwhile, melt the remaining 1 tablespoon butter in a small saucepan over medium heat. Add the flour and cook, stirring constantly, until golden brown, about 5 minutes. Add the shallots and green pepper and sauté until lightly browned, 5 to 7 minutes. Add the wine and cook, stirring constantly, until slightly thickened. Pour into the pot with the tomato mixture and stir to combine. Add the reserved chicken to the pot, cover, and simmer for 45 minutes, or until the chicken is tender. Serve over rice and garnish with avocado slices and parsley sprigs, if you like.

Oysters Rockefeller

2 large leaves Bibb lettuce

5 tablespoons unsalted butter, melted

⅓ cup minced fresh spinach

2 tablespoons minced onion

2 teaspoons minced celery

3 tablespoons fine dry breadcrumbs

½ to 1 tablespoon minced fresh herbs, such as chervil, tarragon, parsley, and chives

¼ teaspoon anchovy paste

¼ teaspoon salt

Freshly ground black pepper

Rock salt for serving

12 oysters on the half shell

Serves 4

Preheat the broiler.

Gently wilt the just-rinsed (damp) lettuce leaves in a dry sauté pan over low heat, turning once or twice. Pat dry and mince.

In a medium bowl, combine the melted butter with the lettuce, spinach, onion, celery, breadcrumbs, herbs, anchovy paste, and salt; season with pepper.

Put a layer of rock salt about ½ inch thick into 2 pie plates and set 6 oysters in their shells into each pan, using the rock salt to hold them level. Place spoonfuls of the spinach-herb mixture on each oyster. Broil until heated through and the oysters have curled, about 5 minutes. Serve immediately.

LOUISIANA

Crêpes "à la Gelée"

½ cup sifted all-purpose flour

1 large egg

1 large egg yolk

¼ teaspoon salt

5 tablespoons milk

2 tablespoons unsalted butter, melted

3 tablespoons currant or
red raspberry jelly

Confectioners' sugar

Makes 12

In a medium bowl using an electric mixer, combine the flour, egg, egg yolk, salt, and milk and beat until the batter is smooth and has the consistency of light cream. Cover and refrigerate for at least 1 hour or overnight.

Heat a crêpe pan or small heavy cast-iron or nonstick skillet over medium-high heat. Brush with a thin coating of the butter. Ladle about 3 tablespoons of the batter into the pan, tilting the skillet to evenly coat the pan with the batter. Cook until golden brown on the bottom and somewhat dry-looking on top, 1 to 2 minutes. Using a rubber spatula, carefully flip the crêpe and cook just until the bottom browns slightly, 30 to 45 seconds. Transfer the crêpe from the skillet to a warm plate.

Repeat the process, beginning with brushing the pan with a little butter, until all the crêpes are made, transferring each finished crêpe to the plate. Cover the plate loosely to keep the crêpes warm while you finish working. When all the crêpes are cooked, spread the center of each crêpe with a thin line of jelly, then roll it up like a cigar. Place the rolled crêpes on a serving platter or inside a large shallow casserole dish. When all the crêpes are cooked, sprinkle them with a little confectioners' sugar. Serve immediately, or place under the broiler to melt the confectioners' sugar, if you like.

Note: The crêpes can be made up to three days in advance and refrigerated in an airtight container separated by layers of waxed paper. They can also be wrapped tightly and frozen for up to 1 month.

DESPITE THE CITY'S MANY fine restaurants New Orleaners love best the parties they give at home. Mrs. Carl Woodward of the Audubon Park District, recognized as one of the outstanding hostesses of the city, plans her own parties and also menus for friends. When the Duke and Duchess of Windsor came to New Orleans for the Mardi Gras it was Molly Woodward who planned the food for the numerous parties attended by the royal couple. One recipe used on two occasions was this cocktail sauce for seafood.

Cocktail Sauce

1 cup mayonnaise

Freshly ground black pepper

Tabasco sauce

1 tablespoon anchovy paste

2 tablespoons ketchup

1 tablespoon tarragon vinegar

Makes about 1 cup

In a large bowl, whisk together the mayonnaise, pepper, and Tabasco. Whisk in the remaining ingredients. Cover and refrigerate for at least 1 hour before serving.

Note: This mayonnaise-based cocktail sauce is best with shrimp or crabmeat.

LOUISIANA

MOLLY'S FAVORITE DINNER FEATURES old ham, hickory-smoked, sugar-cured, and good, surely as pigs are pork. The Woodward ham dinner is served with beaten biscuits, generously buttered, seeming to crumble and vanish instantly as one bites in. There may be a salad of artichoke hearts with tomatoes laid out on lettuce, and over this a homemade French dressing.

Pecan torte for dessert.

Molly Woodward's Pecan Torte

4 large eggs, separated

6 tablespoons (¾ stick) unsalted butter, softened

1½ cups light brown sugar

4 cups ground pecans

½ cup all-purpose flour

1 teaspoon vanilla extract

2 cups whipped cream

Makes one 9-inch layer cake

Preheat the oven to 350 degrees. Grease two 9-inch round cake pans.

In a medium bowl using an electric mixer, beat the egg whites to stiff peaks. In a small bowl, beat the egg yolks.

In a large bowl using an electric mixer, cream the butter and brown sugar. Add the egg yolks and beat until thick and lemon-colored, about 7 minutes. Stir in 3½ cups of the ground pecans, the flour, and vanilla. Fold in the beaten egg whites, one third at a time, just until blended.

Divide the mixture between the 2 prepared pans and bake for about 25 minutes, until golden brown and the cake springs back when touched with a finger. Let the cakes cool in their pans on wire racks for 10 minutes, then invert onto the racks to cool completely. Just before serving, spread the whipped cream between the layers and over the top of the torte. Sprinkle the top of the torte with the remaining ½ cup ground pecans.

MRS. HAMILTON POLK JONES of a celebrated New Orleans family invited me to come for coffee on a Sunday morning. Lift up the latch of the high iron gate. Behold a century-old house of colonial design, banked by camellias, azaleas, and oleanders. I felt awed by its timeless dignity. Once I was in the wide door, my hostess put me at ease with her ready chatter about recipes. There I met Natalie Scott who co-authored with Mrs. Jones *A Gourmet's Guide to New Orleans*. I asked for their three best recipes. Natalie Scott said, "What about chicken pie creole?" Mrs. Jones agreed and added, "Of course, the chocolate sponge."

Mrs. Jones rang for Minnie. "Bring in the Admiral's golden buck. It's an appetizer," she said, "usually served with cocktails, but it goes fine with coffee as well as with salad." A long keeper and a handy one to spread on toasted bread sticks. Just reheat before serving.

Admiral's Golden Buck

LOUISIANA

1 pound sharp cheddar cheese, grated

1 tablespoon unsalted butter, softened

1 large egg, beaten

½ teaspoon salt

1 tablespoon Worcestershire sauce

¼ teaspoon cayenne pepper

12 slices of buttered toast, each cut in half

Makes 2 dozen canapés

In the bowl of a food processor, pulse together the cheese, butter, and egg. Add the salt, Worcestershire sauce, and cayenne and pulse, scraping down the sides of the bowl occasionally, until mixture is totally smooth. Scrape into a small bowl, cover, and refrigerate. Spread the mixture on the toast and broil until the cheese melts. Serve hot.

Note: The cheese mixture may be spread on the toast several hours in advance and broiled just before serving.

Chicken Pie Creole

For the chicken:

1 (5-pound) stewing chicken,
cut into 8 pieces

Salt

For the sauce:

2 tablespoons unsalted butter, melted

¼ cup all-purpose flour

3 cups chicken stock

1 cup half-and-half

½ teaspoon salt

¼ teaspoon freshly ground
black pepper

For the pie:

1 recipe Perfect Pie Crust (page 13)

2 tablespoons unsalted butter, melted

1 large egg, well beaten

1 cup milk

Serves 6

Grease a shallow 2-quart casserole.

In a large stockpot, cover the chicken with salted water and
bring to a boil. Reduce the heat to low, cover, and simmer
for 2 hours, or until tender.

Meanwhile, make the sauce: Melt the butter in a medium
saucepan over medium heat. Whisk in the flour and cook,
whisking constantly, until golden, 2 to 3 minutes. Gradually
pour in the chicken stock and half-and-half and cook,
whisking constantly, 7 to 8 minutes. Add the salt and
pepper and cook, stirring constantly, until the sauce comes
to a boil. Reserve 2 to 3 cups of the sauce for the chicken pie,
and keep the remaining sauce for the gravy bowl; simmer
for 15 minutes to make the gravy.

When the chicken is cooked, set aside until it is cool enough
to handle, then remove the meat from the bones, discarding
the skin and reserving the bones for stock. Spread the
pulled chicken meat over the bottom of the prepared
casserole and pour the reserved sauce over the chicken.

To make the pie: Preheat the oven to 425 degrees. Place
a disc of pastry in a large bowl. In a small bowl, whisk
together the melted butter, egg, and milk. Pour onto the
pastry and, mixing quickly with your hands, loosen to

make a soft dough. Drop the dough by tablespoonfuls over the chicken and sauce in the baking dish. Bake for 15 to 20 minutes, until the top is golden brown and the sauce is bubbling. Serve with the reserved gravy.

HEIRLOOM DISHES FLATTER THE menu when Mrs. John Minor Wisdom entertains in her stately home, over a century old, there on First Street in the Garden District. She serves foods of her father's table, foods that went to parties in her grandfather's time. Here

I give Mrs. Wisdom's favorite luncheon menu with crab timbales first, the main course a chicken and artichoke combination with a rich sauce. With this parsley new potatoes, hot rolls. The dessert—Charlotte Russe wheel.

Crab Timbale

1 cup cooked crabmeat

½ cup minced celery

2½ tablespoons chopped ripe black olives

2½ tablespoons minced pimiento peppers

2½ tablespoons minced green bell pepper

2 (¼-ounce) envelopes unflavored gelatin

1 cup cold milk

1 cup mayonnaise

1 teaspoon minced onion

1 teaspoon Worcestershire sauce

¼ teaspoon Tabasco sauce

¾ teaspoon salt

Pinch of freshly ground black pepper

1 small bunch watercress for serving

6 medium-thick slices ripe tomato

1 cup sour cream

1 tablespoon minced chives

1 (2½-ounce) jar caviar, optional

Serves 6

In a large bowl, combine the crabmeat with the celery, olives, pimiento, and green pepper. In a medium bowl, soften the gelatin in the cold milk, stirring to dissolve; let rest for about 5 minutes, then stir in the mayonnaise. Add the minced onion, Worcestershire sauce, Tabasco, salt, and pepper. Add to the crabmeat mixture. Pour into 6 individual 1-cup molds or ramekins, cover each with plastic wrap, and refrigerate for at least 5 hours or overnight to completely set.

When ready to serve, prepare 6 appetizer serving plates by mounding a small bed of watercress in the center and topping it with a tomato slice. Using a knife, gently loosen the crab custards from the molds or ramekins and invert them onto the prepared serving plates. Dress each timbale with a small dollop of sour cream and garnish with chives. If you are feeling rich, top each with a small spoonful of the caviar. Serve immediately.

"WARREN POSEY WILL COOK you a dinner at the drop of a hat." That's what his friends told me during my New Orleans "good dish" hunt.

When it's a party dinner the Poseys go overboard. Guests are invited to come around at seven-thirty for cocktails and snacks. Dinner seldom gets going before nine o'clock. The menu the evening of our visit included a crabmeat and mushroom soup, something of a trouble to make so it's best made in quantity, then a part frozen for future eating. Or, it might have been the brown oyster chowder. Main course on the Posey menu was breast of chicken served on slices of ham. Spinach for the green vegetable along with the "tipsied yams." The salad, sliced cooked beets on watercress with a tangy French dressing. Dessert a fresh peach ice cream.

Sweet Potato Tipsy

8 medium sweet potatoes

2 pinches of salt

7 tablespoons unsalted butter, softened

½ cup half-and-half

¼ cup dry sherry

3 tablespoons brown sugar

Serves 6 to 8

Preheat the oven to 350 degrees. Grease a medium casserole dish.

Put the sweet potatoes in a large pot, cover with cold water, and add the salt. Place over high heat, bring to a boil, then reduce the heat to medium and cook until soft when pierced with a knife, 30 to 40 minutes. Drain and set aside to cool.

Peel the sweet potatoes and transfer them to a large bowl. Coarsely mash the sweet potatoes with a fork, then add 5 tablespoons of the butter, the half-and-half, sherry, and brown sugar. Beat with an electric mixer on medium speed until light and fluffy, about 2 minutes.

Transfer the sweet potato mixture to the prepared dish, dot the top with the remaining 2 tablespoons butter, and bake until the top is golden brown, about 30 minutes. Serve hot.

LOUISIANA

THE SWEETMEATS YOUNG AMERICA CARRIED

The Creole pecan praline is a true Louisiana confection. The original came from France named for the Maréchal de Plessin whose butler Praslin doted on almonds and who contrived to have them coated with sugar to avoid indigestion. It was reserved for the descendants of the old French in Louisiana to evolve the sugared pecan, a nut that grew wild.

In the days when the white banners of Bourbon France with its three gold fleur-de-lis flew over Louisiana, the ardent lovers of 1795 carried pecan pralines when M'sieur went courting Mam'selle in the Vieux Carré. When in 1766, the Red and White Pavillion of Spain succeeded the flag of Royalist France in the Place d'Armes in New Orleans, dashing caballeros went serenading the sloe-eyed senoritas in moonlit patios and carried *pecarea de garapinadas* (pecan pralines) as their offering of love. After the Star Spangled Banner flew over old New Orleans, in 1803, many changes came to this Hispano-Franco city, but the sweetmeats young America carried when courting the Creole beauties were the same pecan pralines that their grandmothers knew and loved.

A half-century later when the Stars and Bars of the Confederacy flew from the flagstaff in the center of Jackson Square the beaux in their Confederate gray and the belles in their hoop skirts gossiped and laughed and nibbled the pecan pralines. And so it is today.

Pralines have been sold in the streets of New Orleans through all the city's history and always this delicious Creole confection of brown sugar and pecans. Today you can see pralines in the Crescent City in general shops in the Vieux Carré, in department stores, in drugstores, at the airport packaged and ready to mail to friends in far places. The making of the praline is fast reaching the state of big business.

Creole Pecan Pralines

1 pound light brown sugar

½ cup warm water

1 tablespoon unsalted butter

½ pound shelled pecans

Makes 12 large pralines

Line 2 large baking sheets with waxed paper. Place a large bowl of cold water in the sink.

In a large heavy saucepan, combine the brown sugar, warm water, and butter. Place over medium heat and bring to a boil, stirring constantly. Cook, stirring, until the mixture registers 228 degrees on a candy thermometer. This can take up to 40 minutes; the mixture should be thick, bubbly, and golden brown. Add the pecans and continue to boil gently, without stirring, for 3 to 5 minutes, until the mixture registers 236 degrees. Remove the pan from the heat and place the bottom in the reserved pan of cold water to stop the cooking. Cool the mixture to lukewarm (about 100 degrees) without stirring, then beat the candy to thicken it. Using 2 tablespoons, drop tablespoon-size pralines onto the prepared baking sheets, spacing them 1 inch apart; let cool completely.

Note: The pralines can be stored between sheets of waxed paper in an airtight container at room temperature for up to 1 week.

IT WAS MRS. RAY Samuels (her recipe I borrowed for Gumbo d'Zerb) who initiated me into the eating of red beans and rice, a traditional dish in the Louisiana country and filling enough to satisfy harvest hands. Devotees of the rice and bean cult frequently inaugurate luncheon clubs in its honor and meet at set periods to enjoy the old favorite. For rice and red beans are as identical twins as filé and gumbo.

And such notions regarding its service! Some want more beans than rice, some more rice than beans, others say half-and-half. Cooks vary the recipes—one insists on pickled pork, a product I have found only in the South; the next may demand salt pork; another uses ham hock.

Martha Ann Samuels told this story: In the old days Creole merchants would present good customers with a little gift after each order, a sort of thank-you-for-your-trade. The name of this extra was *lagniappe* and so generally accepted was it that the customers named the kind of extra desired. A woman planning a red-bean supper would invariably order a nickel's worth of beans "and lagniappe rice." Whereupon the grocer would dip a hand into the rice barrel and throw in the gratuity.

Red Beans and Rice

1 pound large dried red kidney beans

1 tablespoon unsalted butter
or bacon fat

½ pound salt pork, pickled pork, ham
hock, or bacon, cut into ½-inch pieces

1 tablespoon all-purpose flour

1 large onion, chopped

1 carrot, chopped

6 cups beef stock

3 sprigs parsley

1 bay leaf

Pinch of dried thyme

Pinch of dried sage

2 stalks and leaves of celery

Salt and freshly ground black pepper

Steamed long-grain white rice

Serves 8

Place the beans in a large bowl or pot and cover by 2 inches with fresh cold water. Soak the beans overnight. When ready to use, drain, rinse, and set aside.

Melt the butter in a large heavy saucepan over medium-high heat. Add the meat and brown it, about 5 minutes. Using a slotted spoon, transfer the meat to paper towels to drain. Stir the flour into the fat in pan; cook, stirring, until lightly browned, 2 to 3 minutes. Add the onion and cook for 3 minutes, or until softened and lightly browned. Add the beans, carrot, reserved meat, and stock. Reduce the heat to low and cook for 1 hour, or until the beans are softened, the flavors are melded, and the liquid starts to thicken (if it becomes too thick, add water to the pot). Add the parsley, bay leaf, thyme, sage, and celery and season with salt and pepper. Cook until the gravy is thick and dark and the beans are tender and creamy, about 30 minutes to 1 hour more. Serve with steamed long-grain white rice.

LOUISIANA IS DIVIDED INTO three parts culinarily speaking: Creole, 'Cajun, and Creole-'Cajun combined. One doesn't speak of deep South cooking and omit the 'Cajun country. 'Cajun refers to the Acadian-French, the French-Canadian immortalized in Longfellow's *Evangeline,* who emigrated and settled in Louisiana, then the promised land. I traveled through the vast rice and sugar plantations and finally reached the 'Cajun parish called Terrebone, or the Good Land.

My first stop there was in Franklin to visit with Mrs. Delaware Kemper Vollrath, an authority on Louisiana cooking, Acadian and Creole, born on a plantation in a community where for years the economy largely depended on the sugar industry. Delaware Vollrath was exposed to information on everything from the social side of a sugar-house party to the giant recipe for converting cane into sugar-bowl sweetening. The wild game and seafood native to the section afford wide variety for her culinary experimentation. Loving to cook, she borrowed ideas from neighbors and relatives. Still in her teens, she knew the way of a court bouillon, sauce piquante, how to roast a wild duck.

"Franklin is a wonderful place to live and to cook. So many native seafoods," she told me. "There's a shrimp factory in the basin. Townsfolk can buy shrimp just caught off the boats."

She gave us tips on her way of cooking the shrimp: "I often use a dash or two of Tabasco sauce and fresh tomatoes. Mace, oregano, marjoram, mayonnaise, and curry are all good with shrimp, with almost any fish dish, but not all at once, of course. The choice depends on whatever else is on the menu. Dishes must blend or contrast."

Here we give you her jambalaya and her oyster milk soup and chicken gumbo.

Shrimp Jambalaya

2 pounds shrimp, peeled and deveined

3½ cups cold water

Salt and freshly ground black pepper

3 tablespoons unsalted butter

1 tablespoon all-purpose flour

1 green bell pepper, cored, seeded, and finely chopped

6 scallions, finely chopped

4 stalks celery, finely chopped

2 dozen shucked oysters, with their liquor

1½ cups diced cooked ham

1 cup chopped cooked chicken

4 to 6 cups steamed long-grain white rice

2 tablespoons finely chopped parsley, optional

2 tablespoons diced hearts of celery, optional

2 tablespoons thinly sliced radishes, optional

2 tablespoons chopped scallions, white and tender green parts only, optional

Serves 6 to 8

In a medium pot, cover the shrimp with cold water; season with salt and pepper. Place over medium-high heat, bring to a boil, then reduce the heat and cook until the shrimp are tender, about 5 minutes. Drain, reserving the stock.

Melt the butter in a large Dutch oven over medium heat. Add the flour and cook, stirring, until lightly browned, about 3 minutes. Whisk in the hot shrimp stock. Add the green pepper, scallions, celery, and oysters and simmer for 3 to 5 minutes, until tender and the edges of the oysters begin to curl. Add the cooked shrimp, ham, chicken, and rice and cook, stirring, until piping hot. Turn onto a hot platter and decorate with parsley, hearts of celery, radishes, and scallions, if you like. Serve immediately.

Oyster-Milk Soup

28 oysters, well chilled

6 tablespoons (¾ stick)
unsalted butter

2 teaspoons Worcestershire sauce

½ teaspoon celery salt

1 cup milk

1 cup half-and-half

Salt and freshly ground black pepper

Paprika, mace, and oregano, optional

Serves 4

Shuck the oysters over a medium bowl to catch their liquor and put the shucked oysters into another bowl. Discard the shells.

Melt 4 tablespoons of the butter in a medium saucepan over medium-high heat. Stir in the Worcestershire sauce and celery salt, then add the oysters and bring to a simmer. Add 1 cup of the reserved oyster liquor to the pan (discard any remaining liquor) and bring to a boil. Add the milk and half-and-half to the pan and heat, stirring once or twice, until just about to boil (do not allow to boil or the stew will curdle), 3 to 5 minutes. Season with salt and pepper. Divide the remaining butter among 4 warm soup bowls just before ladling in the soup. Serve hot sprinkled with paprika, mace, and oregano, if you like.

LOUISIANA

Chicken Gumbo

1 cup all-purpose flour

Salt and freshly ground black pepper

2 (3½-pound) chickens,
cut into 8 pieces each

Vegetable oil for frying

Hot water

1 green bell pepper, cored, seeded, and
finely chopped

4 stalks celery, finely chopped

2 large onions, minced

1 pound fresh okra or 20 ounces frozen
okra, cut into ½-inch pieces

1 tablespoon gumbo filé powder

1½ to 2 cups steamed white rice

Serves 8

Pour the flour into a shallow dish and season it with salt and pepper; dredge the chicken pieces lightly in the flour.

Pour about ¼ inch of oil into a large heavy skillet and place over medium-high heat. Heat until hot, then add the chicken and cook until lightly browned, 3 to 4 minutes per side. Drain the chicken pieces on paper towels, then transfer them to a large stockpot. Add enough hot water to the pot to cover the chicken. Add the green pepper, celery, onions, and okra and season with salt and pepper. Bring to a simmer, then reduce the heat to medium-low, cover the pot tightly, and cook until the meat is tender, 30 to 45 minutes, adding more water if necessary. (The meat should taste like stewed chicken but have enough liquid to serve as a soup sauce.)

Place the filé powder in bowls, about ½ teaspoonful to each, then ladle the chicken pieces into the bowls. Ladle in the soup and the rice. A favorite way of serving in the deep South is to serve the gumbo from a soup tureen, the rice in a covered dish, the filé powder in a shaker. Warning: Filé powder makes soup stringy if overheated. Add it to the bowl or soup tureen, but never to the boiling soup.

Note: This is a basic dish for Louisiana cooks. More often than not they add shellfish before the dish is done— 15 minutes for crab or shrimp or 10 minutes for oysters. This is a meal-in-a-dish. Serve with green salad. For dessert fruit—pears, apples, and grapes with Camembert or Gruyère, the right ending. Gumbo blends to perfection when it is stored overnight in the refrigerator. Like many stews, it is better the second day. Cook the rice just before serving.

SMELLIN' AND TASTIN' AND COOKIN' ALL GOES TOGETHER

Deep in the heart of Acadia country at New Iberia, Louisiana, lies a comely little island, kingdom of pepper and salt. This is the United States home of the Tabasco pepper, site of the oldest and thickest salt vein in the Western Hemisphere. Newly added to the scene: fifty-four prolific oil wells knee-deep in the marshes. Avery Island is the name, the private estate of the Avery and McIlhenny clans. A realm family-controlled now into the sixth generation.

My trip to Avery Island was to visit its kitchens, to talk to the cooks who had learned their little miracles at Mama's elbow, cooks who still insist on making things like beaten biscuits. And thank the Lord for such infinite blessings! Mr. Walter McIlhenny, director of this domain, had given permission for me to come and learn first hand the secrets of Creole and 'Cajun cookery.

First day there I spent sight-seeing. I wanted to see the pepper fields, and visit the plant where Tabasco sauce is made. There behind the ivy-covered walls I saw a thousand casks holding the pepper mash, sealed under salt and left to age as fine wine is. The peppers are macerated; no heat touches the fruit except the kiss of the sun. It's after a three-year mellowing period that the mash is ready to blend with the vinegar, then passed through fine sieves and bottled as sauce.

Second day on the island I started my tour, eating my way around from kitchen to kitchen. I learned about "lost bread" at a midmorning breakfast with Mrs. Harold Osborn. This is Rosemary McIlhenny, Uncle Ned's beloved daughter, now married and living in Oklahoma but back to the island for a visit each winter. Uncle Rufus and Aunt Clara left her their place complete with Mary and Levi Dunn—it's their home, too. The Dunns had managed the house and grounds for forty-two years.

It was Mary of the soft voice and the good brown eyes who told me, "Any bread is 'lost' that is more than two days old." It was Mary who gave me the oyster soup recipe, a hand-down from Rosemary's grandmother, Mrs. William Matthews of New Orleans. A secret in the soup: "Put somep'n good in, to get somep'n good out."

I lived in Mr. Walter's guest house, this being two reconditioned slave cabins, a glass-walled living room in between. Here Hazel Whitith is kitchen queen. She gave me recipes in a voice ripe, rich, and rounded. "Never mind about 'how much,' jes' you remember smellin' and tastin' and cookin' all goes together."

A warm February day ten of us were off for a picnic on Mr. Walter's *Heron*, an eighty-five-foot yacht. Down sleepy Petit Bayou Anse, past tremendous oil fields in the marshlands, on to Vermilion Bay, actually a part of the Gulf of Mexico. The tall rozo grass along the way leaned to the wind with a singing sigh. Brahman range cattle grazed the lowlands. Trappers were out for muskrat and nutria. Whirring of wings, as flocks of ducks and geese were off in a breathtaking rush at our approach.

Cooking smells drifted up from the galley enriching the soft spring air. Mmmmm, what a heavenly smell, and I'm off to say hello to Etie Trahan, chef and electrician. I met Captain Fernand Dubois and his brother Joseph, these being Etie's brothers-in-law. All three were keeping an eye on the pot where sauce piquante bubbled with sulky little plop, plop sounds. This 'Cajun dish is to Acadia land as gumbo is to New Orleans. I took notes while Etie described the making, and with such fervor and flavor our anticipation grew until we could hardly wait to eat.

A help-yourself meal; everything was spread on the table in the cabin. Brown rice served as the background for the sauce. We mopped up the last drops with French garlic bread, this piled like cordwood on a big tray. There was a wooden bowl of greens with avocado slices, with tomato quarters and rings of green pepper. A side dish contained stuffed deviled eggs, Tabasco-fired. A jar of jumbles for dessert, each big, thin cookie spilling sugar off its top.

Hazel Whitith's Flannel Cakes

1 large egg, beaten

1½ cups milk

1½ cups all-purpose flour

½ teaspoon salt

2 tablespoons unsalted butter, melted

Makes four 10-inch pancakes

Preheat the oven to 200 degrees.

In a large bowl, whisk the egg with the milk. Using a handheld electric mixer, beat in the flour and salt to make a smooth batter. Stir in the butter.

Heat a large griddle or nonstick skillet over medium-high heat. For each pancake, ladle about ⅓ cup of the batter onto the griddle and spread it evenly with the bottom of the ladle or cup. Reduce the heat to medium-low and cook until the tops of the flannel cakes are covered with small bubbles and the bottoms are golden. Gently turn the cakes over and cook until they are lightly browned. Place the cakes on a baking sheet as they are cooked and keep them warm in the oven while you cook the remaining batter. Serve immediately.

Note: You many serve the flannel cakes rolled with filling of grape jelly, brandy-spiked, and pass a brandied whipped-cream sauce to spoon over the cakes, if you like.

Jumbles

2 sticks (1 cup) unsalted butter, softened	1 teaspoon lemon extract or vanilla extract
2 cups sugar, plus more for sprinkling	5 cups all-purpose flour
4 large eggs, well beaten	1 teaspoon grated nutmeg
2 teaspoons rosewater	

Makes 1 dozen cookies

In a medium bowl using an electric mixer, cream the butter and sugar until fluffy. Add the eggs and mix well, then add the rosewater and lemon extract. Slowly add the flour and nutmeg in batches.

Turn the batter out onto a lightly floured surface and roll it into a disk. Wrap the dough in waxed paper and chill in the refrigerator for at least 3 hours or overnight.

When ready to bake the cookies, preheat the oven to 375 degrees and grease a large baking sheet. Take out just enough batter at a time to roll easily. (The secret of very thin jumbles lies in the dough being kept well chilled.) Roll the batter ⅛ inch thick on a lightly floured surface and cut with a 2½-inch cookie cutter. Transfer the cookies to the prepared pan and bake for 5 to 8 minutes. Cool on the pan on a wire rack for 2 minutes, then transfer the cookies to the rack, sprinkle with sugar, and cool completely.

Mary Dunn's "Lost Bread" French Toast

10 slices 2-day-old bread

3 large eggs, beaten

½ cup milk

1 cup sugar, plus more for sprinkling

½ teaspoon vanilla extract

Unsalted butter or vegetable oil for cooking

Freshly grated nutmeg for sprinkling

Serves 6 to 8

Preheat the oven to 375 degrees.

Remove the crusts from the bread and cut each slice into 4 pieces. In a large shallow dish, whisk the eggs, milk, sugar, and vanilla together. Soak the bread in batches in the egg mixture for 5 minutes, turning the slices halfway through to coat both sides.

Heat a griddle or large nonstick skillet over medium-high heat and grease it well. Add the slices and cook until browned on both sides, 4 to 5 minutes. Transfer to a baking sheet and repeat with the remaining slices. Bake the toasts for 4 to 5 minutes, until slightly crisp to the touch and firm. Sprinkle the toasts with nutmeg and sugar and serve hot with your mid-morning coffee.

Nancy Russell's Baked Grits

2 cups water

Salt

1 cup stone-ground grits

2 tablespoons unsalted butter

1 cup whole milk

1 large egg, beaten

A few drops of Tabasco sauce

Serves 4

Preheat the oven to 375 degrees. Grease a 1-quart casserole.

In a large heavy stockpot or Dutch oven, bring the water to a boil and add salt. Stir in the grits. Cover, reduce the heat to low, and cook for about 20 minutes, stirring frequently, until mixture thickens and the grits are the consistency of thick oatmeal. Stir in the butter, milk, and egg. Add the Tabasco and season with salt.

Turn the mixture into the prepared casserole and bake for 30 minutes, or until the top is nicely browned. Serve with vegetables and meat.

Shrimp Sauce Piquant

2 tablespoons olive oil

1 cup all-purpose flour

2 cups chopped onions

2½ cups chopped fresh tomatoes

1 cup tomato paste

4 stalks celery, chopped

2 cups chopped green bell peppers

1 to 3 tablespoons minced jalapeño peppers

1 teaspoon salt

Dash of Tabasco sauce

¼ cup chopped scallions, white and tender green parts only

2 pounds large shrimp, peeled and deveined

Serves 8

Combine the oil and flour in a large skillet or 4-quart Dutch oven. Place over medium-low heat and cook, stirring to form a pasty consistency and to color it deep brown, 8 to 10 minutes. Add the onions and cook until lightly browned, 5 to 7 minutes. Stir in the tomatoes and tomato paste. Reduce the heat to low, cover, and cook for about 45 minutes, stirring occasionally, until thickened. Add the celery, green peppers, and jalapeño and cook until softened, about 5 minutes. Add the salt and Tabasco. Reduce the heat as low as you can and cook for about 1½ hours, until the flavors are blended, stirring about every 10 minutes to prevent sticking. Add the scallions and the shrimp and cook, stirring occasionally, for 20 to 30 minutes, until the shrimp are cooked through and pink. Serve with garlic bread or over steamed buttered white rice.

LOUISIANA

THE SOUTHWEST

TEXAS

Pleasant are my memories of eating in Texas. Five times I have toured the Lone Star State, notebook in hand, searching for regional dishes. My first taste of Texas was just what I had expected—barbecued beef. I had my bowl of chili, I ate cactus salad, and sampled broiled rattlesnake hips. I was disappointed. Texans, it seemed, aside from a few things, ate just about like the rest of the United States. It was on my second visit I discovered there is a difference, there is such a thing as "The Texas Cuisine."

It was in San Antonio, visiting with Arthur and Bobbie Coleman, that I came to understand why Texans eat what Texans eat. This couple had just published their *Texas Cook Book* and were full of the subject. Texas, they told me, has evolved a cuisine by adoption and adaption, handed down by the people who had pioneered there. It is derived from the good living of the Old South enlivened with contributions made by the French, the Anglo-American colonies, the Indians, the Spanish, the Mexicans, especially along the Mex-Tex border. For good measure it had just a touch of Italian, a bit of Chinese.

The Colemans' house in Alamo Heights is built around the kitchen. The kitchen is a big place with a rocking chair, a sofa, and room for a dozen guests, "because here we spend our free time."

The afternoon of our visit the cocktail glasses were arranged on the long center work counter. A Mexican bowl held little dried shrimp, a popular munch in the Southwest. And tortillas, of course; these in the Border Country are as commonly served as crackers in other states.

On the range was the huge *olla* holding the bean dip, which gave forth with an occasional lazy bubble; cozy warm, not quite to a simmer. Tortillas we dipped in, dipped up. "Isn't that good!"

"It's made with *frijoles*," Bobbie said, showing me a bagful of the uncooked pinto beans.

Arthur explained, "Frijoles stand for the pinto or red beans, not the navies."

Texas Bean Dip

4 cups dried pinto beans

2 cups chopped onion

3 cloves garlic, chopped

2 teaspoons ground cumin

6 tablespoons bacon drippings or vegetable shortening

6 tablespoons chili powder

1 tablespoon salt

1 cup (2 sticks) unsalted butter, softened

½ pound sharp cheddar cheese, grated

Dash of hot sauce

Makes 2 quarts

Wash the beans, discarding any small stones. Soak the beans overnight in a pottery, enamel, or glass pot with enough water to cover.

When ready to cook, add the onion, garlic, cumin, and bacon drippings to the pot. Place over medium-high heat and bring to a boil, then reduce the heat to low and simmer until the beans are very soft, 3 to 4 hours, stirring occasionally with a wooden spoon to prevent sticking. If additional water is needed, use boiling water, as cold water will darken the beans. When the beans are soft but not falling apart, add the chili powder and continue cooking, stirring, for 4 minutes to thoroughly combine. Add the salt. (Salting too soon hardens the beans.)

Transfer the beans to a large bowl and mash in the butter, cheese, and hot sauce, stirring with a fork until the mixture is smooth. Serve warm.

JINGLING SPURS AND CREAKING SADDLES

Beloved by San Antonians, by Texans everywhere, is the historic Menger Hotel. For a century its fabulous table has served as a magnet to draw the traveler. It was in 1858, twenty-two years after the fall of the Alamo, nineteen years before the railroad came to the city, that William A. Menger, a German immigrant, built his two-story hotel of fifty rooms plus adequate stables. "The Finest Hostelry West of the Mississippi," so his advertisements claimed.

San Antonio then was a crossroads of the West. Stagecoach travelers stopped here for refreshment and rest. Trail drivers came with jingling spurs and creaking saddles. Menger's was a green oasis for local ranchers who traveled long distances by wagon to carry home a supply of Mr. Menger's regal beer.

Visitors beelined to Menger's to eat the fine hams so wonderfully cured, to marvel over the highly seasoned sausages, the sauerbraten and *hasenpfeffer* and the rich coffee cakes.

The press of feeding the herd literally forced the building of the hotel—in all the town there wasn't room to bed the guests that came to Menger's to board. A magnificent banquet was given to celebrate the opening. Such a menu! Such a listing of delicacies! Among the meats for instance: wild turkey, quail, and buffalo tongues.

Mint juleps were the drink of the day, served by the hundreds at the long mahogany bar. Since then this bar has been heralded in poetry, fiction, and song. Here O. Henry gathered material for some of his world-famous stories. Here Leonard Wood and Teddy Roosevelt recruited their Rough Riders. Countless heads of cattle have exchanged owners over Menger mint juleps. And the bar is still there. Like the Menger, it has remained through wars, plagues, and floods.

The first hotel is an integral part of the new one, which cost nearly a million dollars. But if William Menger could walk in today I'm sure he would be pleased. The tradition he established for setting the finest table in the West is being upheld as in the old days. Sophisticated dishes are served at the Menger tables and also typical foods of the Border Country.

Our table overlooked the Spanish patio, the backyard of the old kitchen, once zigzagged by a viaduct. It was there Mr. Menger cooled his beer for the bar. A cottonwood tree grew by the water's edge serving as a sort of air-cooled "refrigerator." Meats were hung from the branches: hams, beef, venison, buffalo to be raised and lowered by pulleys. Today this patio is a maze of semitropical trees, shrubs, and flowers.

We ate black bean soup enriched with both red wine and diced frankfurters, a one-course luncheon popular with the businessmen of the town. This is served with crusty bread and a mixed green salad. Something to fill one right to the chin. Besides the bean soup we borrowed recipes for two other Menger specialties, beef picadillo and spinach pudding.

Black Bean Soup with Red Wine and Frankfurters

1 pound dried black beans

3 medium russet potatoes, peeled and diced

¼ cup diced celery

1 medium onion, chopped

2 small carrots, chopped

2 teaspoons salt

¼ teaspoon freshly ground black pepper

2 cloves garlic, chopped

½ pound frankfurters, diced

2 cups red wine, preferably Burgundy

Tabasco sauce

Serves 6

Pick over the beans carefully and wash them; place them in a large stockpot, cover them with water by 2 inches, and soak overnight. The following morning, drain the beans, rinse them again, and cover with fresh water by 2 inches. Place over medium-high heat, bring to a boil, then reduce the heat to low and simmer for 1½ hours, or until the beans are tender. Add the potatoes, celery, onion, carrots, salt, pepper, and garlic. Add enough water to cover, if needed, and cook until the vegetables and beans are tender, about 20 minutes more. Puree the soup in a blender or food processor or with an immersion blender and pour it back into the pot. Add the frankfurters and wine and season with Tabasco. Place over medium heat and cook until the frankfurters are heated through, 5 to 10 minutes. Serve hot.

TEXAS

Beef Picadillo

½ pound ground beef

½ pound ground pork

1 teaspoon salt

¼ teaspoon freshly ground
black pepper

4 medium tomatoes, peeled and diced

2½ cloves garlic, finely chopped

3 scallions, white and tender green
parts only, finely chopped

1 (6-ounce) can tomato paste

3 medium russet potatoes,
peeled and diced

2 jalapeño peppers, chopped

Dash of dried oregano

¾ cup diced pimiento

¾ cup seedless raisins

¾ cup toasted whole almonds

Serves 4

Place the beef and pork in a large stockpot and add water
to cover. Add the salt and pepper, place over medium
heat, and bring to a boil. Reduce the heat to medium-low,
cover, and simmer for 30 minutes, or until the meat is
cooked through and the sauce is thick. Add the remaining
ingredients and cook covered until the potatoes are
cooked through, about 30 minutes more. Ladle into warm
bowls and serve hot.

Spinach Casserole

4 tablespoons (½ stick) unsalted butter, softened

½ small onion, minced

½ green bell pepper, cored, seeded, and minced

1½ cloves garlic, minced

2 (10-ounce) packages frozen chopped spinach, thawed and drained

2 large eggs, beaten

1 teaspoon salt

¼ teaspoon freshly ground black pepper

Dash of grated nutmeg

1½ cups fine breadcrumbs

Serves 6

Preheat the oven to 375 degrees. Grease a 1½-quart baking dish.

Melt 3 tablespoons of the butter in a large deep skillet over medium heat. Add the onion, green pepper, and garlic and cook, stirring, until softened and just beginning to brown, about 8 minutes. Take the pan off the heat and stir in the spinach, eggs, salt, pepper, and nutmeg.

In a small bowl, combine the remaining 1 tablespoon butter with the breadcrumbs. Scrape the spinach mixture into the prepared dish, top with the buttered breadcrumbs, and bake for about 20 minutes, until the spinach is bubbling and the breadcrumbs are golden. Let stand for 10 minutes before serving.

TEXAS

SWEET PERFUME OF A CEDAR-STUMP FIRE

Deep in the heart of Texas, I made "San Antone" my headquarters for junketing jaunts, rustling up ranch recipes. Traveling out, but always coming back to this most hospitable town.

My very first trip yielded two regional treasures: huevos rancheros and chicken guili. We made a caravan procession on the Bandera Highway—four cars in a row, packed with friends of the Searses (Colonel George D. and wife Della). We were invited for Saturday dinner and to stay until Sunday at their Valley View Ranch, in the rolling hill country just beyond Medina.

We drove on the very edge of spring. Late January it was, but the sun had warmed the limestone hills and the mesquite showed in gray-green circles along the ridges. This is the sheep and goat kingdom and there were herds of Holsteins in the fields and the Santa Gertrudis, that relatively new crossbreed.

We crossed the Medina River of strange slate-green color, a lonely country it seemed to us. Then we came to the Searses'.

A bedlam of robust hellos; the barking of Cracker the collie, of Tonkie the terrier. There was the Colonel resting on his stick and well-wrapped in his dignity. There was trim little Della in riding breeches, yellow vest, and checked shirt. Into the thirty-foot living room with the hand-hewn beamed ceiling, a cedar-stump fire was throwing its sparks and giving sweet perfume.

In February, 1946, when the Colonel arrived back from Japan, he had had a heart attack and that was the end of army life. Mrs. Sears, "my city sparrow," as the Colonel likes to call his gay little one, urged that they buy a farm with their savings. This is the ranch, 217 acres of hill and valley, the house a rambling hacienda. A foreman and his wife assist with the work, with extra help hired at harvest periods.

Mrs. Sears makes butter and cottage cheese. She cans and freezes garden stuff. Showing me her well-stocked freezer she said, "I chose this life for us, now I must prove myself a farmer."

But the thing she does best with all her heart is weekend entertaining. "The Colonel likes people," she explained; so does his little "city sparrow."

Chicken guili was the main dish for the Saturday dinner, this served with rice and a green vegetable. A fruit salad for dessert gently mixed with a dressing sweetened with honey and boysenberry juice. The Colonel doesn't like poultry, but he loves the guili sauce and has a special dish of this for himself spooned over shrimp. Mrs. Sears usually makes a double quantity of sauce and puts a part of it in the freezer to use on short order. If it gets thickish thin it with boiling water.

Sunday we had spareribs with barbecue sauce. Liquid smoke had been brushed over the ribs to give an open-fire flavor pitch. The ribs were served with grits and black-eyed peas, the peas from last summer's garden, having spent the winter in the freezer. The Sunday-morning breakfast featured huevos rancheros . . . Hot! Hot! Try it on New Year's Day in the morning when you have celebrated too late and far too well.

Huevos Rancheros

¼ pound bacon

2 large cloves garlic, sliced paper thin

2 medium jalapeño peppers, chopped

1 (14-ounce) can chopped tomatoes

Salt and freshly ground black pepper

4 large eggs

4 slices toast, buttered

Serves 4

Cut the bacon into ½-inch pieces. Fry the bacon in a large skillet over low heat until almost crisp, 8 to 10 minutes. Add the garlic and cook until browned, about 5 minutes. Add the jalapeños and tomatoes and simmer for 10 minutes, stirring constantly with a wooden spoon to press and break up the tomatoes. Season with salt and pepper.

When the mixture is smooth and not too thick, drop in the eggs one at a time and season them with salt and pepper. Cover the skillet and poach the eggs for 3 to 5 minutes, until the whites and center are set. Meanwhile, place 1 slice of buttered toast on each of 4 plates. Ladle an egg with plenty of sauce on top of each of the butter toasts and serve immediately.

TEXAS

Chicken Guili

4 large bone-in, skin-on
chicken breasts

Salt and freshly ground black pepper

½ cup (1 stick) unsalted butter

2 cups chopped celery

1 cup chopped onion

1 cup chopped green bell pepper

6 cloves garlic, chopped

¾ cup finely chopped parsley

2 tablespoons all-purpose flour

2 (14-ounce) cans chopped tomatoes

4 bay leaves

Steamed buttered long-grain white rice
for serving

4 large hard-cooked eggs, chopped

Serves 4

Generously season the chicken breasts with salt and
pepper on all sides. Melt the butter in a large skillet
over medium-high heat. Lower the heat to medium, add
the chicken breasts, and brown them, about 8 minutes
per side, then transfer to paper towels to drain. Add the
celery, onion, green pepper, garlic, and parsley to the
remaining chicken fat in the pan and cook until the onion
becomes transparent, about 3 minutes. Add the flour and
stir slowly until the mixture is smooth, 3 to 5 minutes
more. Add the tomatoes and bay leaves and season with
salt and pepper. Lay in the chicken breasts, cover the pan,
reduce the heat to low, and simmer until the meat is tender,
about 45 minutes. Spoon the chicken and sauce over the
rice and garnish with the chopped hard-cooked egg.

Barbecue Sauce

2 cups tomato sauce

½ cup tarragon vinegar

½ cup firmly packed brown sugar

2 tablespoons powdered mustard

3 tablespoons chopped green onion

2 bay leaves

2 cloves garlic

2 dashes of Worcestershire sauce

2 drops of Tabasco sauce

2 tablespoons unsalted butter

Makes about 2 cups

Combine all of the ingredients in a medium saucepan, place over medium-high heat, and bring to a boil. Reduce the heat to low, cover, and simmer, stirring occasionally, for 1 hour, or until the mixture thickens. Remove the garlic cloves and bay leaves. Serve warm over your favorite meat or cool and store in the refrigerator for up to 2 weeks.

TEXAS

NEXT TRIP OUT OF San Antonio was by plane to the hill country—flying to the Flying "L" Ranch of Colonel Jack Lapham, a five-hundred-acre air resort near Bandera, cowboy capital of the world. Invited to attend a chicken barbecue, I meant to eat chicken, get the great smoky barbecue sauce recipe and right back to town, but with the delicious food cooked open fire, the aromatic sun-warmed air, I stayed for two days.

Flying "L" Chicken Barbecue Sauce

1 cup (2 sticks) unsalted butter

2 (6-ounce) cans tomato paste

1 cup ketchup

1 cup cider vinegar

1 tablespoon brown sugar

3 tablespoons Worcestershire sauce

1 tablespoon hot sauce

1 tablespoon steak sauce

Juice of 2 lemons

Salt and freshly ground black pepper

Makes 4 cups

Melt the butter in a large heavy saucepan over medium heat. Add the remaining ingredients, bring to a boil, then reduce the heat to low and simmer for about 10 minutes, stirring occasionally, until thickened. Serve warm over chicken or store in the refrigerator for up to 2 weeks.

JOY OF THE DAY'S SMALL RITUALS

After eating my way in and out of San Antonio I came to Dallas again, lured by a charming letter I received back in New York City from Mrs. Henry H. Stanton. She had written regarding her mother and her wonderful cooking. "You should have some of her recipes. She is part Greek and part Armenian and puts together foods in weird combinations, but these turn out unbelievably good. Ask for her *dolmades* recipes, and her pilaf, the rice steamed in chicken broth. Please go and see Mama, Mrs. A. L. DeGuire of Greenbrier Lane, Dallas, Texas."

I did go and I met Papa, too, a tall, lean Texan of French descent whose great-grandfather arrived in the Southwest in 1757. Like Frenchmen everywhere Mr. DeGuire takes particular interest in good eating and Mrs. DeGuire never tires of fixing a dish to please Papa's palate.

I found more to interest me in the DeGuire kitchen than a handful of recipes. I learned a lesson in living. These two delightful people make a joy of the day's small rituals. Their happiness revolves around the dinner table, their garden of flowers and vegetables. And there are daughter Ruth's children coming and going.

"Give her our way with the cornbread," Mr. DeGuire said to his wife, then explained. "I taught her how to make it. Couldn't cook much way back then. But was she pretty!" He recollected, "Built like a quarter horse, four foot eleven and a half inches, and she sure set a pace. . . ." Mr. DeGuire's eyes turned to his wife's merry round face, and his smile came gentle as a benediction.

TEXAS

Texas Corn Cake

½ cup fine-ground white cornmeal

½ cup sifted all-purpose flour

½ teaspoon salt

1½ teaspoons baking powder

1 teaspoon sugar

1 large egg, beaten

½ cup buttermilk

1 teaspoon bacon drippings or vegetable shortening

Serves 4

Sift the cornmeal, flour, salt, baking powder, and sugar into a large bowl. Make a well and add the egg and buttermilk; stir until the batter is soft and the lumps just disappear.

Grease a 10-inch skillet with the bacon drippings and place over low heat. When melted, pour in the cornmeal mixture and cook until bubbles form and the corn cake is browned around the edges and somewhat dry on top. Turn the corn cake like a pancake (don't cover the pan or the bread will sweat) and brown on the other side. Transfer to a plate and serve the corn cake with turnip greens and ham hocks or pork jowls with black-eyed peas, if you like.

Chicken Pilaf

3 cups chicken broth

Salt and freshly ground black pepper

1 cup uncooked white or brown rice

1 tablespoon lemon juice

Butter, optional

Serves 6

In a large stockpot, bring the chicken broth to a boil over medium-high heat; season with salt and pepper. Stir in the rice and continue stirring for a couple of minutes. Reduce the heat to very low, cover the pan, and cook until the rice is tender, about 18 minutes. Halfway through the cooking time, add the lemon juice. Don't stir; just slowly cook until all the broth is absorbed and each rice grain stands alone. When the rice is done, let it stand off the heat for 5 minutes. Fluff the rice with a fork and stir in a little butter before serving, if you like.

"Dolmades" (Stuffed Grape Leaves)

3 tablespoons unsalted butter

2 medium onions, finely chopped

1 pound ground lean round steak

1 pound ground pork

4 teaspoons salt

1 teaspoon freshly ground black pepper

1 tablespoon minced parsley

1 teaspoon minced fresh mint or ¼ teaspoon dried mint

½ cup uncooked long-grain white rice

40 brined grape leaves, drained (from one 16-ounce jar)

2 cups water

Makes about 3 dozen

Melt 1½ tablespoons of the butter in a large skillet over medium-low heat. In a large bowl, combine the onions with the ground meats, salt, pepper, parsley, mint, and rice. Place a tablespoonful of the mixture on a grape leaf. Spread the grape leaves, vein side up, on a work surface. Separate the larger leaves; piece together the smaller leaves, overlapping the edges, to approximate the size of the larger leaves. Set 2 tablespoons of the onion mixture in the center of each leaf. Pull the leaf up and over the filling and roll up, folding in the sides as you go. Roll and fasten with a toothpick.

Melt the remaining 1½ tablespoons butter in the water in a large saucepan over medium-high heat, then remove the pan from the heat. Snugly arrange the rolls in the pan in 2 layers. Set a heatproof plate on the rolls to keep them submerged. Cover and cook for 20 minutes, then reduce the heat to low and simmer until all of the liquid has been absorbed, about 10 minutes. Serve hot as a main dish or well chilled as a first course.

WHEN DALLAS, TEXAS, ENTERTAINS, it's in the big-hat manner. There giant steaks go to table dripping raw juices. The shrimp are all jumbo, too big for the mouth. Ears of sweet corn take two hands to heft and the barbecue buns are filled beyond limit. At the table I discovered Dallas remains a man's world. But drop in at a tea party and refreshments go midget. Dallas women want everything biggest until it comes to teatime. Then the demand is for cakes and sandwiches in miniature. Each little tidbit must be no more than mouth-size.

It was Mrs. Roy Braden, cake baker for Dallas social functions, who let us in on this Dallas tea-party quirk. That was some years ago when she was showing me around her newly opened $200,000 bakery on Travis Avenue. There I saw tray upon tray of sweet stuffs cooling. The little cakes no bigger than quarters, cake balls were like marbles, cheese straws like toothpicks. The petits fours were really petits, just half the usual dimensions. We tasted this and tasted that and then asked for recipes; the apricot pinwheels and French nut sticks.

Apricot Pinwheels

1 envelope active dry yeast

¼ cup warm, but not hot, water

¾ cup milk, scalded and cooled to lukewarm

½ cup sugar

1½ teaspoons salt

3 large eggs, beaten

4½ cups sifted all-purpose flour

¼ cup vegetable shortening, melted and cooled

1½ teaspoons grated lemon peel

4 sticks (2 cups) unsalted butter, cut into small bits

½ cup apricot jam

¼ teaspoon ground cinnamon

1 large egg white

1 tablespoon cold water

Makes 6 dozen

In a large bowl, dissolve the yeast in the warm water. Let stand for 5 minutes, then stir in the milk. Add the sugar and salt, stirring until just dissolved. Add the eggs. Add half of the flour, beating with a wooden spoon until smooth and elastic. Beat in the shortening and lemon peel. Gradually work in the remaining flour, blending with your fingers. Turn the dough out onto a lightly floured surface; cover loosely with plastic wrap and it let rest for 1 hour, or until doubled in size.

Using a well-floured rolling pin, roll the dough out into an oblong ⅓-inch-thick disk. Cover two thirds of the dough with the bits of butter. Fold the uncovered portion over half of the buttered portion, then fold over the buttered part, making 3 layers. Repeat this process 2 or 3 more times, rolling and folding. The greater number of times, the flakier the pastry will be. When finished, wrap the dough in plastic wrap and refrigerate overnight.

When ready to prepare the pinwheels, preheat the oven to 400 degrees. Grease 2 or 3 large baking sheets. Divide the dough into 3 equal pieces. Roll each out very thin into an oblong about 15 inches wide. Spread each with a thin layer of the apricot jam; dust lightly with the cinnamon. Roll up the sheets tightly into cylinders, as for a jellyroll.

Cut each into ½-inch slices and place them on the prepared baking sheets.

In a small bowl, beat the egg white with the cold water and brush over the pinwheels. Cover them loosely with plastic wrap and allow to rise at room temperature until they increase in size by about one third, 25 to 30 minutes. Bake for about 15 minutes, until risen and golden on top. Let cool in the pans on wire racks for 5 minutes, then turn out onto the racks to cool. Serve warm or at room temperature.

Note: The pinwheels can be wrapped in foil and stored at room temperature for up to 2 days. Reheat in a 350-degree oven in the foil, then unwrap and bake until slightly crusty, 4 to 5 minutes.

French Nut Sticks

¾ cup (1½ sticks) unsalted butter

2 cups sugar

2 large eggs

3 cups sifted cake flour

1 teaspoon vanilla extract

2 to 3 tablespoons apricot jam

2 large egg whites

Pinch of salt

1 tablespoon all-purpose flour

1 cup chopped pecans

Makes about 3 dozen

Preheat the oven to 350 degrees. Grease a large baking sheet.

In the large bowl of an electric mixer, cream the butter with 1 cup of the sugar until light and fluffy. Beat in the eggs. Gradually add the cake flour a little at a time, beating until smooth. Stir in the vanilla. Roll the dough out onto the prepared baking sheet ¼ inch thick. Spread with a thin layer of apricot jam. Bake for about 6 minutes, until the dough begins to brown and the jam is melted.

Meanwhile, in a medium bowl, beat the egg whites with the salt until frothy. Gradually beat in the remaining 1 cup sugar combined with the all-purpose flour. Beat until the whites form stiff but not dry peaks. Fold in the pecans. Spread the mixture over the jam layer. Cover loosely with plastic wrap and refrigerate to set, about 2 hours.

When ready to bake, preheat the oven to 375 degrees and generously grease a large baking sheet. Cut the mixture into sticks, 2 inches by ½ inch thick. Place on the baking sheet about 1 inch apart. Bake for about 15 minutes, until the meringue is browned. Cool in the pan on wire racks for 2 minutes, then transfer to the racks to cool completely. Serve at room temperature.

Note: These cookies will keep, stored in an airtight container, for up to 3 days.

TEXAS

CANDLELIGHT AND COPPER CHAFING DISHES

I went visiting with a teenage group of Dallas boys and girls, whose idea of fun on the range is the cooking kind. Not chow-wagon grub! This group is the Junior Gourmet Club of Greenhill School who give their spare time and talent to cooking the unusual.

It was an evening in late October, the setting the high-school assembly hall where I was taken to sample their dishes. Imagine my surprise; candlelight, glistening linen, gleaming silver trays, copper chafing dishes. The buffet table was set with a variety of fine fare worthy of an inspired high-bonnet chef. The young people pointed out the specialties—poulet volaille amandine, pheasant roti gremaldo, beef stroganoff, ham timbales bourgeoise. They could rattle off these foreign names with the greatest of ease.

Club members aim at one thing in particular, to learn the preparation of dishes different from the daily habit foods of the family table. These young people want to know the cooking of other countries as well as the best in America. They want to know how to plan menus around the dishes they serve, how to feel at ease in a restaurant, menu in hand.

To cook a fine dish there must be some basic training. Evening meetings were arranged with home economists from commercial food firms teaching the ABC rules. Occasionally a local chef comes to discuss the foods of foreign countries. At periodic intervals the young people dine together in a city restaurant. Then they interview the chef regarding the dishes served, and borrow recipes to try for themselves.

I talked to football player Larry Nichols, seventeen, who was one of the outstanding cooks in the crowd. That spring his chicken cacciatore was voted the best boy-cook dish of the year. Here's a surprise—the boys in the club outnumber the girls. It was in Fort Smith, Arkansas, Larry picked up the recipe when visiting friends with his father. Larry travels often with Dad on cattle-buying trips and Dad's hobby, too, is that of amateur chef. The family has a cattle ranch in Colorado and there Father often prepares a barbecue meal for his men.

Texans love the barbecue. This, one of their most popular ways of entertaining. And our young gourmets go in for this, too, but with what a flourish!

Larry Nichols'
Chicken Cacciatore

12 boneless chicken thighs

1 cup sherry wine

1½ cloves garlic, finely chopped

Salt and freshly ground black pepper

2 tablespoons extra-virgin olive oil

2 cups finely chopped onion

1½ cups finely chopped
green bell pepper

1 teaspoon salt

⅔ teaspoon white pepper

1½ teaspoons curry powder

1½ teaspoons dried thyme

2 (14-ounce) cans chopped tomatoes

1 teaspoon chopped parsley

1 cup currants

1 cup sliced toasted almonds

4 cups steamed long-grain white rice

Serves 6

Place the chicken thighs in a large bowl and toss with the sherry and 1 of the chopped garlic cloves. Cover and refrigerate for 2 hours.

When ready to cook, preheat the oven to 200 degrees.

Remove the chicken from the marinade, reserving the marinade, and season with salt and pepper. Heat the oil in a large deep skillet over medium-high heat. Add the chicken and cook, turning, until lightly browned and crisp, about 8 minutes. Transfer the thighs to a roasting pan, cover with foil, and place in the oven to keep warm. (This is the secret to success.)

Meanwhile, add the onions, green peppers, and the remaining garlic to the fat in the pan, reduce the heat to low, and cook, stirring occasionally, until softened, about 10 minutes. Stir in the salt, white pepper, curry powder, and thyme. Add the tomatoes and parsley and simmer, stirring occasionally, for 5 minutes. Stir in the sherry marinade and simmer for 5 minutes more. Pour the sauce over the chicken thighs, cover the pan, increase the oven temperature to 350 degrees, and bake for 40 minutes, or until the chicken is tender and the sauce is reduced by half. Stir the currants into the sauce and season with additional salt and pepper if needed. Sprinkle the almonds over the top and serve over the rice.

Carroll Cornish's Crabmeat Lorenzo

1½ cups jumbo lump crabmeat, flaked

Salt and freshly ground black pepper

½ cup mayonnaise

½ cup heavy cream, whipped

¼ cup ketchup

1 teaspoon Worcestershire sauce

1 medium head Bibb lettuce, washed, drained, and separated into leaves

2 tablespoons chopped chives

Sweet paprika

3 hard-cooked eggs, sliced

6 lemon slices

Serves 6

In a large bowl, season the crabmeat with salt and pepper. Pour in the mayonnaise, whipped cream, ketchup, and Worcestershire sauce. Cover the bowl with plastic wrap and refrigerate for 2 hours, or until chilled.

When ready to serve, arrange leaves of lettuce on 6 appetizer plates. Mound the crabmeat mixture over the lettuce, and sprinkle with the chives and a little paprika and garnish with the egg and lemon slices. Serve cold.

Burnt Sugar Cake

For the cake:

1 cup sugar

½ cup hot water

3 cups sifted cake flour

1 teaspoon baking soda

½ teaspoon baking powder

¼ teaspoon salt

¾ cup (1½ sticks) unsalted butter, softened

2 teaspoons vanilla extract

2 large eggs, separated

For the frosting:

2½ cups sugar

1 cup milk

2 tablespoons unsalted butter

1 teaspoon vanilla extract

¼ cup half-and-half

Makes one 9-inch layer cake

Grease and lightly flour two 9-inch cake pans. Preheat the oven to 375 degrees.

Heat ½ cup of the sugar in a large skillet over medium-high heat, without stirring, until it just begins to melt. Reduce the heat to low and cook, stirring constantly, until the sugar is golden brown, about 2 minutes more. Increase the heat to medium and very gradually stir in the hot water. Bring the mixture to a boil, then reduce the heat and simmer until the caramel is dissolved and syrupy, another 2 minutes. Remove from the heat and set aside to cool to room temperature.

Sift the flour, baking soda, baking powder, and salt into a medium bowl, then sift them another 3 times (this will help aerate the dough). In a large bowl using an electric mixer, cream the butter with the remaining ½ cup sugar and the vanilla for about 30 seconds to combine. Add the egg yolks, beaten, and cooled syrup.

Add the dry ingredients to the creamed mixture alternately with 1 cup of room-temperature water, adding the flour first and last. In a clean medium bowl, beat the egg whites until stiff and fold them into the batter. Spread the batter evenly into the prepared pans and bake for 25 to 30 minutes, until golden and a wooden pick or skewer inserted into the center comes out clean. Cool the cakes in the pans on wire racks for 10 minutes, then invert the layers onto the racks to cool completely.

While the cake is cooling, make the frosting: Combine 1½ cups of the sugar and the milk in a medium heavy saucepan. Combine the remaining 1 cup sugar and 1 tablespoon of the butter in a large heavy skillet. Place both pans over low heat at the same time. Caramelize the sugar in the skillet, stirring, until amber in color, about 7 minutes. Add the caramelized sugar very gradually to the boiling sugar and milk mixture. Cook, stirring slowly but constantly, until the mixture reaches 230 degrees on a candy thermometer. The frosting should be thick and dark amber. Transfer the frosting to a medium bowl, and using an electric mixer, beat in the remaining 1 tablespoon butter and the vanilla. Add the half-and-half and beat until the mixture is pale, smooth, and creamy, warm but still spreadable.

Frost the cake and serve it in wedges.

Mrs. Grady Strain's Green-Tomato Relish

½ cup cider vinegar

¾ cup chopped green tomatoes

¾ cup finely grated cabbage

½ medium onion, finely chopped

½ medium bell pepper, cored, seeded, and finely chopped

1 hot pepper, finely chopped

¼ cup sugar

1½ tablespoons salt

½ teaspoon dry mustard

¼ teaspoon ground cloves

¼ teaspoon ground cinnamon

¼ teaspoon ground turmeric

¼ teaspoon celery seeds

Makes 1 pint

In a medium heavy-bottomed saucepan, combine all of the ingredients except the celery seeds, place over medium-high heat, and bring to a boil. Boil for 5 minutes. Add the celery seeds. While still hot, pour into a sterilized 1-pint jar; it will keep, refrigerated, for up to 3 months.

MONEY FOR DOODADS

It was ten miles out of Dallas, on the Garland Road, when a huge sign loomed— "Dallas County Farm Homemakers' Market." Big as Texas, a sign almost as long as the concrete market building itself. And it boasted a parking space even larger.

Irene McClelland, the Home Demonstration Agent for the county, had told me about this co-operative project which was started in 1936 by a group of farm women who needed extra money during the depression years. It was a daring adventure for women inexperienced in business, with little "down" money to spend.

The original seventeen members each put up $75 as a first payment on the land. They borrowed $2,000 to buy the building materials and then built the market themselves with their own hands. It's just four walls of concrete blocks and a roof, the measurements twenty-four by fifty-four feet. Bare as a barkless rail, but neat. Oilcloth-covered tables are arranged around the sides to serve as stalls. The market is open two days a week and on these days the big parking space is crowded with shoppers who drive out from Dallas and smaller neighboring towns to buy farm-pantry foods. Homemade, every last thing—cakes, cookies, pies; the preserves and pickles; there is freshly butchered poultry and meats, and all popularly priced. Yet the women make money. This co-operative has helped pay for college educations, has lifted mortgages, reroofed old barns. But mostly the money is used for what the women call doodads, meaning television sets, refrigerators, freezers, washing machines.

I visited the market to beg recipes for bestselling items. Mrs. W. H. Caldwell, then sixty-eight years old, one of the market's charter members, offered me this old-time recipe for her burnt sugar cake. And Mrs. Grady Strain could sell all the green-tomato relish she could carry to market.

TEXAS

A JANUARY MORNING I left Dallas at sunup driving to Fort Worth and on sixteen miles to Eagle Mountain Lake to have second breakfast with Mrs. Marshall Kennady and sample her Christmas gift marmalade. Toast and coffee were served in the sunroom with its glass wall and gorgeous view down the thousand-foot cliff and out over the lake.

This marmalade is really chewy because the fruit is cut in big pieces. It's for the family and to gift-package for friends, and Mr. Kennady, in the insurance business in Fort Worth, liked giving it to his business associates.

Something else Mrs. Kennady makes to send friends at Christmas—her famous dill pickles, the recipe from a Jewish friend. "The original recipe used less pepper," Mrs. Kennady told me, but she likes the pickles hot for serving as a cocktail appetizer. Her way is to chill the pickles well and cut them into big chunks to spear with toothpicks. But when used as a relish, with meat, slice them paper thin.

Kosher Dill Pickles

4 or 5 Kirby cucumbers,
3 to 5 inches long each

1 bunch fresh dill

2 garlic cloves

2 bay leaves

2 grape leaves

2 medium red hot peppers

2 medium green hot peppers

1½ tablespoons mixed pickling spice

1 quart water

¼ cup distilled white vinegar

¼ cup salt

Makes 4 or 5 pickles

Pack the cucumbers into a sterilized 1-quart glass jar. In another jar, combine the remaining ingredients and shake until the salt dissolves. Pour the brine into the jar with the cucumbers, adding more water if the cucumbers are not completely submerged. Refrigerate overnight; the pickles will keep for up to 1 month.

Note: Slice these pickles to use as a relish with meat or cut into thick chunks to serve as an appetizer with drinks and pretzels.

Mrs. Kennady's Marmalade

3 medium grapefruits, well scrubbed

3 medium oranges, well scrubbed

3 medium lemons, well scrubbed

2½ cups sugar

¾ pound whole candied cherries

¾ pound candied pineapple, diced

¼ pound candied ginger, diced

Makes 4 quarts

Fill a large heavy saucepan with water and add the grapefruits, oranges, and lemons. Place over high heat, bring to a boil, then reduce the heat to medium, cover, and simmer for 1 hour, stirring the fruit a few times. Set a colander over a bowl and gently drain the fruit.

When the fruit is cool enough to handle, cut each piece in half and scrape the insides onto a large piece of dampened cheesecloth. Tie the cloth into a bundle. Cut the peels into very thin strips.

In a wide heavy pot, combine the citrus peels with the sugar and 3 cups of water and place over medium-high heat. Bring to a boil, stirring to dissolve the sugar. Add the cheesecloth bundle and boil for 20 minutes, stirring occasionally. Using a slotted spoon, transfer the cheesecloth bundle to a bowl; when cool enough to handle, squeeze out as much liquid as possible. Add the liquid to the pot and discard the bundle. Continue cooking the marmalade until the syrup is very thick and glossy and the temperature registers 220 degrees on a candy thermometer, about 20 minutes longer. Stir in the candied cherries, pineapple, and ginger. Spoon the marmalade into 4 sterilized 1-quart canning jars, leaving ¼ inch of space at the top, and close with the lids and rings. To process, boil the jars for 15 minutes in enough water to cover. Let stand at room temperature for 2 days before using.

Note: The marmalade can be stored in a cool, dark place for up to 1 year. Refrigerate after opening.

NEW MEXICO

It was one of those lucky breaks arriving in Albuquerque, New Mexico, one day ahead of John Snyder of Amarillo, Texas, barbecue king of the great Southwest. John was imported talent, brought in by the New Mexico Company, a building supply concern that stages an annual barbecue for its customers. They came six hundred strong from all parts of the state to eat all they could hold of barbecued beef and lamb, of pinto beans and buns, and the usual barbecue trimmings.

Hearing John was heading into Albuquerque with two truckloads of equipment, two helpers, and 650 pounds of meat, we hurried to the barbecue lot, our chance to see how one of these western meat feasts gets itself organized. First thing, John sets up the pit, this a metal-sided boxlike affair with a bottom resting flat on the ground, its top covered over with fine wire netting but leaving a foot-wide opening along one side so the fire tender could keep shoveling in the fresh coals at his pleasure. Next up was a three-sided metal structure about five feet high, open at the top and with the open side facing the pit. In this wind-protected firebox the logs were laid. John himself is a big part of the day's fun. He held the annual barbecue record of one hundred cattle a year, and with forty years' experience that would be a big trail herd, as such herds went back in trail days.

Five o'clock in the morning the fire was lighted. By six there was a good bed of coals to shovel into that metal-sided barbecue. More logs to the fire, more coals to the pit. By six-thirty the box was hot enough to lay the meat over the woven wire netting and the barbecuing was under way. The meat was cut into pieces ranging from fifteen to forty pounds each and these laid on, piece touching piece. A heavy canvas was spread over all and now the long day of nursing the fire began. In the three-sided fireplace the logs blazed merrily to make more and more coals to shovel under the feast. Long slow cooking—that's the secret of good barbecued meat.

Each fifteen minutes or so the canvas was lifted and John directed his No. 1

helper: "Better turn the end there next. Add a few coals over yonder." The worker wore white canvas gloves and hand-turned the meat. Smoke and steam came from the pits while nearby a second helper sat weeping on the running board of a truck as he sliced fifty pounds of Texas onions. In between onions he tended the fire under two big pots of Paul Bunyan size that held the bubbling pinto beans. Time and slow heat brought the beans to a mealy tenderness.

The barbecue sauce John had made at home and carried with him in gallon glass jars. The making of the sauce he guards as the crown jewels.

The barbecue was eaten at high tables, a stand-up affair, served cafeteria style with a crew of volunteer helpers filling the plates. Everything a barbecue has to offer goes on one dish. "Pile it on, neighbors, pile it on!" John supervised the dishing up. With gloved hands the meat was lifted from carcass to plate; sauce was spooned over, pinto beans next, then comes the salad. There was a spoonful of dried apricot to a serving, the fruit cooked down to a jamlike consistency.

Beer, coffee, and pop for the beverages. The women discussed the pinto beans at great length and without compliments. Every woman in New Mexico has her own way with these beans and is sure as shootin' no other way is as good as her own.

"How do you cook those beans, what's your recipe?" But John wasn't telling.

"You can see what you see," he said tartly. What I saw was that John cooked pintos with plenty of bacon.

Something to behold is the south-westerner's appetite for the pinto. That's the bean called pink, called frijole, called the Mexican strawberry.

The recipes for the pinto are as thick as mesquite on the desert.

The pinto bean is a stranger on the easterner's table. But no Johnny-come-lately! Its popularity in the Southwest and Mexico traces back to the sixteenth century. Pintos for a thousand years have played a leading part in keeping Indian tribes of the West in vigor and health. An official of the Indian Service Nutrition Laboratory estimates that 70 percent of the Spanish-Americans build their basic diet around the pink bean.

Today the pet bean of New Mexico goes to barbecues and banquets, to the everyday table, for in spite of its long history the pinto is no has-been.

In and around Albuquerque I majored in beans, not just beans, but pintos, pedigreed pintos. I asked everybody her way of doing the beans—ranchers' wives, town women, chuck-wagon cooks, and each one gave me her personal conception of the royal flush she adds to the dish. Some, like John, cook the beans with bacon. "Ridiculous," said others, "salt pork is the meat."

"Not at all," another cook answers. "I always use ham." Some soaked the beans overnight; others said no, but to cook the beans the day long.

Ten women, ten recipes, not any two alike. Brand-new rules from domestic science school brides, heirloom "receipts" from old settlers, these last from southerners and away back to Boston pioneers.

I wanted to buy a pinto pot, exactly like those the Indian cooks use. We drove twelve miles to Isleta, a Pueblo village. "What do you use for cooking the beans?" we asked at the door of an adobe home. The mistress of the house opened a cupboard and pointed to the latest model pressure cooker.

And this modernity was borne out by the choice of my long-time friend, the late Elizabeth Dickens Shaffer whom I had gone to Albuquerque to visit. She cooked the pintos every Thursday, maid's day away. Her maid was Cora Sanchez, daughter of a former governor of San Felipe Pueblo, and it was Cora's recipe Mrs. Shaffer followed explicitly. A one-dish, rib-sticking meal it made for three husky young Shaffers. The beans were served with a bowl of sliced Bermuda onions and maybe celery. There was always a great pile of crusty bread to eat with bean gravy. Tomato juice the prelude, fresh fruit the ending to smother the chili's fire.

Elizabeth's Pinto Beans

1 tablespoon extra-virgin olive oil

1 clove garlic, minced

1 tablespoon chili powder

½ pound salt pork or bacon, minced

1 (15-ounce) can pinto beans, with their liquid

2 tablespoons chicken stock or water

Salt

2 tablespoons all-purpose flour

Serves 4

Heat the oil in a medium saucepan over medium heat until shimmering. Add the garlic and chili powder and cook until the garlic is softened, about 3 minutes. Add the salt pork and cook until lightly browned, about 5 minutes. Add the beans and their liquid and the chicken stock and simmer until slightly thickened, 5 to 10 minutes. Season with salt.

About 10 minutes before serving, in a small bowl, stir 2 tablespoons of the liquid from the pot with the flour to make a smooth paste. Add the paste to the beans to thicken the gravy. Serve warm.

IN ARIZONA, NEW MEXICO'S sister state, I acquired two variant recipes for the ubiquitous pinto. First came the ultramodern pressure cooker method, there in the snug Tico Taco Café with the Waldo Contrerases in Scottsdale, "The West's Most Western Town."

Waldo's Pinto Beans

1 pound dried pinto beans

½ cup peanut oil

Serves 4 to 6

Sort and rinse the beans, removing any stones or dirt. Put them in a large bowl, cover with 3 quarts water, and add ¼ cup salt. Let the beans soak overnight.

In the morning, drain and rinse the beans and place them in a pressure cooker. Bring the cooker up to high pressure and cook for 12 minutes. Turn off the heat, then let the pressure come down naturally for about 15 minutes. Remove the lid carefully, opening away from you—the steam will still be very hot. Scrape the beans into a bowl, cool, then cover with plastic wrap and refrigerate overnight.

When ready to cook, remove the beans from the refrigerator and place them in a blender or food processor and puree them to a pulpy mass.

Heat the oil in a large heavy skillet over medium heat. Scrape in the beans and stir quickly for 1 minute. Lower the heat to very low and simmer for 30 minutes, stirring every few minutes to give the dish a smooth texture. Serve warm.

NEW MEXICO

NEXT WAS A GENUINE ranch recipe, T-Dart Pinto Beans, branded by the T-Dart Ranch, located high in the mountains outside Phoenix.

T-Dart Pinto Beans

2 pounds dried pinto beans

¼ cup bacon fat or vegetable shortening

2 cups chopped onion

1 clove garlic, mashed

2 teaspoons salt

Pinch of dried oregano

½ teaspoon red pepper flakes

2 pounds ground beef

Salt

Serves 8

Sort and rinse the beans, removing any stones or dirt. Soak them overnight in a large heavy stockpot in water to cover by 2 inches.

In the morning, drain the beans, add fresh cold water to cover, and bring to a boil over medium-high heat. Reduce the heat, bringing the beans down to a low simmer.

Meanwhile, heat the bacon fat in a large heavy skillet over medium heat. Add the onion, garlic, salt, oregano, and red pepper flakes and sauté until softened and transparent, about 3 minutes. Add the beef and cook until golden brown, 7 to 10 minutes. Add the meat mixture to the pot of beans, partially cover, and simmer for about 4 hours, until the beans are tender and soft. Season with salt and serve hot.

ARIZONA

I asked for the name of the best cook in Phoenix, Arizona, and the answer came, "Ben Projan—that is, when broiling a steak." It isn't so much his method of broiling—it's his steak marinade that has the town talking.

Barbecue cooking is the Projan avocation. Ben takes to the barbecue as some men do to golf, as others to sailing. "I'm a Sunday cook," Ben Projan announced. "I like to invite friends for a Sunday steak supper—nothing like steak to fill the hole of hunger."

Sometimes Ben Projan switches from steak to roast, yes, barbecued. Most of the roasts, he told me, taste better when 'cued than when they come from the oven—superior in the same way that steaks and chops grilled over open coals are superior to kitchen-broiled meats.

"You must come out to my place and see the barbecue setup," Phoenix's gourmet chef was inviting. "Everything's automatic. Even the skewers for the shishkabob turn at the touch of a button."

"How about that marinade for the steaks?" I switched the subject, wanting to get back on the track leading to a good recipe.

"My steaks," Ben Projan said, "get a twelve-hour soak in the marinade. Individual steaks, that's the kind I use, the sirloin, cut New York style, meaning a long narrow steak, the filet taken out. These steaks should be two inches thick and weigh at least one pound."

The meat is placed in a marinade for twelve hours. After that the fat is gashed and slivers of garlic inserted into the cuts. Then to broil, searing first on one side, then the other. Now even slow heat to bring the steaks to medium rare. And all during the broiling the marinade is used as a baster. When the steaks are done, quickly to a hot platter, topping each with a good-sized pat of butter. A few twirls from the pepper grinder, but no salt—the marinade takes care of this matter, its base is soy sauce.

MEXICAN FOOD IS FOUND throughout the Southwest. In Phoenix I ate one of my best Mexican meals at a cubbyhole restaurant called Pancho's Patio. This was operated by Mrs. Elma Van Zandt who learned below-the-border cooking from Pauline Ramirez, a young Mexican woman who took care of Mrs. Van Zandt's children when they were small.

One of the dishes that has come to great popularity is the *albondigas* soup, a meal in itself when served with a green salad.

And popular is the fascinating dessert *almendrado,* done in the colors of the Mexican flag.

"Albondigas"

For the meatballs:

1 pound ground round steak

½ pound ground fresh pork

1 large egg

1 green chili, finely chopped

1 bunch scallions, finely chopped

2 sprigs mint, finely chopped

1 clove garlic, finely chopped

¾ cup yellow cornmeal

¼ cup chopped parsley

½ cup canned chopped tomatoes, drained

¾ teaspoon sage

½ teaspoon ground cloves

Dash of savory thyme

For the soup:

3 quarts water

2 cups beef stock

½ cup tomato juice

Salt and freshly ground black pepper

Dash of savory thyme

¼ cup chopped parsley

½ clove garlic, shaved

1 green chili, finely chopped

Serves 10

First, make the meatballs: In a large bowl, mix together the ground meats with your hands. Add the remaining ingredients, mixing well to combine but taking care not to overhandle. Form into small balls about size of marbles (1 to 2 teaspoons each), arrange on a baking sheet, and cover with plastic wrap. Set aside the meatballs while you make the soup.

To make the soup: In a large heavy-bottom stockpot, combine the water, beef stock, and tomato juice and season with salt and pepper. Place over medium-high heat, add the remaining ingredients, and bring to a boil. Drop the reserved meatballs into the hot soup, reduce the heat to low, cover, and simmer for 1 hour, or until the meatballs are tender, adding water if necessary. Serve hot, ladled into warm bowls.

"Almendrado"

1 tablespoon unflavored gelatin

½ cup cold water

½ cup hot water

½ cup sugar

4 large egg whites

½ teaspoon almond extract

Red and green food coloring

1 cup finely ground almonds

Serves 12

Line an 8 x 8-inch square pan with waxed paper to cover the bottom and sides.

In a large bowl, soften the gelatin in the cold water for 5 minutes. Add the hot water and sugar and stir until dissolved. Set aside to cool. Meanwhile, in another bowl, beat the egg whites until very stiff shiny peaks form. Fold into the cooled gelatin mixture and the almond extract. Using a handheld beater, beat the mixture until it resembles whipped cream, then scrape the mixture with a rubber spatula into 3 small bowls. Leave one uncolored, color the second red, and the third green. Pour the red mixture into the prepared pan and spread to make an even layer; sprinkle with ½ cup of the ground almonds. Pour in the white mixture to make a second layer and sprinkle with the remaining ½ cup almonds. Make a third layer with the green mixture. Cover and refrigerate for 4 hours, or until completely chilled.

When ready to serve, cut into 4 x 2-inch slices. Serve with chilled custard sauce—to stand for the Mexican eagle—or whipped cream, if you like.

FOR ALL THEIR BARBECUE apparatus western women still like to fry beefsteak. It sounds sort of awful but the stuff tastes marvelous. One of the best cooks I met in Albuquerque, Mrs. A. H. Beirne, told me she takes a two-inch steak, pounds in flour with pepper and salt. Meanwhile, she heats vegetable oil in an iron skillet and gets that good and hot, then adds one teaspoon Worcestershire sauce, and in with the steak. One side to fry and then the other, to rare, medium, or well-done as you like it. Serve with a baked potato and a green vegetable and you won't ever turn up your nose again at folks who fry steak.

Steak Marinade

1 quart soy sauce

2 cups beef stock or consommé

½ cup lemon juice

2 teaspoons chipotle chile powder or smoked Spanish paprika

3 cloves garlic, minced

Makes enough marinade for six 1-pound steaks

In a large bowl, whisk together all of the ingredients and pour over the steaks.

Note: This marinade may be refrigerated for up to 1 month.

SWEET TONNAGE

It was the week before Christmas and all through the house came the warm spicy fragrance—cookies were baking. It was just an idea with Mrs. J. V. Guerin that a home-baked present for her dearest friends would mean more than the store-bought kind.

That was twenty years ago. All Esther remembers now about this first baking siege is that she made five kinds of cookies, packed five boxes and that everyone gifted seemed so awfully pleased. "Such heavenly cookies!" "Such a beautiful package: each layer looks pretty as a picture!"

Weeks before Christmas the following year, spurred on by the compliments, Mrs. Guerin began collecting cookie recipes and started her Christmas baking a month ahead of the holiday.

This time she made a few hundred cookies and packed two dozen boxes. Each year since, her Christmas baking has been bigger and better. The cookies are baked, cooled, then stored in large tins with tight-fitted lids. Only one kind is made at a time; this she thinks is the most efficient way of doing the job.

Through the year she saves all the boxes that come to her house, little ones, big ones, anything usable. She borrows from friends. Even so, she seldom has enough containers to carry the sweet tonnage and must buy a few extras. Baking is the big task but packing is no job for lazy hands. Each layer Mrs. Guerin arranges with utmost care for color effect. "Pretty as a picture" is the compliment she likes to hear when the box lids are lifted.

Esther Guerin was born in Colorado but has lived in Arizona since pigtail days. Her father and mother are Italian-born, and as you know the Italians have wonderful recipes for Christmas cookies. Esther's aunt, Mrs. B. Curto of Calumet, Michigan, has given her the family collection of Italian sweets. The *torcetti* is one of the most treasured, a lovely rich cookie, but it takes time to make.

Her aunt, Mrs. Dominic Marta of Ottawa, Illinois, gave Esther the recipe for *zuccarini*. This is a cookie not overly sweet, a sticky dough, a hard one to mix. Best to use your hands for the job; their warmth aids in the blending. If you are making sweets to mail the sugared walnuts travel well.

"Torcetti"

1 cup (2 sticks) unsalted butter, cut into small pieces

½ pound vegetable shortening

4 cups sifted all-purpose flour

½ cup warm milk

1½ teaspoons granulated sugar

1½ teaspoons vanilla extract

1 envelope active dry yeast

2 large eggs, beaten

1 pound confectioners' sugar

Makes 6 dozen

In a large bowl using 2 knives, a pastry cutter, or your fingers, cut the butter and shortening into the flour until the mixture is as fine as cornmeal. In a small bowl, whisk together the milk, granulated sugar, and vanilla; add the yeast and stir until dissolved. Add the yeast liquid to the flour mixture and beat in the eggs. Knead the mixture slightly in its bowl. Cover the bowl loosely with plastic wrap and let the dough rise until doubled in bulk, about 1 hour.

Preheat the oven to 375 degrees. Grease 2 or 3 large baking sheets. Cover a large wooden cutting board, breadboard, or other work surface with the confectioners' sugar. Break off small pieces (1 to 2 teaspoons each) of the dough, roll in the sugar, and shape into figure eights, crescents, twists, or knots. Place the cookies on the prepared baking sheets and bake for 12 to 15 minutes, until golden. Let the cookies rest on the pans on wire racks for 2 minutes, then transfer to wire racks to cool completely.

Note: The cookies may be stored at room temperature in an airtight container for up to 1 week.

Sugared Walnuts

1 cup sugar

⅓ cup orange juice

1 teaspoon lemon extract

2 tablespoons unsalted butter

2½ cups walnut halves

Makes 1 pound

In a large saucepan, combine the sugar and orange juice. Place over medium heat and whisk constantly until the sugar dissolves and the mixture registers 234 degrees on a candy thermometer, about 7 minutes. Add the lemon extract and butter and cook, whisking constantly, until the mixture has a very creamy look and begins to thicken. Add the walnut halves and stir until they are well coated. Pour the mixture onto waxed paper and separate the walnuts to keep them from sticking together. Cool completely.

Note: The walnuts can be stored at room temperature in an airtight container for up to 1 week.

ARIZONA

CACTUS WRENS AND PINK ADOBE

The peace of the place settles down heavily, then melts right into you. This is Camelback Inn in Paradise Valley near Phoenix, Arizona, where I had gone to vacation because friends told me the food there tasted home-cooked, and that even after a month the last meal would taste just as good as the first.

But no one had prepared me for the peace of the valley, a majestic quietness peculiar to areas of vast solitude. I had arrived too late for the evening dinner and gone immediately to my own little "casa." There are seventeen of these pink adobe houses circling the garden.

Before dawn the birds were talking, the cardinals, the cactus wrens, and the robins. The sun came sharp over a rose-colored mountain and my world flamed to a new day. The garden took on the warm dry colors of the desert flowers. Lizards crept out to bask on the warming stones.

Faint whispers stirred the palms. I took a deep breath—it was like drinking wine. Suddenly I was absolutely starved!

I made a beeline to the dining room where Jack Stewart was waiting. He owns the place. Through the glassed side of the main dining room I could see the camel's hump on Camelback Mountain.

Jack Stewart had made an important discovery: that the average American likes to eat French food, Italian food, fiddle with smorgasbord, but just on occasion. For day-after-day menus he likes American cooking, home style, and not overspiced.

The inn's baker, Mrs. Anna Bryan, had baked all her life. This job at Camelback was her first outside her own kitchen. Guests come begging for her recipes!

Like everyone else I went kitchen-visiting. Tell us, please, how you make the mincemeat muffins, the rhubarb pie, that wonderful chocolate sauce.

Fresh Rhubarb Meringue Pie

1 (9-inch) Perfect Pie Crust (page 13)

2 tablespoons unsalted butter

1½ cups plus 6 tablespoons sugar

½ cup all-purpose flour

¼ teaspoon salt

3 large eggs, separated

4 cups diced rhubarb

Makes one 9-inch pie

Preheat the oven to 350 degrees. Line a 9-inch glass pie plate with the pastry. Trim the overhang to 1 inch, fold it under itself, and crimp decoratively, if you like. Refrigerate until chilled, about 15 minutes.

Line the pastry with foil and fill with pie weights or dried beans. Bake for 30 minutes, or until nearly cooked through and dry to the touch. Carefully remove the foil and weights. Bake for about 10 minutes longer, until golden. Place on a wire rack and cool completely. Do not turn off the oven.

In the large bowl of an electric mixer, cream the butter with 1½ cups of the sugar. Slowly add the flour and salt and mix completely. Add the beaten egg yolks. Stir in the rhubarb. Turn the mixture into the prepared pie shell and bake for 30 to 40 minutes, until the rhubarb is tender and the sides of the crust are browned. Transfer to a wire rack to cool slightly.

Increase the oven temperature to 400 degrees. While the pie is cooling slightly, beat the egg whites in a medium bowl until foamy. Add the remaining 6 tablespoons sugar and continue beating until stiff peaks form. Spread the meringue on top of the warm pie and bake for 8 to 10 minutes, until the meringue is nicely browned. Cool completely on a wire rack before serving.

ARIZONA

A HOME OUT OF ANYTHING

This Scottsdale, Arizona, is a boom-town making every effort to create a swashbuckling Western atmosphere. Its main street is garnished with wagon wheels, its windows flash fancy boots, jodhpurs, and saddles. Here's a town determined to be a tourist mecca and it's well on its way.

The town only looks little. New developments stretch out on every side, right into the surrounding cotton fields. Down Orange Blossom Lane, bordered with ranch-style houses and all so new they smell of wet cement and spicy wood shavings, I found Mrs. Harold Holcomb, wife of Rear Admiral Holcomb, retired from the navy. Here is a woman of forthright manner, commanding presence, a sly sense of fun.

But Mrs. Holcomb is no westerner. Buffalo, New York, is her birthplace and she has lived the world over.

"Where are the orange blossoms?" I asked.

"I'm trying to have the street's name changed," Mrs. Holcomb said. "Lizard Gulch would be more appropriate."

She looked at the notebook I carried, at the sharpened pencils stuck in the side of my bag. "I'm not the West's most western cook if that's what you want," she an-nounced. "I don't cook western, my recipes are from everywhere. I have been married to the navy for thirty years and during that period have kept house in ten countries.

"When I got married," Mrs Holcomb said, "I couldn't fry an egg, but I learned in a hurry. A navy wife is supposed to make a home out of anything, and that goes for her menus. One year she may live in a mansion with ten servants, the next year in a shoebox."

Right here I got a word in edgewise. "They say around Phoenix that what you do with a pair of lamb shanks would make Waldorf chefs green with envy."

Mrs. Holcomb said, "My Indian curry is better, and the pineapple chutney that goes with it is simply elegant. It's a recipe from my sister Loraine Kuck who has lived fifteen years in the Orient."

It was in Germany Mrs. Holcomb began collecting recipes for iced vegetable soups. Her iced broccoli is the Admiral's first choice.

Mrs. Holcomb thinks Americans over-season their dishes. She likes seasonings but just enough to point up natural flavors. She leans toward the French style of cooking but admits her Indian curry recipes go best with the family.

Spicy Braised Lamb Shanks

¼ cup all-purpose flour

1 teaspoon salt

½ teaspoon freshly ground black pepper

4 meaty 1-pound lamb shanks

1 cup minced dried prunes

1 cup minced dried apricots

½ cup sugar

½ teaspoon ground cinnamon

½ teaspoon ground allspice

½ teaspoon ground cloves

¼ teaspoon salt

1 cup water

3 tablespoons tarragon vinegar

Serves 4 to 6

Preheat the oven to 350 degrees. Generously grease a deep wide casserole dish or roasting pan.

Pour the flour into a shallow pan, season it with the salt and pepper, and dredge the shanks through it. Place the pieces in the prepared dish, cover the dish with foil, and bake until the lamb is tender, about 2 hours.

Meanwhile, in a large saucepan, combine the remaining ingredients and place over medium heat. Bring to a boil, then reduce the heat and simmer for 5 minutes. Pour the mixture over the shanks, increase the oven temperature to 400 degrees, cover the pan with foil, and bake for 30 minutes more, until the lamb is falling-apart tender and the prune and apricot bits are soft. Let rest, covered, for 10 minutes, then serve.

ARIZONA

Cold Broccoli Soup

1 cup finely chopped onion

½ cup diced celery

¼ cup diced carrots

2 cups water

1 (10-ounce) package frozen broccoli

3 cups chicken stock

1 teaspoon salt

¼ teaspoon cayenne pepper

2 tablespoons rice flour or cornstarch

1 cup heavy cream

1 tablespoon chopped chives

1 teaspoon chopped rosemary

Serves 6

In a large saucepan, combine the onion, celery, and carrots and add the water. Place over medium heat, bring to a boil, then reduce the heat to low and simmer until the vegetables are soft, about 15 minutes. Add the frozen broccoli, then add the stock, salt, and cayenne. Simmer until the broccoli is tender, about 5 minutes more.

In a small bowl, blend the rice flour or cornstarch with 1 tablespoon of water to form a paste. Stir into the soup and bring the soup to a boil, stirring constantly. Turn the heat off and puree the soup in a blender or food processor or with an immersion blender until smooth. Season the soup with salt. Pour the soup into a large bowl, cool to room temperature, then cover and refrigerate for at least 2 hours or overnight. When ready to serve, whip the cream until soft peaks form. Fold in the chives and rosemary. Serve the soup cold in chilled bowls garnished with dollops of the herbed cream.

Pineapple Chutney

1 large fresh pineapple or 2 cans pineapple (1 pound, 13 ounces each), cut into ¾-inch dice

4 cups brown sugar

3 cups cider vinegar

2 cloves garlic

1 pound raisins

1 pound currants

1 pound blanched almonds or walnuts, broken up

2 tablespoons fresh ginger, peeled and chopped

1½ teaspoons salt

⅛ teaspoon freshly ground black pepper

½ teaspoon whole cloves

½ teaspoon ground cinnamon

½ teaspoon ground allspice

Makes four 8-ounce jars

Combine all of the ingredients in a 4-quart saucepan, place over medium heat, and bring to a boil. Boil, stirring occasionally, until thick and syrupy, about 20 minutes. Remove the garlic and cloves. Ladle the chutney into four 8-ounce hot sterilized canning jars and seal according to the manufacturer's directions. Store, refrigerated, for up to 6 months.

Coconut Chicken Curry

3 pounds boneless chicken thighs

1 tablespoon salt

3 tablespoons peanut oil

¾ cup finely chopped onion

1 whole clove

1½ teaspoons curry powder

1½ teaspoons ground turmeric

1½ teaspoons ground ginger

1 teaspoon ground cardamom

1 teaspoon dried marjoram

½ teaspoon dried thyme

1 small bunch fresh parsley, finely chopped

4 chilis, chopped

1½ cups chicken broth

1½ cups coconut water

Serves 6

Wash and thoroughly pat the chicken thighs dry and season them with the salt.

Heat the oil in a large skillet or heavy-bottomed saucepan over medium heat. Add the thighs and sauté, turning as needed, until browned on all sides, about 10 minutes total. Using a slotted spoon, transfer the thighs to paper towels to drain.

Place the onion in the pan with the chicken fat and cook over medium-low heat until softened, lightly browned, and tender, being careful not to let it burn, about 5 minutes. Add the clove, curry powder, turmeric, ginger, cardamom, marjoram, thyme, parsley, and chili, then whisk in the chicken broth and coconut water. Add the reserved chicken to the sauce and simmer for about 15 minutes, until the chicken is cooked through and tender. Serve in warm bowls ladled over steamed rice with pineapple chutney.

Note: In this recipe, it's important to use coconut water, not coconut milk. It's readily available in many groceries, but you can make your own coconut water by soaking 1 cup of grated coconut in 1¾ cups of water for 2 to 3 hours and then draining.

A TWO-DOLLAR, SECONDHAND STOVE

It is only a short drive on into Scottsdale, Arizona, where I found these authentic Mexican foods and borrowed the recipes for making at home. It is Waldo Contreras and wife Emma who dish up this family-style fare in their Tico Taco Café, which feeds around two hundred guests daily at eight oilcloth-covered tables.

Waldo Contreras, with $35, ambition, and plenty of nerve, started a Mexican sandwich stand, selling the taco along with soft drinks. He bought a two-dollar, secondhand stove, added two stools. Cups, saucers, glasses, and cooking utensils he carried from home. His most expensive item was the making of a taco-frying machine. The Mexican sandwich, I should explain, is a thin corn wafer called a tortilla folded over a meat filling, then deep-fat fried. As it comes hot from the fat the sandwich is open just far enough to allow for stuffing in a crisp crunch of shredded lettuce, a sprinkle of grated cheese, a splash of hot sauce. And so to serve!

Opening day the stand had prepared to give away seventy-five tacos, but after the first twenty cash was on the counter and guests ordered seconds. Waldo and Emma were up to their elbows in business.

Taco plate is the menu leader, but other foods are offered also featuring recipes from Waldo's Mexican mother. There is the guacamole plate consisting of two rolled, instead of folded tacos, one chicken-filled, one stuffed with beef, these accompanied by a cup of avocado sauce, to use as a dip. On the same plate is a Mexican green salad and this, too, has the avocado sauce as a dressing.

Mexican food is difficult to write into recipes as each cook's product takes an individual turn.

The tortillas, large, thin corn wafers made in Mexico, are available in cans in Mexican and Spanish shops, ready to fry in hot oil.

ARIZONA

Avocado Dip

3 ripe avocados

½ cup grated sharp cheddar cheese

½ cup grated white Mexican cheese (or a mild cheddar)

1½ tablespoons mayonnaise

½ cup water

1 tablespoon chopped onion

Salt

Makes 5 cups

Peel the avocados, cut them in half, and remove the seeds. Finely chop 2 of the avocados and place them in a large bowl. Scoop out the third avocado into several pieces and place in a blender with the remaining ingredients except the salt. Blend for about 10 minutes, until the mixture is the consistency of thick cream. Scrape the dip into the bowl with the chopped avocado and season with salt. Store in an airtight container, removing any air spaces that could cause browning. Tightly cover the dip and chill until ready to serve. Serve, with a drop of Tabasco, in individual small cups, alongside tortillas or corn chips, if you like.

Mexican Rice

2 cups uncooked long-grain white rice

6 cups chicken or meat stock

1 tablespoon peanut oil

Secret Sauce for Rice (recipe follows)

Makes 6 cups

This is the only Mexican restaurant we have visited ever to feature rice on its menu. Here's how it's done. Clean and wash the rice, put it in a gallon-size pot, and add the chicken stock. Bring to a boil over medium-high heat, then reduce the heat, cover, and cook for 20 minutes, or until the broth is absorbed. Cool for 10 minutes; while still warm, pour into a large jar and shake it around. Cool completely, cover, and refrigerate overnight.

The following morning, heat the oil in a large skillet over medium-high heat. Heat to bubbling and add the rice; cook, stirring constantly, for 2 to 3 minutes. Lower the heat and cook for about 15 minutes, until the rice is chewy and tender and ready to eat. Serve with Secret Sauce for Rice.

Note: Serve on a plate with beans, tomatoes, and enchiladas. The filled plate should go into a 500-degree oven for 3 to 4 minutes. Garnish with more chili sauce, tomatoes, or Secret Sauce. Then a garnish of chopped lettuce, tomatoes, and ripe olives.

Secret Sauce for Rice

2 cups chopped green bell peppers

2 cups finely chopped fresh green tomatoes

2 cups finely chopped ripe tomatoes

½ cup chopped onion

1 tablespoon salt

Pinch of dried oregano

Garlic juice to taste

ARIZONA

Makes enough for 1 recipe of Mexican Rice

Combine all of the ingredients in a medium saucepan and place over medium heat. Bring to a boil, then reduce the heat, cover, and simmer for about 1 hour, until the vegetables are well combined and the green peppers are soft, stirring occasionally. Serve warm over hot cooked rice. It's good anytime, Mexican supper or not.

Enchiladas

2½ cups tomato puree

2½ teaspoons hot sauce

1 teaspoon ground cinnamon

2 teaspoons chili powder

½ cup vegetable oil

12 corn tortillas, soft and at
room temperature

2 cups grated sharp cheddar cheese

1½ cups queso fresco or grated
Monterey Jack cheese

Serves 6

Preheat the oven to 350 degrees. Lightly grease a
9 x 9-inch square casserole or other shallow baking dish.

In a small saucepan, combine the tomato puree, hot sauce,
cinnamon, and chili powder and place over medium heat.
Bring to a boil, stirring occasionally, then immediately
remove the sauce from the heat.

Heat the oil in a medium skillet over medium heat. In
another medium skillet, warm ½ cup of the sauce over
medium heat. Using tongs, dip the tortillas in the oil,
coating both sides, until softened, about 5 seconds. Coat
each tortilla with the sauce and transfer to a plate,
stacking the tortillas on top of each other.

Combine the 2 cheeses in a small bowl. Set a tortilla on a
work surface and spoon ¼ cup of the cheese in the center.
Loosely roll up the tortilla like a cigar and set it in the
prepared baking dish, seam side down. Repeat with the
remaining tortillas. Pour the remaining sauce over the
rolled enchiladas and sprinkle the remaining cheese on
top. Bake the enchiladas for 25 minutes, or until heated
through and the sauce is bubbling. Serve hot.

Pineapple "Sopaipillas"

2 cups sifted all-purpose flour

1 tablespoon baking powder

1 teaspoon salt

3 cups plus 1 tablespoon peanut oil

¾ cup water

3 cups drained crushed canned pineapple, finely chopped

½ cup confectioners' sugar

Makes 20

Sift the flour, baking powder, and salt into a large bowl. Stir in 1 tablespoon of the oil, then stir in the water to make a soft dough. Divide the dough into 4 parts and form them into rounds.

In a medium saucepan over medium heat, bring the pineapple to a simmer and cook for 1 minute, stirring constantly. Set aside to cool slightly.

Heat the remaining 3 cups oil in a large deep skillet to 385 degrees. Roll out the balls of dough on a lightly floured surface to ⅛- to ¼-inch thickness. Cut into pieces 2½ by 4 inches. Fry a few pieces at a time in the hot oil until they puff like pillows, about 1 minute. Turn over and fry until browned on the other side. Remove from the oil and drain on paper towels. While the pillows are still hot, make a slit along two connecting sides of each one. Open up and fill each one with a rounded tablespoonful of the pineapple filling. Dust with the confectioners' sugar and spoon any remaining pineapple over the finished dish. Serve warm.

ARIZONA

HOT GOLD OF THE SAND

The T-Dart Ranch, about two hundred acres, is thirty-two miles out of Phoenix into the desert, into the McDowell Mountains. It is owned and operated as a place for winter guests by a wiry little woman, her face deeply tanned by the desert sun, Mrs. Ruth Phillips.

The drive to T-Dart Ranch I shall remember always. It was an August day, the thermometer registered 112 degrees in the shade. The wide desert seemed asleep under the blistering sun. The unwrinkled blue sky was so blinding it made the eyes drop. Everywhere the hot gold of the sand.

Ruth's kitchen was air-conditioned, but we sat outdoors in the shade of a large mesquite to talk. Peaked brown mountains to stop the eye. A brown thrasher busy eating the seeds of a prickly pear. Strange plants in Ruth's garden—a black cholla, a silver cholla, an ocotillo cactus with its rat-tail spikes, a barrel cactus, all a dusty tired green.

Behind us the main house where the boss lady lived, a long living room, colorful with Navaho rugs, fox pelts on the walls, deer antlers, too, and the skull of a steer. The big kitchen was modern as any city home with electric stove, dishwasher, freezer, a radio. Ruth's sleeping quarters a screened-in porch.

Clustered round the main house like chicks round a mother hen were the guest houses for the visitors from Chicago, New York, San Francisco, come to stay a few days, to stay a few weeks. They came to loll in the sun, they came to ride the long trails, to hunt and to tramp. But what they loved best was eating Ruth's cooking with dinner outdoors prepared at the barbecue grill, built there among the boulders of decomposed granite.

Ruth's cooking was ranch-style and that's what the city folks liked. Luncheon, like dinner, was served outdoors; maybe bacon and eggs with hot dropped biscuits made on a griddle. Sometimes there were pinto beans for the main dish or a stew and often the meal was a huge bowl of this thick vegetable soup.

Beef and Vegetable Soup

2½ to 3 pounds beef short ribs

2 tablespoons salt, plus more to taste

6 large stalks celery, diced

1 large potato, peeled and diced

1 large red onion, chopped

6 medium carrots, diced

1 small head cabbage, shredded

2 white turnips, peeled and diced

2 cups canned diced tomatoes

2 tablespoons chopped parsley

Serves 6 to 8

Place the short ribs in a deep pot and cover with cold water. Add the salt. Place over medium-high heat, bring the water to a boil, then reduce the heat, cover, and simmer for about 2 hours, until the meat is very tender. Remove the meat from the pot, cool slightly, and cut the meat from the bones. Discard the bones and fat and return the meat to the pot. Add the remaining ingredients except the parsley, bring to a boil, then reduce the heat and simmer gently for about 1 hour, until the vegetables are soft and well combined. Just before serving, season with salt and stir in the fresh parsley. Serve hot, ladled into warm soup bowls.

THE

MIDWEST

KANSAS

Sunday dinner is to me the symbol of good eating in the
Middle West. I know those Sunday feasts as of yesterday and
today. I was born and raised in Blue River Valley, now the basin
of the government's great Tuttle Creek Dam. Our farm, before
Alaska's and Hawaii's statehood, was within twenty miles of the
geographical center of the United States.

It was in a yellow limestone church at
Stockdale, Kansas, a crossroads town,
that I sat dreaming during summer
Sunday sermons, not of heaven or hell,
but of the good dinner to come. There
would be fried chicken and gravy,
fresh garden vegetables, green beans,
summer squash or beets. In July came
new peas and new potatoes. There
would be leaf lettuce and cucumbers
with a vinegar-sugar dressing. Always
in summer, homemade ice cream and
invariably this marble cake made from
Grandma Paddleford's recipe.

Grandma Paddleford's Marble Layer Cake

4 cups cake flour

5 teaspoons baking powder

½ teaspoon salt

1 cup (2 sticks) unsalted butter, softened

2 cups sugar

2 teaspoons vanilla extract

4 large eggs, separated

1½ cups milk

2 ounces unsweetened chocolate, melted

Fudge Frosting (recipe follows)

Makes 1 (9-inch) layer cake

Preheat the oven to 350 degrees. Grease and flour two 9-inch cake pans.

Sift the flour, baking powder, and salt into a large bowl. In a separate bowl, cream the butter and sugar. Add the vanilla. Beat the egg yolks well and add to the butter mixture. Add the flour alternately with the milk, beating until smooth after each addition. In a large bowl using an electric mixer, beat the egg whites until stiff peaks form. Fold the stiffly beaten egg whites into the batter.

Divide the batter in half. To one half, stir in the chocolate. Add both batters to the prepared pans, alternating spoonfuls of light and dark batters. Gently drop the pans a few inches onto the counter to settle the batter, then gently smooth the tops of the layers with a spatula. Bake for 18 to 25 minutes, until a toothpick inserted into the center of the layers comes out clean. Let the cakes cool in their pans on wire racks for 20 minutes, then invert onto the racks to cool completely. Frost in between the layers and outside of the cake with the frosting.

Fudge Frosting

4½ cups confectioners' sugar

¾ cup cocoa powder

¾ cup (1½ sticks) unsalted butter, melted

¾ cup hot freshly brewed coffee

1 tablespoon vanilla extract

Makes about 6 cups

Sift the confectioners' sugar and cocoa powder into a medium bowl. Stir in the butter, then the coffee, then the vanilla, mixing well with a wooden spoon after each addition until the frosting is smooth.

NAPKIN-COVERED BASKETS, RED-SPOKED BUGGIES

The Fourth of July Picnic was an important occasion that brought forth the best country eating the Middle West could provide. Go back with me to 1912 in John Sweet's grove.

Farmers' families and the townsfolk were gathered together under the whispering cottonwoods before a rude plank platform, sides swathed in bunting, red, white, and blue. There was a morning program, children speaking pieces and doing a flag drill. Community singing and the voices taking up the words, slightly off pitch: "Oh, say can you see. . . ." Loudly they sang, joyously, knowing that the next number on the program was the great event of the day, the picnic dinner.

Napkin-covered baskets were hauled out from under the seats of the fringe-topped carriages, from backs of the red-spoked buggies, baskets overflowing with delectables. Mounds of fried chicken were flanked by baked hams, chocolate cakes, tall angel foods. Seductive fragrance of fresh cherry pies, their top crusts embellished with fancy scrolls, pink-tinged with the juice. Milk pans held little white navy beans seasoned with plenty of molasses and covered with salt pork baked to a crispy brown. Jars of new pickled beets, no bigger than marbles, flagged the eye to make the mouth water. Cream crocks were mounded with potato salad bedecked with slices of hard-cooked egg.

Bertha Phillips brought those deviled eggs in tomato cases. Showing off, the women knew, to impress the local bachelor banker. It was a trick she had learned at the Kansas State College. And a good trick today. Tops are cut from small tomatoes which are hollowed of their pulp and juice (these saved for a sauce). The inside shell is delicately tinged with a restrained sprinkle of salt, then a half deviled egg pressed in, the tomato top fastened on with a toothpick. This two-in-one is wrapped in waxed paper and chilled well before packing. A salad to eat in the hand.

"Chicken to fry for the Fourth of July" was as traditional as turkey for Thanksgiving Day. At every valley farm the women did handsomely by the picnic bird. Joints were never hacked apart to leave jagged edges. Each piece was wiped dry to avoid spattering in the fat. Riley County women were agreed on a coating of one-third cup flour to one-half teaspoon salt for a bird weighing two pounds. Flour browns more quickly than crumbs, they said. The seasoned flour was patted in evenly with the fingertips.

KANSAS

Honest-to-Goodness
Kansas Fried Chicken

1 (2½- to 3-pound) broiler chicken, cut into 8 pieces, backbone removed, at room temperature

Kosher salt and freshly ground black pepper

⅔ cup all-purpose flour

2 tablespoons unsalted butter

4 tablespoons lard (vegetable shortening may be substituted)

2 cups hot milk, plus more if needed

Serves 4

Preheat the oven to 200 degrees. Wash the chicken pieces and pat them dry with paper towels. Season them generously with salt. Season the flour with a little salt and pepper. Roll the chicken pieces in the flour and pat evenly with your fingertips. Reserve any leftover flour for the gravy.

Melt the butter and lard in a large, heavy skillet over medium heat. When hot but not smoking, add the chicken, largest pieces first. If the skillet won't hold 8 pieces in one layer with room for turning, fry in batches, grouping white and dark meat separately so the white meat stays juicy. Partially cover the skillet so the fat doesn't splatter but the chicken doesn't steam. As chicken pieces brown, turn them. White meat will be finished when the meat close to the bone is light pink; dark meat will be finished when cooked through and fork-tender.

When the chicken is ready, drain it on a rack set in a baking pan. Put the pan in the warm oven while you make the gravy: Pour off all but 2 to 3 tablespoons of fat in the skillet and whisk in 2 tablespoons of the remaining seasoned flour. Cook over medium-low heat for about 1 minute, until the mixture begins to bubble. Then slowly add the hot milk and heat the gravy, whisking constantly, until thickened, about 5 to 7 minutes. For a thicker gravy, continue cooking for a few extra minutes; for a thinner gravy, add more milk. Season the gravy with salt and pepper and serve over the chicken.

Note: When the chicken has cooled, lay the pieces in a big bread pan padded with paper towels. Cover with a tea towel, à la 1912. When the towel is lifted there is chicken in a golden pyramid, piece upon piece, crisp but not crackly, the soft meat finely grained under the coating. Thin slices of homemade yeast bread and plenty of butter are the thing to eat with fried chicken. And pass crisp chunks of watermelon pickle— it adds that something special. As do quince preserves.

TASTING OF SUGAR AND SUN

It was Aunt Mary Blodgett's turnover tarts that men reached for when the coffee was passed. Utility tarts as unadorned as a Grant Wood canvas. But so easy to handle, and chuck full of nectarious goodness. And the crust brown and rich. There was watermelon, that social fruit in which everyone shared.

Men stretched out and bemoaned a great "too much." There was talk of crops and weather. The young folks were busy as beavers tending to the layout for the contests and races. The women cleaned up. Tongues grew warm with the friction of friendly chatter.

The sun was setting behind the cottonwoods before the baskets were packed, the teams hitched, the children herded in. The town folks who had no chores stayed to see the fireworks. Goodbyes were called out. "Quite a celebration, wasn't it?" "It's good to see you neighbors again!"

The old hunger for intimacy is just as real today. And what is patriotism but keeping our faith in one another, a sharing in friendliness, and faith in the flag—the same old flag, and "still there."

The strawberry social is a Middle West institution that survives in country neighborhoods even in our modern world of satellites. For this occasion pick a warm, sweet night in June with moonlight and dew perfuming the honeysuckles. Take two bushels of fat strawberries, a score of baking pans filled with rich biscuit shortcake squares fresh from the oven. Borrow paper lanterns to flutter like jeweled moths against the dark green of tree and shrub. Sparkling white the tables, the planks covered with white paper for tablecloths. Fill low bowls with honeysuckle or the wild roses.

Women counting spoons, women cutting shortcake, women counting noses, women talking of slips and blooms, of hats and setting hens. Voices run high. Men wait in little clusters, quietly, voices low.

"Shortcake's ready!" A scramble for chairs. Shortcakes, on meat platters, are brought whole to the tables to cut before your eyes. The top berries cold and sweet like wine; the crushed berries in between warm and tasting of sugar and sun, the shortcake crunchy and rich with butter.

Old-Fashioned Strawberry Shortcake

3 cups all-purpose flour

5 teaspoons baking powder

⅛ teaspoon grated nutmeg

1 teaspoon salt

1 cup sugar, plus more to taste

½ cup (1 stick) plus 2 tablespoons unsalted butter, chilled and cut into small pieces

1 large egg, beaten

½ cup milk

3 quarts ripe fresh strawberries

Whipped cream for serving, optional

Serves 8

Preheat the oven to 400 degrees.

Sift the flour, baking powder, nutmeg, salt, and ½ cup of the sugar into a large bowl. Transfer to a food processor, add ½ cup of the butter, and pulse until the mixture resembles coarse meal with lumps the size of small peas. Transfer the dough back to the bowl. Make a well and add the egg and milk to it. Knead the dough very gently with your fingertips or a pastry spatula until it just holds together, about 10 seconds. Dots of butter should be visible; do not overwork the dough. Generously flour a work surface and roll the dough out on it to form 2 circles that are ½ inch thick and 8 to 10 inches in diameter. Wrap the disks tightly in plastic and refrigerate.

Set aside 16 of the best-looking strawberries. Hull the rest, then halve them and place them in a bowl with the remaining ½ cup sugar or more, depending on the ripeness of the fruit. Let the strawberries macerate for at least 15 minutes but no more than 45 minutes.

Remove the dough disks from the refrigerator. Place the dough disks on 2 ungreased sheet pans and bake for 12 to 15 minutes, until golden on the outside and just cooked through in the center. Remove from the oven and cool for 10 to 15 minutes.

Slather the remaining 2 tablespoons butter evenly over the disks. Transfer the larger disk to a plate that will accommodate it and the juicy berries running off it. Pile the macerated berries on top and then cover with the other biscuit. Garnish with the reserved whole berries and serve with whipped cream, if you like.

ONCE IT TOOK MANPOWER to make ice cream. One worker relieved another as the cream thickened. The freezers we use today operate at the turn of a switch and they come in all sizes.

In communities where ice was scarce in early years, strawberry ice cream with strawberry sauce was the second pièce de resistance of the June Festival. Ingredients for the ice cream were country born—broad strawberry beds, lush pastures where cows stood in the cool shadows of the willows, to the shady back porches where Father and the older boys took turns at the freezer. As the freezer handle grew stiff and the workers grunted with effort, the ring of children drew closer for the great ceremony of licking the dasher. I remember how my mother pulled it forth adrip with the softly frozen, satiny cream tinted faintly pink of the fruit.

"Somebody bring the oatmeal saucers. We might as well have a little taste now while it's free." That was my father. "This ice cream is for the social," Mother would remind him. She might as well have saved her breath.

At last the lid was on the can, salt and ice packed solidly into the bucket. Dad and "Sonny" carried the freezer to the cellar to let the cream ripen.

Ice cream was sold at ten cents a saucer, fifteen cents with strawberry sauce. Angel cake was a "must have" accompaniment—no charge. Two servings an evening for each member of a family was the usual thing. The money went to pay the preacher, to reshingle the church or revarnish the pews. The minister would say a prayer, thanking both the Lord and the ladies.

KANSAS

Strawberry Ice Cream

3 cups finely crushed fresh
ripe strawberries

4 cups sugar

3 quarts half-and-half

12 large eggs

Dash of salt

3 tablespoons vanilla extract

Makes 1 gallon

Macerate the berries in a bowl with one third of the sugar and let stand in a warm place for 1 to 2 hours, until the juices are drawn out.

In a small saucepan over medium heat, bring the half-and-half to a boil; immediately remove the pan from the heat and set aside to cool. In a large saucepan, beat the eggs well; add the salt and the remaining sugar. Slowly add the half-and-half. Place over low heat and cook for 10 minutes, or until the mixture coats the back of a spoon. Transfer the mixture to a large bowl, set the bowl inside a bowl full of ice, and whisk until cool, then strain it through a fine strainer into a fresh bowl. Whisk in the juice drained from the berries, and the berries themselves if you like the ice cream a bit chunky. Freeze according to the manufacturer's directions for the ice cream maker.

Note: Some like their strawberry ice cream unadorned. Others want more crushed berries ladled over all, to run like rivulets to the saucer to form a crimson lake. For this, slightly crush the fruit as for shortcake, adding as much sugar as the palate dictates, then set to ripen in a warmish place.

COOKING FROM A MAN'S POINT OF VIEW

Today I hear much criticism regarding food in the Middle West. The complaints come usually from tourists who pass through at sixty miles an hour, eating en route in public places, and seldom at the best. I doubt these scorners have ever sat down as a guest at a family table. True, the food of the plains country is forthright as it is in the Northwest, but for the most part it is wholesome and well cooked. It is cooked exactly long enough and served the moment it is ready. It is food to be eaten with real enjoyment.

Allow me to prove my point. Come along visiting. First stop, Manhattan, Kansas, to meet Mrs. Robert Conover, her husband then professor of English and editor of the *Kansas Magazine*. The two young Conovers were at home, Elizabeth twenty and Bob fourteen, and always company coming, company going, front door, back door. There were parties for visiting celebrities, good things cooking.

Mrs. Conover, Darlene her name, a tall willowy woman with an oval face. Around her mouth were fine lines that came from much laughing. Her brown hair was sprinkled with silver, parted in the middle, pulled tightly back. She was neither young nor beautiful, except for her eyes. They were straight-at-you-eyes, gray-blue, which held a joy-in-living look.

Darlene said, "My cooking is from a man's point of view." It shows a southern influence. Her father was Judge V. H. Grinstead, a first judge of the western third of the state, in the short-grass country. Father was opposed to what he called "female food"—and Darlene came to like substantial, sound-eating fare.

A professor's wife hasn't much for extra spending, yet the Conovers, for long years, were elected for considerable official entertaining. Darlene had no help. She planned the menus, cooked and served and cleaned up. To simplify the job she used ten basic recipes. One typical of the basic ten is this sweet roll (recipe follows), which she called her "recipe for anything." She used it in more than a dozen ways with additions and subtractions, as a base for waffles, pancakes, a pastry topping for meat pies, or for sweet desserts, for coffee cakes.

Mrs. Conover's
No-Fail Biscuit Pastry

1½ cups all-purpose flour

4 teaspoons baking powder

3 tablespoons nonfat dry milk

2 teaspoons sugar

½ teaspoon salt

¾ cup lukewarm milk

¼ cup vegetable oil

Makes 12 biscuits or the pastry base or topping for countless treats

Preheat the oven to 400 degrees. Grease a large baking sheet.

Sift the flour, baking powder, dry milk, sugar, and salt into a large bowl. In a small bowl, whisk the lukewarm milk with the oil. Make a well and pour the wet ingredients into the dry. Stir lightly until just blended (about 10 strokes). Turn onto a floured surface and knead gently 10 times. Pat out to ½ inch thick and cut with a floured 2-inch biscuit cutter. Place the dough rounds on the prepared sheet and bake for 10 to 12 minutes, until the biscuits are golden brown. Serve immediately.

Variation: Cheese Biscuits: Makes 2 dozen. Add ⅔ cup finely grated cheese to the dry ingredients, then add the liquid ingredients. Roll out very thin. Cut in tiny rounds; make an indentation in the top with your thumb or a thimble and fill the hole with additional grated cheese, or make cheese sticks or tiny triangles. Bake following the directions above.

Variation: "Niff-Niff": Serves 6. This is Mrs. Conover's word for knickknacks, or trifles. Add 1 teaspoon celery seeds or 2 teaspoons chopped fresh parsley to the dry ingredients. Roll out 1 inch thick and cut into 2-inch squares; use as dumplings for chicken broth, stew, or any favorite pot pie.

Variation: Cinnamon-Crumb Coffee Cake: Makes one 8-inch cake. Preheat the oven to 375 degrees. Grease and flour an 8-inch square cake pan. Add ¼ cup sugar and a dash of grated nutmeg to the dry ingredients. Beat 1 egg lightly; add ¼ teaspoon lemon extract and the liquids from the basic recipe. Add to the dry ingredients, beating until just blended. Pat into the pan. Mix together ¼ cup sugar, 2 tablespoons all-purpose flour, 2 teaspoons ground cinnamon, and 4 tablespoons (½ stick) melted butter. If desired, add finely chopped nuts, currants, or small seedless raisins. Spread over the top of the cake and bake for 30 minutes. Serve hot.

Variation: Apple Delight: Serves 8. Preheat the oven to 375 degrees. Grease and flour two 8-inch pie pans. Add ½ teaspoon grated lemon or orange peel to the dry ingredients. Mix and knead dough. Divide evenly and pat into the prepared pans. Peel and core 4 large baking apples, thinly slice them, as for pie, and press the wedges close together in the dough. Pour over a syrup made by combining 2 tablespoons melted butter, a dash of salt, ¼ cup dark corn syrup, and 1 teaspoon ground cinnamon. Bake for 45 minutes, or until tender. Serve warm, with whipped cream.

THERE IS NO PERFUME in the world like the springtime smell of prairie air. This morning it had a warm green scent that the heat distilled from the endless waves of grass. I took a deep breath of it and turned the car off the main highway up the narrow Spring Creek road.

I had come to visit the Orville Burtis Ranch in Ashland Bottoms. This place, which the Burtises operate, totals seven thousand acres. Once this was a part of the famous Dewey ranch, where mules were raised to work at Fort Riley, twelve miles away. Around 1910, when the seventeen-room house was built, local folks spoke of it in a hushed, awed way. Wealthy Chauncey Dewey brought his friends from Kansas City to party here, to ride and hunt and make merry whole weeks at a time.

The ranch, when I was there a few years back, was still a fun center, but a different kind of fun now from the old days. A gathering spot for daughter Karen Burtis's pals. Karen, then sixteen, a junior in high school with activities unlimited. Young people overran the place and the older crowd, too, Dad and Mother's friends.

Crowd supper parties were a frequent event. Mrs. Burtis would make stew or maybe a tub full of chili. Either dish has a rib-sticking quality that makes you young beyond your time. The meat was taken from her well-stocked thirty-foot locker, and it was home-grown steer beef. The other party foods the guests brought, that is, the salad and dessert.

Butterhorn Rolls

¾ cup milk

½ cup vegetable shortening, melted

½ cup sugar

1 teaspoon salt

1 (¼-ounce) envelope active dry yeast

¼ cup warm water

3 large eggs, beaten

4½ cups all-purpose flour

3 tablespoons unsalted butter, melted

Makes 32

Scald the milk by heating it in a small saucepan over medium heat until bubbles appear around the inside edge of pan and the milk is about to boil. Pour the scalded milk into a large bowl. Add the shortening, sugar, and salt, stir until sugar dissolves, then set aside to cool until lukewarm, about 2 minutes. Meanwhile, in a small bowl, dissolve the yeast in the warm water and set aside until foamy, about 10 minutes.

Add the eggs and yeast mixture to the milk mixture and stir with a wooden spoon until well combined. Gradually add the flour, stirring until the dough comes together. Turn the dough out onto a floured surface and knead until smooth, about 10 minutes. Shape the dough into a ball and lightly dust with flour. Transfer the dough to a large clean bowl, cover with a clean, damp kitchen towel or plastic wrap, and set in a warm spot to let rise until doubled in bulk, about 1 hour.

Lightly grease 2 baking sheets with some of the butter and set aside. Turn the dough out onto a clean surface, divide it in half, then shape each piece of dough into a ball. Roll the dough balls out into 14-inch circles, then brush each with some of the melted butter, and cut each circle into sixteenths, making 32 wedges in all. Starting with the rounded edge and working toward the pointed end, roll up each wedge. Arrange the rolled dough wedges, pointed-end side facing down to keep the wedges from unrolling, on the prepared baking sheets about 2 inches apart. Brush the tops and sides with the remaining butter, loosely cover with a clean, damp kitchen towel or plastic wrap, and set aside in a warm spot to rise for 45 minutes.

Preheat the oven to 350 degrees. Bake the rolls until golden brown and hollow sounding when tapped, about 25 minutes. Transfer to wire racks to cool for at least 15 minutes. Serve warm or at room temperature.

Burtis Ranch Chili

1 pound dry red kidney beans	2½ pounds ground chuck
4 quarts cold water	1 tablespoon vegetable oil
About 5 cups tomato juice	3 tablespoons chili powder
1 tablespoon salt	1 large onion, diced (about 2 cups)

Serves 8

KANSAS

Rinse the beans, place them in a large heavy stockpot, add cold water to cover, and soak overnight.

The next day, cover and simmer in the soaking water for 1½ to 2 hours, until the beans are tender, adding tomato juice from time to time to keep the beans covered as the liquid boils away. If the tomato juice runs out, add more water if necessary to keep the liquid an inch above the beans. Add ½ tablespoon of the salt.

Divide the meat into batches. Heat ½ tablespoon of the oil in a large skillet over medium heat. Add the meat in batches and brown it, stirring the next batch into the earlier one. Add the chili powder. After all the meat is browned, add the remaining ½ tablespoon salt. Remove from the heat.

In a separate skillet, heat the remaining ½ tablespoon oil over medium heat. Add the onion and sauté until golden, about 5 minutes. Add the beef and onion to the pot of beans, place over low heat, and cook, stirring constantly, about 10 minutes longer. Serve with Butterhorn Rolls (page 498), if you like, or crackers.

Osa Nichols's Buttermilk Flapjacks

1¾ cups sifted all-purpose flour

1 teaspoon baking powder

1 teaspoon baking soda

½ teaspoon salt

½ cup buttermilk

1 cup milk

1 small egg, well beaten

Makes 1 dozen pancakes

In a medium bowl, combine the flour, baking powder, baking soda, and salt. In a large bowl, whisk together the buttermilk, milk, and egg. Add the dry ingredients to the buttermilk mixture and stir just until combined.

Heat a griddle or cast-iron skillet over medium-low heat and lightly butter it. For each pancake, gently spread ¼ cup of the batter onto the hot surface to form a 4-inch circle. Cook until the top is set, about 2 minutes. Flip the pancake and continue cooking until golden, about 1 minute longer. Transfer to a large plate and keep warm while you cook the remaining pancakes.

WITH PLENTY OF BUTTER AND SOMETHING SWEET

Sundown I came to Liberal, in the panhandle section of the state, a boom town since the discovery of oil, a town of ten thousand population, self-styled Pancake Hub of the Universe.

Walk down Main Street window-shopping, you are purse-tempted with all manner of pancake novelties: pancake earrings, pancake griddles in china and iron designed for ash trays. A stack of wheats is the center decoration on the checks issued by local banks. Tourists get their picture taken by a six-foot cement mound of pancake on pancake, butter topped. Here is the starting point of the International Pancake Race, an annual Shrove Tuesday event. On this day the fleetest-footed of the local bakers bake pancakes extra heavy to flip safely in the Kansas breeze while they race an S-shaped course. Their racing and flipping skill is pitted against the housewives of Olney, England, who for five hundred years have celebrated Shrove Tuesday with a pancake race.

Contestants for the beauty prize floated by in evening gowns in a wind edged with ice. More beautiful than the beauties were the majestic models of farm machinery. I loved that one-way plow of a size to cover a fifteen-foot strip. There were oil-drilling machines. Hurrah for the pancake tree. Tiny little pancakes, cellophane-wrapped, were thrown helter-skelter to the crowd.

The race came just a few minutes before noon, when Mrs. Binnie Dick beat the world's record and retained the title for the town and the United States. But I didn't come to report on racing records. I wanted to know how this pancake town likes its pancakes. Binnie, the veteran speedster, bookkeeper-housewife, raised in St. James, Missouri, on a dairy farm in the Ozarks, bakes her pancakes by Mama's recipe. She baked a batch of these cakes for me and gave a bit of advice as she beat up the batter. Never overbeat, she said, that makes the cakes tough. She heats the griddle slowly to make for even browning. It's a greaseless griddle she prefers, then to rub clean after each batch with a salt bag. But if you are using a frying pan she suggests "grease it lightly." To test the griddle she dribbles on a few drops of water. If these dance on top, all is well. When the griddle is too hot the little drops explode.

Peggy Tacha of Kismet, Kansas, another racer, gave me her mother's recipe and explained how her family likes their pancakes served: with plenty of butter and something sweet. One favorite is a spread made of brown sugar creamed with butter. Sometimes pancake syrup is heated with butter, this passed warm. And granulated sugar is nice mixed with a sprinkling of lemon rind.

One of the residents of this far west town is Mrs. Osa Nichols who went there as a bride. She is past the age for pancake racing, but no one can beat her when it comes to the baking. Pleased we are to give her recipe.

Mrs. Thornton Scott's Cocoon Cookies

½ cup (1 stick) unsalted butter, softened

⅔ cup confectioners' sugar

1 teaspoon vanilla extract

1 cup all-purpose flour

1 cup finely chopped walnuts

Makes about 3 dozen cookies

In a large bowl, cream the butter with ⅓ cup of the confectioners' sugar until light and fluffy. Add the vanilla. Blend the flour in gradually, ¼ cup at a time, beating well after each addition. Add the walnuts. Cover and refrigerate the dough for 1 hour.

When you are ready to bake, preheat the oven to 350 degrees. Generously grease 2 large baking sheets.

Pinch off small pieces of dough, about 2 teaspoons each, and shape into 1½-inch-long oval "cocoons" with the palms of your hands. Place the cocoons about 1 inch apart on the prepared sheets. Bake for 12 minutes, or just long enough for the cocoons to "dry out" and become golden brown. Let cool on the pans for 2 minutes, then, while still warm, roll in the remaining ⅓ cup of confectioners' sugar. Transfer to wire racks to cool completely.

WHERE NEIGHBOR IS
A COMMON WORD

Anyone growing up in Abilene, Kansas, has what the Midwest calls a "goodly heritage." There the prairie is always within sight and sound, a landscape lovely in its wide monotony. It's a place where neighbor is a common word, where caste or race doesn't count.

It's a place where lunch is the fillingest meal, supper almost as ample, this supplemented by the bedtime snack. It's a place where the best recipes are hand-downs from mothers to daughters, from neighbor to neighbor along with those country counting-out rhymes that children teach to children.

These are the things Mrs. Robert Gemmill told me about her hometown the day I went there, one purpose in mind, to borrow her recipes for the Christmas cookies. I had been eating these cookies, a few each holiday, over a period of years. They were known to me only as "Nina May's present," a box sent annually to our friend Alice Nichols who has always carried a few to my house to share.

"Just thought you'd like some of Nina May's cookies," Alice will say handing me a packet. As I arrange cookies on a plate, Alice explains, "That one she called a Billy Goat, don't ask me why, maybe because it has that whiskery look. These little bundles are cocoons and these with the red and green cherries are the Swedish sweets."

Nina May is an Abilene girl; she has lived there always, her grandparents before her. Grandpa, W. D. Nichols, was mayor of the town for twelve consecutive years. She lives in his old home, built in 1880 by an Episcopalian minister, sold, then resold, going to her grandfather in 1910.

The Gemmills took it over in 1945, remodeled and refurnished it with antiques. All except the kitchen. This room is fourteen by fourteen feet, done in yellow and blue with everything "latest." Family and friends, everybody gravitates toward the kitchen as naturally as water toward a dam.

When I asked Nina May would she part with her cookie recipes, she said, "I'd love to, but of course these aren't really mine. I've borrowed them from friends." Next to collecting antiques, Nina May told me, she enjoys collecting recipes.

These Christmas cookies she makes by the dozens to go into gift packs. She can't remember where she picked up the spicy Billy Goats. The Christmas cookies are from Mrs. Annie Engle who lived in Abilene . . . oh, years ago. When Nina May was little she played with the Engle tribe and loved these cookies their mother made around Christmastime. It was after she married that she wrote to Mrs. Engle, who had moved, to get the recipe. The cocoons are from Mrs. Thornton Scott who lives next door. The Swedish cookies are from friend Mrs. Harry Leonard, Jr.

Billy Goat Christmas Cookies

½ cup (1 stick) unsalted butter, softened

¾ cup sugar

2 large egg yolks

1 teaspoon vanilla extract

1¼ cups all-purpose flour

½ teaspoon baking soda

⅛ teaspoon salt

1 teaspoon ground cinnamon

¼ teaspoon ground cloves

1 tablespoon buttermilk

½ pound walnuts, chopped

½ pound dates, pitted and chopped

Makes 3 to 4 dozen cookies

In a large bowl using an electric mixer, cream the butter and sugar well. Add the egg yolks and vanilla and beat until light and fluffy. Sift the flour, baking soda, salt, cinnamon, and cloves into a medium bowl. Add the dry ingredients to the egg mixture, a little at a time, beating well to incorporate. Beat in the buttermilk, stirring with a wooden spoon. Stir in the walnuts and dates. Cover the bowl and refrigerate the dough until chilled, about 1 hour.

Preheat the oven to 325 degrees and generously grease 2 baking sheets.

Drop the batter by teaspoonfuls about 1 inch apart onto the prepared sheets. Bake for 15 to 20 minutes, until golden brown. Cool the cookies on the sheets for 2 minutes, then transfer to wire racks to cool completely.

IMPERISHABLE IN THE ANNALS of Kansas history are Carry Nation, the Pawnee Rock near the Santa Fe Trail, the cow towns of Abilene and Dodge City, the seven-year curtain raiser to the Civil War—and forever dear to the memory, black walnut cake!

It was in Lawrence, Kansas, I met a black walnut cake that for me held a cumulative wealth of fragrant reminiscences. It awoke memories of the old days of the box social, the Sunday night suppers on Blue Valley Farm. This was a cake baked by Mrs. John Ise, who learned the art of its making by helping her mother in a parsonage kitchen in the eastern part of the state. Mrs. Ise called herself a homebody and that's what she wanted to be. One public character in the family is enough, she told me, referring to

husband John, one of the country's leading economists.

The daily chore of cooking she made a talented hobby. In University of Kansas circles the Ise parties were notable for good talk led by John, good cooking by his lady.

Mrs. Ise shared her husband's interest in collecting antiques. Their home was filled with beautiful pieces of furniture, silver, china, glass bought at bargain values before the antique craze hit the Midwest.

The sterling-silver tea set was one Professor Ise ran across in Atlantic City during the depression years. Mrs. Ise used this when she entertained her Round Table Literary Club at afternoon tea.

And one treat always on deck—her mother's black walnut cake.

Black Walnut Cake

½ cup (1 stick) unsalted butter, softened

1½ cups sugar

2 cups all-purpose flour

4 teaspoons baking powder

½ teaspoon salt

1 cup milk

1 cup finely ground black walnuts

1 teaspoon vanilla extract

4 large egg whites

¼ teaspoon cream of tartar

KANSAS

Makes one 9-inch tube cake

Preheat the oven to 325 degrees. Grease and flour a 9-inch tube pan.

In a large bowl using an electric mixer, cream the butter and sugar well. Sift the flour, baking powder, and salt into a medium bowl. Add the flour mixture to the creamed mixture alternately with the milk, mixing well after each addition. Stir in the walnuts and vanilla.

In a medium bowl, beat the egg whites until foamy. Add the cream of tartar and continue beating until stiff peaks form. Fold the egg whites into the butter-nut mixture. Pour the batter into the prepared pan and bake for 15 minutes, or until the cake begins to rise, then increase the oven temperature to 350 degrees and bake for 30 to 40 minutes longer, until the top springs back when lightly pressed with a finger and a wooden pick or skewer inserted into the center comes out clean. Cool the cake in the pan on a wire rack for 30 minutes, then invert the cake onto the rack, remove the pan, and cool completely. Serve the cake at room temperature with whipped cream or ice cream, if you like, and hot coffee or tea.

GOURMET DINNER CLUBS SPRING up cross-country like mushrooms after rain. The idea is as simple as this: a few friends with a common interest in good eating get together for dinners and eat. They labor lovingly over the planning of the menu, then do the cooking themselves.

It was just such an informal fun group I discovered when I was visiting in Manhattan, Kansas. Five long-time friends, who have made cooking and recipe-collecting a hobby over the years, decided to share their best finds, cook their favorite dishes for each other, and make a party of it.

Meet the gourmets: Clara (Mrs. S. A. McCracken); Irene (Mrs. Hal Harlan); Mary (Mrs. Malcolm Aye); Dorothy (Mrs. Gerald Boone Smith); Marion (Mrs. Marion Kendall Bugbee).

The club was started in September, 1957, with no more planning than a passing remark by Clara saying, "Wouldn't it be fun to have a dinner club?"

"Let's!" came the answer, fortissimo. So the dinners got going, given at each other's homes. The rule is that the hostess of the evening provide only the bread and coffee, but the bread must be homemade.

Each member prepares at least one dish for the dinner. Clara gave us the following skillet cabbage recipe, which we like better than any vegetable dish tasted in a long time.

Irene likes to make desserts, and her apricot pudding is a frequent demand. Marion Bugbee's shrimp chili came originally from Helen Alexander's *Hawaiian Cook Book*, but like all good cooks, Marion has added her personal touches.

Clara McCracken's Skillet Cabbage

½ pound bacon

4 cups shredded cabbage

1 green bell pepper, cored, seeded, and diced

2 cups diced celery

2 large onions, diced

2 ripe tomatoes, chopped

2 teaspoons sugar

Salt and freshly ground black pepper

Serves 6

Cook the bacon in a large heavy-bottomed skillet over medium heat until crisp. Transfer to paper towels to drain. Combine the remaining ingredients with the bacon fat in the skillet, cover, and cook for 5 minutes, then remove from the heat immediatcly and serve warm, garnished with the crumbled cooked bacon.

Note: Whatever else you do, don't overcook this dish. The vegetables should keep their crisp, fresh quality.

KANSAS

GREATEST STRETCH DISH ON RECORD

Busiest young housewife I have met in my travels is Mrs. Robert E. Bogue of Wichita, Kansas. First let me tell you something about this Betty and her doings in home and community, then to talk cooking.

Slim, blonde Betty does her own housework, washing, ironing, cleaning, and cooking for family of five. Betty is family chauffeur, doing the marketing, running the errands, getting three children to and from school.

The Bogues have their own home in a new development on the east side of the city. Robert is a veterinarian, part owner in a small animal hospital with his father and brother.

Such is Betty's homework. Outside activities include church and local club affairs. Betty and Robert work together on the board of governors of the Plymouth Congregational Church. In addition the Bogues find time for fun with their friends and a day a week is left exclusively for the children. Family day is the seventh day. Church

in the morning, then in summer a trip by car to a picnic spot, in winter very often to eat in a restaurant.

Barbecues are the thing with Bob and Betty's crowd. Each couple brings their own steak plus something special. By request Betty is delegated to bring a chili con quesa dip to have with corn chips, a recipe which a friend in the Air Force brought home from Texas.

"But this isn't my greatest specialty," she explains. "I have an economy dish learned in the lean years. It's the greatest stretch dish on record. I can make one chicken feed twenty people."

The Bogues were married while they were still in college, Robert studying on the GI Bill, Betty an art student. But she won her real fame as an artist in stretching the budget. It was in this slim-purse era that Betty learned the meaning of that Hindu proverb, "Five were invited, here come nine; water the porridge, all shall dine." Instead she gives a two-way stretch to a chicken.

Hearty Chicken-and-Stuffing Casserole

Serves 20

Step 1: Chicken (may be cooked a day in advance)

1 (4- to 5-pound) stewing chicken, cut into pieces

1 carrot, sliced into thin rounds

1 onion, quartered

1½ teaspoons salt

Place the chicken, carrot, onion, and salt in deep saucepan. Add water to cover, place over medium-high heat, and bring to a boil. Reduce the heat to low, cover, and simmer until the meat is fork-tender, 3 to 4 hours. Transfer the chicken from the broth to a large bowl. When cool enough to handle, remove the skin and discard it. Pull the meat from the bones and strain the broth. Refrigerate the meat and broth until ready to prepare the casserole.

Step 2: Stuffing

½ cup (1 stick) unsalted butter

1 medium onion, finely chopped

2 large stalks celery with tops, finely chopped

6 tablespoons reserved chicken broth

1 teaspoon salt

1 teaspoon freshly ground black pepper

1 teaspoon dried sage

12 cups soft breadcrumbs or cubes

Melt the butter in a large heavy skillet over medium-high heat. Add the onion and celery and sauté until softened and translucent, about 5 minutes. Add the stock, salt, pepper, and sage and cook, stirring, for 2 to 3 minutes. Stir in the breadcrumbs, remove the pan from the heat, and set aside.

KANSAS

Step 3: Sauce

1 cup (2 sticks) unsalted butter or vegetable shortening

1 cup all-purpose flour

2 teaspoons salt

4 cups reserved chicken broth

1 cup milk

4 large eggs

Melt the butter in a large skillet over medium heat. Add the flour and salt and cook, stirring, to blend into a smooth paste, about 3 minutes. Stir in the stock and milk and cook, stirring constantly, until thick, 8 to 10 minutes. Remove the pan from the heat and cool slightly, about 5 minutes. In a small bowl, beat the eggs. Whisk a little of the sauce into the eggs, then pour the mixture into the pan with the rest of the sauce and whisk to combine. Do not put the pan back on the heat.

Step 4: Casserole

1 cup dried breadcrumbs

4 tablespoons (½ stick) unsalted butter, melted

Preheat the oven to 375 degrees. Grease a 4-quart casserole and pour in the stuffing.

In a small bowl, combine the breadcrumbs with the melted butter. Cover the stuffing with half of the sauce, add a layer of chicken, then cover with the remaining sauce. Sprinkle with the buttered breadcrumbs. Bake for 30 minutes, or until the breadcrumbs are browned and the casserole is bubbling. Let the casserole rest for 5 minutes before serving.

Jezebel Sauce

1 cup apple jelly

½ cup pineapple preserves

¼ cup prepared mustard

1 to 2 tablespoons prepared horseradish

Salt and freshly ground black pepper

Makes enough for 1 meatloaf

In a blender or food processor or using an electric mixer, blend the jelly, preserves, mustard, and horseradish until smooth. Season with salt and pepper. Serve immediately with baked ham or meatloaf, if you like, or use to glaze ribs. Cover and refrigerate the sauce; it will keep for up to 3 weeks.

NEBRASKA

Like "Jewels of India or gems from Samarkand," the wild plum jelly on the grocers' shelf! It shoulders close to a jar of wild plum preserves and next to a jar of warm amber-peach preserves the label reads. All three here from the same farm, the Courtright farm near Beaver City in the Nebraska sand hills.

The ruby juice of the wild plum shines crystal clear, casting its little flames like prairie fires. The thick plum preserves are amethyst, unctuous and solemn, the peach a molten gold. Turn the contents of the jars into cut glass bowls; spill out sunshine and the drone of bees, the wild plum blossom's breath, sweet and strong, coming from a thicket along a deep ravine. Here is fragrance of a peach orchard spreading its pink and white banner of bloom to the soft May breeze. Some crafty kitchen alchemist has caught the blue and gold of summer and turned it into shining jewels to be enjoyed now when days go dull, when snow is falling and icy patterns form on bluish window panes.

These jars mean more to us than the casual shopper knows. Memories lie sleeping in them. Taste the freshness, the zest of the plum preserve, so good with game. The flavor reawakens by exactitude odor memories effaced for years, the sharp smell of plums and sugar cooking into a rich butter, a spread for hot bread. It brings memories of springtime in Kansas and plum thickets in bloom, "earth crammed with heaven and every bush afire with God." The pleasure blazes on for hours in the veins with no more fuel than one small bite and the knowing of how these good things came about.

Bittersweet plum. This jelly-jam making is a family undertaking, a family scattered into far states with the old home place remaining their hub of life; each summer such a trekking back to the farm! The farm started when Clarence Courtright came out of the East and took land in western Nebraska. Today his son, Byron, has the 300-acre stock farm where the wild plums grow along Beaver Creek. The big farm kitchen is the scene of the preserving industry. Marie, that's Byron's wife, she's on the job, but it's Leila Courtright, Byron's sister, who started the operation. Leila is a home economics teacher in Long Island City High School, also in charge of the hospitality class at the Youth and Adult Center Bryant High School, and a kitchenette resident of Manhattan. But back to Nebraska when it's summertime.

It was two years ago, sitting on the porch of the ranch house, the night winds singing through the cottonwoods, a fragrance stealing in from the wild plum thicket, that Leila thought about New Yorkers and what a pity their ignorance of the sandhill plum, its flowery perfume, its goodness cooked into preserves. The beach plum of New England had nothing on this little fruit of the Midwest, its flavor a blending of the bitter and the sweet. These plums, like the pioneer himself, have taken their character from their fight against the rigors of nature. Even in the ripest fruit the bitterness is there.

How many Nebraska acres belong to the Courtrights? The family isn't sure but over a thousand and still not enough plums. The sand plum thickets are fast disappearing in the Midwest, like the black walnuts, like the wild game. In Nebraska and Kansas wheat fields and cattle ranches and the contoured farms roll away into the sunset and no sign of a spot where the draws once gashed the earth, where the plum thickets grew. But riding along a field you may come unexpectedly to a few wild bushes. To meet the growing demand for the plum preserves Leila put an ad in "The Custer County Chief" offering $1.50 a bushel for fresh picked sand plums. She and nephew Leland drove to Broken Bow to pick up the harvest and carried a truckload back to the farm. Everybody worked together as they made up to 1,000 jars, and put up the rest of the plums in half gallon crocks, canned the seed skin-on, these to be made into preserves and jelly as the orders come in.

The jelly is a delicate echo of the more lusty preserves. In the Courtright parlor it is served in a tea sandwich with cream cheese, or as a snack with crusty rolls or crisp crackers or as a garnish with a fruit salad to dot on. Here's a dessert that calls for a second helping among the Courtright tribe. Gingerbread mix is baked, then cut into three-inch pieces spread with the wild plum jelly, topped with whipped cream, and in the center of each piece a dip or jelly as an ornament.

Nebraska Wild Plum Jelly

4 pounds wild plums, halved and pitted

4¾ cups sugar

½ teaspoon ground cinnamon

½ teaspoon grated nutmeg

¼ cup lemon juice

Makes about 8 (8-ounce) jars

Sterilize 8 (8-ounce) canning jars according to the manufacturer's directions. Place a small plate and three metal spoons in the freezer. Place the plums in a wide, non-reactive pan and add enough cold water to barely cover them. Bring to a boil, then lower heat to maintain a lively simmer and cook until very tender, about 45 minutes.

Line a strainer with 4 layers of cheesecloth that you have wet and wrung out, and place over a bowl. Pour the plum mixture into the strainer; cover with the edges of the cheesecloth. Let stand for 30 minutes or until liquid measures 4¾ cups. Return the plum liquid to the pan and stir in the sugar, followed by the cinnamon, nutmeg, and lemon juice. Bring the mixture to a boil and cook for 5 minutes. Skim carefully. If the jelly is foaming excessively, you can add a tablespoon of unsalted butter. Return the mixture to a boil and cook until it registers 220 degrees on a candy thermometer. Check how the jelly is setting by scooping a little of the jelly into one of your frozen spoons. Return the spoon to the plate in the freezer for 2 minutes. After 2 minutes, the jelly should be thick and hold its shape somewhat when you push it with your finger. If the jelly is still thin, boil for another minute and test again on another spoon. Be careful not to overcook, as the jelly will continue to set up as it cools.

Using a funnel, pour the jelly into the prepared sterilized jars. Fill each jar just to the bottom of the funnel, about ⅓ inch from the bottom of the jar threads. Wipe the jar rims with a moist paper towel, checking for any cracks or irregularities as you go. Carefully position lids on each jar. Screw the rings on tightly. You may refrigerate the jars for immediate use or water-bath can them (according to jar manufacturer's instructions) for pantry storage.

THE DAKOTAS

A tall white cake with shadowy chocolate tracings to mark its layers won $25,000 in cash yesterday for its creator, Mrs. Bernard Kanago, of Webster, S.D., one of the 100 finalists from thirty-two states, Puerto Rico, Hawaii, and Alaska who competed in the Pillsbury Mills Fifth Grand National Bake-off. "Queen of Cooks" is the wife of a painter-paper hanger, mother of two children who does her own housework and makes cooking a hobby.

The idea for her prize cake, she said, came "just out of nowhere," and she put it to test, appropriately naming her creation "My Inspiration." Now she calls it, "My Golden Inspiration," for the money will help pay for her children's education and be a family nest egg.

Mrs. Kanago, a small, shy woman, laughed and cried when she learned of her success at the award luncheon yesterday. "I can't believe it! I just can't believe it!" she repeated over and over. Her next thought was: "I've got to get to a phone and tell the folks back home." Her daughter, Cynthia, sixteen-year-old high school student, and her son, Lee, twenty-two, a student at Northern State Teachers' College in Aberdeen, S.D., both had served notice that they intended to cut classes today to watch the bake-off awards on a television program.

Famed first lady of the theater, Helen Hayes, presented Mrs. Kanago with the $25,000 check on the coast-to-coast network to telecast from the Waldorf ballroom. Speaking to the 100 finalists, Helen Hayes said: "The most wonderful part of this is that you have chosen to share your recipes with other women all over America. Certain recipes," said Miss Hayes, "are almost as personal as a woman's age. When a woman gives a recipe that she values to another woman, she gives something of her own self, something of her own home, something of her own background, breeding, and family heritage— something very personal and precious."

A snowbound paper hanger, informed today that his wife had won $25,000 for her championship layer cake, acknowledged both the news and the money were "awfully nice to take." But Bernard Kanago could not say what the family of four planned to do with the prize money. Mr. Kanago said his wife dreamed up the recipe herself. "She reversed the order of usually putting nuts on top and put them in the bottom of the pan. The dough absorbed."

My Inspiration

1 cup finely chopped nuts, such as pecans or walnuts

2½ cups all-purpose flour

4½ teaspoons baking powder

1 teaspoon salt

1½ cups sugar

⅔ cup vegetable shortening

1¼ cups milk

1 teaspoon vanilla extract

4 large egg whites

2 ounces grated sweet or semisweet chocolate (or chocolate chips)

My Inspiration's Chocolate Frosting (recipe follows)

Makes 1 (9-inch) layer cake

Preheat the oven to 350 degrees. Grease and flour 2 (9-inch) cake pans.

Spread the nuts evenly over the bottoms of the pans. Sift the flour, baking powder, salt, and sugar into a large bowl. Add the shortening, milk, and vanilla. Beat for 1½ minutes on medium speed or until the batter is well blended. Add the egg whites and beat for 1½ minutes more. Using an offset spatula, carefully spread one-quarter of the batter into each nut-lined pan, using about half of the batter in total. Sprinkle 1 ounce of the chocolate into each pan. Spoon the remaining batter into the pans, spreading carefully so the chocolate is not disturbed.

Bake for 35 to 40 minutes or until a tester inserted into the cake comes out clean. Cool in the pans for 15 minutes, then turn out onto wire racks to cool completely. Frost the layers nut-side up with the chocolate frosting, then spread the frosting on the sides and top of the cake. Decorate the cake with swirls of the reserved ⅓ cup of white frosting, if you like.

My Inspiration's Chocolate Frosting

4 large egg yolks

½ cup granulated sugar

¼ cup boiling water

2 ounces unsweetened chocolate, finely chopped

½ cup (1 stick) unsalted butter, softened

1 teaspoon vanilla extract

2 cups confectioners' sugar

Makes about 1 cup

In a medium heatproof bowl, whisk together the egg yolks and granulated sugar. Whisk in the boiling water. Set the bowl over a large pot of barely simmering water and heat, stirring constantly, until the mixture reaches 160 degrees on an instant-read thermometer. Remove from the heat and stir in the chocolate until the mixture is smooth. Let cool.

In a medium bowl, cream the butter with the vanilla and confectioners' sugar, adding the sugar slowly and beating after each addition. Reserve one third of this white frosting to decorate the top of the cake with swirls. Add the cooled chocolate mixture to the remaining frosting; beat until smooth.

THE DAKOTAS

A NATIONWIDE RECIPE SWAP

Looking for "cook young" ideas for my "How America Eats" series in *This Week* magazine, I introduced a nationwide recipe swap of time-saving dishes. The result was an avalanche of letters. These came from children under twelve, teenagers, career girls, young brides, mothers, grandmothers. In all, there were over 50,000 recipes, every one using short-cut ingredients—meaning those convenience foods that account for more than 15 percent of today's food sales. Whatever science has developed to make cooking easier "is for us," the letter said. Many reported, "I am a grandmother, but I cook young in heart." A testimony of the times.

The letters indicate that the buffet continues as the best way of entertaining a group, but there is returning interest also in small sit-down dinners. Simple dinners, three courses, for just a few friends. A time for talk and laughter, with the hostess doing the serving. But why should the kitchen see more of her than her guests do? She comes to the table looking gay and relaxed, as if she never had traffic with the kitchen range. Formal meals today belong to the banquet halls.

Meat pokes the biggest hole in the food budget—a number-one problem with brides and career girls. And especially so when it comes to entertaining. Company once a week? Let's not up-end the piggybank. Here is a meat dish quickly done, economical, yet on the elegant side. This is from Mrs. William F. Brennan, of Minot, North Dakota.

Sweet-and-Sour Spareribs

3 tablespoons unsalted butter

1 (5½- to 6-pound) rack of pork spareribs, excess fat trimmed and cut into individual ribs

2 medium onions, chopped

3 tablespoons brown sugar

2 tablespoons cornstarch

½ teaspoon salt

1 (6-ounce) can tomato paste

½ cup water

¼ cup cider vinegar

1 tablespoon soy sauce

1 (8-ounce) can crushed pineapple

Serves 6

Melt the butter in a large heavy-bottom pot over medium-high heat. Brown the ribs on both sides in batches, about 2 minutes per side. Transfer the ribs to paper towels to drain. Add the onions to the pot and sauté until softened, about 3 minutes. Add all of the remaining ingredients to the pot. Bring it to a boil, then reduce the heat to a low simmer, add the ribs, cover, and cook for about 1½ hours, adding more water if necessary, until the ribs are soft and tender and falling off the bone.

MISSOURI

It was Nell Snead, Women's Editor of the *Kansas City Star,* who sent me to visit Mrs. Clarence Decker, her husband at that time President of the University of Kansas City. Nell said, "She has an everlasting cheese pot. She makes a new batch whenever it's needed, adding a part of the old 'make' held back for the purpose. It's bleu cheese and cream cheese with spirits added."

———————————————

This melting pot cheese was started sixteen years ago with French Roquefort as a base. During the war Mrs. Decker switched to American bleu in the absence of French cheese. She makes ten pounds of this spread at a time, using two bleu wheels, four pounds each, and two pounds of cream cheese broken up and placed in a three-gallon bowl of a commercial mixer. The university cafeteria obliged the president's wife by doing the mixing. A most subtle blend, tangy, mellow, and to men irresistible.

Spread this on squares of pumpernickel or whole-wheat bread or a crisp cracker and let appetite take its course.

Mrs. Decker's
Port Wine Cheese Spread

4 pounds blue cheese, softened

1 pound cream cheese, softened

2 cups olive oil

1½ cups sherry wine

3 tablespoons dry mustard

2¼ tablespoons curry powder

3 tablespoons seasoned salt

2 tablespoons garlic salt

1 cup port wine

Makes 1 gallon

Combine the blue cheese and cream cheese in a large earthenware bowl or mixing bowl and beat with an electric mixer until blended. Cover and leave in the refrigerator overnight for the flavors to meld.

When you are ready to make the spread, in a medium bowl, whisk the oil with the sherry, then whisk in the mustard, curry, seasoned salt, and garlic salt. Pour the mixture over the cheese and mix well with a wooden spoon or fork, then beat with the electric mixer until creamy. Place one quarter of the mixture in an earthen crock or airtight jar or pot and pour over ½ cup of the port. Store covered in the refrigerator. (This constitutes the "mother" to be added to the next batch.)

Gash the cheese with a fork and trickle in the remaining ½ cup port. Divide the mixture as desired into crocks or large ramekins. Part of it may be dipped into attractive ceramic jars with wide tops to bring to the table at serving time. Refrigerate for at least a week before serving.

IT'S THE SAUCE THAT'S DIFFERENT

Early April, early morning, a day of receding crispness, old winter reluctantly giving way to spring. Twelve steps heading straight up from the sidewalk to the imposing stone house, twenty feet above the street. Breathless from the climb, I arrived at the front door of the Thomas Hart Bentons' home on Belleview Avenue, Kansas City, Missouri.

Mrs. Benton answered the bell; she's a comfortable woman of immense geniality, her eyes dark and shining with an inner laughter and her voice low, surprising one with its hidden chuckles. Kansas City friends had told me Rita Benton was a superb cook, doing all her own cooking, even baking the family bread.

"They say I'm a natural-born cook," she admitted candidly without a trace of boasting. "How else could I have held an artist husband for all these years?" At thirty-three Thomas Benton, the muralist, married Rita Piacenza, eighteen, an art student in one of his free evening classes. Now Rita practices the art of preparing fine foods for a hardworking husband.

"I was born in Italy," she said, "and every Italian girl must learn to cook. Anyhow I love cooking. But our meals are quite simple; one fine dish followed usually by a salad. Fruit or cake for dessert, maybe a soup for the beginning."

"And your husband's favorite dish?"

"Guinea hens," she said. "And my pecan cake—that's quite outstanding." I asked her about her spaghetti sauce, which I had been told was unbeatable. "I only have that for company," she said, "then only on request. It's too rich for my figure. About the guineas; I buy them frozen and by the dozen and keep them in my cold locker to be ready when needed. It takes one young guinea, two to three pounds, to serve two guests. It's the sauce that's different."

Mrs. Benton's
Roasted Guinea Hens

½ cup all-purpose flour

2 teaspoons salt, plus more
for seasoning the dish

¼ teaspoon freshly ground
black pepper, plus more
for seasoning the dish

2 (2½- to 3-pound) guinea hens,
quartered

5 tablespoons olive oil

1 large onion, diced

1 large green bell pepper, cored,
seeded, and diced

1 clove garlic, minced

1 (16-ounce) can tomato paste

2 cups water

1 pound mushrooms, thinly sliced

1 (14½-ounce) can chopped tomatoes

2 bay leaves

½ teaspoon dried thyme

1 cup white wine

Serves 4

In a shallow dish, combine the flour with the salt and pepper.
Roll the hen quarters in the seasoned flour.

Heat 4 tablespoons of the oil in a large skillet over medium
heat. Add the hen quarters in batches and fry until golden
brown on each side, 10 to 12 minutes total. Transfer the
hen pieces to a Dutch oven.

Add the remaining 1 tablespoon oil to the oil in the skillet,
then add the onion, green pepper, and garlic; reduce the heat
to low and cook until softened, about 10 minutes.

Pour the vegetables into the Dutch oven on top of the
chicken. Add the tomato paste and water to the skillet and
cook, stirring, over low heat to combine, about 3 minutes,
then pour into the Dutch oven. Add the mushrooms, chopped
tomatoes, bay leaves, and thyme to the Dutch oven and
season with salt and pepper. Increase the heat to medium-
high heat and bring to a boil, then reduce the heat to low,
cover, and simmer for about 1½ hours, until the chicken
is tender. Turn off the heat and let the dish stand until 30
minutes before dinner, then add the wine and reheat the
dish. Serve with wild rice, white rice, or buttered noodles
arranged in a copper dish, the guinea pieces laid over them
and the sauce over all, if you like.

Rita's Too-Rich Spaghetti

2 tablespoons olive oil

1 onion, chopped

1 pound pork tenderloin,
cut into very small cubes

½ pound mushrooms, sliced

1 (6-ounce) can tomato paste

1 cup chicken stock or water

1 bay leaf

Salt and freshly ground black pepper

1 pound spaghetti noodles

1 cup grated Parmesan cheese

Serves 4

Heat the oil in a large heavy-bottomed skillet over medium heat. Add the onion and cook until browned, about 15 minutes. Add the pork, mushrooms, tomato paste, stock, and bay leaf and season with salt and pepper. Reduce the heat to medium-low, cover the pan, and simmer for 30 minutes, or until the pork is tender.

Meanwhile, cook the spaghetti in a pot of boiling salted water for 8 minutes, or until al dente. Drain and place into a large serving bowl. Discard the bay leaf from the sauce, pour it on the pasta, and stir to blend. Serve with the cheese.

Pineapple-Glazed Ham

1 (10- to 12-pound) smoked ham, well scrubbed

½ cup firmly packed brown sugar

2 teaspoons dry mustard

½ teaspoon sweet paprika

1 tablespoon whole cloves

1 cup pineapple juice

Serves 25

Soak the ham overnight in a stockpot with cold water to cover.

The next morning, rinse the ham and add fresh water to cover. Place over medium-high heat and bring to a boil, then reduce the heat to medium, cover, and simmer for 25 to 30 minutes per pound, until the meat is tender.

Preheat the oven to 400 degrees. Cool the ham slightly in the stock, then drain. Using a sharp knife, score the top of the ham into diamonds. In a small bowl, make a paste of the brown sugar, mustard, and paprika. Rub the mixture all over the surface of the ham and stud the diamonds with the cloves. Bake the ham uncovered for about 30 minutes, basting every 10 minutes with ⅓ cup of the pineapple juice. Transfer to a cutting board or platter and let the ham rest for 30 minutes. Carve the ham in thin slices and serve warm or at room temperature.

MISSOURI

CHURCHILL IS COMING

When Sir Winston Churchill went to Westminster College in Fulton, Missouri, to speak at President Truman's invitation in March 1946, he was served typical middle western company fare as might be set up at anybody's Sunday table.

Some women, learning they were to be hostess to Mr. Churchill and the President of the United States for two meals all in one afternoon, would have gulped twice and rushed pell mell to Kansas City or St. Louis in search of a caterer. Not the confident straight-thinking Mrs. Frances McCluer, wife of the Westminster College President. She said simply, "Let's just be ourselves. Why put on a poor imitation of entertaining in New York or London with a lot of sophisticated refreshments? We will plan a nice company meal with our own kinds of food. We will serve it our way." And that's what she did.

I flew from New York City to Fulton two days ahead of the great occasion to check in on the cooking. The town was breathless with excitement. Utter strangers gave with big grins as if to say, "You know, of course, that Churchill is coming."

But the trimly cut Mrs. McCluer was the Alpha and Omega of studied calmness. She had been planning the menus since late in December. Everything was but done. She was the one person in Fulton who refused to act excited. No, she wasn't worried. Still, we felt maybe she had a few qualms. What woman wouldn't?

The first thing decided on, the very day that word came Churchill would speak, was to serve the Callaway County ham and fried chicken. These two are the Paul and Virginia of the Fulton party world. Along with this, the twice-baked potatoes. That's what a stuffed baked potato is called in the Midwest.

Mrs. McCluer thought, like many of her neighbors, that a tomato aspic salad was the only right salad to go with a ham. She chose ice cream for dessert, partly because it's so all-American, but especially as an accompaniment for Mrs. Roy Anthony's wonderful angel food cake. She didn't want to bother with tea, but just probably Mr. Churchill would be wanting his tea, and she had better be ready. But how could he refuse her coffee—brown, sultry, pungent, and excellently fresh? We tried a cup.

Four hams averaging twenty-five pounds apiece were prepared for the party. The one for the Churchill-Truman table Mrs. McCluer cooked herself in the big kitchen, its windows looking across the backyard right into Stinson Creek. The famous ham was getting a scrub in the sink when I called, and then to soak overnight. After this, slow simmering for almost six hours. After cooling it was skinned, then plastered over with a paste of mustard mixed with cinnamon and ginger and this pocked with whole cloves in diamond formation. Pineapple juice for the basting sauce, and into the oven to take just long enough to set and brown the crust to perfection. The ham was sliced in the kitchen and truly a pity to deprive Mr. Churchill of the gourmet's joy of seeing the knife slip through the crunchy crust, to watch the pink slices roll down one upon another to the cutting board.

Angel food for celestial company were those eight cakes baked by Mrs. Roy Anthony of light but lavish hand. She had always baked the important occasion cakes for Fultoneans. "Aren't you worried?," we asked the dark-eyed, pretty little woman in the pink housedress. "Worried? Why no," she said, "I've never had a failure with my angel cake, so why would I now it's for the president and Mr. Churchill?" Mrs. Anthony gave me the recipe, one made with a dozen egg whites, which, she told me, are hand-beaten until they hold tight to the bowl when it's turned upside down. Once a cake is in the oven, she advised, never open the door. In exactly one hour it's done, and it's always all right.

Fulton's cooks proved generous with recipes. Here we give you Mrs. McCluer's fruited baked ham, Mrs. Anthony's angel food cake, and Jeff Davis pie.

Another recipe everyone in town was making—Mrs. Truman's Ozark pudding. A Fulton girl, Miss Mary Belle Kerr, who was teaching home economics in Washington, D.C., got the recipe from the Trumans and sent it back to the home folks. "It would have been a nice honor to Mrs. Truman to have served her pudding at the party," Mrs. McCluer confided, "but we figured Mr. Truman had likely had his fill of that dish."

Mrs. Anthony's Angel Food Cake

12 large egg whites

⅛ teaspoon salt

1 teaspoon cream of tartar

1½ cups sugar

1 cup cake flour

1 teaspoon vanilla extract

1 teaspoon lemon extract

Makes one 10-inch cake

In a large bowl, combine the egg whites and salt and beat with an electric mixer until foamy. Add the cream of tartar and continue beating until the whites cling to the bowl and medium peaks form. Gradually fold in the sugar, adding a little bit at a time. Fold in the flour a little at a time, beating well after each addition. Add the vanilla and lemon extracts and continue beating for 3 minutes longer.

Turn into an ungreased 10-inch tube pan, place in a cold oven, and set it to 325 degrees. Bake for 1 hour, or until spongy and a wooden pick or skewer inserted in the center comes out clean. Cool the cake in the pan on a wire rack for 15 minutes, then invert onto the rack to cool completely. Frost or glaze with any favorite frosting, if you like, or serve with whipped cream and berries.

Mrs. Truman's Ozark Pudding

1 large egg

¾ cup sugar

⅓ cup all-purpose flour

1¼ teaspoons baking powder

⅛ teaspoon salt

½ cup peeled chopped apples
(any favorite cooking variety)

½ cup chopped nuts, such as walnuts

1 teaspoon vanilla extract

1 cup heavy cream

¼ cup rum

Serves 8

Preheat the oven to 325 degrees. Grease and flour a 1-quart baking dish.

In a medium bowl, beat the egg well, add the sugar, and beat until light and creamy. Sift the flour, baking powder, and salt into a small bowl. Gradually add to the egg mixture and blend well. Fold in the apples and nuts, then stir in the vanilla. Pour into the prepared dish and bake for 30 minutes, or until a wooden pick or skewer inserted in the center comes out clean. Cool the pudding on a wire rack.

Meanwhile, in a medium bowl, whip the cream until soft peaks form. Pour in the rum and continue beating until stiff peaks form; cover and refrigerate until ready to serve. Serve the pudding warm or at room temperature, with the whipped cream.

EATING A CATFISH IS a cherished memory of my childhood. I caught the fish—Mama fried it in a pan! No other fish ever tasted half so good until I went visiting in St. Louis, that catfish-loving town. I had asked, "Where can I eat catfish?"

"Go to Mrs. Edmonds'," came the answer. "She serves every kind of fish."

Myrtle Edmonds knows fish dishes from around the world. At her table you can order the fish fare of the Maine coast, specialties of Florida, New Orleans, San Francisco, from France, from Italy, from the Philippines.

Mrs. Edmonds, a middle westerner born in Lansing, Michigan, had gone East to school and stayed East for a while. She loved the seafoods and wanted to introduce them to the homefolks. It's over weekends she tries out new dishes, but on the night of my visit to the farm, fried catfish was served along with crisp hush puppies and sour cream cabbage.

Mrs. Edmond's house, logs on the inside, clapboards on the outside, is around 150 years old, with a new part added, this of stone. Antiques in this house deserve spotlight niches in museums.

We talked about the food of the region. Mrs. Edmonds said, "Missouri eats better than any other state in the Union. Southern slave cooks from down the Big River came in the early years to share their secrets of fried chicken, of hot breads, of Creole delicacies. Here you get the thick steaks of the cattle country, the wonderful hams of the nearby South. The large German population has given its knowledge of rich stews and fine pastries. St. Louis has fish equal to that of the East Coast, the West Coast, meaning its sweet-water fish from the local rivers and lakes."

Catfish, of course: heads off, insides out. Wash first in salt water, then dry. Dip in milk, dredge in seasoned flour and fry in shallow fat about one-half inch deep, drippings preferred; fry slowly until golden. Remove from fat, place in a warm oven while the hushpuppies fry.

Enjoy catfish heaven, white, moist meat, thick, crisp crust; the hushpuppies crisply fried and onion-scented; the cabbage cooked with sour cream. Dessert? It doesn't matter. All one needs now, as they say Down South, is "a little nap of sleep."

Sour Cream Cabbage Slaw

4 tablespoons (½ cup) unsalted butter

4 cups grated white cabbage

1 teaspoon salt

1 tablespoon sugar

½ cup sour cream
(not low-fat or non-fat)

Serves 4

Melt the butter in a large skillet over medium heat.
Reduce the heat to low, add the grated cabbage, and cook
for 15 minutes, stirring every 3 minutes, until wilted.
Stir in the salt, sugar, and sour cream. Heat the mixture
through, but do not let boil. Serve hot.

Note: Heavy cream may be made sour by adding
½ tablespoon vinegar or lemon juice to each ½ cup cream
and allowing it to stand for about 5 minutes before
pouring over the wilted cabbage.

FOUND: THE WORLD'S BEST potato salad, twenty cents a side portion on the Speck's menu—that century-old coffeehouse on Market Street in St. Louis. This restaurant-kitchen of the antiquated equipment had been dishing up the salad and other hearty German dishes since before the city's great fire in 1849. Good cooks of the town all had their own versions of the Speck's specialty—but always something was lacking. It took Thelma R. Lison, home economist for an advertising agency, to spy out its secret. Here is Thelma's recipe and the real McCoy, say those in the know. Divine stuff served with baked tongue, with baked ham, with corned beef.

We used this salad recipe in our column in *This Week Magazine.* Then came this letter from a reader who asked to remain anonymous. She wrote, "Having eaten Speck's potato salad for at least fifty years, I can agree with you it is 'the best ever.' But there is one little secret you did not give. Many years ago one of the sons of the founder of the restaurant told me that when the salad was all finished they pour over it the raw white of egg, lightly beaten. That gives it the something that no other potato salad ever had."

Speck's Potato Salad

6 medium russet potatoes, unpeeled

3 slices thick-cut bacon, minced

1 small yellow onion, minced

4 teaspoons sugar

2 teaspoons salt, plus more to season the dish

¼ teaspoon freshly ground black pepper

⅔ cup cider vinegar

⅓ cup water

½ teaspoon celery seeds

3 tablespoons chopped parsley

Serves 6

Place the potatoes in a medium pot and add cold, generously salted water to cover. Place over medium-high heat and bring to a boil, then lower the heat to a simmer and cook until just tender, about 25 minutes. Drain the potatoes and cool slightly, then peel them using a kitchen towel. Slice the potatoes into rounds ¼ to ⅓ inch thick.

Cook the bacon in a medium skillet over medium heat until just crisp. Add the onion to the bacon fat and cook for 1 minute. Add the sugar, salt, and pepper to the bacon mixture. Stir in the vinegar and water. Cook for 5 minutes, then pour the warm dressing over the sliced potatoes and add the celery seeds and parsley. Toss lightly, taste, and adjust the seasoning, adding more salt if necessary. Serve warm.

MISSOURI

CHIFF-CHUFF-CHAFF—the local freight No. 41 on the "Frisco" line drew up at the toylike station of Pacific, Missouri. C. R. Sally, the station agent, looked out the bowed window, gave a nod and a beckon. With a hsh-hsh-hissing, the engine came to a stand and four men in overalls, in denim caps, swung off the local and made straight for the station door. "Chick" Sally reached into a drawer and hauled out a box bulging with candy.

C. R. Sally was the "candy kid" around Pacific, candy his hobby. He figured he made around three hundred pounds of the stuff a year just to give away. "My mother," he recalled, "was an expert candymaker."

Sally was twenty-seven when he left his hometown, Rolla, Missouri, for Pacific to be station agent there and the telegrapher. First thing he did was set up a candy kitchen in the basement of his house. His tools are cooking pots, tablespoons, a marble slab, square cookie tins, a putty knife, a thermometer. "It's no good making candy without a thermometer." If he told me that once he told me twenty times. Christmas he makes eighty pounds of candy and never a failure. He has eight recipes and wants no more.

I drove from St. Louis to Pacific, twenty miles, to meet Mr. Sally and borrow his recipe for old-time horehound. "You will likely have to buy the horehound in an herb shop," he said. "But I pick mine free, over there in Little Ireland." He waved an arm indicating the foothills of the Ozarks.

Vanilla Caramels

2 (12-ounce) cans evaporated milk

4 cups sugar

2 cups dark corn syrup

1 tablespoon unsalted butter

1 tablespoon vanilla extract

1 cup finely chopped black walnuts, optional

Makes about 128 caramels

Grease two 8-inch square layer pans.

In a large saucepan, combine 1 can of evaporated milk with the sugar, corn syrup, and butter. Place over medium-high heat and bring to brisk boil, stirring constantly. Very slowly pour in the second can of milk so the mixture never drops below the boiling point. Never stop stirring or the mixture will scorch. (A long-handled wooden spoon is best for this.) Cook the mixture to the soft-ball stage, about 234 degrees on a candy thermometer. Remove from the heat and stir in the vanilla and black walnuts, if using. Pour into the prepared pans, cool completely, and cut the caramels into squares.

Pecan Brittle

2 cups sugar

¾ cup light corn syrup

¾ cup water

1 tablespoon unsalted butter

1¼ cups chopped pecans

2 teaspoons baking soda

1 tablespoon vanilla extract

Makes 1 generous pound

Generously grease 2 large baking sheets.

Combine the sugar, corn syrup, water, butter, and pecans in a large saucepan. Place over high heat and bring to a boil, stirring until the sugar is dissolved. Reduce the heat to medium and continue boiling, stirring only after the mixture reaches the hard-crack stage (it will be amber colored), about 290 degrees on a candy thermometer. Remove from the heat and gently stir in the baking soda and vanilla. Pour onto the prepared sheets and spread with a rubber spatula until very thin. Cool completely before breaking into pieces.

MISSOURI

OKLAHOMA

The coffee break in midwestern states has blossomed into a social occasion. The bridge luncheon gives way to the *kaffeeklatsch*. "Coffees" are taking precedence over afternoon teas.

The refreshment of the morning: coffee in the cup, juice in the glass, hot bread on the plate. From there on it's all a matter of the hostess' ingenuity—invariably trayloads of novel pickup adventures.

In Tulsa we munched our way through the most unusual "coffee" of a six-state tour. Mrs. Floyd L. Rheam, homemaker and food writer, was entertaining thirty friends at a morning affair.

Corn soup was dipped from a big tureen. This is yellow cream-style corn with milk added, butter, salted to taste, a touch of thyme. Spoon bread came hot from the oven. There was a molded salad, and guests could help themselves. Pick-up garden stuffs; celery cuts, cucumber and carrot sticks. A tray of fruit was prepared. Small clusters of grapes were frosted with sugar, banana cuts were rolled in lemon juice, then in coconut shreds. Frozen pineapple chunks were on hand with toothpick handles; crimson strawberries, stems intact.

The meaty matters: baked ham cubes were paired with sweet potato dandies; mashed sweets were molded around marshmallow pieces, breaded in crumbs and deep-fat fried. Sautéed chicken livers were kept piping hot in the warming oven. Another contender for popularity—the sweetbreads, parboiled in water, seasoned with pickling spices. When cool, these were sliced to dunk in tangy sauce. Hamburger balls helped banish the pinch of hunger. Surprises were passed: Florentine tomatoes.

Mrs. Rheam prepared her party foods in advance to go into the freezer. Spoon bread for example. Batter is made in quantity, poured into throw-away aluminum pans, tightly foiled, and into the freezer, then from freezer to oven. Her antique silver tankard, porcelain-lined, held the coffee. Turn the spigot, help yourself.

Tomatoes Florentine

20 to 24 cherry tomatoes
(each about 1½ inches in diameter)

5 tablespoons unsalted butter

1 bay leaf

1 small clove garlic

1 (10-ounce) package frozen chopped
spinach, cooked and drained

1½ teaspoons lemon juice

¼ teaspoon grated nutmeg

2 drops Tabasco sauce

Salt

2 tablespoons grated
Parmesan cheese

Makes about 2 dozen hors d'oeuvres

Preheat the oven to 350 degrees.

Cut a slim slice off the bottom of each tomato so that they will sit upright. Using a small spoon or melon baller, scoop out the pulp from the tomatoes. Turn the tomatoes upside down to drain.

Melt 3 tablespoons of the butter in a medium skillet over medium heat. Add the bay leaf and garlic and sauté for 2 to 3 minutes, until very fragrant, then discard both the bay leaf and garlic. Stir in the spinach, lemon juice, nutmeg, and Tabasco and season with salt. Place the tomatoes in shallow baking pan; sprinkle their cavities lightly with salt. Stuff the tomatoes with the spinach mixture and sprinkle the tops with cheese.

Melt the remaining 2 tablespoons butter and spoon it over the cheese. Bake for 15 to 20 minutes, until the stuffing is hot and golden brown. Serve immediately.

Smetana Hamburger

1 pound ground beef

1 teaspoon salt

⅛ teaspoon freshly ground
black pepper

½ cup sour cream

1 tablespoon finely chopped fresh dill
or ½ teaspoon crushed dill seeds

Sweet paprika

16 mini buns, optional

Makes 16 mini hors d'oeuvre burgers

Preheat the broiler.

In a large bowl, combine the beef, salt, and pepper.
Shape into 16 equal-sized patties. Broil the patties about
3 inches from the heat, turning once, until done, 4 to
5 minutes total.

Meanwhile, in a small bowl combine the sour cream
and dill. Spoon the mixture over the patties. Return to
the broiler and broil for 2 to 3 minutes to heat the sour
cream. Sprinkle with the paprika and serve immediately,
on mini buns, if you like, or on their own.

Jamie's Spoon Bread

1½ cups milk

1 cup yellow cornmeal

½ teaspoon salt

1 cup water

½ cup (1 stick) unsalted butter

1 large egg, well beaten

Serves 10

Preheat the oven to 350 degrees. Grease a 1-quart
casserole.

Bring the milk to a boil in a small saucepan over medium heat. As soon as the milk begins to bubble, remove it from the heat and set aside. In a medium saucepan, combine the cornmeal, salt, and water. Place over low heat and bring to a simmer; cook, stirring occasionally, for 15 minutes, until thickencd. Remove from the heat. Add the butter to the hot milk and stir to melt it. Slowly pour it into the cornmeal mixture and blend until smooth. Slowly stir the beaten egg into the hot mixture. Pour into the prepared casserole and bake for 35 minutes, or until browned and a wooden pick or skewer inserted into the center comes out clean. Transfer to a wire rack to cool. Serve warm.

Chopped Liver

3 tablespoons unsalted butter

1 pound chicken livers

2 tablespoons minced onion

4 cooked chicken gizzards, cut up

2 hard-cooked eggs, cut into quarters

Salt and freshly ground black pepper

1 tablespoon finely chopped parsley

Serves 8 to 10

Heat 2 tablespoons of the butter in a large skillet over medium heat. Add the livers and sauté until lightly browned, about 8 minutes. Transfer the livers to paper towels to drain. In the same pan, sauté the onion until translucent, about 4 minutes. In a food processor or blender, puree the chicken livers, onion, gizzards, and eggs until thoroughly combined. Melt the remaining tablespoon butter in the skillet and add it to the liver mixture. Season with salt and pepper. Scrape the chopped liver into a large decorative or other nonreactive bowl and garnish with the parsley. Serve the chopped liver with any favorite crackers or buttered toast fingers, if you like.

Note: To make chicken liver balls, after blending in the butter, shape the chicken liver into teaspoon-size balls and roll them in the parsley. The recipe will make about 40 balls. Serve them at room temperature.

OKLAHOMA

THE OLD-FASHIONED CHURCH SUPPER is giving over to a new kind of money-making meal—an affair called a "tasting." This is held at midday and made very social, a short program to follow. It is virtually effortless and the dollars roll in dime by dime!

I heard about this kind of money-making event when I was in Tulsa, Oklahoma, talking to Mrs. W. T. Born, President of the Women's Alliance of the All Souls' Unitarian Church. This group, with a membership of over one hundred women, divided into four units, each taking its turn to manage one tasting a season. Each group member contributes a dish, making it in double amount. A staff of workers do the serving, in bite-size portions. Typewritten recipes are prepared in advance for each specialty on parade, about fifty cards for each dish, these signed by the contributor. After the tasting the guests buy the recipes of their choice. The hand-typed recipe cards sell for ten cents each. Never less than $250 has been taken at a tasting—and that's clear profit, except for the cost of the coffee, cream, and sugar. And one more expense—a babysitter to take over in the church nursery.

Here are a few of the best selling and most popular recipes.

Thelma Brownfield's Citrus Gelatin Salad

1 (4-ounce) package lime-flavored gelatin

1 (4-ounce) package lemon-flavored gelatin

2 cups boiling water

1 cup evaporated milk

2 tablespoons lemon juice

1 pound cottage cheese

2 cups crushed pineapple, drained

1 cup chopped walnuts or chopped celery, or a combination

Serves 12 to 16

In a large bowl, dissolve the lime- and lemon-flavored gelatins in the boiling water, stirring constantly for 3 minutes. Cool to room temperature. Stir in the evaporated milk and lemon juice. Cover and refrigerate until slightly thickened, about 20 minutes. Meanwhile, puree the cottage cheese in a blender or food processor. Take the gelatin mixture from the fridge and fold in the cottage cheese, pineapple, and walnuts or celery. Pour into a favorite 2-quart mold and chill until firm, 3 to 4 hours. When ready to serve, unmold onto a serving plate.

Edith Wharton's Cracker Torte

¾ cup fine soda cracker crumbs

1 teaspoon baking powder

3 large egg whites

1 teaspoon vanilla extract

⅛ teaspoon salt

1 cup sugar

¾ cup chopped nuts, such as hickory nuts or pecans

½ cup heavy cream

1 tablespoon confectioners' sugar

Serves 6

Preheat the oven to 350 degrees. Grease a 9-inch pie pan.

In a small bowl, combine the cracker crumbs and baking powder. In a large bowl, combine the egg whites, vanilla, and salt and beat until stiff. Gradually add the sugar, beating well after each addition; the mixture should be glossy and even stiffer. Fold in the crumb mixture and the nuts. Spread into the prepared pan and bake for 25 minutes, or until light golden brown. Transfer to a wire rack to cool. In a medium bowl, whip the cream and the confectioners' sugar until stiff and spread the mixture over the top of the torte. Cover loosely with foil and refrigerate for 8 hours or overnight. Serve chilled.

OKLAHOMA

Willimae White's Salmon Mousse

---

2 cups smoked or poached salmon

½ cup finely chopped celery

¼ cup minced onion

2 (¼-ounce) packages unflavored gelatin

1 cup water

½ cup tomato paste

¼ cup cider vinegar

1 cup mayonnaise

Paprika

Serves 6 to 8

Grease a 1-quart fish mold.

In a large bowl, flake the salmon into small pieces with a fork; mix in the celery and onion. In a small bowl, dissolve the gelatin in ½ cup of the water.

In a small saucepan, combine the remaining ½ cup water, the tomato paste, and vinegar. Place over medium heat and bring to a boil. Add the softened gelatin; stir until dissolved and immediately remove from the heat. Gently blend the hot liquid with the salmon mixture. Stir in the mayonnaise and turn into the prepared mold. Cover with plastic wrap and refrigerate until firm, at least 8 hours or overnight. When ready to serve, unmold the mousse onto a serving plate and sprinkle with paprika.

Note: Decorate with stuffed olive slices for eyes and a sprig of parsley for a tail, if you like. Mrs. White likes to garnish the mousse with any and all of the following: deviled eggs, tomato quarters, green onions, pickles, carrot sticks, olives, and pickled beets.

Margaret Fisher's Asparagus Bake

2 pounds fresh asparagus, peeled

1 tablespoon olive oil

1 cup finely crushed cheese-flavored cracker crumbs

1 (10½-ounce) can condensed cream of mushroom soup

4 teaspoons water

1 tablespoon unsalted butter or 4 slices cooked bacon, crumbled

Serves 8

Preheat the oven to 350 degrees. Grease a 1½-quart casserole.

Place the asparagus on a large pan or baking sheet, drizzle with the oil, then toss to coat the asparagus completely. Sprinkle ⅓ cup of the cracker crumbs evenly over the bottom of the prepared casserole. Top with a layer of the asparagus. Spread ½ cup of the soup evenly over the asparagus and sprinkle with 2 teaspoons of the water. Repeat the layering, ending with the cracker crumbs. Dot the top of the casserole with the butter or sprinkle with the bacon. Bake uncovered for 25 minutes, or until the crumbs brown and the casserole is bubbly. Let rest for 10 minutes before serving.

OKLAHOMA

THERE IS A BEAUTIFUL place called "Somewhere" and for each of us it's a different place—a personal place where we go to refuel the spirit. You may grow a garden for retreat. Thoreau went to Walden Pond to think. But wherever your wonderful place, it gives you an inner peace.

In Tulsa, I met a woman whose "beautiful place" was an eight- by twelve-foot space—her kitchen. Mrs. R. C. Pigford cooks for relaxation. She peels and chops and mixes to find enriching hours of meditation and happiness.

The Pigfords' two daughters are married and "Doctor husband" retired ten years ago in the prime of his career with a heart ailment. Now the Pigfords live quietly. Once they traveled much and entertained often. Now there isn't as much money as in other years. Today Mrs. Pigford does her own cooking and cuts many a corner, all to the aid of the budget. But cooking is no longer a duty—a job. She works with sure hands and a high heart.

Mrs. Pigford, New Orleans–bred, and her husband, a Mississippian, prefer menus with an Old South flavor. Seafood dishes are to their mutual pleasure. Crab omelet often comes to supper. Crab Savannah is a company dish. Hearty soups are frequently served as a main course along with a salad and dessert. Red bean soup is a favorite.

Summer Cold Tomato Soup

5 cups tomato juice

½ cup minced celery

3 scallions, white and tender green parts only, minced

1 tablespoon soy sauce

2 teaspoons Worcestershire sauce

Few drops of Tabasco sauce

Salt to taste

12 to 16 very thin cucumber slices

12 hot buttered toast points

Serves 4

In a large bowl, combine all of the ingredients except the cucumbers and toast. Puree in a blender or food processor in batches until smooth. Transfer to a bowl, cover with plastic wrap, and refrigerate until cold, at least 3 hours to overnight. Top each serving with a few slices of the cucumber and serve with hot buttered toast points, if you like.

Crab Omelet

¾ pound lump or backfin crabmeat, well drained and picked clean of shells

6 scallions, white and tender green parts only, minced

½ cup minced celery

2 tablespoons minced parsley

⅛ teaspoon salt

Dash of freshly ground black pepper

Few drops of Tabasco

7 large eggs, separated

2 tablespoons unsalted butter

Serves 4 to 6

Preheat the broiler.

In a large bowl, flake the crabmeat into pieces. Add the scallions, celery, parsley, salt, pepper, and Tabasco. In a small bowl, beat the egg yolks well and stir it into the crabmeat mixture. In a large bowl, beat the egg whites until stiff peaks are formed; fold it into the fish mixture.

Melt the butter in a 9-inch ovenproof skillet over medium heat. Pour the mixture into the skillet and reduce the heat to low. Cook until the omelet is set, about 10 minutes. With a spatula or knife, release the omelet from the sides of the pan. Broil the omelet just until the top is puffy and light golden brown, about 5 minutes. Remove from the broiler and put the skillet back on the stovetop; continue cooking the omelet over low heat to finish setting the center, about 5 minutes more. Cut into wedges and serve immediately.

Note: The crab mixture may be prepared in the morning and chilled in the refrigerator until 30 minutes before mixing it with the eggs.

OKLAHOMA

ARKANSAS

"I love these Little Fellows," Robin Woods said, helping herself to number four pie. Into the mouth with it, all in one bite! She had baked these tiny lemon tartlettes just for my pleasure. "Don't you like them?" she asked, generously offering me the last one.

———————————————

"But, Robin," I said helping myself, "I've already had two." Robin's mother is my friend Milly Woods of Little Rock, a newspaper food editor. If Mother has guests, Robin performs. Then she makes her best dishes. Little Fellow Pies for dessert, if they are a taste match for the menu. These she told me—a recipe from her mother's grandmother—should follow highly seasoned foods.

Robin started cooking at the age of eight when the family was living in Lima, Peru. This accounts for her fondness for certain South American dishes.

Little Fellow Lemon Pie Muffins

½ cup (1 stick) unsalted butter	1 tablespoon all-purpose flour
2 cups sugar	⅓ cup lemon juice
4 large eggs	1 Perfect Pie Crust (page 13)

Makes 4 dozen small pies

Preheat the oven to 350 degrees. Grease a 12-cup standard muffin pan.

In a medium bowl, cream the butter and sugar. Add the eggs one at a time, beating to blend after each addition. Add the flour and stir in the lemon juice. Divide the piecrust into quarters and line each hole of the muffin pan with a quarter of the dough, divided into 12 equal pieces. Fill the pastry-lined muffin pans two thirds full with the lemon mixture. Bake for 30 minutes or until the pie muffins are golden brown. Transfer the muffins to wire racks to cool. Repeat with the remaining dough and filling.

Chicken Brazil Stew

1 (4½- to 5-pound) chicken, cut up

1 tablespoon salt, plus more to taste

1 onion, chopped

Juice of 1 lemon

3 celery tops

1 sprig parsley

1 bay leaf

1 cup golden raisins

½ cup dry white wine

2 tablespoons unsalted butter

¼ cup all-purpose flour

2 cups half-and-half

Pinch of cayenne pepper

Pinch of saffron

1 cup blanched almonds

Ground mace or allspice

¼ cup finely chopped pimiento pepper

¼ cup finely chopped green bell pepper

8 cups steamed long-grain white rice

Serves 10

In a large stockpot, cover the chicken with cold water. Add the 1 tablespoon salt, the onion, lemon juice, celery tops, parsley, and bay leaf. Place over medium-high heat and bring to a boil, then reduce the heat, cover, and simmer for about 3½ hours, until the chicken is tender. Transfer the chicken from the broth to a large bowl. When the chicken is cool enough to handle, pull the meat from the bones into bite-size pieces. Set the meat aside. Return the bones to the broth and continue simmering until the broth is reduced to about 3 cups, about 1 hour more. Strain the broth and skim off the fat. Reserve the fat and broth.

In a small bowl, combine the raisins and wine and set aside to plump, about 15 minutes. Heat the butter and 2 tablespoons of the reserved chicken fat in a large heavy skillet over medium heat. Add the flour and cook, stirring, until light golden, about 4 minutes. Add 2 cups of the reserved chicken broth and the half-and-half. Reduce the heat to low and cook, stirring, until the mixture thickens and comes to a boil, about 15 minutes. Season with salt and add the cayenne and saffron. Add the raisins and wine, the chicken, almonds, mace, and green peppers. Bring the mixture to a boil and immediately remove from heat. Serve the stew over the rice.

MIGHTY GOOD VITTLES

There are some mighty good vittles to be enjoyed in and around Fort Smith, Arkansas. This area, it would seem, remains the last stronghold of the conservative American table. Here is food to pleasure the palate, food that sticks to the ribs, food that belongs to the country.

Yet here, as everywhere, women like to do a bit of fancy work when entertaining. And what do they do? They make a production of the vegetables. At luncheons and buffet suppers one meets green beans, broccoli, peas done up with cheese, or combined with chicken or turkey to feature as the main dish.

I went visiting Mrs. Ruth Moss Carroll, catering queen for the town for many years, and we talked about recipes favored for parties. "If it's a dinner," Mrs. Carroll said, "the meat—such as roast beef, roast pork, spareribs, fried chicken—is preferred plain, unadorned." On the other hand the vegetables are apt to be served sauced-up and dressed dramatically. Even mashed potatoes frequently are given an extra touch. And so I discovered at dinner in a Fort Smith home. There I met mashed potatoes beaten feather light and made noble by the addition of finely minced chives and parsley.

Desserts are invariably rich and homemade. A spectacular over the years is Mrs. Carroll's frozen lemon pie, this of her own devising. It was my lucky day when she gave me the recipe. But I was even more interested in her broccoli casserole.

"Everybody here talks about dieting," Mrs. Carroll said, "but they still love their desserts. And eat them, too!" she added jubilantly. Next to her pie the popular fancy is this charlotte russe. This recipe, she was careful to say, was taken from the *Junior League of Memphis Cook Book*.

Frozen Lemon Pie

1 (9-inch) Perfect Pie Crust (page 13)

½ cup lemon juice

1 (14-ounce) can sweetened condensed milk

5 large egg whites

2 tablespoons sugar

1 tablespoon grated lemon peel

Makes one 9-inch pie

Preheat the oven to 350 degrees. Line a 9-inch glass pie plate with the pastry. Trim the overhang to 1 inch, fold it under itself, and crimp decoratively, if you like. Refrigerate until chilled, about 15 minutes.

Line the pastry with foil and fill with pie weights or dried beans. Bake for 30 minutes, or until nearly cooked through and dry to the touch. Carefully remove the foil and weights. Bake for 10 minutes longer, until golden. Let cool completely.

In a large bowl, combine the lemon juice and condensed milk, stirring until a thick, smooth mixture is formed. In a medium bowl, beat the egg whites until foamy. Add the sugar, 1 tablespoon at a time, and beat until stiff peaks are formed. Fold the whites into the lemon-milk mixture. Sprinkle the grated lemon peel on the bottom of the pie shell and turn the filling into the shell. Cover the pie and refrigerate until set, about 5 hours or overnight.

Charlotte Russe

2 (¼-ounce) envelopes
unflavored gelatin

½ cup cold water

2 cups milk

6 large eggs, separated

1 cup sugar

1 teaspoon vanilla extract

18 ladyfingers

2 cups heavy cream, whipped

Serves 12

In a small bowl, dissolve the gelatin in the water. Bring the milk to a boil in a medium saucepan over medium-low heat; immediately remove it from the heat. In a medium bowl, beat the egg yolks and sugar until well blended; stir into the milk. Cook over the lowest heat, stirring constantly, until the mixture coats a spoon, about 7 minutes. Remove from the heat and stir in the gelatin until dissolved. Add the vanilla. Cool completely.

Meanwhile, line the bottom and sides of 10 x 4-inch tube pan with the ladyfingers, making sure there are no gaps in it. In a medium bowl, beat the egg whites until stiff peaks form. Fold the egg whites and cream into the cooled custard and turn into the prepared pan. Cover and refrigerate until set, 4 to 6 hours. When you are ready to serve, gently run a knife around the edges of the mold to make sure nothing has stuck to it, then invert onto a plate and carefully lift off the mold.

GATEWAY TO HEAVEN FOR Susanne Cooley is an open door to a kitchen, groceries waiting, a dinner to cook. Susanne, nineteen when we met, was a freshman at the University of Arkansas. She confided, "I would rather cook than go dancing," although dancing was second-choice fun, swimming was third.

Susanne started cooking when she was knee-high to a table. Five years old, and Susy would push a chair beside Cook, climb up and demand, "Let me stir." No wonder in college she was majoring in Home Economics.

Her father, Wade Cooley, owns the Cooley Drugstore. His wife works with him, which leaves the kitchen free to daughter. During vacations, she did all the cooking, planning the menus, shopping for the groceries, and for a family of six.

This cooking co-ed loved preparing food for her crowd, buffet suppers as

a rule. Twenty she considered just the right number. Her favorite main dish was a precooked ham, reheated, then quilted with cloves and mustard and brown-sugar-glazed.

Susanne was forever experimenting with dishes. The home pantry she kept stocked with ready-to-eat foods, canned stew, for example. Then she went on from there, adding spices to taste, or little white onions, or whatever imagination dictated. Susanne's cookbooks numbered fourteen, her spice shelf collection half a hundred.

Susanne and I sat together on a hot summer evening, drinking colas and discussing favorite dishes. Her curried potato salad, she told me, is to everyone's taste. So excellent with the ham. This unusual chicken ring is an inherited recipe from grandmother Eva Drake. It's a rather complicated dish, but exceptionally good.

ARKANSAS

Chicken and Rice Casserole with Mushroom Sauce

For the casserole:

1 cup diced cooked chicken

2 cups cooked white rice

1 cup dried breadcrumbs

1 teaspoon salt

½ teaspoon sweet paprika

4 large eggs, well beaten

¼ cup chopped pimiento peppers

4 tablespoons (½ stick) unsalted butter, melted

2½ cups milk, chicken stock, or half-and-half

For the mushroom sauce:

½ pound mushrooms, sliced

4 tablespoons (½ stick) unsalted butter

¼ cup all-purpose flour

¼ teaspoon salt

2 cups chicken stock

2 large egg yolks, lightly beaten

¼ cup half-and-half

1 teaspoon lemon juice

1 teaspoon finely chopped parsley

Serves 6

Preheat the oven to 325 degrees. Grease a 1½-quart casserole.

In a large bowl, combine the casserole ingredients in the order given. (Add ½ teaspoon salt if using the chicken stock.) Turn the mixture into the prepared casserole and bake for 1 hour, or until browned and bubbly.

While the casserole is in the oven, make the sauce: Melt 2 tablespoons of the butter in a large skillet over medium-high heat. Add the mushrooms and sauté until lightly browned, about 5 minutes. In another large saucepan, melt the remaining 2 tablespoons butter over medium heat. Stir in the flour just to combine and add the salt. Slowly add the chicken stock, reduce the heat to low, and cook, stirring constantly, until the mixture comes to a boil and thickens, about 10 minutes.

In a small bowl, combine the egg yolks and half-and-half and stir into the hot sauce. Cook for 2 to 3 minutes longer, to thicken slightly and thoroughly combine. Remove from the heat. Stir in the lemon juice, parsley, and sautéed mushrooms. Reheat if necessary.

Let the casserole stand for 15 minutes before serving. Serve warm with the mushroom sauce.

Curried Potato Salad

3 cups water

1½ teaspoons curry powder

2½ teaspoons salt

4 cups diced uncooked russet potatoes

3 tablespoons French Dressing (page 246)

2 tablespoons lemon juice

2 tablespoons minced onion

¼ teaspoon freshly ground black pepper

¼ teaspoon garlic powder

1½ cups diced celery

½ cup diced green bell pepper

3 hard-cooked eggs, diced

¾ cup mayonnaise

Serves 6

In a large stockpot, combine the water, curry powder, and 1 teaspoon of the salt. Add the potatoes, place over medium-high heat, and bring to a boil. Reduce the heat to medium and simmer until the potatoes are tender, about 25 minutes. Drain the potatoes in a colander and transfer to a large bowl.

In a medium bowl, combine the French dressing, lemon juice, onion, remaining 1½ teaspoons salt, the black pepper, and garlic powder. Mix lightly with the potatoes and let stand for 30 minutes. Add the celery, bell pepper, and eggs and stir in the mayonnaise. Serve at room temperature.

ARKANSAS

ILLINOIS

There are many ways to spell glamour—Hollywood stars, opening night at the opera, caviar couched on a glacier of ice— but for glamour at the table spell it "Pump Room," Chicago's Pump Room in the Hotel Ambassador East.

This dining room is patterned after the Pump Room of old Bath in England, the menu written in English Script, the waiters wearing red coats old-time army style. The long back wall is dark blue, a fitting background for the crystal chandeliers holding white tapers. Tables are dressed in the finest of damask, chairs are upholstered in creamy-toned leather.

Fresh flowers float in silver basins topped with silver cupolas with concealed lighting to spotlight the blossoms.

Service here is done the perambulator way. A pastry, perhaps? Up rolls a three-tiered cake wagon with as great a choice as one finds in a pastry-shop window. If it's a salad you order or the cold salmon, the refrigerated cart arrives by magic stealth and instancy, the foods submerged in shaved ice. Hot foods, too, glide by wagon from table to table, served from marmites on alcohol burners.

A baker's dozen of "servitors" carry in blazing foods, six-foot-tall men, dressed in long-tailed green coats. Their turban headdress is plumed with white ostrich feathers. These tall ones bring the chickens, squabs, the breast of duck, the shishkabob and crabmeat brochettes, all manner of foods speared to sword blades and enveloped in flame. Into the sword hilt goes a wadding, alcohol soaked, which is ignited at the moment of serving.

Something we really like, something everyone likes, and which can be served at home for company dinners when roast chicken or duck stars the menu, is this bigarade sauce (recipe follows). It's a French recipe, of course, and designed to give a roasted bird a certain tangy wild flavor.

And the Pump Room's wild rice dressing willy-nilly lifts any barnyard squab or chicken to heavenly levels.

Wild Rice Stuffing

2 teaspoons salt, plus more
to season egg yolks

2 cups wild rice, rinsed

8 tablespoons (1 stick) unsalted butter

1½ pounds chicken livers,
finely chopped

2 large yellow onions, minced

1 pound button mushrooms, cleaned,
trimmed, and chopped

3 tablespoons all-purpose flour

2 cups chicken stock

4 large egg yolks

½ cup dry sherry wine

Freshly ground black pepper

Serves 6 to 8

Bring 5 cups water to a boil in a medium pot over high
heat. Add the 2 teaspoons salt, then slowly add the wild
rice (do not stir). Reduce the heat to medium, partially
cover the pot, and cook, shaking the pot occasionally,
until the wild rice is tender, 35 to 45 minutes. Drain and
transfer the wild rice to a large bowl.

Preheat the oven to 350 degrees. Grease a 2-quart round
or oval baking dish.

Melt 4 tablespoons of the butter in a large skillet over
medium-high heat. Add the livers and cook until lightly
browned, about 8 minutes, then add to rice. Wipe the
skillet clean. Melt the remaining 4 tablespoons butter
in the skillet over medium-high heat, add the onions
and mushrooms, and sauté until the onions are golden,
10 to 15 minutes. Add the flour and cook, stirring,
for 2 minutes. Add the stock and cook, stirring, until
thickened, 4 to 6 minutes, then add to the rice. Whisk the
egg yolks and sherry together in a small bowl, add to the
rice, and season with salt and pepper. Mix well. Transfer
to the prepared dish and cover with buttered foil,
buttered-side down. Bake until heated through, about
40 minutes. Uncover and bake until the top is golden
brown, about 20 minutes more.

If you are stuffing a turkey: Spoon the stuffing into turkey
cavity (put any excess stuffing into a small baking dish,

cover, and put into the oven with the turkey 1½ hours before the turkey is done); then sew the cavity shut using a trussing needle threaded with kitchen twine. Roast the stuffing inside the turkey for 4 to 5 hours in a 300-degree oven, until the turkey temperature is 160 degrees.

AN AUTUMN-RICH SUNDAY morning I meandered down Coyle Avenue in Edison Park to Julius Kasser's house for coffee and jam rolls.

Judy, then nine, and Jimmy, eight, opened the door. "Mother's coming," they said in breathless unison. I was fifteen minutes ahead of schedule and the rolls weren't ready, but right then they were getting their whirligig design in a dribble of frosting.

Here's Mother, bringing coffee, friendly, efficient; wearing slacks and a sweater, sleeves pushed up like any schoolgirl. "Judy, bring the rolls; Jimmy, help Sister." There were we by the fireside table in Irma Kasser's pleasant living room eating "gold ribbon" yeast bread.

These rolls are Hungarian, once baked by Mrs. Kasser's mother, and never a holiday, I was told, but Mom's Jam Surprise showed up for breakfast. Often her mother set the rolls in the early evening, then served them hot from the oven when Irma and her brothers came

in from parties, bringing a crowd of young folks for a midnight lunch.

It was the Christmas after her mother's death that Mrs. Kasser realized Christmas wouldn't be Christmas without the jam rolls. But her mother had left no recipe, and until her marriage Irma had worked as a secretary; she didn't cook much. It was in 1940 she began experimenting with Mom's specialty. She had watched these rolls made a hundred times, yet it took her almost a year to turn them out to perfection. Once they came out right, she typed the recipe in detail and has used it just so ever since.

These are rolls high-raised, feather-light, fine-textured. The outside is nut-crisp with a butter-browned taste, and with little hints of sweetness, thanks to a thin drizzle of icing. Inside, sweet surprise, a golden spoonful of apricot jam. We like these rolls better than any yeast rolls we ever tasted before with one exception—those sticky buns of Philadelphia.

Mom's Jam Surprise Rolls

1 (¼-ounce) envelope active dry yeast

¼ cup warm water

½ cup plus 3 tablespoons granulated sugar

¼ cup scalded milk

4 cups all-purpose flour

1½ teaspoons salt

1 teaspoon grated lemon peel

2 teaspoons vanilla extract

¼ teaspoon ground cardamom

3 large egg yolks

1¼ cups sour cream

½ cup apricot or seedless raspberry jam

½ cup (1 stick) unsalted butter, melted and cooled to lukewarm

¼ pound walnuts or pecans, ground

1 cup confectioners' sugar

¼ cup half-and-half

½ teaspoon vanilla extract

Makes 32 rolls

In a medium bowl, dissolve the yeast in the water. Add 1 tablespoon of the granulated sugar and the scalded milk. Add ½ cup of the flour, beating it in well. Cover the bowl loosely and set in a warm place to rest and rise slightly for 15 minutes.

Meanwhile, sift the remaining 3½ cups flour, ½ cup of the remaining granulated sugar, and the salt into a medium bowl. Add the lemon peel, 1½ teaspoons of the vanilla, the cardamom, egg yolks, and sour cream. Pour the mixture into the dough and beat for about 5 minutes, until very smooth and elastic. Turn the dough into a large greased bowl and cover loosely. Set in a warm place to rise until doubled in size, about 2 hours. Divide the dough into two equal parts; half may be refrigerated if desired and the rolls made up a day or two later. Turn half of the dough onto a well-floured surface and roll to ¼ inch thickness. Cut into 3-inch squares. Place 1 teaspoon jam in the center of each square and pinch the 4 corners together over the jam. Then pinch the protruding 4 corners together to form a ball, rounding smoothly with your hands.

In a small bowl, combine the ground nuts with the remaining 2 tablespoons granulated sugar. Dip each roll into the butter, then into the nuts and sugar. Place the rolls cut-side down into 10-inch pie plates.

Cover the rolls loosely with plastic wrap and let rise in a warm place for about 1½ hours, until more than double in bulk.

Preheat the oven to 375 degrees. Bake the rolls for 15 minutes, then reduce the oven temperature to 350 degrees and bake for 25 to 30 minutes longer, until the rolls are browned and the jam is melted. Let the rolls cool in the pans for 5 minutes.

While the rolls are cooling, make the frosting: In a medium bowl, combine the confectioners' sugar with the half-and-half and the remaining ½ teaspoon vanilla.

While the rolls are still warm, drizzle on the sugar icing in a spiral starting at the center of the cake-like array and working outward. Around the border there should be a double drizzle, as the rolls tend to overbrown at the outside edge. Serve immediately.

Note: Mrs. Kasser makes this apricot jam for the filling: Soak 1 pound dried apricots for 2 hours in cold water, drain, cover with fresh water; cook until tender. Press the fruit through a fine-mesh sieve and add 1½ to 2 cups sugar to the pulp. Cook over low heat until the sugar is dissolved. Makes about 3 cups jam.

IN ALBANY PARK, a north Chicago suburb, I learned of an unusual luncheon club that had started thirty-four years ago and was still being continued. Twelve friends of the Sisterhood of the Beth Israel Temple decided to meet each Thursday to talk, to trade recipes, to sew, to undertake small money-raising projects. All were good cooks, each prideful to show her skill, and each took a turn in preparing the luncheon. Eight of the original group were still meeting together at the time of my visit, with the two new members added in the past decade.

At the very first meeting it was Mrs. William Sturt who prepared the meal, featuring her most talented dish, gefilte fish, along with the proper trimmings. The menu pleased everyone and so many compliments on the fish balls, "so light, so tender and delicate in flavor."

"The girls" loved the baked beets. These are just plain, baked in their skins. "My, oh my—that's real potato pudding." Dessert was an upside-down apple cake served with coffee. When it came Mrs. Sturt's turn to entertain again, the club members begged, "Serve what you had the first time." It's been the same luncheon by request down the years.

I had heard indirectly about this group and the fish-ball luncheon. Traveling through Chicago, I telephoned Mrs. Sturt asking to see the fish balls made.

It was a fascination watching her work so deftly with her hands, so sure and precise. A tall slender woman, Mrs. Sturt, with bright black eyes, dark curly hair parted neatly in the middle. Mrs. Sturt likes keeping to the patterns of the past. She likes living always in the same place. This five-room apartment had been her home for twenty-one years. Her three children grew up and married here. She enjoys her turn entertaining the club, preparing the luncheon exactly as she did the first time the friends had met together.

Potato Kugel

4 large baking potatoes, unpeeled

1 medium carrot, unpeeled

4 tablespoons (½ stick)
unsalted butter

1 large onion, diced

2 tablespoons dried breadcrumbs

1 teaspoon salt

¼ teaspoon freshly ground
black pepper

Serves 6

Preheat the oven to 350 degrees. Grease a 1½-quart casserole.

Using a large box grater, shred the potatoes and carrots into a large bowl.

Melt the butter in a large skillet over medium heat. Add the onion and sauté until golden brown, about 12 minutes. Add the sautéed onion to the grated potatoes and carrots, then add the breadcrumbs, salt, and pepper. Turn into the prepared casserole and cover with foil. Bake for 1 hour and 15 minutes, or until the top is golden, removing the foil for the last 15 minutes. Serve warm.

Gefilte Fish

For the fish balls:

1½ pounds pike

1 pound trout or white fish
or a combination

1 tablespoon fine dry breadcrumbs

1 medium onion, quartered

1 carrot, quartered

1 large egg, beaten

2 teaspoons salt

¾ teaspoon freshly ground
black pepper

For the stock:

Bones and head of the pike and trout
(from the fish balls)

3 cups water

1 teaspoon salt

½ teaspoon freshly ground
black pepper

2 medium onions, quartered

Horseradish-Beet Sauce
(recipe follows)

Serves 8

To make the fish balls: Skin and fillet the fish (or have a fishmonger do it for you), picking over carefully to make sure no bones remain and reserving the bones and heads for the stock (or have a fishmonger do it for you). Pour the fish mixture into a bowl and cover with plastic wrap. Refrigerate for at least 3 hours or overnight.

To make the stock: Combine the bones, water, salt, pepper, and onions in a large stockpot. Cover and bring to a boil over medium-high heat; reduce the heat and simmer for 10 minutes.

Meanwhile, remove the fish mixture from the refrigerator. Wet your hands or use 2 cold spoons and form the fish into 8 even-sized ovals, not too tightly packed. Gently lower the fish balls into the stock. Lower the heat and simmer for 1½ hours, or until the gefilte fish is tender. Check the stock periodically to see if it has enough seasoning. Remove the fish balls from the pot gently using a slotted spoon, place on a platter, cover, and refrigerate. Discard the stock. Serve the gefilte fish chilled with horseradish-beet sauce.

Horseradish-Beet Sauce

¼ pound fresh horseradish, peeled and chopped

1 fresh beet, peeled and chopped

Juice of 1 lemon

½ cup water

1 teaspoon sugar

¼ teaspoon salt

Makes 2 cups

In a large bowl, combine all of the ingredients and coarsely puree them in a blender or food processor, scraping down the bowl or pitcher until combined. Scrape the mixture into a bowl; cover and refrigerate for 1 day before serving.

Apple Upside-Down Cake

For the cake:

1 (¼-ounce) envelope active dry yeast

2 tablespoons warm water

1 cup (2 sticks) unsalted butter, softened

¾ cup sugar

3 large eggs

1 cup sour cream

3 cups sifted all-purpose flour

Pinch of salt

For the filling:

3 tablespoons unsalted butter, melted

3 tablespoons dark brown sugar

2 tablespoons currants

2 tablespoons fine graham cracker crumbs

4 medium apples (any favorite cooking variety)

Vanilla ice cream or whipped cream for serving

Serves 6 to 8

To make the cake: In a small bowl, dissolve the yeast in the warm water. In a medium bowl using an electric mixer, cream the butter and sugar. Beat in the eggs one at a time, beating well after each addition. Beat in the sour cream and dissolved yeast. Blend in the flour and salt. Cover the bowl and refrigerate the dough for at least 3 hours or overnight.

When you are ready to make the cake, pour the melted butter over the bottom of a 9 x 9 x 2-inch pan. Sprinkle in the brown sugar, currants, and graham cracker crumbs. Peel and core the apples and cut into 8 wedges or rings, each about ⅛ inch thick. Arrange the apples on top of the butter mixture.

Take one third of the dough out of the bowl in the refrigerator; reserve the remaining dough (see Note). Roll the dough out on a floured surface into a 9-inch square. Place the dough over the apples and press it against the sides of the pan. Cover the pan loosely and let the dough rise in a warm place until doubled in bulk, about 1½ hours.

Preheat the oven to 350 degrees. Bake the cake for 35 to 40 minutes, until golden and a wooden pick or skewer inserted into the center comes out clean. Cool the cake in the pan on a wire rack for 5 minutes. Run a small knife between the cake and the pan sides to loosen the cake, carefully invert the cake onto a platter, and cool for 15 minutes. Cut the cake into wedges, place on plates, and serve warm with a scoop of vanilla ice cream or whipped cream.

Note: With the addition of enough flour to make a stiffer mixture (about a cup more), the remaining dough may be used for other sweet goods. For example: Roll the dough into a 12 x 8-inch rectangle. Spread with 2 tablespoons of softened butter; sprinkle with 2 tablespoons brown sugar and 2 tablespoons currants. Cut the dough into 3 lengthwise strips and braid. With a sharp knife, cut down the center of the braid. Place on a greased baking sheet and let rise for 2 hours. Bake at 350 degrees for about 30 minutes.

COOKING UP CHRISTMAS

Norvin H. Vaughan of Chicago's Roger's Park area wrote me a three-page letter inviting me to his house to meet wife Adale, a wizard in the kitchen, and especially so with the Christmas sweets.

"Talk about cooking up Christmas!" the words fairly flowed from his typewriter. "Take her cookies, for instance. Adale starts baking them right after Thanksgiving and our home turns into a cookie factory. Last year, for example, she made thirty-four kinds, baking a total of over ten thousand individual pieces, I don't know how many shapes.

"Adale was born in Cedarburg, Wisconsin, a German community, and most of her baking is as it's done in the old country. She inherited a multitude of recipes from her German ancestors. Around the holiday, I find her German cookbooks open to such jaw-breaking names as *springerle, anisplätzchen, teufelszungen, schokoladeplätzchen.*

"It's the last forty-eight hours before Christmas Eve, and no time for sleeping. Our small apartment is filled with a heavenly fragrance, the old-world holiday fruit breads are baking—*stollen, julekake, gugelhupf.*

"My Adale is a rare jewel with a heart as big as a barn door. Come and see for yourself," was the invitation from her husband.

Next trip to Chicago I telephoned Adale and she invited me for tea. Well, friends, she is just as wonderful and amazing as her husband claimed. Nursing was her profession and in World War II she was a First Lieutenant in the Army Nurse Corps in the South Pacific.

"I love cooking next to nursing," Adale told me, "and this pint-sized kitchen just isn't big enough." It was neat as a pin, but crowded with evidence of her baking hobby.

"When we retire I'm going to take six months and card-file my recipes," she said. She talks about her recipes as one would of beloved friends. "My praline kisses are from Tante Ida, Mrs. Paul Kuechle, who lived in Milwaukee until her death. I learned most about cookie baking from her and it wasn't easy. Her standard measures were a coffee cup and a teacup and the words *ein bisschen* (a little) and *ungefähr so viel* (just about that much)."

ILLINOIS

"Schokoladeplätzchen" (Little Chocolate Drops)

3 large egg whites

⅛ teaspoon salt

½ cup sugar

¾ cup almonds, finely slivered (not ground)

4 ounces German sweet chocolate, grated (not ground)

Makes about 50 cookies

Preheat the oven to 275 degrees. Generously grease 3 large baking sheets.

In a large bowl using an electric mixer, beat the egg whites with the salt until firm peaks form. Gradually add the sugar, beating constantly. After adding the last of sugar, beat another 2 minutes. Fold in the slivered almonds and grated chocolate. Drop by teaspoonfuls onto the prepared baking sheets. Bake for 35 to 40 minutes, until the cookies are dry and can be easily removed from the sheet. Transfer to wire racks to cool.

Mrs. Stevenson's Date-Stuffed Oatmeal Cookies

For the filling:

4 cups packed pitted dates

1 cup sugar

1 cup water

1 teaspoon grated orange peel

¾ cup finely chopped walnuts or pecans

For the dough:

1 cup (2 sticks) unsalted butter, softened

1½ cups firmly packed dark brown sugar

2 large eggs

1½ cups quick-cooking oats

3¼ cups sifted all-purpose flour

1 teaspoon baking soda

1 teaspoon cream of tartar

½ teaspoon salt

1 teaspoon vanilla extract

Makes about 7 dozen cookies

Make the filling: In a large saucepan, combine the dates, sugar, and water. Place over medium-high heat, bring to a boil, and boil for about 2 minutes, stirring constantly, until the dates are soft. Transfer to a bowl and using a handheld electric mixer, beat until smooth. Stir in the orange peel and nuts. Cool to room temperature.

Make the dough: In the large bowl of an electric mixer, cream the butter and brown sugar well. Add the eggs, one at a time, beating well after each addition, until the mixture is light and fluffy. Add the oats. In a small bowl, combine the flour, baking soda, cream of tartar, and salt and add to the butter mixture. Add the vanilla. Cover the dough and refrigerate until chilled, at least 2 hours or overnight.

Preheat the oven to 375 degrees. Roll out a quarter of the dough at a time onto a well-floured surface ⅛ inch thick. Cut out cookies with a 2½-inch round or fluted cutter. Spread 1 teaspoon of the date filling on half of each cookie and fold over. (If the filling is too thick to spread, add a little water.) Sealing the edges is not necessary. Place on an ungreased baking sheet and bake in batches for 8 to 10 minutes, until the cookies are a delicate tan

ILLINOIS

color. Let the cookies cool on the sheets for 2 minutes, then transfer to wire racks to cool completely.

Note: This recipe is not from Adale's German collection but one borrowed from the wife of Reverend Roy Stevenson of Summit, a suburb of Chicago. It's a recipe Adale makes not only at Christmas but the year round.

"Zimtsterne" (Cinnamon Stars)

1 cup sugar

1 teaspoon ground cinnamon

1 teaspoon grated lemon peel

3 large egg whites

¼ teaspoon salt

1½ cups almonds, grated (not ground)

A mixture of sugar and flour, or confectioners' sugar for rolling

Makes about 78 cookies

In a small bowl, combine the sugar, cinnamon, and lemon peel. In a medium bowl, beat the egg whites and salt to stiff, moist peaks. Add the sugar mixture gradually, beating constantly. Continue to beat until thick and glossy stiff peaks form. Set aside ½ cup for the frosting. Stir the grated almonds into the rest; cover and refrigerate to chill for 1 hour.

When ready to bake, preheat the oven to 300 degrees and grease 2 large baking sheets.

Roll out the dough in small amounts (it is rather sticky and somewhat difficult to roll) ⅛ inch thick, using a generous amount of a mixture of equal parts sugar and flour, or confectioners' sugar, on a work surface or pastry mat or cloth. Cut out cookies with a small star-shaped cutter. Spread small amounts of the reserved frosting mixture in the center of each cookie. Place on the baking sheets and bake the cookies in batches for 20 to 25 minutes, until dry. Let the cookies cool for 2 minutes on the sheets, then transfer to wire racks to cool completely.

STICK-TO-YOUR-RIBS SOUPS

A queen among the soup makers is Mrs. Cornelius Stob, Lisle, Illinois. The stars in her repertoire are not those delicate brews famed chefs prepare to prelude fine dinners. Mrs. Stob makes stick-to-your-ribs soups, breathing reassurance, loaded with liquid richness, a meal in a bowl. Go prospecting with your spoon—such good things to discover!

Mrs. Stob was born in Amsterdam, Holland, one of twelve children, and brought here as a toddler when Mama and Papa came to live in Chicago. Theodora's earliest memory is of Mama's soup pot, a symbol of her everyday thrifty cooking. And such wonderful soup Mama ladled out to the hungry brood. When soup was served it made the meal. The kinds: the famous Dutch pea soup, the vegetable soup with meat balls, navy bean, the potato soup. Always served as a go-along was homemade bread, great billowy loaves of bread each one as big as a sofa pillow.

A hearty dessert would be the ending—a pudding perhaps, or egg pancakes rolled up tight with brown sugar or a syrup filling.

Theodora showed us the round family table which she inherited from home—sixty inches in diameter to seat twenty-four persons. She keeps this in her dining room and wouldn't part with it for anything. "And we are but two," Mrs. Stob said, "my husband and myself, that is, since our son finished college." He is Dr. Martin Stob teaching in the School of Animal Husbandry of the Department of Agriculture at Purdue University.

Mrs. Stob makes her soups usually for six, which is a big meal for two, but she freezes the leftovers. The Stobs live in an old farmhouse recently remodeled, with five acres of land in orchards and garden. Each year Theodora "freezes the harvest." Look into her freezer—almost as much variety there as in the cold cases at your supermarket. But the soups you won't find anywhere else but in the home pot. Try these "like Mama made them." You will be surprised, and I will, too, if you don't enjoy the results. Real good eating, and such a little cost.

ILLINOIS

Dutch-Style White Bean Soup

1 pound dried navy beans

2 quarts cold water

4 small smoked pork shanks

2 teaspoons salt

2 cups finely chopped onion

2 cups finely chopped celery

1 (6-ounce) can tomato paste

1 teaspoon cider vinegar

Serves 6

In a large saucepan, soak the beans in enough water to cover overnight. When ready to cook, drain the beans and combine them with the cold water and the remaining ingredients. Place over medium-high heat and bring to a boil, then reduce the heat, cover, and simmer until the meat falls from the bones, about 2 hours. Add boiling water as needed to keep liquid at 2 quarts. Remove the bones and serve hot.

Lamb and Barley Soup

⅓ cup pearl barley, rinsed

2 lamb shanks, about 1½ pounds each

2 quarts cold water

2 teaspoons salt

⅓ cup uncooked brown rice, washed

½ cup minced carrots

½ cup minced onion

1 cup minced celery

1 (10½-ounce) can condensed tomato soup

Serves 6

In a large stockpot, soak the barley in enough water to cover overnight.

When ready to cook, drain the barley. Wash the lamb shanks and pat them dry. Combine them in the pot with the barley, cold water, salt, and rice. Place over medium-high heat and bring to a boil, then reduce the heat, cover, and simmer for 1½ hours, or until the lamb is tender at the bone. Add more boiling water as needed to keep the liquid in the pot at 2 quarts. Add the carrots, onion, celery, and tomato soup and simmer for 30 minutes more.

Remove the pot from the heat, cool the soup for 30 minutes, and skim the fat off its surface. Remove the shank bones from the soup and cut the meat from the bones and return it to the soup. Cover and refrigerate the soup overnight. The following day, bring the soup to a boil over medium heat and serve hot.

ILLINOIS

IOWA

Iowa where the tall corn grows! And there I went for a Hawkeye corn roast, to Des Moines in the late summer in the height of the roasting-ear season. My host and hostess, the late Mr. and Mrs. Carl Stewart. It was such a gay party I want the memory of that evening to be included among these eating experiences around the United States. "Stew," as his friends called him, was a wizard at corn roasting, and Wilma, called "Phil," was a wizard at corn picking. The afternoon of the roast Phil telephoned a nearby farmer, then a trip late afternoon to get the ears field-fresh. Back in a hurry before the folks started coming. I went along to see the corn picked. That cornfield was a thing of beauty, a sea of green ripples when the breeze struck.

The party started in Stew's basement den. Stew, his face wreathed in smiles, mixed drinks for the crowd.

"Phil, bring on your smoked almonds," he yelled up the back stairs. Stew tore off to the yard to get busy on the corn. That backyard was a long stretch of green sloping down to the barbecue terrace with its rough picnic table and stone fireplace.

Phil prepared the corn. Stew had no truck with such menial tasks. She cut off the stem end to where it joined the cob; she cut back the silk end right to the corn, pulled off the green husks, but left on the white inner ones. The corn

was laid on the racks or grills, over a bed of flaming hickory. Stew was in attendance, seated on a low bench.

The broiler or racks, he showed me, could be pulled forward off the fire when the corn got too hot. "How do you know when the corn's done?" I asked.

Stew said, "By experience. I can tell by the look." Experience? Stew had been roasting corn this way for forty-odd years.

When it was almost finished, he slipped the husk back and continued the roasting until the kernels shaded from deep gold to brown. The flavor was slightly on the caramelized side.

Then into a pan to pass up and down the long table. Plates of butter for the corn; salt and pepper, of course.

Waiting for the next round of corn, the guests attended to the barbecued pork. Stew barbecued the meat long before the guests put in their appearance; a hickory-flame job with plenty of smoke. The pork was served cold with a spicy barbecue sauce.

Roasting corn Stew's way is going to take practice—if he had secrets he wasn't telling. But Phil shared her recipe for barbecued pork and knew her recipes! Mrs. Stewart was Food Editor of *The Des Moines Register*, and had been cooking ever since she could remember.

Easy Barbecue Pork Sandwiches for Two

1 (1-pound) pork tenderloin

Olive oil or vegetable oil

1 clove garlic, cut in half

1 to 2 tablespoons crumbled sage

Iowa Pork Barbecue Sauce (recipe follows)

Plain soft white sandwich buns

Makes 2 heaping sandwiches

Using a very sharp knife, split the tenderloin lengthwise almost all the way through. Make parallel cuts 1 inch apart down to within 2 inches of the thin end. Take a cleaver and pound the thick end to about the thickness of the tail end (about ½ inch thick). Rub the cut surface with oil and the cut end of the garlic. Sprinkle the sage over the tenderloin, roll it up, and let stand, covered, to marinate for at least 2 hours or overnight.

When you are ready to cook, heat a smoker with hickory wood (or a grill with hickory coals) to 300 degrees. Put the meat in an aluminum pan and place in the smoker for 35 to 45 minutes, until the internal temperature reaches 150 degrees.

During the last 15 minutes of cooking, brush half of the sauce over the meat and put the meat back on the smoker.

Reserve the remaining sauce. Remove the meat from the smoker, cover loosely, and let rest for 10 minutes. Slice ¼ inch thick, pile on top of soft white buns, and serve with a dollop of the remaining sauce.

Iowa Pork Barbecue Sauce

1 cup tomato puree

1 cup water

1 small clove garlic, minced

1¼ teaspoons prepared mustard

¼ teaspoon salt

⅛ teaspoon freshly ground black pepper

⅛ teaspoon sweet paprika

Juice of ½ lemon

1½ teaspoons Worcestershire sauce

2 tablespoons cider vinegar

1 sprig parsley

1 small onion, minced

Tabasco sauce

Makes enough for 2 sandwiches

Combine all of the ingredients except the Tabasco in a large saucepan. Cover, place over medium heat, and bring to a boil. Reduce the heat and simmer for 30 minutes, stirring occasionally. Season with Tabasco to the hotness desired. The barbecue sauce may be stored, covered, in the refrigerator for up to 3 weeks.

WHEN I MET EDITH Davison, a home economics graduate of Iowa State College, she was the managing cateress for the Des Moines, Iowa, Women's Club. From October to May a weekly luncheon was given to serve around four hundred guests. Planning menus without repetition was Edith's big job. But certain dishes, she told me, were always in good favor and used again and again.

One such recipe, which had come down the years in the clubhouse kitchen, was this casserole for macaroni and cheese (recipe follows), almost a soufflé, but easier to handle. Other favorites were dishes Edith had learned from Mama in the big farm kitchen in Mills County. Here are some of the good things she was feeding the "club girls."

Apple Relish

1 pound large red apples

2 dill pickles, finely chopped

1 medium onion, coarsely chopped

½ cup sugar

¼ cup cider vinegar

Makes 1 pint

Core and quarter the apples but do not peel them. Combine the apples, pickles, and onion in a food processor. Pulse until minced and well combined. Add the sugar and vinegar. Pour into a clean pint jar, cover, and refrigerate for 1 day before serving. Serve with pork or turkey. The relish can be stored in the refrigerator for up to 3 weeks.

IOWA

Souffléd Macaroni and Cheese

1 cup soft breadcrumbs

1½ cups milk, scalded

1½ cups grated sharp cheddar cheese

1 cup cooked macaroni

3 large eggs, separated

1 tablespoon chopped parsley

1 tablespoon grated onion

1 teaspoon salt

3 tablespoons unsalted butter, melted

Serves 4

Preheat the oven to 350 degrees. Grease a 1½-quart casserole.

Place the breadcrumbs in a large bowl and pour the milk over them; add the cheese. Cover and let stand until the cheese melts. Add the macaroni.

In a separate bowl, whisk together the egg yolks, parsley, onion, salt, and butter. Beat the egg whites until stiff but not dry peaks form and fold into the mixture. Pour into the prepared casserole and bake uncovered for 25 to 35 minutes, until the top is browned and puffy and the center is set.

French-Style Hot Chocolate

1 ounce unsweetened chocolate

½ cup water

¼ cup sugar

Pinch of salt

¼ cup heavy cream, whipped

3 cups hot milk

Serves 4

Melt the chocolate in the top portion of a double boiler over simmering water. Add the water and stir constantly for about 4 minutes, until smooth. Add the sugar and salt and cook for 4 minutes longer, stirring constantly. Remove from the heat and cool for 20 minutes. Fold in the whipped cream. When ready to serve, place a heaping tablespoonful of the chocolate mixture into each serving cup and pour over the hot milk almost to fill the cup and stir lightly to blend. Serve immediately.

Horseradish Sauce

¼ cup grated horseradish

½ tablespoon prepared mustard

¼ teaspoon salt

Pinch of cayenne pepper

Pinch of sweet paprika

1 tablespoon cider vinegar

½ cup heavy cream, whipped

Makes 1 scant cup

In a medium bowl, mix together all of the ingredients except the whipped cream. Place the whipped cream into another medium bowl and slowly stir the mixture into the whipped cream. Cover and chill for at least 4 hours, until cold. Serve with roast beef, if you like.

IOWA

"THE BEST COOKIES I ever tasted," is how Mrs. Florence Richards of Hartford, Iowa, describes these butterscotch wafers. Originally they were baked by Aunt Mae who lived in a big stone house with a big square range. She baked them twenty dozen at a time around the Christmas season to gift-pack for neighbors and friends.

Then the cookies were made with freshly churned butter, eggs freshly laid and the golden sorghum was from a nearby cane mill. Mrs. Richards has pared down Aunt Mae's recipe to one-egg size and bakes the cookies drop-style. Aunt Mae rolled the dough to cut into a variety of fancy shapes.

Butterscotch Cookies

10 tablespoons (1 stick plus 2 tablespoons) unsalted butter

1 cup firmly packed brown sugar

¼ cup molasses

2½ cups all-purpose flour

1 large egg, well beaten

1 teaspoon baking soda

Dash of ground mace

Makes 3 dozen cookies

Melt the butter in a heavy saucepan over low heat. Add the brown sugar and molasses and stir until the sugar melts. Increase the heat to medium and just as the mixture comes to a rolling boil, remove it from the heat. Cool for 15 to 20 minutes. Add 1¼ cups of the flour, the beaten egg, and then the remaining 1¼ cups flour, the baking soda, and mace. Mix well into a soft dough. Scrape the dough into a bowl, cover, and refrigerate until chilled, about 30 minutes.

Preheat the oven to 375 degrees and grease 2 large baking sheets. Drop the dough by tablespoonfuls onto the prepared baking sheets, about 1 inch apart. Bake for about 10 minutes, until lightly browned. Cool the cookies on the sheets for 2 minutes, then transfer to wire racks to cool completely. When cooled, the cookies are crisp; if stored in an airtight container with a cut apple they will absorb moisture to fairly melt in the mouth.

SWOOSHED OVER HOT BISCUITS

Into our best bib and tucker and off by wing to Ottumwa, Iowa, to keep a dinner date with the John McDermotts. Dr. John is an orthodontist; wife Genevieve makes cooking a "thing."

Genevieve, dark-haired, dark-eyed, slender, has a blackbird's darting way, never idles a minute. When she sits she embroiders or shells peas or peels potatoes. She cooks Iowa-farm style, learned the art from her mother, Mrs. Clara Mincks, whose family has been four generations around Ottumwa.

Genevieve claims "Sunday breakfast is her long suit." It certainly is. Garden-grown raspberries and cream were the superb beginning. Followed fried pork tenderloin, which sells fresh in Iowa, sliced by the pound. The slices are floured, salt-and-pepper-seasoned, then fried golden and passed with a milk gravy made from the drippings. Good, too, swooshed over hot biscuits!

After church, high noon and time for eating again. Here come the chicken in a crisp brown mound, piled on the great platter. Come the mashed potatoes tagged by chicken cream gravy; next a casserole of sweet corn, a bowl of wilted lettuce and new peas fresh from the vine. Ice cream the ending, homemade on the back porch.

The sweet corn was done in a country manner. The corn was picked early morning, dew-wet, the ears stored in a cool place to wait until dinner. After shucking, the kernels were immediately cut from the cob and cut deep, then the blade of a knife run up and down the rows to get out the last drops of milk. Corn into casserole, seasoned to taste with a sprinkle of sugar, with salt and pepper, and top milk to cover. Along with this a great chunk of butter (or margarine) and then into a very slow oven (300 to 325 degrees) for one hour.

Here's Genevieve's way with the wilted lettuce: leaf lettuce from the garden row, one pound for six. Wash well, shake out excess moisture, place in bowl, shred with knife. Add a teaspoon of salt, four green scallions, finely cut, tops included. Into a frying pan go four strips of bacon cut crosswise into one-fourth-inch shreds. When the bacon is crisp, one-half cup cream is added with four tablespoons vinegar.

Heat and whip well to smooth curds. Pour over lettuce, cover bowl with plate ten minutes, and hustle to the table.

Genevieve's Potato Salad

12 medium red potatoes

6 large hard-cooked eggs

1 teaspoon celery seeds

¼ cup finely chopped scallions, white and tender green parts only

Salt

1 cup mayonnaise

Parsley

2 or 3 small young radishes, thinly sliced, for garnish

3 or 4 scallions, white and tender green parts only, thinly sliced

3 pounds cold cuts

Serves 10

Wash the potatoes well and put them in a large heavy stockpot with enough water to cover. Place over medium heat, bring to a boil, and boil until tender, about 25 minutes. Drain, transfer the potatoes to a bowl, cool, then cover and refrigerate until chilled, 3 to 4 hours.

When ready to cook, peel the potatoes and cut them into ½-inch dice; return them to the bowl. Shell the eggs and dice 4 of them. Add to the potatoes with the celery seeds and chopped scallions and season with salt. Mix in the mayonnaise. Mound the potato salad prettily on a large platter. (Never, never sloppy!) Slice the remaining 2 eggs and garnish the platter with them. Sprinkle with parsley. Ring with the young radishes and thinly sliced scallions, alternating them. Make a second ring around the top with your favorite cold cuts.

MINNESOTA

A champion jar lady is Mrs. Leonard W. Scott. This Minneapolis, Minnesota, housewife, a few years ago, startled her neighbors and amazed her family by winning virtually all of the first and second prizes in almost every canning classification at the Annual Fair in the Gopher State. In 1944 she had entered three lonesome little jars and walked off with three firsts. Winning was fun; the next year she decided to go into the competition in a big way and entered something in every class of canned fruits, vegetables, pickles, jellies, and jams.

The family teased her as families will, pretending to worry that there wouldn't be a jar left for the home shelf. Then came the surprise. Mother won the sweepstake; Mother won ribbons and more ribbons and enough cash in hand to buy a dining-room set, just the sort of set she had dreamed of owning all the years since her wedding day.

Mrs. Scott had been canning since she was twelve; first it was helping Mamma in the home kitchen in the small town of Howard Lake, Minnesota.

Then in her own double-windowed workroom on Fillmore Street in Minneapolis.

Mrs. Scott was a "small batch" canner, putting up as the harvest comes along, starting with rhubarb and ending the season with pickles. Her recipes she has collected from everywhere—magazines, newspapers, extension bulletins—but her pickles are hand-downs from Mother Abigail Patrick.

Pickled Pears

2½ cups water

1¼ cups cider vinegar

2 cups sugar

2¼ pounds Bartlett pears, peeled, cored, and cut into quarters

10 to 12 whole cloves

2 sticks cinnamon

Green food coloring and mint flavoring, optional

Makes 2 pints

In a large heavy stockpot, combine the water, vinegar, and sugar. Place over medium heat and bring to a boil, then reduce the heat and simmer for 10 minutes.

Meanwhile, divide the pears between 2 sterilized pint-size canning jars. Divide the cloves and cinnamon sticks between the jars and ladle in the syrup, leaving about ⅛-inch headspace. For variation, add green food coloring to the syrup and a few drops of mint flavoring, if you like. Sterilize the jar lids according to the manufacturer's directions and, using a kitchen towel to handle the hot jars, screw on the rings as tightly as possible. Turn the jars upside down to seal and cool; do not move them until they have cooled completely. Store in the refrigerator for 1 week before serving.

BREATHLESS, GOING PLACES IN a tearing hurry, a warm smile, a hearty handclasp—that's how I remember Mrs. Orren Safford, Virginia Safford to thousands of readers who have followed her columns in the *Minneapolis Tribune.*

Virginia cooks as easily as she writes—and with the same zest.

Simplicity marks even her most important dinners. One menu she serves again and again starts with fillets of herring pickled in white wine, this a "pass-around" with the cocktails.

For the main course, Norwegian meat balls in a rich gravy, served in a ring of wild rice, along with a green salad.

The dessert nine times in ten is crème brûlée with assorted brandied fruits. The brûlée is placed in a glass pudding dish, this centered on a large platter encircled by the fruit—pears, peaches, black cherries, greengage plums—canned fruit which is brandied in a hurry by this simple process: drain off syrup, cover fruit with brandy or kirsch and let stand twelve hours covered in the refrigerator.

About those fillets of herring: drain and place a layer of herring in shallow glass dish. Cover with a layer of peeled, thinly sliced Bermuda onion, over this finely cut chives, and a scattering of capers. Cover with thick sour cream seasoned to taste with salt and a touch of mustard. Chill the dish almost to freezing. Serve on crisp all-wheat crackers. Pass with fork and spoon.

Crème Brûlée

1 quart half-and-half

1 cup dark brown sugar

2 teaspoons vanilla extract

8 large egg yolks

4 tablespoons granulated sugar

Serves 8

Preheat the oven to 300 degrees.

In a medium saucepan, combine the half-and-half and brown sugar. Place over medium heat and cook, stirring, until the sugar melts and small bubbles appear around the rim. Remove from the heat and add the vanilla.

In a medium bowl, beat the egg yolks. Gradually beat in the hot cream mixture, then strain the custard through a fine sieve into a bowl. Set eight ½-cup ramekins in a roasting pan. Pour the custard into the ramekins and add enough hot water to the pan to reach halfway up the sides of the ramekins. Cover with foil and bake for 35 to 40 minutes, until set but still jiggly in the center. Uncover and let cool in the pan. Cover and refrigerate until very cold and firm, at least 5 hours.

When you are ready to serve, preheat the broiler. Place 4 of the ramekins in a baking pan and fill it with ice. Sprinkle about 1½ teaspoons of granulated sugar evenly over each

MINNESOTA

crème brûlée and broil for about 1 minute, until the tops are caramelized. Remove the crème brûlées from the ice water and refrigerate just until chilled, about 15 minutes. Repeat with the remaining crème brûlées. Serve cool as an ice cube.

Note: Alternatively, you may caramelize the sugar with a propane or brûlée torch.

MAKING A MESS OF THE KITCHEN

Terrance Hanold is an up-and-coming young corporation lawyer, but the family friends know Terry best as a successful young father. His children know "Papa" as the greatest cook in the world. Six in the brood and when Daddy takes a turn baby-sitting while his wife gets a breather, he has fun on the job. He takes his young family out for a ride on his hobby. The maid calls it "making a mess of the kitchen." The children call it "helping." The end result is that everyone is eating "high on the hog."

I had never met a corporation lawyer until I met Terry Hanold. I figured interviewing him amid leather-bound books and filing cabinets. The time set for my appointment was a Saturday afternoon and Terrance Hanold said, "Come to the house. I'm keeping the children today."

There I found him in the kitchen, apron draped, bowl in one hand, a mixing spoon in the other, making a banana spice cake.

Maybe you know Terrance Hanold. Hundreds of good cooks do. He is a lawyer for the Pillsbury Mills, Inc., and on many an occasion he combines his legal knowledge and his culinary skill in connection with the cook-ing contests conducted by his firm. He is always on hand at their annual baking bouts.

Terrance Hanold learned to cook because he had to if he wanted to eat. Terry's mother died when he was two, and his father, a traveling salesman, took the child with him from town to town. They kept house together, living in twenty-three different places before Terry had finished eighth grade. Through high school, through college, Terry did the cooking. It was his senior year in high school that Terry decided to take a course in home economics. There were twenty-seven girls in the class, that's how he explains it. "I enjoyed my work immensely. I liked the girls and I liked eating. In fact, this was the very best I had had in years. I even learned how to bake cakes. Ever since I've fought a losing battle with my waistline."

One of Terry's best-liked recipes came from one of his company's contests, though it was not a winner, however, except with Terry. He calls it My Infallible Soufflé. It never collapses, maintaining altitude with airy indifference during the ten to fifteen minutes it takes to get the "widgets" to the table.

Infallible Soufflé

½ cup (1 stick) unsalted butter

¾ cup all-purpose flour

1 teaspoon salt

¼ teaspoon dry mustard

⅛ teaspoon onion salt

1½ cups milk

1½ cups grated sharp cheddar

or other flavorful cheese

¼ teaspoon Worcestershire sauce

6 large egg yolks

6 large egg whites, stiffly beaten

Serves 6

Preheat the oven to 350 degrees.

Melt the butter in a large saucepan over medium heat and sift in the flour, salt, mustard, and onion salt, stirring to combine. Gradually pour in the milk and reduce the heat to low, stirring constantly, until the mixture is thick and smooth, about 8 minutes. Add the cheese, stirring until it is melted, then remove from the pan from the heat. Stir in the Worcestershire sauce. Blend in the egg yolks one at a time, then fold in the egg whites.

Pour the mixture into an ungreased 2-quart casserole. Place in a pan and fill halfway to the top of the casserole with hot water. Bake for 45 to 55 minutes, until the soufflé rises high and is golden brown on top and firm to the touch.

Banana Spice Cake with Banana Frosting

2 cups cake flour

¾ cup granulated sugar

2½ teaspoons baking powder

1 teaspoon salt

1 teaspoon ground cinnamon

1 teaspoon ground allspice

½ teaspoon ground cloves

½ teaspoon grated nutmeg

½ cup firmly packed brown sugar

½ cup vegetable shortening

¾ cup milk

2 large eggs

1 teaspoon vanilla extract

For the banana frosting:

½ cup mashed ripe banana

½ teaspoon fresh lemon juice

4 tablespoons (½ stick) unsalted butter, softened

3 cups confectioners' sugar

Makes one 8-inch layer cake

Preheat the oven to 350 degrees. Grease and flour two 8-inch round cake pans. Sift the flour, granulated sugar, baking powder, salt, cinnamon, allspice, cloves, and nutmeg into a large bowl. Add the brown sugar, shortening, and ½ cup of the milk and beat with an electric mixer for 2 minutes. Add the remaining ¼ cup milk, the eggs, and vanilla. Beat for 2 minutes more, or until the batter is smooth.

Divide the batter evenly between the prepared pans and bake for 25 to 30 minutes, until the cakes are golden and a wooden pick or skewer inserted into the middle comes out clean. Transfer the cakes to wire racks; cool in pans for 20 minutes, then remove from the pans to cool completely on the racks.

While the cake is cooling, make the banana frosting: In a small bowl, combine the banana with the lemon juice. In a medium bowl using an electric mixer, cream the butter. Add the confectioners' sugar alternately with the banana mixture. Frost the top and sides of the banana cake with the frosting.

A SPACIOUS RED-BRICKED ROOM with flagstone floor; a hand-hewn stone fountain in the rear where fresh spring water made a quiet "troubling" over the clean-washed stones of a little pool. Here the brook trout lived. This was Lowell Inn at Stillwater, Minnesota, birthplace of the state.

"Want to catch your fish now?" the waitress asked, handing me a net on a long wooden handle. We netted one brown beauty, then two more; the fish run small. Nell Palmer and her son, the proprietors of the inn, came over to help supervise the fishing. My catch was hurried to the kitchen.

The Palmers told me the story of the famous old inn. Stillwater, they said, was big on the map before St. Paul or Minneapolis were so much as a dot. The inn, white-pillared and majestic, is built on the site of the old Sawyer house.

The Palmers, Nell and her late husband Arthur, a theatrical couple, took over in 1930 when the depression knocked the show business flat. Today this inn is the show spot of the Northwest. It is the Antoine's of the North; the food is superb.

Oh, the trout! Arthur carried my catch to the table. Heads were pillowed on cress, sweet as the spring. I can see these good, fresh trout yet, smell them, taste them, and if there is better food in heaven I am in a hurry to get there.

No recipe. But one I can detail. The Fresh Strawberry Pie, served from May through June.

Fresh Strawberry Pie

1 (9-inch) Perfect Pie Crust (page 13)

1 cup crushed fresh strawberries

4 cups fresh strawberries, hulled

1 cup sugar

1 tablespoon cornstarch

Whipped cream for serving (optional)

Makes one 9-inch pie

Preheat the oven to 375 degrees. Line a 9-inch pie plate with the pastry. Bake until crisp, about 7 minutes. Cool on a wire rack. Pour the crushed strawberries into a large saucepan, place over medium heat, and add the sugar and cornstarch. Bring to a boil and cook until thickened, about 5 minutes. Fill the pie shell with the hulled strawberries, cut in half, and pour the hot berry syrup over the pie. Cover tightly with foil and refrigerate for at least 6 hours, until the filling sets. Serve with whipped cream, if you like.

WISCONSIN

Some of the finest Milwaukee cooking is to be found in the Swiss kitchens. I visited on the North Side with Mr. and Mrs. Joseph A. Gamma. Mrs. Gamma's mother and father, the Greppis, came to Milwaukee directly from Zurich.

"Soup was the great dish with my mother," Mrs. Gamma told me. "She made a hearty vegetable soup and served it over slices of two-day-old bread—that made the meal."

It is this vegetable soup made with a beef-bone stock, the vegetables strained out, then dumplings added, these flecked with nutmeg, that Mrs. Gamma likes better than any other starter to a good dinner.

Here we give you the menu Mrs. Gamma served most often in winter when the son, daughter, and the grandchildren came to spend Sunday. First the soup with dumplings, followed by *g'schnaetzlets,* meaning veal cutlets. This is served with potatoes boiled in their jackets, peeled while hot and browned in shallow hot fat. Carrots for an extra vegetable. Lettuce plain with oil and vinegar dressing. The finish an onion pie and strong black coffee pepped up with cherry brandy.

Beef Bouillon with Dumplings

For the soup:

1 beef marrow bone

2 teaspoons salt

¼ teaspoon freshly ground
black pepper

2 carrots, sliced into ½-inch rounds

1 large leek, white and tender
green parts only, chopped

3 stalks celery, diced

5 sprigs parsley

Freshly grated nutmeg

1 tablespoon chopped parsley, optional

For the dumplings:

2 large eggs

½ cup milk

½ teaspoon salt

1 cup all-purpose flour

Makes 1 quart

Make the soup: Crack the marrow bone; place it in a large stockpot with enough cold water to cover. Bring to a boil over medium-high heat and skim the fat from the surface. Add the remaining ingredients, reduce the heat to low, and simmer for about 1 hour, until the vegetables are soft.

While the soup is cooking, make the dumplings: In a medium bowl, lightly beat the eggs; stir in the milk and salt. Place the flour in a large bowl. Make a well in the center, pour in the liquid, and stir until mixed. Using a handheld electric mixer, beat until smooth.

When the soup is ready, strain it, then drop the dumpling batter by rounded teaspoonfuls into the simmering soup. When the dumplings float, the soup is ready. Serve the soup with about 3 dumplings to each bowl. Dust the soup with nutmeg and sprinkle with chopped parsley, if you like.

Alsatian Onion Tart

1 (9-inch) Perfect Pie Crust (page 13)

2 slices bacon

3 cups chopped onion

2 large eggs

¾ teaspoon salt

1 cup half-and-half

2 tablespoons grated Swiss or Gruyère cheese

1 tablespoon unsalted butter

Serves 6

Preheat the oven to 350 degrees. Line a 9-inch pie plate with the pastry.

In a medium skillet over medium heat, fry the bacon until crisp; reserve the bacon fat in the pan and transfer the bacon to paper towels to drain. Add the onions to the skillet and cook until transparent, 3 to 5 minutes. Take them off the heat to cool for 10 minutes. Add the eggs to the skillet one at a time, beating well after each addition. Add the salt and stir in the half-and-half. Crumble in the bacon.

Pour into the prepared pie shell, sprinkle with the grated cheese, and dot with the butter. Bake for 30 minutes, or until the crust is browned and the tart is set on the outside but still a bit jiggly in the middle. Cool on a wire rack and serve warm.

A POLISH HOUSEWIFE MAY cook American right around the calendar, until the week before Easter: then she's head over heels on a cake-baking spree.

It was Maria, three years out of Warsaw, wife of Michael Laskowski, a biochemistry professor at Marquette Medical School in Milwaukee, who told me how she and the neighbors prepare for the holiday. Mazurka, of course, a cake the Poles consider absolutely necessary to a well-appointed Easter table. Mrs. Laskowski bakes at least three and as many other kinds of cake as her budget will cover.

I begged these cake recipes from Mrs. Laskowski. She gave them to me just as she remembered them made in her home in Warsaw, "a century ago, before the war." Maria came to join her professor husband and college son, direct from a German concentration camp. She came without luggage, she brought only her memories. One memory we translate is the recipe for the *Mazurek* Krolewski. Maria remembers well; the eating is heavenly.

"Mazurek" Krolewski

2 cups (4 sticks) unsalted butter, softened

2 cups sugar

6 large egg yolks

1 cup almonds, chopped

4 cups all-purpose flour

1½ to 2 cups of your favorite chocolate frosting

Slivered almonds, candied orange peel, and diced candied citron, optional

Makes one 13 x 9-inch cake

Preheat the oven to 325 degrees. Generously grease a 13 x 9-inch pan.

In the large bowl of an electric mixer, cream the butter and sugar. Add the egg yolks, one at a time, beating well after each addition. Add the almonds. Sift in 2 cups of the flour, blending thoroughly. Add the remaining 2 cups flour and beat until combined.

Turn the batter into the prepared pan and using a rubber spatula, press the dough into the pan in an even layer about ½ inch thick. Bake for 30 to 35 minutes, until the cake is golden brown and a wooden pick or skewer inserted into the center comes out clean. Cool the cake in the pan on a wire rack, then frost the cake with your favorite chocolate icing. Use slivered almonds, candied orange peel, and diced citron to form flowers on the top of the cake, if you like. The decoration is a matter of each woman's skill.

Polski Torte

For the cake:

6 large eggs, separated

1 cup granulated sugar

1 cup chopped or ground walnuts
or pecans

2 tablespoons graham cracker
crumbs

1 teaspoon vanilla extract

For the chocolate icing:

1 cup (2 sticks) unsalted butter,
softened

1 cup confectioners' sugar

4 ounces unsweetened chocolate

Marmalade or strawberry jam

2 teaspoons sherry wine

Makes one 9-inch layer cake

Preheat the oven to 350 degrees. Grease and flour
two 9-inch round cake pans. In a large bowl, beat
the egg yolks. Gradually add the granulated sugar;
beat until thick and lemon-colored. Add the nuts and
cracker crumbs, then add the vanilla. In a large bowl
using an electric beater, beat the egg whites until stiff
peaks form. Fold the yolk mixture into the egg whites.

Turn the mixture into the prepared pans and bake
for about 30 minutes, until the cakes are golden and a
wooden pick or skewer inserted into the center comes
out clean. Cool cakes in the pans for 15 minutes on
wire racks, then turn onto the racks to cool completely.

To make the chocolate icing: In a medium bowl
using an electric mixer, cream the butter. Add the
confectioners' sugar and whip until light and fluffy;
set aside. Melt the chocolate in the top portion of a
double boiler over simmering water until just melted
and smooth. Pour the melted chocolate into the butter
mixture, blending well.

To assemble the cake: Spread one layer of the torte
with marmalade or strawberry jam to a thickness of
¼ inch. Sprinkle the top with the sherry. Lay the top
layer over it and cover the top and sides of the cake

with the chocolate icing. Decorate the cake as you will
with Easter flowers and salutations.

Note: The cake may be kept in the refrigerator for at least
2 weeks, or without refrigeration for 2 to 3 days.

A BIT OF OLD Milwaukee, that's Mader's
Restaurant. There one goes for the
authentic German dishes that have
been served "just so" in this city since
the turn of the century. It was in 1902
that Charles Mader, who had been
apprenticed in the wholesale grocery
business in the old country, came
to Milwaukee, then "the Munich of
America," to get a job in a restaurant.
He saved his money and started a
place of his own and called it "The
Comfort"—meals twenty cents; beer,
two steins for a nickel.

After his death his boys, George
and Gustave, carried on, and in the
tradition. Kathy, George's wife, keeps
her eye on the menu—she is the
head cook.

Go to Mader's, the first day of
May, drink strawberry May wine—a
festival occasion. Go any day and order
sauerbraten, order potato dumplings,
the German cheesecake.

Here is a popular dish I ate at
Mader's. Kathy Mader gave me the
recipe.

Mader's Cheesecake

For the crust:

3 cups graham cracker crumbs

1 cup sugar

½ cup (1 stick) melted unsalted butter

1 teaspoon ground cinnamon

For the filling:

2½ pounds cottage cheese or farmer's cheese

5 large eggs, separated

2½ cups sugar

1½ teaspoons salt

2 cups milk

5 (¼-ounce) envelopes unflavored gelatin

¾ cup cold water

3 tablespoons lemon juice

1 quart heavy cream, whipped

Serves 20

In a large bowl, mix the graham cracker crumbs, sugar, butter, and cinnamon together. Line a 19 x 11 x 2½-inch pan with the crumb mixture, reserving about ½ cup for topping.

To make the filling: In a blender or food processor, puree the cottage cheese or farmer's cheese until completely smooth. Scrape into a small bowl with a rubber spatula and set aside. In a medium bowl, beat the egg whites until stiff peaks form. In a large bowl, beat the egg yolks slightly. Add the sugar, salt, and milk. Cook in the top portion of a double boiler over boiling water until thickened, stirring frequently, 7 to 10 minutes. Remove from the heat and set aside to cool slightly.

In a small bowl, dissolve the gelatin in the water and lemon juice. Stir the gelatin into the custard until completely dissolved. Cool at room temperature, about 20 minutes. Add the prepared cottage or farmer's cheese and stir until light and fluffy. Fold in the whipped cream and egg whites. Pour into the prepared pan and top with the remaining crumb mixture. Chill in the refrigerator for several hours or overnight before serving.

STOLLEN IS CHRISTMAS EVE bread at tree-trim parties in the F. W. Glantz home in Fox Point, Wisconsin. The Glantzes are German, both sides of the family, but only at Christmas do old-time German dishes get their innings at the table.

Baking the stollen is an annual ritual. It's an all-day job and it has to be perfect, for stollen is as much a part of the family's Christmas festivities as turkey and fixings. The recipe is from Mrs. Glantz's mother, Mrs. Rose Imig of Sheboygan, Wisconsin. In baking these loaves it is well to remember it requires real labor to work in all the fruit. But once the baking job is done there are five big loaves on the table to wrap and let mellow. A bread superb, rich and fruity. It slices paper thin. It keeps, and keeps, and keeps. . . .

Schaum torte is another German sweet Mrs. Glantz bakes at least once during the holiday week. This, too, is made as her mother made it. But the French coffee cake is her own, and one she bakes often. One of the richest coffee cakes I ever set tooth to, a prize of a recipe.

French Swirled-Cinnamon Coffee Cake

❖◦❖

1 (¼-ounce) envelope active dry yeast

¼ cup plus 1 tablespoon warm water

4 cups all-purpose flour

1¼ cups sugar

1 teaspoon salt

2 sticks (1 cup) unsalted butter, chilled and diced

1 cup warm milk

3 large eggs, separated

2 teaspoons ground cinnamon

1 cup chopped nuts, such as hickory nuts or pecans

1¼ cups confectioners' sugar

Water or milk for the icing

❖◦❖

Makes 2 cakes

❖◦❖

Preheat the oven to 350 degrees. In a small bowl, dissolve the yeast in 1 tablespoon of the warm water. In a large bowl, combine the flour, ¼ cup of the sugar, and the salt. Cut in the butter until the mixture resembles coarse meal and the butter is the size of small peas. Make a well. Pour in the warm milk and well-beaten egg yolks, stirring until a soft dough is formed. Add the yeast mixture and beat until combined and the dough is shiny and elastic. Cover the bowl loosely with plastic wrap and let it stand in a cool dry place overnight to rest and double in size.

In the morning, grease 2 large loaf pans. Divide the dough into two equal parts. Roll each half on a floured surface into a rectangle ¼ inch thick. In a medium bowl, beat the egg whites until stiff peaks form and spread the egg whites on top of the dough. Sprinkle with the cinnamon, the remaining 1 cup sugar, and the nuts. Roll as for jellyrolls and place in the prepared loaf pans. Cover the pans loosely and let the dough rise until doubled in bulk, about 1 hour.

Preheat the oven to 350 degrees. Bake for about 45 minutes, until the loaves are browned and a wooden pick or skewer inserted into the center comes out clean. Let cool in the pans on wire racks.

While the cakes are cooling, make the icing: In a medium bowl, combine the confectioners' sugar with enough water or milk for a thin spreading consistency. Brush the glaze over the tops of the loaves while still warm. Slice and serve.

Schaum Torte

8 large egg whites,
at room temperature

½ teaspoon cream of tartar

2 cups sugar

1 teaspoon vanilla extract

1 teaspoon cider vinegar

Berries and whipped cream
for serving, optional

Makes one 8-inch torte

Preheat the oven to 250 degrees. Generously grease an 8-inch springform pan.

Beat the egg whites until frothy. Add the cream of tartar and beat until stiff but not dry peaks form. Slowly add 1 cup of the sugar, the vanilla, and vinegar, beating them in well. Slowly add the remaining 1 cup of sugar, beating until well blended and the mixture is stiff.

Turn the mixture into the prepared pan and bake for about 1¼ hours, until the cake has a marshmallow texture but is still tender and doesn't stick to the fork when gently pricked. Serve topped with berries and heaped with whipped cream, if you like.

Warning: Never bake a Schaum Torte if the day is humid. As Mrs. Glantz told me, "It will be a mess if you do."

WISCONSIN

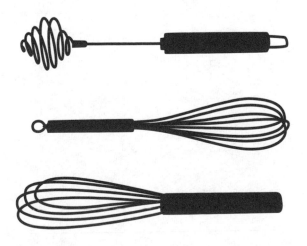

ROLLING POCKET OF EARTH

Drive thirty miles directly west from Milwaukee and you come to writer Edward Harris Heth's house in the Welsh Hills at Wales, Wisconsin.

After a decade in New York City, Ed Heth returned to his native heath. He bought this rolling pocket of earth next door to where his grandpa used to farm. He built this house as a writer's retreat. His joy of simple living he has written into a book, *My Life on Earth.* He writes of the maidenly Litten sisters, Miss Millie, Miss Carrie, and their wonderful sauerkraut dressing for the roasted duck. He tells of the wonders of the dill crock prepared by the commodious, unpredictable Aunt Dell. His characters have fictitious names, but local gossips around Wales have figured out almost exactly who is who and there is no fiction about the recipes, true country kitchen originals.

Here in his House on the Hill (*Y Ty a'r y Bryn,* the Welsh name), Ed Heth started collecting the countryside recipes. It's a job, he told me, getting down amounts to proportions for six.

"Aunt Dell's pork chops for example. When I asked for the ingredients she said gustily, 'Take a dozen pork chops. . . .'" Since Aunt Dell's table is hotel size this was no surprise to Ed. There is always her own voluminous family plus neighbors or even strangers if she can drag anyone in off the street for a meal. Her dish I give here is magnificent in its hearty homespun way. Most of Ed's recipes are. The lamb and cabbage—you don't need a blessed thing else but crusty bread and a green salad. Add home-canned fruit for dessert or make it fresh fruit and cheese.

Aunt Dell's Pork Chops

6 bone-in pork chops,
about ¾ inch thick each

Salt and freshly ground black pepper

1 tablespoon vegetable oil

2 carrots, sliced into thin rounds

6 scallions, white and tender
green parts only, finely chopped

Sweet paprika

¼ cup sour cream

1 (14½-ounce) can creamed corn

¼ cup finely crushed cornflakes

1 tablespoon unsalted butter

Serves 6

Preheat the oven to 350 degrees. Grease a 2-quart shallow baking dish or casserole.

Wipe the pork chops dry and season them on both sides with salt and pepper. Heat the oil in a large skillet over medium heat. Add the chops and brown them in batches, about 5 minutes per side. Transfer the chops to paper towels to drain.

Put a layer of carrots in the bottom of the prepared casserole. Place the browned chops over the carrots. Cover with the scallions and sprinkle with paprika. Pour over the sour cream, then the corn. Season with salt and pepper. Top with the cornflakes and dot with the butter. Cover and bake for 45 minutes, or until the chops are tender and the cornflakes are golden brown.

WISCONSIN

DRIVING IN RACINE COUNTY, Wisconsin, near Sturtevant, I met the youngest farming team in the state—Mr. and Mrs. Riley Green, then aged twenty-three and nineteen. This pair, Gladys and Riley, were running their farm on a partnership basis with Riley's father, five hundred acres in all. They were raising corn, oats, and hay. They had a dairy herd of fifty Holsteins.

Gladys's best dish, now we are quoting young Riley, is her Grandma's "ebleskivers." These are Danish fried cakes that come out round as baseballs, hollow in the middle. "No apple in it," Gladys explains, "the name comes from the shape rather than the content." A skiver pan is required for the making. Buy it in Scandinavian stores. This is a seven-hole affair, the holes nicely rounded. When the morning milking is done Gladys has these Danish fried cakes coming hot from the pan.

Gladys's grandma, Mrs. A. G. Anderson, who was living near Franksville, Wisconsin, always baked a kringle for the holidays. It was Grandmother who taught Gladys how to make *Gron Kaal*. That's green kale soup, something Gladys serves whenever a ham bone is handy, or, you may use a ham butt.

"Gron Kaal" (Kale Soup)

1 (2-pound) smoked ham hock

4 carrots, sliced into thin rounds

1 onion, minced

4 russet potatoes, peeled and diced

2 sprigs parsley, minced

1 cup chopped kale
(middle ribs removed)

Salt and freshly ground
black pepper

Serves 4 to 6

In a large stockpot, cover the ham hock with 2 quarts water, place over medium heat, and bring to a boil. Reduce the heat to low, cover, and simmer for about 1½ hours, until the meat is falling off the bone. Add the carrots, onion, and potatoes and cook for 15 minutes. Add the parsley and kale and simmer for about 15 minutes longer, until the kale is tender. Season with salt and pepper. This shouldn't be a thick soup, but thick enough that the kale stays suspended in the liquid. Discard the bone and serve.

"Chalber Bälleli" (Swiss-Style Meatballs with Gravy)

2½ pounds ground veal

½ pound ground pork

4 large eggs

1 cup half-and-half

1¼ cups milk

¼ cup finely chopped onion

1 teaspoon salt, plus more for gravy

½ teaspoon freshly ground black pepper, plus more for gravy

¼ teaspoon grated nutmeg

6 slices toasted bread, finely crumbled

6 tablespoons (¾ stick) unsalted butter

1 tablespoon all-purpose flour

Serves 6

Preheat the oven to 350 degrees. Generously grease a large casserole or other baking dish.

In a large bowl, mix the meats together with the eggs, half-and-half, and ¼ cup of the milk. Stir in the onion and add the salt, pepper, and nutmeg. Mix in the toast crumbs well and form the meat mixture into tablespoon-size balls.

Melt the butter in a large heavy skillet over medium heat. Brown the meatballs in batches, turning as needed, 5 to 7 minutes per batch. Drain the meatballs on paper towels. When all the meatballs are cooked, turn the meatballs and any remaining fat in the skillet into the prepared casserole. Cover the casserole with foil and bake for about 30 minutes, until the meatballs are sizzling and tender. Uncover the foil and cook until the meatballs turn a deeper brown, about 10 minutes more. Place the meatballs on a platter, reduce the oven temperature to 200 degrees, and keep the meatballs warm.

Pour the fat from the casserole into a large heavy skillet or saucepan. Place over medium heat, stir in the flour, and cook until lightly browned, about 3 minutes. Slowly pour in the remaining 1 cup milk and whisk until slightly thickened, about 5 minutes. Season with salt and pepper. Pour the gravy over the meatballs or serve it passed in a separate bowl.

WISCONSIN

ONE HUGE KETTLE OF CHEESEMAKING

Little Switzerland of America is Green County, Wisconsin, where Alpine costumes and customs abound without benefit of the Alps. Here in the rolling green hills live the descendants of the first Swiss colonists who left overcrowded Canton Glarus in 1845 to establish a New Glarus in the Western World.

They came here to farm, to raise cereal grains, but when the venture ended in failure, they turned to making Swiss cheese as they had made it at home. Today this little county is one huge kettle of cheese-making activity. Its eighty-three crossroads factories produce nearly one-fourth of all the Swiss cheese made in America. Its 24,000 population is less than one third of the number of cows on its farms.

I had come to visit in a Swiss-American kitchen and spend a day at the dairy farm of the Frank Schiessers, Route 1 out of New Glarus. Elda Schiesser, I had heard, was an expert cook, a wonderful manager.

Road signs spoke a welcome to little New Glarus, population 1,224. I thought for a moment this might be Switzerland as I passed the Chalet of the Golden Fleece, an architectural echo of a Swiss mountain house. Next the Swiss museum, a replica of a pioneer cabin, housing a wealth of early-day relics.

A mailbox told us that this was Frank Schiesser's farm. Mrs. Schiesser and eight-year-old Linda opened the door to us. Elda Schiesser was born in this house. She was born of Swiss parents, as was her husband, in this same township. When her mother and dad felt the urge to retire, she and Frank bought the place—120 acres.

The Schiessers had twenty-eight milkers, these the Holsteins, milked twice a day, the milk sold to the local Grove cheese factory a half mile up the road.

The Swiss eat their cheese in amazing amounts. Mrs. Schiesser told me she puts sliced Swiss on the table right along with the salt and pepper shakers and the big sugar bowl. It's cheese for breakfast, lunch, and dinner and in-between snacks. When a chunk of cheese dries then it's used grated to spoon over soups, salads, and sauces. Elda Schiesser bought her cheese at the factory in two-and five-pound pieces. She cut away the rind, then packed her purchase in a plastic bag to store in the refrigerator. If there's no plastic bag handy, she would wrap the cut in a damp cloth, then in waxed paper.

Switzerland Swiss cooking, I learned, is of three distinct types. The northern Swiss of the German section cook with a German accent; those on the French side give the food a French touch. Italian dishes are the rule in the Italian part of the country. But cheese and pastries are on every table.

In New Glarus it's the German influence that seems to be most pronounced, but some dishes are of French and Italian lineage. Add to this a few generations of living in Wisconsin, land of abundance, and Green County cooks offer you a Swiss-American cuisine reminiscent of Switzerland, but modified.

It's on Labor Day weekend that New Glarus celebrates, presenting Schiller's *William Tell* in the Swiss-German language. There is feasting, this too done in the Swiss manner. Hand-down recipes are on every table to delight the gourmet. Here are the recipes Mrs. Schiesser has selected as among the most typical in the country—foods worthy of the festival.

Potato and Swiss Cheese Soup

4 medium russet potatoes

1 large onion

4½ cups water

2 tablespoons unsalted butter

1 tablespoon all-purpose flour

Salt and freshly ground black pepper

Dash of grated nutmeg

2 tablespoons heavy cream

4 teaspoons grated Gruyère or other hard Swiss cheese

Minced parsley

Serves 4

Peel and dice the potatoes and onion and place them in a large saucepan. Cover with 4 cups of the water. Place over medium-high heat, bring to a boil, then reduce the heat to medium-low and simmer until the potatoes are tender, about 25 minutes.

Meanwhile, melt the butter in a large skillet over medium-low heat. Stir in the flour and cook until cream-colored, stirring constantly, about 5 minutes. Stir in the remaining ½ cup water, then stir the mixture into the potatoes and onions. Season with salt and pepper. Add the nutmeg and cream. Increase the heat to high and bring to a boil, then immediately remove from the heat. Puree the soup in a blender or food processor in batches until smooth, then pour back into the saucepan and heat through. Ladle the soup into warm bowls and top each with 1 teaspoon of the grated cheese. Garnish with parsley.

WISCONSIN

Baked Eggs with Bread and Cheese

4 slices buttered thick-cut white or French bread, cubed

1 cup grated Swiss or Gruyère cheese

2 cups milk

2 large eggs, lightly beaten

1 teaspoon salt

Serves 4

Preheat the oven to 350 degrees. Grease a 1½-quart baking dish.

Arrange the buttered bread cubes in the prepared dish and cover with the cheese. In a medium bowl, whisk together the milk, eggs, and salt. Pour the liquid over the cheese and bread. Bake for about 1 hour, until the top is browned and the filling is firm and set.

TWENTY-TWO GUESTS were invited to dinner. The tables were set, one in the parlor, one in the dining room in the farm home of Mrs. Elsie Gerber, one mile down the road west of Monroe in Green County. Again a Swiss meal. Mrs. Gerber is one of the best of the local cooks. Since her husband's death she took in parties by special arrangement and serves the meals in Swiss country style.

Dinner is "dished," dinner is "called," and with much joking and scraping of chairs, the company assembled. Such abundance! *Kalbswurst*—ever eat this sausage of veal? Ample bowls of homemade noodles of rich, nutty flavor. The cauliflower makes a pretty platter, the flowerettes heaped high, well covered with a cheese sauce, the mound circled by nests of diced, buttered carrots, fresh garden peas. There are haycocks of spinach.

I had forgotten how good wilted lettuce could be. Sliced cucumbers in a side dish laved in sour cream.

Homemade yeast rolls; homemade strawberry preserves.

The dried pear bread is almost as fruity as fruitcake. Dessert is the *fastnacht kuechen* and a variety of Swiss cookies. Coffee in big cups. At the very end come the trays of dessert cheese, these laid out on grape leaves; the bleu, Camembert, Liederkranz, and Neufchâtel. No meal in Green County is considered complete if cheese isn't there.

Elsie Gerber's Creamed Spinach

2½ pounds fresh spinach, large stems discarded

1 tablespoon unsalted butter

1 teaspoon minced onion

1 tablespoon all-purpose flour

Dash of grated nutmeg

Salt and freshly ground black pepper

1 cup milk

1 tablespoon heavy cream

Serves 4

Heat a large saucepan over medium-high heat. Add the spinach by the handful and cook, stirring often, until wilted, about 5 minutes. Transfer the spinach to a colander and squeeze it as dry as possible. Finely chop the spinach and return it to the skillet. Add the butter and onions and cook, stirring, until the onions are golden, about 5 minutes. Sprinkle with the flour. Add the nutmeg and season with salt and pepper. Add the milk and bring to a boil. Taste and add more salt and pepper if needed. Just before serving, stir in the cream. Serve piping hot.

WISCONSIN

Swiss Pear Bread

1½ cups dried pears (if not available, double the dried apples)

1½ cups dried apples

1 cup dried currants

1¼ cups raisins

⅓ cup pitted prunes

1 teaspoon finely diced candied citron

3½ tablespoons unsalted butter

½ tablespoon anise seeds

¼ teaspoon ground cloves

½ teaspoon ground cinnamon

½ teaspoon grated nutmeg

8 tablespoons sugar

½ cup walnuts, whole or chopped

½ envelope active dry yeast

2 cups warm water

1 teaspoon salt

About 4½ cups all-purpose flour

Makes 3 loaves

Put the dried pears and apples in a pot with water to barely cover, place over low heat, and bring to a low simmer; cook until very tender, about 10 minutes. Add the currants and raisins. Cook the prunes in water to cover until soft, about 5 minutes, and add to the hot cooked fruit mixture. Add the citron, 2 tablespoons of the butter, the anise seeds, cloves, cinnamon, nutmeg, and 6 tablespoons of the sugar while the mixture is still hot. Cover and let stand overnight.

In the morning, if any water remains, drain it. Then add the walnuts to the fruit mixture. Dissolve the yeast in 2 tablespoons of the warm water and let stand for 5 minutes without stirring. Then mix well and add the remaining 1½ tablespoons butter, the salt, the remaining 2 tablespoons sugar, and the remaining warm water. Let stand until the mixture bubbles. Mix in enough flour, about 4 cups, to make a stiff dough.

Turn the dough out onto a floured surface and work in enough additional flour to prevent sticking, about ½ cup. Cover and let the dough rise until doubled in bulk, about 1 hour. Pinch off 3 pieces the size of a golf ball. Add the fruit-nut mixture to the remainder of the dough and knead it into the dough until there are no streaks of white left. The dough will be quite sticky. Divide it into 3 equal portions. Shape each one into a narrow loaf. Using a generous sprinkling of flour on a work surface and rolling pin, roll each of the small pieces of dough into a very thin sheet (there are likely to be some holes). Wrap a sheet of this plain dough around each loaf. Make it uneven so that the dark fruited roll shows through the gaps and holes. Let the loaves rise in a warm place until nearly doubled in bulk, about 1 hour.

Preheat the oven to 375 degrees. Bake for about 20 minutes, until the dough has come up, then reduce the oven temperature to 325 degrees. Continue baking for 30 to 40 minutes more, until the loaves are golden brown and sound hollow when tapped. Transfer to wire racks to cool completely.

WISCONSIN

THE DINNER-PAIL SPECIAL

obert Neal carved the Cornish pasty. Five quick strokes: once down the middle, four times across. It was a monster pie, bulging with pieces of beef and sliced potatoes, the savory juices ready to run. A wreath of steam rose when the knife sliced through the thick tender crust and the smell came round and gracious to make one feel warm and comfortable. A pleasure to be sitting here at this candle-lighted table in a century-old miner's cottage on Shake Rag Street, Mineral Point, Wisconsin.

The fire snapped and made merry. In the fire shine, the turkey-red tablecloth seemed twice as red. Beet pickles came along with the meat pie. A green salad, too, the tossed kind, and no other vegetable. Dessert was the Devonshire cream.

Mineral Point, population 2,284, in the rolling hills of the southwestern part of the state, was once the most important town in Wisconsin territory. Right here was the heart of the old lead-and zinc-mining region, an Eldorado of the early 1830s for the miners of Cornwall.

Cousin Jennie, wife of Cousin Jack, as the Cornish miners were called, favored the pasty above all dishes, the meat pie born of necessity. At home this meat and vegetable mixture sealed into crust was the dinner-pail special. Baked in the morning, wrapped in paper, it was rushed to the mine shafts to arrive steaming hot for the noon lunch. Today, throughout Wisconsin and Michigan, the pasty comes often to the table and in a dozen variations.

It was in Chicago I heard about the "Shake Rag" restoration project. I was told that three cottages had been opened as dining rooms and guest houses for visitors who come from all parts of the country to see this bit of old Cornwall. The thing that determined me to go was that Cornish food was served, prepared by hand-down recipes of the housewives who cooked in these cottage kitchens more than a hundred years ago.

Having dinner by the fire, I heard the story of the project from the man most responsible for the undertaking. The street is actually a narrow road meandering along a ravine. The cottages, of native limestone, are built with walls eighteen inches thick, hugging close to the protecting ridge.

These houses were built exactly as those the Cornish left behind in Cornwall and are restored so perfectly they may well be more Cornish than the real thing.

"Over there," Robert Neal was explaining indicating the ridge across the ravine, "were the 'diggings.' Midday the miners' wives would go to their front doors, wave a white cloth to signal the men home for dinner. So the street got its name."

The rich surface deposits of lead had begun to peter off before the Cornish got here. They didn't get rich quick and home again as they had planned. The Cornish stayed until the mines were worked out, then some turned to farming; others moved on to the gold fields of the West. Shake Rag's little stone houses were left to decay. They settled, stones separated; roofs tumbled in, gardens grew wild.

Robert Neal, of Cornish ancestry, born in Mineral Point, knew the street as a boy. Even then the houses were coming to ruin.

One little house he dreamed of owning some day, with a garden in the rear, a candle in the window, and from the chimney a violet spiral of smoke. He told me about it, this house we were sitting in. Robert Neal of Mineral Point became Robert Neal the decorator of Chicago, New York, London. The house was forgotten. In 1935, he returned to visit his boyhood home. He walked down Shake Rag Street and fell in love with "his" house all over again. He learned it was offered for taxes and bought it on impulse, the price was ten dollars.

Edgar Hellum came to the street, looking for old stone to restore a house in his hometown, Stoughton, Wisconsin. He met Neal and listened to his planning and instantly saw the possibilities in the undertaking.

The two pooled their shoestring resources and started work immediately to recondition the house to use as a shop for antiques. To help finance the venture, tea was served, tea with scones and plum preserves, and scalded cream and saffron cake.

In the midst of restoring their house came the opportunity to purchase the houses right and left. So, the idea took form for a typical Cornish historical grouping, comparable, in a small way, to the restoration of Williamsburg. It's a long story and the end isn't yet. Meanwhile the Cornish dishes, prepared by the old recipes, help pay the bills. The pasty recipe I give here is from Neal's Cornish grandmother, Mary Rogers Neal. I copied it exactly from an old beat-up cookbook.

Cornish Pasties

For the dough:

2¼ cups all-purpose flour

1 tablespoon salt

6 tablespoons vegetable shortening

½ cup cold water

For the filling:

10 ounces shoulder or chuck steak, trimmed and cut into ¼-inch dice

1 small onion, diced

1 small russet potato, peeled and cut into ¼-inch dice

2 tablespoons salt

1 teaspoon freshly ground black pepper

1 large egg, lightly beaten

Serves 6

To make the dough: In a large bowl, combine the flour and salt. Cut in the shortening with a pastry blender or 2 knives until half the mixture resembles coarse cornmeal and half the mixture is the size of small peas. Pour in the water and stir the dough together. Knead briefly until the pastry is smooth with no cracks. Press into a flattened disk and cover with plastic wrap; refrigerate the dough for at least 30 minutes or overnight.

When ready to assemble, remove the dough from the refrigerator and unwrap it. Roll the dough out onto a lightly floured work surface ¼ inch thick. Using a small plate or saucer as a guide, cut out six 6-inch rounds. (The scraps may be combined and reformed if you cannot get 6 rounds out of the first batch.) Stack the pastry rounds onto pieces of plastic wrap with plastic between each round to keep them from sticking together. Refrigerate while you prepare the filling.

To make the filling: Preheat the oven to 400 degrees. Grease a large baking sheet.

Combine all of the filling ingredients except the egg in a large bowl. Place the pastry circles on a lightly floured work surface and place about ½ cup of the filling in the center of one side of the pastry. Using the beaten egg, brush the edges of the pastry and then bring the unfilled side over the filled side so that the edges meet. Press the edges together to seal and then crimp them with the fork tines. Repeat with the remaining pastry rounds, then transfer them to the prepared sheet. Brush the tops of the pasties with the remaining egg and cut several slits into the top of each. Bake for 20 minutes, or until the pasties are golden brown around the edges. Reduce the oven temperature to 350 degrees and continue to bake until the pasties are golden brown. Remove from the oven, transfer to wire racks, and cool for 10 to 15 minutes before serving.

Note: To be truly Cornish, the pasty will go long on the potatoes and short on the meat. Just a touch of the onion and no other vegetable, as it is so frequently met on other folks' tables.

Cornish Scones

2 cups all-purpose flour

1 tablespoon baking powder

1 teaspoon salt

4 tablespoons sugar

2 tablespoons vegetable shortening

2 large eggs

⅓ cup milk, plus more if needed and for brushing the scones

½ teaspoon lemon extract

Clotted cream and fresh raspberries for serving, optional

Makes 1 dozen scones

Preheat the oven to 375 degrees. Grease 2 baking sheets.

In a large bowl, combine the flour, baking powder, salt, and 2 tablespoons of the sugar. Using a pastry cutter or 2 knives, cut in the shortening until the mixture resembles the texture of coarse meal. In a small bowl, beat the eggs and milk; stir in the lemon extract. Add to the flour mixture and stir just enough to make a soft and moistened but not sticky dough. Add a few more drops of milk to the dough if necessary.

Gather the dough into a ball and knead it gently on a lightly floured surface for a few seconds. Pat the dough out into a ½-inch-thick round. Using a 2-inch square cookie cutter, stamp out as many scones as you can. Gently gather the scraps, press them together, and cut several more.

Transfer the scones to the prepared baking sheets, moisten the edges, and pinch together to form triangles. Brush the scones lightly with milk. Sprinkle with the remaining 2 tablespoons sugar. Bake for 20 to 25 minutes, until light golden brown. Transfer to a wire rack to cool. Serve warm or at room temperature with clotted cream, softly whipped cream, and fresh ripe berries, if you like.

WISCONSIN

MICHIGAN

It was a happy day when I met the Corbetts. I had driven out of Detroit to Grosse Ile early on a Sunday morning in time for breakfast.

––––––––––

Both Lucy and Sid are gone now, but I shall tell the story of my visit, for that remains a bright memory.

Their kitchen was a room of three stoves—gas, electric, and wood-burning—this room Sid commanded from his wheelchair. It was there he did his writing, spinning yarns of the old days when Detroit was a young and leisurely tree-shaded town. Here Lucy tested her recipes, which she added to Sid's stories as a sort of cap-sheaf. Mouth-watering dishes, many of which had their roots in old France, for Detroit, remember, was originally French.

Some of Lucy's dishes were English. She had a grandma from Prince Edward Island, way down in the Canadian Maritime. "Some of her cooking," Sid said, "is just good American grub."

Sunday breakfast starred pancakes made paper-thin and the width of a dinner plate. The batter was the same as that used for the crêpes suzette of the French cuisine.

Came fresh Michigan blueberries with a bowl of sour cream. The blueberries were spooned across the middle of the buttered hot cake,

then sour cream spooned over, next a sprinkle of sugar, the cake was rolled using fingers or fork. A bowl of currant jelly for those who might prefer a filling more sweet. Next came a platter of crisply fried bacon.

Here is the way Lucy made the pancakes: four whole eggs were broken into the mixing bowl and three-fourth teaspoon salt added, a pinch of sugar, then as Sid said, "beat the be-jeepers out of them with a rotary egg beater." Next she sifted in about one-half cup of all-purpose flour and continued beating until smooth. Slowly whole milk was added, just enough to thin the batter to heavy-cream consistency (about one-fourth cup). Two tablespoons of melted butter were stirred in and the cakes were ready to bake.

The baking was done one cake at a time in an eight-inch heavy iron frying pan. In went one tablespoon butter, the heat high so the butter came to a quick sizzle and turned golden brown. At this moment Lucy poured in about three tablespoons of batter, she tilted the pan to and fro so it spread quickly over the pan bottom. After a moment she lifted the edge and peeked. We have been taught not to peek at a pancake's downside, but Lucy did. When golden brown she flips it over. The cakes were served directly from pan to plate, soft, never crisp. Would I stay for dinner? Lucy would make the "painless borscht." Did I like kidneys in white wine? This in a border of mashed potatoes was one of Sid's favorite meals. Frenched snap beans, a tossed salad, and dessert a cherry pie with marriner crust.

Painless Borscht

1 (14½-ounce) can beef stock

1 (14½-ounce) can chopped beets

1½ cups water

3 tablespoons grated onion

2 tablespoons tarragon vinegar

1 teaspoon coarse salt

½ teaspoon garlic salt

¼ teaspoon freshly ground black pepper

⅛ teaspoon cayenne pepper

2 tablespoons sour cream

Serves 6

Combine all of the ingredients except the sour cream in a large heavy skillet and place over medium heat. Bring to a boil, then reduce the heat to low and simmer for about 5 minutes to thoroughly combine. Ladle the soup into warm bowls and serve topped with sour cream, a teaspoonful added to each bowl.

Marriner Pie Crust

1 cup sifted all-purpose flour

¼ pound cream cheese, softened

½ cup (1 stick) unsalted butter, softened

Makes one 8-inch double pie crust

Place all of the ingredients in a large bowl and work together with your fingers, 2 knives, or a pastry cutter to form a putty-like mass. Pat the dough into a disk, wrap it tightly in plastic wrap, and refrigerate overnight. When ready to use, remove the disk and let it stand at room temperature for at least 2 hours. (Otherwise, Lucy says, you must roll it with a sledgehammer. That pastry is solid until baked, then a tender, flaky delight.) Divide the dough into 2 equal pieces. Roll one of the pieces onto a floured surface ⅛ inch thick.

Lightly grease an 8-inch pie pan and line the pan with the dough. Fill the pie with your desired filling, such as the cherry pie filling (recipe follows). Roll out the remaining pastry and cut it into 8 strips 1 inch wide; twist the strips and lay across the filled pie shell.

Sour Cherry Pie

1 quart fresh sour cherries, pitted

2 tablespoons quick-cooking tapioca

1½ cups sugar

⅛ teaspoon salt

2 drops almond extract

1 (8-inch) Marriner Pie Crust (recipe opposite)

Makes one 8-inch pie

Preheat the oven to 450 degrees.

In a large bowl, toss together all of the ingredients except the crust. Turn the mixture into the pie shell and cover with the twisted pastry strips to make a lattice design. Bake for about 10 minutes, until the top begins to brown. Reduce the oven temperature to 350 degrees and bake for 20 to 30 minutes, until the pie is golden brown and the filling is bubbling. Transfer to a wire rack to cool completely. Serve warm or at room temperature.

VISITING THE FAMOUS HENRY Ford homestead in Dearborn, Michigan, I was invited to have dinner with Edith B. Crumb, an interior decoration writer. But get to know Edith and discover a far greater talent—her bona fide enthusiasm for good friends and good food.

The high cupboard in her small apartment kitchen there in Greenfield Village on the Ford property held files of old recipes as carefully treasured as her blue and white English Staffordshire pottery. Her recipes she had collected in New England where she vacationed each autumn after the foliage had turned to its glory.

When Edith put forth her best efforts getting a dinner the menu invariably started with cream of corn soup as made by her grandmother, this served with toast fingers. Followed the ham loaf passed with hot mustard sauce. Next the parsley potatoes, the buttered asparagus.

"A businesswoman must make the most of shortcuts," she confided and with the next breath announced, "I like to bake my own bread." This is a hundred percent whole-wheat bread, coarse-textured, heavily crusted, giving the mealy savor of ripe wheat in the mouth. The sweet, dark taste? That's molasses.

The green salad is a course to itself. The ending, lemon ice cream passed with pecan balls. The ice cream is the easiest to make of any I ever tried and it comes smooth as a petal, a joy to eat.

The pecan balls are rich to grease the fingertips; one swift bite, a shower of nut-sweet crumbs crumble in the mouth.

Lemon Ice Cream

1 cup sugar

3 tablespoons lemon juice

2 teaspoons finely grated lemon peel

1 pint half-and-half

2 drops yellow food coloring, optional

MICHIGAN

Makes about 3 cups

Place a deep baking dish in the freezer.

In a large bowl, combine the sugar, lemon juice, and lemon peel, mixing well. Slowly stir in the half-and-half and food coloring, if using. Chill the bowl over a large bowl full of ice for about 30 minutes, until cold.

Transfer the mixture to the prepared pan in the freezer. After 45 minutes, open the door and check it. As the ice cream starts to freeze near the edges, remove it from the freezer and stir it vigorously with a rubber spatula or a handheld electric mixer, taking care to break up any frozen sections. Return to the freezer. Continue to check the mixture as it's freezing every 30 minutes, stirring vigorously with a spatula or a handheld electric mixer, until the ice cream is frozen. It will likely take 2 to 3 hours. Transfer to a storage container and cover until ready to serve.

Pecan Balls

1 stick (½ cup) unsalted butter, softened

1 teaspoon vanilla extract

2 tablespoons granulated sugar

1 cup sifted all-purpose flour

1 cup finely chopped pecans

½ cup confectioners' sugar

Makes about 2 dozen cookies

In a large bowl using a handheld electric mixer, cream the butter and vanilla until smooth. Blend in the granulated sugar and flour and stir in the pecans. Cover and refrigerate the batter for 1 hour.

Preheat the oven to 350 degrees. Scoop out the batter 1 tablespoon at a time, rolling each spoonful between your palms to form balls. Place the balls on ungreased baking sheets and bake for about 15 minutes, until the balls are browned. Cool on the sheets for 3 minutes, then roll the balls in the confectioners' sugar and cool completely.

A SALT-SWEET TASTE

Clara Bryant Ford's two hands were as talented at the baking board as her famous husband's clever fingers were in dealing with machines. She too had a "Model T," one of her own designing, a low-cost family model of a tea wafer. With sly good humor she named her dollar-sized cookie for her husband Henry's fast-dollar-earning model, America's first "family class" car. Proud she was of her wafer, made with wheat germ, which she served for afternoon occasions when the ladies got together.

Mrs. Ford was no faddist, but long before the world had gone diet crazy she was a wheat-germ enthusiast. She used this vital part of the kernel in many, many ways, but her favorite way was in this "Model Tea" recipe. The mixture is rolled thin, it is baked crisp, and because the wheat germ has been toasted it gives a salt-sweet taste. Model Teas are high in nutritive values, low down in calories, something to satisfy the afternoon school crowd, sophisticated and unsweet enough to serve with cocktails.

All her life Mrs. Ford was an excellent cook and housekeeper. She knew every detail of running a home, and knew by first-hand experience. Until her husband came into riches she had done her own work. She went to market, basket on arm, to choose bargain buys. Always she kept a tight rein on the budget, so much for food, so much for rent. Even when the money rolled in, she continued to spend long hours in her kitchen.

She collected cookbooks and recipes. She was an ardent year-around canner. The jellies, jams, pickled fruit, and relishes that appeared on the Ford table were Clara's homemade specialties. Her green-tomato relish became a family tradition but this "Model Tea" wafer is the most esteemed hand-down in the Dearborn kitchen of the young Mrs. Henry Ford of this generation. Its method of making is easy, the results always exactly what they should be.

Model Teas

½ cup cake flour

¼ cup all-purpose flour

2 teaspoons baking powder

½ teaspoon salt

¾ cup wheat germ

2 tablespoons unsalted butter, chilled and cut into small dice

¼ cup ice water

Makes about 30 wafers

Preheat the oven to 325 degrees.

Sift the flours, baking powder, and salt into a large bowl. Add ½ cup of the wheat germ. Using your fingertips, 2 knives, or a pastry cutter, cut in the butter until the mixture resembles coarse meal with some pea-sized lumps. Add the water, blending well without too much handling. Turn the dough onto a floured surface and shape into a ball. Roll out lightly to about ½ inch thickness. Sprinkle the dough with the remaining ¼ cup wheat germ and continue to roll out the dough until it is wafer thin, keeping the wheat germ spread evenly over the top.

Cut out wafers with a 2-inch rectangular or square cutter. Place the wafers on ungreased baking sheets and bake for 12 to 15 minutes, until the wafers are lightly browned and crisp. Cool in the pans on wire racks for 2 minutes, then transfer to the racks to cool completely.

TWIN TABLES STRETCHED ACROSS the broad lawn of the farmhouse of apple grower Arnold Schaefer, Sr., in western Michigan. A sight to behold. Each table a plethora of delicacies, 120 different apple dishes made with the local apples—the Northern Spy, McIntosh, Jonathan, Delicious, and a few of the early Wealthy.

The occasion was the Annual Apple Smorgasbord prepared by the wives of the Peach Ridge Fruit Growers'

Association which has some 150 members. The orchards range in size from forty to four hundred acres, covering most of Kent and Ottawa Counties with a few in Muskegon.

Here came the women, their cars loaded with food in baskets—apple salad, apple meatloaf, apple bread, relishes, and desserts—each dish made by a favorite family recipe. While the ladies are at work, their menfolk are busy taking guests touring the orchards.

Once Peach Ridge was noted especially for its peaches, so the name. Now it has turned to raising apples— the little apple kingdom running eight miles long, four miles wide. The day of my visit, apples flamed the land, branches bent low with the weight of harvest.

The smorgasbord wasn't all. There were sampling booths set around the lawn where visitors could overeat before the real eating started. I tried the apple punch one, two, and three times. Next booth under the elms, four women— Mrs. Herbert Reister, a fruit grower's wife was chairman of the team—were all working furiously, frying apple fritters in deep-fat electric fryers. You could have your fritter plain or rolled in powdered sugar or in cinnamon-sugar. I milled through a flock of children to find the center of interest—a booth handing out candied caramel apples.

The long tables were made of planks laid over sawhorses covered with white wrapping paper. Baskets of autumn fruits were centered at intervals down the vast stretch.

Here are a few of the good things. I'm not saying the best—I didn't taste a fourth of the foods presented, for the choice was inexhaustible.

Applesauce Meatloaf

For the meatloaf:

1½ pounds ground meat, such as beef, pork, or veal, or a combination

2 large eggs, beaten

2 tablespoons chopped onion

2 teaspoons salt

½ teaspoon ground allspice

¾ cup rolled oats

1 cup strained applesauce

For the topping:

1 large red apple, peeled, cored, and cut into thin rings

¼ cup brown sugar

⅛ teaspoon ground cloves

1 tablespoon water

MICHIGAN

Serves 8

Preheat the oven to 350 degrees. Grease a 9 x 5 x 3-inch loaf pan. In a large bowl, combine all of the meatloaf ingredients. Pack firmly into the prepared pan. Press the apple rings into the top of the loaf. In a small bowl, make a glaze by whisking together the brown sugar, cloves, and water. Using a brush, glaze the top. Bake for 1 hour and 15 minutes, or until the glaze is browned and a meat thermometer inserted into the center of the loaf reads 160 degrees. Let stand for 5 minutes, then cut into slices and serve.

Apple Duffle

For the apple duffle:

2 cups sifted all-purpose flour

2½ teaspoons baking powder

¼ cup vegetable shortening

½ cup sugar

¼ teaspoon salt

1 large egg, beaten

1 cup milk

4 cups peeled, diced apples

For the crumb topping:

½ cup sugar

⅓ cup all-purpose flour

½ teaspoon ground cinnamon

4 tablespoons (½ stick) unsalted butter, chilled and cut into pieces

Serves 12

Preheat the oven to 350 degrees. Grease an 8 x 12-inch pan. Sift the flour and baking powder into a small bowl. In a medium bowl using an electric mixer, cream the shortening and sugar. Beat in the salt and egg, then beat in the flour alternately with the milk. Spread the batter into the prepared pan and completely cover the top with the apples.

Make the topping: In a medium bowl, combine the sugar, flour, and cinnamon. Using your fingertips, cut in the butter. Sprinkle the topping over the apples. Bake for 45 to 50 minutes, until the topping is browned. Serve with any favorite hard sauce, whipped cream, or ice cream.

OHIO

Ohio does more sophisticated eating than any other state in the United States outside California. Here I found much cooking with herbs, with wine. Restaurants in her larger cities can match our finest restaurants anywhere.

One of the state's glamorous eating places is the Gourmet Room, Terrace-Hilton Hotel in Cincinnati, a dining spot high in the sky. This is a fish-bowl room of circular construction, glass walled on three sides. Here the Caesar salad is made a big thing.

André Ballestra, manager of the restaurant, took my order and described the view. Over to the left he pointed out the downtown area of the city, a little to my right Mount Auburn, nudging Mount Adams, home of the Passionist Fathers and the famous Church of the Immaculate Conception. There at the far right one could see across the Ohio into Kentucky.

My host was saying, "But at night it's really beautiful, almost as beautiful, but in a different way, as the view from the Rainbow Room in New York City." André Ballestra should know. For eight years directly after he came from France to the United States, he worked in that famous room. He came to Cincinnati when the Terrace-Hilton opened in 1948.

The salad table rolled to my elbow with all the makings for the famous Caesar. André was telling me that there are as many Caesar salads as men who put them together. "But ours really works."

The ingredients are never mixed in advance—this salad must always be made at the table. Use one or more flavorsome greens, like romaine, endive, or escarole but no ordinary lettuce—that's too bland.

Gourmet's Caesar Salad

For the garlic oil:

1 cup olive oil

3 cloves garlic, smashed with
the side of a knife

For the croutons:

1 baguette, crust removed,
cut into 16 cubes

⅔ cup garlic oil (see above)

For the salad:

½ teaspoon salt, plus more to season
the salad

1 large clove garlic, cut in half

5 anchovy fillets, minced
(about 2 teaspoons)

Juice of 2 lemons (about ¼ cup)

5 drops Worcestershire sauce

2 large eggs, coddled for
2 to 3 minutes and cooled to
room temperature

⅓ cup garlic oil (see above left)

2 heads romaine lettuce

¼ cup finely grated Parmesan cheese

Freshly ground black pepper

Serves 4

To make the garlic oil: In a small bowl, combine the oil
and garlic and let it sit at room temperature for several
hours or overnight, then remove the garlic.

To make the croutons: Heat the ⅔ cup garlic oil in a
medium skillet over medium heat. Add the bread cubes
and fry them until well scented and golden, 5 to 7
minutes. Transfer the cubes to paper towels to drain.

To make the salad: Sprinkle the salt over the inside of a
wooden bowl. Rub with the cut clove of garlic. Add the
anchovies, lemon juice, Worcestershire sauce, and eggs,
stirring to combine, and then drizzle in the ⅓ cup garlic
oil. Blend with a whisk, breaking up the cooked egg
whites if chunky.

Break the heads of lettuce into 2-inch pieces and drop
them into the bowl. Add the cheese and croutons. Toss
to combine all of the ingredients and season with salt
and pepper.

I HAD PLANNED ALWAYS to go someday to France—the village of Issel, overlooking the Castelnaudary plain, and learn firsthand the way of making the *cassoulet*—a baked-bean dish. That's what it is, but a far-distant cousin to the one we call Boston. The fame of the *cassoulet* is to Castelnaudary as the gumbo file is to New Orleans, as sauerkraut to Milwaukee.

Here is the recipe. Guess where we found it. Not in Castelnaudary but in Cincinnati, Ohio. Inquiring for the names of good cooks around that city, I was told Mrs. George M. Guest, a doctor's wife, "does wonderful dishes with wine." Work takes the doctor to France frequently, and Mrs. Guest goes along.

Each trip she returns with some rare recipe in hand; a recent summer it was this *cassoulet* of Castelnaudary.

When Dr. Guest, a professor of pediatrics at the University of Cincinnati, introduced his bride to his friends, he said, "Meet M.L., she writes beautiful poetry but can't fry an egg."

A challenge to the bride. She started cooking next day and learned by the book. Evidence of her reading is a seven-shelf bookcase in her kitchen, crowded from floor to ceiling with the cookbooks of many nations; cookbooks old and cookbooks new. Her recipes she card-filed by subject—appetizers, soups, entrées—a third of these at least being French in their origin, wine- and herb-scented.

Cincinnati Cassoulet

1 pound dried kidney beans

1 medium onion, thinly sliced

4 slices bacon

Salt and freshly ground black pepper

½ pound sweet Italian sausage meat

1 pound boneless veal, cut into small pieces

2 cloves garlic, crushed

1 teaspoon minced parsley

½ teaspoon crushed fresh rosemary

1 cup dry red wine

Serves 6 to 8

Rinse the beans and soak them overnight in a large saucepan with enough water to cover. In the morning, remove the floaters, but do not drain the pot. Add the onion and bacon and season with salt and pepper. Add more water to cover if needed. Place over medium heat and bring to a boil, then reduce the heat to low, cover, and simmer for 1½ to 2 hours, until the beans are tender but not broken, stirring occasionally and adding water as needed.

Meanwhile, brown the sausage in a large skillet over medium-high heat, about 10 minutes. Remove the sausage and all but 2 tablespoons of fat from the pan. Add the veal to the skillet. Add the garlic, parsley, rosemary, and wine and season with salt and pepper. Reduce the heat to low, cover, and cook for about 1 hour, until the veal is tender and falling apart. Remove from the heat and reserve the veal.

Preheat the oven to 350 degrees. Grease a 3-quart Dutch oven or high-rimmed baking dish. Remove the pot from the heat. In the casserole, layer the beans and meat with the sauce, using 3 layers of beans and 2 layers of meat (combine the veal and sausage in 1 layer). Cover and bake for 1½ hours, removing cover during the last 30 minutes of baking to form a brown crust on top.

Tarragon Chicken

½ cup dry white wine

1 bunch minced fresh tarragon, or 2 teaspoons dried tarragon

1 cup all-purpose flour

Salt and freshly ground black pepper

1 (3- to 3½-pound) chicken, quartered

4 tablespoons (½ stick) unsalted butter

Serves 4

Preheat the oven to 375 degrees.

In a small bowl, combine the wine and tarragon and set aside. Pour the flour into a shallow dish, season with salt and pepper, and dredge the chicken pieces in the flour.

Melt 2 tablespoons of the butter in a large heavy-bottomed skillet over medium heat; add the chicken and brown lightly, about 10 minutes, turning occasionally. Drain the chicken on paper towels, then transfer to a roasting pan. Pour the tarragon-wine mixture over the chicken and dot the chicken pieces with the remaining 2 tablespoons butter. Cover tightly and bake for about 40 minutes, basting once or twice, until the chicken is tender and still moist and the wine sauce is bubbling. When serving, spoon the pan sauce over the chicken.

THE BAKING STARTS AT FOUR

The Virginia Bakery," I said, stepping into a taxi in downtown Cincinnati, Ohio.

"Okay, lady." The driver slammed the door and was off without waiting for the address.

"Oh, you know the place?" I asked him.

"Everybody here knows the Virginia, out on Ludlow near Clifton. Folks go there from all over just to get the Thies' coffee cakes.

"Grandma Thie is still on the job." The driver was one of those friendly talkative fellows. "There every day," he was saying. "She's along in her seventies and working hard as the young ones."

So that was the Virginia, all slick and shiny with glass cases and lighted signs shouting "Birthday Cake," "Wedding Cake," "Angel Food." Blue inlaid linoleum, smart leather davenport. I sat down there to look things over a minute before introducing myself.

It was mid-afternoon, supposedly the quiet hour, the noon rush over, and too early for the dinner stampede. But, good gracious, there were at least ten people in the place and four clerks busy. That small angular woman with the gray hair and blue-gray eyes, that would be Hattie Thie. She was greeting everyone, asking about family affairs, and "How is Mary's chicken pox?"

Across the counter there was a broad view into the open daylight cake shop where four bakers worked. Mrs. Thie spied me scribbling a note. "Are you that party from the paper?" she wanted to know. I nodded and she came from behind the counter, hand outstretched. "Let's go upstairs, I have my apartment there."

"It wasn't always like this," Mrs. Thie told me. "When we started here, it was just a little kitchen with one oven and one mixer. Now we have six bakers besides ourselves."

Over weekends, the baking starts at four on Friday morning, no stopping until six o'clock Saturday evening. Shoppers come from as far away as Dayton, Ohio, and from across-the-river Kentucky towns. In a year as many as 200,000 customers push in and out of the bakery door.

A vast collection of sweets but here are two coffee cakes Mrs. Thie claims Cincinnati loves best.

OHIO

"Bundkuchen"

1 envelope active dry yeast

1 cup plus 1 teaspoon sugar

½ cup warm, but not hot, water

1 cup warm milk

2 cups plus 6 tablespoons sifted all-purpose flour, plus more if needed

1 cup (2 sticks) unsalted butter, softened

⅛ teaspoon salt

12 large egg yolks

Thinly sliced almond halves

Makes one 9-inch tube cake

In a large bowl, dissolve the yeast and 1 teaspoon of the sugar in the warm water; let stand until the mixture bubbles, about 5 minutes. Add the warm milk and 2 cups of the flour and beat well. Lightly cover and let stand in a warm place until light and bubbly, about 2 hours.

Generously grease a 9-inch tube pan. In the large bowl of an electric mixer, cream the butter with the remaining 1 cup sugar until well blended and light yellow; add the salt. Then add the egg yolks, two at a time, beating well after each addition and adding 1 tablespoon of the flour between each addition of yolks. Pour in the yeast mixture and beat well. The dough should be stiff enough to hold a spoon upright. If necessary, add more flour. Line the prepared pan with as many almond halves as you like. Turn in the dough, cover loosely with plastic wrap, and let rise in a warm place until doubled in bulk, about 1 hour.

While the dough is rising, preheat the oven to 275 degrees. Place the dough in the oven and bake for about 1 hour and 45 minutes, until golden and a tester inserted in the center comes out clean. Cool the cake completely in the pan on a wire rack, then unmold and serve.

German Coffee Crumb Cake

For the cake:

1 envelope active dry yeast

½ cup warm but not hot water

4 cups all-purpose flour

1 cup milk

1½ cups (3 sticks) unsalted butter, melted and cooled

⅔ cup sugar

1 teaspoon salt

6 large egg yolks

For the streusel mixture:

2 cups all-purpose flour

¼ pound confectioners' sugar

¼ cup brown sugar

Pinch of salt

¼ teaspoon ground cinnamon

4 tablespoons (½ stick) unsalted butter, melted

¼ cup vegetable shortening, melted

Makes two 8-inch cakes

Grease two 8-inch square pans.

To make the cake: In a medium bowl, dissolve the yeast in the warm water and let sit until foamy, about 5 minutes. Sift 2 cups of the flour into a large bowl. In a small saucepan, bring the milk just to the boiling point over medium heat; remove from the heat immediately and cool for about 10 minutes. Make a well in the flour and pour in the milk along with the dissolved yeast and stir into a smooth batter. Cover loosely with plastic wrap and let rise in warm place until doubled in bulk, 1½ to 2 hours.

Using a rubber spatula or wooden spoon, add the melted and cooled butter, the sugar, salt, and egg yolks. Stir in the remaining 2 cups flour until well blended. Divide the dough into the prepared pans. Cover loosely with plastic wrap and let rise in a warm place until doubled in bulk, 1½ to 2 hours.

While the dough is rising, preheat the oven to 325 degrees.

Make the streusel: Sift the flour, confectioners' sugar, brown sugar, salt, and cinnamon into a large bowl. Stir in 3 tablespoons of the melted butter and the shortening until little balls or crumbs are formed and sprinkle

OHIO

over the cakes. Sprinkle the cakes with the remaining 1 tablespoon melted butter and cover with the streusel mixture. Bake for about 25 minutes, until the tops are golden. Cool the cakes completely in their pans on wire racks, then cut into squares.

Note: German butter cake is made with the same basic dough but without the crumb mixture. Instead, sprinkle the cakes with melted butter, then drop lumps of butter over the surface of the batter and lightly cover with powdered sugar. Let stand until the batter rises, 1½ to 2 hours. Bake at 350 degrees for 25 minutes.

THE SUN GREW PALE as a frosted penny; slowly the color drained out of the western sky. Mist came creeping across the Ohio River from the low-curved Kentucky hills. I was the tea-time guest of Mrs. Horace F. Tangeman in her fire-lit living room on Tusculum Avenue. This is a section of Cincinnati once a part of the great vineyards of Nicholas Longworth, eulogized, you may remember, by Henry Wadsworth Longfellow.

Mrs. Tangeman was saying, "These cookies are left from my Christmas baking. I make twenty-nine kinds of German sweet stuffs and keep each in a box to itself and the boxes are always filled, winter and summer."

Early November Mrs. Tangeman starts making the cookies for the Christmas giving—the cinnamon stars, the vanilla *kipfel,* the linzertorte, the *spitzbuben,* and more and still more. Her recipes are collected from family cookbooks, from friends, and the very best ones came from Grandma Louise Rodenberg's kitchen across the Ohio in Alexandria, Kentucky.

Some are taken from a collection of more than two hundred cookbooks. Mrs. Tangeman brought in her loose-leaf notebook of cookie and cake recipes. Remember this, she warned, wherever nuts are called for, always grind them a day in advance to help get out the oiliness. One more bit of advice: store the cookies in the refrigerator, each kind to itself in a tight-lidded tin to retain the fresh, delicate flavor.

Vanilla "Kipfel"

½ cup (1 stick) unsalted butter, softened

¼ cup sugar

½ teaspoon salt

1 cup sifted all-purpose flour

1 cup ground almonds

½ cup confectioners' sugar

⅛ teaspoon vanilla bean pulp

Makes about 3 dozen crescents

In a large bowl using a handheld mixer, cream the butter, sugar, and salt. Add the flour, a little at a time, stirring it in thoroughly. Add the almonds. Cover loosely with plastic wrap and refrigerate until the batter is chilled, about 30 minutes.

Preheat the oven to 400 degrees. Generously grease 2 large baking sheets.

Remove the batter from the refrigerator and scoop out 1 teaspoonful at a time, roll in the palm of your hand to a fat coil, then bend the ends to form a crescent. Lay the crescents in rows on the prepared sheets. Bake for 2 minutes, then reduce the oven temperature to 300 degrees and bake for about 10 minutes longer, until the cookies are a pale yellow color. Let cool on the sheets for 2 minutes, then transfer the cookies to wire racks to cool slightly.

In a shallow dish, combine the confectioners' sugar with the vanilla bean pulp. When the cookies are cool enough to handle but still warm, roll them in the sugar mixture.

OHIO

Grandmother Tangeman's Meringue Thumbprint Cookies

1 cup (2 sticks) unsalted butter, softened

2 cups sugar

6 large eggs, separated

2 cups all-purpose flour

1 teaspoon baking powder

2 cups blanched almonds, thinly sliced

¼ cup currant jelly

Makes about 5 dozen cookies

In a large bowl using a handheld electric mixer, cream the butter with ½ cup of the sugar. Beat in the egg yolks. Sift the flour and baking powder into a medium bowl and add to the egg-butter mixture, stirring in a little at a time. Cover the dough loosely with plastic wrap and refrigerate for about 1 hour, until firm enough to roll out (very important).

Preheat the oven to 425 degrees. Generously grease 2 large baking sheets.

In a medium bowl using a handheld electric mixer, beat the egg whites until they form stiff but not dry peaks, then fold in remaining 1½ cups sugar. Take a small piece of dough from the refrigerator—one piece at a time, as the dough is hard to handle when soft. Turn onto a floured kitchen towel and, using a well-floured rolling pin, roll out ¼ inch thick. Using a floured favorite cookie cutter (Mrs. Tangeman prefers the diamond shape), cut out cookies and transfer to the prepared pans. To each diamond add 2 teaspoons meringue, sprinkle with the almonds, and make a slight indentation in the center of the meringue with your thumb. Bake the cookies for 5 to 7 minutes, until the meringue begins to brown, then reduce the oven temperature to 300 degrees and bake for 5 to 10 minutes more to set the meringue. Let the cookies cool on the sheets for 2 minutes, then transfer to wire racks to cool completely. Spoon a dab of jelly in the indented center of each cookie.

IT'S ONE THING TO have a green thumb, but to have a green thumb for growing "green enchantment" ensures long hours of happiness. Mrs. Harold F. Downing of Lebanon, Ohio, wife of a pediatrician, has a talent for the growing of herbs, and something more, cooking with herbs has become her special art.

Ruth Downing told me that, in the State of Ohio, Grandmother's herb patch has staged a remarkable comeback. She didn't tell me, but her friends did, that much of the credit for this herbal renaissance is due to Ruth's work. She was one of the first to take her herb garden seriously; one of the first to put herbs to work in everyday cooking.

I made a surprise visit to the Downing farm one drizzly March morning. Ruth had just come in from an hour of fishing in the farm pond. Bluegills were in the creel; fish stew for dinner.

Downing Farm Fish Stew

2 cups water

2 cups white wine

½ lemon, sliced

2 sprigs parsley

1 tablespoon salt

¼ teaspoon freshly ground black pepper

2 raw shelled lobster tails

2 pounds shrimp, peeled and deveined

3 pounds red snapper fillets

4 tablespoons (½ stick) unsalted butter

4 medium onions, finely chopped

1 small green bell pepper, cored, seeded, and finely chopped

1 tablespoon minced parsley

2 cloves garlic, minced

½ teaspoon crushed red pepper

2 tablespoons all-purpose flour

3 pounds boned bluegill fish (5 to 6 fish; also called "bream"; sunfish and yellow perch may be substituted)

2 (12-ounce) packages frozen oysters

1 tablespoon saffron threads

OHIO

Serves 6 to 8

In a large heavy stockpot, combine the water, wine, lemon, parsley, salt, and pepper. Place over medium heat and bring to a boil. Add the lobster tails, cover, and simmer for 7 to 8 minutes, until tender, adding the shrimp during the last 3 minutes of cooking. Remove the lobster and shrimp to a bowl. Cut the lobster meat into large pieces, return to the bowl with the shrimp, and loosely cover. Add the red snapper to the stock, cover, and simmer for 5 to 7 minutes, until tender. Remove the fish from the stock to the bowl with the lobster and shrimp. Strain the fish stock and reserve it.

Melt the butter in large heavy skillet over medium heat; add the onions, green pepper, parsley, garlic, and crushed red pepper and sauté until the onions and green pepper are tender but not browned, about 4 minutes.

In a bowl, blend the flour with ¼ cup of the fish stock to make a paste; add the paste to the stock and pour it into the skillet. Cook over medium heat, stirring constantly, until thickened, 3 to 5 minutes. Add the bluegill and oysters and simmer for 3 to 5 minutes, until the bluegill are tender and the oysters are plump. Add the reserved lobster, shrimp, and red snapper and cook for 1 minute longer, until the fish is heated through. Stir in the saffron. Serve immediately with hot garlic bread and a green salad.

POETRY OF THE OLD WORLD

Middle West women have a reputation for their church suppers. The best I ever ate was dished up in Ohio, a Hungarian dinner cooked by the women of the Magyar Evangelical and Reformed Church on West River Street in Elyria. This is an industrial town; some ninety factories are busy here. The population of 36,000 is made up of many foreign groups, but Hungarians predominate.

Life for them centers around their church, especially so since 1939 when the Reverend Louis Novak and his young wife Irene came to the parsonage. The Novaks, second-generation Hungarians, sensed a need among their people to keep the best of the old in their cultural background to blend with the best of the new in their adopted America. Gifts brought from the Old World must not be lost. Through the activities of the church, the Novaks tried to preserve the poetry of the Old World, its folklore, the love of the dance.

It was the women of the church who said, ". . . and the cuisine of our native Hungary is as important as its music." No festival or holiday is complete without the traditional dishes. These women wanted their daughters, who were beginning to be real American girls, to inherit their own talent as cooks. So it was that whenever a community supper or picnic was in the making, the foods were prepared the Hungarian way.

Outsiders began to hear of this fabulous eating—they wanted to come. Eventually organizations planning get-togethers would ask one of the nine Magyar Women's Guilds to prepare a chicken paprika dinner. The church needed many things and the women saw a way to help earn the needed money. They charged $2.50 a plate and served the dinner family style. This dinner is always the same, that is, until you come to dessert—then it's take your choice among the many pastries. Each woman contributes the thing that she does best, baking at home and donating the product.

Guests began coming from all directions, from Oberlin College seven miles away, they came from Cleveland and from local towns.

I had written to the Dorcas Guild and asked if they would let me know when a supper was on the calendar—I would like to visit and come early to see the dishes made. Instead I was invited as the honored guest, supper prepared just for me.

Mrs. Alex Miko was making *palacsintas*. She smiled and I smiled, as she deftly flipped a big thin pancake to the work board. Mrs. Grace Ballas laid on the filling of sweetened cottage cheese, then rolled the golden, brown-spotted pancake. The rolls she arranged in glass pie plates to be sauced later with sour cream, then into the oven until heated through all-a-bubble, that was a main-course dish that I mistook for dessert and had two helpings!

Mrs. Al Wyszynski was making the tiny dumplings, the *nokedli* to go with the chicken *paprikas*. Mrs. Mary Messaros was busy with the sour-cream gravy. Mrs. Louis Ignatz stuffed the cabbage leaves and showed me how the ends can be tightly closed to prevent a leakage, all without string or toothpicks.

Three girls from the Youth Fellowship group served the supper, a sit-down meal for thirty guests. After the grace, chicken *paprikas* arrived. The chicken was cooked tender but not overdone and delicate the dumplings. Pass the chicken gravy to spoon over the *nokedli* and cabbage meat-stuffed, the big pancakes, the sour-cream sauce delicious.

Then dinner was over, and came the surprise. The table was seven feet long and four feet wide and every square inch a maze of sweetness. I counted twenty-three desserts, each one made with loving care just for me to taste. The bakers were there, all twenty-three of them to see that I tasted, to watch while I sampled, ears cocked for praise.

First I forked into a slice of poppy-seed cake, next a long strip of strudel; the tortes followed, three kinds in a row. There were the celestial crusts, the open-face cheese cakes. I was unprepared for this super-abundance of richness.

"Palacsintas"

For the cottage cheese filling:

1 pound dry cottage cheese or farmer's cheese

1 large egg, well beaten

¼ cup sugar

¼ teaspoon vanilla extract

For the pancakes:

2 cups sifted all-purpose flour

2 teaspoons granulated sugar

1 teaspoon salt

4 large eggs

2 cups milk

2 tablespoons unsalted butter

Confectioners' sugar

Sour cream for serving

Preserves for serving

Makes 24 pancakes

To make the cheese filling: In a small bowl, combine all of the filling ingredients and set aside while you make the pancakes.

Preheat the oven to 300 degrees. Grease a large shallow baking dish.

In a large bowl, combine the flour, granulated sugar, and salt. In a small bowl, beat the eggs with the milk. Make a well in the flour and gradually pour in the milk mixture, beating to form a smooth batter without lumps; the batter should be very thin, about the consistency of heavy cream.

Heat a 6- to 7-inch skillet over medium heat and melt the butter. Spoon 3 tablespoons of batter onto the hot greased skillet, tilting the pan so the batter is distributed to the edges (the pancakes will be very thin). Brown lightly on both sides; you know it's time to flip the pancakes when the edges begin to brown, about 45 seconds on the first side and 15 to 30 seconds on the flipside. Continue making pancakes until the batter is used up.

Stack the finished pancakes on a warm plate, spread with the cottage-cheese filling, and roll them up. Place them in the prepared dish and sprinkle with confectioners' sugar. Place in the oven and heat through, about 10 minutes, until the filling is bubbly. Serve topped with sour cream and preserves.

Stuffed Cabbage

1 large head cabbage
(about 3½ pounds)

3 tablespoons vegetable shortening

1 large onion, minced

¾ pound ground pork

¾ pound ground beef

2 tablespoons salt

1 tablespoon sweet paprika

1 teaspoon freshly ground
black pepper

¾ pound uncooked rice, washed well

1 (15-ounce) can sauerkraut

1 (12-ounce) can tomato juice

1 cup sour cream, optional

OHIO

Serves 6

Bring a large saucepan of water to a boil. Remove any damaged outer leaves from the cabbage. With a sharp knife, core the cabbage, cutting a hole at least 1 inch wide and 1 inch deep. Place the cabbage in the saucepan, cored end down, and boil for 12 minutes, until the cabbage is crisp-tender and wilted but not overly soft. Transfer the cabbage to a large bowl of ice water and shock briefly to keep it from become mushy. Carefully peel off as many softened leaves as you can without tearing them; you need about 16 whole leaves. With a sharp knife, trim the thick center vein of each cabbage leaf.

Melt the shortening in a large skillet or saucepan over medium heat. Add the onion and sauté until browned, about 7 minutes. Add the pork, beef, salt, paprika, pepper, and rice, mix well, and cook until heated through, 2 to 3 minutes. Remove the seasoned mixture from the heat and cool slightly.

Place a heaping tablespoon of filling on each cabbage leaf; roll up by folding the rib end of each leaf up over the stuffing and then folding the top of the leaf down over it. Using both index fingers, tuck in the ends of each cabbage roll to form a packet. Lay the cabbage packets into a large casserole, arrange the sauerkraut over it, and pour the tomato juice on the top. Cover, place over low heat, and cook for about 1 hour, until the cabbage packets are soft and tender and the sauerkraut and tomato juice have formed a thick sauce. Ladle into soup bowls and pass with the sour cream, if you like, or pour the sour cream over the top and cook for 5 minutes more to melt it, then ladle and serve.

Chicken "Paprikas"

3 pounds bone-in, skin-on chicken pieces

1 tablespoon salt, plus more for seasoning the chicken

1 teaspoon freshly ground black pepper, plus more for seasoning the chicken

¼ cup vegetable shortening

1 onion, chopped

1 tablespoon sweet Hungarian paprika

1½ cups chicken stock or water

1 cup sour cream

1 cup half-and-half, optional

Serves 4

Pat the chicken pieces dry with paper towels and season with salt and pepper. Heat the shortening in a Dutch oven over medium-high heat and brown the onion, about 5 minutes. Add the paprika, salt, and pepper. Add the chicken pieces and brown on both sides, about 10 minutes total. Transfer the chicken to paper towels to drain and cool. Slowly pour the stock into the pan, stirring with a wooden spoon to scrape up any browned bits in the bottom of the pan, and bring to a boil. When the chicken is cool enough to handle, remove the skin (which becomes rubbery when braised). Add the chicken to the pan, reduce the heat to low, cover, and simmer until the chicken is tender, 20 to 25 minutes. Remove the pan from the heat and stir in the sour cream. If more gravy is desired, add the half-and-half. Serve ladled over the dumplings (recipe follows), if you like.

Dumplings "Nokedli"

3 large eggs, beaten

½ cup water

2½ cups all-purpose flour, plus more if needed

2 teaspoons salt

Makes about 1 dozen dumplings

OHIO

In a large bowl, beat the eggs with the water. Add the flour and salt and stir to make a stiff batter, adding more flour if necessary. Drop by tablespoonfuls into a pot of boiling salted water. Reduce the heat to a simmer and cook the dumplings until puffed and cooked through, about 10 minutes. Drain the dumplings in a colander and rinse with cold water. Add to any favorite soup or stew.

"WURST" HUNGRY

If you are "wurst" hungry, be it for *mettwurst*, or *Bratwurst*, or *blutwurst*, Cleveland's the town. If you have a palate for the flavor of pigs' knuckles with sauerkraut, for cider-cured *hasenpfeffer*, for *Koenigsberger klops*, Cleveland's the town.

Gruber's, I had been told, was a German restaurant, a landmark of old Cleveland. Today there is no smarter place to dine in or around the city, but the menu reads French except for one item—there it is, under the appetizers, a true German dish. What's more, to the Gruber brothers' amazement, a very best seller.

"Try an order of our sauerkraut balls," an old-school German waiter said softly in my ear. Then Max Gruber told me the story of the great "little" favorite. The Gruber brothers are lawyers and this restaurant is a side business just to keep the family name in the restaurant world. Modern Gruber's has nothing but name in common with the old place downtown. Here there is Continental dining leaning heavily toward the French. And Cleveland approves. On Saturday nights often several hundred people are turned away and the place is no pocket patch either, having a seating capacity for three hundred guests.

It was old customers who started asking for those sauerkraut balls "like your father used to serve."

The chef decided to give them a trial. He prepared a few dozen one evening to pass at the bar and repeat orders followed. Sauerkraut balls disappeared as dew before the sun. Now their making is a major daily production.

Patrons, two out of three, order this treat. Cleveland at heart is true to its German traditions.

Sauerkraut Meatballs

1½ tablespoons vegetable shortening

½ medium onion

½ teaspoon minced parsley

½ pound ground lean pork

¼ pound ground beef

1 cup all-purpose flour

1 teaspoon dry mustard

1 teaspoon salt

1 cup milk

1 pound sauerkraut, drained

1 large egg, lightly beaten

1 cup dry breadcrumbs

Vegetable oil for frying

Makes about 4 dozen meatballs

Melt the shortening in a large heavy skillet over medium heat. Add the onion and sauté until soft and translucent, 3 to 5 minutes. Add the parsley, pork, and beef and brown the meat, 8 to 10 minutes. Add the flour, mustard, salt, and milk. Cook, stirring constantly, until thick, 5 to 7 minutes. Add the sauerkraut and cook for 2 more minutes to combine. Puree the mixture in batches in a blender or food processor until smooth. Return the mixture to the skillet and cook over medium heat, stirring constantly, until very thick, about 7 minutes. Pour the mixture into a bowl, cool to room temperature, then cover with plastic wrap and refrigerate for 1 hour to chill.

Form the mixture into tablespoon-size balls, dip each one in the egg, and roll in the breadcrumbs. Pour vegetable oil to the depth of ¼ inch in the skillet and heat to 370 degrees. Fry the meatballs in batches until browned on all sides, turning carefully with a fork or spatula, about 5 minutes. Transfer to paper towels to drain. Serve hot speared onto toothpicks, as an appetizer or hors d'oeuvre.

OHIO

MRS. STANLEY H. WATSON of South Park Street in Cleveland is typical of the sophisticated middle western hostesses who entertain with great ease. The logs crackled and snapped in the big fireplace and we settled down to tea and talk.

Mrs. Watson told me she loves entertaining: teas, cocktail parties, barbecues for small groups of twelve to twenty. In winter her parties are most often midnight buffets given after concerts.

Here is one of her many clever ideas. Take a No. 2½ tin of baby beets, drain off the juice, and soak the beets in herb-tinctured vinegar. Before serving, drain and stick a toothpick into each. These are arranged around a bowl of sour cream well seasoned with curry, with a dash of grated horseradish, with salt and pepper to taste. The eater dunks the beet into the sauce, into the mouth. These miniatures average about forty marble-size beets to a can.

This liver spread, Mrs. Watson said, was a favorite with her crowd, never a smitch left. Take one pound chicken livers and drop into boiling water one minute. Slice two onions; sauté in butter until golden. Onions and livers are put into a wooden bowl along with three hard-cooked, shelled eggs and four tablespoons of chopped parsley, and the whole mixture finely chopped. If the spread seems dry, add olive oil or butter and a splash of brandy. This tastes best spread on rye bread triangles or on crisp little crackers.

Let the applause go to this Watson luncheon menu. The main dish is a noodle and cottage cheese casserole to serve with baked Canadian bacon and a sweet pickled-fruit relish. A tart green salad to follow and pears baked in wine sauce for the dessert.

A buffet menu Mary Watson suggests for summer is roast beef, cold, or ham with asparagus Caesar (recipe follows), a green salad, and a Watson version of cherries jubilee, meaning cherries in frost instead of flame.

About the cherries first: take a large tin of the Bings and turn into the freezing tray of the refrigerator. Freeze until the syrup gets mushy. Then dip cherries into dessert dishes, and dollop with whipped cream, using about three-fourths cup for four portions and adding to this one jigger of brandy—no more.

Roasted Asparagus Caesar

2½ pounds white asparagus, peeled (or substitute green asparagus)

½ cup (1 stick) unsalted butter, melted

3 tablespoons lemon juice

Dash of sweet paprika

½ cup grated Parmesan cheese

Serves 4 to 6

Preheat the oven to 400 degrees. Grease a large flat-bottomed shallow casserole or rimmed baking dish.

Lay the asparagus in 1 layer in the prepared dish. Pour the melted butter over the asparagus, drizzle over the lemon juice, and sprinkle with the paprika and cheese. Bake for 15 minutes, or until the asparagus is crisp and charred in spots. Serve warm.

Creamy Copy-Cat Noodle Casserole

1 pound medium egg noodles

1 pound cottage cheese

2 cups sour cream

1 small onion, grated

2 teaspoons salt

¼ teaspoon freshly ground black pepper

Dash of cayenne pepper

OHIO

Serves 8 to 10

Preheat the oven to 350 degrees. Generously grease a 2½-quart casserole dish.

Cook the noodles in a large pot of boiling water until tender, 7 to 8 minutes. Drain in a colander and rinse with cold water. Transfer to a large bowl.

In a blender or food processer, combine the remaining ingredients and puree them. Pour over the noodles and toss to coat. Pour into the prepared casserole dish and bake for 30 to 45 minutes, stirring the mixture about halfway through, until the top is nicely browned and the casserole is bubbling. Let rest for 15 minutes before serving.

IN A TAILORED BLUE SATIN SUIT

I taxied nine miles to west-side Cleveland to find the modest little home of Mrs. Anthony J. Celebrezze, first lady of the city. The Mayor's wife answered my ring dressed in a tailored blue satin suit. It was ten o'clock in the morning.

"I'm ready for a luncheon," she explained her dressed-up appearance. "We will talk first, then I'll drive you back to town." She had finished her morning chores. Everything about the house was clean as a freshly washed dinner plate. She had baked whole-wheat bread, its fragrance was everywhere. Luncheon for the children was ready waiting in the refrigerator, a heat-and-eat meal. The evening dinner was planned.

The telephone rang. Mrs. Celebrezze sighed. "It seems to ring all the time."

Anthony Celebrezze was Cleveland's first foreign-born mayor. The other thirty-nine were native Americans, so Anne Celebrezze was telling me, ". . . but my husband missed being American-born by only two years, his family coming here in 1912."

"You live a long way from Main Street," I said to my hostess.

"We've owned this home now for twelve years," she explained, "and we like living here. Seven rooms, besides the basement. These are our children." She showed me a picture album—Anthony, Jr., Jean Anne, Susan Marie.

The Celebrezzes are first-generation Americans and their table features all American food except for a now-and-then Italian dinner and certain Old-World holiday dishes beloved by the Mayor.

Mrs. Celebrezze was Anne Marco who learned cooking from her mother. One of the best of her recipes is this ravioli. She makes the stuffed dough cushions big, with a generous filling. A dozen pieces are allowed to a serving when ravioli is the main dish; six pieces are enough, she said, when used as a course between soup and meat. The fillings can be varied but the Celebrezzes prefer ricotta cheese with freshly grated Parmesan.

Ravioli

For the ravioli:

6 cups all-purpose flour

¾ teaspoon salt

4 large eggs

1 cup warm water

Grated Parmesan cheese for serving

Tomato Sauce (page 94) for serving

For the filling:

1 pound ricotta cheese

2 large eggs, lightly beaten

½ cup grated Parmesan cheese

1 tablespoon finely chopped parsley

Salt and freshly ground black pepper

Makes about 4 dozen ravioli

To make the ravioli: Sift the flour and salt into a large bowl. Make a well in the mound, crack in the eggs, and combine lightly with your fingertips. Then mix the eggs into the flour with a folding-in-and-lifting motion of the hands until they are well absorbed. Gradually add the warm water and start shaping the dough into a large ball. Knead the dough just 3 or 4 turns, adding a little more water if it seems too dry. (Alternatively, you can make the dough in a food processor: First pulse the flour with the salt, then add the eggs and pulse until incorporated, then turn out and form a ball and continue with the rest of the steps.) Cover the bowl loosely with greased plastic wrap and let rest at room temperature for 30 minutes.

Meanwhile, make the filling: In a large bowl, break up and mash the ricotta with a fork. Add the remaining ingredients and mix until smooth.

Cut the dough into 4 equal pieces and cover with plastic wrap. Work with 1 piece at a time: Flatten the dough into a 5 x 4-inch oval about ½ inch thick. Roll the dough through a hand-cranked pasta machine at the widest setting. Fold the dough in thirds (like a letter), then run it through the machine at the same setting, folded edge first. Repeat the folding and rolling once more. Roll the dough through at successively narrower settings, two times per setting, until it is thin enough for you to see the outline of your hand through it. Lay the dough out on a lightly floured work surface.

OHIO

Drop teaspoonfuls of the filling about 2 inches apart on half of the dough. Cover with the other half. Using your fingertips, gently press around each mound of filling to form little filled squares. Cut the squares apart with a pastry wheel. Cook by dropping the squares into a very large pot of boiling salted water. Ravioli must have ample room so they can be stirred occasionally while they are boiling. The water will stop boiling for a little while when the squares are dropped in, but stir anyway so they will not settle in the pan. After the water comes back to a boil, continue to stir occasionally and cook until desired tenderness is reached, 3 to 5 minutes. Drain and place one at a time on a serving platter; sprinkle each layer with cheese and cover with tomato sauce.

Zucchini Squash and Tomatoes with Egg and Cheese Dumplings

2 tablespoons olive oil

½ small onion, chopped

4 or 5 large fresh tomatoes, coarsely chopped

Salt and freshly ground black pepper

2 leaves basil

1 large or 2 small zucchini, peeled and cut into ½-inch cubes

1 large egg, lightly beaten

1 cup finely grated Parmesan cheese

Serves 4

Heat the oil in a large skillet over medium heat. Add the onion and sauté until softened and just beginning to brown, about 6 minutes. Add the tomatoes and season with salt and pepper. Add the basil. Cover, reduce the heat slightly, and simmer for about 20 minutes, until well combined and saucy. Add the zucchini and continue to simmer until it is transparent and tender, about 15 minutes more.

While the squash is simmering, prepare the dumplings:
In a large bowl, combine the egg with the cheese. Season
with pepper. When the squash has finished cooking,
drop the batter by tablespoonfuls (there should be about
12) onto the hot cooked zucchini and tomato mixture.
Cover and simmer until the dumplings are firm, about
5 minutes. Serve hot.

SOME OF THE FINEST, the richest baking in the world is done in Jewish home kitchens for the feast days. When I learned that Mrs. Norman Less, of Cleveland, was one of the excellent "old-school" pastry bakers, I invited myself for coffee and cake.

"The *Hamantaschen*," said my hostess, passing a plate of three-cornered turnovers puffy with a stuffing of finely ground poppy seeds, "are traditional for Purim, but we like them just any time—for the Sabbath dinner, a bridge-club supper, and whenever the grandchildren are coming to call."

"Funny little things," I said, biting into a pastry. "I like the surprise in the middle," she said.

"Try another one," Mrs Less urged. "This one has an apricot filling."

Mrs. Less bakes these sweets on a moment's notice, keeping always a quantity of the pastry on hand in the refrigerator along with jars of the fillings.

"Hamantaschen"

For the dough:

2½ cups sifted all-purpose flour

½ teaspoon salt

1 cup (2 sticks) unsalted butter, at room temperature

3 large egg yolks

½ cup sugar

3 tablespoons distilled vinegar

3 tablespoons cold water

For the poppy-seed filling:

¾ cup ground or whole poppy seeds

½ cup milk

¼ cup honey

2 tablespoons chopped pecans

2 tablespoons sugar

⅛ teaspoon ground cinnamon

For the apricot filling:

1 cup dried apricots

¾ cup water

¾ cup sugar

Makes about 25 cookies

To make the dough: In a medium bowl, combine 1½ cups of the flour with the salt. Add the butter and rub it into the flour with your fingers. In a separate bowl, mix the egg yolks and sugar with a fork. Add the vinegar and water. Sift the remaining 1 cup flour into the egg mixture, mixing together lightly. Combine the 2 mixtures and blend well with a fork. Cover and refrigerate for at least 6 hours or overnight. When ready to use, the dough will be sticky; work quickly while it is cold.

Meanwhile, make the filling. For the poppy-seed filling, place the seeds in a fine strainer and run water through it again and again; if using whole poppy seeds, grind in a coffee grinder. Place in the top portion of a double boiler with the milk and cook over hot water until all of the milk is absorbed, 10 to 15 minutes; the filling should thicken considerably. Add the honey, pecans, sugar, and cinnamon and cook for about 4 minutes, stirring until the sugar is dissolved and the honey is blended. Cool, cover, and store in the refrigerator until ready to use.

For the apricot filling, wash the apricots and coarsely chop them. Place them in a small saucepan, add the water, and cook over low heat until very soft, about 7 minutes, adding more water if necessary. Add the sugar and heat, stirring constantly, until the fruit comes to a boil, about 12 minutes. Cool, cover, and store in the refrigerator until ready to use.

Preheat the oven to 400 degrees.

To form the *hamantaschen*, pick off dough the size of a walnut and roll on a well-floured surface into a 3¼-inch round. Place a level teaspoonful of filling in the center. Pinch the sides together, forming a closed triangle over the filling. Cut the pinched edges about ¼ inch deep at ½-inch intervals to give a scalloped top when baked. Place on an ungreased baking sheet and bake for 20 minutes, or until browned.

Note: The fillings make 2 cups, more than enough for the 25 turnovers in the pastry recipe. You can use either of the remaining fillings as a substitute for prune puree in any recipe in this book. The poppy filling will keep for 3 days in the refrigerator and the apricot for 2 weeks.

OHIO

MRS. GUY ROCKWELL WAS up to her elbows in party preparations the Saturday morning I rang the doorbell of her comfortable colonial home on Farmington Road, East Cleveland. Five couples were coming for dinner.

"I'm busy," she said, "but come in— we can talk while I work."

It's a sit-down dinner Mrs. Rockwell likes best. Her dining-room table pulls out to seat twelve, then after dinner three tables for bridge. The Saturday I was there the menu included tomato-juice cocktails with baked Cheddar-cheese balls, a new idea then, and going great guns.

The main course was pork tenderloin with mushroom sauce, candied sweet potatoes, Brussels sprouts, brown-and-serve rolls. No salad, instead a relish tray of celery, green and black olives, pickles and jelly.

Dessert is important at these mixed parties; men like something rich and filling, Mrs. Rockwell explained, and opened the refrigerator to show me her fresh coconut mold, this to be served with a caramel sauce. It looked wonderful; it tasted still better.

Mrs. Rockwell showed us the cheese balls chilling for last-minute baking. The recipe calls for one-eighth pound of butter or margarine brought to room temperature, blended with a six-ounce crock of a neutral sharp Cheddar spread, or you could use the bacon-Cheddar spread that is around in the markets. Into the cheese add butter, work in three-fourths cup of all-purpose flour, form the mixture into balls to refrigerate several hours. Just before serving, into a hot oven for 10 minutes' baking. Serve piping hot. Crusty on the outside, soft within. Don't burn your tongue!

At luncheon parties and no men to consider, Mrs. Rockwell dispenses with dessert, serves fruit salad instead. The luncheon dish she prefers above all others is a cheese fondue to pass with hot rolls, then the salad with a French dressing a little on the sweet side.

Chilled Coconut Cream with Caramel Sauce

For the coconut cream:

1 (¼-ounce) envelope unflavored gelatin

¼ cup cold water

1 cup milk

1 cup sugar

2 cups heavy cream, whipped to stiff peaks

2 teaspoons vanilla extract

2 cups grated unsweetened coconut

For the caramel sauce:

2 cups brown sugar

1 cup half-and-half

1 tablespoon unsalted butter

½ cup chopped nuts, such as walnuts, pecans, or peanuts

Serves 6

In a small bowl, dissolve the gelatin in the cold water. In a medium saucepan, bring the milk to a boil over medium-low heat. Whisk in the gelatin and sugar. Let stand to cool and slightly thicken, 10 to 15 minutes. When gelatin mixture begins to set, fold in the whipped cream and vanilla, then fold in the coconut. Place in a mold or bowl, cover tightly with plastic wrap, and refrigerate overnight.

Meanwhile, make the caramel sauce: Combine the brown sugar, half-and-half, and butter in a medium heavy saucepan and place over low heat. Cook for about 5 minutes, stirring constantly, until the sauce is syrupy and smooth.

Serve the coconut cream in chilled bowls topped with warm caramel sauce.

Cheese Fondue Soufflé

1 cup milk

¼ pound sharp cheddar cheese, diced

1 cup soft breadcrumbs

1 teaspoon unsalted butter

½ teaspoon salt

3 large eggs, separated and yolks lightly beaten

Serves 4

Preheat the oven to 350 degrees. Grease a deep 1½-quart casserole or other deep baking or soufflé dish.

Bring the milk to a boil in a large heavy saucepan over medium heat. As soon as the milk begins to boil, turn the heat down to low. Add the cheese and stir constantly to melt. Add the breadcrumbs, butter, salt, and beaten egg yolks to the mixture. Remove from the heat and let cool slightly. In a medium bowl, beat the egg whites until stiff peaks form. Fold into the melted cheese mixture. Pour into the prepared casserole, set the casserole in a roasting pan, and pour in enough hot water to come halfway up the sides. Bake for 50 minutes, or until the casserole is puffed and browned and a knife inserted into the soufflé comes out clean.

OHIO

INDIANA

It's "punkin" time in Indiana; it's "punkin" pie de luxe in the Hawthorn Room, Indianapolis. Hawthorn is the tree of the state, pumpkin its most important vegetable, and pumpkin pie its most renowned dessert. To eat pumpkin pie at the Hawthorn Room, I made a 250-mile detour from Detroit to Indianapolis en route to New York.

The Hawthorn is a brag place with the Hoosiers who claim it can equal best eating anywhere. The chicken I ate there was done to perfection in Midwest style; the mashed potatoes were whipped to snowy lightness; not a lump in the milk gravy made in the pan in which the chicken was fried. The butterscotch rolls can be described in three little words—yum, yum, yum. But "big punkin" on the menu was the "punkin" pie, tasting even finer than the sour-cream raisin. Pumpkin pie feasting here keeps going long past the season, right into the spring.

Hoosier "Punkin" Pie

1 (8-inch) Perfect Pie Crust (page 13)

1½ cups canned or fresh pureed pumpkin

1 cup milk

1 cup sugar

¼ teaspoon salt

¼ teaspoon grated nutmeg

¼ teaspoon ground cinnamon

2 large eggs, lightly beaten

1 tablespoon melted unsalted butter

Makes one 8-inch pie

Preheat the oven to 400 degrees. Line an 8-inch pie pan with the pastry and make a fluted standing rim.

Place pumpkin in a large bowl; gradually add the milk, stirring constantly. Add the remaining ingredients in the order given and beat well with an electric mixer to combine. Pour into the prepared pie pan and bake for 35 to 45 minutes, until a knife inserted into the custard comes out clean. Transfer to a wire rack to cool completely. Serve at room temperature or chilled.

Cherry Cobbler

1 quart frozen sweetened sour cherries

3 tablespoons all-purpose flour

1 cup sugar

Pinch of salt

2 tablespoons unsalted butter

1 Perfect Pie Crust (page 13)

Vanilla ice cream or whipped cream for serving, optional

Serves 6

INDIANA

Preheat the oven to 400 degrees. Grease an 8 x 8-inch baking dish.

In large bowl, combine the cherries with the flour, sugar, and salt. Turn into the prepared dish and dot the top with the butter. On a lightly floured surface, roll out the pie crust and lay it over the cherries, making a fluted edge, or cut the pastry into strips and make a latticework top by placing half of the strips in one direction and weaving the other half in the other direction. Bake for 45 minutes, or until the pastry is browned and the cherries are completely cooked and bubbly. Transfer to a wire rack to cool a little. Serve warm, with vanilla ice cream or whipped cream, if you like.

THE NAME MARIAN SCHLEICHER, I learned, was known boundary to boundary in the state of Indiana. She was a cooking school teacher, Home Service Director for a large corporation conducting classes in sixty out of the state's ninety-two counties. I asked Marian to give me a line on the dishes Indiana women liked best. She said, "What I serve at home is typical. Sunday dinner is the big meal at our house. We favor Swiss steak."

Broccoli is a good vegetable with this, or any strongly flavored green. Add snowflake potatoes, whipped light as a cloud, a background for gravy. Bring on the Waldorf salad, the Hoosier Sunday-dinner delight.

Our hickory-nut cake would be the ideal dessert. The recipe is a hand-down from fifty years back, coming from Marian's grandmother, Mrs. Reba Carey. This is a cake to bake when you have plenty of time, not because the baking is so tedious, but those hickory nuts are a devilish business to get out of their shells. The cake bakes light and fluffy, is made with all-purpose flour and can be put to all purposes. That is, serve it as a dessert with coffee, serve it with fruit or ice cream. It's a long-keeping loaf.

Scrapple is a frequent dish at the Schleichers' table and hundreds of Indiana women have Marian's recipe. This dish is a meal when served with syrup and a green salad. Let's have canned apricots for dessert.

Swiss Steak

½ cup all-purpose flour

1 teaspoon salt

3½ pounds round steak or beef bottom round, cut 1 inch thick and trimmed of excess fat

½ cup bacon drippings or vegetable shortening

¼ cup chopped onion

¼ cup chopped celery

1 tablespoon finely chopped green bell pepper

1 (15-ounce) can chopped tomatoes

Serves 6

In a small bowl, combine the flour with the salt. Cut the meat with the grain into ½-inch-thick slices. Place the slices of meat on a board, sprinkle half of the seasoned flour on one side, and pound with a meat hammer for 1 minute. Turn over, sprinkle with the remaining flour, and pound for 1 minute more.

Heat the bacon drippings in a large heavy-bottomed skillet over medium-high heat. Add the meat and cook until golden brown on each side, about 2 minutes per side. Remove the steaks to a plate until all of the slices have been cooked. Add the onion to the pan and cook for about 1 minute to soften, then add the remaining ingredients, stirring to combine. Return the meat to the pan and submerge it in the liquid. Cover the pan, reduce the heat to low, and cook for about 1½ hours, until the meat is falling apart. Serve immediately.

Note: If the liquid isn't sufficient, open a can of tomato juice and add as needed.

INDIANA

Indiana Scrapple

1 (2½-pound) soup bone with about 1½ pounds of meat on it, such as a pork shoulder or pork back bones

2½ quarts boiling water

2 cups yellow cornmeal

2 teaspoons salt

½ cup grated carrots, optional

½ cup bacon fat, pork drippings, or vegetable shortening

Serves 10

Place the soup bone in a large saucepan and add the boiling water. Place over medium-high heat, cover, and bring to a boil. Reduce the heat and simmer until the meat begins to fall away from the bone, 2½ to 3 hours. Add more water to the bone as it cooks to keep it covered. When the meat is done, remove it from the stock and cut it into very small pieces. Increase the heat to medium-high and reheat the stock to boiling. Slowly stir in the cornmeal and salt. Add the diced meat and grated carrots, if using. Cook uncovered until the mixture is very thick, stirring occasionally, about 10 minutes.

Pour the mixture into two 9 x 5 x 3-inch loaf pans. Press down with a spoon to form 2 even, solid loaves. Cover the loaves with plastic wrap and refrigerate for at least 4 hours or until set, chilled, and solid.

When ready to cook, turn the loaves out of the pans and cut into ½-inch-thick slices. Melt the bacon fat in a large heavy skillet over medium heat. Fry the slices until golden brown and crusty on both sides, 5 to 7 minutes on each side. Serve as a main dish with syrup.

Hickory-Nut Layer Cake

3 cups all-purpose flour

4 teaspoons baking powder

1 teaspoon salt

1 cup (2 sticks) unsalted butter, softened

1¾ cups sugar

1 teaspoon vanilla extract

¼ cup maple syrup

4 large eggs

2 cups chopped hickory nuts or pecans

¾ cup milk

Maple Frosting (page 12)

Makes one 9 x 13-inch sheet cake or one 9-inch layer cake

Preheat the oven to 375 degrees. Grease a 9 x 13-inch pan or two 9-inch round cake pans.

Sift the flour, baking powder, and salt into a medium bowl. In the large bowl of an electric mixer, cream the butter and sugar until very light and lemon-colored. Add the vanilla and maple syrup. Beat in the eggs one at a time, beating well after each addition. Stir in 1½ cups of the nuts. Add the dry ingredients alternately with the milk, beginning and ending with the dry ingredients. Turn the batter into the prepared pan or pans and bake for 35 to 40 minutes, until a wooden pick or skewer inserted into the center of the cake comes out clean. Transfer the pans to wire racks to cool. Cool for 15 minutes in the pans, then turn out onto the racks and cool completely. Frost with maple frosting or another favorite icing and sprinkle with the remaining ½ cup nuts.

INDIANA

A **POPULAR PLACE TO** lunch in Indianapolis is the L. S. Ayres Co. Department Store. Nearly six thousand people eat there daily in the tearoom and the downstairs luncheonette. And no wonder: for years the management had been borrowing recipes from the guests. When Veronica Morrissey was in charge she started the idea.

Mrs. Margaret Legge, a local golf champion, said to Miss Morrissey, "I have a recipe that makes a better tomato aspic than the one you serve." Miss Morrissey said, "Loan it to me. I'll trade you our strawberry whip." It was a deal and the new aspic worked dandy.

The story was told at a bridge club table and word got around. That started things. Soon the tearoom was getting over fifty letters a week asking for recipes on the trade plan. The rub: it was taking one secretary's full time to handle the mail. A recipe service was started, guests giving recipes received in return menu favorites, card printed.

Here are three of the recipes most in demand.

Orange ginger-ale punch is a top favorite. It was developed during the war when points were at a premium and the tearoom had a double line waiting for tables. To keep the standees happy a fruit juice mixture was served. A bothersome thing, keeping one employee busy the full morning squeezing oranges and lemons, mixing grape juice and sugar. Then a friend suggested a jiffy punch she had seen served at a house party in Louisville, Kentucky. "Just orange ice and ginger ale," she explained. No squeezing of fruit, no nothing.

Place the orange ice cream or sherbet, three-fourths of a gallon, in large chunks in a well-chilled punch bowl, then pour over five quarts of chilled ginger ale, garnish with mint leaves and maraschino cherries and serve it at once. Yield: 55 cups.

Strawberry Whip

¾ cup frozen and thawed strawberries

1 large egg white

½ cup sugar

½ tablespoon freshly squeezed lime juice

Serves 10

Combine all of the ingredients in the large bowl of an electric mixer and whip for 20 minutes or longer, until the mixture is stiff. Serve immediately or chill and serve with a thin custard sauce or whipped cream, if you like.

WHEN DONALD C. DRAKE of Indianapolis started his dog talk and began his gun cleaning, his wife would get busy on the telephone. Six lucky friends received the invitation, "Come for a pheasant dinner, Don's going hunting."

Mrs. Drake, in the mood of the season, would drag out the big casserole, the one she kept just for company occasions. A look for the blue pudding bowl—this just the right size to make persimmon pudding for eight.

The pheasant in casserole she did with sour cream. Cranberry juice cocktail for the first course. Mashed potatoes taste wonderfully right with the rich pheasant gravy. Succotash is the vegetable, green salad a go-along; persimmon pudding for dessert.

The Drakes are a pair of Buckeyes from Cincinnati who moved to Indiana and liked it so well they came to call themselves Hoosiers.

Yes, Hoosiers all right, but many of Mrs. Drake's recipes go back to her mother's Cincinnati kitchen. One such is the oatmeal sausage she makes for giving at the holiday season.

Mrs. Drake told me, "There are as many sausages in Cincinnati as there are butchers but this particular sausage is one of the best I ever met anywhere."

The mincemeat is a gift item, too, but an old English recipe with personal touches. This persimmon pudding originated in Hendricks County, Indiana, and dates back seven generations.

INDIANA

Persimmon Pudding

⅓ cup unsalted butter, softened

2 cups sugar

2 large eggs, beaten

2 cups persimmon pulp (about 5 or 6 medium ripe persimmons, peeled and seeded)

1 teaspoon baking soda

¼ cup hot water

2½ cups sifted all-purpose flour

3 cups milk

1 cup whipped cream, optional

Serves 12

Preheat the oven to 275 degrees.

In a large bowl using an electric mixer, cream the butter and sugar. Add the eggs and persimmon pulp. In a small bowl, dissolve the baking soda into the hot water and beat it into the persimmon mixture. Beat in the flour alternating with the milk.

Two methods of baking: In northern Indiana, the batter is poured into a greased 16 x 10 x 2-inch pan and baked for about 1¾ hours, until set and browned. In southern Indiana, the preferred way is to pour the batter into a greased baking bowl, place in a pan of water, and bake for about 3 hours, stirring once every 20 minutes, until set and browned. In both places, you may serve it with whipped cream, if you like.

Pheasant Casserole

3 (3-pound) pheasants

1 cup all-purpose flour

Salt and freshly ground black pepper

1 cup (2 sticks) unsalted butter

3 cups sour cream

Serves 8

Preheat the oven to 300 degrees. Grease a large ovenproof casserole.

Cut each pheasant into 8 pieces, as you would for a chicken, or ask a reliable butcher to do it. Season the flour with salt and pepper and dredge the pheasant pieces through the seasoned flour. In a large heavy-bottomed skillet, melt the butter over medium-high heat. Brown the pheasant pieces in batches, turning, 7 to 8 minutes per side. Transfer to the prepared casserole and pour the sour cream over the pheasant pieces. Bake for 1 hour, or until the pheasant pieces are tender and release clear juice when pierced with a fork. Let the casserole rest for 10 minutes before serving. Serve hot.

INDIANA

Indiana Mincemeat

1 pound suet

2 pounds beef-neck meat,
cut off the bones into ⅛-inch dice

4 pounds apples (preferably Winesap),
peeled, cored, and diced

1½ pounds quince, peeled and diced

½ pound citron, diced

½ pound raisins

½ pound currants

1 pound sugar

2 cups molasses

1 tablespoon salt

2 tablespoon ground cinnamon

1 tablespoon ground cloves

1 tablespoon ground allspice

2 teaspoons grated nutmeg

2 teaspoons freshly ground
black pepper

1½ cups boiled apple cider

Makes 3 quarts

Place the suet and neck meat in a large heavy stockpot,
add water to cover, and place over medium-high heat.
Bring to a boil, then reduce the heat and simmer until the
meat is tender, about 3 hours.

Meanwhile, in a large bowl, combine the apples, quince,
citron, raisins, sugar, molasses, salt, cinnamon, cloves,
allspice, nutmeg, and black pepper.

When the meat is tender, remove the stockpot from the
heat and allow it to cool, about 1 hour. Add the reserved
fruit and the cider to the pot. Place over medium heat,
bring to a simmer, and cook for about 1 hour, until all
the fruit is tender. Blend the mixture in a blender or food
processor in batches until completely smooth. Use as
filling for pies or turnovers, or baked into muffins.

Note: Those who like a "stick" in their Christmas pie may
add a cup of brandy.

Oatmeal Sausage

2 pounds pork shoulder

2 pounds beef-neck meat,
cut off the bones

1½ cups steel-cut oats

1 tablespoon brown sugar

2 tablespoons salt

1 teaspoon poultry seasoning

½ teaspoon ground cinnamon

½ teaspoon ground cloves

½ teaspoon ground allspice

½ teaspoon ground ginger

½ teaspoon ground mace

½ teaspoon grated nutmeg

½ teaspoon freshly ground
black pepper

½ teaspoon sweet paprika

½ teaspoon garlic salt

3 tablespoons unsalted butter

Makes 2 loaves

Wipe the pork shoulder and beef neck meat with a damp cloth. Place the meat in a large stockpot, add water to cover, and place over medium heat. Bring to a boil, then reduce the heat to a simmer and cook until tender, about 3 hours. Remove the meat from the stock, reserving the stock, and finely grind the meats in a meat grinder.

Generously grease two 9 x 5 x 2½-inch loaf pans.

Add the oats to the meat stock, place over medium heat, and bring to a simmer. Cook for 25 to 30 minutes, until smooth and creamy. Add the ground meat to the oatmeal, then add the remaining ingredients and stir to combine. Turn mixture into the prepared pans, cover, and refrigerate overnight to set.

To serve, cut the sausage into ¼-inch slices. In a large skillet, melt the butter. Fry the slices until golden brown, about 3 minutes on each side.

INDIANA

YOURS FOR CELEBRATION—canned whole peaches, but not what you think. Look! No pit in the middle, instead a rich stuffing of candied fruits. This recipe was developed by home economist Gladys Kimbrough of Muncie, Indiana. The idea came, she told me, at Christmas when she was working on a recipe for stuffing oranges to go with holiday meals. Peaches, she decided, would be equally good with a fancy filling and could be put to more uses.

Filled peaches may be served in the manner of cherry jubilee. A sumptuous dessert is to sandwich a peach between meringue shells and pour over the sauce in which the peaches are canned. Slice the peaches and use as a garnish over ice cream, or to decorate a fruit salad or a fruit cup. The peaches, just as they come from the jar, make an interesting relish with cold meats and fowl.

Gladys tells me the clingstone peach looks neatest in the jar and holds together best, if properly pitted. But the freestone gives the best flavor.

She warns, don't try to pit the clingstone without a pitting spoon, a handy, inexpensive little tool costing around a dollar.

Home-Canned Stuffed Peaches

For the peach stuffing:

1 large slice candied pineapple

2 or 3 pieces candied orange peel

¼ cup citron

⅓ cup candied cherries

2 or 3 candied ginger slices

For the orange syrup:

5½ cups sugar

1 cup orange juice

2 teaspoons grated orange peel

4 cups water

½ teaspoon salt

For the brandied syrup:

5 cups sugar

3 cups water

2 cups peach brandy

For the peaches:

2 quarts water

1 tablespoon salt

9 or 10 medium-large clingstone or freestone peaches

Makes two 1-pint jars

658

Make the peach stuffing: Finely chop all of the stuffing ingredients and combine them in a small bowl, mixing well so the fruits can hold together when pressed.

If you are making the orange syrup, in a large saucepan, whisk together all of the ingredients and place over medium heat. Bring to a boil, then reduce the heat and simmer for 5 minutes. Remove from the heat, cover the pan, and keep the syrup warm.

If you are making the brandy syrup, in a large saucepan, whisk together the sugar and water, place over medium heat, and bring to a boil, stirring constantly. Reduce the heat and simmer for 5 minutes, then stir in the brandy. Cover the pan and keep the syrup warm.

Sterilize the pint jars according to manufacturer's instructions.

Pour the water into a large deep saucepan, add the salt, and bring to a gentle boil over medium-high heat. Score each peach with a shallow X on the underside. Fill a large bowl with ice water. Dip the peaches 4 at a time into the boiling water and scald them for about 30 seconds, then plunge them into the ice water to shock. Slip the skins off, cut the peaches in half, and gently remove the pits. If the skins are tough to remove, use a very sharp paring knife to cut them off. If the peaches do not release easily from the pit, try quartering them to get a better handle on them.

Tightly pack ½ to ¾ cup of the stuffing into the centers of the peaches. Pack the peaches upright in the prepared jars. Add syrup to cover, 1 to 1½ cups, leaving ¼-inch headroom at the top of the jars. Run a knife down between the jars and the peaches to release any air bubbles. Seal the jars according to the manufacturer's directions. Process the peaches in a large stockpot of boiling water for 30 minutes. Keep the water boiling steadily but not so hard as to shake the jars. Store in a cool dry place.

Note: If the peaches rise to the top, let the jars stand until cooled, then put them on their sides. Let them stay in this position for a week; turn the jars daily and the peaches will have a better appearance. The peaches may be stored in their jars for up to 6 months.

INDIANA

Note: After the syrups are cooked, cover the pan and keep them hot but do not let cook further. The yield for each depends upon the rate of boiling, but these recipes generally make 5 to 6 cups syrup. The peach stuffing makes about 1 cup. If you have extra syrup, add it to sparkling water or seltzer; any leftover stuffing can be used as an ice cream topping.

A CREAM PIE GONE WRONG

The world's first butterscotch pie was a cream pie gone wrong. Its birthplace was the kitchen of the Wheeler Creamerie Exchange in the little town of Connersville, Indiana, sixty-five miles from Indianapolis.

"It happened fifty-odd years ago and I know," W. O. Wheeler was saying. "It was my mother, Sarah Wheeler, who burned the custard that turned into butterscotch."

I was spending the afternoon with Bill and Goldie Wheeler at their home in Castleton, having driven out to see their orchids.

After talking flowers for a full hour, I was invited into the house to have pie and coffee. It was butterscotch pie and unusually good, and I said so. Then came the story that this pie was the original butterscotch pie, Mother Wheeler's invention.

Sarah Wheeler ran a bakery in Connersville, specializing in breads, rolls and pies.

One day, Mr. Wheeler recalls, his mother was making cream pie when a customer came in and stayed overlong. When Mom got back to her cooking, the cream-pie filling had scorched. Before Mrs. Wheeler could dump her failure, her sons were at their favorite pastime—licking the pan. They raved about the sticky mess tasting so good and Mother tasted it too. "Why," she said, "it's exactly like butterscotch candy."

That scorched custard started Mrs. Wheeler experimenting to get the same taste into a pie. She never did count how many cream fillings were ruined before she had a perfect production. After that she had plenty of practice. All Connersville started eating that new pie.

Mrs. Wheeler made her butterscotch filling in a skillet. We found it was apt to curdle that way. We did it double-boiler style to make it foolproof.

Sarah Wheeler's Butterscotch Pie

1 (8-inch) Perfect Pie Crust (page 13)

2½ cups milk

2 large eggs, separated

¼ cup all-purpose flour

1 cup firmly packed dark brown sugar

½ cup water

⅛ teaspoon salt

1½ tablespoons unsalted butter

1 teaspoon vanilla extract

¼ teaspoon cream of tartar

¼ cup granulated sugar

Makes one 8-inch pie

Preheat the oven to 350 degrees. Line a 9-inch glass pie plate with the pastry and make a fluted standing rim. Refrigerate until chilled, about 15 minutes.

Line the pastry with foil and fill with pie weights or dried beans. Bake for 30 minutes, or until nearly cooked through and dry to the touch. Carefully remove the foil and weights. Bake for 10 minutes longer, until golden. Let cool on wire racks completely. Increase the oven temperature to 400 degrees.

In a medium bowl using an electric mixer, beat ½ cup of the milk with the egg yolks and flour. In a large heavy-bottomed saucepan, scald the remaining 2 cups of milk. In a medium heavy-bottomed saucepan or skillet, combine the brown sugar, water, and salt, place over low heat, and bring to a gentle boil, whisking constantly. Cook until the mixture thickens and a few bubbles break, sending up not whiffs but puffs of smoke. Add the caramelized sugar very slowly to the scalded milk, stirring constantly until smooth. Gradually stir in the egg-yolk mixture and cook, stirring constantly, until thick, about 5 minutes. Remove the pan from the heat and whisk in the butter and vanilla. Cool the filling and pour it into the cooled pie shell.

In a medium bowl, beat the egg whites until foamy; add the cream of tartar and granulated sugar and beat to form stiff peaks. Spread the meringue over pie and bake for 8 to 10 minutes, until delicately browned. Transfer to a wire rack to cool; refrigerate until ready to serve.

INDIANA

THE

FAR WEST

WYOMING &
COLORADO

This is the main road through Grand Teton National Park, two miles from Jenny Lake, Wyoming. Turn the car left into a bumpy woodland. Cross a low plank bridge with a rumble like thunder and into a bright meadow of sweet, dry smells. Honk the horn. Here we are at the vacation home of Mr. and Mrs. Harold Fabian, a place of two cabins within shouting distance. One is for living and sleeping, one for cooking and eating, and a cottage to accommodate friends from the world over, a few thousand in a decade by "guest book" count.

Harold Fabian is the Salt Lake City lawyer retained by John D. Rockefeller in the twenties to handle the land-acquisition program for the creation of this park now administered by the U.S. Government.

The twin-cabin place at the foot of the peaks is the only spot in the valley where every peak in the Grand Teton Range is visible. Look to the left: Buck Mountain, next Mt. Wister, follows Nez Percé, South Teton, Middle Teton, Grand Teton, Mt. Owen, Teewinot, then to the far right, the St. John's Group. After this, Mt. Moran. All are within the swivel of the eyes.

This was a busy day for Mrs. Fabian, with friends arriving by private plane from San Francisco, and unexpectedly here I was underfoot. But Josephine Fabian is a natural-born hostess. Her friendliness, it would seem, comes straight from the heart. Wearing her welcome smile, wearing Western riders, a handwoven shirt and calfskin jacket, she stood at the built-in wall bar taking cocktail orders. The fire made a great shine and a crackle.

I tagged Mrs. Fabian to the kitchen-dining cabin where she made a last check on the progress of dinner.

The dinner this evening was roast ribs of beef with horseradish sauce (whip a half pint of cream, fold in one-fourth cup prepared horseradish). There was a spinach-rice ring filled with buttered baby beets as the main dish accompaniment. And hot biscuits, thank heaven! A tossed green salad and for dessert this night, sherry-almond pudding with a pompadour of whipped cream.

Mrs. Fabian's rib roast of beef, and always a seven-rib roast, has made her reputation as a fabulous cook. Whether it's the way she does the beef or the quality of the meat she buys that has the guests cheering is very hard to know. She makes a sort of ritual of the preparation. She herself visits the meat man asking him to saw off the heavy bone at the top of the ribs, then with string she ties this on again. "Not to lose any of that good bone flavor," she explains. Near the end of the cooking, off with the bone. When Mr. Fabian carves, there is no protruding bone to get in the way.

Before the meat goes into the oven, bottom and top ends are covered with a thick coating of salt, then seared top stove, to seal in the juices. The roast is started in a 400-degree oven. After thirty minutes, the heat is reduced to 350 degrees and so left until thirty minutes before serving. Now out it comes, cut the string, remove the bone and back with the roast into a 400-degree oven for twenty minutes. The total time allowed is twelve minutes to the pound for a rare to medium roast. This comes crusty brown on the outside, quite pink within.

Buttered Leeks

⬦⬦⬦

12 medium leeks, white and tender green parts only, sliced ½ inch thick

1½ quarts chicken stock or water

7 tablespoons unsalted butter

Salt and freshly ground black pepper

3 slices thick-cut country-style white bread, toasted, buttered, and cut in half

Finely chopped shallots, optional

Marigold heads, optional

⬦⬦⬦

Serves 6

⬦⬦⬦

Place the leeks in a large saucepan and add the chicken stock. Place over medium-high heat and bring to a boil, then reduce the heat to low and simmer until the leeks are tender, 30 to 40 minutes. Strain the leeks and pour them back into the saucepan. Stir in 6 tablespoons of the butter and season with salt and pepper.

Serve the leeks hot with the buttered bread halves in warm soup bowls. Garnish with chopped shallots and marigolds, if you like.

Note: For a tasty variation and a light luncheon, make a simple broth by dissolving 3 to 4 bouillon cubes in chicken stock and stirring in these buttered leeks just before serving.

TEENAGE KITCHEN QUEENS ARE seldom met in my travels, but I found one for sure in Denver, Colorado, Carol Jean Byma her name, a girl wonder of a cook. The evidence of her prowess as a young homemaker is a stack of prize ribbons won in five years of 4-H Club work, twenty-two in the collection. All the blue ribbons are for cooking.

Carol Jean, then fourteen, a sophomore at South High School, had warm brown eyes inviting your friendship. She gave a smile for a smile. A confident miss, but not one to brag except when boasting of Sally, her ten-year-old sister. Little Sally could sling a mean onion; she knew her hamburger. Carol Jean was long past the Sloppy Joe and hot dog stage. She could sling a mean pizza, she could bake a fine cake or a superb loaf of French bread, or a fruited tea loaf.

I drove from the Brown Palace Hotel into southeast Denver to meet the H. G. Byma family. Father was on his job at the city post office, but Mama was there. Mrs. Byma's mother was born in Scotland and came here at sixteen with Old Country convictions that every girl must learn to cook and sew before she marries. Her daughter Alice believes the same way.

It was Lois Humphrey, Denver 4-H home-demonstration agent, who told me about Carol Jean's fine work and that pile of "prize" ribbons. This Carol wasn't just a sometime cook. She gave a hand always with the family meals and in summer vacation did dinner by herself two or three times a week assisted by Sally.

Bread baking is this young cook's greatest talent and this French bread recipe is one of her best. But when the neighborhood gang gathered for ping-pong in the Bymas' basement, the big moment of the evening was forking into a Carol Jean pizza.

PIONEER-DISH RECIPE FILE

Colorado still can claim high rank for its Rocky Mountain cooking done in the grand tradition of the Old West." It was Caroline Bancroft of Denver who told me this, and she ought to know. Caroline is a third-generation Coloradan, author of a score of books and booklets on the history of the state and historic personalities. Among her most recent books: "Gulch of Gold," the story of Central City; and the history of "Colorful Colorado."

Ever since college days Caroline has been digging into Colorado's past glories. Her research has turned up data galore on the foods of early days. "The most fascinating of these dishes," Caroline said, "came to Central City with the arrival of the Cornish miners around 1862."

Caroline lives in "Mile High Denver," the name of one of her many booklets—her home on Capitol Hill, the house where she was born. It was there she invited me to dig into her pioneer-dish recipe file.

Caroline's father, George J. Bancroft, a mining engineer, wrote extensively on Colorado mining and reclamation affairs. When Caroline was in her teens she traveled with Father to various mining camps and there met Cornish miners he counted best friends.

Caroline loves staging parties with a historic background. The best party she has ever given was a Cornish supper for the Colorado Folklore Society held on the Eve of St. Piran's Day. This St. Piran was a delightful character who lived around 550 A.D., his special mission in life to bring to miners revelations about metallurgy. Caroline's Cornish party menu headed off with leek soup—pasty the main course, *figgie 'obbin* the dessert.

Cousin Jack's pasty was the most important dish—a midday meal with the Cornish miners. The "pie" originated in the mining districts of Cornwall in the predinner-pail era.

Caroline explained that the name "cousin" was used first in derision. The Cornish liked America and could live better here than they ever did at home. Whenever the boss mentioned an available job a Cornishman was quick to suggest a "cousin" back in Cornwall, ideal for the place. And so they came, bringing a world of food, music, wit, and laughter. Soon Jack and Jennie were beloved "cousins."

Here is a recipe used to this day on Colorado home tables.

COLORADO

667

Carol Jean's Pizza

For the dough:

1¼ cups lukewarm water,
plus more for brushing the crust

1 (¼-ounce) envelope active dry yeast

3½ cups bread flour

1 tablespoon salt

1 tablespoon olive oil

For the sauce:

1 tablespoon olive oil

6 cloves garlic, chopped

2 medium yellow onions, chopped

1½ teaspoons salt

1 (28-ounce) can whole
peeled tomatoes

For the toppings:

1 cup shredded mozzarella cheese

2 tablespoons Parmesan cheese

1 teaspoon dried oregano

Serves 4

Make the dough: In a small bowl, combine ½ cup of the warm water and the yeast. Let rest for about 5 minutes, until foamy, then add the remaining ¾ cup water.

In a food processor, pulse the flour and the salt until combined. Slowly add the water and oil and pulse until the dough just forms a ball. Form the dough into a disk, place it into an oiled metal bowl, cover with plastic wrap, and leave at room temperature for at least 2 hours (24 hours is best), until tripled in size.

Meanwhile, make the sauce: Heat the oil in a large saucepan over medium heat. Add the garlic and sauté, stirring, for 1 minute. Add the onions and lower the heat to medium-low. Sprinkle with the salt and sauté for 15 minutes, or until lightly browned. Add the tomatoes and crush them using a wooden spoon or spatula. Increase the heat to medium-high and bring to a boil. Reduce the heat and simmer, stirring occasionally, for 10 minutes. Puree the sauce in batches in a blender or food processor until well combined. Set aside. Note: You will have plenty of leftover sauce for other uses.

To prepare the pizza: Place a pizza stone in the oven and preheat the oven to 550 degrees for at least 30 minutes.

Punch the dough down and cut off one third of it. (You may store the remaining dough covered in the refrigerator for up to 3 days; there is plenty of sauce and enough dough to make additional pies. You may also use the sauce and dough to make finished pies and store these, wrapped in plastic wrap and then aluminum foil, in the freezer for up to 1 month.)

Roll out the dough into a round that is 12 to 14 inches in diameter. Brush a little lukewarm water around the entire rim of the dough. Fold over and press to form a "lip." Brush the tablespoon of olive oil around the lip of the crust. Place a sheet of parchment paper on a peel, then place the crust on top of the parchment paper. Spread 2 tablespoons of the sauce on the bottom of the dough, then top with the mozzarella, and, finally, sprinkle on the Parmesan and oregano.

Slide the pizza from the peel directly onto the heated stone in the oven. Bake for 6 minutes, or until the cheese begins to brown.

Remove the pizza from the stone using the peel. Let cool for 3 minutes, then serve.

COLORADO

French Bread

2 (¼-ounce) envelopes active dry yeast

½ cup warm, but not hot, water

2 cups lukewarm water

1 tablespoon salt

6 cups bread flour

¼ cup yellow cornmeal

1 large egg yolk, beaten with
1 tablespoon water

Makes 2 large loaves

In a large bowl, dissolve the yeast in the ½ cup warm water and let stand for 10 minutes. Add the 2 cups lukewarm water, the salt, and 2 cups of the flour and, using an electric mixer fitted with the dough hook, beat until the dough just comes together and is still quite wet and sticky. Add the remaining 4 cups flour and beat well. The dough should still be sticky enough to come off the sides of the bowl and crawl up the dough hook.

Grease a large bowl and turn the dough into it. Cover with a clean kitchen towel and let rise in a warm place for about 1½ hours, until it doubles in size. Remove the dough from the bowl and turn out onto a well-floured surface. Divide the dough into 2 equal portions and pat each portion into a large rectangle about ¾ inch thick. Roll up the dough, beginning with the short side and stopping after each full turn to press the edge of the roll firmly into the flat sheet of dough to seal. Press with your fingertips. Tuck and roll so that any seams disappear into the dough.

Sprinkle a large baking sheet with half of the cornmeal. Place the loaves on the baking sheet and sprinkle them with the remaining cornmeal. Cover the loaves with a clean kitchen towel and let rise until doubled in size, about 1 hour.

Preheat the oven to 375 degrees.

With a sharp knife, make diagonal slashes about 1 inch apart on the top of each loaf. Using a pastry brush, brush the egg wash evenly over each loaf. Place a cup of hot water in an ovenproof container on the baking sheet with the loaves.

Bake the bread for about 45 minutes, until the loaves are golden brown. Remove from the oven and cool on wire racks. Slice and serve.

MRS. JESSIE SPRAGUE CLAYCOMB lives on a ranch twelve miles to the closest telephone and fifty miles from town, smack in the center of the famed uranium district at Gateway, Colorado. Jessie's particular talent is in cooking wild game. She constantly bewails the fact that so much game killed is wasted because women don't know how to prepare it in tempting ways.

This sauerbraten is one of her most borrowed recipes, one commonly used for venison in her neck of the woods.

Venison Sauerbraten

1 (3- to 4-pound) roast of venison

2 cups chopped onions

1½ cups red wine vinegar

3 cups beef stock

2 teaspoons salt

⅛ teaspoon freshly ground black pepper

3 bay leaves

15 allspice berries

12 whole cloves

6 to 10 tablespoons unsalted butter, bacon drippings, or vegetable shortening

Serves 6

Wipe the roast with a damp paper towel. Place in an earthen-ware crock or large bowl with the onions, vinegar, stock, salt, pepper, bay leaves, allspice, and cloves. Cover and refrigerate for 24 hours to marinate.

When ready to cook the venison, remove the meat from the marinade and wipe it dry, reserving the marinade. In a 4-quart pressure cooker, melt the fat. Sear the meat on all sides until browned, about 12 minutes. Strain the marinade liquid and pour it over the meat. Cover the cooker, raise the pressure to high, and cook for 50 minutes. Release the pressure using natural pressure release (just let the pressure cooker cool down), about 30 minutes. When the pressure drops, remove the cover, transfer the meat to a platter, and cover loosely with foil to rest. Remove the bay leaves. Pour the sauce into a blender or food processor and puree until smooth. Cut the meat into thick slices and serve topped with the sauce.

COLORADO

UTAH

Utah cooks use just as many potatoes as their sister cooks in Idaho. Shortly after my jaunt around the Potato State I arrived in Salt Lake City hunting recipes typical of the area. "Go to a church party," Mormon friends advised. "Eat potato salad served with baked ham. That's church supper fare."

Money-making suppers in the Mormon city are thirteen to a dozen. Usually the food is contributed, then the members pay to eat their own contributions, and pay very well, from five to ten dollars a plate, a little less for the children.

I went to a church potluck supper given for the Highland View Ward Choir of the East Mill Creek Stake of the Mormon church. Seven potato salads contributed by seven different cooks stood bowl nudging bowl on the kitchen counter. I started interviewing as I tasted. Here I learned several fine points regarding the way of a potato in a salad. When a potato salad is a matter of planning, the potatoes should be newly boiled, they say, and any firm potato will do the job. Little new "spuds" give a sweet waxy taste; the older potatoes have a more mealy consistency. Cover potatoes with boiling salted water and cook until just tender. Drain, cool in colander, skins on. When cold, peel and cut in slices a little less than one-fourth inch thick or cut into one-half-inch dice, and marinate in French dressing.

After the main course ice cream with butterscotch cookies. My favorite of the seven salads is the one given here.

Adele Milczarck's Potato Salad

12 hard-cooked eggs plus
1 large raw egg

6 cups diced cooked potatoes

½ onion, finely chopped

¼ cup French Dressing (page 246)

2 tablespoons cornstarch

1½ cups water

¼ cup vegetable oil

2 tablespoons cider vinegar

1 teaspoon prepared mustard

2 tablespoons sugar

3 teaspoons salt, plus more
for seasoning

¼ teaspoon sweet paprika

½ cup evaporated milk

Freshly ground black pepper

Serves 8

Dice 6 of the hard-cooked eggs. In a large bowl, combine
the potatoes, the 6 diced hard-cooked eggs, the onion,
and French dressing. Cover and refrigerate until ready
to serve.

In a medium saucepan, combine the cornstarch and ½
cup of the water, place over medium heat, and whisk to
form a paste. Whisk in the remaining 1 cup water and
stir constantly until clear. Remove from the heat and set
aside. In a medium bowl, combine the raw egg, the oil,
vinegar, mustard, 1 tablespoon of the sugar, 1 teaspoon
of the salt, and the paprika. Mix well and gradually add
to the hot cornstarch mixture; beat until smooth. Add
the evaporated milk, the remaining 1 tablespoon sugar,
and remaining 2 teaspoons salt and whisk until smooth.
Cool the sauce to room temperature, then pour it over the
chilled potatoes. Season with salt and pepper. Put half
of the potato mixture into a serving bowl. Slice 3 of the
remaining hard-cooked eggs and lay them over the salad.
Add the remaining potato mixture. Cut the remaining
3 hard-cooked eggs into wedges and add as a garnish to
the top of the salad. Cover and refrigerate until chilled
before serving.

THIRTY-THREE STOCKINGS

Utah brags that the State's best crop is its children, that the average family runs a baker's dozen. So we were not in the least surprised on Christmas Eve to find Mr. and Mrs. Cleo D. Wright filling thirty-three stockings for the Wright boys and girls.

It's a hunt for the stockings. These are around everywhere: on door knobs and sofa arms, dangling from curtains, looped over picture frames. Mama and Papa had retired to the kitchen, knee-deep in candy, in oranges and apples. The table was a glitter of papers silver and gold; silver dollar "toe-fillers" were stacked in a high pile.

The Wrights then had fifteen children, eleven boys and four girls. Five of the family were married, but all living nearby, and at the last counting, fifteen grandchildren, the oldest one five. Every last Wright comes home for Christmas. The roof of the house is all but lifted by laughter and song.

Celebration begins with Christmas Eve supper. Read the menu: chicken à la king made thick with mushrooms, served with a vegetable salad and hot yeast rolls. Mrs. Wright's recipe makes a hundred rolls, each the size of a bun. The finish, ice cream with fruitcake. After supper the children pop corn, they set up tables for rook, they sing themselves hollow, so refreshments again!

Each Christmas Mr. Wright, who is a sheep raiser, slaughters two lambs for the holiday. He gives a quarter to each of his married children and plenty left over for the home feast. Two legs of lamb are roasted the day before the dinner, then reheated while the potatoes roast in the pan drippings. Relish plates go to dinner filled with celery, green onions, and radish roses. There are great platters of Mom's hot rolls to pass and repass.

Mrs. Wright's Christmas Fruitcake

For the fruitcakes:

1 cup vegetable oil

1½ cups brown sugar

4 large eggs

3 cups all-purpose flour

1 teaspoon baking powder

2 teaspoons salt

2 teaspoons ground cinnamon

2 teaspoons ground allspice

1 teaspoon ground cloves

1 cup fruit juice (apple, pineapple, or orange)

1 cup chopped candied pineapple

1½ cups whole candied cherries

1 cup raisins

1 cup chopped figs or dates

3 cups chopped walnuts

Glacéed fruits and nuts, optional

For the glaze:

2 tablespoons brown sugar

1 tablespoon corn syrup

2 tablespoons water

Makes two 9-inch cakes

Make the fruitcakes: Preheat the oven to 275 degrees. Grease two 9 x 5 x 3-inch loaf pans.

In a large bowl, combine the oil, brown sugar, and eggs and, using an electric mixer, beat for 2 minutes. Sift 2 cups of the flour, the baking powder, salt, cinnamon, allspice, and cloves into a medium bowl. Stir the dry ingredients into the oil mixture, then add the fruit juice. In a medium bowl, combine the remaining 1 cup flour with the candied pineapple, candied cherries, raisins, figs, and nuts. Add to the batter and mix well. Pour the batter into the prepared pans and bake for 2½ to 3 hours, until the cakes are cracked down the center, golden on top, and a toothpick inserted into the center comes out clean. Let the cakes cool in the pans on wire racks for 10 minutes, then unmold them onto the racks to cool completely.

While the cakes are cooling, make the glaze: In a small saucepan, combine the brown sugar, corn syrup, and water. Place over medium-high heat, bring to a boil, and

UTAH

boil for 2 minutes. Pour over the cake tops while the cakes are still hot, so the glaze may seep into the cake and help keep it moist. Decorate with glacéed fruits and nuts, if you like.

Mrs. Wright's Potato Rolls

1 large russet potato

3 envelopes active dry yeast

¾ cup warm, but not hot, water

4 tablespoons (½ stick) unsalted butter

¾ cup sugar

1 tablespoon salt

3¼ cups milk, scalded

3 large eggs, beaten

15 cups bread flour

Melted butter for brushing the rolls

Makes about 45 rolls

Preheat the oven to 400 degrees.

Wash and dry the potato, prick it a few times with a fork, and bake it in the oven directly on a rack for about 1 hour, until the sides give when squeezed gently between your fingers. Wrap the potato in aluminum foil and let rest for 5 minutes. Do not turn the oven off. When the potato is cool enough to handle, cut it in half and scoop out the meat with a spoon. Mash the potato with a fork and stir in enough hot water to make about 2 cups; set aside.

In a small bowl, dissolve the yeast in the warm water and let sit until foamy, about 10 minutes. Meanwhile, combine the butter, sugar, salt, and milk in a medium saucepan. Place over medium heat and stir until the butter is melted; take the pan off the heat and cool to lukewarm. Add the eggs and mix well, then stir in the potato mixture.

Grease 2 large baking sheets.

Pour the flour into a large bowl and make a well in the center. Add the milk mixture and mix vigorously for about 8 minutes to form a silky, slightly soft dough.

Knead the dough until it is smooth and elastic. Transfer the dough to a lightly oiled bowl, cover loosely with a damp cloth, and let rise in a warm place until doubled in bulk, 1½ to 2 hours. Gently punch down the dough in the bowl several times, cover the bowl, and let the dough rise again until doubled, about 40 minutes. Punch down the dough again and divide it into 5 equal pieces. Cut 1 piece of dough into 9 equal pieces. Roll each piece into a ball to form rolls and transfer each to the prepared baking sheets. Brush the tops of the rolls with a little bit of melted butter and set aside in a draft-free spot until doubled in size, about 1½ hours.

Preheat the oven to 400 degrees. Bake the rolls for 10 to 15 minutes, until golden. Let rolls rest for about 5 minutes on a wire rack and serve warm.

THE WASATCH MOUNTAINS circling Salt Lake City were silver-fretted with snow that sharp-edged winter day when I went calling on Mrs. Ezra Taft Benson, wife of the Secretary of Agriculture.

Her husband, her children, and the Mormon church are Flora Benson's profession, her hobby, her life. Heavy-scheduled her days, unending appointments, she keeps her own house. "Never had a maid," she said. "My girls must learn to work, cook, sew, and clean."

The Benson family operates as an organization, each member of the household sharing the work. "We believe the best way to raise children," Mrs. Benson told me, "is for parents and children to work and plan together. Except when it has been absolutely necessary we have never had hired help in the house. One year's supply of food," she told me, "is kept in the stockroom of every faithful church home."

Daughter Barbara, then a student at the University of Utah where she was studying home economics, did much of the baking. Prune cake, she said, was her best recipe, and she gave it to me (recipe follows).

"But it isn't ours," Mrs. Benson said. "It's Mrs. William Bracy's recipe. I'll telephone to ask permission for its use."

"Go ahead," said Mrs. Bracy.

Barbara said, "Oh man, it's really a honey!"

UTAH

Mrs. Benson has always liked cooking. Although the daughter of an affluent pioneer jeweler, like all Mormon daughters she was taught how to work.

Secretary Benson says, "My wife is a wonderful cook." Mrs. Benson says, "Barbara cooks just as well as I do."

"Bankaken"

1 tablespoon unsalted butter

½ cup vegetable oil

1 (3- to 4-pound) thin round steak, sliced into strips about ¼ inch thick

1 cup grated onions

2 tablespoons all-purpose flour

1½ quarts beef stock or water

1 bay leaf

1 tablespoon salt

½ teaspoon freshly ground black pepper

Serves 6 to 8

Melt the butter in the oil in a large heavy skillet over medium heat. Add the steak and cook on both sides until deep golden brown, 4 to 5 minutes. Transfer the meat to paper towels to drain. Add the onions to the fat in the pan and fry until golden, about 15 minutes. Pour the onions into a bowl and reserve them. Add the flour to the pan and, stirring constantly, brown it well, about 7 minutes. Slowly add the stock, whisking constantly to make a gravy. Stir until the gravy is smooth, bring it to a boil, and remove it from the heat.

Place the meat in a 2-quart Dutch oven and cover it with the onions. Pour the gravy over the top and add the bay leaf, salt, and pepper. Put the pot over low heat, cover, and cook until the meat is tender, about 1½ hours. Serve with mashed potatoes, a green vegetable, and a fruit salad, if you like.

Mrs. Bracy's Buttermilk-Prune Cake with Creamy Vanilla Frosting

2¼ cups all-purpose flour

1 teaspoon baking soda

1 teaspoon ground allspice

1 teaspoon ground cinnamon

½ teaspoon ground cloves

¼ teaspoon salt

½ cup (1 stick) unsalted butter, softened

1½ cups sugar

2 large eggs

1 cup prune puree (sometimes called *lekvar*)

1 cup buttermilk

Creamy Vanilla Frosting (recipe follows)

Makes one 10-inch square cake

Preheat the oven to 350 degrees. Grease a 10-inch square baking pan.

Sift the flour, baking soda, allspice, cinnamon, cloves, and salt into a medium bowl. In another medium bowl, cream the butter and sugar until smooth. Blend in the eggs, then the prune puree. Add the flour mixture alternately with the buttermilk, adding a small amount at a time and beating well after each addition. Pour into the prepared pan and bake for 40 to 45 minutes, until the top is browned and a wooden pick or skewer inserted into the center of the cake comes out clean. Cool the cake in the pan on a wire rack for 20 minutes, then invert onto the rack, remove from the pan, and cool completely. When cooled, frost the top and sides with the frosting.

Creamy Vanilla Frosting

4 tablespoons (½ stick) unsalted butter, softened

2 cups confectioners' sugar, plus more if needed

3 tablespoons evaporated milk, plus more if needed

1 teaspoon vanilla extract

Makes enough to frost one 10-inch cake

In a medium bowl using an electric mixer, cream the butter well. Add 1 cup of the confectioners' sugar and beat until smooth. Pour in the evaporated milk and cream well. Add the remaining 1 cup confectioners' sugar and the vanilla and beat until the frosting is creamy and of spreading consistency. More confectioners' sugar or evaporated milk may be added for desired thickness, if you like.

Sweet Carrot Casserole

1 cup all-purpose flour

1 teaspoon baking soda

1 teaspoon ground cinnamon

½ teaspoon ground cloves

½ teaspoon grated nutmeg

½ teaspoon ground allspice

1 cup dried breadcrumbs

1 cup sugar

1 cup pureed carrots

1 cup mashed potatoes

1 cup beef stock

1 cup raisins, chopped

1 tablespoon dark molasses

Serves 6 to 8

Preheat the oven to 400 degrees. Grease a wide, shallow 1½-quart casserole.

Sift the flour, baking soda, cinnamon, cloves, nutmeg, and allspice into a large bowl. Stir in the breadcrumbs and sugar. Add the carrots, potatoes, beef stock, and raisins to the dry ingredients, then stir in the molasses. Pour the mixture into the prepared casserole and bake for about 25 minutes, until browned and bubbly. Serve hot.

IN SALT LAKE CITY you cook to satisfy the hunger of growing boys and girls; large families are the rule—five to fifteen children. There I found the kind of cooking which relies more upon content than upon any subtle techniques. Good plain food is put together in the honest old-fashioned manner to give dishes of flavor and savor and toothsomeness.

It's just such cooking that is done by Mrs. Thomas W. Jensen, mother of eight sons and one daughter, all grown and married. When I was there Mrs. Jensen was doing more cooking than ever. "I have twenty-three grandchildren, all living nearby."

"Some days," she said, "there's nobody here, just Mr. Jensen and myself. Then within ten minutes there may be fifteen visitors waiting to be invited for a meal."

At least three times a week these apple dumplings are dished for dessert. That's what the Jensen boys like and not a daughter-in-law can make dumplings so good; they admit it themselves. Even Mrs. Jensen's own daughter can't compete with mother.

Mrs. Jensen is equally proud of her starch cake. This is a traditional celebration cake in Sanpete County, a little Denmark in itself; 90 percent of the population is of Danish descent. Never a birthday that starch cake isn't served.

UTAH

Sanpete County Starch Cake

6 large eggs, separated

1 cup sugar

1 cup potato starch

2 teaspoons baking powder

¼ teaspoon salt

3 tablespoons water

1 teaspoon lemon extract

Makes one 9-inch tube cake

Preheat the oven to 300 degrees. Grease a 9-inch tube pan.

In a large bowl, beat the egg yolks until they are a pale yellow color. Very slowly add the sugar, a little at a time, and beat well until ribbony. Sift in the potato starch, baking powder, and salt, then add the water and beat well. In a medium bowl, beat the egg whites until stiff but not dry and fold into the mixture along with the lemon extract. Pour the batter into a 9-inch tube pan and bake for 1 hour, or until a wooden pick or skewer inserted in the center comes out clean. Cool the cake on a wire rack in the pan for 30 minutes, then unmold onto the rack to cool completely. Have it plain, have it frosted, or serve with a tart lemon sauce.

Mrs. Jensen's Apple Dumplings

1 cup all-purpose flour

2 teaspoons baking powder

¼ teaspoon salt

2 large eggs

⅓ cup half-and-half

2 cups water

3 medium unpeeled
Golden Delicious apples, sliced

4 tablespoons (½ stick)
unsalted butter

½ cup sugar

1 teaspoon lemon juice

Whipped cream for serving, optional

Serves 6

Sift the flour, baking powder, and salt into a large bowl. Beat in the eggs and half-and-half. In a wide saucepan, bring the water to a boil over medium heat. Add the apples, butter, sugar, and lemon juice and return to a boil. Drop the flour mixture by tablespoonfuls into the sauce, reduce the heat to low, cover the pan, and cook for about 15 minutes, until the dumplings are soft and tender and the sauce is syrupy. Serve just warm in bowls topped with whipped cream, if you like.

UTAH

CURRY POWDER BY MAIL

When old-timers around Salt Lake City get to reminiscing about the good eating of yesterday, they invariably mention the Finch Rogers Café. Then Miss Nancy's name pops up sure as anything—"A chip off the old block, just as good a cook as her dad."

Nancy and her sisters, Margaret and Florence, learned to cook helping father, Harry L. Finch, prepare his little home suppers for friends. Father loved cooking on his day off from business. He'd have the house in one delicious confusion. Nancy still lives in the home place and the same delightful dishes are served at her table.

Nancy, like her father, made a business of food. Eleven years she was home economist for the Utah Power and Light Company. Then to run her own show, a public secretarial service. Spare hours, and Miss Nancy's in her kitchen cooking for pleasure, maybe cooking for company, or just for herself. It's her father's dishes she serves most often. But exotic foods, too, find a way to her menus. She sends to far places for unusual delicacies. Her curry powder travels by mail from New York City. Macadamia nuts she orders from San Francisco. Macaroons she buys from the kitchen of San Francisco's St. Francis Hotel.

Relaxation to Nancy after a day at the office is to come home and get dinner. Just-a-minute cook? Heaven forbid! She takes time, all the time she needs to prepare a good meal. She likes eating late.

A party dinner with Nancy usually means eleven friends and herself. The dinner is more often a supper given after a concert with the artist invited as the honored guest. One favorite meal is built around this robust Scotch broth.

Miss Nancy's Scotch Broth

1 (1½-pound) piece chuck beef

1 (1½-pound) piece rump beef

1 (1½-pound) beef-leg bone, cracked

2 quarts water

2 quarts beef stock

2 bay leaves

2 tablespoons salt, plus more to taste

Freshly ground black pepper

1 tablespoon chopped onion

1 cup diced carrot

1 cup diced turnip

1 small parsnip, diced

1 tablespoon barley

1 cup navy beans

1 cup cooked garbanzos

Dash of Tabasco sauce

Serves 8

Place the meats and bones in a large stockpot. Add the water, stock, bay leaves, salt, pepper to taste, and the onion. Place over medium-high heat and bring to a boil. Reduce the heat to low, cover, and simmer for 3½ to 4 hours, until the meat is very tender. Strain and cool the meat, reserving the broth in the saucepan. Add the carrot, turnip, parsnip, and barley to the strained broth and cook over medium heat until tender, 25 to 30 minutes. When cool enough to handle, cut the meat into bite-size pieces. Add the beans and the meat to the pot and bring to a boil. Remove from the heat and season with salt, pepper, and the Tabasco. Ladle into bowls and serve hot.

UTAH

Harry Finch's Welsh Rabbit

8 slices toasted sandwich bread,
crusts removed and lightly buttered

¾ pound sharp aged cheddar cheese,
grated

¼ cup beer, preferably ale

2 tablespoons unsalted butter

¼ teaspoon dry mustard

Cayenne pepper

Salt

Serves 4

Preheat the broiler. Lay the toast slices on a baking sheet.

Combine the cheese and beer in a medium pot. Place over medium heat and melt the cheese into the beer, stirring slowly. Mix in the butter and mustard and season with cayenne and salt. Stir constantly until thickened into a smooth sauce, about 5 minutes. Ladle the mixture over the buttered toast, place the pan under the broiler, and broil until the cheese turns golden brown. Sprinkle the toasts with cayenne and salt and serve hot.

Warm Braised Beef
with Horseradish Sauce

4½ pounds beef short ribs,
cut into 2-inch pieces

6 quarts water

1 cup chopped onion

8 small carrots, cut in half crosswise

1 bay leaf

2 tablespoons salt

Freshly ground black pepper

1 tablespoon all-purpose flour

Horseradish Sauce (recipe follows)

Serves 6

Place the meat in a large stockpot and cover with the water. Add the onion, carrots, bay leaf, salt, and pepper to taste. Place over medium heat and bring to a boil. Reduce the heat to low and cover; simmer for 3½ hours or more, until the meat is tender. Turn the heat off the meat and let the pot cool to room temperature. Skim the fat off the broth, reserving 1 tablespoon.

In a small saucepan, melt the reserved tablespoon of fat over medium heat; stir in the flour and cook, whisking constantly to make a smooth paste, 3 to 5 minutes. Add a cup of the broth to the pan and whisk constantly until thickened into a sauce-like consistency, 7 to 8 minutes more. When ready to serve, divide the meat and vegetables into soup plates, ladle the sauce over them, and serve with the horseradish sauce on the side.

Note: This dish tastes even better when you cook the beef a day in advance of serving it.

Horseradish Sauce for Braised Beef

1 cup sour cream

1 teaspoon prepared horseradish

1 teaspoon red wine vinegar

Pinch of sugar

Dash of Tabasco sauce

Salt

Makes 1 cup

In a medium bowl, combine the sour cream, horseradish, vinegar, and sugar. Add the Tabasco and season with salt. Cover and refrigerate until ready to serve.

UTAH

IDAHO

Next to Maine, Idaho is the nation's largest potato-growing state; California is third. So into Idaho to hunt for new ways to serve the potato. Easy to find, we imagined in our innocence. But women there never give a thought to any such thing. They boil the potato, bake, stew, cream, and mash it, and know that an Idaho potato is a perfect thing without any folderol. Here is Mrs. Hollis Becker at her front gate with a welcome committee; sister-in-law Mrs. Raymond Holmer, who lives down the road, daughters Janna and Joeena, then eleven and five. And two dogs barking like crazy—Rags, a sheepdog, and a black cocker named Puddles.

The Becker farm is in Oakland Valley in the New Sweden area six miles from the National Reactor Testing Station. In the distance I could see the Teton Range.

Mrs. Becker knew I was coming but she couldn't believe her ears when I told her why I was there—just to ask how the family likes its potatoes. She and her sister-in-law exchanged a sly glance, thinking perhaps I was a little "tetched" in the head. Mrs. Becker said politely, "We like potatoes every day." Mrs. Holmer added, "And every meal, because that's what our men want— meat and potatoes."

"But how do you cook potatoes?" I persisted, and I could see I was getting nowhere fast, so I inquired instead about the farm. It totals 160 acres, forty in potatoes, the rest in grain and hay for the cattle. We took a walk down the garden path.

"But how do you like your potatoes best?" I interrupted, not forgetting the reason for my visit. "Baked," Mrs. Becker said.

Mrs. Holmer said, "Fern, for goodness sake, don't forget the potato boiled pudding." This is a recipe from Mrs. Becker's mother, Mrs. H. C. Dopp, who lives in Boise. It's a pudding she steams in a coffee tin, making several puddings at a time.

The sisters both together said, "Oh yes, our layered casserole!" We were at the kitchen table writing recipes lickety-split. Mrs. Becker laughed, "After all, you did find recipes."

Mom's Cinnamon-Raisin Potato Pudding with Old-Fashioned Caramel Sauce

1 cup grated carrots

1 cup grated potatoes

1 cup raisins

1 cup sugar

2 large eggs, well beaten

2 cups all-purpose flour

1 teaspoon baking soda

½ teaspoon salt

1 teaspoon ground cinnamon

½ teaspoon grated nutmeg

½ teaspoon ground allspice

¼ teaspoon ground cloves

3 tablespoons unsalted butter, melted

Old-Fashioned Caramel Sauce
(recipe follows)

Serves 10

Grease a 6- to 8-cup steamed pudding mold or 2-quart casserole or soufflé dish.

In a large bowl, combine the carrots, potatoes, raisins, and sugar. Stir in the eggs. In a small bowl, combine the flour, baking soda, salt, cinnamon, nutmeg, allspice, and cloves. Stir into the carrot-potato mixture, adding more flour if needed to make the consistency of a cake batter.

Pour the batter into the prepared pan, cover the pan tightly with aluminum foil, and secure it with a rubber band. Set the pudding on a rack inside a large pot. Pour enough boiling water into the pot to reach two thirds of the way up the side of the pudding, cover the pot, and bring to a boil. Reduce the heat to low and simmer for 2 hours; add more boiling water if the water evaporates. Carefully remove the pudding from the pot and let cool slightly. Uncover the pudding and invert it onto a plate. Slice the pudding and serve warm, with the caramel sauce.

Old-Fashioned Caramel Sauce

2 cups sugar

½ cup hot water

½ cup heavy cream

Makes enough for one 2-quart pudding

Melt 1 cup of the sugar in a medium heavy skillet over medium heat. Cook, stirring constantly, until browned. Gradually and carefully stir in the water and cook, stirring, until dissolved. Stir in the remaining 1 cup sugar until dissolved. Add the cream, stirring constantly. If a thicker sauce is desired, thicken with a paste made with a little cornstarch and heavy cream. Serve warm over pudding or ice cream.

Delicious Chocolate-Potato Layer Cake

¾ cup (1½ sticks) unsalted butter, softened

2 cups sugar

4 large eggs, separated

2 cups all-purpose flour

2 teaspoons baking powder

1 teaspoon ground cinnamon

½ teaspoon ground cloves

½ teaspoon grated nutmeg

½ cup milk

½ cup hot mashed potatoes

2 tablespoons cocoa powder

1 cup chopped nuts, such as walnuts or pecans

Caramel Icing (page 453)

Makes one 9-inch layer cake

Preheat the oven to 375 degrees. Grease two 9-inch layer cakes.

In a large bowl, cream the butter and sugar well. Beat in the well-beaten egg yolks. Sift the flour, baking powder, cinnamon, cloves, and nutmeg into a medium bowl. Add to the creamed mixture alternately with milk, beating well after each addition. Beat in the mashed potatoes, cocoa powder, and nuts until blended. In a medium bowl, beat the egg whites until stiff peaks form. Fold the stiffly beaten egg whites into the cake batter. Pour into the prepared pans and bake for about 25 minutes, until the cake springs back when lightly touched with a finger and a wooden pick or skewer inserted in the center comes out clean. Cool the cakes in their pans for 10 minutes on wire racks, then unmold onto the racks to cool completely. Frost with caramel icing.

Hamburger, Potato, and Tomato Bake

1½ pounds ground beef

3 teaspoons salt

1 teaspoon freshly ground black pepper

3 tablespoons unsalted butter

2 medium onions, thinly sliced

7 medium russet potatoes, thinly sliced

1 quart canned tomatoes

Serves 4

Preheat the oven to 400 degrees. Grease a large shallow baking dish.

In a medium bowl, gently mix the meat with 2 teaspoons of the salt and the black pepper. Without overhandling the meat, shape it into 8 equal-size patties. Melt the butter in a large heavy-bottomed skillet over medium-high heat. Cook the burgers in batches, browning them

IDAHO

on both sides, about 12 minutes total. Transfer the cooked burgers to the bottom of the prepared casserole, making sure it's large enough to hold the burgers in one layer. Pour any fat remaining in the skillet over the burgers. Layer the sliced onions and sliced potatoes over the burgers evenly. Pour the tomatoes over the top of the onion-potato layer and sprinkle with the remaining 1 teaspoon salt. Cover the casserole and bake for about 1 hour, until the potatoes are tender. Remove the cover and bake for about 30 minutes longer, until the casserole is browned and bubbling. Let the casserole rest for 15 minutes and serve hot.

THE ROSY-TINTED VEGETABLE

The seasonal-event dinner is an old-country custom dating from the days when each fruit and vegetable had its little great moment. Now, modern transportation and cold storage and freezers make a joke of the calendar. Yet in some rural families that old custom still prevails.

So without surprise I listened to Mrs. Lily W. Hansen tell of the family's rhubarb custard pie supper enjoyed each spring when the first slender pipes of the rosy-tinted vegetable came from the slowly yielding earth. And the new potato supper—that's another seasonal event with the Hansen family. Take the little new potatoes before they grow big, boil with skins on, and pass with a pitcher of heavy cream mixed with finely cut chives. Pour over potatoes and mash it in. Eat with gusto.

The Idaho bakers Mrs. Hansen serves with a bowl of sour cream, one of finely cut scallions, and sometimes a bowl of crisply fried bacon bits.

It was to talk potato dishes I drove five miles out of Idaho Falls to the Hansens' 485-acre farm. Since her husband's death, then eight years previous, Lily Hansen had managed the place with the help of her two sons, Norman and Reed. John, the youngest, was attending law school, and worked home during summer vacations. More help was required, but this was seasonal. Potatoes here are one of the important crops—one hundred acres.

Lily Hansen, of Swedish parents, has lived in the country thirty-one years, the last fifteen on this farm in the ten-room house she and her Danish husband built facing the Tetons. Now, after eight years alone, Mrs. Hansen was planning a move to a smaller place but still facing the Tetons, "so beautiful when the sun rises, so beautiful when the sun sets."

She gave me this potato whirl recipe, the one most used in the area, as well as daughter-in-law Donna's potato salad.

Potato-Cheddar Pinwheels

1 Perfect Pie Crust (page 13)

½ cup grated cheddar cheese

For the mashed-potato filling:

1 cup mashed potatoes

1 teaspoon chopped parsley

½ teaspoon salt

¼ teaspoon freshly ground black pepper

1 large egg, beaten

1 teaspoon minced onion

Serves 6

Preheat the oven to 450 degrees. Generously grease a large baking sheet.

Roll out the pastry onto a well-floured surface into a 9-inch square. Sprinkle the grated cheese all over it.

Combine all of the filling ingredients and spread the filling on top of the cheese. Roll up the dough tightly, as for a jellyroll. Cut into 6 slices and place cut-side up on the prepared sheet. Bake for about 25 minutes, until the rolls are browned and the cheese is melted. Serve the pinwheels with creamed vegetables or leftover meat, if you like.

IDAHO

Donna's Creamy Dill Potato Salad

6 medium potatoes, peeled, boiled, and diced

6 hard-cooked eggs, sliced

½ cup minced onion

1 tablespoon chopped parsley

¼ cup chopped dill or sweet pickle

1 tablespoon salt

¼ teaspoon freshly ground black pepper

1 tablespoon prepared mustard

1 tablespoon mayonnaise

1 tablespoon French Dressing (page 246)

1 tablespoon dill-pickle juice

¾ cup half-and-half

Sweet paprika for garnish

Makes 2 quarts

In a large bowl, lightly toss together the potatoes, 5 of the sliced eggs, the onion, parsley, pickle, salt, and pepper. In a small bowl, combine the mustard, mayonnaise, French dressing, pickle juice, and half-and-half. Gently toss with the potato mixture. Arrange in a bowl, place the remaining egg slices around the top, and sprinkle with paprika. Serve immediately.

DARK AND LOVELY, THE purple plums of the Northwest. Amber-fleshed this plum, and a free-stone. A delicious plum to eat in the hand; a wonderful cooker, excellent when canned. Excellent, too, when made into a fresh plum chutney as I sampled in the kitchen of the Governor's mansion, Boise, Idaho.

Rich, dark, and fruity, this chutney dips from the cooking pot. It is of spicy pungency, of peppery sharpness, exotic in fragrance. Royal purple the color, a delight to the eyes.

The recipe is one developed by Mrs. Robert E. Smylie, the First Lady of Idaho, developed to serve as an accompaniment to the lamb curry her husband likes to make on those certain occasions when close friends gather.

The Governor was so pleased with his wife's creation he changed his curry recipe, adding half a cup of the chutney as one of the ingredients, serving it also as an accompaniment. Use it as a relish with hot or cold meats. Try it with cream cheese as a dessert.

Idaho Purple Plum Chutney

1 cup firmly packed light brown sugar

1 cup granulated sugar

¾ cup cider vinegar

1½ teaspoons crushed red pepper

2 teaspoons salt

2 teaspoons mustard seeds

2 fat cloves garlic, thinly sliced

1 small onion, thinly sliced

½ cup pickled ginger, cut into thin slices

1 cup golden raisins

3½ cups fresh purple plums, cut in half and pitted (about 20)

Makes 3 half-pint jars

In a large heavy stockpot, combine the sugars and vinegar and bring to a boil. Add the remaining ingredients except the plums and mix well, then stir in the plum halves. Reduce the heat to low and simmer until thickened, about 50 minutes, stirring gently and frequently. Ladle the mixture into hot sterilized jars, seal, and store in a cool dark place.

IDAHO

Governor Smylie's Lamb Curry

2 tablespoons unsalted butter or vegetable shortening

4 pounds lamb, cut into 1½-inch pieces (if the meat is from the shoulder or leg pieces, save the bones for stock)

2 tablespoons curry powder

2 tablespoons all-purpose flour

1 small clove garlic, mashed with 1 tablespoon salt

1 large onion, diced

1 small tart apple, peeled, cored, and sliced

Grated peel of 1 small orange

6 small sweet pickles, sliced

½ cup Idaho Purple Plum Chutney (page 695) or other plum preserves

1½ cups chopped tomatoes

2 cups water or stock

Serves 8

Melt the butter in a large heavy-bottomed skillet over medium heat. Add the lamb and brown it on all sides, 10 to 12 minutes total. Sprinkle the curry powder and flour over the meat and stir until well coated. Add the remaining ingredients and bring the lamb to a boil. Cover the pan tightly, reduce the heat to low, and cook until the lamb is tender, stirring occasionally, about 2 hours. (Add more liquid if the lamb begins sticking to the pan along the way.)

Note: Serve the lamb curry with steamed rice, plum chutney, and a salad of crisp greens. For dessert, fruit sherbet and cookies.

THIRTY-MILE TRIP TO THE GROCERY STORE

A great lady of the sheep world is Mrs. Robert Naylor of Emmett, Idaho. She is a woman beloved by neighbors and friends, a woman trusted by the hundreds of workers in the greatest sheep kingdom of the Northwest, built by her famous father Andrew Little. Since her father's death Jessie has operated the place assisted by husband and two brothers, but Jessie at the helm.

Sheep buyers from everywhere are proud to know Mrs. Naylor who, it is claimed, knows more about sheep than anyone else in the field. And Jessie likes parties. A party without Jessie is never quite as much fun. The day before I met Mrs. Naylor she had driven two hundred miles for an afternoon of bridge with the girls. She is a willing worker in local civic programs. She can always find time for committee duties for her church. She has a ten-room house, without maid, without cook.

"Nothing to cooking," she said. "I keep the freezer well stocked, and we are but two." She didn't mention the many parties when "we are but twelve."

Jessie's busiest time is the selling season from the tenth of July into early August. Then she and Mr. Naylor go weekly to their camp in the mountains a hundred miles out of Emmett, there to park the car and off by pack horse to headquarters camp. No phone, a thirty-mile trip to a grocery store.

At the headquarters camp during the buying season, there are seldom fewer than twenty people at mealtime. It's a varied crowd—commission men, foresters, truckers, regular employees. Lamb steak is the most frequent dish, one of Jessie's best. The lamb is cut from the leg, and very thin. And camp stew is favored by the Basque cooks because it's expendable. Ribs of lamb are covered with water and simmered until almost tender, then rice is added and canned tomatoes along with seasoned tomato sauce. The rib meat puts real flavor into the rice.

Roasted Lamb Saddle Stuffed with Curried Rice

1 (5½- to 6-pound) boneless saddle of lamb, with side flaps of meat intact

Salt and freshly ground black pepper

1½ tablespoons minced onion

¾ cup uncooked rice

1 tablespoon unsalted butter

2 cups beef stock

1 teaspoon salt

½ teaspoon curry powder

Serves 8

Preheat the oven to 350 degrees.

Spread the saddle of lamb on a work surface, fat side up. Using a sharp knife, lightly score the fat in a crosshatch pattern. Turn the saddle over and trim any excess fat from the loin, tenderloin, and flap pieces. Season the lamb all over with salt and pepper and set aside.

To make the stuffing, melt the butter in a large saucepan over medium heat. Add the onion and rice and sauté, stirring frequently, until the rice is golden, 5 to 6 minutes. Add the stock, salt, and curry powder. Cover, reduce the heat to low, and steam for 20 minutes, or until the rice is dry. Pour the filling over the inside of the lamb. Roll up the roast, wrapping the flaps around the outside to form a neat cylinder, then tie at 1-inch intervals with kitchen string. Season the outside of the roast with salt and pepper, place the roast on a rack in a roasting pan, and roast the lamb for about 1 hour, until an instant-read thermometer inserted into the center of the roast registers 120 degrees. Transfer to a carving board and let rest for 15 minutes. Thickly slice the roast crosswise and serve.

Smoked Lamb Shoulder

4 tablespoons (½ stick) unsalted butter

2 medium onions, chopped

Salt and cayenne pepper

2 (6-ounce) cans tomato paste

2 cups water

¼ cup brown sugar

½ cup lemon juice

6 tablespoons Worcestershire sauce

¼ cup cider vinegar

1 (2½- to 3-pound) boneless shoulder of lamb

Serves 4 to 6

To make the marinade, melt the butter in a large skillet over medium heat. Add the onions and sauté until golden brown, about 15 minutes. Season with salt and cayenne, then stir in the remaining ingredients. Bring to a boil, then reduce the heat to low, cover, and simmer for 30 to 40 minutes, until thick.

Place the lamb shoulder in a large aluminum roasting pan. Pour half of the marinade all over the meat, turning it to coat. Cover and refrigerate for at least 3 hours or overnight.

When you are ready to cook the meat, heat a smoker to 275 degrees. Place the pan uncovered on the smoker for 2 hours. Remove the pan from the smoker and pour the remaining half of the marinade over the meat, brushing it on. Cover the pan with aluminum foil and put it back on the smoker for about 2 more hours, until the temperature of the shoulder reaches 175 degrees. Uncover the lamb and let it rest for 10 minutes. Remove the lamb from the pan and transfer it to a cutting board. Slice and serve warm or at room temperature.

IDAHO

GEORGE OTTEN OF PORTLAND, Oregon, I found a quiet fellow with a quiet sense of humor. A landscape architect and a handy man with an Oregon potato, Mr. Otten was prouder of his potato-pancake wizardry than of his skill with flower, shrub, and tree arrangements. His pancake recipe is one so simple he claimed to be downright embarrassed to detail the ingredients. But, "Yes ma'am, I'd be happy to eat potato pancakes every supper—that is, if I made them myself."

And to Mrs. Otten a merry side glance. She was quick to pick up the long-standing argument. "Your pancakes aren't a bit better than my clam fritters." And both sides of the family agree on plum shortcake.

Mr. Otten's Potato Pancakes

6 medium russet potatoes

3 large eggs, beaten

1½ teaspoons salt

3 tablespoons bacon fat or vegetable shortening

3 tablespoons unsalted butter

Serves 4

Preheat the oven to 200 degrees.

Peel the potatoes and grate them on a box grater (6 medium potatoes should yield about 1 quart grated). In a large bowl, mix the grated potatoes with the eggs and add the salt. Melt the bacon fat and butter in a large skillet over medium heat. Turn in half of the potato mixture, press it down until it is one thin layer the size of the bottom of the pan, and fry until golden brown on one side, about 5 minutes. Flip with a spatula and fry the other side until crisp and well browned, adding more fat if needed, about 3 minutes. Remove to a heatproof platter and keep warm in the oven. Fry the remaining half of the potato mixture and serve immediately.

Note: Dill pickles are a must as an accompaniment to potato pancakes.

Plum Shortcake

1 cup all-purpose flour

¼ cup plus 1 tablespoon sugar

1 teaspoon baking powder

½ teaspoon salt

3 tablespoons vegetable shortening

1 large egg, beaten

About 1 tablespoon milk

12 halves fresh purple plums or
10 cooked pitted whole prunes

½ teaspoon ground cinnamon

2 tablespoons unsalted butter

½ cup coarsely chopped walnuts

Whipped cream for serving, optional

Serves 6

Preheat the oven to 375 degrees. Grease an 8-inch square pan.

In a medium bowl, combine the flour, ¼ cup of the sugar, the baking powder, and salt. Using 2 knives or a pastry cutter, cut the shortening into the flour mixture until well blended and the consistency of coarse meal, with some lumps about the size of small peas. Stir in the egg and milk to make a soft dough. Turn the mixture into the prepared pan and press the plums into the dough. Dust the top of the cake, plums, and any visible batter with the remaining 1 tablespoon sugar, then sprinkle with the cinnamon, dot with the butter, and cover with the walnuts. Bake for 30 minutes, or until golden and a wooden pick or skewer inserted into the center comes out clean. Cool to room temperature and serve in wedges with whipped cream, if you like.

IDAHO

THE FILBERT FOLKS

One beautiful morning I left Portland around eight o'clock, heading for breakfast at the Rosa B. Connell ranch. The purpose of my trip was to see her filbert grove, five acres of orchard, and to learn first-hand how the filbert folks use these nuts on their menus.

Breakfast was a hearty meal: orange juice, poached eggs on toast, bacon and applesauce, and more toast with three jelly molds quivering on a cut-glass plate. There was coffee and for a climactic ending warm apple pie. A thick coating of chopped filberts had been sprinkled over the crust, these to bake crisp and give extra richness.

"Eat hearty," Mrs Connell urged; "you will be hungry before we finish tramping the grove." Beyond the dining-room windows stretched the green avenues of trees.

"This orchard," she told us, "will be twenty-seven years old this spring, planted by my first husband, H. T. Bruce, when we started housekeeping."

After her husband's death she went to work on the ranch. She can run a tractor—I saw her do it—with the same efficient ease that she baked this applesauce cake.

Rosa's second husband was sheriff of the county and had enough to keep him busy, so she kept right on the job managing the orchard. Since Mr. Connell died she has spent even more time out in the open. The house seems lonesome now "and one doesn't bake a pie just to eat by oneself."

Filbert waffles were a frequent Sunday night supper dish. Take any waffle recipe and add one cup of ground nuts and one-half cup of crushed, drained pineapple.

After I finally got my fill of filberts Mrs. Connell gave me a free choice among her filbert recipes, more than fifty in her collection. It was hard to decide which to take among such richness.

First give warm appreciation for this filbert applesauce cake.

Filbert Applesauce-Prune Cake

½ cup vegetable shortening

1 cup sugar

1 large egg, beaten

1 teaspoon vanilla extract

1 cup prune puree (*lekvar*)

1½ cups applesauce

1 cup raisins

1 cup filberts, finely chopped

½ teaspoon ground cinnamon

½ teaspoon ground cloves

2 cups all-purpose flour

2 teaspoons baking soda

Makes one 10-inch loaf cake

Preheat the oven to 350 degrees. Grease and flour a 10½ x 5½ x 3-inch loaf pan.

In a large bowl, cream the shortening and sugar well. Beat in the egg and add the vanilla. Stir in the prune puree, applesauce, raisins, filberts, cinnamon, and cloves. Sift the flour and baking soda into a medium bowl and add to the mixture, stirring in well to form a smooth batter. Turn the batter into the prepared pan and bake for 1 hour, or until a wooden pick or skewer inserted into the center of the cake comes out clean. Transfer the pan to a wire rack and cool for 15 minutes, then turn out onto the rack to cool completely. Cut into slices and serve.

Note: The cake can be wrapped in plastic and refrigerated for up to 1 week.

IDAHO

COOKING FOR PAPA HEMINGWAY

Miss Mary," she is called lovingly by her famed husband Ernest Hemingway and their many friends. Papa is his nickname, but Miss Mary quite often calls him "Lamb."

Mary has been a newspaper reporter and a foreign correspondent. She knows her way around the world. She is a talented woman in many fields. Her husband has described her as "charming and witty, an excellent fisherwoman, a fair wing shot, a strong swimmer, an amateur astronomer, a student of the arts..." and that's just his beginning. But he always ends by saying with square-toed positiveness, "She is a really good cook and a good judge of wine."

Mary didn't learn her cooking at Mama's elbow in Walker, Minnesota. Like everything she has learned to do, she learned when she needed to know. She started cooking during World War II when she was living in England and food was closely rationed. "The first thing I decided," she told me, "was to pay great attention to flavors to make the most of a little."

Married to Ernest Hemingway in 1946, Mary has lived in many places—in Spain, in Africa, and now in Cuba where the Hemingways have a lovely old farm eleven miles from the center of Havana. She cooks to please Papa and he enjoys Spanish dishes and has a great love for game.

I was in Sun Valley to attend a wine tasting and learned that the Hemingways were in nearby Ketchum, virtually in hiding so "Papa" could work without too many interruptions. And the climate, they figured, would be an invigorating change from the tropics. Here too was good hunting—deer, bobcats, pheasant, duck...

I called them up right out of the blue and asked Miss Mary if she would tell me her husband's favorite dishes. She said, "It was codfish yesterday. He likes whatever I plan. Come and taste that fish; I have some left over from dinner last night."

I taxied to Ketchum where the Hemingways lived in a half-completed house rented from a Sun Valley employee, yet a house wonderfully friendly. The living room had a picture window with a mountain view; it had a log-burning fireplace and Black Angus steer scatter rugs to help keep your feet warm. The two comfortable armchairs were occupied two winter cat tenants—Big Boy Peterson and Miss Peterson, his pretty sister.

Here Miss Mary and I started talking recipes, but quickly moved to the kitchen to taste that leftover dish. She was wearing black stretch pants, a black jersey blouse and diamond-pearl earrings. This Mary is slim as a wand, agile as a teenager, and can talk intelligently about almost anything. But today the subject was food. This past winter she did all the cooking and with careful menu planning had trimmed her husband to a youthful 200 pounds.

"Here he comes," she said. "He's been bobcat hunting with Gary Cooper." There he was, looking his slimmest and brimmest, his face rugged, his beard neatly trimmed. His greeting was, "What are we going to have for dinner tonight?"

Mary cooks with high adventure, likes experimenting, likes cooking the kill in ways to please Ernest. In Idaho she shot her deer of the season. Some of the meat she had smoked—cocktail appetizer. The round she had ground and frozen to use for deerburgers. Six years ago on a safari in Africa she killed a lion, served the tenderloin grilled. The meat is almost pure white, delicious as veal, but firmer textured.

The codfish dish the Hemingways fancy is from Marcelino's Café in Pamplona, Spain, a workingman's restaurant. Mr. Hemingway discovered it first in 1926 when he was there writing *The Sun Also Rises*.

The ratatouille is from Provence, France. Mary serves it to accompany pheasant, likes it as a stuffing for turkey, too. When planned as a dressing, cook but two-thirds done, then into the bird.

Salt Cod Pamplona

1 pound salt codfish

2 tablespoons vegetable oil

2 cloves garlic, minced

2 tomatoes, sliced

1 large onion, thinly sliced

1 green pepper, thinly sliced

1 tablespoon hot sauce

2 bay leaves

½ teaspoon sugar

¼ teaspoon cumin seeds

¼ teaspoon dried oregano

¼ teaspoon dried marjoram

Fresh ground black pepper, to taste

½ cup white wine

12 ounces jumbo lump crabmeat

1 cup raw peeled shrimp

8 ounces thinly sliced mushrooms

Serves 6

IDAHO

Prepare the codfish the night before: In a large shallow baking dish or bowl, cover the cod with fresh cold water and let it stand for 20 minutes to soften. Drain the fish and cut it into pieces. Add more cold water to cover the fish; cover with plastic wrap and refrigerate overnight. When ready to cook, simmer the cod in its soaking water for 45 minutes or until soft and tender. Drain the fish thoroughly.

Meanwhile, heat the oil over moderate heat in a large skillet. Add the next 12 ingredients. Bring to a boil, then reduce the heat to a simmer and cook, covered, for 30 minutes or until flavors are well combined.

Add the drained cod and simmer, covered, for 20 minutes more. Add the crabmeat, shrimp, and mushrooms; simmer covered for 10 minutes. The fish will absorb the liquid and the resulting dish should be the consistency of a fish stew. Serve with Cuban-style black beans, if you like.

Layered Ratatouille

2 cups cubed yellow summer squash	½ teaspoon dried oregano
1½ teaspoons salt	3 medium onions, sliced
3 cloves garlic, minced	2 green peppers, cut in thin strips
⅓ cup vegetable oil	½ teaspoon dried marjoram
½ teaspoon cumin seeds	3 medium tomatoes, sliced
2 cups cubed and peeled eggplant	½ teaspoon dill seeds

Serves 6

Preheat the oven to 350 degrees. Grease a 2½-quart casserole. Cover the bottom of the prepared casserole with the squash cubes. Sprinkle with ⅓ of the salt, garlic, and oil. Add the cumin seeds.

Make a second layer with the eggplant. Sprinkle with ⅓ of the salt, garlic, and oil. Scatter the oregano on top.

Make a third layer with the onion slices. Make a fourth layer with the green pepper. Sprinkle with the remaining ⅓ of the salt, garlic, and oil. Scatter the marjoram on top. Cover the casserole. Bake for 1 hour, or until the vegetables are soft and tender.

Add a layer of sliced tomatoes to the top. Sprinkle with the dill seeds. Bake uncovered for 15 minutes more, until the tomatoes have blended into the dish. Serve hot or cold.

IDAHO

Planked Porterhouse
with Whipped Potatoes

For the steak:

1 (2-pound) porterhouse steak, about 1¾ inches thick

Salt and freshly ground black pepper

Prepared plank (see Note)

3 tablespoons vegetable oil

For the whipped potatoes:

2 russet potatoes, peeled and cut into about 6 pieces each

2½ teaspoons salt

3 large egg yolks, lightly beaten

6 tablespoons heavy cream, half-and-half, or whole milk

3 tablespoons butter, melted

⅛ teaspoon black pepper

3 large egg whites, beaten to stiff peaks

Serves 2 to 4

Allow the steak to come to room temperature, about 45 minutes before serving. Wipe the steak dry and cut off superfluous fat. Season the steak heavily with salt and pepper on both sides at least 10 minutes and up to 30 minutes before cooking.

Meanwhile, prepare the whipped potatoes: Place the potatoes in a medium pot with cold water to cover and 1 teaspoon of the salt. Place over high heat, bring to a boil, and boil until the potato pieces are fork-tender, 15 to 30 minutes. Drain and mash with a potato masher or put through a food mill for a finer texture. Set aside.

In a medium bowl, beat the egg yolks with the cream, butter, remaining 1½ teaspoons salt, and the pepper, then add to the warm potatoes. Allow the mixture to sit for 10 minutes, or until cooled. Adjust the seasonings and fold in the egg whites.

Meanwhile, preheat the broiler. Heat the vegetable oil in a large heavy cast-iron skillet and sear the steak evenly on each side, about 7 minutes total, turning the steak over once about halfway through the cooking time. Transfer the steak, in the skillet, to the broiler and cook until firm to the touch and browned, about 7 minutes. Set aside, loosely covered.

To serve: Using a pastry bag, pipe a border of whipped potatoes about 1 inch from the edge of prepared plank. Place the steak in the center of the plank. Place the plank in the broiler and broil until the potatoes are browned on top, about 1½ minutes, rotating the plank once during broiling for even browning. Rest the meat for about 10 minutes before serving, keeping the potatoes loosely tented with foil. Sprinkle with salt and pepper and serve on the plank, if you like.

Note: To prepare the plank: Soak an untreated 12-inch square hardwood board—avoiding cedar—which may be purchased at a lumberyard, in hot water for at least 30 minutes. Dry and oil with vegetable oil.

OREGON

Portland was home base for several weeks while I made side trips here and there around the state and went visiting in the country. It was in Tigard, ten miles out of the city, I spent a day in Nana's kitchen, a kitchen that laughs out loud. The blue shelves wear laughing calico ruffles in gay red and yellow—little kick-skirts decorously jubilant. Blue dishes, yellow dishes in the open cupboard. Painted woodenware on the walls. Here was a bit of Old Sweden in the Northwest.

Nana's kitchen and dining room opened wide, one to the other. No door closed the kitchen away from the living room. Guests in this house never stay put—they tag Nana around to watch while she cooks.

Nana, born in Filipstad, Sweden, came to America at the age of ten. Now her name is Mrs. Wesley C. Heise and her friends call her Nan. Her menus are American except when it's Christmas and except for those certain year-around dishes a Swedish palate demands.

Then supper is spread on the round dining-room table. It's smorgasbord, a Swedish holiday specialty. First the glugg, steaming and spirituous. Every last guest has *skal'd* with the hosts. The smorgasbord, the groaning-with-pleasure board. See what I see? The pickled ham, the spareribs and potato sausage, these three meats a part of

a ritual dish called dunk-in-the-kettle. There are flatbreads and a homemade rye loaf. Nan's pickled herring is there and a rolled sausage called *rullkorv*, and *kalv sylta*, this last jellied veal, and delicious.

Dessert is rice porridge, *risgrynsgrot*. I spelled it—you can pronounce it.

Dunk-in-the-kettle starts with half a fresh ham, this soaked in salt brine two days before preparation, then cooked in fresh water, just enough to cover, simmered slowly three to four hours. Fresh spareribs are added after the ham has cooked for 1½ hours, then the potato sausage goes in, this a homemade creation added the last hour of cooking. The meats are removed to one big platter, the sausage and ham sliced, the spareribs divided.

The eating ritual is the important thing. Guests take a slice of Swedish rye bread on a fork and with plate in hand go to the kitchen to dunk the bread into the hot stock in which the meats simmered. Bread on the plate, back to the table to load up with the meats and other good things.

Creamy Rice Pudding ("Risgrynsgrot")

1½ cups long-grain white rice

1¼ cups water

1 teaspoon salt

5 cups milk

½ cup sugar

1 teaspoon ground cinnamon

Serves 6

Thoroughly rinse the rice and place it in the top portion of a double boiler. Pour the water in the bowl with the rice, add the salt, and cook over boiling water, adding milk as the rice absorbs the moisture, for 1 hour, after which all of the milk should have been absorbed. Stir in the sugar and cinnamon. Cover and cook for about 2 hours, until the pudding sets. Cool slightly and serve warm.

Note: The consistency of the rice pudding should be about that of blancmange. Nan serves the pudding in wooden bowls, adding a spoonful of lingonberries, or again plain, a jug of thick cream for the sauce.

Holiday Glugg

¾ pound raisins

1½ cups water

¾ cup sugar

2 teaspoons ground cinnamon

2 teaspoons whole cloves

12 cardamom pods

½ gallon red Burgundy wine

2 cups brandy or bourbon

Makes 2 quarts

In a large heavy stockpot, combine the raisins with the water. Add the sugar, cinnamon, and cloves. Crack the cardamom pods and drop them in the pot with their shells. Bring to a boil, then reduce the heat to low, cover, and simmer for 2 hours, or until the raisins swell. If necessary, add more water from time to time. Remove the pot from the heat, stir in the wine, and put the pot back on the stove. Turn the heat to medium and bring almost to a simmer, not quite, and then keep hot at about 160 degrees for 2 hours. Cool the mixture and leave the spices in the brew overnight.

In the morning, drain the liquid and squeeze the raisins to get out every last drop of wine. Pour the liquid into bottles until ready to use. Reheat when ready to serve, adding the brandy or bourbon.

PURPLE MASSES UNDER THE TREES

Again Tigard, Oregon, where the purple plum trees went marching up Bull Mountain in blue-green columns. Hot the sun, the wind was still; a scent-quiet morning. Ripe plums lay in purple masses under the trees.

This is the orchard of S. Elton Lasselle, a grower and packer of plums. His blonde, blithe daughter Kathleen, then sixteen, was my companion. "Eat a plum?" she invited, picking up a few of the dark, oval beauties.

Kathy said, "We used to call these plums, prunes. Now the packers call them purple plums, and prunes only when they have been dried. You know all prunes are plums, but not all plums can be prunes, just certain kinds. Here comes Paddy, he can explain."

Mr. Lasselle, president of the newly founded Purple Plum Association, said that up to the year previous, these plums, when canned, were sold under twenty-three different names, such as tart plums, red Ital-ian plums, Idaho prune plums, fresh Italian prunes. . . . Now all the packers by cooperative agreement use the purple plum name.

Suddenly beyond the trees the Lasselles' house thrust itself out from the hillside like a new spring flower—flowers edged the driveway and the garden walks. Mrs. Lasselle opened the door and invited us into the dining room for a little tasting bee of desserts made with canned plums.

"Kathy made the pie," she told me, "by Grandmother Lasselle's recipe." Grandma, she said, lived to be ninety-six and spent most of her life cooking for the family. "The cake is one of Kathy's hurry-ups; the cobbler is something we have been making for years. The soufflé is my own idea."

Kathy, it turned out, was a fine cook, a 4-H Club member and winner of cooking and sewing prizes. Kathy loves to cook, and when she and mother turn loose, they often bake the day long.

OREGON

Oregon Double-Crust Purple Plum Pie

2 (8-inch) Perfect Pie Crusts (page 13)

2 (15-ounce) cans whole plums in syrup

½ cup sugar

2 tablespoons all-purpose flour

¼ teaspoon salt

¼ teaspoon ground cinnamon

1 tablespoon unsalted butter

1 tablespoon heavy cream, half-and-half, or whole milk

Makes one 8-inch pie

Preheat the oven to 425 degrees. Line an 8-inch pie pan with one of the piecrusts, reserving the other for the top.

Drain the plums, reserving ¾ cup of their juice. Pit, halve, and lay the plums on top of the crust. Pour in the plum juice. In a small bowl, combine the sugar, flour, salt, and cinnamon, and sprinkle into the pie; dot the pie with the butter. Add the top crust, seal, make vent openings with a sharp knife, and brush the top of the pie with heavy cream. Bake for 30 to 40 minutes, until golden brown. Remove from the oven and cool on a wire rack for several hours or overnight.

Quick-to-Make Plum Cake

2 (15-ounce) cans whole plums in syrup

½ cup (1 stick) unsalted butter

2 teaspoons baking soda

2 cups sifted all-purpose flour

1 cup sugar

½ teaspoon salt

½ teaspoon ground cinnamon

½ teaspoon ground cloves

½ cup raisins or chopped citron

½ cup chopped walnuts

Whipped cream or coffee for serving

Makes one 9-inch cake

Preheat the oven to 350 degrees. Grease a 9 x 5 x 2½-inch loaf pan.

Drain the plums and put them in a large saucepan; pit them and use a fork to mash them to a pulp. Add the butter to the pan and heat over medium heat, stirring, until the butter is melted and the mixture thickens. Stir in the baking soda, remove from the heat, and cool. Stir in the flour and the remaining ingredients; mix well.

Pour the batter in the prepared pan and bake for 60 to 70 minutes, until the top is browned and a wooden pick or skewer inserted in the center comes out clean. Cool the loaf on a wire rack in the pan for 20 minutes, then turn out onto the rack to cool completely. Serve warm with whipped cream or at room temperature with coffee.

OREGON

Any-Day Plum Cobbler

2 (15-ounce) cans whole plums in syrup

⅔ cup sugar

1 cup plus 2 tablespoons all-purpose flour

¼ teaspoon ground cinnamon

½ teaspoon plus ⅛ teaspoon salt

3 tablespoons unsalted butter

1 teaspoon baking powder

¼ cup milk

Whipped cream or ice cream for serving, optional

Serves 6

Preheat the oven to 450 degrees.

Drain the plums, reserving their juice. Pit the plums and place them in a 1½-quart casserole. Add the drained juices. Sprinkle with ⅓ cup of the sugar, 2 tablespoons of the flour, the cinnamon, and ⅛ teaspoon of the salt and dot with 1 tablespoon of the butter.

Bake in the oven for 10 minutes while mixing the top crust: In a large bowl, combine the remaining 1 cup flour, the baking powder, the remaining ½ teaspoon salt, and the remaining ⅓ cup sugar. Coarsely cut in the remaining 2 tablespoons butter. Stir in the milk until a ball of dough is formed.

Pat the dough into the shape of casserole, remove the casserole from the oven (the plums should be gently bubbling), and cover the fruit mixture with the dough. Bake for 25 to 30 minutes, until the dough is golden and the filling is bubbling. Rest for 10 minutes. Serve warm with whipped cream or ice cream, if you like.

SOFT AS A BUTTERFLY'S WING

The number was 395 Jerris Avenue, the town Salem, Oregon, the time, early morning, November 1948. Mrs. Douglas McKay, the new Governor's wife, was at home as usual and busy with her baking. A pleasant motherly woman exuding vitality, she dusted the flour from her hands and welcomed us. She knew exactly what we wanted without palaver. "I have everything ready, if you want to watch while I bake my angel food cake."

From 1933 to 1940, the McKay cake had taken the first prize annually at the state fair. In 1941 it came off with the grand prize and Mrs. McKay retired from the contest to give other good bakers a chance. Then, after seven years out of the running she entered the cake again, just to see how it rated. It was a first-prize winner!

"The recipe is not a secret," Mrs. McKay told me. "It's just a good angel food cake, but it's my way of whipping it together that makes the big difference." The cake is built on a huge turkey platter, a wire whisk for a beater. And the same platter then as for twenty-five years.

Sometimes the cake was given a lemon-butter frosting, or again a thick spreading of seven-minute chocolate icing. Mrs. McKay however preferred angel food plain, or served with whipped cream and folded into this, ground peppermint candy. But her late husband preferred his cake topped with ice cream and over this quick-frozen sliced and sweetened strawberries.

We had talked the morning away. The cake was baked, it had cooled. Now Mrs. McKay turned her prize from the pan. It stood tall, oven-tanned to pale gold. With two forks she broke out a piece for us to try. Snow-white the crumb, fine-textured, soft to the touch as a butterfly's wing. So light in the mouth. "How in the world do you do it?" Here are the directions exactly as she gave them to us.

OREGON

Mrs. McKay's Prize-Winning Angel Food Cake

1½ cups egg whites (about 13 large)

Pinch of salt

1¼ teaspoons cream of tartar

1½ cups sugar

1 cup plus 1 tablespoon sifted cake flour

1 teaspoon vanilla extract

Serves 12

Dust a 10-inch aluminum tube pan with flour.

Turn the egg whites into a very large bowl and add the salt. Beat with a wire whisk until the whites are frothy. Add the cream of tartar and continue beating until the mixture forms soft peaks. Sift the sugar into a small bowl and aerate it well; add it to the egg whites 1 tablespoon at a time, folding it in gently, so gently. Sift the flour 6 times to aerate it well, and add it 1 tablespoon at a time. Add the vanilla.

Pour the batter into the prepared tube pan and place it in a cold oven. Set the oven to 150 degrees and bake for 10 minutes, then increase the oven temperature to 200 and bake for another 10 minutes. Then increase the temperature 25 degrees every 10 minutes until the oven is at 300 degrees. Now give the cake another full 10 minutes, and at this point increase the temperature to 350 degrees and leave it in for 10 minutes longer to take on that delicate macaroon color. In all, 1 hour and 10 minutes and out comes the cake. Turn upside-down onto a wire rack and let cool for 2 hours. Remove the cake from the pan, frost with your favorite frosting, or leave plain.

IT'S MOTHER'S SOUR MILK chocolate cake that daughter Mary Lou, then a senior at Oregon State, asked to have made and mailed to Corvallis for midnight feasting. A second daughter, Mrs. Wayne Hadley, who lived just around the corner, favored the coffee cake.

Buttermilk-Chocolate Cake

½ cup (1 stick) unsalted butter, softened

1½ cups sugar

2 large eggs, well beaten

2 ounces unsweetened chocolate, melted and cooled

2 cups cake flour

1 teaspoon baking soda

1 teaspoon salt

1 cup buttermilk

1 tablespoon sour cream

1 teaspoon vanilla extract

Favorite frosting

Makes one 9-inch layer cake

Preheat the oven to 350 degrees. Grease two 9-inch layer cake pans.

In a large bowl using an electric mixer, cream the butter and sugar well. Beat in the eggs, then the melted chocolate. In a small bowl, combine the flour, baking soda, and salt. Add to the creamed mixture alternately with the buttermilk and sour cream, beating well after each addition. Add the vanilla.

Divide the batter evenly between the prepared pans and bake for about 30 minutes, until the cakes are springy and a wooden pick or skewer inserted in the center of the cakes comes out clean. Transfer the cakes to wire racks and let cool completely. Turn the cakes out of the pans and frost the middle, top, and sides with any favorite frosting.

OREGON

PIE TIMBER COUNTRY—APPLES, PEACHES, PLUMS, AND PEARS

WASHINGTON

In Washington, the Evergreen State, I found plenty of "pie timber" along with the pine timber. A fruity state with apples, apricots, pears, purple plums, and peaches—peaches that Mrs. Mayor Clinton of Seattle likes to make into her husband's pet peach glaze pie.

I gave the taxi driver the address. "The Mayor's house," I said, thinking he'd surely know where. He grunted, "Oh, yeah."

We drove a long piece, coming at last to one of those streets of all identical houses in a neighborhood of identicals. Here we are before a trim little cottage, the name Clinton spelled in metal letters on the screen door.

Deborah, age five, in a white flannel nightgown answered my ring. Behind Deborah came slender mother. "We are expecting you," she said. Behind her was father, Gordon S. Clinton, a boyish-looking mayor, mid-thirties, no more.

The little house was full of living. There was sewing in a basket, a pair of roller skates, a bowl of garden flowers. Supper was over but something lingered as a friendly reminder, a fragrance not unlike hamburger and onions. The living room opened wide to a small dining space. Mrs. Clinton suggested we sit at the table to talk—

more room there to spread out my notebook and her recipes.

The Mayor settled himself in a deep chair, the day's newspapers piled at one side, an extension telephone within easy reach.

"What does your husband like best in desserts?" The answer came from the deep armchair. "Tell her about your peach glaze pie. Tell her about your mother's ox-blood cake, but remember I like it with chocolate fudge frosting half an inch thick, not that sugar dusting."

"What do you cook at the summer place?" Now the older children, Barbara, eleven, Gordon, nine, had joined the interview. "Tell her, Mama, about the crab burgers." "Tell her about our picnics when Daddy cooks," piped little Deborah.

Mayor Clinton said, "Tell her about the crab mold you make for the bridge club." And so I added it to the crab lore I had brought back from Alaska.

Seattle Oxblood Cake

⅔ cup shortening

2 cups sugar

2 large eggs

2½ cups all-purpose flour

1 cup buttermilk

¾ cup cocoa powder

2 teaspoons baking soda

1 teaspoon salt

¾ cup hot water

Fudge Icing (recipe follows)

Makes one 13-inch cake

Preheat the oven to 350 degrees. Grease a 13 x 9 x 2-inch pan.

In a large bowl using an electric mixer, cream the shortening and sugar. Beat in the eggs one at a time, beating well after each addition. Add the flour and buttermilk alternately. In a small bowl, combine the cocoa powder, baking soda, salt, and hot water. Fold into the batter and stir just until smooth. Pour the batter into the prepared pan and bake for about 1 hour, until springy and a wooden pick or skewer inserted in the center comes out clean. Cool completely in the pan on a wire rack. Frost with fudge icing and serve in squares.

Fudge Icing

2¼ cups confectioners' sugar

5 tablespoons cocoa powder

6 tablespoons (¾ stick) unsalted butter, melted

5 tablespoons hot coffee

1½ teaspoons vanilla extract

Makes enough to frost one 13-inch cake

Sift the confectioners' sugar and cocoa into a medium bowl. Stir in the butter, then the coffee, followed by the vanilla, mixing well with a wooden spoon after each addition, until the frosting is smooth. Ice the top and sides of your cake with frosting.

Mrs. Clinton's Peach Glaze Pie

1 (9-inch) Perfect Pie Crust (page 13)

4 cups sliced fresh peaches

¾ cup water

1 cup sugar

3 tablespoons cornstarch

1 tablespoon lemon juice

1 tablespoon unsalted butter

Pinch of salt

Whipped cream and peach slices for serving, optional

Serves 6 to 8

Preheat the oven to 350 degrees. Line a 9-inch glass pie plate with the pastry. Trim the overhang to 1 inch, fold it under itself, and crimp decoratively, if you like. Refrigerate until chilled, about 15 minutes.

Line the pastry with foil and fill with pie weights or dried beans. Bake for 30 minutes, or until nearly cooked through and dry to the touch. Carefully remove the foil and weights. Bake for 10 minutes longer, until golden. Cool the crust completely.

Place 1 cup of the peaches in a large saucepan. Add the water, place over medium heat, and cook to soften, about 4 minutes. In a small bowl, combine the sugar and cornstarch and add to the peaches. Cook until the liquid is thick, clear, and syrupy, stirring occasionally, about 10 minutes. Add the lemon juice, butter, and salt; stir them in and then immediately remove the pan from the heat and cool. Arrange the remaining 3 cups peaches in the cooled pie shell and pour the cooled peach glaze over. Cover with foil and refrigerate for at least 4 hours or overnight. Top with whipped cream and a few peach slices, if you like.

Crabmeat Melts

½ cup cottage cheese

½ cup mayonnaise

1 cup jumbo lump crabmeat, flaked

¼ cup diced celery

2 tablespoons chopped onion

4 hamburger buns, cut in half

Butter for the buns

Serves 4

Preheat the broiler.

In a blender or using a handheld mixer, blend the cottage cheese and mayonnaise until smooth. Stir in the crabmeat, celery, and onion. Butter both sides of the buns. Toast the top halves of the buns and set aside. Spread the mixture on the bottom half of the buns and transfer to a small baking sheet. Broil until hot and browned, about 5 minutes. Top with the toasted bun halves and serve hot.

Note: A slice of fresh, juicy ripe tomato is excellent on these sandwiches.

WASHINGTON

BOATS OF GIBLET GRAVY

ome For Thanksgiving" means a family get-together for the Langlie clan of Olympia, Washington. During the twelve years Arthur B. Langlie was Governor, the annual harvest dinner was served in the gracious dining room of the State Mansion. This is a beautiful Georgian-Colonial house, family reunion size, with ballroom, dining room, great hall, and library. The Langlies are an old-fashioned family preferring foods traditional to the day. Always a mammoth roast turkey filled with bread stuffing, redolent of onions and sage. There are boats of giblet gravy, the giblets cut fine, as Mrs. Langlie likes them. There are two kinds of potatoes, a snowy butter-rilled mountain of the mashed and a bowl of golden glazed sweets. Green beans on the menu from the backyard garden by way of the freezer.

There are always two kinds of cranberry relish—the whole-berry sauce and the raw-berry mixture ground with fresh orange and sweetened with honey. Always a hot bread—usually popovers, Mr. Langlie's favorite.

Comes dessert and the dinner breaks with tradition. It's pudding, not pie, two puddings, these alternating year by year. One is persimmon, the other a Scandinavian dessert from Mr. Langlie's mother.

The Scandinavian pudding is a pretty sight, decorated with whipped cream and sprinkled with grated nuts or with small snippets of preserved ginger, or, if you wish, with red and green maraschino cherries.

Mrs. Langlie has cooked since she was a young girl at home in Pittsburgh when she and her sister pitched in together to help prepare meals for the family of seven. But music, not housekeeping, was her planned career. It was on a summer trip through the West that Miss Evelyn Baker of Pittsburgh met the young attorney Arthur B. Langlie of Washington. Then came housekeeping in earnest. Young attorneys have budgets to mind. Even today Mrs. Langlie plans all meals and for tea parties bakes this apricot bread.

Apricot Raisin Bread

½ cup dried apricots

1 large orange

½ cup raisins

2 tablespoons unsalted butter, softened

1 cup sugar

1 teaspoon vanilla extract

1 large egg

½ cup chopped walnuts

2 cups all-purpose flour

2 teaspoons baking powder

½ teaspoon baking soda

¼ teaspoon salt

Makes 1 loaf

Preheat the oven to 350 degrees. Grease and flour a 9 x 5 x 3-inch loaf pan.

Cut the apricots into small pieces, about ¼ inch each. In a small bowl, soak the dried apricots in enough water to cover until softened, about 30 minutes; drain. Peel and zest the orange, reserving the zest. Squeeze the juice from orange into a measuring cup and add enough water to make 1 cup. In a small bowl, combine the drained apricots, orange zest, and raisins. In a large bowl, cream the butter and sugar. Add the vanilla and beat in the egg. Stir in the fruit mixture and the walnuts. In a small bowl, combine the flour, baking soda, baking powder, and salt. Add it to the fruit mixture, alternating with the orange-juice mixture, stirring well after each addition.

Pour into the prepared pan and bake for 50 to 60 minutes, until a wooden pick or skewer inserted into the center comes out clean. Transfer the pan to a wire rack and cool for 15 minutes, then turn out onto the rack and cool completely. Cut into slices and serve.

Scandinavian Lemon Pudding

1 (¼-ounce) envelope unflavored gelatin

½ cup hot water

5 large eggs, separated

¾ cup sugar

Juice of 1 lemon

1 teaspoon grated lemon peel

Pinch of salt

Whipped cream and maraschino cherries or finely ground toasted almonds, optional

Serves 8

Dissolve the gelatin in the hot water and let sit for 5 minutes, until cooled to lukewarm. In a large bowl, beat the egg yolks well. Add the sugar a little at a time, beating constantly, until ribbony. Add the lemon juice and lemon peel and continue beating. Add the cooled gelatin mixture and beat again to combine; set aside. Place the egg whites in a medium bowl, add the salt, and beat until stiff. Fold into the egg-yolk mixture. Pour the mixture into a 1½-quart compote or other serving bowl. Cover and refrigerate until firm, at least 4 hours or overnight. Serve with whipped cream and maraschino cherries or finely ground toasted almonds as a garnish, if you like.

A GOLDEN SILKY HEAT lay over the valley. The car traveled full speed along the beautiful road by the side of the ripple-reefed Wenatchee River. Ahead the rugged Cascades lifted in a jagged rim rising straight up, it seemed, from the valley floor. Follow anyone of these little canyons opening so slyly into the narrow valley and you are in apple land. Through the town of Cashmere, Washington, and one mile beyond, up a steep and winding hill road to keep a tea date with Mrs. Kenneth Bixler.

Fern and Kenneth are apple growers; forty-five acres they have of the red and golden Delicious, a few of the Winesaps. Fern is Kenneth's right-hand helper—she keeps the books, pays the help, writes the letters, and keeps the business end of things running as well as her house. She learned about apples before she married. Her father, an orchardist, died the year Fern finished college and she came home to help run the family business.

Around a curve of the road Fern is waiting. Slim, blonde, tanned, a woman golden and silky as the day itself.

"The muffins are done, the tea is ready," and Fern led the way. "Let's eat on the terrace." What a view! The rustic house is built into the side of a mountain; it's a 400-foot drop into the valley. In a matter of minutes I was sipping flowery tea and eating apple muffins confected just for me. The oblique evening sun nibbled at the edge of the table. Once it stretched a warm finger as far as the muffin basket.

Apple Muffins

1½ cups all-purpose flour

1 cup sugar

1 teaspoon salt

1¾ teaspoons baking powder

½ teaspoon grated nutmeg

1 large egg, beaten

¼ cup milk

⅓ cup vegetable oil

½ cup firmly packed grated apple

1 tablespoon ground cinnamon

4 tablespoons (½ stick) unsalted butter, melted

Makes 9 medium or 12 small muffins

Preheat the oven to 400 degrees. Grease and flour a muffin pan.

In a large bowl, combine the flour, ½ cup of the sugar, the salt, baking powder, and nutmeg. In a medium bowl, combine the egg, milk, and oil. Make a well in the flour mixture and pour in the egg mixture. Mix just until moistened. Add the grated apple. Spoon the batter into the muffin pans and bake for 20 to 25 minutes, until a wooden pick or skewer inserted in the middle of a muffin comes out clean.

WASHINGTON

In a small bowl, combine the remaining ½ cup sugar and the cinnamon. Let the muffins cool in the pan on a wire rack for 5 minutes, then invert the muffins onto the rack. Brush the top of each one with the melted butter, then roll in the sugar-cinnamon mixture. Serve warm.

DARK AND SPICY DEPTHS

In this pine timber state the best holiday pies are stuffed crust to crust with "The Dean's Mincemeat." That's the word of a few hundred good cooks of Spokane who buy this "pie timber" sold each autumn as a moneymaker for the Cathedral of St. John the Evangelist.

It's made by the Dean's Guild, one of fourteen units of the women's division of the church, which holds its annual bazaar in early November.

The recipe belonged originally to Mrs. Charles A. Power. She told me about it one afternoon when we had a leisurely talk on the terrace of her newly built home with its spectacular view overlooking the city. Far beyond I caught glimpses of Kaniksu and Bitterroot Mountains.

When Anna Mae married Charles Power and came to Spokane to live in 1937, the Cathedral needed funds. It occurred to her to make her mother's mincemeat as a donation for the annual bazaar. Women took one look into its dark and spicy depths and bought jars by the half dozens.

The first year's sales were so phenomenal that ever after the mincemeat was made in quantity, six gallons at a time, in stone crocks, and allowed a few weeks to mellow, later to pack into pint and quart jars.

The church ladies make it according to a recipe without liquor, but if you like mincemeat with a bit of spirit give the crocks a brandy drink and let sit in a cool place for a lengthy time, adding more brandy as it's needed.

Instead of expensive beef, sometimes the guild ladies substitute chicken. Old hens are boiled until tender enough to slip the meat from the bones, then run through the grinder.

Bleu Cheese Dressing

3 egg yolks

½ teaspoon salt

½ teaspoon sweet paprika

¼ teaspoon dry mustard

3 cups vegetable oil

¼ cup cider vinegar

¼ cup sugar

¼ teaspoon salt

3 ounces bleu cheese, crumbled

½ teaspoon minced garlic

¼ cup tomato paste

¼ teaspoon celery salt

Makes about 3 cups

In a large bowl, beat the egg yolks; add the salt, paprika, and mustard. Whisk in 1½ cups of the oil very slowly and continue beating constantly until the mixture is thick. Whisk in the vinegar a little at a time, alternating with the remaining 1½ cups oil. In a small bowl, combine the sugar, salt, bleu cheese, garlic, tomato paste, and celery salt. Blend into the oil mixture. Cover and refrigerate until ready to serve over any favorite salad or vegetable.

WASHINGTON

WHEAT MAN, SEED MAN

On my travels around America I like to get out of the cities and visit on farms. So on a golden morning of warm sun I spoked out of Spokane, through the Palouse Hills. This is wheat country and it was near the harvest time. On either side of the highway was a golden ocean of ceaseless motion and flow. Momentarily it would flow asunder to show brown spaces where fields were fallowing . . . spring-harrowed, tooth-combed. Ahead we see the Moscow Mountains across the state line in Idaho. Into Pullman and out on Route 2 looking for the mailbox of wheat man, seed man, Max Hinrichs. But it's Mrs. Hinrichs we have come to visit, begging recipes.

Marge was having threshers the day we were there. Fourteen men sat down at the long kitchen table. Six dozen orange rolls disappeared before dinner was done. We had arrived mid-morning and Marge was in the kitchen with a high-school girl for a helper. At least one car every half hour came into the driveway. A knock at the door to pick up orange rolls or the bleu cheese dressing. Marge does a real business in these items, not just for money but to oblige the neighbors and because she thinks it's fun.

I stayed for luncheon and ate what the men ate. It was a banquet: fried chicken, broccoli with a bleu cheese sauce, boiled new potatoes and chicken gravy. Kidney bean salad was passed; a pickle relish in the mixture. We had leaf lettuce fresh from the garden with French dressing. Dessert was gelatin with banana slices and pineapple chunks. Also a boysenberry pie topped with ice cream. And as we said, the orange rolls—these but sun-kissed rapture.

Celery Seed Dressing

1¼ cups sugar

2 teaspoons salt

2 teaspoons dry mustard

½ medium onion, grated

½ cup cider vinegar

2 cups vegetable oil

2 tablespoons celery seeds

Makes 1 quart

In a large bowl, combine the sugar, salt, mustard, onion, and ¼ cup of the vinegar; beat well. Gradually add the oil, whisking constantly. Gradually whisk in the remaining ¼ cup vinegar. Add the celery seeds and beat until the mixture is thick. Cover and refrigerate until ready to use.

Note: This superb sweet dressing is perfect poured over a fresh fruit salad.

I FELT STRANGELY AT home in the Palouse Country in Spokane County. There where the wheatlands stretch over rolling hills, I was reminded of Kansas, my home state. And I was strangely at home in the ranch-house kitchen of Mrs. Jacob Rohwer. As farm women everywhere, Pauline Rohwer talked weather, talked crops and local politics, she talked recipes for cookies and cakes. Through the kitchen window she pointed out the family farmlands—160 acres of meadow and pasture yonder, there 160 acres of wheat and off beyond the horizon 120 acres more of pastureland.

"This isn't the home place," she told me. "Our son Earl took that over when he married and he and his brother Scotty, both agriculture graduates of Washington State College, farm it together."

We had morning coffee with Mrs. Rohwer and sampled two of her prize

products. First the brownies, rich and chewy like candy, so easy to make. Mrs. Rohwer told us she can stir up a batch in five minutes flat. These are the brownies that took a first prize one year at the Southwest District County Fair. The gingersnaps are prize winners too, and these made with sorghum. A drop snap and quicker to do than the rolled-and-cut kind.

Gingersnaps

⅔ cup sugar

¼ cup shortening

1 large egg

1 teaspoon vanilla extract

½ teaspoon baking soda

¼ teaspoon salt

1 teaspoon ground ginger

½ teaspoon ground cinnamon

¼ cup sorghum or molasses

1½ cups all-purpose flour

Makes about 50 cookies

In a large bowl using an electric beater, cream the sugar and shortening well. Beat in the egg and vanilla. In a small bowl, combine the baking soda, salt, ginger, cinnamon, and molasses. Blend into the creamed mixture. Add the flour, stirring well. Cover the bowl and chill the dough for 1 hour.

Preheat the oven to 400 degrees. Line several baking sheets with parchment paper. Drop the batter by teaspoonfuls onto the prepared sheets and bake for 10 to 12 minutes, until the cookies are browned and set. Cool for 2 minutes on the baking sheets, then transfer to wire racks to cool completely.

Mrs. Rohwer's Best Brownies

4 ounces unsweetened chocolate

6 tablespoons (¾ cup) unsalted butter, melted and kept hot

6 large eggs

3 cups sugar

2 cups all-purpose flour

½ teaspoon salt

½ cup chopped walnuts

2 teaspoons vanilla extract

Makes 4 dozen brownies

Preheat the oven to 450 degrees. Oil two 14 x 10-inch pans.

In a large bowl, combine the chocolate and hot melted butter, stirring constantly until the chocolate is melted. In a medium bowl, beat the eggs with the sugar. In a small bowl, combine the flour and salt; beat into the egg mixture. Add the melted butter–chocolate mixture, the walnuts, and vanilla and stir to form a batter.

Turn the batter into the prepared pans and bake for 12 to 15 minutes, until the top is shiny and lightly cracked, the edges are set, and the center is still a bit jiggly. Transfer the pans to wire racks and cool. Cut into squares while still warm and serve.

WASHINGTON

CHERRY TIME

It's in cherry time Mrs. John Van Hees of Vera Community, Washington, makes cherry omelets by dozens and half dozens—if not every day, at least three times a week and for any occasion, be it Sunday breakfast, a lunch for "the girls" or just to please John.

It is then she is pitting fresh Montmorency cherries to put away in the freezer for omelets to come and cherries for soup, the cold kind of the Continent so good in hot weather. Her recipe is from Germany, it belonged to her mother.

Irmgard Van Hees, born in Germany, came here with her family in 1910 when she was eighteen. She learned cooking in the Old Country and many such dishes show up on her menus, this sweet and sour spinach being an example. She cooks also in Dutch, having married a Hollander with a homesick palate. She cooks in American, the sons and daughters wanting the home table to be like that of their friends.

These cherry omelets are on occasion a full meal for a gathering of the Van Hees clan. It's just as I remember in strawberry time when our family had strawberry shortcake for supper and not a thing else but shortcake soaked in sugar and milk—and plenty of berries! So with the omelets. The Van Hees family has plenty of cherries—they can count seventy-five acres of orchard.

The work today is the business of the sons. Mother and Dad retired from the farm a few years ago to grow flowers commercially on a two-acre plot ten miles out of Spokane.

Cherry Omelet

6 large whole eggs

6 large eggs, separated

¾ cup all-purpose flour

¾ cup milk

Pinch of salt

1 tablespoon unsalted butter

3 cups pitted fresh tart cherries, sugared to taste

Serves 12

In a large bowl, combine the 6 whole eggs with the 6 egg yolks; beat until blended. Add the flour, milk, and salt and mix until smooth. In a medium bowl, beat the 6 egg whites with the salt until they form stiff but not dry peaks.

Heat an 8-inch cast-iron skillet over medium heat and melt the butter in it. For each omelet, pour in one twelfth of the batter (about ¼ cup), tilting the pan to cover the bottom. (The batter should be thin; if it thickens, thin with milk.) Let the omelet brown for about 1 minute. Spread one twelfth of the egg whites (about ½ cup) over half of the omelet. On the other half, sprinkle ¼ cup of the cherries. Fold the egg-white area over the cherries and cook over medium heat for another 60 seconds; turn and bake for 60 seconds longer. Serve immediately or transfer to a low oven to keep warm until all of the omelets are cooked.

Cold Cherry Soup

1 quart pitted fresh tart cherries

1½ quarts plus ⅓ cup cold water

⅓ cup cornstarch

Dash of almond extract

1 to 2 teaspoons sugar to taste, according to the ripeness of the cherries

Tiny macaroons

Serves 6

In a large saucepan, combine the cherries and the 1½ quarts cold water. Place over medium heat and bring to a boil. Reduce the heat to low and simmer for 3 to 4 minutes, until the cherries are softened and cooked through but not falling apart. Drain the cherries and return the juice to the saucepan. In a small bowl, make a paste of the cornstarch and the remaining ⅓ cup water; stir the paste into the hot cherry juice and cook, stirring constantly, until the mixture is smooth, about 5 minutes. Add the almond extract. Add the cherries and sugar.

Cover and refrigerate until chilled, at least 4 hours or overnight. Serve in soup plates with tiny macaroons sprinkled over each portion.

Sweet-and-Sour Red Cabbage

1 cup cider vinegar

1 tablespoon salt

2 tablespoons unsalted butter

1 large head red cabbage, shredded

1 cup sugar

2 medium Granny Smith apples, peeled and grated

Serves 6 to 8

In a deep pot, combine the vinegar, salt, and butter. Place over medium heat and bring to a boil. Add the cabbage, cover, reduce the heat to low, and simmer for 1½ hours, or until the cabbage is tender but still has some bite. Add the sugar and the apples; simmer for 30 minutes more. You may serve the dish warm or transfer it to a bowl, cover, and refrigerate until chilled.

PEAR COUNTRY

The trip started at dawn, out of Seattle over the Chinook Pass to Yakima, Washington, 138 miles to keep a lunch date—the menu, canned pears. Rugged mountains, fir-clad, laced with silvery waterfalls; peaks snowcapped. Mt. Rainier was lost in a veil of clouds. At the top of the pass we entered Yakima County, into the fruit valley. Here the climate is dry and water is a precious thing. The orchards growing on the hilltops thrive by irrigation. Into Yakima, a city of 41,000, where the canneries flourish, on through the town to a new section skirting the pear orchards. Here my hostess was waiting.

Mrs. Alva Strausz, wife of a leading pear grower of the region, had invited me for what she called "a canned-pear-dish sampling." At the time this seemed a queer notion. Why canned pear dishes when hundreds of acres of Bartlett orchards hung heavy with the harvest? But Bartletts, I soon learned, although fine to eat fresh, are the world's best pear for processing.

Olive Strausz, tall, slender, her raven hair streaked gray, pridefully showed me around her new home. The house was all on one level with picture windows enough to bring the garden indoors. The rose arbor seemed a part of the dining room.

The table was a pretty sight. It was set for twelve, soft pink the cloth, the centerpiece pink roses and blue delphinium. The guests were bigwigs of the pear world.

"Come see my kitchen and meet my mother." Mother was Mrs. Amanda Turner, supervising the last-minute details of the luncheon. Right-hand helper was Mary, wife of Bob Strausz, in business with Dad.

The meal was sit-down after helping ourselves to the buffet dishes. A turkey-sized platter was piled high with fried chicken and alongside this a great bowl of rice, accompanied by chicken gravy, the kind made with the giblets. "Help yourself to the pear fritters. Take two, eat them hot, there are more on the way." The relishes were on the table: apple jelly, pickles, stuffed celery and divine pickled pears.

The pear salad was a picture piece. This is served often in the Strausz home as a dessert-salad course to complete a rich dinner. For each salad plate halve a thin slice of orange to lay on a lettuce leaf. Soften cream cheese with cream, mold into balls, roll in chopped black walnuts. Drained, canned pear halves are next on the list, one for each portion. Place a half pear, cavity down, over a nut-crusted cheese ball. The dressing used is a half-and-half combination of the home-boiled, blended with a commercial mayonnaise. A little whipped cream is folded in for extra fluffiness. Over this a big sprinkle of wet-pack canned coconut. At Christmas build the salad on a slice of cranberry jelly instead of the orange.

Mrs. Fred Westberg contributed pear fritters. Her husband was the commission manager. Doris Westberg is Norwegian, and like most Scandinavian women, a very fine cook. These fritters are delicate in flavor with a thin batter coating that turns golden brown in the hot fat. The Pearadise Pie Doris made at home and carried still warm to the luncheon party. The recipe, she said, was originated by Mrs. George Eschback who grew up in the pear country and has developed many interesting Bartlett dishes.

WASHINGTON

Mrs. George Eschback's Pearadise Pie

2 (8-inch) Perfect Pie Crusts
(page 13)

8 fresh ripe Bartlett pears (about
4 pounds), peeled, cut in half,
cored, and sliced ½ inch thick

¾ cup sugar

1 tablespoon cornstarch

½ cup half-and-half

1 tablespoon orange juice

1 tablespoon lemon juice

1 tablespoon unsalted butter

⅛ teaspoon ground cinnamon

⅛ teaspoon grated nutmeg

Ice cream for serving, optional

Serves 6

Preheat the oven to 425 degrees. Line an 8-inch pie plate
with one disk of the pastry.

Arrange the pear slices in the bottom of the crust. In a
medium bowl, combine the sugar and cornstarch, then
stir in the half-and-half. Add the orange juice and lemon
juice and mix well. Pour the mixture over the pears and
dot with the butter. Sprinkle the cinnamon and nutmeg
over the top.

On a lightly floured surface, roll out the remaining crust
and cut it into ½-inch strips. Arrange the pastry strips
in a lattice pattern on top of the pear slices and seal the
edges. Bake for 35 minutes, or until the crust is browned
and the pears are tender when pierced with a knife. Serve
warm. Top with ice cream, if desired.

ALASKA

One adventurous summer I took a short course majoring in salmon in the Northwest. I followed salmon in their tearing hurry from river's mouth to spawning grounds, from river's mouth into nets, into boats; then to the canneries. I spent time in Washington, Oregon, and on into Alaska. By late August I was on intimate terms with the whole luscious pink-meated tribe from pale Coho to sister Silver, to big brother Chinook, king of the clan. I got chummy with light rosy Chum, so inexpensive, and met brilliant red Sockeye.

I was ready now for the climax of my visit, a Salmon Derby weekend on the Columbia River. We left Portland before sunrise up the long road to Sunset Highway. We were in a procession of cars, most of them with trailers hitched behind loaded with boats, and boats in turn loaded with tents and beds and fishing gear and food—supplies for the long weekend.

On the opposite side of the great river, the Washington fishing folks were bumper to bumper heading for the fishing grounds. Rosy the dawn—rosy the salmon. Everyone was talking about the derby windup. I should say derbies, four of these were going on at once, and enough boats in the Columbia River to jump your way across and never get your feet wet.

I was with Catherine Laughton of the *Oregon Journal* and her husband Charles and photographer Edmund Y. Lee. Katie pointed out the sights along the way: the Tillamook Burn of 1933, the biggest fire the white man had ever known in this area. "Three days Portland was in darkness," she said. Now the barrenness has been reforested, mostly with the help of the school children. Helicopters spread the fir seed. Tillamook County is the home of fine cheeses, home of fir trees and ocean breezes, lush grass and dairy herds.

We talked about the derby. What do these folks do with all the salmon they catch? Katie said, "Some have it custom-canned. There are companies who do this year by year. It is quite a business out here. Others clean their own fish and put it in the home freezer."

We came to the town of Astoria clinging to the green hills, now a resort town, once the frontier stop where Lewis and Clark spent a winter in 1805–6. Five years later at this point John Jacob Astor's fur trading company founded a colony. The Columbia River here is five miles wide and no easy crossing—it's a maze of sand bars.

The yacht we boarded to join the derby was owned by Thomas H. Sandoz. Young Tom Sandoz, Jr., and John McGowan were our hosts this day. The pilot was E. L. Matthews, general helper Henry Swanson, Jr. And every last one of us determined to do a little serious fishing.

Across the river from the deck we could see the Washington shoreline as we entered the main ship channel, leaving the western tip of Oregon. Through spyglasses we take turns viewing the scene, noting four to five thousand tents, homes of the derby entrants. Now the derby is discontinued. Sports fishermen in the country were taking one-fourth of the catch needed by the canneries.

This day the river is alive with boats, rowboats, life rafts, little dories, outboards. There are gill net boats, the kind that catch most of the commercial salmon, these chartered for derby use. Also commercial boats rented for parties. Coast patrol boats: we counted nine. The fishing area ran about twenty miles in length. Our motor was cut off; we drifted with the current, chumming, using frozen herring for bait with two hooks. Sun and clouds, boats yellow, red, blue. We waved at neighbors' boats who shouted their catch—we shouted ours.

Not everyone fished. Hotels in Astoria were filled with groups of wives and friends of entrants who were along for the ride. Cocktail parties were in session and canasta tournaments.

"What will you do with the salmon your husband brings home?" was my question to every woman I met. "Freeze it or can it," was the usual answer, "it's fish for a year." "But do you have special recipes?" Here are the best I gathered from both sides of the river.

Salmon Mousse

1 tablespoon unflavored gelatin

⅓ cup cold water

2 large egg yolks, lightly beaten

1 teaspoon salt

1 teaspoon dry mustard

1½ tablespoons unsalted butter, melted

¾ cup milk

2 tablespoons white wine vinegar

1½ pounds skinless salmon fillet, cut into 1-inch pieces

½ cup sliced green olives

Lettuce for serving

Serves 6 to 8

Grease a 1-quart mold. In a small bowl, dissolve the gelatin in the water and let sit until foamy, about 10 minutes. In the top portion of a double boiler, combine the egg yolks, salt, mustard, and butter. Gradually stir in the milk. Cook over hot water for 5 to 6 minutes, until thickened, stirring constantly. Add the gelatin and stir until dissolved. Remove from the heat and add the vinegar, salmon, and olives. Pour into the prepared mold, cover, and refrigerate until firm, at least 4 hours or overnight. Serve on a bed of lettuce.

ALASKA

Salmon Burgers

1½ pounds skinless salmon fillet, cut into 1-inch pieces

4 large eggs

2 tablespoons heavy cream

⅓ to ½ cup dried breadcrumbs, plus more for coating

½ teaspoon salt

Pinch of freshly ground black pepper

2 tablespoons cold water

3 tablespoons unsalted butter

½ cup finely chopped celery

4 toasted buttered buns

Serves 4

In the bowl of a food processor or in a blender, combine the salmon, 2 of the eggs, lightly beaten, the cream, breadcrumbs, salt, and pepper. Pulse until combined but not pureed. Transfer the mixture to a bowl. In a small bowl, lightly beat the remaining 2 eggs with the cold water. Form the salmon into 4 round burger shapes, taking care not to overhandle. Dip the cakes into the egg and coat lightly with breadcrumbs.

Melt the butter in a large skillet over medium heat. Add the salmon patties and sauté until well browned on both sides, about 4 minutes per side. Serve on the buns.

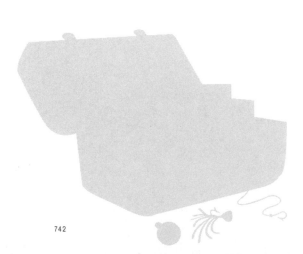

LAND OF INFINITE VARIETY

When the pioneers turned their eyes toward the Pacific Northwest reaching westward from Montana to include Idaho, Washington, and Oregon, they found a land of great natural resources. Rich was the soil, giant the timber, abundant the water. A land of infinite variety, and a lavishly stocked larder. The lush valleys, swift rivers, and great orchards yielded a wealth of good eating.

Here the fruit is the biggest, the berries the juiciest, the steak is the thickest, the salmon the freshest. Here is a man's world; appetites are hearty and food is cooked to satisfy. Yet, the Northwest hasn't any such thing as a regional cookery to call its own, Mrs. David Gaiser of Spokane, Washington, told me. "There are regional foods certainly," she explained. "Fresh salmon is our greatest delicacy. But this is a young and growing country and everyone has come from somewhere else bringing her own recipes, her own ideas of seasonings, which make the cooking a blend.

"Fresh salmon, for example, I like stuffed for a big dinner party, but the stuffing I use came from my sister who lives in Kalamazoo, Michigan. She uses it to fill any large fish and there it's usually a freshwater lake variety."

Salmon for dinner and Mrs. Gaiser picks a big one, weighing ten to twelve pounds, and serves the "king" stuffed. Parsleyed potato balls a good choice for a vegetable; add frenched green snap beans topped with sautéed chopped almonds. A dramatic ending, a watermelon basket filled with melon balls and fresh fruits, capped with scoops of raspberry ice.

ALASKA

743

Roasted Whole Stuffed Salmon

1 (10- to 12-pound) wild salmon, scaled, boned, and cleaned

1 tablespoon plus 1 teaspoon salt

3 tablespoons lemon juice

4 tablespoons (½ stick) unsalted butter

1 cup chopped celery

1 cup chopped celery leaves

2 small onions, finely chopped

½ pound mushrooms, thinly sliced

1 loaf whole-wheat bread, crumbed

2 teaspoons poultry seasoning

⅛ teaspoon freshly ground black pepper

8 ounces pimiento-stuffed olives, chopped

Serves 12 to 15

Preheat the oven to 425 degrees. Grease a very large rimmed baking sheet.

Rub the fish well inside and out with 1 tablespoon of the salt and sprinkle with the lemon juice. Lay the salmon diagonally on the prepared baking sheet.

To prepare the stuffing, melt the butter in a large skillet over medium heat. Add the celery, celery leaves, and onions and sauté until the onions are transparent, about 5 minutes. Add the mushrooms and cook for 5 minutes longer. Remove from the heat and add the breadcrumbs. Add the poultry seasoning, the remaining 1 teaspoon salt, the pepper, and olives. Lay the stuffing on one side of the salmon and tie the salmon with kitchen string at 3-inch intervals. Bake for about 1 hour, basting the salmon frequently with its juices, until just cooked through and an instant-read thermometer inserted into the thickest part registers 135 degrees.

Remove the salmon from the oven and preheat the broiler. Broil the salmon for about 3 minutes, until it is richly browned. The fish should be tender but not dry. Serve with a rich white sauce combined with hard-cooked egg slices.

A CRAB TUCKED TIGHT WITH SWEET EATING

In Ward's Cove, Alaska, I went to a new kind of party—called a crab feast. And some crab! The *bluestocking* of the Pacific Northwest, his everyday name Dungeness, his scientific name *Cancer Majister*. It is a crab tucked tight with sweet eating, meat in all the eight legs, in the two claws. There is body meat, too, moist and tender.

This was a late-summer party given near Ketchikan, Alaska, where I had traveled before for the salmon run and to visit the canneries. The Brindle Brothers, salmon packers of Ward's Cove, said, "You can't leave the North without eating the Dungeness, better by far than any Maine lobster." A party was arranged and I was invited to help pick the crabs fresh off the boat.

Before sunup we were down on the pier of the Pacific Pearl Alaska Canning Company, packers of the Dungeness. The crew of the *Five Brothers* was unloading its haul of 150 dozen crabs from the live boxes.

Winn Brindle picked twenty-four crabs and each one a beauty, the average weight two pounds apiece. Quickly now to Ward's Cove by car, and to the mess house where chef Royland Ryder-Smith took over with the boiling.

It was 108 steps, I counted, up the wooden stairway fastened to the cliff side right to the front door of Winn Brindle's house.

The sun poured a level flow of light through the picture windows into the living room, which is three hundred feet above the inlet. Across the green water I could see the spruce-covered points and beyond, the rose-haloed mountain peaks.

This was a family party—the four Brindle brothers who are in business together, and their young wives and a half dozen children.

Everyone pitched in to help. Winn and I cracked the cooked crabs on the back terrace. We shook out the body meat to heap on big platters.

Came the come-and-get-it call. We squeezed in around the table stretched its full length. Three platters were piled high with the crab. There were bowls of mayonnaise, vinegar, salt and pepper. There were munch stuffs: celery, green onions, radishes. Don't forget the garlic bread. A bottle of beer by every plate. Tossed salad was passed. After the feast was done, black coffee for dessert.

You can't repeat this crab party *au naturel* unless you live in the Northwest. But you can enjoy dishes made with canned Dungeness. Or you can use the meat of the blue crab of the East Coast and be happy in the eating! Especially the crab dip, which turns out something creamy that fairly melts in your mouth.

Miniature Deviled Crab Casseroles

¾ cup flaked crabmeat

1½ cups dried breadcrumbs, plus more for topping

½ cup heavy cream

½ cup milk

½ teaspoon salt

¼ teaspoon dry mustard

⅛ teaspoon freshly ground black pepper

¼ teaspoon Worcestershire sauce

1 pimiento pepper, chopped

2 teaspoons unsalted butter

Serves 4

Preheat the oven to 375 degrees.

In a large bowl, combine all of the ingredients except the butter. Spoon into four 5-inch crab-shell casseroles or 6-ounce baking dishes. Dot each casserole with the butter and sprinkle each lightly with breadcrumbs. Put the casseroles on a baking sheet and bake for 20 to 25 minutes, until the casseroles are browned and bubbly. Serve piping hot.

Dungeness Crab au Gratin for Two

2 tablespoons unsalted butter

2 tablespoons all-purpose flour

1 cup milk

½ teaspoon salt

⅛ teaspoon freshly ground black pepper

¾ cup flaked Dungeness crabmeat

½ cup grated Parmesan cheese

Dried breadcrumbs for topping

Serves 2

Preheat the oven to 425 degrees. Grease a 1½-quart casserole.

Melt the butter in a large skillet over medium heat. Whisk in the flour and cook until a paste forms and it turns slightly brown, about 4 minutes. Whisk in the milk and cook, whisking constantly, until thick and smooth, about 7 minutes. Add the salt and pepper. Remove the sauce from the heat and stir in the crabmeat. Pour the mixture into the prepared pan and sprinkle with the cheese and the breadcrumbs. Bake for 10 minutes, or until the mixture is hot and the breadcrumbs are browned. Serve hot.

Brindle Brothers' Crab Dip

1 cup sour cream

¼ cup mayonnaise

¾ cup flaked Dungeness crabmeat

1 tablespoon capers

1 tablespoon minced onion

1 tablespoon fresh lemon juice

Salt and freshly ground black pepper

Makes 2 cups

In a large bowl, combine all of the ingredients. Cover and refrigerate for at least 3 hours before serving. Use as a dip for crackers, toast, pretzels, cauliflowerettes, and celery sticks.

ALASKA

Pacific Crab Salad

½ cup sour cream

¼ cup minced celery

2 tablespoons chopped olives

1 tablespoon minced onion

1 tablespoon chopped parsley

2 tablespoons tomato sauce

1 tablespoon brown sugar

1 teaspoon cider vinegar

⅛ teaspoon ground cinnamon

Dash of ground cloves

Dash of ground allspice

¼ teaspoon salt

4 cups shredded romaine lettuce

2 large ripe tomatoes, peeled and cut in half crosswise

¾ cup flaked Dungeness crabmeat

1 hard-cooked egg, thinly sliced

Serves 4

In a medium bowl, combine the sour cream, celery, olives, onion, parsley, tomato sauce, brown sugar, vinegar, cinnamon, cloves, allspice, and salt. Cover and refrigerate to blend the flavors and chill, about 3 hours.

When ready to serve, arrange small beds of lettuce on 4 salad plates; put a tomato half on each. Pile the crabmeat on each tomato and spoon the chilled dressing over the top of each. Garnish with the sliced egg.

A COMPACT CUBICLE

It was a long way down to eat the sour-dough pancakes. The rungs of the iron ladder were two feet apart and it was a straight-up-and-down ladder from dock-side to water. Below, I could see the deck of the *Narada*, a seventy-two-foot cannery tender. I saw an upturned face, a waving hand, bandy legs well braced. That was Chef Phil Kerr.

I took a firm grasp on the top rung, took a last look at the green-clad mountains jut-ting behind the town of Ketchikan, Alaska.

Step by step down I hung on to those chilly rungs with hands, toes, teeth, and pure determination. Then a jolly "Hello!" from Phil Kerr, his bald head scrubbed to the shine of a McIntosh apple, his cheeks flamed to match. Phil was wearing his best black-and-white-checked pants, exactly like those worn by the top chefs in France. A nifty outfit topped with a sweatshirt and fancy suspenders.

"Come in, come in," he invited, leading the way to the galley, a compact cubicle. Here Phil cooks and feeds five to seven men during the salmon-brailing season as the boat cruises from one to another of the eleven traps owned by the Ketchikan Packing Company. When the tender's in port, the bosses come often, guests in tow, just to eat sourdough pancakes.

Fishermen eat big breakfasts. That morn-ing of my visit there was a choice of melon or fruit juice. There were eggs sunny-side-up, fried potatoes, thick slices of fried ham, a pile of buttered toast. A. great pot of cof-fee was purring gently on the back of the stove. Pancake reinforcements flapped my way about every four minutes.

"Eat up," Phil kept urging. "You ain't had any. Once I had an engineer who could eat fourteen in a row. But most of the fellows stop with six or seven."

Phil chewed on a toothpick, his face red now as a turkey's wattle. He dipped up bat-ter, let it trickle down, one cake, two cakes to bake at a time. The baking was done on the grid of the stove, this scoured between batches with a wad of brown paper. The grid was but medium hot, that is, a drop of water flicked on would dance gently with-out sputter and hiss. No grease, not if you want the cakes to be an even brown.

Sourdough is a staple of the Far North, and in the early days, Phil told me, was used throughout the Northwest and California, providing pancakes, biscuits, and other such products. This fermented dough came into use as a substitute for the fresh leav-ening in the pioneering days. A sourdough starter then was worth its weight in gold to those who lived far from a trading post. In the Klondike the trappers and miners and prospectors were so dependent on this forever-keeping dough they became known as "sourdoughs." Even today this is used to denote an old-timer.

Visitors to the Northwest who eat the sourdough products invariably ask for a starter recipe, determined to have these regional specialties passed on the home table. Results are seldom up to the beguil-ing memory. It's quite a job to keep a start-er going unless the temperature can be kept at a constant coolness. In olden days sourdough pots were kept going for years, but the need then was of real importance. A housewife would speak of her starter naming the years it was old. Brides took starters from their mother's sourdough when they set up for housekeeping.

Today there is a dehydrated starter sold by mail from Fairbanks, Alaska, but why bother with a starter? Make Phil Kerr's pancakes and a fresh start each time. Mix the batter the night before to finish in the morning.

Phil's Sourdough Pancakes

2 (¼-ounce) envelopes active dry yeast

4 cups plus ½ cup warm water

6 cups all-purpose flour

2 teaspoons salt

1 teaspoon baking soda

3 tablespoons molasses

5 large eggs, beaten

Vegetable oil for cooking the pancakes

Makes about 40 pancakes

Preheat the oven to 200 degrees.

In a large bowl, dissolve the yeast in 4 cups of the warm water until foamy, about 10 minutes. Stir in the flour. Cover the mixture and let stand at room temperature for 24 hours. When ready to cook, stir in the salt, baking soda, molasses, and remaining ½ cup warm water. Add the eggs; mix well but don't beat them. Let the batter stand for 30 minutes.

Heat a large heavy skillet over medium to medium-low heat and lightly oil the surface. Pour ¼ cup of the batter into the skillet for each pancake, spreading it slightly. Cook until the edges look dry, about 3 minutes. Turn the pancakes and cook for 1 minute. Transfer the pancakes to a cookie sheet and keep warm in the oven while making the rest.

CALIFORNIA

Gentlemen prefer cooking. Every other man I meet can shake an omelet with one hand and cut parsley with the other. They are inclined to the unusual dishes, elaborate concoctions to make your gastric juices thumb noses at La Belle France.

Once a man cooks he wants to talk about it, so sooner or later he writes a book. Nevertheless, it is still something of a sensation when a brigadier general makes cooking his hobby and writes a book to boot.

Brigadier General Frank Dorn is the man. He has lived in nineteen places in thirty years. It was in the Philippines that he first tried his hand at serious cooking, and started his world-wide collection of recipes. This recipe for halibut was the first of the lot, a dish rich in memories. It was a favorite with the men who dined in the bottle-lined bachelors' mess at Fort McKinley, a few miles from Manila. There the sliding window panels were of latticed shell; enormous trees shaded the long low building. Gone now since the bombing. But for General Dorn a legacy, this recipe taken from Francisco the cook.

It was a Geraldine who ran General Dorn as well as his kitchen when he was stationed at the Presidio in Monterey. She introduced the boss to the joy of baked ham well sauced in beer. In San Antonio, Texas, Berta Herrera spent her day in his kitchen chopping exciting hot mixtures, blending them artfully with mortar and pestle. One of her simplest creations, this Mexican chicken is the dish General Dorn liked best (recipe follows).

It was a surprise stop in St. Ignace on the upper peninsula of Michigan during the whitefish season that the General was served broiled whitefish livers at the Blue Bell Café. He developed the recipe using chicken livers and the liver of duck.

Broiled Spiced Chicken Livers

1 cup dry white wine

½ cup brandy

2 dashes of Tabasco sauce

2 tablespoons Worcestershire sauce

8 whole cloves

1 teaspoon caraway seeds

1 teaspoon minced fresh ginger

4 bay leaves

8 peppercorns

½ cup (1 stick) unsalted butter

Salt and freshly ground black pepper to taste

1 pound chicken or duck livers

1 tablespoon all-purpose flour

White radishes, optional

Serves 2 to 4

Combine all of the ingredients except livers and flour in a large saucepan. Place over medium-high heat, bring to a boil, and boil for 2 to 3 minutes. Place the livers in a large bowl, pour the liquid over the livers, cool to room temperature, then cover and refrigerate to chill for at least 6 hours or overnight.

When ready to cook, preheat the broiler. Remove the livers from the marinade to a broiler pan, draining off and reserving the marinade. Broil the livers until golden brown, about 3 minutes. In a small bowl, combine 1 tablespoon of the marinade with the flour and stir to make a thin paste. Pour the marinade into a large saucepan, place over medium-high heat, and bring to a boil. Reduce the heat to medium-low, gradually stir in the paste, and cook, whisking constantly, until thickened, about 7 minutes. Pour the sauce over the livers. Garnish with white radishes, if you like.

Mexican Chicken with Almonds, Raisins, and Oranges

1 (5-pound) chicken, cut into pieces

Salt and cayenne pepper

4 tablespoons (½ stick) unsalted butter

¼ cup blanched almonds

⅓ cup raisins

½ cup pineapple chunks

⅛ teaspoon ground cinnamon

⅛ teaspoon ground cloves

1½ cups orange juice

2 tablespoons all-purpose flour

¼ cup water

1 avocado, sliced

2 oranges, sectioned

1 bunch watercress

Serves 6

Preheat the oven to 200 degrees.

Wash and pat the chicken pieces dry. Season the chicken pieces well by rubbing them with salt and cayenne. Melt the butter in a large deep skillet over medium heat. Brown the chicken on all sides in the hot fat, turning as needed, 10 to 12 minutes total. Transfer the chicken pieces to paper towels to drain. Add the almonds, raisins, pineapple, cinnamon, cloves, and orange juice to the skillet and stir to deglaze the pan. Return the chicken pieces to the pan and cover with the sauce and fruits. Cover the pan, reduce the heat to low, and simmer for 1 hour, or until the chicken is tender. Remove the chicken, fruits, and almonds to an ovenproof serving platter and keep warm in the oven.

In a small bowl, make a smooth paste of the flour and the water and add to the liquid in the pan. Cook, stirring constantly, until thickened, 5 to 7 minutes. Pour the pan sauce over the chicken. Garnish the platter with avocado wedges, orange sections, and watercress. Serve with steamed rice and a green salad, if you like.

CALIFORNIA

Roasted Halibut with Onions and Bacon

½ cup (1 stick) unsalted butter

1 cup white wine

1 (2½-pound) halibut, skinned

6 slices large red onion

12 half slices of bacon

Salt and freshly ground black pepper

Serves 6

Preheat the oven to 400 degrees.

Melt the butter in a large roasting pan over medium heat. Add the wine, whisking constantly, and bring the mixture to a boil. Lay the fish in the wine sauce. Place the onion slices over it and cross its surface with the bacon slices. Season the fish with salt and pepper.

Bake uncovered for 15 minutes, then cover the pan with foil, reduce the oven temperature to 350 degrees, and continue baking for 20 minutes, or until the fish is tender. Transfer the halibut with its cooking juices to a platter and serve immediately with tartar or another favorite fish sauce, if you like.

HER ACRE OF GOLD

I found Lillian Johnson tending her acre of gold. It was a midafternoon in hot July that I came into the driveway of the Johnson farm out of Hollister, California. No one answered. My knock at the kitchen door, but a buzz of talk came from the apricot orchard. Heading that way I came to the cutting shed where women and girls were busy halving the fruit, laying the golden globes, pit-side up, over big trays.

Miss Lillian, they told me, was out on the drying grounds and there I found her marching up and down the avenues of trayed treasure. Two acres of fruit were spread out to the sun—one golden acre the apricots, one ebony acre the prunes.

Lillian Johnson waved; she came to meet me with a hearty handclasp. "One hour to finish and get the help paid," she said. "Then we can talk."

Lillian had no intention of being a rancher. She was born on the place but, eager for a business career, she took her home economics degree at the University of California and then Kansas State College for a master's degree in institutional management.

Her first commercial job was in the testing kitchen of General Foods, headquarters New York. It was during the war that her mother became seriously ill and there was no help available; Lillian returned home. The mother died and shortly after, her father, W. A. Johnson, came to poor health and Lillian stayed on to help her brother Carol manage the place—thirty acres of apricots, thirty-two acres of prunes. Some of these trees were among the first to be planted in that part of the state over fifty years back.

The father died and Lillian took the place to her heart. The ranch offered a better way of life than any city she had found.

Knowing Lillian to be a trained home economist, the purpose of my visit was to learn her ways with dried fruit. Each harvest she puts aside fifty pounds of dried apricots and the same of dried prunes for her own table. The apricots are stored in big galvanized cans with tight-fitted lids. The prunes are dipped first in hot water, one-half to one minute for the Imperials, two minutes for the French variety, then into a wire basket and a slow oven until the fruit dries. It is packed while still warm into cartons, paper bags, or into jars.

Apricot pulp Lillian makes in quantity and keeps on hand as a ready filling for cookies. She folds it into stiffly beaten egg white for a delicate fruited dessert, allowing one-half cup pulp to each egg white used. Delicious as a chocolate-cake filler, this made by folding pulp from one pound apricots into one cup whipped cream. Split two layers of chocolate cake to make four layers and sandwich together with the puréed fruit.

Pulp: Take a pound of apricots, soak two hours with water to cover, then cook in the same water until mushy and thick. Press through a strainer, measure, and add half as much sugar as purée.

Easy again this apricot confection: steam dried fruit in a sieve over hot water five minutes until warm but not overly moist. While still hot, roll in granulated sugar. Dry on waxed paper and serve as a confection—not quite a candy but very, very good.

CALIFORNIA

Deluxe Prune Cake with Mocha Cream Frosting

2 cups all-purpose flour

1 teaspoon baking soda

½ teaspoon salt

2 teaspoons ground cinnamon

1 teaspoon grated nutmeg

½ cup cocoa powder

½ cup (1 stick) unsalted butter, softened

1½ cups sugar

1 large egg

2 cups prune puree

½ cup prune juice

1 cup raisins

1 cup dried currants

1 cup coarsely chopped walnuts

Creamy Mocha Frosting (recipe follows)

Makes one 10-inch cake

Preheat the oven to 350 degrees. Grease a 10 x 7 x 2-inch baking pan.

In a medium bowl, combine the flour, baking soda, salt, cinnamon, nutmeg, and cocoa powder and set aside. In a large bowl using an electric mixer, cream the butter and sugar well. Add the egg and beat until well blended. Add the flour mixture, the prune puree, and prune juice alternately, beating thoroughly after each addition. Stir in the raisins, currants, and walnuts.

Pour into the prepared pan and bake for about 1¼ hours, until a wooden pick or skewer inserted in the center of the cake comes out clean. Cool the cake completely in the pan on a wire rack. Frost the top with the frosting directly in the pan, cut into squares, and serve.

Creamy Mocha Frosting

2 cups confectioners' sugar

1 tablespoon cocoa powder

3 tablespoons unsalted butter, softened

3 tablespoons hot coffee

Makes about 2 cups

In a small bowl, combine the confectioners' sugar with the cocoa powder. In a medium bowl using an electric mixer, cream the butter, gradually adding ½ cup of the sugar-cocoa mixture. Add the remaining sugar-cocoa mixture alternately with the hot coffee, beating until the mixture is of an easy spreading consistency.

CALIFORNIA

"**THERE IS A CENTRAL** Court into which carriages can be driven rising the full seven stories of the hotel past balustraded galleries to an opaque glass roof." This excerpt from a San Francisco newspaper dated 1875 described the entrance to the incredible halls of the newly opened Palace Hotel.

The Palace Hotel is still a world-famous hostelry but less amazing to this generation, surrounded as we are by architectural miracles. Yet no gourmet even today would think of visiting San Francisco and not dining at the Palace. I went knowing exactly what I wanted to eat: the Palace Court Salad.

Salad base is shredded lettuce cut fine as fine—use the scissors. Make a half-inch-thick mattress of the shreds to almost cover the plate. Center on this a thick slice of tomato, now a large heart of artichoke (these you buy canned), turn cup side up resting on tomato. Fill the cup with cooked crabmeat, cooked shrimp, or diced white meat of chicken marinated in French dressing and very well drained. Build the tower spoonful by spoonful to a peak five inches tall from the base of the artichoke. Over this dip three or four tablespoons of Thousand Island dressing as it is made at the Palace. Add two tablespoons sieved yolk of hard-cooked egg to trim the base of the salad like a golden wedding band. Umm—a good dressing!

Thousand Island Dressing

2 cups mayonnaise

1 (6-ounce) can tomato paste

½ cup chili sauce

¼ teaspoon sweet paprika

1 tablespoon tarragon vinegar

1 tablespoon chopped parsley

2 teaspoons chopped chives

1 teaspoon chopped tarragon

Makes about 3 cups

In a large bowl, combine all of the ingredients and gently mix until completely blended. Cover and refrigerate overnight to blend the flavors.

YOU HAVE HEARD, of course, of the green goddess dressing? *This* originated at the Palace but today there are as many versions of the goddess as ways to make apple pie. Here's the original recipe.

Green Goddess Dressing

4 anchovy fillets, minced

2 tablespoons minced onion

1 tablespoon minced parsley

1 tablespoon minced tarragon

4 teaspoons very thinly sliced chives

1 teaspoon tarragon vinegar

1½ cups mayonnaise

Salt

Makes about 2 cups

Combine the anchovies, onion, parsley, tarragon, chives, and tarragon vinegar in a medium bowl. Add the mayonnaise and gently whisk together until combined. Season with salt. Cover and refrigerate until ready to serve.

Note: Serve Green Goddess over greens tossed together in a salad bowl rubbed with a cut clove of garlic.

CALIFORNIA

WHATEVER THE DAY'S CATCH SUPPLIES

San Francisco's blue bay stirred in uneasy ripples. Little fishing boats cast purple shadows as they rocked themselves to sleep there by Fisherman's Wharf. Gill netters, purse seiners, trollers, crab boats, day's work done, were bedded down for the night.

I sat in a corner of Tarantino's Restaurant, its outer wall of clear glass, overlooking the harbor, looking into the West, all America at my back.

"What's this ?"

"Your bib, madam," said the waiter, tying a cloth of white around my neck. In red-stitched lettering the bib announced, "I'm eating cioppino." The words were scarcely digested when the stew arrived. The first fragrant fumes wreathed up to make friends with the nose.

I poked into the dish with an exploring fork, a strange gathering of seafare—oysters, lobsters, crab, clams. Then the first rapturous taste of the sauce-steeped garlic bread—delectable sauce.

This cioppino, pronounced "cho-PEEN-o," is a bouillabaisse of sorts, a kissing cousin of the bouillabaisse of Mediterranean cities, but this is a California creation, found nowhere else. Dan Sweeny, Jr., and Gene McAteer, the Erin lads who operated Tarantino's, told me the name is a corruption of the Italian word *cuoco*, which means "cook." A fisherman's concoction made first by the Genoese who man the small fishing boats that chug in and out of the harbor.

The dish is made over charcoal braziers, made of whatever the day's catch supplies. It may be shellfish entirely, or seafood and shellfish, the various kinds washed, cleaned, layered in the pot; then a rich garlicky tomato sauce added and the collection cooked. The fishermen usually leave the shellfish in the shells; restaurants and home cooks more often remove the meat. It's a matter of taste.

Visit San Francisco and eat cioppino or make it at home using the day's market catch. Here we give you the recipe exactly as it's made in the Tarantino kitchen.

Those who live inland may not be able to get the full assortment of shellfish mentioned, but never mind, do as Western cooks do—add what you please. As to seafood, boned striped bass and halibut, cut in two-inch pieces, are favorites for cioppino. Start the layering with the fish on the bottom, then tuck in the rest, any which way, but layered as to kind.

Tarantino's Cioppino

3 sprigs fresh thyme

1 fresh bay leaf

3 tablespoons olive oil

4 cloves garlic, minced

1 medium onion, minced

1 green bell pepper, cored, seeded, and diced

1 leek, white and tender green parts only, minced

3 green onions, minced

Salt and freshly ground black pepper

Dried red pepper

2 tablespoons tomato paste

1 (28-ounce) can whole tomatoes, tomatoes minced and juice reserved

2 cups white wine

20 uncooked littleneck clams in the shell, scrubbed

4 medium uncooked oysters in the shell, scrubbed

2 fresh live Dungeness crabs (about 2 pounds each) or 4 live blue crabs (about 1 pound each)

12 large uncooked shrimp, peeled and deveined

Garlic-toast fingers for serving, optional

Serves 4

Wrap the thyme and bay leaf in cheesecloth and secure with string. Set aside.

Heat the oil in a large heavy stockpot over medium heat. Add the garlic and sauté, stirring, until the garlic is light golden brown, about 2 minutes. Add the onion, green pepper, leek, and green onions, season with salt, pepper, and dried red pepper, and cook until softened, about 5 minutes. Add the tomato paste and cook for about 3 minutes, then add the chopped canned tomatoes. Add the wine, reserved tomato juice, and herb sachet and simmer to reduce by about half, 20 to 30 minutes. Reduce the heat to low, cover, and cook for about 1 hour, adding a little water if necessary, until the stew is thick and juicy. Check the seasoning and add more salt and pepper if needed.

Add the clams, oysters, and raw crab to the simmering stew, cover, and cook until the oysters and clams begin to open, about 5 minutes. Remove the oysters and clams to

CALIFORNIA

a large serving platter as they open. Season the shrimp with salt and add it to the pot. Cover and cook until just cooked through, 2 to 3 minutes.

Discard the herb sachet, adjust the seasoning, and return the oysters and clams to the pot to reheat. Check the consistency again, adding a little water if necessary and adjusting the seasoning before serving.

In the kitchen, heap the stew into soup plates, seeing that each bowl has some kind of each kind of seafood and a big helping of sauce. Garnish with garlic-toast fingers, if you like, and serve.

SLIVERS OF TRUFFLE UNDER THE SKIN

Blazing hot the sun there on the Bay Shore Road out of San Francisco. Past the orchards of pears, apricots, prunes. Past walnut groves and into the Almaden Vineyard gate to be welcomed by our host and hostess, Mr. and Mrs. Louis A. Benoist.

This occasion was a luncheon for the Benoists' friends among the wine growers of the Valley and a few guests from away. Quite a company—places were set for thirty-two guests at the long table under the wide spread of the lace-leafed pepper trees.

Grapevines opulently green stretched from the edge of the terrace far into the valley. There was a shimmer of heat over the vineyard, and beyond, the Santa Cruz Mountains reared their heads in a soft haze of changing blues.

The farmhouse, Mrs. Benoist told me, was built in 1852 by Etienne Thèe, a Bordeaux farmer. His son-in-law, Charles Lefranc,

who later came to own the farm, doubled its acreage, naming it Almaden after the quicksilver mine on an adjacent hill.

In this old house, Anna Held had that famous champagne bath as a change-off from milk. Then as now champagne was the vineyard's pride. Almaden Brut champagne was the drink on the terrace while a foursome of Mexican minstrels in native costume entertained with their sad-gay Spanish melodies.

Then luncheon came. Pink-cheeked Louis Benoist presided at one end of the thirty-foot table, with gracious blonde Katherine opposite. Waiters hurried from the house across the lawn with tray loads of glasses, trays of food.

Salad the first course in the California manner. Garlic-tinctured croutons had been tossed along with the dressing and the medley of greens. The dressing was the quintessence of simplicity, made of California olive oil with red wine and tarragon vinegars. A cold-meat plate accompanied the salad, the ham sliced leaf-thin (the hogs raised right here on the home place), stuffed eggs for the platter and sliced tomatoes. Came the garlic bread hot from the oven.

Baby turkey, with creamed green beans for the main course. The turkeys, seven-pounders, boned the day before cooking and slivers of truffle inserted just under the skin, then left overnight in the refrigerator to allow the truffle perfume to permeate the meat. Broiling was the method of cooking; butter for basting. At the last, the addition of a gourmet sauce, a creation too difficult for the average cook to make.

The beans were a dish anyone might do. These garden-fresh, cut frenched style, cooked until just tender in boiling, salted water barely to cover, drained and heavy cream added. Over this a sprinkling of grated Parmesan and Gruyère cheese and into the oven until the cream thickened into a rich sauce and the cheese had melted and delicately browned.

Fresh freestone-peach halves for dessert; these had been peeled and sprinkled with cognac and left in the refrigerator for an hour before serving, or use champagne.

Louise Savin cooked this luncheon, each detail a perfection, and she a woman totally blind. Daughter-in-law Sally was her right-hand helper. But without Sally, Louise could have managed the meal. She has learned by touch every inch of the big kitchen. She knew the location of each pot, of each wine and liqueur, each condiment, each kind of spice. She gave us details for Chicken Raphael Weill, a dish served often to Almaden guests and easier than the boned turkey broilers.

Chicken Raphael Weill

3 (2-pound) chickens, cut into pieces

½ cup (1 stick) unsalted butter

2 tablespoons minced shallots

½ cup white wine

2 cups heavy cream

4 large egg yolks

Pinch of fresh or dried parsley

1 teaspoon minced chives

Dash of grated nutmeg

Cayenne pepper

Salt

Serves 6

Wash the chicken pieces and pat them dry. Melt the butter in a large deep skillet. Add the chicken pieces in batches and sauté until they are golden in color, about 10 minutes. Drain the chicken on paper towels. Add the shallots to the pan and sauté for 3 to 4 minutes more. Stir in the wine and deglaze the pan. Add 1½ cups of the cream and stir. Put the chicken back in the pan, cover with the sauce, reduce the heat to low, cover, and simmer to thicken the sauce, about 20 minutes.

In a medium bowl, beat the egg yolks with the remaining ½ cup cream and add it to the chicken. Shake the pan to mix the ingredients. Increase the heat to medium and heat to just under boiling. Keep shaking the pan gently until the sauce thickens. Add the parsley, chives, and nutmeg and season with cayenne and salt. Serve immediately.

Note: The chicken is turned to a platter and served garnished with small bundles of frenched string beans. The beans are sliced lengthwise on a slight bias, tied with string into one-portion bundles and boiled in very little salted water until tender; now drain and sauté a moment in butter. Not too done—keep the beans nice and green. Usually potato marbles are Louise's choice for a second vegetable, the balls sautéed golden in butter, then lid on the pan and the potatoes get tender before serving.

THE STURDY REDWOOD HOUSE built on a hillside, built on three levels, is claimed to be the oldest house in Piedmont, California. A long flight of steps led up to the door and to a rambling porch that extended over a flowering garden. A magnificent view; the city of Oakland below and beyond the Golden Gate Bridge, strong and lovely in the morning sun.

Mrs. Richard S. Wright was waiting at the top of the steps, her gray-blue eyes smiling a welcome. "Let's talk in the kitchen and have coffee and toast." This was a comfortable large room opening to a sunlit patio. "It's here I hold my cooking classes," she said. "Just a few hours each week. I do it for fun. The extra money buys little surprises for my two girls. Both are married. There is only my youngest child Jack and my husband to cook for now, so I have time on my hands."

Her greatest pleasure is in the creation of new recipes. She uses wine with a generous hand, she is clever in seasoning with herbs. Many of her vegetable dishes are of original devising.

She does a delicious broccoli piquante that would make the most virulent enemy of this vegetable its devoted friend for life. Try her baked spinach, the stuffed zucchini.

Roasted Spinach-Stuffed Zucchini

6 small-to-medium zucchini (about 2¼ pounds), ends trimmed

1 cup fine soft breadcrumbs

½ cup finely chopped well-drained cooked spinach

½ cup grated Parmesan cheese

1 tablespoon minced onion

2 large eggs, lightly beaten

2 tablespoons olive oil

¼ teaspoon dried thyme

Salt and freshly ground black pepper

Garlic salt

Sweet paprika

Serves 6

Preheat the oven to 350 degrees. Grease a large shallow baking dish.

Wash the zucchini and cut each in half crosswise, making 12 cylinders 4 to 5 inches long. Using a melon baller or small spoon, scoop out the flesh to form cups with a ¼-inch-thick shell. Finely chop the scooped-out pulp and place it in a large bowl. Add the breadcrumbs, spinach, ¼ cup of the cheese, the onion, eggs, oil, and thyme and season with salt and pepper. Fill the half shells with the mixture. Place in the prepared baking dish, sprinkle the tops with the remaining ¼ cup cheese, and season with garlic salt and paprika. Bake for 40 to 50 minutes, until the zucchini is tender and heated through. Serve hot or at room temperature.

CALIFORNIA

Baked Spinach with Bacon

2 tablespoons unsalted butter or bacon fat

1 (10-ounce) package frozen chopped spinach, thawed

Grated nutmeg

Salt and freshly ground black pepper

2 large eggs, lightly beaten

3 tablespoons fine dry breadcrumbs

4 bacon slices

Serves 4

Preheat the oven to 350 degrees. Grease a 1½-quart casscrole dish.

Melt the butter in a large skillet over medium heat. Add the spinach and sauté until heated through and tender, 3 to 4 minutes. Season with nutmeg, salt, and pepper. In a small bowl, combine the eggs and breadcrumbs and stir into the spinach. Scrape the mixture into the prepared casserole and cover the top with the bacon. Bake for about 45 minutes, until the mixture is bubbly and brown. Remove the bacon, dice it, and mix it into the casserole. Serve hot.

Note: If desired, ½ cup chopped nuts or chopped mushrooms or grated cheese may be mixed into the spinach with the breadcrumbs and eggs.

Creamy Broccoli Casserole

1½ tablespoons unsalted butter

1½ tablespoons all-purpose flour

½ cup warm milk

2 cups chopped cooked broccoli
(if using frozen, thawed)

½ cup mayonnaise

1 tablespoon minced onion

3 large eggs, well beaten

Salt and freshly ground black pepper

Serves 6

Preheat the oven to 350 degrees. Grease a 1-quart casserole.

Melt the butter in a medium saucepan over medium heat. Stir in the flour to make a paste and cook until lightly browned, 4 to 5 minutes. Slowly whisk in the warm milk, a little at a time, whisking constantly. Cook, whisking, until the sauce thickens, about 7 minutes, then take the pan off the heat and reserve the sauce.

In a large bowl, combine the remaining ingredients and stir in the warm sauce. Pour into the prepared casserole, set the casserole in a roasting pan, and pour in enough hot water to come halfway up the sides of the casserole. Bake for about 45 minutes, until browned and firm. Rest for 10 minutes before serving.

Note: Spinach, Swiss chard, artichoke hearts, or asparagus may be substituted for the broccoli with equally good results.

CALIFORNIA

THE PARTIES AT EKBACKEN, that's Mama Gravander's house, make Christmas really Christmas in Mill Valley. We speak for the children. Then comes their annual meeting with *Julbocken*, the straw ram, the steed that *Tomte*, the Swedish Santa Claus, rides when he travels packloaded with presents for the good boys and girls.

Christmas at Ekbacken means cookies, hundreds of dozens of cookies all baked by Mama herself. Weeks before the holiday she is busy creating the gingerbread figures. Christmas to Mill Valley youngsters means storytelling around the hearth at Ekbacken and Mama telling the tales of how it was at Christmas when she was a child long ago in Sweden. Each holiday she observes the Old Country customs for the pleasure of her neighbors and the excitement of the little ones.

Two parties are given, the last on Twelfth Night; the first, December 13, darkest day of Sweden's year when Santa Lucia, the Goddess of Light, is feted. In Sweden, it's a national celebration observed in homes, offices, hospitals, and Santa Lucia is impersonated. Refreshments follow—a vast array of sweets and the flowing bowl. Mama Gravander's galas are for the neighborhood only.

She greets her guests in her native dress, full-skirted, tight-bodiced, with hand-woven apron and white shawl. She wears a tiny felt bonnet.

Each autumn the little girls in the neighborhood get in a tizzy of excitement. "Which of us," they wonder, "will Mama choose this year to be Santa Lucia," to wear the flowing white robes and the candlelighted headdress? Santa Lucia is the cookie bearer. She will enter the studio on the party evening bearing a great tray of sweets.

Holiday Walnut Meringues

3 cups sugar

12 large egg whites

Dash of salt

1½ cups finely chopped walnuts

Makes about 6 dozen cookies

Preheat the oven to 250 degrees. Line several baking sheets with parchment paper.

In the top portion of a double boiler, combine the sugar, egg whites, and salt. Place over boiling water and beat with a handheld beater until the mixture holds its shape and medium peaks form. Remove from the double boiler and fold in the walnuts. Butter a baking sheet and dust lightly with flour. Drop the mixture onto the prepared sheet using 2 teaspoons, one to dip, one to push the dip.

Bake for 1 hour, or until the meringues are lightly browned and completely dry. To test, remove one meringue from the oven, let cool for 1 minute, then taste; it should be dry and crisp all the way through. Let the meringues cool completely on the pans.

Note: The meringues may be stored in an airtight container for up to 3 days.

Almond Fingers

1 cup (2 sticks) unsalted butter, softened

⅓ cup plus 2 tablespoons sugar

½ teaspoon almond extract

2½ cups all-purpose flour

1 large egg, beaten

15 blanched almonds, chopped

Makes about 5 dozen cookies

In a large bowl, cream the butter and ⅓ cup of the sugar until fluffy. Add the almond extract and flour and mix thoroughly to form a batter. Cover the bowl with plastic wrap and refrigerate until chilled, about 1 hour.

When ready to cook, preheat the oven to 350 degrees and line several baking sheets with parchment paper.

On a lightly floured surface, roll out the dough ½ inch thick and cut into 2 x ½-inch strips. Brush with the egg and sprinkle with the almonds and remaining 2 tablespoons sugar. Place on the prepared baking sheets and bake for 8 to 10 minutes, until the fingers are golden yellow. Cool in the pan on wire racks for 2 minutes, then transfer to the racks to cool completely.

CALIFORNIA

TOO RIPE FOR THE LONG HAUL TO MARKET

It was the Fourth of July, 1921, that Helen Power, a California fruit grower's bride, made up her mind to do something about a bad situation. Overnight had come a hot spell—the plums and figs ripened, and too ripe, for the long haul to market.

A busy day on the highway—young Helen had an idea. Why not set up a stand under the black walnut tree and sell what she could to passers-by? Grandfather Josiah Allison had planted that tree by the road in 1859 on the old Immigrant Trail. The tree would bring them luck! Edwin, her husband, made a table of planks to lay over sawhorses. Helen covered this with a best tablecloth. At either end a bowl of flowers and an American flag, in the middle of the table a six-foot tray of the beautiful figs and plums.

Edwin carried out a rocking chair and a magazine for his lady to enjoy when she had time on her hands. She didn't get much reading done—this proved to be the busiest day Helen can ever remember. Ed had to help. Together they sold over $50 worth of fruit, all in driblets.

Fall came; the Powers had found a new way to make farming pay. They borrowed $1,500 to build a roadside shack and they began serving sandwiches, bacon and eggs at a short-order counter. They sold dried fruits and nuts from the farm. Thereafter each year the place was expanded.

Today the Nut Tree is one of California's most spectacular roadside restaurants and marketing centers. It's located at Vacaville, between Sacramento and San Francisco. Now there are five dining rooms, with facilities for three hundred guests at one seating.

The shopping area is divided into many departments—toy shop, flower shop, fresh fruits, candies. People come to eat and shop from miles around.

Today the entire Power family is engaged in the operation, employing 150 people in addition. Helen's husband, Edwin I. Power, manages the orchards and is buyer of the delicacies. Mary Helen, a daughter, is the personnel manager. Ed Junior is in charge of the toy and gift shop. Robert, a graduate of the restaurant division of the City College of San Francisco, does the food planning. Many of his menu items are spectaculars. Example: the fabulous sandwiches served with green potato salad.

Among the most famous of the pastries is a chess pie that has been on the menu thirty years, a recipe from Helen's sister, Edith Harbison. But plain bread gets the most compliments, real homemade bread by an easy-to-do recipe that was developed by Grandmother Hester Harbison who died only a few years ago when she was ninety-five.

The Nut Tree's Signature Bread

1 cup warm water

1½ tablespoons sugar

1 (¼-ounce) envelope active dry yeast

3 cups bread flour

1½ teaspoons salt

Makes one 9-inch loaf

Pour the water into a large bowl. Add the sugar and yeast and stir until dissolved; set aside for about 5 minutes. Add 1½ cups of the flour and the salt; beat hard with a spoon for about 2 minutes. Gradually add the remaining 1½ cups flour, mixing first with a wooden spoon, then with your hands to make a smooth, springy ball of dough, about 5 minutes. Cover the dough bowl with a towel and allow to stand in a warm place until doubled in bulk, about 45 minutes.

Preheat the oven to 425 degrees. Grease a 9 x 5 x 3-inch pan.

Flatten the dough out on an oiled board. Shape into a loaf and put into the prepared pan. Cover and let rise in a warm place until tripled in bulk, about 30 minutes. Bake for 25 to 30 minutes, until the loaf is golden brown and sounds hollow when tapped. Cool in the pan on a wire rack for 10 minutes, then turn out onto the rack to cool completely.

Note: If you prefer, the dough may be divided into 4 individual loaves and baked in 5 x 2½ x 1½-inch pans at 400 degrees for 20 minutes.

CALIFORNIA

Frosty Green Potato Salad

4 pounds unpeeled potatoes (about 12 medium), cut into quarters

½ cup chopped parsley

¼ cup chopped green bell pepper

¼ cup chopped celery tops

¼ cup chopped green onions

¼ cup chopped dill pickle

1 cup mayonnaise

¼ cup French Dressing (page 246)

2½ teaspoons salt

1 teaspoon dry mustard

½ teaspoon freshly ground black pepper

Sprigs of watercress or chopped celery tops for garnish, optional

Serves 8

In a large stockpot, boil the potatoes in water to cover until tender, 20 to 30 minutes. Drain and set aside until cool enough to handle. Peel the potatoes, then cut them into ½-inch cubes and put them into a bowl. In a small bowl, combine ¼ cup of the parsley, the green pepper, celery tops, green onions, and pickle.

Take out about ½ cup of the mixture, place it in a small bowl, and add the remaining ¼ cup parsley. Add the potatoes to the vegetable mixture. In a small bowl, combine the mayonnaise, French dressing, salt, mustard, and black pepper. Add to the salad and toss to mix well. Pack the potato salad into an 8 x 8 x 2-inch pan or shallow 2-quart baking dish. Sprinkle the reserved parsley mixture over the top. Cover the mixture with plastic wrap and refrigerate until chilled, 3 to 4 hours. Lift out servings with a flat spatula and garnish each serving with sprigs of watercress or chopped celery tops, if you like.

A DAY OF TURQUOISE sky, we headed out of Sacramento, up the river valley straight into the pear country around Placerville. Destination was the George Volz Ranch, six miles out, down the Carson Road; object a pear party, Mrs. Volz our hostess. This was to be a sampling of pear dishes to show how wives of the pear country use their native fruit—as commonly, I discovered, as other women use apples, in puddings, pies, in a sauce to substitute in applesauce cake.

My guide for this trip was F. W. Read, Assistant General Manager of the California Fruit Exchange, which is located in Sacramento. Mrs. Read was along, bringing her frozen pear salad, which made the trip in dry ice. With my appetite in high gear we reached Placerville. Pear orchards here spread on every side in even spaced lines over the rolling foothills. Beyond rose the mountains, slate-colored, darkly silhouetted against a pale morning sky.

A quick look now into the world's largest pear-packing plant owned by the Placerville Fruit Growers Association and built especially for handling pears for Eastern cities. But my visit to the Volz Ranch was much more exciting. Here the orchards average a pear yield per tree of around two thousand fruit.

We stayed a long time in that orchard watching the pickers busy on ladders, listening to their shouts, their wisecracks, hearing the gentle thud of fruit into picking sacks, watching how the bowed branches, released of their burden, rose high again to the sky.

"Luncheon's ready," came the call down the orchard row. I hurried back to the house. Fruit made the table centerpiece, a long low arrangement of Bartlett pears, nectarines, red Malaga grapes, the ribiers, and the Thompson seedless.

Noodle-meat casserole was the mainstay dish, which Mr. Volz fancies and had asked his wife to have for me. Other things were homemade yeast rolls, these a base for the pear and cherry jelly. Snap beans the green vegetable and the big jellied-pear salad molded in a ring, garlanded with romaine, the center filled with a cream dressing. After this a pear pie.

CALIFORNIA

Mary Read's Old-Fashioned Creamy Chilled Pear Salad

6 large Bartlett pears, peeled, cut in half, and cored

About 24 maraschino cherries

6 ounces cream cheese, softened

10 tablespoons mayonnaise

1 cup apple juice

1 small head romaine lettuce, large tough outer leaves removed

½ cup heavy cream

Serves 12

Arrange the pears, cavity up, in bottom of a flat-bottomed gelatin mold. Place the cherries in the cavity of the pears and between the pears. In a large bowl, blend the cream cheese and 5 tablespoons of the mayonnaise; slowly beat in the apple juice. Pour the mixture over the pears. Cover the mold with plastic wrap and freeze until firm, at least 4 hours or overnight. When ready to serve, arrange the lettuce on a serving dish. Unmold the salad in the center of a plate. In a large bowl, whip the cream until stiff and fold in the remaining 5 tablespoons mayonnaise. Fill the center of the mold with the dressing. Serve cold as a luncheon or brunch dessert.

MID-HARVEST IN THE CLING PEACH ORCHARDS

It was mid-harvest in the great cling peach orchards of the Sacramento Valley. The air was a murmurous hot haze; the roads thundered to the traffic of cannery trucks and trailers stacked high with boxes of the beautiful fruit.

At Yuba City I asked my way to the Blazer Ranch. Earnest Blazer, I knew, was the largest peach grower in the valley with two thousand acres. I knew, too, that Mrs. Blazer was called a wonderful cook and especially clever at baking.

The Blazers' rural Eden is built of brick, a ranch-style house, eight rooms, utterly modern. The kitchen is twenty feet long, a dining nook at one end with wide windows facing toward the orchards.

Mrs. Blazer said, "It's the home Earnest and I have talked about having since we were married in 1918. We started housekeeping in two rooms, surrounded by twenty acres in Thompson grapes." Their house grew with the family, a boy, a girl, and finally six rooms with all the modern extras. Now the children are married and in nearby homes. And at long last, just a few years ago, Eleanor and Earnest built the house of their dreams.

In Mrs. Blazer's big kitchen we had peach cake and coffee and talked recipes. Fresh clings she had used in the cake, but the canned she likes better. Each season she puts up some 150 quarts for home use— halves, slices, and whole fruit. She pickles the small sizes, a few dozen jars; she freezes at least thirty pints.

Along with the peach cake Mrs. Blazer passed the cookie jar. "I keep it filled for the grandchildren," she explained. "Our son, Earl, who lives half a mile down the road has three. My daughter, Mrs. Karl Staple," she nodded toward a house almost in her backyard, "has three more."

The family has a summer place at Cisco Cove, Sierras, near Dorner Summit on Lake Tahoe. It was there one evening, planning to make a peach cobbler, Mrs. Blazer discovered she was out of everything needed except the peaches. She used a ready-mix pancake flour. It turned out perfect. The recipe is a cinch to make.

CALIFORNIA

Peach Upside-Down Cake

½ cup (1 stick) unsalted butter

1 cup brown sugar

4 large ripe peaches, peeled, pitted, and sliced

2 tablespoons large whole pecans or walnuts

1 cup sifted all-purpose flour

1 teaspoon baking powder

½ teaspoon salt

3 large eggs, separated

1 cup granulated sugar

5 tablespoons peach juice (from canned peaches) or canned pineapple juice

Whipped cream for serving, optional

Serves 12

Preheat the oven to 375 degrees.

Melt the butter and pour it into a 12 x 8-inch pan. Spread the brown sugar evenly in the pan. Arrange the peach slices on top of the brown sugar; fill any spaces with the nuts.

In a large bowl, combine the flour, baking powder, and salt. In a small bowl, beat the egg yolks until light colored. Gradually beat in the granulated sugar and blend in the peach juice. Make a well in the flour and pour the egg yolk–peach mixture in and stir together to form a batter. In a medium bowl, beat the egg whites until stiff peaks form and fold the egg whites into the batter.

Pour the batter over the peaches in the cake pan and bake for 30 to 35 minutes, until a wooden pick or skewer inserted in the cake comes out clean. Cool the cake in the pan on a wire rack for 5 minutes, then invert the cake onto a platter to cool completely. Cut into squares and serve topped with whipped cream, if desired.

OVER DESERT, OVER MOUNTAIN a little red plane was finding its way. I was with Stafford Wentworth, olive grower of Palermo, California. He had flown to Bakersfield, in the southern part of the state, to carry me north for a day's visit to learn about olives. Higher now, to ten thousand feet to fly over mountains. Scattered over the foothills were the olive groves; northeast of Tulare a vast acreage. Into Butte County, there to see the first Stafford Wentworth orchard of 125 acres, a solid mass of green from the air.

The plane circled, glided to a meadow and taxied to the Wentworths' barn. Young sons Franklin and Brandon came running and there was Mrs. Wentworth to welcome us to the house built in 1897 by Phoebe Hearst, mother of William Randolph.

Mrs. Wentworth and I sat on the steps of the high front porch that circles three sides of the house to talk recipes. She uses olives, every day, every way; cuts them into salads, adds them to cheese rabbits and into this mixture, which is used as a dunk for pretzels, for celery spikes:

Take six ounces of cream cheese, add milk to soften, stir in one-eighth teaspoon curry powder, one-fourth teaspoon grated lemon rind, one-half cup chopped ripe olives with a dash of pepper.

Olive Rabbit

◇◇◇

1 tablespoon unsalted butter	¼ teaspoon dry mustard
1 tablespoon all-purpose flour	¼ teaspoon Worcestershire sauce
½ cup milk	Dash of freshly ground black pepper
2 cups grated sharp cheddar cheese	½ cup pitted black olives, quartered
½ teaspoon salt	Hot buttered toast for serving

Serves 4

In the top portion of a double boiler, melt the butter over hot water and whisk in the flour. Gradually add the milk and cheese; stir until the cheese melts. Add the salt, mustard, Worcestershire sauce, pepper, and olives. Pour over hot buttered toast and serve immediately.

CALIFORNIA

Black Olive, Chicken, and Spaghetti Bake

1 (5-pound) chicken, cut into pieces

¼ cup olive oil

6 cups hot water

1 tablespoon salt, plus more
for seasoning the dish

¼ cup chicken fat

⅓ cup chopped onion

⅓ cup diced green bell pepper

2 cups sliced celery

½ cup diced pimiento peppers

1 pound spaghetti

1½ cups whole and halved
black olives

2 cups grated sharp cheddar cheese

Salt and freshly ground black pepper

Serves 6

Heat the oil in a large heavy skillet over medium heat. Brown the chicken pieces in the hot oil, 10 to 12 minutes. Pour in the hot water and add the salt. Reduce the heat to a simmer, cover, and simmer until the chicken is tender, about 30 minutes. Remove the skillet from the heat and transfer the chicken to a platter. From the broth left in the pan, skim off the fat and reserve ¼ cup of it. When the chicken is cool enough to handle, remove the skin and bones from the chicken, leaving the meat in large pieces. Return the chicken to the broth in the skillet.

Melt the chicken fat in a medium saucepan over medium heat. Add the onion, bell pepper, and celery and sauté until tender, about 3 minutes. Stir the vegetable mixture into the chicken and broth; add the pimiento peppers. Bring to a boil. Break up the spaghetti to fit into the pan and cook until the spaghetti is tender, adding more water if necessary, about 7 minutes. Stir in the olives and cheese and heat slowly until the cheese is melted. Season with salt and pepper. Serve immediately.

Pissaladière

1 Perfect Pie Crust (page 13)

3 tablespoons olive oil

¾ cup chopped onion

1 clove garlic, minced

1 green bell pepper

2 pounds ripe tomatoes, chopped

½ pound red cherry tomatoes,
cut in half

1 teaspoon salt

⅛ teaspoon freshly ground
black pepper

4 tablespoons grated Parmesan cheese

3 tablespoons chopped good-quality
black olives

1 (3-ounce) jar anchovy fillets, drained

Serves 6

Preheat the oven to 425 degrees.

On a lightly floured surface, roll out the dough ⅛ inch thick and transfer it to an 8-inch-wide x 4-inch-high cake pan. Place parchment paper over the dough and spread ¼ cup dried beans over the parchment to keep the pastry from bubbling. Bake for 15 minutes, or until golden. Remove the beans and cool completely on a wire rack before adding the filling.

Heat the oil in heavy cast-iron skillet over medium heat. Add the onion and garlic and sauté until golden, 10 to 12 minutes. Meanwhile, cut the pepper in half, remove the core and seeds, and cut into strips about ¼ inch wide. Add to the onion and cook until softened, about 3 minutes. Add both tomatoes, the salt, and pepper. Reduce the heat to very low and cook until the sauce has thickened, about 2 hours, stirring occasionally with a wooden spoon.

Preheat the oven to 300 degrees. Remove the skillet from heat and stir in 3 tablespoons of the cheese and the chopped olives. Turn into the pastry shell. Arrange anchovy fillets in spoke-of-wheel fashion, allowing one to a portion. Sprinkle with the remaining 1 tablespoon cheese. Bake until the mixture is heated, the cheese is lightly browned, and the crust is crisp, about 30 minutes. Cool for 5 minutes, then cut into squares. Serve as an hors d'œuvre.

CALIFORNIA

THE KING OF BARBECUE KINGS

Sunday dawned in a golden haze. At ten o'clock with Helen Selleck driving, we turned into the narrow road that curves the steep mountainside to Dr. Raoul Blanquie's little house perched on the edge of a canyon in the Los Angeles Mountains sixty miles from San Francisco. In the rear was a small amphitheater enclosed by live oaks, bays, firs, and madronas.

All preliminaries had been taken care of, and by the time we arrived the business of a barbecue was already in full swing: three massive structures of brick and stone, one the rotisserie with revolving spit, operated by a clock-wound spring such as the French use for fireplace spit cooking. The rotisserie was mounted on a raised stone base three feet high, the fire pit at its back, beneath a shallow pan to catch the dripping fat. A three-sided sheet-metal affair, insulated with asbestos, covered the spit, its open side toward the heat, a door in the front so the cook could reach in to tend to his basting. The last touch, a smokestack and damper.

A few steps to the left a barbecue pit built of brick, maybe four feet high, the fire bed about one and one-half feet deep with an adjustable grate. The third structure was a domed brick oven for baking anything from bread to soufflé.

Dr. George Selleck, a San Francisco dental surgeon and King of Barbecue Kings, was in chef's coat and spotless white pants, standing one inch taller than his five foot nine. When the doctor cooks he grows in height and power. Friend Dr. Raoul Blanquie, a fellow dentist whose home and barbecue pit were the scene of action, served as flunky. I watched while the doctor cooked.

"Where are the lemons?" he shouted. "Bring the lamb," he called to Jeanne Blanquie. "No matter what kind of grill or pit or fireplace or coal bucket you use, learn to use it before you bring on the guests," he said to me. "You have to learn to gauge those outdoor fires as you do a cookstove."

The lamb loomed on the horizon. A forequarter, the complete rack, nine chops, four neck chops. "There's the classical noisette." The Doctor pointed with his knife to the choice piece of the shoulder blade region. He had ordered the meat man to cut through the center of each rib bone to make carving easy. The shoulder had a nice outer layer of fat and plenty of protective fat in the fiber; this would act as a moistener bringing out the savory, succulent flavor. The doctor doesn't approve of boned meat to barbecue. The bone serves as a matrix to hold the piece together and keep in the juices.

The night before he had treated the lamb to a stimulating herbal marinade. Nothing complicated except that first you must catch your fresh herbs, including one sprig marjoram, one long sprig rosemary, three short sprigs of thyme, three cloves garlic. These are finely cut. Next, add a dozen cracked peppercorns. The doctor means *cracked,* not ground—placed in a heavy cloth and whacked with a hammer. Grinding, he says, evaporates the oils, dissipating the flavor. Enough olive oil, about half a cup, was added to the mixture to make a thick paste.

Lamb in hand he had rubbed the surface with the cut side of a lemon, then the herbal mixture spread on and rubbed generously between each rib. On the skin side of the forequarter the doctor had cut three wide pockets under skin and fat and into these he stuffed the remaining paste. The lamb had been wrapped in butcher paper and stored overnight in a cool place, but not in the refrigerator. A too-low temperature and the volatile oils congeal, do not permeate the meat.

Oak was the wood used in the barbecue pit. After several hours of firing, there it lay, a smooth smokeless bed of gray-eyed coals giving a steady, searing heat. The adjustable grate was placed about two and one-half feet above, and the lamb laid on, skin side down to liquify the heavy layering of fat and get a seared surface. The fat dripped and the flames danced. The doctor sprinkled on a handful of water. A big smudge of smoke. "Fine," he said, "the smoke adds to the flavor."

Drop by drop the grease melted like candle wax while the doctor set to work preparing the guinea hens. The birds, each about two and one-half pounds, he had ordered dressed. "Truss the little critters well," he said, tying the legs and wings tight to the body with long skewers and string to make a solid bundle.

He rubbed the birds over with olive oil, dusted on pepper and salt. A piece of salt pork, one fourth of an inch thick and three inches long, was placed over the center of the breast, another strip down the back.

Into the cavity of each went a sprig of fresh sage and a stalk or two of celery. It is best, the doctor believes, not to stuff animals or birds for the spit, that is, beyond the few necessities needed for flavor. When heat is applied, stuffing extracts the juices and the meat will be dry. The steel spit he ran through the guineas like a sword, directly through the center so the weight would be balanced.

The spit clock wound, the spring released, slowly the birds turned golden, their juices dripping into a tin-lined drip pan. This held the basting liquid, two cups of a stock made from guinea giblets and necks. A stalk of celery had been diced and laid in with top leaves, two sprigs parsley, one quartered onion, one diced green pepper, and two whole carrots. The drippings added their own savory touch. Four to six times the birds were basted during the cooking. At the last the juices in the pan were added back to the finely cut giblets and this reheated and passed as sauce.

Dr. Selleck doesn't believe in barbecue sauces of the hot-temper breed. He spends hours of loving care in handling the meat to bring it to a final point of perfection and considers it heresy to lather a masterpiece with a multitude of fiery spices masking the true flavor.

After the birds were well seared, the heat was decreased and the cooking continued at a slower pace. In spit cooking, the doctor pointed out to me, the meat cooks as steadily on the inside as the outside because the metal spit acts as a heat conductor. Guinea or chicken, spit-cooked, will be done in forty-five minutes to an hour.

The doctor talked while he made the torta, a baked dish of zucchini and spinach that can be served hot or cold. Just the right dish, he thinks, for a barbecue because it needs no attention during that important moment when the cook is carving. This recipe is given exactly as the doctor gave it to me.

After an hour the lamb had turned mahogany brown, almost done. The doctor moved it to one end of the grate, parking the bone side down, the bone to serve as a warming agent. With a few deft cuts he lifted out the shoulder blade, seared the cut side to seal in the juices, then left this over the heat twenty minutes longer to make sure this thicker portion was done.

Marinated Chayote Squash Sticks

4 chayotes (½ to ¾ pound each),
cut in half lengthwise, pitted,
then cut lengthwise into 24 slices

1 quart water

2 teaspoons salt

3 tablespoons tarragon
wine vinegar

3 tablespoons olive oil

Makes 10 to 12 appetizers

Place the chayote strips in a medium saucepan,
cover with the water, and add the salt. Place over
medium heat and bring to a boil, then reduce the
heat and simmer for 15 to 20 minutes, until tender.
Drain. Spread the strips out on a platter, and while
still warm, sprinkle with the vinegar. Cool and
dress with the oil. Serve as appetizer with thin slices
of prosciutto or your favorite dip.

Garden Torta

3 pounds spinach

1 cup water

4 medium zucchini, sliced into ¼-inch circles

¼ cup olive oil

3 tablespoons grated Parmesan cheese

4 large eggs

2 slices white, wheat, or other favorite sandwich bread, crusts removed

¼ cup half-and-half

⅛ teaspoon freshly ground black pepper

Pinch of dried thyme

Salt

¼ cup chopped parsley

3 green onions, sliced

Serves 10

Preheat the oven to 350 degrees. Grease a 12 x 8 x 2-inch baking dish.

Wash and pick over the spinach. Combine the spinach and water in a large saucepan. Place over medium heat and steam the spinach for 5 minutes; immediately drain and finely chop it, then transfer to a large bowl. Heat the oil in the same saucepan over medium heat. Add the zucchini and cook for 2 minutes to soften, then cover the pan to steam the zucchini for 3 minutes; do not cook thoroughly! Stir the cheese into the spinach. Add the eggs, one at a time, beating well after each addition. In a small bowl, soak the bread in the half-and-half, then whip it into the mixture. Add the thyme and season with salt. Add the parsley. Fold in the zucchini and green onions. (Be careful not to break the slices of squash.)

Turn the mixture into the prepared pan and bake for about 45 minutes, until a wooden pick or skewer inserted into the center of the torta comes out clean. Let rest in the pan for 5 minutes, then cut into large squares and serve hot or at room temperature.

Camembert and Sherry Masterpiece Spread

1 pound ripe Camembert cheese

½ cup Amontillado sherry

2 cups (4 sticks) unsalted butter, softened

Crackers and toasts or 3 tablespoons dry breadcrumbs for serving

Makes 2 cups

Remove the rind from the Camembert, place it in a large bowl, and cover it with the sherry. Cover and let stand overnight in a cool, dry place to soften and ripen. When ready to use, cream the butter in a medium bowl using a handheld beater. Drain the sherry from the cheese and reserve it. Mash the cheese with a fork, scrape the butter into the bowl, and cream well with the beater. Blend in the reserved sherry, scrape the mixture into a small ramekin or bowl, cover, and refrigerate until the cheese sets, about 3 hours.

When ready to serve, place the ramekin on a platter surrounded by various crackers and toasts, or immerse the bowl to the rim for 1 minute in warm water, then unmold the cheese neatly to a serving plate and garnish it with the dry bread crumbs.

HERE WE FEAST

California eats better at home and in her restaurants than any other state, or so it seems to me. In any case it is doubly golden because of the cornucopia of homegrown luxuries—fruits, nuts, wine. What more can one ask? The women there love to talk about cooking, they love to cook—and do. The barbecue may have had its big start in the South, but it took Californians to make it a national recreation. On my first eating trip into the state I started in the south to eat my way north. I wanted to know about the pioneer foods and was told to talk to Ana Begue de Packman, California's leading authority on the state's early-day cuisine.

Here was a woman who knew the food of her state backwards from now right down to yesterday when the Spaniards moved in. She said, "Before we start talking about cooking get this straight. Early California food wasn't Mexican, nor was it pure Spanish. Those first early settlers, Spanish descendants, tried the best way they could to duplicate home dishes but their cooking had to be done with the food at hand and that made the difference. They used the native foods of the western Indians but tastefully improved to satisfy the palate of the Spanish colonists. These first settlers carried with them a limited supply of beans, corn, and dried meal to which were added wild greens, seeds, and roots and the edible fruits of the region. They found an abundance of watercress, wild onions, wild oats, grasses, herbs, and wild grapes." And to cultivate these they recruited their Indian converts into a land army to work the soil with crude implements.

Occasionally Manila-bound galleons and later the Boston clippers rounded the Horn bringing seeds and cuttings. Soon, around every mission sprang a variety of young trees and vines—the foundation of California's agricultural economy.

It was of such things Ana Begue de Packman spoke as we sat together in her small square living room—a little patch out of the past, and Hollywood but a few miles to the west.

A delicious fragrance wafted down the hall. "What are you cooking?" My curiosity had to be satisfied.

"Pollo con arroz, chicken and rice. This was one of my mother's favorites prepared by Chona, the family's Indian cook for many years. I'm also preparing carne con chili."

"What's that?" I wanted to know.

"It's what some call chili con carne, but that's a misnomer. Meat, you know, is the main ingredient and therefore deserves the honor place in the name."

Carne con Chili

2 pounds beef chuck,
cut into 1-inch cubes

3 teaspoons salt

1 teaspoon plus a dash of freshly
ground black pepper

4 tablespoons vegetable oil

4 large dried ancho chiles,
stemmed and seeded

1 quart boiling water

1 tablespoon all-purpose flour

1 clove garlic, minced

1 tablespoon cider vinegar

1 cup ripe black olives, quartered

Serves 4 to 6

Pat the cubes of meat dry and season with 2 teaspoons of
the salt and 1 teaspoon of the pepper. Heat 2 tablespoons
of the oil in a large skillet over medium heat and brown
the meat on all sides, 8 to 10 minutes, turning as needed.
Transfer the meat to paper towels to drain.

Meanwhile, make the chili sauce: Put the chiles and
water in a medium pot. Place over medium heat and
bring to a boil, then reduce the heat and simmer until
the chiles are soft, about 10 minutes. Transfer the
chilis and their simmering liquid to a blender and puree
until smooth.

Heat the remaining 2 tablespoons oil in a large skillet
over medium heat; stir in the flour and garlic and cook,
stirring, until the flour is a light golden color, about 5
minutes. Pour in the chili purée and the vinegar. Add the
meat, bring the mixture to a boil, then reduce the heat to
low and simmer until the meat is tender and the flavors of
the sauce have melded, at least 1½ hours or up to 5 hours.
Season with the remaining 1 teaspoon salt and dash of
black pepper. Serve garnished with the olives.

Note: Chili con carne gets better upon standing, so you
could let the pot simmer all day and then bring up the
heat just before you're ready to serve the chili. And it's
even better the next day.

Salsa Verde

1 clove garlic, coarsely chopped

1 teaspoon salt

1 small onion, minced

2 or 3 fresh serrano or jalapeño chiles, coarsely chopped

6 to 8 tomatillos (about ½ pound), husked and quartered

3 large ripe tomatoes

Makes about 2 cups

In a food processor or blender or using a heavy mortar, process or pound the garlic and salt to a paste. Add the onion, chiles, tomatillos, and tomatoes; either pulse in the food processor to make a chunky purée or pound and mash the ingredients together as finely as possible for the same result. Serve immediately.

Note: A delicious sauce and ready to serve with barbecued and broiled meats.

CALIFORNIA TAKES PRIDE IN setting fashions in food. If New York, for example, has a favorite dish, California cooks may be eager to copy but will do the thing differently. Take cherries jubilee, which every fine eastern restaurant lists among its desserts, an idea borrowed from France. Now jubilee goes western and the fruit flamed is the orange.

California cuisine is many things, most of them spectacular. So is this dessert. It's a dish sweet as the drip of orange honeycomb. Its fragrance is so strong you can feel the touch of it like an indefinable sugar in the air. The syrup for this can be prepared in advance, the fruit added at serving time.

Oranges Jubilee

1 cup fresh-squeezed orange juice

1 cup water

¾ cup sugar

1½ tablespoons cornstarch

6 navel oranges, sectioned

½ cup toasted slivered almonds

½ to ⅔ cup brandy, heated slightly, optional

Rich vanilla ice cream for serving

Serves 4

In a large saucepan, combine ¾ cup of the orange juice with the water and sugar. Place over medium-high heat and bring to a boil; reduce the heat to low and simmer for 5 minutes. In a small bowl, mix the remaining ¼ cup orange juice with the cornstarch into a smooth paste. Add the paste slowly to the hot mixture, stirring constantly. Cook until slightly thickened and glossy, about 10 minutes, stirring occasionally. Place the orange sections in a chafing dish and cover with the thickened syrup. Sprinkle with the almonds. Heat until just warm. Add the brandy, and ignite, if desired. Serve hot, ladled over rich vanilla ice cream.

EVEN A TRIED-AND-TRUE RECIPE like the baked Alaska gets a new twist—it's baked à l'orange. Here is California's way with this dish.

Individual Baked Alaskas à l'Orange

8 navel oranges

¼ cup grenadine syrup

3 egg whites

½ cup sugar

1 pint very firm vanilla ice cream

Serves 8

Slice off the tops of the oranges. Scoop out the fruit with a spoon, taking care not to damage the shells, which you want to leave whole and round and which you need to reserve. Cut the fruit into bite-size pieces, removing the membranes. Pour the fruit into a bowl and pour the syrup over it. Cover with plastic wrap and refrigerate for about 1 hour to chill.

Preheat the oven to 400 degrees. Line a shallow baking pan several times with aluminum foil.

Stuff the chilled orange filling into the scooped-out orange "cups." In a medium bowl, beat the egg whites until foamy. Gradually beat in the sugar until the mixture forms stiff but not dry peaks. Top the oranges with a small scoop of ice cream. Immediately cover the ice cream with the meringue to the edge of the shell; completely seal the cream inside the white. Place the filled cups on the prepared pan. Bake 3 to 5 minutes, until the meringue is browned. Serve immediately.

CALIFORNIA

SWEETER FOR A BIT OF THE SOUR

Lemons are as important as the orange to the Golden State. We stop to pick a lemon and talk with Mrs. Thomas F. Knight, Jr., of La Canada, who picks no fewer than a dozen a day winter and summer. Always a lemon handy in her kitchen, for the Knights grow their own.

Tom Knight is a grandson of Jesse Knight who planted the first extensive citrus grove in this area back in 1889. Tom's father, Tom Senior, a business executive, took the ranch over in 1908 as a sideline.

Mrs. Knight uses lemons in every possible way. She adds lemon as a garnish zester to the fish platter, to salads, to the jellied soup bowl. Talk about gilding the lily, Jean even garnishes the garnish, sprinkling the lemon slices with minced meat, parsley, pimiento. She thinks lemon juice enhances the flavor of fresh garden vegetables and frequently serves fat wedges with beets, with new cabbage, and always with spinach.

Someday try Jean's way of giving little new potatoes the kiss of a lemon. Boil twelve tiny spuds, these really new. Drain and cover with one-fourth cup lemon juice blended well with six tablespoons of browned butter.

Many foods, Jean finds, are sweeter for a bit of the sour. Example: lemon quarters with melon to bring out the melon's natural sweetness. And tender young carrots—shredded, with raisins, with lemon juice added along with a dash of salt when combined in a salad.

Here's an idea to borrow: take the day-by-day grocery-store tea and give it the taste of a rare and expensive blend. Before steeping, add 1 teaspoon of grated lemon peel to the pot. What a delicate flavor! Such a flowery aroma!

Jean Knight gave me her best lemon recipes. When this pudding comes to supper every child, she says, licks his dish clean.

Daddy Knight's favorite is the lemon mist pie, a recipe that came to Mrs. Knight from her friend Mrs. Daniel B. Miller. "My most borrowed recipe is for lemon sours," Jean told me. This is a pastry of sorts but almost a confection. Children eat it like candy.

Lemon Pudding

1 cup sugar

¼ teaspoon salt

3 tablespoons lemon juice

2 teaspoons grated lemon peel

3 large eggs, separated

⅓ cup sifted all-purpose flour

2 tablespoons unsalted butter, melted

1½ cups milk

Whipped cream for serving, optional

Serves 6

Preheat the oven to 350 degrees. Grease a 2-quart casserole.

In a large bowl, combine the sugar, salt, lemon juice, and lemon peel. Add the egg yolks and beat. Add the flour, mixing well. Blend in the melted butter and milk. Beat the egg whites until stiff peaks form and fold into the egg-yolk mixture. Pour the pudding into the prepared casserole, set the casserole in a larger pan, and pour hot water halfway up the sides of the casserole. Bake for 45 to 50 minutes, until the edges are firm but the center is still a bit soft. Remove from the water bath and cool completely. Serve with whipped cream, if you like.

Note: The lemon pudding may be stored covered in the refrigerator for 3 days.

CALIFORNIA

Lemon Squares

¾ cup all-purpose flour

5 tablespoons plus 1 teaspoon unsalted butter, softened

2 large eggs

1 cup brown sugar

¾ cup shredded sweetened coconut

½ cup chopped walnuts

⅛ teaspoon baking powder

⅛ teaspoon vanilla extract

1 teaspoon grated lemon peel

1½ tablespoons lemon juice

⅔ cup confectioners' sugar

Makes 2 dozen squares

Preheat the oven to 350 degrees.

In a large bowl, mix together the flour and butter with your fingers to the consistency of fine meal. Sprinkle the mixture evenly into the bottom of an 11 x 7-inch pan. Bake for 10 minutes, or until browned.

Meanwhile, in a medium bowl, beat the eggs; mix in the brown sugar, coconut, walnuts, baking powder, and vanilla. Spread on top of the flour mixture as you take it from the oven; return to the oven and bake for about 20 minutes longer, until set.

In a small bowl, mix lemon peel and lemon juice and stir in the confectioners' sugar until creamy. Spread over the top as soon as the pan is taken from oven. Cool completely on a wire rack, then cut into squares and serve.

THE NATURAL CHARM OF AN ORANGE

My first visit to a California orange grove was the afternoon I went calling on Mrs. John Powell, twenty-five miles out of Los Angeles. The low stone house nestled among a tangle of flowers at the foot of Mt. Wilson. Below stretched the valley of San Gabriel with its manicured acres of citrus groves, twenty-eight of those acres belonging to the Powells' ranch. Oranges and lemons and avocados they counted their big crops.

"I have already started the citrus spareribs for dinner," Mrs. Powell said, opening the door into the kitchen. She knew we had come to talk cooking, to learn how oranges are used at home in the orange-growing country. "We like our oranges best just as they are," she was explaining. "I section the fruit, cut the sections in halves, dust with powdered sugar. That's the way to enjoy all the natural charm of an orange."

Mrs. Powell's very best tricks with citrus are in preparing meat and fish dishes. Baking a fish she covers it over with slices of orange, then slices of onion and over all bacon, allowing one piece for each serving. Her pot roast done with orange deserves the Cordon Bleu. The roast is seasoned with salt and pepper, dredged with flour, browned on all sides in hot fat, then one sliced onion added and one sliced orange, the peel left on, two bay leaves, two peppercorns, four cloves, and a small amount of liquid, the pot covered tightly, the roast let simmer until the meat tenders. Cook it on top of the range or in a slow oven. As the liquid cooks away, add more boiling water, but only a little.

Warming to the subject, Mrs. Powell described orange meat loaf and the winter chiffon pie that her husband favors.

Citrus Spareribs

1 (4-pound) rack of pork spareribs, excess fat trimmed

Salt and freshly ground black pepper

1 large unpeeled lemon, thinly sliced

1 large unpeeled orange, thinly sliced

1 large onion, thinly sliced

1 (6-ounce) can tomato paste

2 cups water

1 teaspoon chili powder

1 teaspoon salt

⅓ teaspoon Worcestershire sauce

2 dashes of Tabasco sauce

Serves 4

Preheat the oven to 450 degrees.

Season the ribs all over with salt and pepper. Place the ribs in a shallow roasting pan, meaty side up. Arrange slices of lemon, orange, and onion on the top of the rack. Bake for 20 minutes, or until the meat begins to sizzle and render fat.

In a medium saucepan, combine the remaining ingredients, bring to a boil, and pour the mixture over the ribs. Reduce the oven temperature to 350 degrees and continue baking until the ribs are tender and richly glazed, about 1 hour more, basting a few times during the cooking. Let the ribs stand for 15 minutes. Using a chef's knife, cut the rack into ribs and arrange on a platter.

THE LATE MRS. DOROTHEA Dalton cooked a meal for me in the fashion of early day California families. Mrs. Dalton was quick to explain that she comes from Missouri. "But my husband's family," she said, "has lived here seven generations."

Her husband was the late Roger Dalton, a citrus grower in the San Gabriel Valley. His grandfather Henry came to the West from England to build the great domain known as Rancho de Azusa. To ride its boundaries by horse took three days, a distance of seventy-five miles through the wilderness. English grandpa married a southern California Spanish girl and that was the beginning of Spanish eating at the Dalton table. One should be awfully empty to sit down to this meal. A salad first, in the modern California manner, and along with the salad hot buttered tortillas. Soup followed, *albondigas de carne*, a sturdy broth in which delicately flavored meatballs came,

four to a portion. Next, *frijoles con queso*, meaning beans with cheese. And with this *salsa*, a tomato relish.

Carne con chili was the main dish at dinner, just such a recipe as Ana Begue de Packman gave. The vegetable was the *colachi*, a savory medley of garden wares. Let's not forget the pickled Mission pears, spicy and tender. Early-day tables had few desserts. The pumpkin was often preserved, *dulce de calabaz*a, to be eaten as a dinner sweet. We had instead a fresh lemon meringue pie.

"Frijoles Con Queso"

1 pound dried pinto beans

5 strips bacon, diced

¼ cup grated sharp cheddar cheese

Salt

Makes 4 cups

Wash and pick over the beans. Place them in a large stockpot, cover with cold water, and place over medium-high heat. Bring to a boil, then reduce the heat to very low and cook for 5 to 6 hours, until the beans are tender, making sure the beans are always covered by water and adding more hot water as needed. Drain and place in a large bowl. Using a potato masher, mash the beans well. In a medium skillet over medium heat, fry the bacon bits until crisp. Stir the mashed beans into the skillet, add the cheese, and stir until melted. Season with salt and serve hot.

"Colachi"

1 tablespoon olive oil

3 strips bacon, diced

1 medium onion, sliced

1 clove garlic, minced

1 pound zucchini, cut into
½-inch slices

1 ripe tomato, chopped

1½ cups corn niblets

1 cup cooked green beans,
cut into 1-inch pieces

1 teaspoon cider vinegar

1½ teaspoons salt

½ teaspoon sugar

Serves 6

Heat the oil in a large skillet over medium heat. Add the
bacon, onion, and garlic and sauté until golden brown,
about 15 minutes. Add the remaining ingredients, reduce
the heat to low, cover the skillet, and cook for 35 to 40
minutes, until all the vegetables are tender and the
mixture is thick and juicy. Serve hot.

California-Style Salsa

1 quart canned chopped tomatoes,
drained

2 medium onions, very finely chopped

1 (1-ounce) can green medium-hot
chiles, chopped

1 clove garlic, minced

1 teaspoon sugar

Salt to taste

1 tablespoon olive oil

1 tablespoon cider vinegar

Makes about 4 cups

In a large bowl using a mortar or in a food processor, mash the tomatoes. Add the remaining ingredients, mixing well if using a mortar or pulsing a couple of times if using a food processor. Cover the salsa and refrigerate until chilled, at least 2 hours. Serve over beans or tortillas.

WHEN I MET CAROL Jean Ackley she was a sophomore at Chaffey College, not far out of Los Angeles, in Claremont. She was a popular coed, a belonger, a doer, and more. She was a capable little homemaker, mistress since her mother's death a year previous of the eight-room house she and Daddy called home. Daddy is Harold J. Ackley, advertising manager of Sunkist Growers. Since then Carol has married and has written to tell me, "I now have two men to keep happily fed."

When I met Carol I asked, "When did you learn cooking?"

"I've never quite learned," she said, "but I started as long ago as the seventh grade and Mother always let me bake. When she was sick I cooked and she directed, so I learned her dishes, the things Daddy likes. She taught me to plan menus and market so groceries and dinners somehow came out even. Yet I'm no wonder cook," Carol repeated.

"A few things I do extra well. Daddy likes my veal cutlets, macaroni and cheese, and tunafish casserole. I make Mother's wonderful lemon ice-box pudding. And for picnics I take along savory lemon pats for the hamburgers. I pretend the recipe is very secret but it isn't and I'll tell you how it's done. We like this butter at home and have it often on our broiled steaks.

"And Mother's sand tarts—that's a recipe you should have. Trimmed with frosting they look like a million."

Carol Ackley's Sand Tarts

For the sand tarts:

1 cup plus 1 tablespoon unsalted butter, softened

¼ cup confectioners' sugar

1½ to 2 cups all-purpose flour

⅛ teaspoon salt

1 tablespoon plus 1 teaspoon cold water

½ teaspoon vanilla extract

30 walnut halves

For the icing:

¾ cup confectioners' sugar

2 tablespoons hot milk

¼ teaspoon vanilla extract

Confetti-colored sugar or other candy decorations for garnish, optional

Makes 30 cookies

Make the sand tarts: In a large bowl, cream the butter and confectioners' sugar. Beat ½ cup of the flour and the salt into the creamed mixture. Add the water and vanilla and work in the remaining flour. Cover and refrigerate the dough until chilled, about 1 hour.

Preheat the oven to 375 degrees. Pinch off small amounts of dough and roll into ½-inch balls. Top each with a walnut half. Place the balls on an ungreased baking sheet and bake for about 10 minutes, until light golden. Reduce the oven temperature to 325 degrees and continue baking for 15 to 20 minutes, until browned. Transfer the sand tarts to wire racks to cool.

While the sand tarts are cooling, make the icing: Combine all of the icing ingredients and mix until smooth. Run the icing through a pastry tube, making a thread-like line around the top of each cookie. Sprinkle with confetti-colored sugar or other candy decorations, if you like.

Lemon-Parsley-Rosemary Butter

½ cup (1 stick) unsalted butter, softened

2 teaspoons grated lemon peel

3 tablespoons fresh lemon juice

1 teaspoon seasoned salt

2 tablespoons finely chopped parsley

⅛ teaspoon minced fresh rosemary

Makes about one 5-inch log

In a medium bowl, beat the butter with the lemon peel and juice until the butter has absorbed the juice. Stir in the seasoned salt, parsley, and rosemary. Turn out the butter onto waxed paper and mold into a log, twisting the ends. Chill the butter in the freezer until firm, about 3 hours. When ready to use, slice the butter and serve pats on broiled steaks, hamburgers, roast chicken, and fish.

NEXT TO THE CITRUS fruits, the grapes and pears and other orchard bounty, walnuts are a leading kitchen crop in California. Everybody, but everybody, in both the southern and northern part of the state, has walnut recipes. Maxine Thorpe of Hollywood gave me some of her favorites. When I met Maxine and her husband Carlyle Thorpe, he was general manager of the California Walnut Growers Association and had been for thirty-five years. As she said, "I'd just better know how to use walnuts." She gave me a hatful of tips.

Having baked potatoes for dinner? Split across one side with a sharp pointed knife, fork-stir the potato to a light fluff, add a big lump of butter and stir it again. Sprinkle over ground walnuts and into the oven till piping hot.

Always creamed onions on Maxine's Christmas menu. The onions are cooked not quite done, drained and one tablespoon of butter added, then placed in a casserole and over this mushroom sauce. The sauce requires one cup condensed mushroom soup plus one-fourth cup heavy cream and folded into

CALIFORNIA

this one-half cup English walnut meats; grated cheese is sprinkled on and again to the oven until the cheese melts.

A holiday hors d'oeuvre uses one package of cream cheese mashed with one teaspoon grated onion with Tabasco sauce to taste, this mixed with enough ground walnut meats to make a thick paste. Roll into small balls. Take walnut halves, twice as many as there are cheese balls, and run into the oven until toasted and brown. Sandwich each cheese ball between walnut halves and serve hot.

I visited Mrs. Thorpe in her Hollywood kitchen. She knew I was coming and baked a banana-nut loaf. Each year in November she makes this bread and in quantity, six loaves, two pounds each, to wrap in foil paper and into the home freezer to keep for holiday parties.

Banana-Walnut Bread

10 tablespoons plus 2 teaspoons unsalted butter, softened

1 cup sugar

2½ cups sifted all-purpose flour

1 teaspoon baking powder

1 teaspoon baking soda

½ teaspoon salt

2 large eggs, beaten

1 ⅓ cups mashed ripe bananas

½ cup sour cream or buttermilk

1½ cups chopped walnuts

Makes one 2-pound loaf or two 1-pound loaves

Preheat the oven to 350 degrees. Grease a 2-pound loaf pan or two 1-pound loaf pans. In the large bowl of an electric mixer, cream the butter and sugar well. In another bowl, sift the flour with the baking powder, baking soda, and salt, not once but four times. Place the bowl with the butter and sugar under the electric mixer. Add 1 beaten egg with about 1 tablespoon of the sifted flour mixture and beat at low speed until smooth. Add the second beaten egg with another 1 tablespoon of the sifted flour mixture and beat again until smooth. Add the mashed bananas and beat again. Add the sour cream alternately with the remaining sifted flour mixture. Remove the bowl from electric mixer and stir in the chopped walnuts. Transfer the batter to the prepared pan or pans and bake for about 1¼ hours for the 1 large loaf or 1 hour for 2 loaves, until a wooden pick or skewer inserted in the center of the cake comes out clean. Cool slightly on a wire rack, then remove to the rack to cool completely.

A LITTLE DINNER FOR THIRTY

hef Joseph Leopoldo Milani is giving a party. No, not on television. No, it isn't over radio. Just a quiet little dinner at his home in North Hollywood." I was in Los Angeles, scarcely had my hat off when this invitation came in by telephone.

I knew it was an honor to be Chef Milani's guest. On the West Coast "Milani" was a kitchen byword.

This Chef Milani had spent his lifetime in kitchens. He started as a "shavetail" at the Bertolini in Naples, one of Europe's finest restaurants, and worked his way up through the ranks. He had operated successful restaurants in this country both east and west. He had won distinction as a high-powered Hollywood caterer, doing elaborate dinners for movie stars, the price a small fortune. He had been retained as consultant for numerous food firms. Such facts I knew.

But this had not prepared me for the whimsical, kindly man who cooked what he called "a little dinner for thirty."

Mrs. Milani—her name Rosina—left all the party cooking strictly to the master, but she attended to every other detail.

Maybe you would like to have the menu the great one served to his guests the evening I sat down to dinner. Pecan soup the beginning but that soup is a nuisance to make. The chicken à la cacciatora was the heart and soul of the meal or you might substitute his meatloaf supreme. We helped ourselves to eggplant casserole, to green salad, and each made his own dressing, anointing the leaves with California olive oil and native wine vinegar.

Dessert was a choice of fruits in season or the spumoni ice cream, a supply always at hand in the Milanis' freezer.

Swiss Cheese–Stuffed Meatloaf Supreme

1¾ pounds ground beef

¼ pound ground veal

1 cup dried breadcrumbs

½ cup sherry wine

3 tablespoons minced parsley

2 large eggs

2¼ teaspoons salt

Freshly ground black pepper

½ pound Swiss cheese, grated

¼ pound ham, minced

¾ cup chopped onion

3 tablespoons olive oil

1 (15-ounce) can tomato sauce

Serves 8

Preheat the oven to 325 degrees. Grease a 10½ x 5½ x 3½-inch loaf pan.

In a large bowl, combine the beef, veal, breadcrumbs, sherry, 2 tablespoons of the parsley, the eggs, 2 teaspoons of the salt, and a good pinch of pepper. In a medium bowl, combine the cheese, ham, remaining 1 tablespoon parsley, the onion, remaining ¼ teaspoon salt, and pinch of pepper.

Line the bottom and sides of the prepared pan with half of the meat mixture and fill with the cheese mixture. Top with the remaining meat mixture and seal the edges so that the cheese filling is enclosed inside the loaf. Brush the top with the oil and bake for 1 hour, or until an instant-read thermometer inserted in the center registers 140 degrees. Pour the tomato sauce over the meatloaf and bake for 45 minutes longer, or until the internal temperature is 160 degrees and the meatloaf is cooked through. Serve hot.

A FLYING CLOUD OF GLEAMING STARCH

ars were lined bumper to bumper a mile down the road from the gateway of Rancho Marinero. The neighbors were coming. Old friends were here from all the little towns in San Gabriel Valley; they came from Los Angeles.

The Stuart Coulters were holding year-end open house; it's held every year, the Sunday afternoon before Christmas Day. The ten rooms of the ranch home and its wide patio were elbow to elbow with convivial friends. In a five-hour period more than three hundred guests had plate and cup filled and refilled at the bounty table. This was a crowd young and old; the Coulters' sons, Fred and Bill, had invited their own crowd.

The dining-room table was stretched its full length and laden to groaning with heaped platters of food, every last bite a specialty of the Coulter kitchen. No caterer is called when the Coulters entertain.

Open House Day Mattie Thomas, Mrs. Coulter's right hand, was a flying cloud of gleaming starch as she carried the good things from kitchen to table. At one end of the feast board rested the festive ham, opposite a turkey beautifully bronzed. And more of the same waited in the kitchen. Tiny cream puff shells were filled with a variety of savory mixtures, these to accompany the Tom-and-Jerrys. Mattie had ready a thousand cocktail sausages each rolled in pastry to bake as needed and bring snapping from the ardent oven.

The brandy balls Mrs. Coulter had made in spare hours over several weeks; these to disappear literally by the hundreds. So did the tiny mincemeat tarts. They were filled with an uncooked mincemeat, its many different ingredients stirred to a perfect unity. It's a recipe Mrs. Coulter had from her mother, Mrs. William Bowring who lived next door.

Mrs. Coulter's father, William Bowring, planted this citrus and avocado grove when he came from England in 1889. From the north Old Baldy looked down, snow on his topknot.

If it's refreshments for "the girls," Mrs. Coulter likes serving her angel cake with the peanut-brittle topping, everyone saying, "We shouldn't eat this; oh well, we can make up for it tomorrow."

Mrs. Coulter's Brandy Balls

2 (4¾-ounce) packages vanilla wafers, crushed

¼ cup brandy

¼ cup rum

½ cup honey

1 cup confectioners' sugar

Makes about 54 cookies

In a large bowl, combine all of the ingredients except the confectioners' sugar and mix thoroughly. Using a level tablespoon for each, form into balls. Roll the balls in the confectioners' sugar. Store in a tightly covered stone jar or other cookie jar.

Note: Brandy balls keep moist and fragrant for as long as 6 weeks.

Angel Food Cake for the Girls

1 (10-inch) angel food cake

1 tablespoon unflavored gelatin

¼ cup cold water

2 tablespoons bourbon

8 large egg yolks

1 cup confectioners' sugar

1 pint heavy cream, whipped

½ pound peanut or pecan brittle (page 533), crushed

Makes one 10-inch cake

Slice the cake crosswise into 3 layers. In a small bowl, dissolve the gelatin in the cold water; add the bourbon. In a large bowl, beat the egg yolks until thick, then beat in the confectioners' sugar. Stir in the gelatin mixture and fold in the whipped cream. Cover the bowl and refrigerate until the mixture is chilled and begins to stiffen, 1½ to 2 hours. Spread the mixture between the cake layers, sprinkling each layer with brittle. Cover the entire cake with the cream mixture and sprinkle the top with brittle. Refrigerate for several hours and serve cold.

MRS. HUGH B. MCDUFFEE of Long Beach, California, told me she loves everything there is to love about Mexico. She will drive an extra ten miles to shop in a Mexican market to find just the right spice, the right heat in a pepper. Living in Southern California, there is no need to cross the border to find Mexican groceries.

Olive McDuffee said, "I cook Mexican about once a week, having learned the art from a Mexican friend." The learning was easy. Olive had a feeling for below-border food. "I may be a reincarnated Mexican," she likes telling her husband. He doesn't mind, he likes her cooking. Together they go sampling in Mexican restaurants to compare Olive's version of various dishes with the originals.

Her favorite company menu starts with a guacamole appetizer and pomegranate-juice cocktail. The chicken *mole* follows. Spanish rice with this, and a little of the sauce. Olive says it takes a brave cook to try her recipe, and when it's served she advises, "Don't tell what goes in it until the last bite is gone." Red beans for the main course, also *chilis rellenos*. The salad is not Mexican. Olive, as most Californians, prefers the Caesar toss-up. A red wine with the meal, one lighter than burgundy and not so dry—a California wine, that's understood.

For dessert a lemon sherbert and almond cookies. Instead of bread, there are crackers or the corn tortillas or hot potato chips, or a hot garlic loaf. Too much starch, of course, our hostess admits, "But it's awfully good!"

CALIFORNIA

Guacamole

3 very ripe avocados

1 clove garlic, minced

1 tablespoon lemon juice

½ teaspoon salt, optional

Serves 4

Cut the avocados in half, remove the pit, and spoon out the flesh into a medium bowl. Using a fork, mash and whip until smooth. Add the garlic, lemon juice, and salt. If not using immediately, cover with plastic wrap pressed directly on the surface of the guacamole and refrigerate—preferably not more than a few hours.

Chicken "Mole"

1 (4-pound) chicken, cut into pieces

½ cup plus 2 tablespoons minced onion

1 slice white toast, broken into pieces

2 tablespoons seedless raisins

¼ ounce (¼ square) unsweetened chocolate

3 tablespoons blanched almonds

3 tablespoons vegetable oil

2 tablespoons all-purpose flour

1 tablespoon chili powder

½ teaspoon salt

¼ teaspoon ground cinnamon

¼ teaspoon ground cloves

2½ cups chicken stock

½ cup tomato juice

Warm tortillas and steamed rice for serving, optional

Serves 4 to 6

Place the chicken in a large stockpot and add cold water to cover. Add ½ cup of the onion, place over medium-high heat, and bring to a boil. Reduce the heat to low, cover, and simmer until the meat is tender, 1½ to 2 hours. Transfer the chicken from the pot to a bowl to cool.

In a food processor, combine the toast, raisins, chocolate, and almonds and grind to form a paste. Heat the oil in a large skillet over medium heat. Add the remaining 2 tablespoons onion and sauté until golden brown, about 12 minutes. Stir in the flour, chili powder, salt, cinnamon, and cloves. Add the toast mixture and stir in the chicken stock and tomato juice. Cook until slightly thickened, 5 to 7 minutes. Pull the chicken meat from the bones, discard the skin, and add the chicken to the pot. Simmer over low heat for about 30 minutes, until well combined. Serve with warm corn tortillas and steamed rice, if you like.

"Chilis Rellenos"

6 medium poblano chilis (about 3 ounces each)

1 tablespoon vegetable oil

½ small onion, minced

1 garlic clove, minced

1 jalapeño, seeded and minced

6 ounces Monterey Jack cheese, shredded (about 1½ cups)

¼ cup freshly grated Parmigiano-Reggiano cheese

Salt

Salsa (page 796) for serving

Serves 6

Preheat the broiler.

Place the poblanos on a broiler pan and roast them, turning, until they are charred all over, 3 to 5 minutes Transfer the poblanos to a bowl, cover with plastic wrap, and cool. When cool enough to handle, peel the charred skin off of the poblanos. Make a small lengthwise slit in each one near the stem end. Using kitchen scissors, cut out the core and seeds, then remove the core and seeds without tearing the poblanos or enlarging the opening.

Preheat the oven to 425 degrees. In a small skillet, heat the oil over medium heat. Add the onion, garlic, and jalapeño and cook, stirring occasionally, until softened, about 5 minutes. Let the vegetable mixture cool, then stir in the cheeses.

Lightly season the insides of the poblanos with salt. Carefully stuff the cheese filling into the poblanos and press them closed. Place the stuffed poblanos on a baking sheet and bake for about 12 minutes, until the cheese is melted. Transfer the chilis rellenos to plates, spoon the salsa on top, and serve.

THIS RECIPE WAS THE $25,000 First
Grand Prize Winner in Pillsbury's 17th
Busy Lady Bake-Off. It is by Mrs. John
Petrelli of Las Vegas, Nevada.

Golden Gate Snack Bread

For the bread:

2 envelopes active dry yeast

1 cup warm water

4 to 4½ cups all-purpose flour

1 cup cream cheese, softened

2 tablespoons sugar

2 tablespoons unsalted butter, softened

1 teaspoon salt

For the filling:

½ cup (1 stick) unsalted butter, softened

1 packet onion soup mix

Makes 2 long loaves

Preheat the oven to 350 degrees.

In a large bowl, dissolve the yeast in the warm water until foamy, about 5 minutes. Add 2 cups of the flour and the remaining ingredients. Beat for 2 minutes with an electric mixer at medium speed. By hand, gradually beat in the remaining flour to form a stiff dough. Cover the bowl loosely with a clean kitchen towel or plastic wrap and let rise in a warm place until light and doubled in size, about 30 minutes. Generously grease a large cooking sheet.

Meanwhile, prepare the filling: In a small bowl, combine the butter and the onion soup mix until well blended.

Roll out the dough on a lightly floured surface to a 20 x 14-inch rectangle. Spread with the filling.

NEVADA

Starting with the 14-inch side, roll up in a jelly-roll fashion. Seal the edges and ends. Using a knife or kitchen scissors, make a lengthwise cut down the center to form 2 loaves. Place cut-side up on the prepared cookie sheet. Cover loosely with plastic wrap or a clean kitchen towel. Let rise in a warm place until light, about 45 minutes.

Bake for 25 to 30 minutes, until golden. Serve hot or freeze and reheat.

HAWAII

At a cocktail party in New York City I met the William Hardy Hills of Hilo, Hawaii. "Do let us know when you come our way." I accepted their invitation with eagerness, having a trip to the Islands already in the planning. I knew also that Ouida Hill, born in Roanoke, Va., was one of the Hawaii's most experienced hostesses.

Helen of Troy's face may have launched a thousand ships, but Mrs. Hill's efficient hands have launched more than a few thousand parties since her husband was elected to the Territorial Senate in 1927. (Currently he is the President of the State Senate.)

The Hills live on Hawaii, the largest island of the group. There they have two homes, both ocean side, one in Hilo, the other in Kailua-Kona; the latter a teach-type place, Japanese in style. Senator Hill is the island's leading industrialist. His largest operation is the realty investment company he organized 40 years ago. He is president of the Hilo Light and Power Company. We could go on about the Senator's busy world, but it's his right-hand helper, Ouida, I want you to meet.

A tiny woman, just over five feet with gray-green eyes and reddish-golden hair. Her voice is animated and warm, especially when she talks about her hobbies: riding, swimming, growing orchids. But she has a job as well: official entertaining. Three and four times a week the Hills have company for dinner; there are buffets, beach parties, barbecues.

Many a Stateside governor remembers with pleasure the party the Hills gave in June, 1961, for the 53rd Annual Governors' Conference. And the Governors' wives were a bit surprised that the tidbits with the cocktails were not too, too different from hors d'oeuvres served mainland. Like most "haoles" in the Islands (Senator Hill was raised in Idaho) the foods of home are served, plus Oriental touches. Local produce offers variety to mainland eating. Snow peas are one of Mrs. Hill's great favorites. She prefers taro to potatoes when the root is ground and made into cakes, then fried. She is partial to guava ice cream, but it's a banana dessert of her own invention which everyone loves.

Ripe bananas are peeled and wrapped in wax paper, the ends twirled for a tight closing. Into the deep freeze. Just before serving the frozen bananas are thin sliced, sprinkled with sugar and enough cold heavy cream poured on to coat the fruit. The cream immediately freezes to the slices.

Barbecue parties are popular with the Hills. In both homes they have built-in barbecues, large enough to accommodate 28 chickens when halved. The basting sauce for the chicken is made with ½ pound butter, ¼ cup soy sauce, ¼ cup fresh lime juice, with a little of the grated peel.

Ouida Hill's Frozen Bananas and Cream

5 ripe bananas

About 1¼ cups heavy cream

¼ cup sugar, or more to taste

Serves 6

Peel the bananas. Wrap each in waxed paper, twirling both ends to create a tight seal. Place in the freezer until very firm, overnight or at least 3 to 4 hours.

Chill 6 wide-mouthed dessert glasses or shallow bowls in the freezer for 5 to 10 minutes. Remove the glasses from the freezer and pour 1 tablespoon of the cream into each. Unwrapping the bananas one by one, slice half of them ¼-inch thick, and then distribute the slices evenly among the glasses. Sprinkle 1 teaspoon of the sugar over the bananas in each glass. Then drizzle 1 tablespoon of the cream atop the sugared bananas. Slice and divide the remaining bananas among the glasses and repeat the process, sprinkling each serving with 1 teaspoon of the sugar and then topping with an additional 1 tablespoon of the cream. Serve immediately.

IT WAS IN HONOLULU I listened in on a beginners' class in Japanese cooking conducted by Mrs. Takeo Isoshima. Stateside visitors and servicemen's wives flock to her classes at the YWCA. These sessions are a pleasure, as "teacher" speaks perfect English and uses only standard measurements in the recipes.

Born in Tokyo, Yoshie (meaning "Sweet Branch") came with her parents to Hawaii at the age of five. The family set a Japanese table and little daughter learned cooking. Shortly after her graduation from the University of Hawaii, Yoshie married the son of a successful merchant in the gift line business. With four children to mother and a house to manage, Mrs. Isoshima was a busy woman with no thought for careering. She was content, doing the cooking at home. Every so often she entertained her husband's golf club, a buffet composed of nine to ten dishes.

Twelve years ago she went back to Japan to take care of her ailing mother-in-law. She stayed two years; her four children and their father managed alone. Needing outside interests in the strange country, she entered the cooking school run by Tokumitsu Tsuji in Osaka. This famous school has 11

branches throughout the island. When Mrs. Isoshima returned to Hawaii she decided to make sure of her food training and applied at the YWCA to open Japanese cooking classes.

Lessons are given one morning and four evenings a week. The students eat what they cook, sitting together at a long table and having a delicious time. Then the class buckles down and does K.P. duty.

Ask anywhere in Honolulu for a good Japanese cookbook and the answer is the book prepared by the Hui Manaolana Club, a group of second-generation Japanese women who have translated their family recipes as a sort of memorial to their mothers. The purpose—to perpetuate foods familiar to the average Japanese family. It was Mrs. Isoshima who put the ingredients into standard measurements, and through her cooking classes she has been able to test the dishes in the YWCA kitchens.

Here are but two of the recipes most popular with stateside women. The book, "Japanese Foods," is in its third edition, the profits to promote the philanthropic work of the Hui Manaolana Club.

HAWAII

Barbecued Shrimp

1 pound medium shrimp

½ cup soy sauce

¼ cup sugar

1½ teaspoons grated fresh ginger

1½ teaspoons sake

Serves 2 to 4

Remove the legs from the shrimp, leaving the shells and tails on. Cut along the back of the shrimp, through the shell, to remove the vein. Flatten the shrimp into butterflies.

Make the marinade: In a large bowl, combine the soy sauce, sugar, ginger, and sake and whisk to dissolve the sugar. Cover and marinate the shrimp until chilled, about 1 hour.

Preheat the broiler. Transfer the shrimp and marinade to a small heavy ovenproof casserole and broil for 5 minutes, or until the shrimp are pink. Serve immediately.

Stuffed Japanese Eggplant

3 small Japanese or Chinese eggplants, about 3 inches long and 3 inches wide, or 1 large eggplant, about 9 inches long

Salt

½ pound ground pork

¼ teaspoon grated fresh ginger

1 tablespoon chopped onion

1 large egg, lightly beaten

1 teaspoon salt

⅛ teaspoon seasoned salt

1 tablespoon vegetable oil

Kuzu An Sauce (recipe follows)

Serves 4

Preheat the oven to 400 degrees. Cut off 1½ inches from bottom of the eggplant and discard. Move a knife ¼ inch from the cut side and cut almost but not all the way through the eggplant (this is the pocket). Move the knife ¼ inch from the pocket cut and cut a slice free from the eggplant. Make 7 more slices with pockets in the same manner. Sprinkle the inside of the eggplant with the salt.

In a medium bowl, combine the pork, ginger, onion, egg, salt, and seasoned salt and stir with a fork. Spread 1 tablespoon filling in each eggplant pocket. Transfer the eggplant to a large baking sheet and brush the eggplant on the top and bottom with the oil. Bake for about 45 minutes, until the filling is browned and the eggplant is tender. Serve with the Kuzu An Sauce.

Kuzu An Sauce

¾ cup chicken stock

2 tablespoons soy sauce

4 teaspoons cornstarch

4 teaspoons warm water

4 teaspoons sugar

¼ teaspoon seasoned salt

Makes about 1 cup

In a medium saucepan, whisk the stock, soy sauce, sugar, and seasoned salt together. In a small bowl, dissolve the cornstarch in the water. Bring the stock mixture to a boil, stir in the cornstarch mixture, reduce the heat to low, and simmer, stirring, until the mixture thickens to a syrupy consistency, about 7 minutes. Remove from the heat and serve.

HAWAII

Conversion Chart

ALL CONVERSIONS ARE APPROXIMATE.

Liquid Conversions		Weight Conversions		Oven Temperatures		
U.S.	METRIC	U.S./U.K.	METRIC	°F	GAS MARK	°C
1 tsp	5 ml	1/2 oz	14 g	250	1/2	120
1 tbs	15 ml	1 oz	28 g	275	1	140
2 tbs	30 ml	1 1/2 oz	43 g	300	2	150
3 tbs	45 ml	2 oz	57 g	325	3	165
1/4 cup	60 ml	2 1/2 oz	71 g	350	4	180
1/3 cup	75 ml	3 oz	85 g	375	5	190
1/3 cup + 1 tbs	90 ml	3 1/2 oz	100 g	400	6	200
1/3 cup + 2 tbs	100 ml	4 oz	113 g	425	7	220
1/2 cup	120 ml	5 oz	142 g	450	8	230
2/3 cup	150 ml	6 oz	170 g	475	9	240
3/4 cup	180 ml	7 oz	200 g	500	10	260
3/4 cup + 2 tbs	200 ml	8 oz	227 g	550	Broil	290
1 cup	240 ml	9 oz	255 g			
1 cup + 2 tbs	275 ml	10 oz	284 g			
1 1/4 cups	300 ml	11 oz	312 g			
1 1/3 cups	325 ml	12 oz	340 g			
1 1/2 cups	350 ml	13 oz	368 g			
1 2/3 cups	375 ml	14 oz	400 g			
1 3/4 cups	400 ml	15 oz	425 g			
1 3/4 cups + 2 tbs	450 ml	1 lb	454 g			
2 cups (1 pint)	475 ml					
2 1/2 cups	600 ml					
3 cups	720 ml					
4 cups (1 quart)	945 ml					
	(1,000 ml is 1 liter)					

Index of Recipes

3 1901 04997 9687